Digital Crossroads

Digital Crossroads
American Telecommunications Policy
in the Internet Age

Jonathan E. Nuechterlein and Philip J. Weiser

The MIT Press
Cambridge, Massachusetts
London, England

First MIT Press paperback edition, 2007

©2005 Massachusetts Institute of Technology

MIT Press books may be purchased at special quantity discounts for business or sales promotional use. For information, please email special_sales@mitpress.mit.edu or write to Special Sales Department, The MIT Press, 55 Hayward Street, Cambridge, MA 02142.

This book was set in Sabon and was printed and bound in the United States of America.

Library of Congress Cataloging-in-Publication Data

Nuechterlein, Jonathan E.
Digital crossroads : American telecommunications policy in the Internet age / Jonathan E. Nuechterlein and Philip J. Weiser
    p. cm.
Includes bibliographical references and index.
ISBN 978-0-262-14091-1 (hc. : alk. paper)—978-0-262-64066-4 (pb. : alk. paper)
1. Telecommunication policy—United States.   2. Telecommunication—Deregulation—United States. 3. Internet. 4. United States. Telecommunications Act of 1996. I. Weiser, Phillip J. II. Title
HE7781.N84 2005
384'.0973—dc22

                                                                                          2004061063
10 9 8 7 6 5 4

To Stephanie and Heidi, for their support and encouragement; and
To Zoe, Kate, and Aviva, our own next generation

Contents

Acknowledgements

Many friends and colleagues in the telecommunications policy field played essential roles in the completion of this project. We are particularly indebted to Dale Hatfield and Lynn Charytan. Dale is not only a legend in this field, but also an extraordinary teacher and friend. He carefully read every chapter and offered extremely helpful feedback. Lynn, despite her crushing work schedule, found time to read almost the entire manuscript as well, and her comments were equally indispensable and exactly on-target. She has been our partner in the very best senses of the term.

We are indebted to many others as well. One of our goals has been to integrate the distinct perspectives of the various communities of academics and practitioners involved in shaping telecommunications policy. To that end, we enlisted the help of reviewers from each such community, and they responded with very constructive comments on one or (usually) more chapters of the manuscript. In the academic community, we benefited from the suggestions and insights of Paul Campos, Nestor Davidson, Alison Eid, Gerry Faulhaber, Ellen Goodman, Melissa Hart, Clare Huntington, Alfred Kahn, Marty Katz, Sarah Krakoff, Mark Loewenstein, Tom Lookabaugh, Patrick Ryan, Scott Savage, Doug Sicker, Jim Speta, Jane Thompson, Molly van Houweling, Kathy Wallman, Kevin Werbach, and Chris Yoo. Equally valuable were the comments of practitioners, jurists, and former policymakers, some of whom are accomplished scholars in their own right. These included Brad Bernthal, Brad Berry, Marc Blitz, Dan Brenner, Craig Brown, John Flynn, Jon Frankel, Ray Gifford, Paul Glist, John Harwood, Roy Hoffinger, Samir Jain, Bill Lake, Jeff Lanning, Marsha MacBride, A. Richard Metzger, Melissa Newman, Tom Olson, Adam Peters, Bill Richardson, Dorothy Raymond, Joel Rosenbloom, Nan Thompson, and Steve Williams. Of course, none of these reviewers will agree with every proposition in the finished book. Also, as is always the case, the authors bear responsibility for any remaining errors.

We are also immensely grateful to Elizabeth Murry, our own editor of genius at the MIT Press. Liz gave this project her vote of confidence, was instrumental in acquiring the manuscript on behalf of the Press, and then read it from start to finish, providing invaluable insights throughout. She is one of the best in her profession. Also at MIT, Krista Magnuson and Erica Schultz provided very helpful editorial support.

Several other individuals were invaluable in the production process. To shorten the interval between the manuscript's final draft and the book's ultimate publication, we opted to do the typesetting ourselves. That would have been impossible without the indefatigable Lynn Caban, who shepherded the manuscript from Microsoft Word files to a camera-ready version. We are awed by her talents, dedication, and apparent lack of need for sleep. A number of research assistants played important roles in cite checking, proofreading, creating the appendices (including the index), and developing the diagrams. These included Mary Beth Caswell, Sarah Croog, Joel Dion, Michael Drapkin, Lisa Neal Graves, Daniel Houlder, Todd Hoy, Cory Jackson, Tom Kerner, Emily Lauck, Yen Le, Travis Litman, Jenny Loyd, Wyatt Magee, John Meehan, Alison Minea, Rita Sanzgiri, Siddharth Sheddy, Cindy Sweet, Carole Walsh, and Dion West.

We also wish to express deep gratitude to our respective institutions— Wilmer Cutler Pickering Hale & Dorr LLP and the University of Colorado—for supporting us in this project. Wilmer once again proved its storied commitment to public interest projects by enthusiastically encouraging our undertaking from conception to time-consuming completion. Similarly, CU provided an intellectually supportive environment, a wealth of research assistants, and a platform—the Silicon Flatirons Telecommunications Program—for the exchange of ideas between academics and practitioners throughout the field.

Last but certainly not least, we both owe an enormous debt to our families. Our parents gave us the curiosity, drive, and discipline needed to undertake this ambitious project. And our wives, Stephanie Marcus and Heidi Wald, showed remarkably good humor in bearing with us while we secluded ourselves on innumerable nights and weekends to write and revise the manuscript. We look forward to getting reacquainted with them now that the task is done.

Preface to the Paperback Edition

Just as one cannot step in the same river twice, neither can one take two successive snapshots of the same telecommunications industry; in each case, the only constant is change. True to form, the telecommunications policy field has evolved since the original hardcover edition of this book was published in January 2005. We have thus written this new preface to bring this new paperback edition up to date. In substance, however, this preface is more an afterword than a foreword, in that it presupposes familiarity with the main text of this book. First-time readers may wish to read the relevant chapters first before turning to the discussion below.

Industry consolidation

As foreshadowed in chapter 13, Bell company SBC merged with long-time rival AT&T Corp. in 2005 to form a new company called "AT&T Inc." Although it adopted AT&T's better-known brand name, SBC achieved a rare corporate feat: a company's acquisition of its former parent. In early 2006, the combined company announced further plans to merge with BellSouth, a move that will reunify many elements of the original Bell System in nearly two dozen states spanning the Sun Belt and Midwest. Meanwhile, the other Bell company with global ambitions, Verizon, merged with MCI, which for years had been AT&T's only true peer in the retail market for the sophisticated voice and data services purchased by enterprise business customers. Through these mergers, SBC (now AT&T) and Verizon obtained the assets and expertise they needed to become preeminent communications firms not just in their traditional service regions, where they had focused most of their efforts since their inception, but in major metropolitan areas throughout the country and the world.

A number of industry groups and consumer advocates fervently opposed the SBC-AT&T and Verizon-MCI mergers when they were announced in early 2005. The opponents argued that, by reconstituting the local and long-distance operations of the original Bell System within SBC's local service region, the SBC-AT&T merger would recreate the discriminatory evils that the 1984 divestiture was designed to prevent (see chapter 2). And the opponents likewise resisted the merger of Bell offspring Verizon with longstanding AT&T rival MCI. The merging parties responded that radical changes in the telecommunications marketplace during the ensuing 20 years had erased those discrimination concerns. They argued that the Bell companies, which faced no local exchange competition to speak of in 1984, now confronted greater local competition than ever before from wireless, wireline, and voice over Internet Protocol (VoIP) providers, and that such competition would itself discipline any anticompetitive conduct. More generally, they added, regulators in 2005, unlike regulators in 1984, had developed effective regulatory safeguards against discrimination in local exchange markets.

The merging parties essentially won this debate: the Justice Department and FCC not only approved both mergers in late 2005, but imposed less onerous conditions on the merging parties than many industry analysts expected. Because AT&T and MCI had recently stopped marketing services to new residential customers in response to the regulatory developments discussed in chapter 3, the merger-review authorities focused instead on whether these combinations would unduly increase concentration in the business-oriented market for "special access" services: for example, last-mile fiber-optic links between individual office buildings and long-distance voice and data networks. The Justice Department ultimately conditioned its approval on the merging parties' commitment to divest fiber-optic capacity on designated routes to rival special access providers.[1] The FCC followed up with a few conditions of its own, extracting from the merging parties, among other "voluntary" concessions, a commitment to comply for at least

---

1 *E.g.*, United States v. SBC Communications, Inc., Civil Action No. 1:05CV02102, Final Judgment (D.D.C. filed Oct. 27, 2005). As of this writing, a federal court is reviewing Tunney Act claims that the Justice Department should have imposed stricter conditions on the merging companies, but that proceeding appears unlikely to result in major new obligations for those companies.

two years with the FCC's Net neutrality "policy statement" (discussed later in this preface).[2]

Quite apart from their commercial impact, these mergers marked the end of a 20-year era in regulatory advocacy. Since AT&T's 1984 divestiture of its local exchange operations (described in chapter 2), the wireline telecommunications industry was characterized by disputes between the regional Bell companies, of which Verizon and SBC had become the largest, and their wireline competitors, of which the traditional long-distance giants AT&T and MCI were the most prominent and politically influential. The elimination of those two companies as independent actors has thus reshaped not merely the commercial landscape, but the political dynamics of telecommunications policy.

A trend toward increasing consolidation characterized other segments of the telecommunications industry as well in 2005–06. Cingular's acquisition of AT&T Wireless in 2004 (see chapter 8) was followed in 2005 by Sprint's merger with Nextel. These mergers reduced from six to four the number of mobile wireless providers with national networks of their own (the other two are Verizon Wireless and T-Mobile). The Justice Department and the FCC approved both mergers without imposing any particularly onerous conditions, reasoning in each case that the wireless market would remain robustly competitive despite these incremental increases in concentration. The cable industry continued to consolidate as well, as Time Warner and Comcast acquired and divided up the assets of Adelphia, a scandal-wracked cable provider. That set of transactions, which the FCC approved with programming-related conditions in 2006,[3] further cemented the leadership position of those two companies in the cable industry.

---

2 *E.g.,* Memorandum Opinion and Order, *SBC Communications Inc. and AT&T Corp. Applications for Approval of Transfer of Control,* 20 FCC Rcd 18,290 (2005). As this paperback edition goes to press, the Justice Department has approved the AT&T-BellSouth merger without conditions, but a politically divided FCC is mulling proposals to impose conditions similar to those it imposed on the SBC-AT&T merger.

3 Memorandum Opinion and Order, *Applications for Consent to the Assignment and/or Transfer of Control of Licenses, Adelphia Communications Corp., Assignors,* MB Dkt. No. 05-192, FCC No. 06-105 (July 21, 2006).

Network access and "Net neutrality"

When we submitted our manuscript two years ago, we devoted much of chapter 5 to a discussion of "Net neutrality" even though that issue had not yet become what it is now: the fiercest battle in telecommunications policy. Indeed, the FCC's only foray into the area came in the form of then-Chairman Michael Powell's 2004 speech exhorting broadband providers to observe vaguely defined "Internet Freedoms," such as the freedom of consumers "to run applications of their choice" over any broadband platform, except where doing so "exceed[s] service plan limitations or harm[s] the provider's network" (see p. 178 below). Since then, few policy disputes in any field have generated as much controversy as this one, not just at the FCC but, more recently, in Congress itself. Before turning to those developments, we first place this Net neutrality debate within the larger context of present-day network access disputes.

For decades, telecommunications policymakers have debated whether and when the government should force the owners of last-mile transmission facilities to give rivals access to their networks. When Congress passed the Telecommunications Act of 1996, the debate focused on the rights of new entrants to lease physical elements of the telephone network (see chapter 3). In June 2006, after ten years of litigation, that debate neared closure when the D.C. Circuit upheld the FCC's *Triennial Review Remand Order,* the Commission's fourth major attempt to define network element rights (see p. 109 below).[4]

Meanwhile, in the late 1990s, a new dispute had arisen about whether the government should give unaffiliated Internet service providers rights of access to cable modem networks (see chapter 5). The Supreme Court effectively ended that "open access" debate when, in 2005, it decided the long-running *Brand X* case.[5] By a vote of 6–3, the Court reversed the Ninth Circuit and affirmed the FCC's determination that cable modem service should be classified as a Title I "information service" without any Title II "telecommunications service" component. The Court thereby undermined any argument that current law requires a cable company to give unaffiliated ISPs common-carriage-type access to its cable modem platform.

---

4 Covad Communications Co. v. FCC, 450 F.3d 528 (D.C. Cir. 2006).

5 National Cable & Telecomm. Ass'n v. Brand X Internet Servs., 125 S. Ct. 2688 (2005).

The resolution of this dispute about how to characterize cable modem service prompted the FCC to announce its long-delayed *Wireline Broadband Order* concerning the proper regulatory treatment of the competing DSL-based Internet access offered by telephone companies.[6] First, the FCC affirmed its tentative conclusion that DSL Internet access, like cable modem service, is an "information service" without a "telecommunications service" component. The FCC further announced that, after a transition period, it would eliminate all *Computer Inquiry* "unbundling" obligations in this context (see pp. 153, 166–67 below): in other words, that it would allow telephone companies to offer broadband Internet access without offering the underlying transmission component as a common carrier service to unaffiliated ISPs and other willing buyers. In short, the FCC relaxed the major "legacy" obligations that the telephone companies, but not their cable rivals, had faced in the broadband market.

In March 2006, a four-member FCC—shorthanded by one commissioner—split 2–2 on whether to grant a Verizon forbearance petition seeking similar deregulation of an expansively defined class of business-oriented "broadband" services beyond the basic Internet access services at issue in the *Wireline Broadband Order.* Because the Communications Act provides that any forbearance petition "shall be deemed granted if the Commission does not deny" it within fifteen months, the Commission issued a short press release announcing that its 2–2 deadlock operated to grant Verizon's petition by default.[7] The other Bell companies have now filed forbearance petitions of their own seeking the same relief Verizon has won. But the precise scope of that relief is unclear in the absence of any substantive FCC order granting Verizon's broadly worded forbearance request.

At the same time that it eliminated the telcos' regulatory obligation to deal with unaffiliated ISPs, the FCC sought to address any ensuing concerns about the "openness" of the Internet by issuing a non-binding "policy statement" that, in substance, embraced Michael Powell's "Internet Freedoms."

---

6 Report and Order and Notice of Proposed Rulemaking, *Appropriate Framework for Broadband Access to the Internet over Wireline Facilities,* 20 FCC Rcd 14,853 (2005).

7 *See* 47 U.S.C. § 160(c); *see generally* p. 215 below (discussing forbearance mechanism). A trade group representing competitive carriers has challenged this unprecedented deregulation-by-default on constitutional and administrative law grounds. COMPTEL v. FCC, No. 06-1113 (D.C. Cir. filed Mar. 29, 2006).

The policy statement provides, among other things, that consumers are "entitled to run applications and use services of their choice," such as VoIP or video, "subject to reasonable network management" and "the needs of law enforcement."[8] And the policy statement applies not just to telcos, but more broadly to all broadband providers, including the cable companies that had never been subject to any remotely similar obligations under federal law. Although the FCC stressed that it was "not adopting rules" on the subject, this policy statement signaled a critical shift in regulatory focus from the now moribund, ISP-oriented "open access" debate to a new generation of "Net neutrality" disputes (see pp. 168–79 below).

The term "Net neutrality" means different things to different people. Broadly speaking, it refers to rules that forbid broadband network owners to discriminate against unaffiliated providers of applications and content. But the devil is in the details. As of this writing, the debate about those details has moved from the FCC to Congress, which is considering several competing proposals. One of the less interventionist of these, approved by the House of Representatives in mid-2006, would formally authorize the FCC to enforce its 2005 policy statement but bar the Commission from expanding on that policy statement or even adopting rules that flesh out what it means. Another proposal, sponsored by Senate Republicans, would accomplish much the same thing, except that it would replace the FCC's policy statement with a longer "consumer bill of rights." Most major network owners have reluctantly signaled their readiness to acquiesce in such proposals in exchange for legislative relief on other issues, such as video franchising requirements (see below).

In contrast, sizable minorities in the House and Senate support a "strong" form of Net neutrality legislation that would greatly limit the freedom of network owners to give more favorable quality-of-service assurances to some application providers (say, those willing to pay for them) than to others. Such preferential treatment can make the difference between, for example, high and low quality streaming video. Advocates of strong Net neutrality rules argue that permitting network owners to divide applications providers into "tiers" this way would unfairly favor entrenched economic interests, including the network owners' affiliates, and would suppress

---

8 Policy Statement, *Appropriate Framework for Broadband Access to the Internet over Wireline Facilities,* 20 FCC Rcd 14,986, ¶¶ 4–5 & n.15 (2005).

upstarts innovating at the edge of the network.[9] These advocates are unlikely to win majority support in either house of Congress in the near term. But they may have enough political strength to forestall the passage of any comprehensive telecommunications reform legislation that omits "strong" Net neutrality guarantees.

Discussions of Net neutrality tend to be long on rhetoric and short on practical considerations. Part of the reason is that, with rare exceptions, broadband providers have not discriminated in any plainly abusive sense against unaffiliated applications or content providers.[10] But the issue will come to a head when telcos and the cable companies begin running all of the services they provide consumers, including both voice and video, as applications over a unified IP platform.

We address the economic dimensions of this debate in chapter 5. Policymakers, we observe, must weigh the asserted *need* for prospective Net neutrality rules to prevent market failures against the potential costs of such preemptive intervention, and we conclude that this cost-benefit analysis is difficult to resolve in the abstract because so many of the economic variables

---

9 See pp. 169–71 below. For example, the key Senate sponsor of "strong" Net neutrality legislation, Oregon Senator Ron Wyden, has condemned access tiering for its "chilling effect on small mom and pop businesses that can't afford the priority lane, leaving these smaller businesses no hope of competing against the Wal-Marts of the world." News Release, "Wyden Moves to Ensure Fairness of Internet Usage with New Net Neutrality Bill," (Mar. 2, 2006) (http://wyden.senate.gov/media/2006/03022006_net_neutrality_bill.html). In contrast, he says, "[n]eutrality in technology enables small businesses to thrive on the Internet, and allows folks to start small and dream big[.]" *Id.* By focusing more on small business interests than on the ultimate consumer welfare effects of his policy, Senator Wyden signaled disagreement with the modern antitrust principle that the government should interfere with free market dynamics only for "the protection of *competition*" in the sense of overall market efficiency, "not *competitors*" as such. Brunswick Corp. v. Pueblo Bowl-O-Mat, Inc., 429 U.S. 477, 488 (1977) (emphasis added; internal quotation marks omitted).

10 See pp. 173–74 below. The most prominent exception in the United States has been the short-lived decision of a rural telephone company, Madison River Communications, to block the ports that its DSL customers used for VoIP services. Madison River quelled the ensuing public furor by agreeing, in a consent decree, to unblock the ports. *See* Consent Decree, *Madison River Communications LLC,* 20 FCC Rcd 4,295 (2005). Significantly, the FCC's authority to regulate port blocking and similar broadband practices remains uncertain because it depends on open questions about the scope of the agency's "ancillary jurisdiction" (discussed at pp. 216–23 below and later in this preface).

remain unknown. At bottom, we address the issue the way antitrust law would address any other concern that a firm's market power in a platform market might lead it to harm consumer welfare by discriminating inefficiently against unaffiliated providers of complementary applications.

It is worth noting that many proponents of Net neutrality rules resist viewing these issues from the perspective of traditional competition policy, or at least would weigh the costs and benefits of market intervention differently from the way antitrust law would weigh them. Some of these advocates might favor strict Net neutrality rules even if there were little risk that, in the absence of such rules, platform owners would discriminate among applications providers in *anticompetitive* ways that would harm overall economic welfare as measured by conventional antitrust analysis. To these advocates, the problem lies in the very fact of discrimination, even when it might be economically efficient. They believe that any differential treatment among similarly situated applications providers threatens the core attribute that makes the Internet a uniquely valuable global resource: the equal opportunity that the end-to-end principle guarantees for all fledgling innovators at the edge of the network. Net neutrality opponents, in contrast, tend to view the Internet the same way they would view any other marketplace. Thus, absent a demonstrated market failure, they are no more inclined to support government intervention in the terms of network access than in any other set of business disputes between large and small companies. This fundamental difference in perspective, coupled with differing assessments on the level of competition in broadband Internet access, helps to explain why the two sides of this debate tend to talk past one another, and why the Net neutrality debate often generates more heat than light.[11]

A second, less discussed, aspect of the Net neutrality dispute concerns the set of institutional competence issues we explore in chapter 13. In June 2006, the Federal Trade Commission officially claimed jurisdiction to police "unfair methods of competition" involving most types of broadband Inter-

---

11 For a discussion of these competing viewpoints, and a proposal for a new approach to the issue, see Robert D. Atkinson and Philip J. Weiser, *A "Third Way" on Network Neutrality* (2006) (http://www.itif.org/files/netneutrality.pdf). For a provocative economic critique of Net neutrality proposals, see Benjamin E. Hermalin and Michael L. Katz, *The Economics of Product-Line Restrictions With an Application to the Network Neutrality Debate* (2006) (http://repositories.cdlib.org/iber/cpc/CPC06-059).

net access.[12] That announcement reinvigorated a debate about who is better positioned to enforce competition policy principles related to potentially anticompetitive conduct in broadband markets: the FCC, which has traditionally overseen the industry through prescriptive regulation, or an antitrust authority such as the FTC, which operates on a more retrospective, case-by-case basis?[13] That institutional question is as fundamental as the substantive debate about the content of any Net neutrality rules. As of this writing, policymakers do not appear to be approaching a consensus on either issue.

Video franchising reform

The current Congress might never have taken Net neutrality legislation seriously if the telcos—the most politically powerful opponents of such legislation—had not themselves sought intervention on a different issue: video franchising requirements.

Since the dawn of cable television several decades ago, the states and thousands of local governments have played a critical role in deciding the terms on which cable companies can use public rights of way to provide multi-channel video services to end users. Originally, policymakers tended to view cable television as a natural monopoly market, and many states and localities granted exclusive franchises to particular companies in exchange for heavy regulatory oversight. Over time, as we discuss in chapter 11, policymakers recognized that the public would benefit from competition in this market—from direct-to-home satellite providers such as DirecTV and EchoStar, cable overbuilders such as RCN, and traditional telephone companies. The telcos never seriously threatened to enter this market until, with the growth of broadband Internet access, they began deploying fiber-optic

---

12 *See* Prepared Statement of the FTC Before the Senate Judiciary Committee on FTC Jurisdiction Over Internet Access Services (June 14, 2006). The FTC reasoned that, because *Brand X* and the *Wireline Broadband Order* hold that most Internet access services are information services rather than common carrier services, most such services fall outside the statutory "common carrier exemption" to the FTC's jurisdiction. *See id.* at 3 n.4 (citing 15 U.S.C. §§ 44, 45(a)(2)).

13 *See* Raymond L. Gifford, Testimony to the U.S. Senate Judiciary Committee on "Reconsidering Our Communications Laws: Ensuring Competition and Innovation" (June 16, 2006) (http://www.pff.org/issues-pubs/testimony/060616gifford_com.pdf) (arguing for FTC oversight).

cables deeper and deeper into the nation's residential neighborhoods—
cables with enough capacity to support not just fast access to the public
Internet, but high-quality video programming as well. Although that fiber
build-out remains a work in progress, the largest telcos—AT&T and Verizon—contend that they will deliver the benefits of widespread video competition as soon as they are assured of freedom from any cumbersome
obligation to obtain thousands of franchises to use public rights-of-way for
that purpose.

It was one thing for cable companies to negotiate such franchises with
municipalities over a period of many years when, for all practical purposes,
they were literally the only multi-channel video providers in town. It is quite
another thing for a new video entrant to negotiate thousands of franchises
when it must build up a big footprint quickly enough to cover the prodigious
cost of programming and the enormous capital expenditures needed to bring
fiber close to the home, all before it wins any significant market share. Thus
the telcos claim that they could provide price-lowering competition to the
cable incumbents much faster if Congress or the FCC stepped in to impose
national rules for telco entry into the video market.

In late 2005, the FCC opened an inquiry into whether it could and
should adopt national rules forcing local authorities to streamline the process for obtaining video franchises.[14] But the FCC soon put that proceeding
essentially on hold pending congressional consideration of video franchising reform. In early 2006, different bills began circulating in the House and
Senate that, depending on the bill, would either (i) give the FCC explicit
authority to grant video franchises for new entrants on a national level or (ii)
formally leave franchising authority in the hands of localities but subject

---

14 See Notice of Proposed Rulemaking, *Implementation of Section 621(a)(1) of the
Cable Communications Policy Act of 1984 as amended, by the Cable Television
Consumer Protection and Competition Act of 1992*, 20 FCC Rcd 18,581 (2005).
Section 621 of the Communications Act generally requires any "cable operator providing a cable service" to obtain a franchise from local authorities. 47 U.S.C. § 541.
In 2005, a controversy arose concerning whether an IP-based video-delivery system,
such as AT&T's "Project Lightspeed," is a "cable system" subject to that franchise
obligation in the first place, an issue that turns on several abstruse statutory definitions. *See* 47 U.S.C. §§ 522(5) (definition of "cable operator"), 522(6) (definition of
"cable service"), 522(7) (definition of "cable system"), 522(20) (definition of "video
programming"). That issue, too, was placed on the back burner when Congress and
many states in AT&T's region began considering franchise reform legislation in
earnest.

those localities to severe federal limitations on their ability to withhold franchise applications.

As with any other highly regulated market that is suddenly subject to new entry, much of the video franchise debate concerns questions of regulatory parity. One such question is whether telcos and other new entrants should be subject to the same build-out and anti-redlining obligations that franchising authorities have long imposed on the cable companies: that is, obligations to serve most households in a geographic area over time, not just those in the neighborhoods containing the highest concentration of wealthy individuals who are most likely to order premium packages.[15] The cable companies argue that it would be unfair to exempt the telcos from such obligations; the telcos disavow any interest in redlining but add that upstarts in any regulated market often are, and should be, exempt from public-service obligations traditionally imposed on incumbents. As a case in point, they note that incumbent telcos (ILECs) are subject to carrier-of-last-resort obligations and various forms of economic regulation, whereas new telco entrants (CLECs) are generally subject to relatively modest government oversight (see pp. 46 and 78 below).

Cable companies also fear that franchise relief would tilt the playing field in favor of the telcos by exempting them from various benefits the cable companies have traditionally bestowed on local governments. These range from revenue-based franchise fees to the miscellaneous obligations that cable incumbents have long undertaken for municipalities in exchange for the issuance (or renewal) of a franchise, such as providing institutional networks or wiring fire stations and other local government buildings for free. The telcos argue that, as a philosophical matter, they should not have to pay states or localities any fees in addition to those they already pay for use of the same rights-of-way to provide broadband services, given that municipalities incur no extra costs or disruption when telcos shoot video-related packets through the same pipes used for conventional Internet access. To achieve a political compromise, however, the major telcos support legislation that would require them to pay essentially the same franchise fees that their rival cable incumbents pay, typically about 5% of revenues.

As of this writing, video franchise legislation has at least temporarily stalled in the Senate, where proponents have not yet won enough support to

---

15 *See* 47 U.S.C. § 541(a)(3), (4).

block a threatened filibuster from senators who oppose any telco-friendly telecommunications reform legislation that excludes Net neutrality requirements. And the telcos may soon lose much of their incentive to compromise on Net neutrality in order to win federal franchise relief, because while Congress stands idle, an increasing number of states, beginning with Texas in 2005, have given the telcos much of the franchise relief they need on a state-by-state basis. It thus remains unclear whether and when Congress will finally achieve the political consensus needed to take action.

Other developments

Intercarrier compensation. Completed in late 2004, chapter 9 concludes with an all-important question: whether policymakers in general, and the FCC in particular, have the political will to adopt comprehensive intercarrier compensation reform. The jury is still out. After the collapse of the Intercarrier Compensation Forum plan (see p. 330), the core members of the ICF, with the encouragement of state regulators, began negotiating with representatives of the nation's mid-sized and rural carriers to forge a consensus plan that might win broad-based political support. The result of this collaborative effort is the 83-page "Missoula Plan," named after the site of key negotiations. Among other things, the Plan proposes a rationalized calling-network-pays regime that would reduce access charges over time and ultimately unify the call-termination rates of all carriers except the smallest rural telephone companies. In July 2006, the National Association of Regulatory Utility Commissioners, on behalf of state regulators, filed this plan with the FCC but stopped short of endorsing it. Shortly thereafter, the FCC invited comment on the plan. Various industry groups oppose the plan, however, and it remains unclear when the FCC might take decisive action in this politically sensitive area.

Incremental regulation of VoIP. Relying in part on its "ancillary" authority under Title I (see chapter 6), the FCC ordered each VoIP provider interconnected with the public switched network to upgrade the emergency dialing features of its service and inform its customers of any remaining deficiencies.[16] The FCC further adopted, and a split panel of the D.C. Circuit

---

16 First Report and Order, *IP-Enabled Services, E911 Requirements for IP-Enabled Service Providers,* 20 FCC Rcd 10245 (2005).

upheld, new CALEA rules requiring interconnected VoIP providers to facilitate official wiretaps of VoIP calls.[17] Both measures confirm that, even as the FCC emphasizes the need to keep the Internet free of traditional common carrier regulation, it will impose non-economic regulation of Internet-based services in the name of particular social welfare objectives.

Universal service contributions. In the same vein, the FCC required interconnected VoIP providers to contribute to the federal universal service fund for the first time, and it further increased the contribution obligations of wireless carriers.[18] The FCC took these steps to accommodate not just a steady increase in the fund's size, but also the increasing use of VoIP and wireless services as substitutes for wireline long-distance service, which had borne a disproportionate share of the contribution burden. The FCC also acted to avoid a sudden shortfall of its own making: In the *Wireline Broadband Order,* it had exempted DSL service from contribution obligations in order to bring DSL into parity with cable modem service, which has never borne such obligations (see pp. 350–51, *infra*). But these are mere band-aids. As we explain in chapter 10, the FCC will never bring lasting stability to the federal fund until it fundamentally reforms its contribution methodology to avoid arbitrary regulatory classifications.

FCC ancillary jurisdiction. In 2005, the D.C. Circuit reminded the FCC, in the quite different context of the digital television transition (see chapter 12), that its Title I authority has limits. In particular, it invalidated the FCC's "broadcast flag" order (see pp. 403–05) as the product of an excessively expansive view of the Commission's ancillary jurisdiction, holding that, "at most, the Commission only has general authority under Title I to regulate apparatus used for the receipt of radio or wire communication while those apparatus are engaged in communication."[19]

---

17 American Council on Education v. FCC, 451 F.3d 226 (D.C. Cir. 2006); see pp. 222–23 below (discussing CALEA).

18 Report and Order, *Universal Service Contribution Methodology,* 2006 WL 1765838 ¶¶ 52–53 (June 27, 2006). The FCC imposed a rebuttable presumption that 64.9% of VoIP calls are "interstate" and thus subject to assessment under the current revenue-based contribution methodology. See pp. 348–49, 607 n.49 below. The FCC raised the comparable figure for mobile wireless services from 28.5% to 37.1%.

19 American Library Ass'n v. FCC, 406 F.3d 689, 704 (D.C. Cir. 2005). In its *Brand X* decision, the Supreme Court hinted at a more generous view of the FCC's ancillary jurisdiction. *See* 125 S. Ct. at 2711.

Digital television transition. There is finally light at the end of the tunnel for the transition from analog to digital television. Congress set a date certain—February 17, 2009—for the completion of that transition and agreed to help subsidize the provision of converter boxes to analog TV set owners that would otherwise be stranded by end of analog broadcasting.[20] Several disputes about the DTV transition remain unresolved as of this writing, including whether the government should require multicast must-carry (see pp. 401–02), and whether any rules will govern cable companies' decisions about "down-converting" local signals (in other words, carrying them in a lower quality format, see pp. 401–02). We hope that Congress will reach closure on these (and other) issues in time for our next preface.

J.N. and P.W.
Washington, D.C., and Boulder, Colorado
October 2006

---

20 *Digital Television Transition and Public Safety Act of 2005,* Pub. L. 109-171, Title III, §§ 3001 *et seq.,* 120 Stat. 21 (2006) (codified in part at 47 U.S.C. §309(j)(14)(A)).

Preface

This book is about the regulation of competition in the telecommunications industry. Our purpose is twofold. First, we aim to help non-specialists climb this field's formidable learning curve as efficiently as possible. Second, we seek to make substantive contributions to the major policy debates within the field. We have given equal priority to these two quite distinct objectives, and we believe that telecommunications policy veterans as well as newcomers to the field will benefit from our analysis.

Each of us knows from first-hand experience about this discipline's intellectual barriers to entry. When we first met more than eight years ago in the Justice Department, we were generalist lawyers who knew very little about the nuts and bolts of telecommunications regulation. But we needed to become specialists quickly because our respective jobs—in the Solicitor General's office and the Antitrust Division—required us to explain and help formulate federal telecommunications policy in the wake of the Telecommunications Act of 1996. After learning the field the hard way—through years of intensive first-hand immersion—we resolved to shorten the process for others by writing a book that clearly explains telecommunications competition policy in the Internet era. This book is the result.

We offer a few points of clarification up front about the nature of our project. First, this book addresses competition policy issues in the United States, with particular emphasis on the regulatory dimensions of (i) competition in wireline and wireless telephone service, (ii) competition among rival platforms for broadband Internet access and video programming distribution, and (iii) the Internet's transformation of every corner of the telecommunications industry, particularly through the emergence of voice over Internet protocol (VoIP). Except where relevant to our discussion of competition policy, we do not address issues concerning, for example, consumer privacy, government regulation of broadcasting content, or international matters.

Second, while lawyers and law students may find this book particularly useful, it is not a typical "law book" designed exclusively for a legal audience. We examine legal issues and court decisions insofar as they have significantly altered the shape of the telecommunications industry. Our analysis of the industry's deep structure, including its peculiar economic characteristics and rapidly changing technology, drives our analysis of legal developments, not vice versa. We have ordered the discussion this way precisely because we expect that many of our readers will be lawyers, whose understanding of this field is often distorted by too much exposure to legal details and too little exposure to the economics and technology of the industry.

At the same time, for the benefit of practitioners, scholars, and students, we have included extensive endnotes and tables that canvass the most relevant court decisions, orders of the Federal Communications Commission (FCC), and academic commentaries. For students—of business, engineering, economics, journalism, law, or mass communications—we have developed a website (http://spot.colorado.edu/~weiserpj/dc/) with teaching and study aids. For all readers, we have included a glossary of acronyms, a detailed index, and a statutory addendum containing the most important provisions of federal telecommunications law. (Before relying on that addendum in court filings, of course, practitioners are advised to consult the most recent version of the United States Code.)

Third, we have worked hard to explain in clear, accessible prose the many complexities of telecommunications regulation. To balance the needs of a general readership with the needs of readers with more specialized interests, we have included detailed endnotes for each chapter and written two appendixes that supplement our main focus in the text. Appendix A elaborates on the FCC's current methodology ("TELRIC") for pricing a new entrant's access to the elements of local telephone networks, and appendix B addresses the FCC's enforcement regime under the 1996 Act.

Fourth, we hope to earn the trust of our readers by remaining objective and strictly non-partisan throughout our analysis. This is no small challenge. When we searched for a reliable explanatory book in the early years after passage of the 1996 Act, we were told that no such book *could* exist because the only people who truly understood the nuts and bolts of telecommunications competition policy were already beholden to one industry faction or another. One of our central ambitions in writing this book is to disprove that proposition. For the sake of full disclosure, one of us, Jon Nuechterlein, is a practicing lawyer in this field, and his clients currently include incumbent local exchange carriers. From late 1995 through early 2001, however, he represented the FCC itself, often against the interests of these incumbent carriers. Phil Weiser is a law professor who does not generally represent private telecommunications clients, although, most recently, he consulted with the consumer plaintiffs (against the same incumbent carriers) in the *Trinko* Supreme Court case discussed in chapter 13. No opinions expressed in this book should be attributed to any of these clients, past or present; these views are ours alone. In all events, our analysis focuses on how, as a threshold matter, policymakers should conceptualize the basic trade-offs presented in current policy debates. With a few exceptions, we steer clear of advocating any precise outcome for such debates.

Fifth, technological and marketplace developments in the telecommunications industry move very quickly, and there is of course no way to keep any discussion of this industry fully current once the manuscript has been sent to press. For this reason and others, readers should not view this book as a source of specific legal or investment advice. We have nonetheless sought to guard against premature obsolescence by focusing as much on the first principles of telecommunications policy in the Internet age as on the fleeting controversies of the moment. And we plan future editions that will take full account of the changing face of the industry.

Finally, readers should feel free to contact either of us with substantive reactions to the text. Those reactions will prove helpful in revising the text for future editions. We can be reached, respectively, at jon.nuechterlein@wilmerhale.com and phil.weiser@colorado.edu.

J.N. and P.W.
Washington, D.C., and Boulder, Colorado
November 2004

1

The Big Picture

The word "telecommunications," a twentieth century amalgam of Greek and Latin roots, literally means the art of conveying information "from a distance." For millennia, people had to rely on messengers to perform this task, which was as costly per message sent as it was time-consuming. When the Greeks repelled the Persians at Marathon in 490 B.C., the legendary messenger Pheidippides could not shout the good news back to Athens, for it was 26 miles away, nor could he call anyone up, for there were no telephones; instead, he had to run. Several hours later, Pheidippides arrived in Athens, gasped out the news, and died of exhaustion. There had to be a better way—but, for the next 2300 years or so, sending a flesh-and-blood messenger on a trip was the normal method of delivering information from one place to another.

One dramatic break from that convention appeared in post-revolutionary France. In the early 1790s, Claude Chappe invented a system of relaying *visual* messages hundreds of miles across the French countryside over a network of towers spaced about 20 miles apart. For example, someone in Paris would manipulate the mechanical arms at the top of one of these towers to spell out a coded message; his counterpart in another tower 20 miles away would read the message and duplicate it for the benefit of the person manning the next tower down the line, and so on. Weather permitting, this system could be used to transmit a message from Paris to the border of Germany within ten minutes. Other societies had used visual communications techniques before, such as ship-to-ship semaphore signals and such land-based mechanisms as smoke signals and torches. But the French, quickly joined by several other European countries, improved greatly on the idea by developing a nationwide communications *network*. By the Napoleonic era of the early 1800s, the French had developed a sprawling system of towers with six arms radiating from Paris to such far-flung destinations as Cherbourg, Boulogne, Strasbourg, Marseille, Toulouse, and Bayonne.[1]

Before long, these networks, which could be used only in daylight and good weather, confronted the first revolutionary technology in telecommunications: the telegraph. Developed by Samuel Morse in the 1830s, the telegraph sent encoded messages down copper wires by rapidly opening and closing electrical circuits. The telegraph dominated telecommunications until it too was gradually replaced by the next revolutionary technology: the telephone system, invented by Alexander Graham Bell in 1876 and widely deployed throughout much of the United States within a generation. In the 1890s, Guglielmo Marconi exploited the discovery that the airwaves, like copper wires, could propagate electromagnetic signals, and "radio" technology was born.

Today, although precise definitions differ, "telecommunications" is broadly defined as the transmission of information by means of electromagnetic signals: over copper wires, coaxial cable, fiber-optic strands, or the airwaves. This technology—which underpins radio and television, the World Wide Web, e-mail, instant messaging, and both wireless and wireline telephone service—is the *sine qua non* of contemporary global culture. But telecommunications is also a uniquely volatile field, economically, technologically, and politically. The disputes that arise within and among the different sectors of the telecommunications industry, often in response to these rapidly changing conditions, have triggered some of the fiercest public policy wars ever waged. In the United States, the very structure of the industry turns on the decisions of various regulatory authorities, most notably the Federal Communications Commission (FCC).

As Nicholas Lemann wrote not long ago in the *New Yorker*: "Of all the federal agencies and commissions, the [FCC] is the one that Americans ought to be most interested in; after all, it is involved with a business sector that accounts for about fifteen percent of the American economy, as well as important aspects of daily life—telephone and television and radio and newspapers and the Internet."[2] The policy questions answered at the FCC and elsewhere influence not just how we communicate with one another and what we do or don't watch on TV, but the fate of an industry that, in the United States alone, accounts for hundreds of billions of dollars in annual revenues and more than a million employees.[3]

As Lemann notes, however, "[i]t's an insider's game, less because the players are secretive than because the public and the press—encouraged by the players, who speak in jargon—can't get themselves interested."[4] Non-specialists also confront a vexing conundrum in trying to learn this field: to comprehend the whole of telecommunications policy, one must first understand its parts; but to understand the parts, one must first comprehend the whole. This chapter aims to overcome these difficulties by covering the major themes of telecommunications competition policy in enough depth, and with spare enough use of jargon, to help non-specialists understand how each of the policy issues discussed in subsequent chapters fits into the big picture. To this end, the first part of this chapter introduces the peculiar economic characteristics of the telecommunications industry that drive most forms of regulation in the United States. The second part then introduces the market-transforming phenomenon of "convergence"—the competitive offering of familiar telecommunications services through unconventional technologies, such as the provision of telephone service over high-speed cable connections to the Internet.

I. Economic Principles

Why does competition in the telecommunications world—unlike, say, competition in the world of home appliance manufacturing—present public policy issues of such importance and dizzying complexity? To answer that question, we must ask a still more basic question: What would happen if the government just left the telecommunications industry alone—no regulation of the retail rates charged by telephone companies, no antitrust enforcement against monopoly abuses, no government intervention whatsoever?

The answer to this question is controversial. Some free market proponents claim that, if only Congress were to abolish the FCC and stand out of the way, Adam Smith's invisible hand would trigger a consumer-friendly explosion of diverse telecommunications products at efficiently low prices.[5] Others claim that the government needs to intervene much more than it already does to protect consumers against consolidation and monopoly.[6] As will become clear in the pages that follow, we stake out a middle ground. Our thesis is that facilities-based competition will warrant comprehensive deregulation of the telecommunications industry over time, but that deregulating it now, completely and instantaneously, would produce serious market failures and harm consumers.

Understanding this debate requires a familiarity with the basic economic phenomena that regulators have long cited to justify government intervention in telecommunications markets. At the risk of some oversimplification, we will sum up the most important of these phenomena in three concepts: network effects, economies of scale and density, and monopoly leveraging. We address each of those concepts in turn.

A. Network effects and interconnection

Flash back about 100 years to the infancy of the U.S. telephone industry. Different telephone companies often refused to interconnect with one another, and each had its own set of subscribers. Few consumers, of course, wanted to buy several telephones—and pay subscription charges to several telephone companies—simply to make sure they could reach anyone else they wished to call. Unfortunately, this was the choice many consumers faced in the early 1900s.

Such arrangements are quite wasteful in that they misallocate society's scarce resources away from their most productive uses. To be sure, the prospect of extra profits from the successful deployment of a closed (non-interconnected) telephone network may well have encouraged some entrepreneurs to build a better product and reach customers more quickly than they otherwise would.[7] Apart from those incentive effects, however, consumers typically received little added value from multiple subscriptions that they would not have received from one subscription to a single carrier if the various networks were interconnected and exchanged traffic at reasonable rates. For the most part, consumers simply paid more money for the same thing, which meant that they had less money to spend on purchasing things of value in other markets.

In the absence of any interconnection obligation, virtually every telephone market in early twentieth century America reached a "tipping point," in which the largest network—the one with the greatest number of subscribers—became perceived as the single network that everyone had to join, and the rest withered away. The potential for certain industries to slide into monopoly in this manner illustrates an economic phenomenon known as *network effects*. In many markets, individual consumers care very little how many *other* consumers purchase the same products that they buy. For example, the bottle of shampoo you just bought does not become significantly more or less valuable to you as the number of other purchasers of the brand increases or falls. The telecommunications industry, like several other "network industries," is different: the value of the network to *each* user increases or decreases, respectively, with every addition or subtraction of *other* users to the network.

Suppose, for example, that you lived in a midwestern American city in 1900, and there were two non-interconnecting telephone companies offering you service. You would be much more inclined (all else being equal) to select the company operating 80% of the lines rather than the one operating 20% because the odds would be much greater that the people you wished to call would be on the larger network. The absence of interconnection arrangements among rival networks thus creates a cut-throat race to build the largest customer base in the shortest time frame—and then put all rivals out of business by pointing out the dwindling value of their shrinking networks. Economies of scale—a carrier's ability to reduce its per-customer costs by increasing its total number of customers—further accelerates this process by permitting larger carriers to undersell smaller ones in the market.

By the early twentieth century, the U.S. telephone market had "tipped." In most population centers, the victor was the mammoth Bell System: a collection of very large "operating companies" that provided local exchange services and were eventually bound together by a long distance network known as Long Lines. All of the far-flung operations of the Bell System were owned by American Telephone & Telegraph (AT&T), which maintained its own equipment manufacturing arm (Western Electric) and also, for a time, held the rights to patented technologies developed by the Bell System's creator and namesake.

In the areas AT&T did not control, which typically were the less populous ones, the so-called "independent" local telephone companies vied for market share. In many cases, AT&T sought to coerce these independent companies into joining the Bell System by refusing to interconnect them to AT&T Long Lines, which was then the only long distance network in the United States. The independent companies were in no position to build a rival long distance network. Even if they could have cooperated to construct the needed transcontinental facilities (and done so without infringing any remaining AT&T patents), they still could not have used that shared network to send calls through to the increasing majority of Americans who were served by local exchanges owned by the non-interconnecting Bell System. As a result, without interconnection rights, these independent companies could not provide their customers with satisfactory telephone service—i.e., service extending beyond the local serving area—unless they could somehow duplicate the nationwide physical infrastructure the Bell System had built up over several decades of sharp dealing and self-reinforcing good fortune. That was an economic impossibility.

AT&T's coercion of the independent companies ultimately aroused the attention of the Justice Department's antitrust authorities. In the Kingsbury Commitment of 1913, AT&T resolved the dispute by agreeing to interconnect its Long Lines division with these independent local companies and to curb its practice of buying up independent rivals.[8] In exchange, the government placed its effective imprimatur on AT&T's monopoly control over all U.S. telecommunications markets in which it was already dominant. This incident is noteworthy not just because it illustrates the monopolistic tendencies of an unregulated telephone industry, but also because it provides an instructive contrast to the anticompetitive conduct that ultimately led to the breakup of the Bell System 70 years later into its local and long distance components. In 1913, AT&T used its control of the *long distance* market to suppress other *local* carriers. As explained below, AT&T would later leverage its control of most *local* markets to suppress the *long distance* competition that technological advances had made possible by the 1960s.

The network effects phenomenon presents different competitive questions in different industries, and reasonable people can disagree about when the government should require a firm to share access to its customer base. But when such intervention is deemed necessary, the usual solution is an interconnection requirement. Suppose you own a telephone network and one of your subscribers wants to place a call to someone who subscribes to Provider X's network. If Provider X's network is larger than yours, it may have the incentives just described to refuse to interconnect, in which event your subscriber learns that the call has failed—and considers defecting to Provider X. But if the government forces Provider X to take the call onto its network and route it to the intended recipient, your customer remains satisfied, and you stay in business. Interconnection obligations work the other way as well: Provider X cannot preclude its subscribers from reaching yours.

If dealing with network effects were as simple as decreeing that all competing carriers "must interconnect," telecommunications regulation would not be so complex. But many critical details need to be worked out to ensure that two networks cooperate efficiently. For example, when you, the owner of the smaller network, hand off calls for completion by the larger network, how much—if anything—should that larger network be able to charge you for this task? That may seem like a simple question, but it is theoretically quite complex, and answering it incorrectly can have debilitating consequences, as chapter 9 explains.

The physical details of interconnection arrangements can also raise a number of thorny issues. There are many subtle ways in which a larger network operator can disadvantage a smaller one through shoddy interconnection arrangements, such as providing only limited capacity within its interconnection facilities for the receipt of calls from you, the smaller carrier. Your subscribers might then receive an "all circuits busy" signal when they try to call the larger carrier's subscribers during peak calling periods—leaving them, once more, dissatisfied and tempted by the prospect of defection. To prevent such problems, regulators often need to develop rules to govern the operational details of interconnection arrangements and penalize non-compliance.

Although we have focused so far on the telephone industry, network effects are endemic to information technology industries generally, and there are ongoing debates about when, if ever, the government should step in to address any anticompetitive consequences. Consider the market for instant messaging. The key to instant messaging technology is a centralized database, known as a "names and presence directory," which allows a service provider to tell its subscribers when their designated "buddies" have logged on to the same provider's network and are available for a kind of e-mail exchange in real time. So long as each such directory is proprietary to a particular firm and unshared with others, subscribers are likely to value an instant messaging service in direct proportion to the number of their "buddies" who are also subscribers to the same service. This dynamic tends to favor the service provider with the largest customer base, which, in the United States, has traditionally been America Online (AOL).

When it approved AOL's merger with Time Warner in 2001, the FCC expressed concern that the instant messaging market was tipping and that AOL's instant messaging systems—and particularly, in the U.S., "AOL

Instant Messenger"—had accumulated such a large subscriber base that users of instant messaging would feel compelled to choose AOL as their provider. The FCC was particularly alarmed that AOL had dragged its feet in designing an interconnection mechanism that would enable the subscribers of other services to make use of AOL's proprietary names and presence directory and communicate with AOL's subscribers as freely as with each other. Some people cited AOL's reluctance to interconnect as conclusive evidence that the company itself perceived the instant messaging market as likely to tip and produce a lucrative AOL monopoly. As the FCC's then-chief economist later explained: "If it is a more competitive market, the incentive is for all the players to interoperate. There is a mathematical proof on that one."[9]

In the end, the FCC stopped short of ordering AOL to interconnect with its rivals for the generation of instant messaging services that had become familiar to many American consumers. Controversially, however, the FCC did impose an "interoperability" condition for any "advanced," video-oriented applications of instant messaging using high speed Internet services.[10] Instant messaging programs, the FCC reasoned, can be modified to serve as "information platforms" for all sorts of communications applications, including video conferencing; indeed, some people believed that instant messaging would gradually supplant the telephone as the dominant means of person-to-person communication. The FCC feared that, unrestrained by interconnection obligations, AOL's proprietary systems would become *de facto* standards and would become indispensable to residential and business users over time. The FCC thus worried that AOL would end up monopolizing portions of the telecommunications market much as AT&T's Bell System had done almost one hundred years before and would raise consumer prices dramatically once it had succeeded. As AOL's share of instant messaging users steadily declined in the early 2000s, these concerns began to seem overblown and the FCC lifted the interoperability requirement.[11] But such concerns reveal the unusual sensitivity of regulators to the monopolization threat posed by network effects in the communications industry.

One of AOL's fiercest opponents in the instant messaging debate was Microsoft, which offered its own proprietary brand ("MSN Messenger") and had repeatedly tried and failed to interconnect with AOL's instant messaging network. There was no small irony here, for Microsoft was simultaneously defending itself in court against the Justice Department's claims that, in subtly similar ways, it had abused its dominance in the market for personal computer operating systems.

The dominance of Microsoft Windows in today's personal computer market arises from network effects and, specifically, from what antitrust courts have called the *applications barrier to entry*.[12] At some point in the 1980s, software designers realized that more users were choosing Microsoft's operating systems than the alternatives, a choice cemented by Microsoft's eventual development of the Windows "graphical user interface." In response, more and more applications developers created programs only for Windows, leaving would-be rivals (like IBM) to sell operating systems that did not have as many programs designed for them and were therefore less popular. As a result, Microsoft won an increasing share of the operating system market. That, in turn, reinforced the software designers' predictions about the dominance of Windows and their desire to produce applications for it, often to the exclusion of applications for rival operating systems.[13]

In these and other contexts, reasonable people can disagree about whether network effects create any problems for which the government should offer a solution. The proponents of government intervention argue that monopolization is virtually always an evil to be avoided, reasoning that monopolization of any industry necessarily produces higher consumer prices, less product variety, and lower quality. Opponents of government intervention, by contrast, point to a theory of competition, first developed by economist Joseph Schumpeter, that focuses on the "creative destruction" of old incumbents by new insurgents, who are rewarded with monopolies of their own until knocked off their perch by the next round of insurgents.[14] Under this theory, the most significant competition takes place not *within* a market—in the form of price wars or incremental increases in quality—but *for the market itself*: i.e., in establishing the next great invention that will displace the old monopoly with a new one.[15]

The first key premise of the modern-day Schumpeterian perspective is that, in high-tech industries, the next industry-transforming technology could arise at any moment to eclipse the products of today's monopolists.[16] This threat is said to give current monopolists powerful incentives to keep their products as efficient and consumer-friendly as possible. The second key Schumpeterian premise is that the best way to induce entrepreneurs to risk enormous sums in developing revolutionary technologies is to welcome the prospect of a temporary monopoly when those technologies succeed. Because they view temporary monopolies favorably, modern-day Schumpeterians argue for strong intellectual property protection and freedom from both competition-oriented regulation and aggressive antitrust enforcement.[17] As Richard Posner has put it: "The gale of creative destruction that Schumpeter described, in which a sequence of temporary monopolies operates to maximize innovation that confers social benefits far in excess of the social costs of the short-lived monopoly prices that the process also gives rise to, may be the reality of the new economy."[18]

Although network effects can dramatically influence the course of competition in information industries, the arguments for and against government intervention to counteract that influence are subtle and specific to each individual market. Nonetheless, today there is broad consensus that the government should impose interconnection obligations on ordinary telephone networks. One reason for this is that the telephone market, with its high fixed costs, is characterized not just by network effects, but also by enormous *economies of scale and density* (which we discuss below). Without interconnection rights, a new provider could not offer its customers effective telephone service—i.e., service capable of reaching all the people those customers wish to call—unless the provider first builds a new, ubiquitous physical network whose geographic scope rivals that of the dominant network, and then finds some way of underwriting that network without passing on its unusually high per-customer costs to its initially small customer base. To articulate this challenge is to reveal the economic near-impossibility of meeting it.

B. Economies of scale and density

Although our discussion treats "network effects" and "scale economies" as two separate phenomena, they are in fact closely related. Each describes a characteristic of markets in which, all else held constant, increasing the scale of a firm's operations improves the ratio of (i) the value of the firm's services to each customer, and thus the revenues the firm can obtain from that customer, to (ii) the per-customer cost to the firm of providing those services. Network effects improve this ratio by increasing the value of the service to each customer, whereas scale economies improve it by decreasing the per-customer cost of providing that service. In the absence of regulation, each result would play a powerful role in favoring larger scale telecommunications firms over their smaller rivals.

Interconnection obligations significantly lower the entry barriers posed by the combination of network effects and scale economies because, as discussed, they exempt a new entrant from the need to build a ubiquitous network before competing for the dominant carrier's customers. But interconnection obligations do not eliminate those entry barriers altogether. Although they reduce any advantage that incumbents derive from network effects, they do not ensure that new entrants will benefit from the enormous scale economies enjoyed by a provider with a large, established customer base. As discussed below, the lion's share of controversy about the Telecommunications Act of 1996 stems from disagreement about how best to deal with this concern.

Any telecommunications carrier contemplating the construction of a new network faces immense initial costs, including, for example, the costs of digging trenches and laying thousands of miles of cable to reach different customer locations. These costs are both *fixed*, in that the carrier must incur them up front before it can provide any volume of service, and *sunk*, in that, once made, the investment cannot be put to some other use—a fact that makes the investment particularly risky.[19] In contrast, the marginal cost of providing service to each additional customer, once the network is up and running, is often tiny by comparison. Given these enormous fixed costs and negligible marginal costs, the carrier's long run average costs within a defined geographic area—i.e., its long run costs per line in service—may well decline with every increase in the size of its network, all else held constant. Put differently, it is often cheaper per customer for a carrier to provide service to the one millionth customer than to the one thousandth customer.

Closely related to such economies of scale are economies of density. These are best explained by way of example. Imagine a 1000-unit beach condominium complex that is both distant from any telephone company switching station and, because of zoning restrictions, isolated from other buildings. If the fixed costs of laying a cable from the nearest switch to that complex were $100,000, a single telephone provider serving the entire complex could spread the recovery of those costs among all 1000 sub-scribers for a cost of $100 per subscriber. But if ten providers divided up that customer base equally after laying their own cables to the same com-plex—each digging up the streets at different times and incurring the same fixed $100,000 cost—the average cost of that ten-fold effort would rise to $1000 per customer, for each provider could spread its $100,000 costs only over 100 customers rather than 1000.* In this respect, economies of density can be roughly conceptualized as scale economies within a partic-ular geographic area, such as the condominium complex in our example. For ease of exposition, we will use the term "scale economies" broadly to include these economies of density.[20]

Of course, high fixed costs and low marginal costs lead to large scale economies in many industries, from auto manufacturing to applications software production, and most such industries have never been subject to pervasive schemes of prescriptive economic regulation. The difference is one of degree. In some settings, scale economies do not increase "over the entire extent of the market,"[21] for there are diminishing returns to scale at some level of production. In other settings, however, scale economies keep increasing until a provider is serving all customers in the market. In that context, because a single firm can serve the whole market (however defined) with lower overall costs per customer than could multiple firms, the market is said to be a *natural monopoly.*[22]

The government has traditionally addressed such a market by award-ing a monopoly to a single firm and heavily regulating it, on the theory that

---

* Economies of density also explain why telephone service is much more costly to provide in rural than urban areas. Suppose your company runs a telecommunica-tions network on a rigidly fixed budget. Would you rather (1) build one line to each of 1000 customers living on widely dispersed farms or (2) 1000 lines to one apart-ment building with 1000 units? Even if the average line length were the same in each example (say, because the apartment building is farther away from your switching station than half of the farms), you would still much rather serve the apartment building because you would only have to dig up the ground once to lay the lines needed to serve those 1000 units. If you picked the farms option, you would need to dig up the ground many more times to lay 1000 different cables, and you would have to pay far more to obtain the rights of way as well (although the lower rural land values would slightly offset those higher costs).

this is the best way to keep consumer prices low. As Richard Posner once explained, in describing a similar phenomenon in the cable television business:

You can start with a competitive free-for-all—different cable television systems frantically building out their grids and signing up subscribers in an effort to bring down their average costs faster than their rivals—but eventually there will be only a single company, because until a company serves the whole market it will have an incentive to keep expanding in order to lower its average costs. In the interim there may be wasteful duplication of facilities. This duplication may lead not only to higher prices to cable television subscribers, at least in the short run, but also to higher costs to other users of the public ways, who must compete with the cable television companies for access to them. An alternative procedure is to pick the most efficient competitor at the outset, give him a monopoly, and extract from him in exchange a commitment to provide reasonable service at reasonable rates.[23]

Similar considerations led regulators for many years to conclude—somewhat controversially in hindsight—that the whole telephone market was a natural monopoly in this sense and that the "alternative procedure" Posner described would be the optimal means of ensuring dependable service at low rates.

This natural monopoly premise provided a convenient solution to the problem of network effects as well. Because (the thinking went) there was no reason to allow a second or third provider into the same geographic market to begin with, since that would only dilute the incumbent's economies of scale, there was no need to worry about forcing the incumbent to interconnect with competitors. The principal exception, illustrated by the Kingsbury Commitment, seems almost trivial in this light: different geographic regions would be served by different monopoly providers of local service, and the government would ensure simply that neighboring monopolists interconnected with each other for the exchange of calls between their respective regions and that the national monopoly provider of long distance service (AT&T) allowed all of these monopolies access to the rest of the country.

Relying on this natural monopoly premise, many regulators not only refused to order interconnection among potential rivals, but straightforwardly prohibited new market entry by granting exclusive franchises to the monopolists. In part, policymakers resisted competition not just because they believed in the economics of natural monopoly theory, but also because they relied on regulated monopolies to advance various social policies, most notably "universal service." For example, regulators deliberately kept prices for business customers high (compared to the underlying cost of serving them) as a means of cross-subsidizing affordable rates for other users, such as residential customers in rural areas where economies of scale and density are low.[24] As we will discuss later, this scheme can work over the long term only to the extent that rival providers are barred from competing for the business customers who pay the above-cost rates that subsidize low rates for others.

For many years, AT&T's Bell System invoked "universal service" concerns to persuade regulators to bar competition in all telephone-related markets, including equipment manufacturing as well as local and long distance services. Its long-lived regulatory success in this respect provides a classic case study in *public choice theory*—the economic analysis of relations between market participants and the government officials they seek to influence.[25] Public choice theory holds that private economic actors will exploit regulatory schemes to extract "rents" from policymakers: i.e., special benefits that arise from political influence rather than economically valuable contributions to social welfare. Successful rent-seeking need not, and usually does not, take the form of outright bribery. Instead, private actors look for ways to match their own pecuniary interests with the political goals of regulators. In the case of telephone regulation, the suppression of competition in the name of "universal service" gave AT&T what it wanted—formally protected monopoly status—and gave the regulators what they wanted: a hidden scheme for underwriting low residential rates that avoided all the political costs presented by a more explicit and tax-like system.[26] The victims of such Faustian bargains are consumers, who in the long run might well be better off, at least in the aggregate, if regulators made the hard political choices necessary to remove barriers to competition.

Starting in the 1970s, policymakers began questioning the natural monopoly assumptions that had been conventional wisdom almost since the inception of the industry.[27] This process followed a predictable pattern, as we will discuss in chapter 2. After the FCC adopted rules allowing competition in the provision of telecommunications equipment, the markets that next fell prey to competition were the ones in which overall call volumes were so huge, and the incumbent's retail prices were so far above economic cost, that a competitor could efficiently build a rival network and earn large profits even though it had only a small share of the total customer base. The first such market was for business-oriented long distance services between major cities, a market that MCI and other firms entered in the 1970s and 1980s with the help of both microwave technology and the courts. The second was the market for so-called "access services": the high-speed links between local networks and long distance networks. In each case, the companies that owned the core "natural monopoly" assets—the local exchanges, with their "last mile" connections to every home and business in a given calling area—tried to thwart this nascent competition by (among other things) refusing to interconnect with the upstarts or by making interconnection unnecessarily burdensome. In each case, the U.S. government stepped in and mandated non-discriminatory interconnection.

Finally, in the Telecommunications Act of 1996, Congress seemed to dispense with the natural monopoly premise altogether. It abolished all exclusive franchises, ordered all telecommunications carriers to interconnect with any requesting carrier, and declared all "local exchange" markets—in addition to the long distance and "access" markets—open for competition. But Congress could not repeal the laws of economics. In many settings, it remained commercially infeasible for new competitors to build redundant "local" wireline networks bridging the last mile to all of their subscribers' buildings. The main exception to this rule lay in some local exchange markets—such as densely populated, downtown business districts—where high volumes of voice and data traffic enabled new entrants to exploit fiber-optic technology by building telecommunications networks all the way to their customers. In less densely populated areas, however, such as many suburbs and most rural areas, call volumes could not support the efficient construction of wholly duplicative networks replete with thousands upon thousands of wired connections to all homes and businesses. To be sure, firms were successfully building new *wireless* telephone networks in these areas, but, until recently, disparities in price and service quality have kept customers from replacing, rather than merely supplementing, their landline phones with wireless ones.

This tension—between (i) the competitive aspirations of the 1996 legislation and (ii) the stubborn economic characteristics governing the last mile—is a central focus of the next two chapters. Congress attempted to resolve that tension in part by granting new entrants rights to *lease capacity* on the facilities owned by the incumbent telephone company, enabling them to "participate" in the incumbent's economies of scale by availing themselves of the same low per-unit costs. But Congress left all of the major decisions about such compelled leasing arrangements to federal and state regulators. Almost a decade later, there is no consensus about the most basic questions: which facilities a new entrant should be entitled to lease from incumbents, for how long, and at what price; and what to do if the relevant regulations are violated. These abiding controversies remain important to the future of the telecommunications industry, and chapter 3 and appendixes A and B address them in detail.

C. Monopoly leveraging and the concept of "information platforms"

So far, we have addressed the regulation of *horizontal* relationships within the telecommunications industry: the relationships between competing providers of substitutable services. Now we introduce the equally complex set of issues presented by *vertical* relationships between providers of communications-related goods or services in complementary ("adjacent") markets. These relationships arise across the economy: between, for example, wheat farms and bakeries, and between bakeries and grocery stores. Vertical integration by a firm across different markets is often desirable because it can produce significant *economies of scope:* cost efficiencies obtained by producing several products at once. In most industries, moreover, competition in each of the adjacent markets liberates these vertical relationships from the need for heavy governmental oversight. To the extent the government gets involved, it is typically through ad hoc enforcement of the antitrust laws.

The telecommunications industry has historically been different for reasons relating to the nature and regulation of the market for last mile services. Telephone companies and cable companies are often vertically integrated: they provide not just various last mile transmission services—the markets in which they are often dominant—but a variety of complementary services as well, such as Internet access, long distance voice service, and video programming. Competitive concerns arise when such companies are asked to bargain with rival providers in those adjacent markets about the terms of access to their last mile facilities. Although many firms wish to sell you telecommunications-related services—say, long distance, Internet access, or video programming—you may not be able to accept any of their offers unless the local telephone or cable company agrees to transmit these firms' signals into your home or business. And your local telephone or cable company *may* have incentives to discriminate against these unaffiliated firms if it is simultaneously trying to sell you competing long distance, Internet access, or video programming services of its own.

The reason a monopoly provider of last mile transmission services might want to discriminate against providers of complementary services is not as obvious as it might seem. It is instructive to contrast such last mile providers with a monopoly firm like Microsoft. Although Microsoft has a monopoly in the operating system market (Windows), it lets other companies write a variety of software applications that ride on top of the Windows platform. Since the government does not regulate Microsoft's price for Windows, Microsoft can maximize its monopoly profits simply by charging supracompetitive prices in the operating system market that it monopolizes. Microsoft thus would not normally benefit from using its Windows monopoly to exclude unaffiliated software companies from designing applications that enhance the consumer value of Windows.

This scenario illustrates an economic insight, known as the *one monopoly profit* principle, identified with the nineteenth century French economist Antoine Cournot. This principle holds, among other things, that the total profits a monopolist could earn if it sought to leverage its monopoly in one market by monopolizing an adjacent market are equivalent to the extra profits it could earn anyway simply by charging more for the monopoly product itself.[28] Cournot illustrated this point by hypothesizing the relationship between separate zinc and copper monopolies and its effect on the "downstream" market for the alloy of those two elements: brass. As recently summarized by Berkeley economist Hal Varian: "If the copper producer cuts its price, brass producers will buy more zinc, thereby increasing the profits of the zinc producer. But the zinc producer's additional profits are irrelevant to the copper producer, making it reluctant to cut its price too much. The result is that the copper producer sets a price that is higher than the price that would maximize joint profits."[29] This means, among other things, that the zinc monopolist may well benefit from competition

in the copper market because, as the price of copper falls, it can appropriate more of the profit-maximizing price that is paid in the aggregate for the
two constituent elements of brass.

Microsoft likewise benefits from encouraging other firms to develop
new applications that run on Windows because so doing will drive additional demand for Windows and cement its monopoly grip on the operating system market. Put in economic terms, the benefit that a platform
provider gains from added applications for its product is a *complementary
externality*, which means the platform itself will be valued in direct proportion to the proliferation of complementary products, no matter what their
source. Perhaps counterintuitively, the high-profile antitrust case against
Microsoft is entirely consistent with these observations. Microsoft decided
to crush Netscape not because Netscape had designed an ordinary Internet
browser that could run on top of Windows (and thus enhance its value),
but because Netscape had designed an Internet browser that could radically decrease the value of Windows. Microsoft feared that Netscape could
eventually serve as a rival platform in its own right, on top of which end
users could run software applications, regardless of the underlying operating system. Netscape, in other words, threatened to tear down the "applications barrier to entry" that protects Windows' monopoly: it could
potentially reduce both the need for software companies to design applications specifically for Windows and the need for consumers to purchase
computers with Windows installed.[30]

The telecommunications industry gives rise to similar issues. The basic
question, which recurs in many different forms, is whether a dominant
provider of a given telecommunications platform—such as last mile transmission to homes and offices—has appropriate incentives to let independent firms compete freely in adjacent markets, such as long distance service
or Internet access.[31] One critical variable in answering that question is
whether the dominant provider, like Microsoft, has reason to fear that an
independent firm in an adjacent market could develop a product that
threatens to supplant the platform monopoly itself. Another key variable is
whether the platform service is—unlike Microsoft Windows—subject to
price regulation. If so, the "one monopoly profit" phenomenon will not
apply, and the provider may well have incentives to discriminate against
firms in adjacent markets, because it will be unable to recoup all otherwise
available monopoly profits from the sale of the platform itself and will
need to extract them instead from those other markets.

This latter exception to the "one monopoly profit" rule is sometimes called *Baxter's Law* in honor of William Baxter, the Justice Department official who cited it, in the early 1980s, as a reason for breaking up AT&T's Bell System to keep it from leveraging its monopoly in local markets to suppress competition in the adjacent long distance market. The problem arose largely because, as discussed, AT&T was allowed to charge above-cost prices for long distance service, telecommunications equipment, and various other products to compensate for the very low rates its Bell affiliates were forced to charge for local residential service. This scheme could work only if other firms could not compete for the customers that were paying above-cost prices. Thus, when new entrants such as MCI sought to enter the long distance market to compete for those customers, AT&T opposed MCI's efforts on the ground (among others) that it would endanger the traditional commitment to "universal service" by removing the source of support for the local services it was sometimes required to provide below cost.

The efforts of AT&T's pre-divestiture Bell System to disadvantage these rivals led to an antitrust suit by the federal government that changed the face of telecommunications regulation. After many years of litigation, AT&T ultimately entered into a consent decree under which it divested the regional Bell companies in January 1984. The new corporate entity that inherited the AT&T name kept Long Lines, the research and equipment manufacturing arms later spun off as Lucent Technologies, and a few other units. The Bell operating companies kept the local exchanges but were subject to various restrictions on the lines of business they could pursue, including a ban on the provision of long distance services and the manufacture of telecommunications equipment. This quarantine was an aggressive remedy—but, as discussed in chapter 2, the antitrust authorities concluded that it was necessary to counter the tendency of AT&T's vertically integrated Bell System to discriminate against long distance and equipment manufacturing competitors. The individual Bell companies began winning approval to enter the markets for long distance service and equipment manufacturing fifteen years later, after proving to the FCC on a state-by-state basis that they had opened their local exchange markets to competition and had set up separate long distance affiliates as a structural safeguard against discrimination. This process, governed by sections 271 and 273 of the Communications Act, is described more fully in chapter 3.

During the same general period as the AT&T divestiture, the FCC adopted somewhat less radical measures to deal with the perceived threats of monopoly leveraging that telephone companies posed to "enhanced service providers," which include such companies as Lexis-Nexis, voicemail providers, and—most important of all—what we now call "Internet service providers" (ISPs). In orders known collectively as the *Computer Inquiries*, the FCC required each telephone company, among other things, to sell enhanced service providers whatever basic transmission services it provides to its own enhanced service operations and on the same terms. Until recently, this policy could be justified as another straightforward application of Baxter's law. The telephone company's transmission services were price-regulated, and its network was long considered an indispensable bridge between enhanced service providers and their customers.

In the late 1990s, however, the emergence of broadband (high-speed) Internet access began drawing that justification into question. Such access is *not* generally subject to price ceilings. Just as important, it is offered not just by telephone companies, but by competing providers with technologically dissimilar transmission platforms as well, such as the "cable modem" service offered by cable television companies. As discussed in chapter 5, a key dispute in telecommunications policy today is the extent to which traditional anti-leveraging rules will remain appropriate as broadband eclipses traditional dial-up connections as the Internet access method of choice.

Our discussion of monopoly leveraging has focused so far on the last mile transmission services provided by telephone companies because, until recently, there was little doubt that those companies owned the only feasible path to consumers for certain telecommunications-related services. But leveraging issues have also cropped up in various other settings within the communications industry.

For example, the FCC has struggled for years to justify caps on the size of cable television companies. (Related limits, which the Commission controversially relaxed in June 2003, also apply to the ownership of television broadcast stations, as discussed in chapter 11.) The theory underlying these "horizontal ownership restrictions" is that the local cable company is dominant in any given geographic area in the provision of multi-channel video programming to the home. Congress and the FCC feared that, if any one cable company (say, Time Warner) served too large a share of the American public, that company could exert undue influence in the market for television programming by, for example, giving preferential treatment to its own affiliated studios (say, HBO).[32] By adopting rules to limit the extent to which a single firm can own multiple cable systems, the FCC sought to limit the creation and exercise of "monopsony" power (i.e., dominance in the purchasing market) that could doom independent programming studios, which cannot finance the creation of television shows unless those shows can be expected to reach a critical mass of the viewing public.

In 2001, the D.C. Circuit[33] invalidated the FCC's decision to limit the subscribership of any one cable company to 30% of the total number of subscribers to multi-channel video programming services (i.e., cable plus satellite). The court concluded, among other things, that the FCC's underlying economic reasoning—dubbed "antitrust lite" by its critics—had underestimated the emerging significance of satellite television services as an alternative platform for independent programming. Even though the number of cable subscribers dwarfs the number of satellite subscribers, Judge Stephen Williams, writing for the court, explained that "a company's ability to exercise market power depends not only on its share of the market, but also on the elasticities of supply and demand, which in turn are determined by the *availability* of competition. . . . If [a cable company] refuses to offer new programming, customers with access to [satellite service] may switch."[34] That possibility, in turn, may cause even very large cable companies to worry less about dominating the programming market than about reinforcing the value of their cable "platform" by purchasing attractive programming for its viewers—without regard to which studio created it.

Throughout this book, we will return to this basic scenario: a firm that dominates a platform market, and is regulated on the premise that it could leverage that platform dominance to control an adjacent market for applications, becomes subject to competition from the provider of a new alternative platform made possible by technological innovation. Such competition can suddenly arise to confront any dominant platform, from the conventional cable television platform we have just discussed (now contested by satellite TV services), to the telephone platform used for Internet access (now contested by cable companies), to AOL's instant messaging platform (threatened by Microsoft's and Yahoo's instant messaging products), to Microsoft's operating system platforms (threatened by "open source" operating systems such as Linux).

The unpredictable growth of such *cross-platform* competition in previously monopolistic industries presents policymakers with several critical challenges.* Despite political pressures and bureaucratic inertia, they must (i) judge how strongly entrenched a proprietary information platform might be; (ii) weigh the benefits of anti-leveraging regulation against the costs of dampened incentives to innovate in a sometimes Schumpeterian world of "serial monopolies"; (iii) calibrate any regulations they do adopt to the actual leveraging threat the platform poses to applications markets; (iv) act promptly in modifying or withdrawing those anti-leveraging regulations once platform competition develops; and (v) remain wary of the administrative costs inherent in market intervention and of the unintended consequences of poorly designed regulation. On the one hand, regulators understandably want to adopt policies that will promote welfare-maximizing competition over the long term. On the other hand, they do not want to interfere with market forces in a way that will undermine the incumbents' own efforts to create consumer value. Incumbents often stand in the best position to develop valuable new products for consumers, and excessive regulation can stop that innovation in its tracks. Similarly, if regulators react too slowly in modifying regulations that mistakenly presuppose that a once-monopolistic platform has no rivals, they will artificially advantage the rival platform provider in its efforts to steal customers off the incumbent platform. We now turn to this question of *regulatory parity* in a world of rapidly evolving telecommunications technology.

---

* Many commentators and the FCC use the term "intermodal competition" to describe competition among technologically dissimilar platforms. We prefer the somewhat broader term "cross-platform competition." From a competition policy standpoint, the most important issue is whether an incumbent faces facilities-based competition in the form of a rival platform, not what particular technology ("mode") the rival might use. At the same time, the particular technology used to enter the platform market may have important consequences under any regulatory regime, since the new technology may well be immune from legacy regulations applicable only to the traditional platform provider.

II. Convergence

Very roughly speaking, most forms of telecommunications fall into one of two general categories. *Point-to-point* communication involves the transmission of content—e.g., the placement of a "call"—from a person or machine to a discrete recipient. Examples include ordinary telephone calls and fax transmissions. *Broadcasting* involves the transmission of content to the world at large, or at least anyone who cares to watch or listen. Examples include television and radio programming. This dichotomy has always been a bit of an oversimplification, and the Internet—with its mass e-mails and simultaneous webcasting—has blurred the distinction still further. But most forms of telecommunications today still fall into one of these two categories, particularly if we broadly construe the "points" in "point-to-point" communications to include moving cellular telephones.

For most of the twentieth century, people closely identified each of these categories of service with a particular medium of transmission. In particular, they assumed that commercial point-to-point voice services ("telephony") would be conveyed over the copper wires of the telephone system, and that radio and television broadcasting services would be provided over the airwaves. The Communications Act of 1934 was originally written with this assumption in mind. Congress designed Title II of the Act to govern wireline "common carriers"—i.e., the companies that provided telephone service indiscriminately to the public at large. And it designed Title III to govern "radio communications," a category that grew to encompass both radio and television broadcasting. Under Title III, the FCC licensed radio and television stations to use the airwaves to broadcast programming "in the public interest."

And so the world remained until the 1960s, when something peculiar happened: companies increasingly began to transmit television signals not over the airwaves, but over wires. For a long time, such "cable television" service provided no new programming; it was designed only to transmit stronger signals of conventional broadcast programming to people whose homes were too far away from a transmission tower to receive clear pictures (or any pictures). Even so, the seeming anomaly of wires being used for broadcasting threw the regulatory world into tumult, for it raised questions about how the FCC could legally follow through on its expressed intent to regulate this new creature and preempt contrary state and local regulation. After all, Title II addressed common carriage, not broadcasting, and Title III addressed use of the airwaves, not wires.

The FCC ultimately asserted what it called its "ancillary jurisdiction" to regulate anything that affected the explicit subjects of its regulatory authority. In this case, the FCC concluded that because cable television transmissions affected commercial over-the-air broadcasting, the Commission had the right to regulate them under the general enabling authority provided in Title I of the Act. In 1984, long after the Supreme Court upheld the exercise of this strikingly open-ended regulatory authority (in 1968),[35] Congress stepped in and added a new Title VI to the Communications Act to govern federal, state, and local regulation of cable television services.

In the 1980s, "cellular" wireless technology gave consumers an altogether new means of placing telephone calls. This technology uses the radio spectrum—long the province of specialized broadcasts by taxi dispatchers and policemen in addition to television and radio stations—for regular communications among members of the public at large. This development produced another anomaly unanticipated in the structure of the 1934 Act: the use of the *airwaves* to provide a common carrier-type service. Congress eventually patched this hole by adding provisions to Title III to govern the regulation of this new service.

The use of radio signals to carry telephone calls, and of wires to carry broadcast programming, are examples of *technological convergence*: the coming together of different technologies to provide similar services. But the examples of convergence just discussed are tame in comparison to the upheavals triggered by the Internet. By placing a "call" over your Internet connection to a distant website, you can listen, along with the citizens of Prague, to the broadcast of a Czech radio station. With a click of the mouse, you can sign on to Launch.com, an interactive Yahoo!-sponsored music service that keeps track of the music you like and sends you—and you alone—a personalized stream of songs. With another click of the mouse, you can chat with a friend across the world through instant messaging. Alternatively, by plugging special telephone hardware into any broadband connection, you can speak to the same friend using *voice over Internet protocol* (VoIP) services that are so clear and refined that, for all practical purposes, you may as well be talking over a traditional telephone circuit. And, so long as you have a broadband connection of some type, you can do all these things no matter how the Internet signals come into your home: whether through your telephone line ("digital subscriber line" or "DSL"), your television cable ("cable modem"), a high speed wireless connection, or someday even your electric power line.

The contemporary forms of convergence are largely the result of digital technology, which came of age commercially in the 1980s and 1990s. As chapter 4 discusses in depth, digital technology provides concise mathematical representations of the world, in the form of 1s and 0s, that software inside your computer decodes and converts into everything from voice conversations to photographs to documents to Prague radio broadcasts. The Internet forms a convenient means of transporting those 1s and 0s, also known as *bits*, between computers (or other devices with data processing capability). The computers on each end of a data session do not "care" what physical conduits link them together, so long as the bits are delivered quickly enough for the relevant software programs to run properly. And, for the most part, the Internet's physical infrastructure has not traditionally "cared" what software programs those bits are associated with; it just delivers the 1s and 0s and lets the computers do the rest. In part because "a bit is just a bit" in this sense, the Internet severs any strong logical or practical link between communications *services* and the physical *media* over which they are transmitted to consumers.

For the telecommunications market to function efficiently, this comprehensive technological convergence must be matched by an equally comprehensive *regulatory* convergence. Except where lingering natural monopoly conditions make one provider dominant in a particular market, like services should generally be regulated alike, no matter what physical medium is used to provide them. Consider a rough analogy. Perhaps it made sense to regulate the incumbent railroad operators heavily in the days when railroad tracks were genuine monopoly facilities, before the interstate highways made trucking a feasible alternative for many customers with long haul transportation needs. But it made less sense to regulate the railways as heavily once trucking became a vibrant source of competition.

Similar considerations apply in the telecommunications industry. Take, for example, the case of telephony, the transmission of ordinary voice conversations between two or more people. Cable television companies have begun invading the telephone companies' core markets by offering subscribers voice services of their own, most recently in the form of VoIP applications that ride on top of the cable companies' broadband Internet platform. Even when cable companies do not themselves offer voice services, stand-alone VoIP providers like Vonage are happy to sell them directly to consumers as one broadband application among many. And wireless telephone service adds another dimension of cross-platform competition to the mix. Increasing numbers of Americans have begun "cutting the cord" by relying *entirely* on their wireless phone for all of their voice communications, a development facilitated by the FCC's recent decision to enable consumers to take their wireline telephone numbers with them when they sign up for wireless service, as discussed in chapter 8.

Eventually, cross-platform competition may so thoroughly deprive the wireline telephone companies of their traditional market power that it will no longer make sense to think of them—or regulate them—as natural monopoly providers of voice services. As it happens, Congress anticipated in 1996 that cable companies would begin providing ordinary telephone service to their customers, and it took steps to make sure that they would receive no special advantages or disadvantages in so doing. What Congress did *not* foresee is that telephone companies and cable companies would soon compete in a different and potentially more important market: the market for providing broadband Internet access. Cable companies provide their version of such access (cable modem service) over the same facilities they use to provide ordinary cable television service. Similarly, telephone companies provide their version (DSL) over ordinary telephone lines. The two services are market substitutes, and they are offered to the public in fierce head-to-head competition. But they are not regulated alike: telephone companies providing DSL are currently subject to burdensome wholesale regulations to which cable companies providing cable modem service are not subject, even though cable providers have a larger share of the U.S. residential broadband market than telephone companies.

The story of broadband regulation, discussed in chapters 5 and 6, is important not just because it exemplifies the tenacious influence of obsolete regulatory assumptions in the age of convergence, but also because the government's resolution of the "regulatory parity" debate, whenever it comes, will dramatically affect the future of the telecommunications industry as a whole. Data traffic used to constitute a tiny percentage of the signals flowing over a voice-centric network; soon, however, voice traffic will become just a small minority population of bits flowing over a data-centric network. More generally, the last link between technological platforms and particular services will be weakened, if not severed, once all applications are carried as indistinguishable bit-streams over different platforms. As we approach that date, a regulatory regime that still treats substitutable platforms differently will distort the marketplace by, among other things, creating artificial regulatory advantages for one set of competitors over another. For the most part, policymakers know this. But, as we shall see, the entrenched commercial interests that benefit from the regulatory status quo make it politically difficult for policymakers to fix the problem by overhauling the rules.

* * *

One of the more dispiriting moments in the writing of this book came in a local Starbucks, where a friendly middle-aged woman pointed at the laptop on which these words were written and asked what the book was about. Upon learning that it was about telecommunications policy, she made a face. Then, when prompted to explain herself, she volunteered that she found the whole telecommunications industry confusing: she missed the simpler times, when one company—Ma Bell—served all needs and sent out unitary bills that ordinary people could understand. She is not alone. Millions of Americans wonder whether all this technological and regulatory upheaval is "worth the candle," as Justice Stephen Breyer (a former professor of regulatory law) has mused.[36]

In essence, this question asks whether the benefits of introducing competition to this previously monopolized industry warrant the tumult that such competition entails. In general, government management of a monopoly regime inevitably produces not just waste, but also a maze of politically expedient yet economically artificial regulatory distinctions. Economic competition finds and destroys each such distinction and destabilizes the whole regulatory house of cards. For example, as discussed in chapters 2 and 10, competition in the markets for business and long distance services has undermined the traditional universal service regime of implicit cross-subsidies. Business and long distance customers traditionally paid the telephone monopolist above-cost rates to subsidize below-cost rates for basic local service in some areas. But once business and frequent long distance callers have a choice of telecommunications carriers, and once they learn they can send by e-mail what they would otherwise send through expensive hour-long fax transmissions over traditional telephone networks, they will no longer buy the erstwhile monopolist's services at the inflated prices that traditionally supported other people's low phone rates. The ultimate result is either an increase in those rates or a proliferation of confusing tax-like fees that appear on telephone bills. From an economic perspective, either result is much more efficient than the cross-subsidy regime. But each is politically quite unpopular. In the short term, overt price hikes and new line-item fees tend to attract far more controversy than adherence to a quietly inefficient (albeit ultimately unsustainable) scheme in which retail rates stay at more or less the same levels but, unbeknownst to the ordinary consumer, bear no rational relationship to underlying costs.

To be sure, today's regulatory climate would be simpler if Congress had acted more decisively in drafting the Telecommunications Act of 1996, a crazy-quilt of ambiguous provisions designed, as we shall see, to leave many of the important questions unanswered so as to offend no powerful interest groups. And the world would also be simpler if Americans had kept their perspective during the Internet gold rush of the late 1990s, instead of cheering on massive overinvestment in certain types of telecommunications infrastructure—such as the unused fiber-optic capacity known as "dark fiber"—on the catastrophically misguided assumption that "supply will create its own demand." The result of that overinvestment, as everyone knows, was a string of corporate scandals and bankruptcies several years later. But even if Congress and the business community had exercised better judgment in the waning years of the twentieth century, the growth of competition still would have generated litigation and economic displacement. The question remains: is facilitating competition worth the candle?

In the long run, the answer is surely yes. The very premise of capitalism is that a competitive market, as compared to a monopolistic one, creates more innovation, greater product variety, increased efficiency, lower costs, and lower average prices. The telecommunications market is no exception to this rule. For example, AT&T deployed very little optical fiber in its long distance network until its new rivals—specifically, MCI and Sprint—placed a bet on that new technology, ordered materials and equipment from Corning, and advertised the "pin drop" clarity of their long distance services as compared to AT&T's. Moreover, competition not only keeps monopolists from complacency, but removes any incentive they may have to withhold the deployment of new services that could "cannibalize" their less efficient but more profitable old services. For example, the growth of cable modem service and other broadband options appears to have helped induce incumbent telephone companies to roll out broadband DSL services more vigorously than they otherwise might because, in the *absence* of competition, they would make more money if they continued to sell the previous generation of often less efficient transmission technologies.

Even apart from technological improvements, competition also leads to marketing innovations. For example, competition among wireless companies has not only driven wireless prices down, but also revolutionized the very structure of pricing for voice services. Depending on your expected usage, you can choose a wireless plan with a low monthly fee, relatively few "free" minutes, and extra charges for roaming and long distance; or you can buy a plan with a higher monthly fee, a bucket of virtually unlimited "free" minutes, and no extra charge for roaming or long distance; or you can purchase any number of plans with variations on these pricing themes. What's more, if you're reasonably happy with your wireless service, you can, as noted, "cut the cord" of your conventional wireline service, as many people, most of them young, have already done. Indeed, wireless offers a key feature that, by definition, landline service cannot: mobility.

This raises an intriguing question. As discussed in chapters 7 and 8, wireless services have not yet made wireline voice services superfluous. This is mostly because of quality concerns stemming from, first, zoning restrictions on the placement of antennas and, second, the government's limitations on the radio spectrum available to commercial wireless carriers. These quality concerns will probably abate over time, however, with innovations in both wireless technology and federal spectrum policy. Once a critical percentage of customers in a given market considers wireless service (at least) a substitute for wireline service, why would it make sense to continue regulating any wireline service in that market more than wireless service, which is regulated hardly at all?

That question points to light at the end of the regulatory tunnel. The cut-throat rivalry among multiple companies in the wireless market promotes the interests of consumers in that market far better than any regulator could. The ultimate aspiration of telecommunications policy is to do for the telecommunications industry *generally* what the FCC's deregulatory policies have helped do for the wireless sector *specifically*. Imagine a world in which neither the telephone company nor the cable company nor any other company could exercise market power in the provision of any telecommunications-related service because technological innovation has supplied alternative, facilities-based platforms for each such service. In that world, little regulatory significance would attach to categories like "local," "long distance," "voice," or "data"—or even "telephone" or "cable." A call would just be a call, a carrier would just be a carrier, and a bit would just be a bit. Getting from here to there is every bit as complicated as it is important. Illuminating that path is the project of this book.

2

Introduction to Wireline Telecommunications

In March 2002, the FCC renamed the "Common Carrier Bureau," one of its largest and most important operating divisions, the "Wireline Competition Bureau." The term is a bit of a misnomer because this Bureau regulates some wires but not others. For example, the Bureau oversees broadband Internet services when offered over the copper loops of telephone companies, whereas the "Media Bureau"—which has general responsibility for cable regulation and broadcasting—oversees competing broadband Internet services offered over the facilities of cable television companies.

For present purposes, however, we will go along with the FCC and use the term "wireline" to specify those landline networks—such as ordinary telephone networks—that are designed chiefly to provide point-to-point voice and data services. As we have explained, local telephone companies were long deemed natural monopoly providers of "last mile" transmission for high quality voice and data services. Today, cross-platform competition—ranging from wireless telephony to VoIP services offered over cable modem platforms—has drawn into question many of the regulations designed to curb wireline telephone companies' now-fading monopoly power.

Understanding the debate about the continuing need for such regulations requires some familiarity with the basic technology and regulatory history of traditional telephone networks. Part I of this chapter addresses the technology; part II addresses retail rate regulation of telephone service; and part III discusses the advent of competition in telephone markets from the 1970s to the eve of the Telecommunications Act of 1996. Chapter 3 will then discuss the current rules governing competition among wireline carriers. And chapters 4-10 will discuss, among other matters, the policy issues raised by competition between wireline telecommunications carriers and their *non*-wireline rivals, such as cable companies and wireless carriers.

I. A Primer on Wireline Technology

Placing a telephone call is so routine that it is easy to forget how astonishingly complex the process is. By picking up the receiver and punching some numbers, you can reach anyone with access to a telephone anywhere in the world. This is an uncanny feat: the global telephone system must locate that person among a billion other telephone subscribers—and then establish a connection with her that twists and turns through aerial wires and underground cables and a succession of computerized switches, all within an instant or two. And even this description oversimplifies the matter because the call may well be handled not by one network but by several, and the companies that own those networks must arrange the multiple transfer of your voice signals like a baton in a very, very fast relay race.

But this brief sketch is merely the beginning, for the technological accomplishments just described take us only up to around 1980. Then came the rise of the Internet, which relies on many of the same facilities as the telephone network, but uses the power and versatility of digital technology to convert a telecommunications infrastructure originally designed for voice calls into a worldwide network of networked computers. With a few keystrokes, you can use your personal computer or other "smart" device to reach one of millions of other computers across the globe. As the 1s and 0s generated by a single webpage flit unpredictably along different paths across the Internet, the sights and sounds of foreign countries come streaming into your home at the speed of light.

Chapter 4 describes this digital overlay we call the Internet. Until then, keep the following in mind. The Internet is not some mysterious set of wires unrelated to the local and long distance networks over which we place ordinary voice calls. The telephone line you may use to connect your computer to the local Internet service provider is the same telephone line you use to call up your friends. And although many providers buy dedicated lines solely for data traffic, your long distance company may well use the same fiber-optic routes to transmit your voice across the country that it uses to transmit music downloads, webpages, and e-mail messages to dozens of other people over the Internet. When you conceptualize the difference between the public telephone network and the Internet, you should think not so much about any differences in the underlying physical facilities (although, to be sure, there are some important ones), but about the differences in how those facilities are used. While the analogy is imprecise, Internet services and ordinary voice services each "ride on top of" wireline network facilities in much the same way that cars and bicycles ride on many of the same paved roads, albeit often in different lanes.

The telephone network and the Internet are examples of switched networks: from any given point on the network, you can direct calls or data to any other single point on the network. At the most fundamental physical level, such networks consist of *transmission pipes*, including copper wires and fiber-optic cables, and the *switches* that route calls from one such pipe to another. The pipes are further subdivided into (i) the *loops* that connect customers to switches and (ii) the high capacity *transport* links (sometimes known as "trunks") that connect switches to other switches. Although the distinctions can blur at the edges, these three elements— *loops*, *switches*, and *transport*—are the fundamental building blocks of any point-to-point telecommunications network.[*]

A. Transmission pipes: loops and transport

Loops are so-called "last mile" facilities: the wires or cables a telecommunications company uses to connect its customers to the nearest switch and thence to the rest of the world. Strung through the air or laid underground (sometimes in tubes called "conduits"), loops constitute by far the costliest portion of most telecommunications networks and are thus the most difficult facilities for an upstart company to duplicate. For that reason, they are often described as "bottleneck" facilities, with major regulatory consequences.

The basics of wireline transmission

The most traditional form of the loop—a typical telephone line—consists of a twisted pair of copper wires used to establish an electrical con-

---

[*] When reviewing the following discussion, readers may wish to glance forward to Fig. 1, which appears on p. 41 at the conclusion of our description of the traditional telephone network.

nection with the telephone company's switch. When a customer lifts the receiver off the hook to place a call, the switch sends her a dial tone to confirm that the circuit has been established and is available to carry her call. When someone else calls her, the switch sends another electrical current down the line, this time to trigger the ringing of her telephone. The electrical currents come from giant batteries at the telephone company's switching station, known as a *central office*—usually identifiable as a bland-looking building with few windows and the telephone company's logo outside. For public safety reasons, the electricity that powers ordinary telephone service is independent of the electricity that provides power in the rest of your home. Thus, when the electric grid fails, you can still use your phone unless, of course, it is a cordless one whose base station requires ordinary AC power.

Suppose that you place a telephone call to someone whose loop is connected not to your local switch, but to a neighboring one. To get from your switch to hers, your voice signals must travel along a high capacity transport link. Most modern transport facilities use *optical fiber* technology; to some extent, as explained below, telephone companies have begun using that technology in loop facilities as well. In effect, a fiber-optic cable is an extremely thin glass tube that transmits light over long distances through various forms of internal reflection. Laser-originated light waves, carrying signals, bounce from one end to the other. (One common, though quite rough, analogy compares fiber optic technology with shining a flashlight down the interior of long tube with a mirrored surface on the inside; although the tube may bend and twist, the light shines out of the other end.) Attached to each fiber strand are expensive electronic devices that aggregate all of the signals from different customers' individual lines onto the same physical strand of optical fiber. This is called *multiplexing*. Copper wires often carry multiplexed signals too, but not with the phenomenal capacity of fiber.

In the traditional wireline telephone world, the most common form of multiplexing—known as "TDM" for *time division multiplexing*—"samples" the signal for a given call many times a second and transmits those samples along with the corresponding samples taken of other calls. A "sample" is a kind of digital snapshot of the signals in a call at any given moment, much as a frame in a movie is a snapshot of the action in progress. Each call is preassigned time slots in the multi-call transmission; at the other end, this aggregated signal is "de-multiplexed" back into individual signals. By means of this multiplexing technology, a single strand of fiber thinner than a human hair can carry thousands of simultaneous voice conversations. This aspect of telecommunications technology often comes as a surprise to people outside the industry: the calls you place to your friends across the country typically coexist on the same fiber strand with many other calls taking place between people you don't know.

The use of optical fiber is routine on any transport route where extremely high numbers of calls need to be transmitted at once, such as between cities or between most central offices. The use of fiber to connect central offices to customers—i.e., in loops—is less predictable. Sometimes, optical fiber is used only in the aggregated multi-loop *feeder* cables closest to the central office, and copper wires remain the medium of choice for the more diffuse *distribution* portion of the loops closest to the customers. (Think of feeder cables as the main branches of a tree and of distribution cables as the smaller branches and twigs.) But telephone companies sometimes use optical fiber all the way from the central office to the locations of certain customers with very high call and data volumes, such as large businesses.

Whether it makes economic sense to use optical fiber rather than copper wires in new loop facilities is often a complex question. Fiber provides more capacity and lower long term maintenance costs, but also considerably higher up-front costs in the form of the necessary electronic equipment. The choice between copper and fiber thus depends on, among other things, the length of the loop and the "line density" of a particular area: i.e., the number of homes and businesses in close proximity. Fiber-optic technology is most prevalent in the major cities, where fiber "rings" pass beneath the streets in downtown business districts to collect the enormous call volumes coming from large office buildings. On a smaller scale, fiber also has become increasingly popular in densely populated residential areas, both because its long term maintenance costs are lower and because it enables telephone companies to provide broadband Internet services to more customers, and at faster speeds, than is possible using purely copper loops.

The last point warrants some elaboration. Fiber has exceptionally high *bandwidth*—i.e., data carrying capacity—that does not vary significantly with the distance between the telephone company's central office and a customer's home. One industry study found that an all-fiber ("fiber-to-the-home") loop would enable residential customers to download a high quality copy of the movie "Braveheart" onto their computer hard-drives in less than half a minute (if only there were commercially available computers capable of keeping up with the task).[1] The bandwidth of copper wires is much more limited and varies inversely and dramatically with length. The major "broadband" Internet access service now offered over copper loops is known as *digital subscriber line* (DSL) service, which we will discuss in chapters 4 and 5. The speediest, most expensive variants of DSL—which still offer only a fraction of fiber's bandwidth—are available only to customers living in very close proximity to the telephone company's central office or other specialized data-handling facility. And even the slower, more standard versions of DSL are generally unavailable to customers more than 18,000 feet away.

The fiber glut

Not too long ago, media coverage of the telecommunications industry focused on the "fiber glut" that sent high-flying long distance companies such as WorldCom (now MCI) and Global Crossing into bankruptcy. Along *long distance* transport routes, this glut is real,[2] and is the result of two basic factors. First, in the 1990s, many companies racked up huge debts laying redundant fiber-optic cables over the same city-to-city routes on the mistaken—and, in retrospect, wildly unrealistic—assumption that demand would keep pace. That assumption was memorably encapsulated in a turn-of-the-millennium Qwest commercial, in which a weary traveler shows up at a hotel in the middle of nowhere, asks the desk attendant what movies are for rent, and learns that, through the miracle of fiber optics, he can watch (on demand) any movie ever made in any language.

In reality, such exponential growth in the demand for long distance telecommunications capacity would take many years to materialize, in part because too little fiber has been deployed *in the last mile* to generate demand from individual customers for bandwidth-consuming products, and in part because content providers fear that making such products available on the Internet will lead to widespread illicit copying.[3] As a result, people have continued renting movies in hard copy or watching them on cable (or satellite) television—and are likely to keep doing so in the near term. In the not-so-distant future, the broadband vision depicted in the Qwest commercial may well become a reality, at least in some areas. Making that vision a reality, however, will require overcoming obstacles both (i) to the deployment of high speed connections to a critical mass of customers and (ii) to the wide dissemination of digital content that will encourage customers to order those connections.

The second primary reason for the fiber capacity glut is technological. In recent years, advances in "wavelength division multiplexing" have dramatically and unexpectedly increased the signal-carrying capacity of optical fiber, including some fiber that had been in the ground for years. Among other innovations, engineers have greatly expanded the bandwidth of a given fiber strand by finding new ways to send signals within that strand simultaneously over multiple wavelengths of light—colloquially known as "colors," even though the signals at issue lie outside the visible spectrum. The result of such technological advances, combined with the manic overinvestment of the late 1990s, led to an extreme surplus of *dark fiber,* so named because no electronics have been placed at either end to "light" the fiber up with laser-guided signals. True to the laws of supply and demand, this overcapacity slashed the rates that debt-saddled telecommunications carriers could charge for providing transmission services along the major routes.[4]

Significantly, the routes subject to this overinvestment were those with the highest volumes of conventional voice calls and Internet traffic: the *long distance transport* routes between major population centers. Again, there was little fiber overinvestment *within* any community, except for the most densely populated, and there is no fiber glut—and sometimes no fiber at all—in the last mile *loop* facilities to most homes and small businesses. Those facilities retain some "bottleneck" characteristics in many areas, at least if one does not count the alternative last mile facilities of cable or wireless companies. Policymakers have thus tended to agree that competition in the provision of local wireline telephone services would develop quite slowly for all except the highest volume customers unless new entrants enjoy a regulatory entitlement to rent at least some of the loop facilities of established telephone companies. By contrast, because a number of national providers own long distance transport networks, a thriving wholesale market for leased capacity on those networks arose without heavy government intervention. As discussed in chapter 3, many of today's regulatory battles about leasing rights are waged in the territory between these two extremes: in the market for "local transport," including the links connecting two of a telephone company's central offices.

Regulatory distinctions among transmission pipes

People in the telecommunications industry use broad-brush terms like "local" and "long distance," and "loops" and "transport," as useful short-hands to describe the different ways in which transmission pipes are used in telecommunications networks. But it is important to keep these distinctions in perspective. As we shall see, regulators attach great significance to the difference between "local" and "long distance" services. Until quite recently, they fenced the largest "local" wireline carriers out of the "long distance" market altogether, and they still draw bright geographical lines to identify when a call qualifies as "long distance."[5] From an engineer's perspective, however, there is no clear demarcation point between "local" and "long distance" transport: pipes run the spectrum from long to short and from higher capacity to lower capacity. This is *not* to say that regulators have wholly contrived the distinction between local and long distance services on the basis of arbitrary criteria. Distance remains relevant from a business and technological perspective insofar as it corresponds to commercially significant phenomena like traffic volumes and their associated economies of scale. But once a telecommunications network is up and running, a carrier incurs little, if any, extra cost to send a call a thousand miles to its destination rather than ten miles.

The rigid long distance-local distinction that characterized the market in the last two decades of the twentieth century is increasingly giving way to these underlying economic and technological realities. As local telephone companies enter the long distance market, and as long distance companies enter the local telephone market, the distinction between these two markets has inevitably blurred. As in wireless markets, wireline consumers are increasingly able to purchase pricing plans with large buckets of interchangeable "long distance" and "local" minutes. And the providers of "voice over Internet protocol" (VoIP) almost always offer consumers the same option.

There is also no firm engineering distinction between a "transport" facility and a "loop." Remember that both are simply transmission pipes. By definitional tradition, a "loop" connects a switch and a customer location rather than, as with a transport link, a switch and a switch. But suppose that the customer connects its end of the loop to a switch of its own. For example, the customer may be a large business with its own private internal switch, known as a *private branch exchange* (PBX); or a competing telecommunications carrier with its own switch; or an Internet service provider with a "modem bank" connected to a router that in turn leads into the Internet. In each of these cases, the distinction between "loops" and "transport" breaks down somewhat. It is useful to keep this point in the back of your mind as you think about telecommunications issues, even though regulators normally designate the facilities as one or the other.

One final point before we move on to switching technology: the loop facilities described in this chapter are the main ones used by "wireline" telecommunications carriers, a somewhat arbitrary category consisting of the companies that built wired networks for the primary original purpose of providing point-to-point voice and data services. But cable companies now lead the residential market in the provision of *high speed* point-to-point *data* services, and they have begun entering the market for point-to-point voice services as well. As discussed in chapter 4, their "loops" are the same cables—usually a combination of optical fiber and, in the portion nearest the customer, coaxial cable—used to bring television signals into American homes.

Conventional wisdom holds that, to prevail in the market for fixed (non-mobile) residential services over the long term, a communications provider must find a way to offer consumers the so-called "triple play" of voice, data, and video services. The battle for this market—which ultimately pits wireline telephone companies against cable companies—will likely be won by the providers that find ways to cover the exorbitant costs of pushing more fiber-optic cable into more residential neighborhoods closer to the ultimate consumers. We will defer a full discussion of that cross-platform competition, and its highly controversial regulatory dimensions, until chapters 4-6, below. And, in chapters 7 and 8, we will address another critical alternative means for bridging the last mile to the customer: *wireless* connections between a customer's mobile telephone and the nearest tower on her cellular network.

B. Switches

A network is defined by its switches (or routers, as they are typically called in the Internet world). Imagine trying to connect every home or business in the United States to *every other* home or business without the use of a switch. The number of required lines, and thus the cost, would be astronomical. In fact, if we estimated the number of wireline telephones in the United States as roughly equivalent to the number of Americans, the tangled mess of lines criss-crossing the country to connect each telephone to every other would amount to more than 40 *quadrillion* lines.[6]

Switches are built to solve this problem in the most economical way. They direct a voice or data call from one transmission pipe (a loop or transport link) to another en route to the call's destination. Although the distinction can blur at the margins, there are two basic kinds of switches—*circuit switches* and *packet switches*—that are used, respectively, in conventional voice networks and more advanced data networks, including the Internet. As mentioned, the physical infrastructure of wireline telephone networks overlaps significantly with that of the Internet. The major exception to this rule lies in switching technology, for reasons we discuss below.

Circuit switches

Circuit switches include the early hand-operated switchboard and its modern-day functional equivalents in virtually every conventional telephone network. A circuit switch sets up a dedicated transmission path from the calling party to the recipient for the duration of a call. At any point during the call, a particular increment of capacity is reserved for that call on the loop, switch, and transport pipe, even if no one is talking and no information is being sent.[7] To save money, a telecommunications carrier does not build enough capacity on its switches and inter-switch transport links to carry calls from all customers at once. Instead, like a bank, it keeps just enough in reserve to cover the greatest reasonably expected demand. The size and cost of switches and transport links are thus determined by the expected capacity needs of the network at peak calling hours. This is one reason why many callers in the nation's capital received "all circuits busy" signals when calling home on September 11, 2001: telephone engineers had not built in enough network capacity to serve this unexpectedly high call volume.

Modern circuit switches are essentially very large computers that, in addition to establishing circuits for given calls, perform a variety of other "intelligent" functions, including call forwarding, caller identification, and call waiting—known collectively as *vertical switching features*—as well as billing. A modern circuit-switched network is usually shadowed by a par-

allel, packet-switched *signaling network,* which tells the circuit switches
how to route particular calls to avoid network congestion and how to
implement specific customer requests, such as where 800 number calls
should be directed and how calling card calls should be handled. The
"brains" of a circuit-switched network are said to reside in the switch and
the parallel signaling network, not at the "edge" of the network in an end
user's computer, and they are centrally owned and controlled by the
telecommunications company. As a result, it is difficult, if not impossible,
to introduce new intelligent features to the circuit-switched network (as
distinguished from the customer's own PBX) without first obtaining the
permission of the telephone company that owns the switch.

Finally, circuit switches are often arranged "hierarchically" to minimize
the number of switches and transport links needed to keep a circuit open
during the duration of a call from one place to another (see Fig. 1). At the

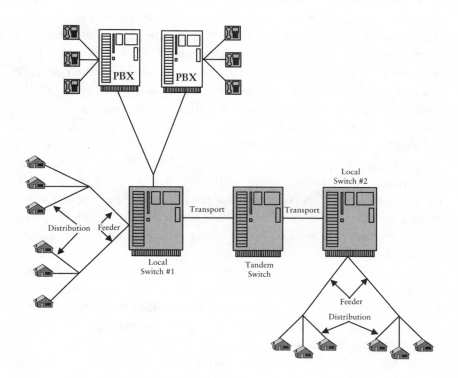

Figure 1. Traditional telephone network architecture

low end of the hierarchy, established long ago by AT&T's Bell System, are the so-called *local* (or "Class 5") switches, to which most loops are connected. The next level up consists of the *tandems*, which, among other things, route large call volumes from one local switch to another. In the years before the break-up of the Bell System in 1984, the switches higher in the hierarchy were associated with the routing of long distance calls. After 1984, AT&T kept those switches, and the newly independent Bell companies kept the local and tandem switches.

Packet switches

Packet switches, unlike circuit switches, do not set up a dedicated circuit for the duration of a call. Instead, the transmitted information is converted into discrete digital packets, and the packet switch sends each of them separately from the others, potentially along different transmission paths. As noted in chapter 1, these packets are encoded strings of 1s and 0s that could contain information of any kind, ranging from a webpage to a photograph embedded in an e-mail to the sound of a human voice. Each packet may be held in queue at the packet switch while yet other packets, from unrelated "calls" (or "sessions"), pass through the switch. All the packets in a given transmission ideally end up at the same place because each of them has an "address header" that tells the network's packet switches ("routers") who is supposed to receive it. At the receiving end, the recipient's computer unjumbles the packets and displays the message (e.g., a webpage). The difference between circuit-switched and packet-switched networks has been roughly compared to the difference between, on the one hand, sending an envelope down a chute intact and, on the other, ripping the envelope into pieces, sending the pieces through different chutes, and reassembling them at the other end.

Why would anyone ever prefer this second option? For most (but not all) data communications, a packet-switched network is more efficient than a circuit-switched network because it does not dedicate capacity for the duration of a particular call or session, including the many portions of the call that include the transmission of no information. In concrete terms, the circuit that remains dedicated to you during even short pauses in an ordinary voice call is a waste of network capacity because the facilities carrying the call are standing idle instead of carrying someone else's transmissions. So the real question is why any provider would ever prefer a more wasteful circuit-switched network to a more efficient packet-switched one, even for voice calls.

The main reason that circuit switches remain widely used is that, until very recently, packet-switching technology did not lend itself easily to managing voice calls and certain other real-time applications. The flip side of a packet-switched network's efficiency can be perceptible delays, known as *latency*. Such delays result from the unpredictable and sometimes slow transmission of jumbled packets through the network and their final reorganization into a coherent "message" that can be understood and translated by the recipient's applications software. One-second delays are barely noticeable when someone is downloading a webpage, but they are quite distracting in an ordinary telephone conversation. These latency challenges are surmountable, however, as we will explain in chapter 6. Indeed, a number of private businesses have already begun converting their internal telephone networks to packet-switched technology. And providers of "voice over Internet protocol" (VoIP) have shown that such technologies have much broader commercial potential.

In contrast to circuit-switched networks, where the intelligence resides in the telephone company's network, the intelligence in a packet-switched network resides mostly in the computers or other "smart" devices hooked up to the end of the loop on a customer's premises. To the network, only the addressing function of a packet-switched stream of bits has significance. Otherwise, the network does not typically "know" what the series of 1s and 0s means or even what kind of thing (a photo or a voice call) those 1s and 0s describe. Encoding and decoding that information is the province of specialized software owned by the sending and receiving parties.

This *end-to-end* customer control over packet-switched networks, and the indifference of those networks to the services provided by digital bitstreams, dramatically expanded the uses to which data networks could be put and triggered the explosive growth of the Internet. On the other hand, the anarchy of this end-to-end ethos has led the owners of some packet-switched networks to build greater intelligence into them for various purposes, such as filtering out pornography and helping law enforcement officials identify threats to national security. Network owners have also begun giving "quality of service" priority to some types of services, such as VoIP, by marking the packets associated with those services and advancing them to the head of the queue in the event of network congestion. By reserving capacity for these preferred services, this approach enables packet-switched networks to perform high quality real-time functions (such as videoconferencing or voice telephony), mainly by placing more intelligence in the center of network and thus blurring the distinctions between packet switching and circuit switching.

We began this chapter by noting the significant overlap between the physical infrastructure underlying the Internet, on the one hand, and local and long distance telephone networks, on the other. Switches, as noted, mark the major exception to this rule. To be sure, you can gain access to the Internet through a conventional circuit switch by placing an ordinary "local" call to your Internet service provider, which will in turn convert the signals into packets and route them over the packet-switched Internet. But the circuit switch at the threshold of that transmission is more a hindrance than a help, even though it connects you to the ISP. That switch was designed with the almost single-minded purpose of carrying high quality voice traffic as efficiently as possible. Although the switch ensures real-time dependability by holding a dedicated circuit open for the duration of each call, it makes up for all the capacity "wasted" by that *temporal* reservation of bandwidth by limiting the *amount* of bandwidth allocated to each circuit held open. Specifically, it filters out all but the core frequencies associated with the typical human voice; as a result, the person on the other end of the line sounds more or less like herself, but the music you hear while being placed on hold sounds tinny. Economizing on bandwidth this way keeps network costs down, but it makes circuit switches inefficient processors of most data transmissions, for which high bandwidth is essential. Just as a conventional circuit switch squelches the acoustic texture of tubas and piccolos, it also excludes the myriad frequencies on which computer data can be exchanged.

Depending on what they are made of, loops have limited bandwidth too, but not nearly as limited as that of a conventional circuit switch. As explained in chapter 4, a key challenge for telecommunications engineers is thus to find ways of *bypassing the circuit switch* by connecting the loop directly to a packet-switched network linked to the Internet. Sometimes this involves connecting a customer's loop at the central office directly to a high speed transport link en route to the network of a company that, like AT&T or MCI, serves as a long distance transporter of both voice calls and data traffic. Similarly, providing broadband Internet access to homes or small businesses sometimes involves a different means of bypassing the circuit switch—the DSL technology we mentioned above and describe more fully in chapter 4. For their part, cable television, satellite, and wireless companies also provide customers with direct links to the Internet by way of their alternative (non-"wireline") loop facilities. Chapter 5 addresses the complex regulatory implications of such cross-platform competition.

II. Traditional Telephone Rate Regulation

Roughly speaking, telecommunications policy issues fall into two broad categories: (1) state and federal *retail* regulation of the terms on which telecommunications carriers can provide retail service directly to end users, and (2) state and federal *wholesale* regulation of the relationships among telecommunications providers. Although this book focuses on the latter rather than the former, understanding wholesale regulation requires a basic familiarity with retail regulation. Accordingly, we continue our discussion of the wireline telephone industry with the basic retail regulatory framework that came of age in the 1920s and 1930s: a framework that, as we shall see, can work as intended only if there is very little competition in telecommunications markets.

A. The basics of price regulation

In ordinary, non-monopolized markets, companies compete against one another for customers, and this competition theoretically keeps the price of goods and services at reasonably efficient levels. By definition, however, there is no competition in a market that regulators treat as a natural monopoly, as the market for telecommunications was treated for most of the twentieth century. And, if left to their own devices, monopoly providers of any product, including wireline telephone services, can be expected to maximize their profits by raising their retail prices to inefficiently high levels. These high prices include monopoly profits that enrich the monopolist at the expense of consumer welfare, artificially reducing the demand for telecommunications services and keeping total output (i.e., sales volume) below optimal levels. In markets without formidable barriers to entry, monopoly profits tend to be a temporary phenomenon, for upstart firms will enter the market and undercut the incumbent's prices. Federal and state policymakers have long treated local telephone markets differently, however, because of the traditionally high entry barriers discussed in the previous chapter. In particular, they have relied on rate regulation—and not Adam Smith's invisible hand—to protect consumers from monopoly pricing.

The regulatory compact

Some foreign governments have addressed the problem of monopoly pricing by owning the telephone system outright, an approach that many of them are in the process of undoing.[8] In the United States, by contrast, virtually every telephone network has been privately owned and operated. At the same time, such networks have traditionally been regulated as *public utilities*—i.e., as commercial enterprises charged with providing an essential public service and subject to pervasive regulation to protect the public interest. The Supreme Court explains: "At the dawn of modern utility regulation, in order to offset monopoly power and ensure affordable, stable public access to a utility's goods or services, legislatures enacted rate schedules to fix the prices a utility could charge. As this job became more complicated, legislatures established specialized administrative agencies, first local or state, then federal, to set and regulate rates."[9]

Like other public utilities, an incumbent local telephone company has made a kind of regulatory compact with the government. In exchange for agreeing to serve consumers at affordable rates as the carrier of last resort, the company is given an opportunity to earn a "reasonable rate of return" on its overall regulated investment. No similar arrangement exists for long distance carriers or new entrants into the local exchange market. Those carriers face fierce enough competitive pressures, from one another and from the dominant local telephone company, that they already have adequate incentives to keep their rates low and their service quality high.

The regulatory mechanisms for setting a dominant local telephone company's retail rates are baroque in their complexity. To make matters still more complicated, these mechanisms changed significantly in the 1980s and early 1990s, as regulators began moving from *rate-of-return* regulation to an alternative *price cap* model for the largest local carriers. We address these regulatory schemes in turn, beginning with the traditional rate-of-return approach.

Under a rate-of-return regime, federal and state regulators give dominant local telephone companies an opportunity to charge retail rates sufficient, in the aggregate, to cover their anticipated expenses plus a reasonable return on their net investment. As discussed more fully in appendix A, this involves, among other things, calculating a company's "historical costs"—the costs it has actually incurred and lists on its books—and making various judgments about them. Such judgments include (i) the extent to which these costs were "prudently incurred"; (ii) how quickly the telephone company should be able to recover the total costs of given facilities (through its monthly retail rates)—a judgment that in turn depends on estimates of how long those facilities will be in service ("depreciation lives"); and (iii) how much of a return on investment ("cost of capital") the company needs to continue attracting capital to finance new investment.

Regulatory agencies resolve such issues in long and complex "rate cases." If dissatisfied with the result, the telephone company can file suit for "just compensation"—in the form of increases to its retail rates—if it believes that its current rates are so low that they leave the company "insufficient operating capital" or "imped[e] [its] ability to raise future capital."[10] Although this is an important backstop in theory, courts are unlikely in practice to find that a public utility has suffered such a "regulatory taking," as the Supreme Court showed once more in 2002.[11]

Dual jurisdiction

To this point, we have kept the identity of the rate-setting regulators anonymous. Now it is time to unveil another layer of complexity: the arcane division of labor between the federal government and the states in retail telephone regulation. Since the 1930s, the FCC and the states have shared responsibility for ensuring a "reasonable return" on investment and regulating the retail rates the dominant local telephone company may charge consumers.

Because every aspect of telecommunications can be characterized as an instrumentality of interstate commerce, Congress could have preempted all state regulation in this area under the Commerce Clause of the U.S. Constitution and placed the entire industry within the exclusive province of a federal regulator. When it enacted the Communications Act of 1934, however, Congress chose a model of *dual jurisdiction*—which gave the newly created FCC plenary jurisdiction over interstate services and, under section 2(b) of the Act,[12] precluded the Commission from intruding on state regulation of intrastate services. Importantly, this particular federal-state division of authority applies only to retail services, such as those addressed in this section, and to the *access charges* that a long distance company pays the local telephone companies on each end of a long distance call, as described below. Wholesale "local competition" issues, discussed in subsequent chapters, have been governed by a very different jurisdictional arrangement since passage of the Telecommunications Act of 1996.

The federal government and the states divide their traditional retail rate-setting responsibilities roughly as follows. The FCC and the states first allocate a percentage of a telephone company's total costs into "interstate" and "intrastate" categories for purposes of ensuring a reasonable return. The interstate costs are recovered by rates for interstate services regulated by the FCC, and the intrastate costs by rates for intrastate services regulated by the states. The process of dividing up costs this way is called the *jurisdictional separations* process and dates back to the Supreme Court's 1930 decision in *Smith v. Illinois Bell*.[13] The criteria used can be quite arbitrary because many facilities, such as the loop and switch, are typically used for both interstate and intrastate calls. For example, all calls leaving one's house, whether they cross state lines or not, use the same pair of copper wires. How, for cost-recovery purposes, should the cost of installing and maintaining those wires be divided between the federal government and the states? The general rule, rooted more in political compromise than in technological reality, is that 75% of the cost of that loop is assigned to the "intrastate" side of the cost ledger and the remaining 25% to the "interstate" side.[14]

Incumbent local telephone companies are entitled to a "reasonable" rate of return on costs allocated to each side (interstate and intrastate) of the cost ledger, considered independently. The FCC and the states have met this responsibility in similar ways. Each set of regulators enables a telephone company to recover costs through a combination of flat and usage-sensitive rates. Subscribers pay two flat monthly fees—one set by the states, the other by the FCC—to receive basic local telephone service, which normally includes unlimited "local" calling. The federal fee, called the *subscriber line charge*, is similar to the monthly "local service" fee set by state regulators, but it is designed to permit the telephone company to recover the portion of loop costs allocated to the interstate side of the cost ledger.[15]

"Usage-sensitive" rates take two general forms. First, a telephone company collects per-minute *toll charges* from its subscribers for certain types of calls. Second, the company collects *access charges* from long distance carriers whenever it (i) hands off *to them* a call placed by one of its subscribers or (ii) completes calls delivered *by them* to one of its subscribers. Understanding the critical role of access charges in the cost-recovery equation requires some brief background.

Access charges

During the period when AT&T owned most of the local telephone exchanges and the only long distance network, it relied on regulated accounting mechanisms to allocate the costs of long distance calls within the Bell System: i.e., the costs of long distance transport itself and the costs of "accessing" the local networks on each end of the call. When long distance competition developed in the 1970s, regulators had to devise a more formal mechanism—access charges—for allocating these two categories of costs.[16] To see how this system works today, suppose that you are an ordinary residential subscriber living in Atlanta, your local telephone company is BellSouth, your long distance provider is MCI, and you call a friend served by SBC in Dallas. The call begins with a brief trip through BellSouth's local network before it hits MCI's long distance network, and it then ends with a brief trip through SBC's local network in Dallas en route to your friend. The local companies on each end of the call— BellSouth and SBC—collect from MCI an access charge for the right to use their respective networks for this purpose. MCI, in turn, passes those charges along to you and the rest of its customers in its long distance rates.

At this point, it is important to understand the distinction between two different types of access charges: those for *switched access* and those for *special access*. A long distance carrier pays access charges, and passes them on to its customers, on a per-minute basis for all "switched access" calls: i.e., calls that pass through the local carrier's switch en route to the long distance network. As noted above, many business customers place enough long distance calls to justify dedicated lines that bypass the switch and link the business directly to the long distance carrier's network. If those lines belong to the local telephone company, it charges the long distance carrier a flat monthly fee for this "special access" arrangement.

We now return to the role of access charges in the recovery of a telephone company's total "costs." For switched access, the FCC regulates the interstate access charges that local telephone companies may charge long distance companies for calls that cross state lines, and the states regulate the intrastate access charges levied for calls that stay within state lines. The division of authority for the regulation of special access rates is more subtle, because the "service" at issue is not the completion of a single call, but the provision of a dedicated line that, like an ordinary loop, can be used for either local or long distance calls. Under a longstanding FCC rule, a special access circuit is deemed interstate in character, and subject to regulation by the FCC, if it is used to carry at least 10% interstate traffic.[17] In recent years, through a policy called *pricing flexibility*, the FCC has largely deregulated special access charges in a number of urban areas where it has determined that competition has arisen in the provision of direct links to long distance networks.[18]

Tariffs

Incumbent local telephone companies are not usually permitted to enter into wholly private contractual arrangements with individual consumers in traditional telephone markets. Instead, the basic premise of the incumbents' common carriage commitment is that each customer should have the same opportunity as any other similarly situated customer to buy the same services on the same terms. Thus, when an incumbent wishes to introduce a new service, it normally must file a *tariff* with the relevant regulatory authority, spelling out the terms and conditions of its services and offering them for sale to the public at large. Often, such tariffs are permitted to take only temporary effect while regulators conduct an inquiry into the reasonableness of their terms.[19]

Once approved, the terms of these tariffs govern the retail relationships between carriers and their customers, even if a carrier offered different terms in a sales call. In theory, this *filed rate doctrine,* which allows companies to charge only tariffed rates and (to their great benefit) shields them from litigation concerning the legitimacy of those rates,[20] protects consumers by ensuring that they receive the prices, terms, and conditions approved by the regulators. In practice, however, requiring tariff filings creates significant social costs by slowing down the rough and tumble of free market competition and facilitating collusion between rivals by enabling them to see one another's prices before they go into effect.[21] As we will discuss in chapter 6, the FCC has thus freed "non-dominant" carriers from tariffing obligations in many markets and has sometimes, over their opposition, affirmatively forbidden them to file tariffs.

Price caps

Up to this point, our discussion of telephone company cost recovery has presupposed the use of rate-of-return regulation, in which federal and state policymakers set their respective retail rates and access charges at levels designed to guarantee each local telephone company an opportunity to earn, overall, a reasonable return on the prudently incurred costs attributable to its regulated activities. But traditional rate-of-return regulation tends to give any public utility perverse incentives to "gold plate" its assets: that is, incentives to spend more than is efficient or necessary simply to increase the rate base on which it earns its profits. Rate-of-return regulation also can make it easier for firms to engage in monopoly leveraging by over-assigning joint and common costs to its monopoly markets and thereby *cross-subsidize* its operations in competitive markets—a phenomenon we discuss in part III of this chapter. In the 1980s and 1990s, federal and most state regulators sought to address these incentive problems by adopting a *price cap* scheme for retail rate regulation of the largest local telephone companies.

A price cap analysis starts with the retail rates produced in a given year under traditional rate-of-return regulation. In succeeding years, however, retail rates will be determined on the basis not of new rate-of-return proceedings, but of mathematical adjustments designed principally to reflect (a) expected industry-wide increases in efficiency (known as the "X-factor") due to technological and other innovation and (b) fluctuations in inflation and other macroeconomic variables.[22] A price cap approach, unlike a traditional rate-of-return regime, rewards the incumbents for their efficiency over time by entitling them to keep much of the extra profit they generate as the result of cutting unnecessary costs.[23]

Although the size of the X-factor is a source of lively debate and often successful litigation,[24] price caps have proven quite effective in balancing the financial needs of the incumbents against the consumer welfare interest in lower retail rates.[25] The retail rates of the largest incumbent telephone companies, as well as their access charges, are now generally subject to price cap rules. Smaller incumbents are often still subject to rate-of-return regulation.

B. Introduction to universal service policies

The sum of an incumbent telephone company's retail rates in the aggregate is mostly determined by the mechanics of rate-of-return or price cap regulation. But this calculation does not answer the question of which categories of customers will end up paying what percentages of these costs. One straightforward approach would be to estimate the cost of providing particular services, add a reasonable allocation of the regulated company's "joint and common costs," such as the CEO's salary, and use that number as the basis for setting rates for those particular services. But that is not generally what happens because, as public choice theory predicts (see chapter 1), telecommunications regulators are motivated by political objectives in addition to purely economic ones.

In particular, regulators have traditionally set rates for certain services, such as residential service in many areas, below the cost of providing them—although, to be sure, the precise measure of "cost" in this context, and the extent to which an incumbent local exchange carrier actually provides service to residential customers "below cost," have always been topics of debate. To cover the difference between these discounted rates and the actual cost of providing service, regulators have historically allowed the monopolist to set the rates for other services, such as those provided to business customers, above the cost of providing them. Theoretically, the regulated monopolist receiving these rates in the aggregate should be indifferent to such *implicit cross-subsidies* because—so long as it faces no competition for the customers paying the above-cost rates—its books come out even in the end.

The term *universal service* is used somewhat overbroadly to describe the regulatory manipulation that produces low residential rates, even though such manipulation may be completely unnecessary to ensure that the beneficiaries actually remain hooked up to the network. Chapter 10 discusses the changing face of universal service in some detail, but it is important to cover the basics here at the outset.

The telecommunications industry is riddled with different types of implicit cross-subsidies justified as necessary for "universal service." If you live in a highly populated urban or suburban neighborhood, the odds are that you are paying the same basic rate for telephone service as someone living deep in the countryside an hour down the state highway.[26] This itself is a form of implicit cross-subsidy. Because of economies of density, it costs much less to provide service to you than to your rural counterpart. This practice of setting the same rate for all residential customers in a large geographic region such as a state—known as *geographic rate averaging*—means that you are in effect paying a hidden surcharge on your telephone bill to enable the rural customer to receive service at a rate well below the cost incurred in providing it to him.

On the other hand, you should not complain too much if you are an urban residential customer, for the corner grocery down the street from your apartment has even greater cause for dissatisfaction: it is likely paying up to twice as much for a telephone line as either you or the rural inhabitant. That may seem odd, since it may well cost the telephone company no more to provide that service to the grocer than to you. But this is another way in which regulators have typically kept residential rates low: by authorizing the telephone company to maintain artificially high rates for "business lines." In effect, when the grocer orders telephone service, he may be signing a tacit agreement to pay more than a 100% tax on that service to underwrite low rates for rural subscribers.

Long distance calls are another principal source of implicit cross-subsidies. The reason is somewhat complex. Before the 1980s, when there was very little competition in the long distance market, regulators set per-minute rates for such calls far above cost. Those rates helped underwrite low monthly rates on the bill for local telephone service. Throughout the 1980s and 1990s, as robust competition developed in the long distance market, long distance rates dropped significantly. But they often remained (and still remain) higher than "cost." How is this possible, given the inter-city fiber glut and the strength of competition in the long distance market?

The primary answer lies in access charges, first discussed above. Let's assume there is perfect competition in the market for city-to-city transport and other long distance services. There remains imperfect competition in the market for "access" services: i.e., for connecting end users to the networks of their chosen long distance carriers, a task normally performed by the traditional local telephone companies.[27] As a result, these "access" charges are still generally capped by regulators, and they too are often set above any rigorous measure of "cost," in part to offset the losses such companies are said to incur when they are forced to provide basic local service to residential customers at low rates. Since local companies impose access charges on long distance carriers, which in turn pass them on to their own subscribers, the net result is that long distance rates exceed the underlying costs of providing long distance service. Those who place many long distance calls therefore end up subsidizing below-cost rates for "basic" local service. Since the 1996 Act, the FCC has reduced the levels of interstate access charges, but there is no consensus that it has succeeded in reducing all such charges down to levels that reflect a strict calculation of "cost." And there is little dispute that many states continue to set significantly above-cost access charges for intrastate long distance calls.

Yet another fertile source of implicit cross-subsidies is the sale of "second lines" to residential customers. Second lines have long been popular among families with teenagers and people with home business offices. In the late 1990s, the number of second lines skyrocketed as people discovered dial-up Internet access yet wanted to avoid tying up the telephone for voice calls when on-line. The rates that state and federal regulators have imposed for these second lines are often twice as high as the rates for primary lines, even though the extra copper wires needed for this service are usually already installed alongside the primary ones and cost very little to activate. In this respect as well, regulation has imposed, in effect, a surcharge on heavy users of telephone service to help telephone companies afford the low rates they charge light users of that service. While politically expedient, such arrangements subvert a principle of economic efficiency called *Ramsey pricing*, which prescribes, for firms with large fixed costs, higher rates for essential services such as primary lines and lower rates for more discretionary services such as second lines or long distance services.[28]

All these implicit subsidies—geographic cost averaging, above-cost business rates, above-cost access charges, above-cost second lines, among others—are politically convenient. They are all economically equivalent to a special tax imposed on some customers or services to subsidize below-cost rates for other customers or services. And, precisely because they are "implicit" rather than "explicit," they come without the political baggage of an explicit tax or universal service fee.

But these are "taxes" with a special drawback: customers can avoid paying them altogether if they can find a provider *other than* the regulated local telephone company to perform the same services at a lower price—i.e., without the implicit tax inherent in the regulated rate. New entrants in any market know this, and they will make it their first priority to cherry-pick the very customers who are paying the largest implicit taxes. This cherry-picking is a form of *arbitrage*—a low-risk profit opportunity arising from arbitrary distinctions. The new entrants that exploit such opportunities inexorably undermine the whole scheme of implicit cross-subsidies, but they are doing nothing wrong. They are merely delivering the message that this traditional scheme, designed for monopoly market conditions, is unsustainable in a competitive era.

As discussed in chapter 10, the competitive entry stimulated by the 1996 Act will force regulators to find a more competitively neutral scheme for keeping residential telephone rates low. After all, regulators cannot deficit-finance their universal service policies indefinitely by requiring the incumbent local telephone companies to continue providing below-cost services without *any* source of subsidy. In the long run, as we shall see, the only options are higher residential rates for high cost customers or more explicit, tax-like fees for all customers. Neither option is politically appealing, which explains why regulators have dragged their heels for so long in response to calls for genuine universal service reform.

III. Wireline Competition Policy Before 1996

To review, a market is said to have "natural monopoly" characteristics if, because of high fixed costs and large scale economies, a firm's long run average costs "over the entire extent of the market"[29] always decline with any increase in output. Throughout most of the twentieth century, the entire wireline telecommunications industry in the United States was treated as a natural monopoly. The principal beneficiary of that policy was AT&T's Bell System. AT&T and its subsidiaries were permitted to monopolize the market for telephones and telephone equipment (Western Electric), the market for long distance services (AT&T Long Lines), and most major local exchange markets (the Bell operating companies). And those calling areas not served by the Bell System's local exchange operations were nonetheless served by some other state-sanctioned monopoly, such as GTE.

In chapter 1, we briefly introduced the major story in wireline communications since 1970: the slow but steady peeling back of this natural monopoly premise from one market to the next until only fragments of the local exchange market were left. Over time, often as the result of technological advances and the efforts of reform-minded regulators, policymakers repeatedly recognized that some segments of the telecommunications industry do not exhibit natural monopoly characteristics and should not be left as the exclusive preserve of the local telephone company. Each time, the government—either telecommunications regulators or antitrust authorities—adopted one means or another of ensuring that local telephone monopolies could not leverage their ownership of bottleneck facilities to preclude fair competition in adjacent markets for wireline telecommunications-related services. The result was a hodge-podge of antitrust and regulatory responses to different monopoly leveraging concerns, which persisted until partially superseded by the Telecommunications Act of 1996. Today, most public policy disputes about wireline competition are battles about how to implement the amorphous competitive objectives of the 1996 Act. We address those battles in chapter 3; this section sets the stage for that discussion by summarizing the development of wireline competition policy from 1970 through the eve of the 1996 Act.

Before 1996, as in more recent years, three basic opportunities tended to invite upstart carriers into particular telecommunications markets. First, competitors were attracted to markets in which call volumes were great enough that they, like the incumbent, could enjoy significant scale economies while serving only a fraction of the total customer base. Second, competitors were also attracted to any market, such as those that traditionally generated implicit cross-subsidies, in which the incumbent could be expected to hold a *price umbrella* over new entrants by charging its own retail customers rates higher than cost. This price umbrella enabled the entrants to undersell the incumbent while nonetheless earning substantial profit margins of their own. Finally, competitors were eager to fill niche markets—particularly for the provision of sophisticated data services—that AT&T's Bell System had largely disregarded through its century-long focus on ordinary voice telephony and its desire to avoid cannibalizing its existing revenues.

Between 1970 and 1996, competition arose in the markets that most clearly met one or more of these conditions: the "long distance" market for intercity transport, the "access" market for connecting large business customers directly to a long distance carrier's network, and the emerging markets for computer-to-computer data transmission services. In each case, what the upstarts needed most from the government were robust interconnection guarantees, in the form of "equal access" requirements, to keep incumbents from leveraging their dominance in the local exchange markets to exclude all rivals from adjacent markets. In the pages that follow, we summarize the history of competition in the long distance and access markets and the relevant regulatory measures. We then turn briefly to the first, pre-1996 regulatory initiatives for bringing competition to local exchange markets. We begin, however, with the industry segment that fell prey to competition before any service market did: the market for telecommunications equipment. The debate about competition in that market centered not so much on natural monopoly theory, for no one seriously suggested that equipment manufacturing itself had natural monopoly characteristics, but on the technical consequences of letting customers attach "foreign" (i.e., non-AT&T) devices to the telephone network.

A. Telecommunications equipment manufacturing

In the telecommunications world, the market for *customer premises equipment* (CPE) includes not just ordinary telephones themselves, but also the sophisticated private switches (PBXs) used in large office buildings, the "modems" that enable computers to communicate with each other over telephone lines, and a variety of other devices. For decades, AT&T had cited dubious technical concerns as a pretext for prohibiting its customers from attaching to its network so-called "foreign" devices manufactured by companies other than Western Electric, its equipment manufacturing unit. As AT&T's chairman warned as late as 1973, "If consumers can plug anything they want into the network—any old piece of junk made who knows where—the system will break down. A faulty telephone in one house could conceivably disrupt service to an entire city."[30] As may seem obvious in retrospect, such concerns did not support AT&T's argument for granting it an exclusive franchise to manufacture all telephone equipment. Instead, they supported, at most, the adoption of industry-wide standards that multiple manufacturers could follow in ensuring that use of their products would not harm the telephone network. But it took regulators decades to recognize this fact, to overcome AT&T's lobbying prowess, and to write the rules needed for robust competition in the equipment manufacturing market.

AT&T's motives for resisting competition warrant a brief recap. As discussed in chapter 1, an unregulated platform monopolist ordinarily recovers all supracompetitive profits in the sale of the platform itself (here, telephone service) and thus welcomes competition in the applications market (equipment manufacturing). This is because the more attractive and less expensive the applications are, the more valuable the underlying platform monopoly becomes. One wrinkle in telecommunications markets is that retail rate regulation has long limited the price the monopolist may charge consumers for use of the platform. Such regulation thus gives the monopolist strong incentives to leverage its platform monopoly to obtain supracompetitive profits in adjacent, less price-constrained markets. The market for customer premises equipment fell into this category. As with long distance and business services, regulators had permitted the price of telephone equipment—which often took the form of monthly lease rates—to remain well above its underlying cost in order to subsidize inexpensive local service for residential customers.[31]

AT&T's monopolistic hold on the equipment market showed its first signs of erosion in the 1950s and 1960s. During the multi-year *Hush-A-Phone* controversy, AT&T prohibited its customers from attaching an independently manufactured cup-like device to a telephone receiver for the modest purpose of limiting background noise. The FCC absurdly agreed with AT&T's submission that the use of such "foreign devices" threatened the integrity of the telephone system, even though the practical effect of the device was equivalent to covering the receiver with one's hand.[32] A bemused court of appeals reversed the FCC's decision in 1956 on the ground that it made no sense.[33] The FCC eventually learned its lesson: in 1968, after much hand-wringing, it rejected AT&T's efforts to bar the use of the "Carterfone," a device that connected a telephone line to a two-way radio, so that people using the radio could gain access to the telephone network and those on the network could communicate with those using the radio.[34]

Throughout the 1970s, the FCC built on these precedents in two basic respects. First, in 1975, it created the *Part 68 rules,* a set of technical standards that, once met, entitle any equipment manufacturer to sell its wares to the public and demand cooperation from the telephone companies.[35] The Part 68 rules supplanted AT&T's last-gasp efforts to discriminate against equipment manufacturing rivals by forcing them to purchase, from AT&T, various "protective coupling devices." The ostensible purpose of those devices was to protect the integrity of the telephone network, but their actual effect was to raise rivals' costs and hamstring competition in violation of the antitrust laws, as the courts later found.[36]

Second, in connection with a set of orders in the 1970s and 1980s known as the *Computer Inquiries*, which we discuss more fully in chapter 5, the FCC required telephone companies for a time to sell equipment through structurally separated subsidiaries and to "unbundle" such sales from their telephone service offerings. This "separate subsidiary" requirement was designed (i) to keep telephone monopolies from anticompetitively linking their products in these two markets and (ii) to help regulators detect any effort by these monopolies to cross-subsidize their equipment operations by allocating excessive joint and common costs to their regulated telephone service rate base. (We discuss cross-subsidization concerns and the nature of joint and common costs in greater detail below.) By facilitating competition in the equipment market, the FCC's new rules triggered not just an enormous decline in prices for telephones and other equipment, but also an explosive growth in the variety of end user devices. These included computer modems, whose proliferation helped launch the Internet into public life.

Finally, when it broke up AT&T's Bell System in 1984 under the consent decree discussed below, the antitrust court prohibited the seven newly independent regional Bell companies (the "Baby Bells" such as Bell Atlantic, Ameritech, and BellSouth) from manufacturing telecommunications equipment. This line-of-business restriction included not just customer premises equipment, but also the very core of the telephone network, such as central office switches. In section 273 of the Communications Act,[37] added by the 1996 legislation, Congress replaced that antitrust prohibition with similar, statutory line-of-business restrictions, but it enabled the Bell companies to escape many of those restrictions once they satisfied certain conditions for opening their local markets to competition, as they now have.

B. Long distance competition and the AT&T consent decree

Much of telecommunications policy in the final quarter of the last century involved efforts by the Justice Department's Antitrust Division and a federal district court to keep AT&T's Bell System and, after divestiture, its Bell company progeny from leveraging their control over *local* markets to dominate the *long distance* market. Throughout most of the twentieth century, this was no issue at all because AT&T owned the only significant city-to-city transport facilities (AT&T Long Lines). For quite some time, these facilities were also considered part of the vast natural monopoly of telecommunications, and the FCC permitted AT&T to charge above-cost rates for long distance service as one mechanism among many for subsidizing low residential rates for basic service.

The assumption that the long distance market was a natural monopoly changed when, in the late 1960s and early 1970s, a small upstart called Microwave Communications, Inc.—now famous as MCI—first offered business customers city-to-city services using a new technology, microwave relay towers, to bypass AT&T's Long Lines. It is no surprise that the first major competition in the telecommunications industry came in the long distance market. As discussed, long distance rates were priced far above cost, and the call volumes between cities are typically great enough to provide large economies of scale to more than one carrier. A third factor was at work as well. The birth of modern computing had made businesses across the economy hungry for new data services involving communication between distant computers over telephone lines. For example, a given business might need ready access to airline flight schedules, financial market data, or the databases of Lexis-Nexis. Like most monopolies, the Bell System had been slow to adapt to the demand for these innovative data services, which then occupied only a niche market, and had continued to focus on its bread and butter: providing ordinary voice service. The entry of specialized data carriers like Datran, Telenet, and Tymnet, which designed specialized digital networks to carry computer traffic, came as a welcome contrast to Bell's continued reliance on outdated analog technology.

The vanguard of competition, however, was MCI, and its first ambitions were modest. It began by offering "private lines"—i.e., closed, point-to-point circuits—connecting the branch offices of large businesses in different cities. In granting MCI's application as a "specialized common carrier," the FCC noted the unmet demand for these private lines, including for use in data communications. Over time, MCI persuaded the FCC to let it go one step further and provide so-called FX ("foreign exchange") lines to its business customers.[38] These were private lines with a twist: one end connected to the Bell System's local exchange. Thus, MCI's FX line might connect two offices of the same company—say, one in New York and one in Chicago—but in New York, the line was assigned a local telephone number, and calls to that number appeared, from the perspective of the Bell company switch, to be ordinary local calls. Equipped with an access code, the company's employees could dial that number from anywhere in New York and, for the cost of a local call, be connected to the company's office in Chicago. Similarly, a ski resort in the Rocky Mountains might purchase a private line with the "open" end in Denver. The line would permit Denver residents to dial a local number to reach the resort and would enable the resort itself to place seemingly local calls to its own Denver suppliers. In each case, AT&T's Long Lines division would receive no toll revenues, and MCI would charge only a flat rate for the private line.

The final step in MCI's development, which marked its full emergence into the long distance (and not just private line) market, came in the form of a controversial new service called Execunet, first offered in 1975 and judicially validated in 1978.[39] Execunet involved, among other things, the use of private lines that were "open"—i.e., connected to Bell's local exchange—on *both* ends rather than just one. To take the example above, this meant that anyone authorized to gain access to the private line could call from anywhere in Chicago to anywhere in New York and vice versa, without paying toll charges to AT&T. Before long, MCI used such lines to make general-purpose long distance services available to the public at large: i.e., not just to the employees of large subscribing businesses, but to individual consumers as well that signed up with MCI. Separately, MCI also sought and received regulatory enforcement of the right to purchase AT&T's long distance services in bulk at the standard volume discounts available to AT&T's large business customers and then resell those services to customers of its own.[40]

AT&T's effective cooperation in providing non-discriminatory access to its local exchanges was essential to MCI's prospects in the long distance market. Because MCI could not possibly duplicate the Bell System's local facilities, its long distance network would be of little use if, because of Bell System recalcitrance, MCI had no feasible way to connect its network to its customers *and* to the parties those customers wished to call. AT&T understood that the denial of effective interconnection was a powerful anticompetitive tool, just as it had understood the same fact 60 years before, during the events leading up to the Kingsbury Commitment (see chapter 1). Consequently, AT&T fought tooth and nail to deprive MCI of effective access to its network. At one point, AT&T even unplugged from its local networks the supposedly "open" ends of the FX lines MCI had sold to its customers.[41] AT&T sought to justify its anticompetitive conduct on several grounds. Most fundamentally, it argued that permitting MCI to cherry-pick AT&T's highest margin customers in the long distance market—those who had been paying supracompetitive rates for many years—would undermine the commitment to "universal service" and would require substantial increases in local service rates in order to support the maintenance of the nation's telephone network.

In several different contexts, courts and regulators rejected AT&T's policy justifications and awarded its competitors a series of incremental victories until, in 1982, AT&T and the Justice Department entered into an antitrust consent decree (consummated in 1984) that required the complete divestiture of the Bell System's local exchange facilities from AT&T.[42] The decree also prohibited the newly independent Bell companies from providing long distance services themselves until they had satisfied the antitrust court that doing so posed no threat of anticompetitive behavior.

There were two basic rationales for splitting up AT&T and for quarantining the Bell companies, for the most part, to local telecommunications markets. The first was a concern about operational *discrimination*. AT&T had already agreed to interconnect with MCI's long distance network—i.e., to allow the use of its local exchange facilities to originate calls bound for MCI's network and to complete calls on the other end. But, as noted in chapter 1, there are many subtle ways in which a dominant carrier can create interconnection problems for new entrants. For example, it can reserve insufficient capacity on its interconnection trunks to meet customer demands for access to the rival long distance company's network during peak calling periods. AT&T Long Lines had given customers good reasons to perceive that, because of its affiliation with the Bell companies, they would get more dependable service from AT&T than from MCI. The fear was that, if the newly independent Bell companies were permitted to enter the long distance market, they—like the integrated AT&T before them—would find ways to discriminate in favor of their own long distance operations.

For good measure, the antitrust decree further subjected the Bell companies not just to this line-of-business restriction, but to affirmative *equal access* obligations as well. These requirements directed the Bell companies to upgrade their equipment to give AT&T's long distance rivals the same access as AT&T itself to the Bells' local networks. For example, in the 1980s, many subscribers that wished to avail themselves of MCI's low rates had to dial an access code first to reach MCI's network, wait for a second dial tone, and only then enter the digits of the party they wished to call. These extra dialing steps, which AT&T's long distance customers never confronted, inconvenienced MCI's customers and thus disadvantaged MCI in the long distance market. *Dialing parity* requirements, a type of equal access obligation, fix that problem by directing each local telephone company to reconfigure the connections between its switches and the networks of various long distance companies so that an end user can "pre-subscribe" to the long distance provider of her choice and need dial only "1" plus the called party's number to have her long distance calls carried by that provider.[43]

The other basic concern underlying the Bell companies' exclusion from the long distance market related to predatory *cross-subsidization*, to which we referred in the equipment manufacturing context. Under traditional rate-of-return regulation, the rates that the pre-divestiture AT&T could charge its local customers for particular services were set, in part, on the basis of the "costs" that appeared in its accounting books in connection with those services, plus a reasonable profit. But AT&T had a great many costs and a great many services, and matching particular costs to the particular services that "caused" them was an exercise in extreme subjectivity. Costs that were "joint and common" to a number of services—such as loop costs—were especially subject to manipulation because they did not truly belong to any one service category. Thus, whenever competition arose, AT&T enjoyed considerable discretion to assign costs away from competitive markets—thereby lowering prices and underselling rivals—and to attribute those costs instead to its operations in uncontested markets, where its captive customers would be forced to pay marginally higher rates. If successful, these surgical strikes on new entrants would enable AT&T to retain its monopoly position in most markets without threatening its ability to maintain relatively low residential telephone rates over the long term. Here again, the fear was that, if permitted to enter the long distance market after their separation from AT&T, the Bell companies would exploit the same anticompetitive opportunities as AT&T's integrated Bell System.

In the years following entry of the consent decree, these twin concerns—operational discrimination and predatory cross-subsidization—gradually became less compelling as a justification for the Bells' line-of-business restrictions. First, price cap regulation, both on the federal level and in many states, significantly alleviated the risk of predatory cross-subsidization. In particular, it prevented the Bell companies from obtaining near-automatic recovery of their book costs and thereby reduced their incentive to allocate all joint and common costs to their regulated operations while slashing prices to undercut competition in contested markets.[44] Indeed, the many local exchange carriers throughout the country that were *not* the offspring of AT&T's Bell System *were* permitted to offer long distance service during this period, and the FCC had developed accounting and other safeguards to protect unaffiliated long distance carriers from predatory conduct.[45] As for concerns about operational discrimination, years of successful administration of the equal access rules—in both Bell and non-Bell territories—had raised questions about the need for full-blown line-of-business restrictions to protect competition in the long distance market.[46]

Citing these developments, the Bell companies argued to the antitrust court in the years preceding 1996 that the decree's outright restriction on their entry into the long distance market was no longer warranted. In 1996, Congress largely rejected these arguments by perpetuating these line-of-business restrictions in statutory form—but it did give the Bell companies a statutory mechanism for overcoming those restrictions, as we discuss in the next chapter.

C. Competitive access services

Telecommunications competition first arose in the long distance market largely because the enormous call volumes *between* population centers, as opposed to *within* them, were adequate to support profitable entry by more than one carrier. Just as it is much cheaper (all else being equal) to deploy a single cable to a 100-unit apartment building than 100 different cables to 100 farms, it is also much cheaper to run a single multi-circuit transport pipe from one city to another than to disperse an equivalent number of circuits among many smaller pipes into hundreds of neighborhoods. In the 1980s, the next site of facilities-based competition predictably appeared in the market for special access links. This was not just because the Bell incumbents were sometimes providing technologically inferior access services, and not just because they were often providing access services at rates well above cost, but also because high traffic volumes in the access market enable competing carriers to enjoy large scale economies even if they serve only part of the customer base.

As noted earlier in this chapter, special access circuits are leased high capacity lines that directly connect businesses with large call volumes to the networks of long distance voice and data carriers, bypassing the incumbent telephone company's local switch (though not necessarily its network). Until the 1980s, these access services were provided overwhelmingly by the incumbent local telephone companies themselves and were priced well above cost. In the 1980s, *competitive access providers,* sometimes known as "CAPs," began enabling long distance carriers to bypass not just the incumbents' switches en route to their business customers, but also the incumbents' transport pipes (i.e., the links between the long distance network and the individual central offices serving given customers) and occasionally their loops as well. Beneath the streets of America's major cities, these providers laid extensive fiber "rings" that offered not just enormous bandwidth, but also critical "self-healing" properties that ensured network reliability: because signals could move in either direction around a given "ring" en route to a network node, customers remained connected even if a line was cut; the signals would simply move in the opposite direction. Thus, if a long distance company wished to provide its customers with a range of voice and data services, it could bypass the Bell networks in whole or in part by contracting with a competitive access provider. In so doing, the long distance company would avoid Bell's above-cost access charges, at least to some extent,[47] pay lower rates to these competitive access providers, receive more responsive service, and enjoy higher quality performance from the state-of-the-art digital technology that the Bells themselves were slow to provide.

In the years immediately preceding passage of the 1996 Act, the predominant "local competition" disputes in the telecommunications industry concerned the terms on which these competitive access providers could demand interconnection at an incumbent's central office when scale economies did not permit them to lay their own cables all the way to each individual end user. In the early 1990s, the FCC issued its *Expanded Interconnection Orders*, in which, among other things, it entitled these new providers to "collocate" (i.e., "co-locate") their own equipment for this purpose in specially designated areas within a central office.[48] As discussed in the next chapter, that initiative sparked a round of legal wrangling that extended through 1996, when Congress codified the collocation rights of competing carriers, and even then persisted for another six years until, in 2002, the courts finally upheld FCC regulations defining exactly how far those rights should go.

D. The first steps towards "local exchange" competition

By the mid-1990s, regulators had taken their first tentative steps towards promoting competition not just in *local access* markets, but also in *local exchange* markets. That distinction warrants a brief explanation at the outset. Let's say that you own a large suburban hotel. When guests punch 8 before dialing a long distance number, your hotel's internal switching equipment (its PBX) will pass their calls along to the access line that leads to the network of whatever default long distance carrier you have chosen for them. Suppose that a portion of that access line—typically the link between the telephone company's central office and the long distance network—is operated by a competitive access provider, which can undersell the incumbent for some portion of the access charges the incumbent would otherwise impose. This is *access* competition (sometimes described as a subcategory of "local" competition), but not *local exchange* competition. Punching 8 will not enable your guests to place local calls. Instead, the access provider's sole function is to connect guests to a single, predetermined long distance network.[49]

To place a local call, your guests must press 9, which directs the hotel's internal switching equipment to pass their calls along to the local telephone company's own lines, which lead in turn to its central office. Local exchange competition arises only when you, the hotel's owner, have a meaningful alternative to the incumbent local exchange carrier as the telephone company to which such calls are passed. As we discuss in later chapters, there are two different ways in which carriers might compete to offer you such a choice, and each presents different regulatory issues. A *facilities-based* competitor will arrange for these local calls to be routed to a switch of its own suitable for processing local traffic, and it may also own the high capacity loop connecting your hotel to that switch. The competitor will then need to obtain "interconnection trunks" linking its local switched network to that of the dominant incumbent carrier because it will need to hand off most of these outgoing local calls to the incumbent. A *non-facilities-based* competitor will lease capacity on the incumbent's switch (and loop) or otherwise resell the incumbent's local exchange services. Either way, if you choose a competing carrier to route your local exchange traffic, you will likely choose the same carrier to route your long distance traffic as well, just as you almost certainly use the same wireless company to handle your "local" and "long distance" cellphone calls.

Regulatory interest in promoting local exchange competition first arose in three principal and complementary contexts. First, a number of states, such as New York and California, began experimenting with creative schemes under which new entrants could interconnect with the incumbent's network and lease capacity on its facilities at low wholesale rates to provide competing local exchange services. Such leasing arrangements were indispensable to local exchange competition in all but the most densely populated business districts because there was generally little economic justification for building lines all the way out to each customer location. Among the first carriers to take advantage of these opportunities were the competitive access providers, which had already built transport networks (i.e., fiber rings) throughout many of the major downtown business districts.

Second, as part of the *Computer Inquiries,* the FCC devoted several years in the late 1980s and early 1990s to the development of complex regulatory schemes—known by the names "comparably efficient interconnection" and "open network architecture"—designed to give data carriers and other information service providers "unbundled" access to an incumbent's local network services on the same terms enjoyed by the incumbent's own information services affiliate. These are briefly noted in chapter 5. Third, in 1995, the Justice Department and Ameritech (a midwestern Bell company) entered into an agreement, quickly aborted after the 1996 Act became law, under which the Department promised to seek relaxation of the consent decree's line-of-business restrictions if Ameritech submitted to various requirements for leasing network capacity to rivals.[50]

The immediate practical consequences of all this regulatory experimentation were meager. By early 1996, the incumbent telephone companies still provided nearly all local exchange services throughout the United States. But the legacy of these early initiatives was nonetheless profound. When Congress—or, more precisely, the interested parties—sat down to write the 1996 Act, their immediate influences were these three regulatory experiments: by the states, by the FCC, and by the Justice Department. The result was the set of "local competition provisions" of sections 251 and 252, which we cover in the next chapter.

3

Wireline Competition Under the 1996 Act

The previous chapter presented the backdrop for the Telecommunications Act of 1996,[1] the most important telecommunications legislation—and arguably the most important regulatory legislation of any kind—since the New Deal. The Act's importance is matched only by its opacity. As Justice Antonin Scalia wrote for the Supreme Court in 1999: "It would be gross understatement to say that the 1996 Act is not a model of clarity. It is in many important respects a model of ambiguity or indeed even self-contradiction. That is most unfortunate for a piece of legislation that profoundly affects a crucial segment of the economy worth tens of billions of dollars."[2] And, as we shall see, the Act has already become anachronistic in key respects, in part because the statutory drafters did not fully anticipate the Internet's radical reordering of the telecommunications industry. Until Congress steps back into the fray, however, the Act's existing terms, however ambiguous and outdated they may be, will govern wireline competition policy in the United States.

This chapter's discussion of the 1996 Act is divided into three parts, which progress from the more general to the more specific. Part I summarizes the Act's broad-brush competitive objectives. Part II surveys the nuts and bolts of Act's major provisions. Part III then focuses on the central facilities-leasing disputes that have dominated wireline competition policy since 1996.

I. The Objectives

The Act's foremost aspiration is greater competition in local telecommunications markets.[3] In essence, Congress sought to accelerate the defining trend of telecommunications policy throughout the second half of the twentieth century: the steady roll-back of the portions of the network deemed subject to natural monopoly economics. This roll-back began with the long distance market, as MCI and others showed that more than one carrier could profitably compete for a share of the city-to-city transport market. The roll-back then continued, in the 1980s and 1990s, with the emergence of a market for competitive "access" services, which enable long distance companies to bypass some or all of the incumbent company's local network in connecting with large business customers for voice and data transmission.

A core principle of the 1996 Act is that the natural monopoly assumption can and should be rolled back even further into the local exchange market itself, and not just the high volume transport markets (such as long distance or "access"). To that end, Congress added a Part II, entitled "Development of Competitive Markets," to Title II of the Communications Act of 1934. The key provisions within Part II are sections 251 and 252, which mandate interconnection between rival carriers and give new competitors vaguely defined rights to lease the incumbents' network facilities, or capacity on those facilities, as a means of providing competing local services.*

There is some consensus, though not unanimity, that Congress designed these provisions to produce, *in the long term*, local competition that is largely "facilities-based." This term means different things in different contexts, but we use it here to denote any form of competition in which each carrier provides service at least partly over its own local facilities rather than leasing all relevant facilities from the incumbents or reselling the incumbent's finished services. The Act presupposes that, with the right regulatory jump start, technological innovations and increased traffic volumes will someday make it economical for multiple carriers in the same local markets to provide telecommunications services over their own local

---

* The 1996 Act formally "amends" the Communications Act of 1934. For the most part, the section numbers used to denote provisions added by the 1996 Act are technically sections of the amended Communications Act itself, not of the 1996 Act. Most, but not all, of the major sections of the Communications Act correspond to the sections of Title 47 of the United States Code. Readers may assume that correspondence when we discuss a particular section number without providing a formal Code citation.

switches and, in many cases, over their own last mile connections to the customer. A few carriers contend, to be sure, that the natural monopoly characteristics of local markets are so durable that widespread facilities-based competition is neither possible in many markets, even over the long term, nor particularly important. These carriers believe that regulators should thus indefinitely allow them to lease all aspects of the incumbents' local networks at regulated wholesale prices to foster a shallower type of competition in which, with few exceptions, new entrants offer essentially the same services as incumbents and distinguish themselves by offering those services at lower prices or in different bundles. But this is a minority view. Eventual deregulation of the telecommunications industry is a long-term objective of the 1996 Act, and that objective will remain out of reach until there is widespread facilities-based competition.

Some of the most important regulatory disputes today concern how much and how long of a regulatory jump start is needed to ensure an eventual transition to such competition. At the risk of some overgeneralization, there are two warring sides in this debate: (i) the Bell companies and other incumbent telephone companies, called *ILECs* ("EYE-lecks") for "incumbent local exchange carriers" and (ii) their new local exchange rivals, which are known as *CLECs* ("SEE-lecks") for "competitive local exchange carriers," and which were led, during the Act's first decade, by the traditional long distance giants AT&T and MCI.* Since 1996, the incumbent local providers have argued that regulators should focus primarily on encouraging facilities-based competition sooner rather than later and that, to achieve this objective, regulators need to restrict new entrants to leasing options that are both less extensive and more expensive than what the entrants themselves propose. The incumbents reason that unlimited leasing rights undermine incentives for investing in new facilities, both for new entrants (because, incumbents say, anyone would prefer short-term leases at guaranteed low rates over risky capital expenditures) and for incumbents (because liberal leasing rights mean having to share the fruits of any

---

* To keep the acronyms in this chapter to a bare minimum, we often refer to ILECs as "incumbents" and to CLECs as "competitors" or "new entrants." Of course, ILECs are themselves the competitors of CLECs and, as discussed in later chapters, of cable companies, wireless carriers, and other providers of alternative transmission platforms.

capital expenditures that succeed while still bearing the full loss on capital expenditures that fail). The new entrants counter that, without expansive leasing rights, many residential and small business consumers will see no local wireline competition of any kind, now or in the foreseeable future.

A related objective of the 1996 Act is the elimination of *regulatory*, and not just economic, barriers to entry. This goal is expressed most directly in section 253, which formally preempts any state or local law that protects monopoly franchises from competition. Congress likewise sought to bring greater competition to all telecommunications markets by breaking down the explicit line-of-business restrictions that had artificially protected long-standing incumbents in those markets. Most significantly, section 271, added by the 1996 Act, creates a procedure for knocking down the wall between "local" and "long distance" providers of wireline services.

As discussed in chapter 2, the 1984 AT&T consent decree barred the largest incumbent telephone companies—the regional Bell companies spawned by the break-up of the Bell System—from providing most long distance services within their traditional local service regions. The Bells had long sought relaxation of that line-of-business restriction from the antitrust court on the ground that it was no longer necessary to protect fair competition in the long distance market. But the incumbent long distance companies, including AT&T and MCI, opposed that request, and it was unclear when, if ever, the Bells would win judicial relief. The 1996 Act struck a grand political compromise between the two sides by permitting each Bell company to provide long distance service after persuading the FCC (rather than the antitrust court) that it had opened its local exchange market in a given state to competition and that the Bell's entry into the long distance market would serve the public interest. Because AT&T and MCI were expected to rank among the primary providers of local exchange competition, the 1996 Act triggered a race between the Bells, on the one hand, and the long distance companies, on the other, to see who would be the first to provide a complete "bundle" of local and long distance services to given consumers.

Congress likewise sought to lower the regulatory barriers that kept a given telephone company and cable company from competing on each other's turf. Section 253 preempted any state or municipal laws that kept cable companies out of the telephone business, and a separate provision relaxed federal restrictions on the provision of video programming over a telephone company's lines.[4] For many years, though, neither the cable industry nor the telephone industry showed much interest in entering the other's traditional markets. With a few notable exceptions,[5] cable companies concluded that the cost of upgrading their systems to provide ordinary circuit-switched voice services normally exceeded the expected revenues from those services, particularly since telephone companies already served many residential customers at subsidized, below-cost rates. Only recently have cable companies broadly reconsidered that cost calculus, now that it has become feasible for them to provide high quality voice services over cable Internet connections at comparatively low incremental cost (see chapters 1 and 6). Finally, the copper telephone lines that serve most residential subscribers normally have too little bandwidth to provide a widespread competitive alternative to conventional cable TV service. Not until the first years of the new millennium did the major telephone companies express serious interest in deploying new fiber-optic facilities to provide meaningful video competition to the cable companies (see chapters 4 and 5).

Although Congress took limited steps to ensure competitive parity between telephone and cable companies in the provision of voice and video services, the real competition between wireline and cable platforms arose in a market that hardly existed in 1996: the market for broadband Internet access. Because Congress did not foresee that cable and telephone companies would compete in this market, it did not set forth a clear regulatory framework for that market—let alone contemplate how to ensure regulatory parity between these competing platforms, as chapter 5 explains in depth. More generally, Congress largely left in place the arbitrarily compartmentalized regulation of the industry reflected in the multiple "Titles" of the Communications Act. That approach, as discussed in chapters 1 and 6, subjects distinct last mile transmission platforms to radically different forms of regulation on the assumption that those platforms will not be used in competition with one another. Now that the growth of Internet technologies has undermined that assumption for good, the shortcomings of this approach have assumed enormous significance.

A third key objective of the 1996 Act is to maintain low-priced telephone service for residential customers in sparsely populated areas even though greater competition will erode the source of traditional implicit price subsidies. This third objective can be challenging to reconcile with the first two goals. As we explained in the previous chapter, the above-cost rates that once-captive business customers and others had to pay incumbents in the absence of effective competition had long underwritten inexpensive telephone service for "high cost" customers. But those business customers, who often pay twice the rates of residential customers even though they are no costlier to serve, are the very customers that the competitors are most likely to cherry-pick from the outset. In the long run, as such competition develops, the incumbents will gradually forfeit these customers altogether or will be forced to lower their rates in order to keep them. In either event, they will eventually lose the source of the implicit cross-subsidies that allowed them to serve other customers at a loss and still balance their books.

There are essentially three long-term outcomes to the drying up of traditional cross-subsidies: first, the incumbents could go bankrupt; second, regulators could let the incumbents charge more for services previously sold below cost, in a process known as "rate rebalancing"; or, third, regulators could come up with some other means of artificially holding down telephone rates below the cost of providing service in high cost areas. Because the first option would be politically unsustainable and probably unconstitutional,[6] and because the second is politically unattractive as well, Congress focused on the third. In section 254 of the newly revised Communications Act, Congress ordered the FCC to set up a competitively neutral "universal service fund" that operates like a specialized taxation system. Under this system, as currently implemented, carriers contribute money into the fund on the basis of their retail "interstate" revenues, and a federal administrator then doles out the money, in the form of explicit subsidies, to ensure "affordable" and "reasonably comparable" rates throughout the country. As we will discuss in chapter 10, the 1996 Act gave the FCC and state public utility commissions considerable leeway in managing the transition to competitively neutral subsidy mechanisms, and this transition has moved quite slowly. For now, the important point is that implicit cross-subsidies are still commonplace, and many residential rates remain below cost because of them rather than because of any explicit funding alternative.

II. The Wireline Competition Provisions

We now turn to the nuts and bolts of the key provisions added by the 1996 Act. Arguably the most fundamental of these provisions is section 253(a), which provides that "[n]o State or local statute or regulation, or other State or local legal requirement, may prohibit or have the effect of prohibiting the ability of any entity to provide any interstate or intrastate telecommunications service." In that one sentence, Congress drove the last nail into the coffin of exclusive franchise arrangements in the telecommunications industry, which, in a number of areas, still protected telephone monopolies against competitive entry.[7]

Apart from section 253, the main wireline provisions of the 1996 Act are contained in sections 251 and 252, sometimes called the *local competition provisions*, and in section 271, which enables the Bell companies to apply for entry into the long distance market.[8] We have reprinted these provisions, along with several others, in the Statutory Addendum. If you look at them now, before reading on, you will discover why telecommunications law is so daunting to newcomers. The provisions are a confusing laundry list of several dozen rights and obligations, all expressed in specialized industry jargon.

The simplest way to conceptualize these provisions is to refer back to the three basic economic attributes of this industry, discussed in chapter 1: *network effects*, virtually unparalleled *scale economies*, and *monopoly leveraging* opportunities. Much of the 1996 Act can be understood as a systematic effort to deal with each of these three concerns in the world of wireline communications. Sections 251 and 252 address network effects by granting new entrants expansive rights to interconnect their networks with those of the incumbents and by regulating the terms on which multiple carriers are compensated for the costs of calls that cross more than one carrier's network. Sections 251 and 252 separately address the disparity in scale economies between incumbents and new entrants by allowing the latter (i) to lease capacity on certain of the incumbents' network facilities and (ii) to resell the incumbents' retail services to customers of their own. Section 271, in turn, addresses leveraging concerns by conditioning entry of the Bell companies into the long distance market upon a showing that they have loosened their monopoly grip on the local market (essentially by complying with sections 251 and 252) and have set up separate long distance affiliates to preclude anticompetitive practices against unaffiliated long distance companies. We address each of these statutory mechanisms in turn, after a brief introduction to the major terms and players.

A. A taxonomy of carriers and services

Sections 251 and 252, like the rest of Title II of the Communications Act (into which they were inserted), address the relationships among "telecommunications carriers." These are the carriers that provide "telecommunications services," defined as basic transmission services offered "for a fee directly to the public, or to such classes of users as to be effectively available directly to the public, regardless of the facilities used."[9] The term "telecommunications service" is essentially synonymous with the more traditional term "common carriage service."[10] Under the usual test, a "common carrier" is a provider of transmission services that (i) holds itself out to serve all customers interested in buying any services the carrier offers and (ii) allows customers to transmit whatever content they wish by means of its facilities.[11] Stated simply, common carriers—as opposed to "private carriers"—do "not make individualized decisions, in particular cases, whether and on what terms to deal."[12] Moreover, many carriers—such as traditional telephone companies—are not normally permitted to act as private carriers in their traditional service markets, but face regulatory obligations to act as common carriers whether they would like to do so in a particular context or not.[13]

Not every service that involves telecommunications is a "telecommunications service" or "common carriage service." For example, when the telephone company sells you broadband access to the Internet through a DSL connection, it is providing you an "information service" by means of telecommunications.[14] But, under the FCC's traditional view of the relevant statutory definitions, now drawn into question by a 2003 court decision,[15] the carrier is not providing you a "telecommunications service" and is therefore not acting as a "telecommunications carrier" when it sells you broadband Internet access. Keep this esoteric detail in the back of your mind as you read through the following chapters; it will reappear with a vengeance in chapters 5 and 6 below.

"Local exchange carriers" (LECs) are a species of "telecommunications carriers" and are defined as companies that provide either local exchange service or "access" services or both.[16] Not all telecommunications carriers are local exchange carriers; for example, pure long distance companies are telecommunications carriers, but not local exchange carriers. By special statutory fiat, mobile wireless carriers are also not local exchange carriers, unless and until the FCC says otherwise, but they are "telecommunications carriers."[17]

The world of local exchange carriers, as noted above, is subdivided into incumbents (ILECs) and competitors (CLECs). The largest incumbents by far remain the regional Bell Operating Companies, also known as *RBOCs* or *BOCs*.[18] We usually refer to them simply as "Bell companies." There were seven regional Bell companies in 1996, but now, as the result of consolidation, there are only four: (i) Verizon, a combination of Bell Atlantic and NYNEX (plus the non-BOC GTE); (ii) SBC, a combination of Southwestern Bell, Pacific Telesis, and Ameritech (plus the formally non-BOC Southern New England Telephone); (iii) BellSouth; and (iv) Qwest, a long distance company and Internet backbone provider that purchased the former U S WEST in 2000 and inherited its regulatory obligations. There are hundreds of smaller ILECs throughout the country, particularly in rural areas, that were never part of the Bell System and remain "independent carriers." Many of these independents are small enough to qualify as "rural" carriers, a characterization that entitles them to larger universal service subsidies than the Bell companies and, under section 251(f), special statutory exemptions from the most intrusive requirements that the 1996 Act imposes on incumbents generally.

There are many CLECs as well, of which the largest, as of this writing, include the traditional long distance companies AT&T and MCI (formerly WorldCom). CLECs are defined by their customers, which, at the highest level of generality, fall into two different categories. The first such category consists of *enterprise customers:* large businesses, often with multiple branch offices, that generate massive voice and data traffic on a daily basis (think Merrill Lynch or General Electric). Carriers like AT&T and MCI typically connect an enterprise customer directly to their networks over fiber-optic transport pipes. In downtown urban areas, they commonly own these transport pipes outright—both AT&T and MCI purchased competitive access providers in the late 1990s—or lease them on the open market. For areas outside the major business districts, these carriers often connect business customers to their networks by leasing capacity on the incumbent's transport pipes. A central question is what price they must pay to lease that capacity. Must they pay the incumbents relatively high rates for the traditional "special access" services discussed in chapter 2? Or may they instead lease capacity on the underlying transport facilities at the significantly lower "cost"-based rates applicable to network elements? For the time being, the answer turns on complex, somewhat artificial regulatory distinctions between "local" and "long distance" services and between

"CLECs" and "long distance carriers," an issue further considered at the end of this chapter.

The second major category of CLEC customers consists of smaller business and residential subscribers, known as *mass market customers*, to whom long distance carriers like AT&T and MCI have sold conventional long distance services for many years. Such carriers have entered the local mass market by leasing, directly from the incumbents at regulated rates, whatever local facilities they need to provide these smaller customers with the same "bundles" of local and long distance services that the Bell companies have offered since winning authorization to enter the long distance market throughout the United States. As we discuss later in this chapter, recent regulatory developments have made this strategy more difficult for CLECs and have led AT&T and others to announce plans to phase out their "mass market" operations over the long term.

Finally, although we have focused on AT&T and MCI, there are dozens of other CLECs as well that vie to enter local markets under the 1996 Act. Many of these focus their business plans on particular market niches. For example, Covad leases lines from incumbents mostly to provide high speed Internet access through DSL technology. Sometimes such competitive data providers team up with more conventional CLECs like AT&T and MCI to provide complete bundles of voice and data services to consumers.

The basic distinction between CLECs and ILECs, statutory definitions aside, is that the latter have traditionally possessed market power in the local exchange market. ILECs are therefore regulated much more heavily than CLECs, and ILEC-specific obligations are the focus of this chapter. Nonetheless, in sections 251(a) and (b), Congress imposed a handful of obligations on all local exchange carriers, including all CLECs, with potential exceptions only for certain rural carriers.[19] For example, section 251(b)(2) directs CLECs and ILECs alike to cooperate with regulatory efforts to make telephone numbers "portable" for customers that change carriers (see chapter 8). Section 251(b)(4) requires all local exchange carriers to share their "poles, ducts, conduits, and rights-of-way" with other telecommunications carriers. All local exchange carriers must further allow other carriers to purchase their services for resale to the public (section 251(b)(1)); interconnect with other carriers (section 251(a)); and strike "reciprocal compensation" deals to ensure mutual recovery of the costs of calls involving the networks of more than one carrier (section 251(b)(5)).

Apart from critical questions about the "reciprocal compensation" mandate (see chapter 9), however, the lion's share of controversy about the 1996 Act involves the provisions, all set out within section 251(c), that specify obligations imposed only on the incumbents. The rules we are about to describe are *default rules* only. In theory, incumbents and competitors are free to negotiate whatever arrangements they like, so long as they do not discriminate against third parties. But, given the inability of incumbents and competitors to agree on very much, in part because no company has any incentive to agree to outcomes less favorable than what it could receive from regulators, these default rules end up governing the most important aspects of local competition.

B. Addressing network effects: interconnection and collocation

Although section 251(a) requires all "telecommunications carriers" to interconnect with one another on *some* terms, incumbents alone are subject to a highly specific set of rigorous interconnection obligations. Under sections 251(c)(2) and (c)(6), competing local exchange carriers may demand interconnection with the incumbent's network at "any technically feasible point," not just a location of the incumbent's choosing, and may assert rights to "collocate" (i.e., "co-locate") their facilities on the incumbent's property at tightly regulated rates based on "cost."

In plain English, this means, among other things, that any competitor may rent space in an incumbent's central office (the building that houses the incumbent's switch); place its equipment there to interconnect with the incumbent's network; and purchase various related services, such as power and air conditioning, from the incumbent. A competitor may also place its equipment in the incumbent's central office if it has leased some of the incumbent's loops for purposes of serving the customers at the other end and needs to link all these loops, via a high capacity transport pipe, to its own switch.

For many years, the FCC and the courts engaged in a game of legal ping-pong about the legal limits on the Commission's authority to impose liberal collocation rules at the expense of the incumbents' property interests. The ultimate result, reached in 2002, is that competitors may demand room to place necessary equipment in an incumbent's central office so long as (i) the primary function of the collocated equipment is to allow interconnection or access to an incumbent's transmission facilities, (ii) any additional functions are logically related to that primary function, and (iii) the additional functions do not increase the relative burden on the incumbent's property interests.[20]

The rights described here are those of a competitor to interconnect with an incumbent by placing its equipment on the incumbent's property (or, in an arrangement known as "virtual collocation," by directing the incumbent to dedicate some its own equipment to the same task). Under section 252(d)(1), regulators normally limit the rates a competitor must pay for such interconnection to the incumbent's costs of hosting the relevant equipment in its central office. These collocation rights are distinct from the "intercarrier compensation" rules governing how much a carrier that originates a given call owes the carrier that completes it for the latter's cost of delivering the call from the point of hand-off to the called party. We discuss the latter rules in chapter 9.

C. Addressing scale economies: "network elements" and "resale"

The interconnection obligations just described go a long way towards reducing any anticompetitive advantage that network effects might otherwise give incumbents in the local exchange market. But, as discussed in chapter 1, these obligations do very little to help new entrants match the overwhelming scale economies that incumbents enjoy by virtue of having built up a ubiquitous network over many decades of regulated monopoly. The next two statutory rights discussed here, the rights of new entrants (i) to lease capacity on an incumbent's network facilities at regulated prices and (ii) to "resell" an incumbent's retail services, are designed to enable new entrants to share in those scale economies—up to a point.

Leasing an incumbent's network elements

Suppose that you manage an upstart telecommunications carrier and wish to provide both local and long distance service to residential customers in a suburban neighborhood. Precisely because your customer base is small and your scale economies low, it might well be financially infeasible for you to incur the enormous fixed costs needed to build a complete new wireline network out to your prospective new subscribers. One way out of that Catch 22, which we introduced in chapter 1, is to lease existing lines from the incumbent, so long as the lease rates are low enough. Over time, if your customer base grows, increased scale economies might then justify the construction of your own network.

In sections 251(c)(3) and 252(d)(1), Congress facilitated this process by giving new entrants a right not just to interconnect with incumbents, but to obtain "access to [the incumbents'] network elements on an unbundled basis"—i.e., to lease capacity on the incumbents' network facilities—at regulated "cost"-based rates. These unbundled network elements are called *UNEs* (pronounced YOO-neez). In this context, to say that network elements are available "on an unbundled basis" is simply to say that the competitor may, if it wishes, lease them individually at separate rates or in combinations of its choosing. It does not mean, however, that the incumbent may unilaterally disconnect requested facilities from one another for the purpose of inconveniencing the competitor, a point the Supreme Court confirmed in 1999.[21]

Although we will often use the phrase "leasing the incumbent's facilities" as an intuitive shorthand for the statutory concept of "obtaining access to network elements," the latter phrase is sometimes technically more accurate.[22] What a competitor receives when it invokes rights under section 251(c)(3) is not always a discrete physical "facility" as such—although it can be, as in the case of a copper loop. Often, the competitor receives only *capacity* on such a facility, along with its "features, functions, and capabilities."[23] For example, when a competitor leases "dedicated transport" as a network element from an incumbent, it does not normally lease an entire fiber-optic strand; instead, it leases a fixed increment of capacity on that strand. Indeed, the FCC went one step further and until recently permitted competitors to lease, as "network elements," not just *fixed* increments of capacity, but *variable* (per-minute) increments as well—as in the case of access to an incumbent's switch (discussed in part III of this chapter).

A related provision, section 251(d)(2), directs the Commission to limit the network elements subject to unbundling under section 251(c)(3) by "consider[ing], at a minimum, whether . . . the failure to provide access to such network elements would impair the ability of the telecommunications carrier seeking access to provide the services that it seeks to offer."[24] This statutory mandate is known as the *impairment standard*. In essence, this provision tells the FCC to identify, at some level of generality, the network elements that a competitor truly needs in order to compete, and to limit the unbundling obligation to those elements alone. As noted in chapter 5, the FCC construes the "at a minimum" language to give it some discretion to impose or withhold unbundling obligations in the service of larger statutory goals even when doing so may be in tension with the formal outcome of the "impairment" inquiry.

For eight years after 1996, when the FCC issued its massive *Local Competition Order* adopting the first rules implementing sections 251 and 252,[25] the Commission generally followed a permissive reading of the "impairment standard." As this book goes to press, despite this policy's multiple setbacks in court, a competitor can still sometimes lease from an incumbent essentially all facilities and network functionalities to provide telephone service, including the loop and capacity on the incumbent's switches and inter-switch transport links. This arrangement, which the FCC began phasing out in late 2004, has come to be known as *the UNE platform* or *UNE-P.*

Alternatively, a competitor might bring some of its own local exchange facilities to the table and lease others from the incumbent. For example, it might lease the incumbent's loops by themselves and connect them to its own switch. Or it might lease those loops in combination with fixed capacity on the incumbent's transport facilities, again for purposes of connecting its customers ultimately to its own switch. That entry strategy is known as *UNE-L,* with the "L" (for loop) distinguishing it from "UNE-P." We discuss the regulatory debates concerning these two entry strategies later in this chapter. In chapter 5, we address the now quite limited circumstances in which a competitor may lease an incumbent's facilities for the provision of broadband Internet access.

The TELRIC pricing standard. Rights to lease network elements will promote welfare-enhancing competition only if the rates for those elements are set appropriately. Section 252(d)(1) provides that such rates, like the rates for collocation arrangements, "shall be based on the cost . . . of providing" them. As discussed below, individual state public utility commissions set actual carrier-to-carrier rates on the basis of the FCC's rules implementing this "cost" standard.

In 1996, just after the Act was passed, the FCC construed this standard to require states to base network element rates on *forward-looking cost* rather than "historical" or "embedded" cost. This means that when a competitor leases an incumbent's network assets to provide services of its own, the rates it pays the incumbent are calculated on the basis of what it would cost today to obtain those assets or their functional equivalent, not what it actually cost the incumbent to obtain the particular facilities at issue, as recorded on its books. Suppose, for example, that a new entrant seeks to lease capacity on a switch that actually cost the incumbent $10 million to purchase and install five years ago but that would cost only $5 million to purchase and install today. Under the FCC's approach, which aims to reflect the dynamics of a competitive market, the latter figure would form the starting point for determining how much the entrant must pay the incumbent for leasing that capacity. Because technological innovation has caused many unexpected declines in the value of certain telecommunications assets, such as switches, the conventional wisdom (which may be wrong in various contexts) is that rates would generally be higher under an historical cost methodology than under a forward-looking approach.

Since 1996, the FCC has required the use of a forward-looking methodology it has dubbed "total element long run incremental cost," or *TELRIC*. Controversially, this methodology instructs state agencies to base their forward-looking cost estimates not on the incumbent's network design and technology mix, but on what it would cost a hypothetical "most efficient" carrier to build an entirely new network from scratch today, taking as given only the locations of the incumbent's existing switches.[26] In its 2002 decision in *Verizon Communications Inc. v. FCC*, after six years of litigation and uncertainty, the Supreme Court finally upheld TELRIC against claims by the incumbents that this methodology *necessarily* produces network element rates so low that they unlawfully "strand" (deny recovery on) past investments and undermine the incentives of incumbents and competitors alike to invest in new facilities.[27]

TELRIC's history and theoretical rationale are complex, and readers interested in a comprehensive exposition will find it in appendix A to this book. Here we emphasize two points, each of which helps explain our abbreviated treatment of the issue in this chapter.

The first point relates to the concern, neatly summarized by Judge Frank Easterbrook, that "[p]rices for unbundled elements affect not only the allocation of income among producers but also new investment and innovation: if the price to rivals is too low, they won't build their own plant (why make capital investments when you can buy for less, one unbundled element at a time?), and the incumbents won't maintain or upgrade their facilities (why make costly capital investments if you have to sell local loops to rivals for less than it costs to produce them?)."[28] Although there is much debate about whether, in application, TELRIC dampens ILEC and CLEC investment incentives in these respects, the more fundamental disagreement in that debate often concerns the FCC's implementation of the underlying impairment standard for unbundling. TELRIC applies to a network element only once the FCC decides, under section 251(d)(2), that the element should be subject to mandatory leasing in the first place. And, in making such decisions, the Commission purports to take into account the same types of issues: whether CLECs can feasibly duplicate the element in question and whether subjecting the element to sharing obligations would harm investment incentives. This is not to say that TELRIC's methodological details are unimportant to the "price signals" that CLECs and ILECs receive about when it would or would not make sense to build new facilities, but rather that those details must be viewed in the larger context of the FCC's implementation of section 251.

Second, it is unclear how much the theoretical details of any FCC pricing methodology matter to the actual rates that state commissions end up assigning to particular network elements. As Eli Noam explains, with only slight exaggeration: "Regulators do not really care about theory but about outcomes, along the lines determined by the political system. . . . [P]rices are the tool; economic theorists merely provide the rationale."[29] Or, as one former state commissioner argues, the FCC's pricing methodology is, in the hands of state regulators, just a malleable means of inviting entry into selected markets by "creating a margin between wholesale and retail rates."[30] To be sure, the FCC's methodological choices do provide some guidance to the state regulators charged with implementing them. But that guidance is far less outcome-determinative than the rhetoric about TELRIC would suggest.

Reselling an incumbent's retail services

To address the scale economies problem through another means, Congress added one more entry right to the mix that is ostensibly (though not ultimately, as we shall see) independent of the debate about leasing network elements. Section 251(c)(4) permits a new entrant to sign up large numbers of local service customers with the stroke of a pen by reselling an incumbent's "retail" services under its own brand name. That way, it can build up customer loyalty, develop an established base of customers for a particular geographic area, and only then—when the economies of scale are great enough—serve these customers using at least some facilities of its own. Indeed, MCI followed this very strategy while building its long distance business in the 1970s and 1980s.[31]

Entering the local market by reselling an incumbent's services would seldom be a very effective tool for a competitor if it had to pay the incumbent the full retail price for those services. The competitor's retail rates must cover its own costs of sales, marketing, and billing. But the incumbent's underlying rate usually reflects *its* own retail-specific costs, so tacking on a surcharge for competitor-specific retail functions effectively double-charges the ultimate customer. And, most of the time, customers would be uninterested in paying the competitor more for the same local telephone service that they could purchase instead from the incumbent at a lower price.

To make resale a more plausible entry strategy, Congress entitled competitors to obtain, for resale, an incumbent's "retail" services at retail rates *minus* the retail-specific costs (of marketing, billing, etc.) that the incumbent will "avoid" by virtue of no longer providing retail service to the customers at issue. This pricing formula, found in section 252(d)(3), is known as "retail minus avoided cost" or "the avoided-cost discount." (Although competitors are separately required under section 251(b)(1) to allow other carriers to resell *their* services, they need not provide any such discount.) In theory, at least, the avoided-cost discount should permit the competitor to charge its customers no more than the incumbent charges them, and so build up its brand identification and customer base at relatively low risk. In practice, the attractiveness of this resale option to new entrants dimmed once a regulatory consensus emerged, solidified by a 2000 court of appeals decision,[32] that incumbents "avoid" only a limited portion of their retail-specific costs when they lose retail customers to resellers. After all, even if an incumbent loses customers to rivals, it still must typically keep all of the same systems in place to serve its remaining customers. So applied, the avoided-cost discount has often proved insufficient to make the resale option a successful entry strategy in local markets.

D. Procedures for implementing the local competition provisions

The text of the 1996 Act is notoriously unclear on the respective roles of the FCC and the states in giving practical effect to the local competition provisions. In October 1996, the Eighth Circuit, sitting in St. Louis, stayed many of the FCC's implementing rules, including the TELRIC pricing methodology, on the ground that the Commission had no statutory authority to adopt such rules. The court believed that, in designing the 1996 Act, Congress had largely meant to follow the traditional "dual jurisdiction" framework of the Communications Act of 1934. As discussed in chapter 2, this framework, where applicable, divides the subject matter of telecommunications law into separate "interstate" and "intrastate" spheres and, under section 2(b), fences off the FCC from the latter. The Eighth Circuit concluded that matters relating to local exchange competition are essentially intrastate in character and that Congress meant to give individual state public utility commissions, not the FCC, authority to resolve most of those issues. In the Eighth Circuit's words, section 2(b) "is hog tight, horse high, and bull strong, preventing the FCC from intruding on the states' intrastate turf."[33]

This barnyard metaphor remained the law until January 1999, when the Supreme Court reversed the Eighth Circuit in *AT&T Corp. v. Iowa Utilities Board*.[34] By a 5-3 margin, the Court ruled that Congress had implicitly given the FCC general jurisdiction to adopt preemptive regulations fleshing out the local competition provisions. The Court relied for this conclusion on section 201(b) of the original Communications Act, which provides that "[t]he Commission may prescribe such rules and regulations as may be necessary in the public interest to carry out the provisions of this [Act]." Writing for the majority, the Court held that this provision "means what it says: The FCC has rulemaking authority to carry out the 'provisions of this Act,' which include §§ 251 and 252, added by the Telecommunications Act of 1996."[35] In the sphere of local competition, the Court thus replaced the dual jurisdiction framework with a new model of cooperative federalism, which erases the distinction between "interstate" and "intrastate" matters and directs the FCC and state commissions to work together in complementary capacities to implement the local competition provisions. In particular, the FCC establishes the basic rules governing local competition matters, and state public utility commissions apply those rules in resolving specific carrier-to-carrier disputes.[36]

The resolution of such disputes is governed by the procedural provisions of section 252. The process begins when a competitor asks an incumbent to enter into an "interconnection agreement" containing the key terms that will govern the relationship between the two carriers for a period of years (typically about three). One of two things might happen. First, the two carriers might resolve all relevant issues without regulatory intervention. In that event, they simply file their completed agreement with the relevant state commission, which in turn must approve it so long as it does not harm third parties or otherwise threaten the public interest. The state commission may not conduct a more searching inquiry into whether one side or the other might have gotten a better deal if it had pressed its section 251 rights to the mat.[37]

Alternatively, the negotiations might break down, either because the parties disagree about what each side owes under the governing law or simply because one side or the other believes that it can achieve a more favorable outcome by taking the matter to litigation. In that event, the state commission arbitrates the disputed issues under procedures spelled out in section 252, applying the rules of the 1996 Act, the FCC's implementing regulations, and any supplemental (and consistent) rules of state law.[38] Either side may appeal the state commission's order by filing suit in the relevant federal district court.[39] The court then reviews the order for compliance with federal law and (under its pendent jurisdiction) with state law too, if necessary. If it finds problems, it remands the matter to the state commission for further proceedings. In appendix B, we address the complex jurisdictional and procedural issues presented by a party's subsequent efforts to enforce the terms of such interconnection agreements.

Section 252(i) requires a carrier to "make available any interconnection, service, or network element provided under an agreement approved under this section to which it is a party to any other requesting telecommunications carrier upon the same terms and conditions as those provided in the agreement." The FCC interpreted this provision in 1996 to allow competitors, with minor limitations, to mix and match provisions from any of the incumbent's existing interconnection agreements, choose the provisions most favorable to them (and least favorable to the incumbent), and reject other provisions in the same agreements. This *pick-and-choose rule* was controversial because many in the industry believed that it discouraged private negotiations as an alternative to arbitration. Incumbents were concerned that, if they made special concessions to competitor X on one issue to win corresponding concessions on another, competitor Y could come along and demand the same special concessions on that first issue while spurning competitor X's concessions on the second.[40] In 2004, the FCC eliminated the pick-and-choose rule in favor of a new *all-or-nothing rule*, which requires a competitor "seeking to avail itself of terms in an interconnection agreement to adopt the agreement in its entirety."[41] The Commission reasoned that the new approach "will promote more 'give and take' negotiations, which will produce creative agreements that are better tailored to meet carriers' individual needs."[42]

E. Addressing monopoly leveraging concerns: section 271

As we noted in part I of this chapter, the political quid pro quo for saddling incumbents with the "local competition" obligations of sections 251 and 252 was liberation of the Bell companies from the line-of-business restrictions of the AT&T consent decree. In section 271, Congress replaced the decree with *statutory* line-of-business restrictions and created a mechanism for the Bell companies to apply to the FCC for authorization, on a state-by-state basis, to enter the wireline long distance market within their traditional service regions. To win such authorization, the Bells needed, in effect, to demonstrate full compliance with the underlying local competition requirements within the relevant state and also needed to set up a separate long distance affiliate, as required by section 272.[43]

In 1996, the Bell companies served about 80% of U.S. lines. The only other incumbent of comparable size was GTE; the rest of the nation's incumbents spanned the range from single-exchange family-owned carriers in remote towns to the "mid-sized" incumbents, such as Southern New England Telephone in Connecticut, and hybrid carriers such as Sprint, whose long distance operations tended to overshadow its nonetheless significant local exchange operations. Congress subjected the Bell companies alone to special regulatory restrictions on the provision of services in markets adjacent to the local exchange markets that they dominated. These included not just the long distance market, but also the markets for telecommunications equipment manufacturing, "electronic publishing," and "alarm monitoring."[44] These three additional line-of-business restrictions were much less competitively significant than the primary restriction on entry into the long distance market, and we do not address them here.

The stated reason for treating the Bell companies more strictly than all other incumbents, including GTE, was the special nature of their local markets: they served by far the greatest number of densely populated urban areas, and their "footprints" (service areas) were large and contiguous. Conditioning long distance entry on satisfaction of the underlying local competition obligations was considered necessary to keep the Bell companies from leveraging their traditional dominance in these key markets to win anticompetitive advantages in the market for long distance voice and data services.[45] The animating discrimination and cross-subsidization concerns were similar to those that had led to the Bell System's break-up in 1984, although the cross-subsidization concern was largely allayed by the advent of price cap regulation (see chapter 2). Another reason for treating the Bells differently was maintenance of the industry status quo. They were already subject to comprehensive restrictions under the 1984 AT&T consent decree, and their immediate entry into the long distance market would have threatened the livelihoods of stand-alone long distance carriers like AT&T and MCI. Also, no one seriously suggested that Congress should have imposed important *new* restrictions on the smaller ILECs (or GTE) just to bring them into regulatory parity with the Bell companies.

The Bells spent several years in the late 1990s arguing in various courts that this specially disadvantageous treatment violated, among other constitutional provisions, the ban on "bills of attainder"—i.e., legislative "punishments" imposed against named entities. These arguments ultimately failed,[46] although the Bells did manage to pick up some dissenting votes along the way. The notable weakness in their constitutional challenges was that, with trivial exceptions, section 271 and its companion provisions made the Bells better off than they would have been under continued enforcement of the AT&T consent decree, which Congress simultaneously lifted. The courts thus concluded that these provisions could hardly be characterized as "punitive." Also, the Bell companies themselves had lobbied hard for congressional enactment of the 1996 Act. Their subsequent attack on the constitutionality of section 271 thus struck some observers, including perhaps the reviewing courts, as disingenuous and at odds with common sense. As the Fifth Circuit remarked, section 271 gave the Bell companies "a clear delineation of what they needed to do to achieve a lifting of all the old [consent decree] restrictions in the future—certainly a step up, from the [Bell companies'] perspective, from being under [the consent decree court's] perpetual supervision. It is perhaps for this reason that the [Bell companies] have apparently consistently represented, outside of litigation, that they were pleased with the Act."[47]

Having failed in court to invalidate section 271 altogether, the Bell companies recommitted themselves to the hard work of earning section

271 authorization on a state-by-state basis. The essential challenge was to show the FCC (i) that competitors had in fact entered the local market in a given state, (ii) that the relevant Bell company would cooperate in permitting them to keep doing so, and (iii) that the Bell company had established a structurally separated long distance affiliate to make it more difficult to engage in (and easier to detect) anticompetitive conduct of the kind that had led to the AT&T break-up.[48] In most but not all cases, the most important disputes concerned the second of these showings. Section 271 sets up a 14-point checklist—the regulatory equivalent of an exceptionally rigorous auto inspection—to judge the Bell companies' compliance with their interconnection, network element, and resale obligations under sections 251 and 252. The central issues in most section 271 proceedings related, first, to the Bell companies' demonstrated proficiency in processing and completing competitors' orders for network elements (largely by means of automated systems) and, second, to the consistency of the Bell companies' rates for those network elements with the FCC's TELRIC methodology.

Before filing a section 271 application with the FCC, a Bell company typically spent several years improving its wholesale performance in a given state and earning the recommendation of the relevant state public utility commission.[49] Theoretically, the Justice Department—which had developed an expertise in this area by helping to administer the AT&T consent decree—played an important role in the section 271 process by submitting, for each application, a recommendation of its own, to which the FCC was required to give "substantial weight."[50] Starting in 1999, however, the FCC ended up deferring much more to the state commissions than to the Justice Department.

By the end of 2003, the four Bell companies—Verizon, BellSouth, SBC, and Qwest—had all secured section 271 authority to offer long distance services for all states in their respective regions. Their success in this process now allows them to offer long distance services at very low incremental cost to their existing base of local exchange customers. Even more important, completion of the section 271 process entitles the Bell companies to provide lucrative voice and data services to nation- and region-wide "enterprise" customers: large businesses with far-flung branch offices. AT&T, MCI, and (to a lesser extent) Sprint have traditionally led this market for essentially three reasons. First, the technological expertise required to provide complex telecommunications services to large businesses is quite sophisticated, and these carriers have spent years mastering it. Second, a carrier's name recognition and perceived reliability count for a lot from the perspective of an enterprise customer's chief technology officer, given the ruinous damage that a major service outage can do to its business. And, third, the line-of-business restrictions at issue—which prohibited the Bell companies from carrying either voice or data transmissions across pre-scribed regulatory boundaries—kept them from competing for the most profitable contracts with these enterprise customers. The Bell companies' new ability to compete for that business is likely the greatest benefit to them of entering the long distance market.

Section 271 remains important to the industry, although far less so than in 1996, when the Bell companies had not yet received long distance authorization for their states. The FCC retains the authority to rescind section 271 approval from, halt future long distance marketing by, or (more realistically) impose substantial fines on any Bell company that falls out of compliance with the substantive standards of section 271.[51] The threat of such sanctions gives the Commission extra leverage in compelling the Bell companies to play fairly even after they have won section 271 approval. Also, as discussed below and in chapter 5, the Commission has construed the section 271 checklist to impose on the Bell companies limited leasing obligations even for certain network elements that do *not* meet the "impairment" standard for unbundling under section 251, which applies to incumbent local exchange carriers generally. Section 271 was chiefly designed to play a transitional role, however, and that transition has taken place.

III. UNEs and the "Impairment" Standard

Having summarized the key wireline provisions of the 1996 Act, we now turn to the specific policy disputes to which they apply. By far the most contentious and expensively litigated of these disputes relate to the scope of a competitor's rights to lease an incumbent's unbundled network elements (UNEs) at regulated cost-based rates. Here we address the scope of a competitor's right to lease components of the *traditional telephone network*. In chapter 5, we will address the distinct set of issues relating to leasing rights for *next generation broadband facilities*.

A. Network element entry strategies

As we have noted, the FCC has traditionally erred on the side of granting new entrants expansive rights to lease most elements of an incumbent's traditional telephone network on favorable terms, and wireline competition debates tend to focus on the wisdom of this policy. The best place to begin in understanding these debates is to imagine a hypothetical world in which Congress and the FCC adopted instead a far more restrictive policy.

In the complete *absence* of leasing rights, a new entrant into the local exchange market would have to obtain its own last mile pipes connecting each of its customers to a switch suitable for handling local traffic, and it would then need to arrange for the mutual hand-off of "local" traffic with the incumbent by means of dedicated "interconnection trunks" (see Fig. 2). Except where the customers in question are tightly clustered in office complexes or massive apartment buildings, however, economies of scale and density are often too low and call volumes too inadequate to cover the costs of deploying lines all the way to their disparate addresses. All else held constant, it usually costs far less *per customer* to serve 100% of the customers within a circumscribed area than 10% of them. Unless those 10% are all closely quartered (say, in a new industrial park), it is not even close to ten times cheaper *in total* for a carrier to lay an alternative network

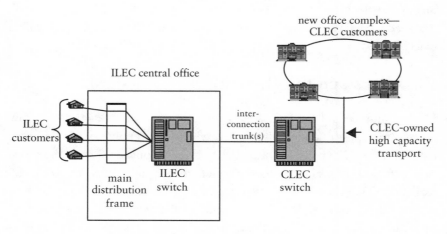

Figure 2. Interconnection—no leasing

of loop facilities to serve a tenth of the available customers than to serve all of them. And, relying on their own facilities, new wireline entrants could not hope to rival the customer base of the incumbents, except over the long term.

One regulatory response to this concern would be to entitle a new entrant to lease ordinary copper loops from the incumbent at "cost"-based rates, but force it to connect those loops to its own remote switching facilities (via a collocation arrangement in the central office, as shown in Fig. 3). If the FCC had taken just that step, the effect would have been to ratify, for the telecommunications industry, the controversial *essential facilities doctrine* of antitrust law.[52] Under that doctrine, a monopolist violates section 2 of the Sherman Act if it unreasonably denies rivals "access" to facilities that they cannot feasibly duplicate but without which they cannot compete. In the telecommunications industry, enforcement of such "access" rights could mean one of two things. In its weaker form, it could mean merely that the incumbent must *interconnect* its own local networks with its rivals' networks, such that it agrees to exchange voice or data "calls" with them and assess any related charges on a per-call or per-minute basis. This was arguably the theory under which, in 1983, the Seventh Circuit held AT&T's Bell System liable for refusing to make its local networks gen-

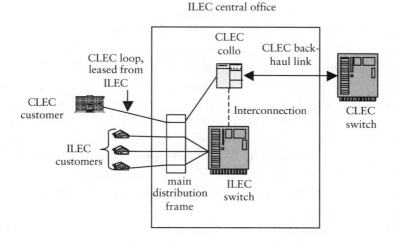

Figure 3. Collocation with leased loops

uinely available for the origination and completion of calls over MCI's long distance network.[53] In its stronger form, the essential facilities doctrine would require an incumbent not just to interconnect with its rivals for the mutual hand-off of telecommunications traffic, but also to lease its loops to the rivals and let them provide a full suite of local, long distance, and data services to the customers served by those loops.

If the 1996 Act had never been enacted, most courts probably would have steered clear of ordering this strong form of antitrust relief on their own. Such remedies can raise a host of difficult pricing and other policy issues—including those addressed in this chapter and in appendix A—that are more properly resolved by specialized agencies than by generalist judges. That is a key reason why, in 2004, the Supreme Court rejected any broad role for antitrust litigation in achieving the same sorts of market-opening objectives as the 1996 Act itself, as we will discuss in chapter 13.[54] Nonetheless, parties opposing expansive leasing rights often argue that Congress intended the underlying natural monopoly logic of the essential facilities doctrine to serve as a critical limiting principle on the scope of the unbundling rights ordered under the 1996 Act. As the D.C. Circuit explained in 2002, "scholars have raised very serious questions about the wisdom of the essential facilities doctrine as a justification for judicial mandates of competitor access, and accompanying judicial price setting. But a doctrine that is inadequate for that purpose may nonetheless offer useful concepts for agency guidance when Congress has *directed* an agency to provide competitor access in a specific industry."[55]

The hypothetical leasing regime we have just described, in which an entrant may lease loops from the incumbent but must connect them to its own switch, permits the entrant to follow the "UNE-L" entry strategy we noted earlier in this chapter. The same term describes a similar arrangement in which, if regulators permit, the entrant leases both loops and transport links from the incumbent at TELRIC-based prices. These loop-transport combinations, known as *enhanced extended links* (EELs), enable the entrant to serve customers over a wide area, and connect them all to its remote switching facilities, without incurring the expense of setting up col-location equipment in each of the central offices serving those customers (see Fig. 4).

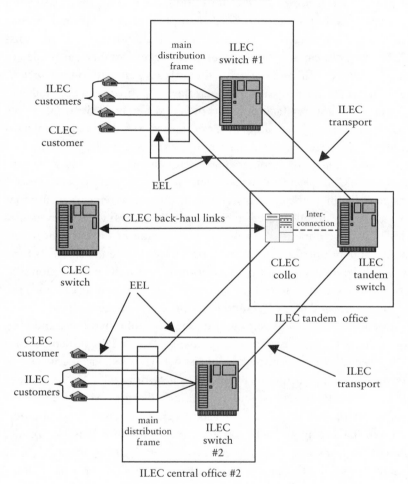

Figure 4. Enhanced extended links (EELs).
(Note: The CLEC and ILEC transport links between two ILEC
offices occupy different circuits on the same facility.)

In contrast, when regulators permit a new entrant to follow a *UNE-P* entry strategy, as they broadly did until 2004, the entrant may lease from the incumbent *all* of the elements needed to provide conventional circuit-switched telephone service. Those elements include loops, "shared transport" (i.e., variable capacity on an incumbent's transport links, as needed to handle the entrant's fluctuating call volumes), and capacity on the *incumbent's* switches.[56] Under this arrangement, the competitor need not, and usually does not, deploy any facilities of its own to differentiate its local service technologically from the incumbent's, nor does it even dispatch technicians to set anything up. As a general matter, it just sends an order to the incumbent, usually by means of automated ordering systems, indicating a desire to lease all of the UNE platform's constituent facilities as "network elements." For its part, the incumbent simply adjusts its billing systems to ensure that it replaces the retail bills it used to send the relevant end users with wholesale bills for the competitor that has won the retail business of those end users. And it continues operating the network for those end users as before; the major difference is that the retail relationship with them now belongs to the competitor rather than to the incumbent. The competitor rebrands the service as its own and may offer innovative pricing packages that the incumbent does not offer, such as flat monthly fees for unlimited local and long distance services. But, with rare exceptions,[57] a "UNE-P" competitor does not offer its end users a technologically distinct *type* of service because it is, for the most part, just using the incumbent's network.

If this UNE-P strategy sounds very much like the section 251(c)(4) "resale" entry option discussed earlier in this chapter, it is. The main differences lie in marketing and wholesale prices. First, UNE-P, unlike resale, frees a competitor to *package* its services differently from the incumbent. Rather than reselling the exact services offered by the incumbent, a UNE-P competitor can use the network capacity it has leased to sell its customers, say, a $50 per month bucket of unlimited local and long distance minutes whether or not the incumbent does so.

The other major difference lies in the *rate* the competitor must pay the incumbent for the use of its network. Again, a competitor choosing the resale option must pay the incumbent a rate based on the incumbent's own *retail prices* minus whatever small amount the incumbent is deemed to save by virtue of no longer being a retail provider for the customers in question. In contrast, an incumbent's retail prices theoretically never enter into the cost equation for the network element platform because the competitor pays a regulated rate based on the constituent elements' forward-looking "cost." Which pricing scheme would the competitor prefer: the "retail-minus-avoided-cost" scheme for resale, or the "cost-based" scheme for leasing the UNE platform?

For complex reasons relating to the implicit cross-subsidies still embedded in retail rates and access charges, the calculation of wholesale costs for the UNE platform option is, in most but not all settings, more attractive to competitors than the calculation of retail rates minus avoided costs.[58] Also, some states have been accused of gaming the process of setting TELRIC-based rates for the UNE platform by determining in advance what sorts of margins competitors need to compete in particular markets—and then reverse-engineering their "cost" determinations to produce that result. Most state commissions have not similarly jury-rigged the avoided cost discount, in part because identifying avoided costs (which are booked to particular accounts) is a more mechanical process than quantifying all costs. Until the FCC began phasing it out in 2004, therefore, the UNE platform eclipsed resale as the entry strategy of choice for competitors seeking to enter local markets without providing any facilities of their own.

The UNE-P option may likewise have deterred at least some competitors from pursuing a UNE-L strategy, in which, as discussed, they lease the incumbent's loops, and perhaps capacity on its transport links, but connect those leased facilities to their own switches. As of June 2003, the number of loops leased together with capacity on an *incumbent's* switches—the hallmark of a UNE-P arrangement—increased by 27% from six months earlier (13.0 million compared to 10.2 million). The number of loops leased *without* switching decreased about 1% over the same period (about 4.2 million compared to 4.3 million).[59]

Of course, statistics can tell only a part of the story, and these numbers may or may not suggest that competitors were broadly forgoing a UNE-L strategy *because* favorable regulatory decisions at the time enticed them to rely instead on the lower risk UNE-P strategy. To the extent, however, that the continued availability of the UNE platform at low TELRIC-based rates did cause CLECs to forgo a UNE-L strategy they would otherwise have successfully pursued, it came at a cost. Unlike a UNE-P strategy, under which CLECs normally provide the same types of service as the ILEC, a UNE-L strategy frees up the CLEC to provide a range of services that the ILEC does not offer and thus helps effectuate one of the main consumer benefits promised by the 1996 Act: greater product variety as well as lower prices.

B. The rise and fall of UNE-P

Traditionally, the hardest fought leasing-rights battle has concerned whether competitors should be entitled to lease the elements specific to UNE-P—i.e., switching and shared transport—at TELRIC-based rates. Incumbents claim that UNE-P competition is a sham; that it adds no value to the industry; that it imperils the incumbents' financial integrity; and that it undermines the incentives of incumbents and competitors alike to invest in value-adding new facilities. Some new entrants claim, in contrast, that the alternative to UNE-P is a complete absence of any local exchange competition for most residential and small business customers (for practical reasons discussed below); that those customers have benefited significantly from the innovative retail pricing plans that UNE-P makes possible; that UNE-P does not threaten the incumbents' profitability; and that, as an empirical matter, UNE-P either increases investment or, at worst, has little effect on it. These entrants portray UNE-P as a much-needed means of unprying the *retail* operations of a vertically integrated telephone monopolist from its *wholesale* network operations and forcing the latter to provide cheap and equal commodity services to all rival retail providers. Viewed in this light, UNE-P is but one step removed from these entrants' preferred regime: formal *structural separation* between an incumbent's retail and wholesale arms, an idea that AT&T, a few other local competitors, and some commentators unsuccessfully advocated in the early 2000s.[60]

Of course, at the right price, the incumbent can profit from receiving wholesale revenues for the use of any of its facilities, just as it profits when it receives retail revenues for their use. When incumbents object to UNE-P obligations, they are largely complaining about the low TELRIC-based rates that regulators force them to charge for providing that wholesale service to their rivals (see appendix A). Over the long term, this regulatory dispute may be overtaken by new commercial realities, at least in some markets. As voice over Internet protocol (see chapter 6) and wireless services (see chapter 8) enable more and more end users to cancel their traditional wireline telephone subscriptions, an incumbent will be better off with *some* wholesale revenues for the UNE platform (so long as they exceed avoidable costs) than with *no* revenues for the use of the UNE platform's constituent facilities. Some industry observers contend that the entrenched culture of certain incumbents will cause them, against their economic self-interest, to "limit the growth and profitability of their infrastructure businesses to protect their customer relationship businesses."[61] Only time will tell whether that assessment is correct. But based on experience in the long distance and wireless markets, it seems likely that, as competitive pressure from rival platforms increases, at least some companies will take the economically rational step of offering attractively priced wholesale services to resellers as a means of filling up their networks with traffic, lest they otherwise lose that traffic and all associated revenues to rival facilities-based providers.[62]

In the shorter term, however, there is no question that incumbents are financially worse off, and that many entrants are commensurately better off, if the latter retain rights to lease the UNE platform at TELRIC-based rates. That fact has led incumbents and entrants to wage a uniquely vociferous legal and public relations battle on this topic. That battle persisted for almost a decade after enactment of the 1996 Act until, with the prodding of the D.C. Circuit, the FCC finally awarded victory to the incumbents in late 2004 and began phasing out UNE-P rights across the nation. That prolonged period of uncertainty arose both from Congress's unwillingness to specify the scope of unbundling rights in the text of the 1996 Act and from repeated judicial invalidation of the FCC's own efforts to exercise its broad statutory delegation of authority on the issue. That the telecommunications world could remain in this regulatory limbo for so long exemplifies the exceptionally lawyer-driven nature of this industry. Because such regrettable indeterminacy has "ma[de] it impossible for companies to make 'capital and customer decisions' with any competitive certainty," it has also driven some investors away from this sector of the economy.[63]

The early terms of the UNE-P debate

In its 1996 *Local Competition Order*, the FCC granted new entrants in local telephone markets essentially unlimited rights to lease the UNE platform, and the incumbents went to court to challenge that decision on a number of grounds. They argued, for example, that the UNE platform is resale by another name and that allowing competitors to lease, at "cost," all elements needed for telephone service, as the FCC had done, amounts to an unlawful end run around the retail-minus-avoided-cost pricing standard for resale prescribed by sections 251(c)(4) and 252(d)(3).[64] At the end of the day, however, the only challenge that stuck was the argument that the Commission's particular rationale for making the switching element available violated a proper interpretation of the "impairment" standard of section 251(d)(2). As noted, this standard directs the FCC to "determin[e] what network elements should be made available for purposes of [section 251(c)(3)]" by "consider[ing], at a minimum, whether . . . the failure to provide access to such network elements would impair the ability of the telecommunications carrier seeking access to provide the services that it seeks to offer."[65] Although the "at a minimum" language provides some interpretive discretion, the FCC must still make basic judgments about which network elements are *needed* for competition, and it must generally restrict leasing obligations to those elements alone.

That is not quite what the FCC had done in 1996. As the Supreme Court found in *Iowa Utilities Board*, the Commission's half-hearted efforts to implement section 251(d)(2) in 1996 "began with the premise that an incumbent was obliged [under section 251(c)(3)] to turn over as much of its network as was 'technically feasible,' and viewed subsection (d)(2) as merely permitting it to soften that obligation by regulatory grace."[66] But, the Court made clear, "[s]ection 251(d)(2) does not authorize the Commission to create isolated exemptions from some underlying duty to make all network elements available. It requires the Commission to determine on a rational basis *which* network elements must be made available, taking into account the objectives of the Act and giving some substance to the . . . 'impair' requirement[]."[67] Consequently, the Commission had improperly disregarded that requirement by "assum[ing] that *any* increase in cost (or decrease in quality) imposed by denial of a network element . . . 'impair[s]' the entrant's ability to furnish its desired services."[68]

In effect, the Court directed the Commission on remand to start from scratch and apply a more rigorous understanding of the "impairment" standard—one that recognizes that the mandated sharing of facilities gives rise to costs as well as benefits. But the Court did not specifically preclude the Commission, at the conclusion of its inquiry, from once again requiring incumbents to make any given element available at cost-based rates, including those elements that together constitute the UNE platform.

In November 1999, nine months after the Supreme Court ruled, the Commission produced the so-called *UNE Remand Order*, its second effort to implement the "impairment" standard.[69] Although the Commission relieved incumbents of their preexisting obligation to provide "operator services" and "directory assistance" to competitors as "network elements," it generally kept the key UNE platform elements—loops, switching, and shared transport—on the mandatory unbundling list. The one exception, known as the "switching carve-out," applied only in limited business settings in several dozen urban areas, and only when the incumbent relinquished its right to invoke otherwise applicable restrictions on competitors' rights to lease loop-transport combinations as network elements. Indeed, the Commission separately *added* several non-platform-related elements to the national unbundling list. These included "dark fiber" (fiber-optic lines to which no electronics have yet been attached), the "subloop" (the "distribution" portion of the loop closest to the customer, which previously could be leased only as part of the entire loop, except where a given state had ordered otherwise), and the "high frequency portion" of the copper loop (used for the provision of competing DSL services in an arrangement known as "line sharing," discussed in chapter 5).

The text of the Commission's order paid at least superficial obeisance to the "impairment" standard as interpreted by the Supreme Court. But that was not enough. In 2002, the D.C. Circuit invalidated the crux of the order on the ground that the Commission had once more observed section 251(d)(2) only in the breach.[70]

The premise underlying this D.C. Circuit decision, now known as *USTA I*, is that "unbundling is not an unqualified good," for it "comes at a cost, including disincentives to research and development by both [incumbents] and [competitors] and the tangled management inherent in shared use of a common resource."[71] The role of the "impairment" standard, the court suggested, is to ensure that the "completely synthetic competition" facilitated by too-liberal leasing rights—a thinly veiled reference to the UNE platform—does not undermine "incentives for innovation and investment in facilities."[72] The court concluded that the Commission still had not come to grips with this basic statutory concern, had not struck an appropriate balance between too few and too many leasing rights, and had overgeneralized about the "need" of competitors for particular elements without conducting any market-specific analysis of this issue. Finally, although the Commission had sought to justify its permissive leasing policies on the ground that new entrants would otherwise lack the incumbents' scale economies during the early stages of competitive entry, the court responded that "average unit costs are necessarily higher at the outset for any new entrant into virtually *any* business."[73] The "impairment" standard, the court ruled, precludes "[a] cost disparity approach that links 'impairment' to universal characteristics, rather than ones linked (in some degree) to natural monopoly"—that is, linked specifically "to cost differentials based on characteristics that would make genuinely competitive provision of an element's function *wasteful*" over the long term.[74]

Once again, however, the court did not explicitly *preclude* the Commission from ordering any particular set of leasing rights. Instead, the Commission remained technically free on remand to adopt whatever bottom line it wished so long as it could justify the results under the "impairment" standard as now interpreted by the Supreme Court and the D.C. Circuit.

The *Triennial Review Order* and *USTA II*

This brings us to the FCC's *Triennial Review Order* in 2003, in which a 3-2 majority decided, over the dissent of Chairman Michael Powell, to preserve the UNE platform as an entry strategy in most markets by delegating much of the issue to the states, which were widely perceived as sympathetic both to that objective and to the competitors generally.[75] Spanning 485 pages and some 2,447 footnotes, the *Triennial Review Order* addresses many wholesale leasing issues, but focuses heavily on the availability of the circuit-switching element—the *sine qua non* of the UNE platform. (As discussed in chapter 5, a different 3-2 FCC majority—this one pitting the three Republicans, including FCC Chairman Michael Powell, against the two Democrats—concluded that less expansive leasing rights should prevail with respect to next generation broadband investments, such as high capacity fiber lines leading all the way to the premises of mass market customers.)

The Commission framed its general analysis with a refined interpretation of the "impairment" standard. A competitor is "impaired," it said, "when lack of access to an incumbent['s] . . . network element poses a barrier or barriers to entry, including operational and economic barriers, that are likely to make entry into a market uneconomic. That is, we ask whether all potential revenues from entering a market exceed the costs of entry, taking into consideration any countervailing advantages that a new entrant may have."[76] Applying this standard to the UNE-P debate, the majority established a national presumption that disabling competitors from leasing capacity on an incumbent's switches at cost-based rates would "impair" their ability to serve "mass market" (i.e., residential and small business) customers.[77]

In creating this presumption of impairment, the FCC did not conclude that switches are natural monopoly facilities that exhibit declining average costs over the entirety of the market. Instead, it based the presumption on the more mundane premise that an incumbent would often be incapable of performing the operational tasks, known as *hot cuts*, needed to disconnect large numbers of leased loops from its own switch and promptly reconnect them to the competitor's switch without inflicting unexpected service outages on the customers at the end of those loops.[78] And, hoping to address the D.C. Circuit's prohibition on unbundling requirements designed to alleviate entry barriers found in ordinary competitive industries, the Commission reasoned that the considerable costs of hot cuts—for which competitors must theoretically reimburse incumbents up front—arise because the incumbents' "networks were designed for use in a single carrier, non-competitive environment," a phenomenon found in few other parts of the economy.[79] The majority recognized, however, "that a more granular analysis may reveal that a particular market is not subject to impairment in the absence of unbundled local circuit switching."[80] It delegated that "granular analysis," however, to the individual state commissions with few concrete limits on their discretion to frame the inquiry as they saw fit.

When the *Order* came out in 2003, the bottom-line consensus of industry analysts was that the Commission's various findings and delegations would operate to ensure the availability of the UNE platform in virtually all residential and small business markets for the indefinite future. Most state commissions, they reasoned, had grown to view UNE-P as essential to immediate widespread local competition in mass markets and would now exercise their discretion to promote UNE-P-based competition into the indefinite future. Indeed, a broad coalition of state regulators had filed papers with the FCC indicating their intention to do just that if the Commission so allowed.

The losers in this struggle—the Bell companies—were soon back before the D.C. Circuit, claiming that the *Triennial Review Order* violated the court's prior mandate in *USTA I*. In *USTA II*,[81] decided in March 2004, the D.C. Circuit again vacated the Commission's UNE platform-related unbundling rules, this time on two grounds, one procedural and one more substantive.

The court first held that the Commission had violated its statutory obligations by subdelegating much of the market-specific impairment inquiry to the states. "[T]he cases," it found, "recognize an important distinction between subdelegation to a *subordinate* and subdelegation to an *outside party* [such as a state agency]. The presumption that subdelegations are valid absent a showing of contrary congressional intent applies only to the former. There is no such presumption covering subdelegations to outside parties. Indeed, if anything, the case law strongly suggests that subdelegations to outside parties are assumed to be improper absent an affirmative showing of congressional authorization."[82] The court deemed it inconsequential that "the subdelegation in this case is to state commissions rather than private organizations."[83] Congress, it held, is generally free to delegate federal power to the states as it likes, but a federal agency may not subdelegate to the states whatever responsibilities Congress gives it "absent an affirmative showing of congressional authorization."[84] Otherwise, the court concluded, "lines of accountability may blur, undermining an important democratic check on government decision-making," and the states "may pursue goals inconsistent with those of the agency and the underlying statutory scheme."[85]

The court's reaction was in some ways unsurprising. The context of the *Triennial Review Order* suggested to critics of UNE-P that the Commission was punting its section 251(d)(2) obligations to the states as a means of evading legal and political accountability for what, in practice, amounted to a decision to keep UNE-P alive as an entry option. But the court's rationale swept more broadly than was necessary to its bottom line. Although the court suggested (without quite holding) that the FCC could delegate only "fact gathering" authority to the states in the service of the Commission's own policy decisions,[86] that is unlikely to emerge as the general rule, and it is unclear that the D.C. Circuit meant to suggest that it should. The FCC cannot be expected to resolve, as soon as they arise, all of the myriad regulatory issues involving local competition. And, of course, whenever the FCC does not decide such issues, it has effectively "subdelegated" them to the states, whether or not it says so explicitly, and whether or not it even focuses on them. The states must often resolve those issues themselves if they are to discharge their own statutory role under section 252 in overseeing the negotiation and arbitration of interconnection agreements. Whatever the uncertain precedential implications in other contexts, however, the court made clear that the FCC's sweeping subdelegation in the *Triennial Review Order* was impermissible.

The court then turned to the merits and rejected the substance of the FCC's own truncated impairment inquiry. The court observed that, in several passages of the *Order*, the FCC itself had acknowledged that its national presumption of "impairment" in the absence of switching rights, "without the possibility of market-specific exceptions . . . , would be inconsistent with *USTA I*."[87] The court agreed and, noting that it had just invalidated the Commission's mechanism for making those "market-specific exceptions," invalidated the national "impairment" finding as well. More generally, the court expressed skepticism that the Commission had any strong basis for concluding that ILECs as a whole would be unable under any circumstances to keep up with escalating hot cut orders as CLECs lost access to the switching element: "One can imagine the Commission successfully identifying criteria based, for example, on an ILEC's track record for speed and volume in a market, integrated with some projection of the demand increase that would result from withholding of switches as UNEs. The Commission, however, has made no visible effort to explore such possibilities."[88]

The aftermath of *USTA II*

Many industry observers expected the D.C. Circuit's decision to fade into historical irrelevance because, they predicted, the government would take the case to the Supreme Court. Supporters of UNE-P were particularly encouraged by the tenor of the Supreme Court's 2002 decision in *Verizon Communications Inc. v. FCC*,[89] which not only upheld the FCC's TELRIC pricing rules, but seemed to endorse the Commission's aggressively pro-competition agenda more generally. Their hopes were thwarted when, in June 2004, Solicitor General Theodore Olson, acting for the Bush administration, decided not to seek Supreme Court review of *USTA II*. As a practical matter, this decision all but doomed any prospect of Supreme Court intervention, even though the private carriers aggrieved by the D.C. Circuit's ruling filed certiorari petitions of their own (which the Supreme Court denied several months later).

The D.C. Circuit issued its "mandate" in June 2004 and thereby formally removed switching from the FCC's list of network elements subject to unbundling obligations. As a practical matter, however, UNE-P may remain available as an entry method in some areas, at least for a while. First, a carrier's rights and obligations under the 1996 Act are ultimately governed by state-approved interconnection agreements between individual incumbents and competitors. Some of these agreements, signed in the months or years before *USTA II*, may operate to preserve a competitor's access to the constituent elements of the UNE platform, at least for the life of the agreements. Second, in remand proceedings that were still pending at press time, the FCC sought to help competitors make an orderly transition from UNE-P to UNE-L by entitling them to lease (for existing customers) the switching element for an additional twelve months at TELRIC-based rates plus a small premium.[90] Relatedly, even when switching is formally removed from the list of network elements subject to unbundling under *section 251* at low TELRIC-based rates, the FCC has construed *section 271* to compel the Bell companies to make switching available at "just and reasonable" rates—a flexible and amorphous standard whose application in this context remains unclear.[91]

Finally, some states may try to preserve inexpensive, highly regulated access to the UNE platform under state law even in markets where the FCC, following the D.C. Circuit's guidance, has concluded that switching does not meet the "impairment" standard. Such state-level efforts will raise significant issues of *federal preemption*.

Normally, any regulation the FCC is "statutorily authorized" to adopt "will pre-empt any state or local law that conflicts with such regulations or frustrates the purposes thereof."[92] The preemption analysis is somewhat complicated by the proliferation of vague "savings clauses" throughout the Act protecting various categories of state-level regulation.[93] The best known of these is section 251(d)(3), which bars the FCC from preempting any state interconnection or network element rule that "does not substantially prevent implementation of the requirements of [section 251] and the purposes of [the 1996 Act's local competition provisions]." The prevailing view today, however, is that these savings clauses are designed primarily to foreclose any claim that the federal scheme preempts the field of local competition regulation and thereby precludes the states from adopting *complementary* rules of their own to fill the interstices in that scheme.[94] But state law that poses an outright conflict with federal policies is still preempted.[95]

In the unbundling context, this means that state efforts to preserve the UNE platform's broad availability over the long term are preempted to the extent that they are found to subvert the federal policies that led Congress to include an "impairment" limitation on unbundling rights. Those policies include, in the words of the *USTA I* court, the concern that excessive unbundling would inflict disproportionate "costs of its own, spreading the disincentive to invest in innovation and creating complex issues of managing shared facilities."[96] Thus, as the FCC puts it, if "state law were to require the unbundling of a network element for which the Commission has either found no impairment—and thus has found that unbundling that element would conflict with the limits in section 251(d)(2)—or otherwise declined to require unbundling on a national basis, . . . it [is] unlikely that such decision would fail to conflict with and 'substantially prevent' implementation of the federal regime, in violation of section 251(d)(3)(C)."[97] On the other hand, the FCC often remains vague enough about its policy conclusions that it leaves plenty of room for litigation about the preemptive consequences of those conclusions in other forums.

Two more practical points are worth making about the fate of the *Triennial Review Order*. First, whatever its substantive merit, the *Order* was not the FCC's finest moment as an institution. What the industry most needed, in the wake of the D.C. Circuit's invalidation of the *UNE Remand Order* in 2002, was certainty about the scope of network element leasing rights. The FCC's UNE-P majority seemed less concerned about meeting that objective than about avoiding direct responsibility for keeping UNE-P available to competitors. The result was a legal regime that, had it survived judicial review, would have kept hundreds of advocates fully employed for many months (if not years) in state-by-state disputes about access to the UNE platform. The *Order* was embarrassing for the Commission on a procedural level as well. It was announced six months before it was finally released, the substance had changed noticeably in the interim, and it came accompanied by an almost intemperate dissent by the Commission's own chairman. Moreover, the two Democratic commissioners initially indicated that, in forging a grand political compromise with renegade Republican Kevin Martin to preserve the UNE platform, they had betrayed their own better judgment by voting against the long term rights of competitors to lease only the high frequency portion of the loop to provide broadband Internet access (see the "line sharing" discussion in chapter 5).[98] In the words of Alfred Kahn, a prominent regulatory economist, the *Triennial*

Review Order was "an abomination, purely political in the worst sense of the term and grounded in neither good economics nor honorable regulatory practice."[99]

Second, one should not infer from the rhetorical intensity of the UNE platform debate that its outcome carries enormous significance for the telecommunications industry in the long run. To be sure, the phasing out of UNE-P rights may have striking consequences in the shorter term. For example, it led AT&T to announce in July 2004 that it will stop seeking new customers in the mass market for conventional telephony services, and other carriers may soon follow suit. But the future of this industry lies in packet-switched, Internet-oriented technology, not in conventional circuit-switched telephony. UNE-P is by definition a narrowband, circuit-switched platform and is thus aptly characterized as yesterday's technology.

For the same reason, the incumbents' victory in the UNE-P debate will preserve a limited profit stream in the near term, but it can do nothing to solve their more fundamental and long term problem: the convergence of voice and data services over broadband Internet connections. As the ink lay drying on the D.C. Circuit's mandate in the summer of 2004, the incumbents began contemplating how they could preserve market share in the long run against providers of voice over Internet protocol (VoIP).[100] Such providers include stand-alone VoIP firms such as Vonage and AT&T itself, both of which offer high quality voice services over any broadband Internet access platform,and cable companies like Comcast and Time Warner, which offer VoIP along with their own cable modem services. If anything, the defeat of AT&T and other CLECs in *USTA II* strengthened their resolve to compete with the ILECs on this more promising playing field. We discuss this set of competitive issues in chapters 4 through 6.

C. Loop-transport combinations

We close this chapter with the story of an equally significant, though less publicized, legal controversy: the circumstances in which carriers may lease high capacity dedicated circuits for business customers as "network elements" priced at TELRIC rather than as more expensive "special access" services. Although the details of this dispute may seem esoteric, they probably affect carriers' bottom lines as much as the UNE platform controversy does. This dispute is significant for a more conceptual reason as well: it marks a critical point in the industry's transition from legacy regulation, where the distinction between "local" and "long distance" markets and carriers is clear, to the regulatory model of the future, in which industry changes have irreversibly eroded such distinctions.

There are two basic dimensions to the controversy about leasing rights for high capacity dedicated circuits. The first concerns the circumstances in which transport and high capacity loops should be available as network elements at all. In the *Triennial Review Order*, the FCC delegated much of that question, like the switching impairment inquiry, to the individual state commissions. Although it took the highest capacity pipes off the table, it entered a national finding of "impairment" for all remaining transport and loop facilities and granted the state commissions broad discretion to decide when the existence or feasibility of competitive alternatives warrants a more "granular" finding of "no impairment" in particular areas.[101] In *USTA II*, focusing on the transport issue specifically, the D.C. Circuit invalidated the FCC's delegation of this discretion to the states for the same reasons it invalidated the Commission's delegation of the switching inquiry, and it also expressed doubts about the FCC's ability on remand to justify a national "impairment" finding.[102] Among other things, the court held that, at least in some contexts, the FCC could no longer categorically disregard a competing carrier's ability to purchase special access services from the incumbent in analyzing whether denying the same carrier's access to the incumbent's underlying transport facilities as lower priced *network elements* would "impair" that carrier's competitive position. On remand in late 2004, the FCC announced new rules that somewhat narrowed the geographic markets in which defined categories of high capacity loops and transport links can be leased as network elements.[103]

The second and equally controversial dimension of this controversy involves the *purposes* for which a carrier may lease capacity on an incumbent's transmission pipes on the routes where such capacity is otherwise available as a network element. When a competing local exchange carrier leases the loop-transport combination known as the enhanced extended link (or EEL), it receives a dedicated high capacity circuit connecting its network to a high volume business customer. Again, this is essentially the same circuit it would receive if it were a long distance carrier purchasing a special access line on behalf of that customer. The principal difference is price. As noted, a loop-transport combination normally costs much less when leased in the form of network elements (the EEL) than as a special access circuit. When the 1996 Act was passed, long distance carriers instantly sensed an opportunity to increase their margins with business customers by invoking rights to lease loop-transport combinations not for the provision of local exchange service at all, but simply to provide themselves with a less expensive version of special access.

If the long distance carriers had succeeded in exploiting this arbitrage opportunity, they would have denied the incumbent local carriers recovery of billions of dollars in special access revenues. After an initial period of legal uncertainty, the FCC has sought since 1999 to keep pure long distance carriers from obtaining access to these loop-transport combinations at the TELRIC-based rates applicable to network elements. But carriers providing some minimum quantum of local exchange services are nonetheless free to lease those same combinations at those very rates. This rule is often characterized as a *use restriction,* although that term is slightly inapt: if a carrier maintains the prescribed quantum of "local" traffic, it is free to use the circuit for long distance traffic as well.

This variation in treatment between local and long distance carriers presented the FCC with a legal problem. As the FCC saw it, Congress did not create wholesale leasing rights to help lower the costs of long distance carriers *qua* long distance carriers. Special access services generate billions of dollars in annual revenues for the incumbents, and those revenues have steadily risen since the mid-1990s with industry-wide increases in data traffic. The Commission was politically unwilling to sacrifice those revenues in the absence of much clearer direction from Congress. But Congress never quite expressed the desired limitation on network element rights in the text of the Act. Section 251(c)(3) extends such rights to "telecommunications carrier[s]" generally, not only to carriers committed to the development of local exchange competition. And, in all events, Congress defined a "local exchange carrier" as one that provides either "telephone exchange service" or "exchange access," which includes both switched and special access.[104] So how could the FCC justify greater wholesale leasing rights for "local exchange" services than for "exchange access?" The policy answer used to relate to the maintenance of universal service subsidies.[105] But, as discussed in chapter 10, the FCC's *CALLS Order* purported to remove such subsidies from access charges and to fill the universal service need through other mechanisms.

In June 2000, the FCC found another route to the same outcome. It suggested, without formally ruling, that loop-transport combinations fail the "impairment" test as to long distance carriers, but not as to genuine local exchange competitors.[106] On review, the D.C. Circuit agreed that, "[b]y referring to the 'services that [the requesting carrier] seeks to offer,' [section 251(d)(2)] seems to invite an inquiry that is specific to particular carriers and services."[107]

Resolution of that abstract legal question, however, provided no answer to a vexing problem of implementation. Since the bits flying over these loop-transport combinations are simply bits, and since nothing readily identifies them as "local" or "long distance" traffic, what rules are necessary to ensure that carriers are not using these facilities, leased at cost, "primarily" for the provision of long distance service? Remember, for these purposes, that many carriers are both long distance companies and competing local exchange carriers. To what extent must such carriers show that they are using these facilities for the provision of ordinary local exchange traffic, rather than simply for long distance traffic?[108] Questions like these prompted the FCC to establish *safe harbors* that define the circumstances in which a carrier is demonstrably providing enough "local" services to a given customer that it should be entitled to lease these facilities as cost-based "network elements" for all purposes. As initially framed in 2000, these safe harbors required a carrier availing itself of these network element rights to certify, roughly speaking, either (i) that it was the sole provider of local service to a particular customer or (ii) that the amount of local exchange traffic flowing over the loop-transport circuits at issue met certain percentage thresholds.[109] The first safe harbor was difficult for competitors to meet because many business customers order at least a few backup lines from the incumbent for use in the event of trouble with the competitor's network.

The problem with the second type of safe harbor—involving the relative percentages of "local" and "long distance" traffic—was the artificial distinction it erected in the face of technological change. Such safe harbors are most straightforwardly applied to traditional voice networks, in which one can theoretically identify what kind of "call" (local or long distance) is exclusively occupying a given circuit at any particular moment. They are less easily applied to packet-switched networks, in which voice and data signals often coexist on the same circuit in a continuous stream of 1s and 0s. Indeed, some carriers argued, the FCC's original emphasis on this type of safe harbor not only imposed insurmountable measurement problems, but also perversely discouraged new entrants from using efficient "compression" techniques to conserve the bandwidth consumed by voice signals within that bitstream. After all, these carriers explained, they were subject to higher "special access" rates—rather than lower "network element" rates—once those techniques drove "local" voice-related bandwidth below a prescribed minimum percentage of the circuit's total use.

In the *Triennial Review Order,* the FCC adjusted its safe harbors to address this and other practical concerns.[110] But those adjustments were a short term patch (and a controversial one) for a more conceptual problem. Presumably the reason why loop-transport combinations are subject to TELRIC-priced wholesale leasing rights at all is that, for purposes of the impairment analysis, competitors need such rights to provide "local exchange" services. But, again, these are the exact same circuits, on the exact same facilities, that long distance carriers lease at higher rates for access to local markets. Why should some carriers pay more than others to exercise the same leasing rights? Or, to flip the same question around, if long distance carriers can afford to pay special access rates, presumably because they earn enough in long distance revenues to cover the extra costs, why should the government favor competing "local" carriers whose business plans, by hypothesis (under the "impairment" standard), might not survive if they also had to pay special access rates? That question is especially perplexing when one considers that almost no carrier provides *only* "local" services; virtually any competitive "local" provider also provides these supposedly profitable "long distance" services to the same customers over the same leased pipes.

The FCC's distinctions in this setting seem designed for an earlier regulatory era, when voice traffic dominated the market and it was comparatively easy to divide the world into "local" and "long distance" (as well as "interstate" and "intrastate") communications. But those days are over. In today's network, data traffic eclipses voice traffic in total volume, and competition promises to destabilize any distinction among carriers that is based on legacy regulation rather than engineering or economic imperatives. So long as companies' balance sheets continue to turn on a *regulatory* distinction between "local" and "long distance" traffic, this distinction will lead only to arbitrage opportunities, as carriers learn how to reconfigure their networks to make traffic look more like the former than the latter.

The artificial distinction between EELs and special access is only one manifestation of this phenomenon. As we will discuss in chapter 9, policymakers have created similarly perverse incentives by varying the compensation that a calling party's carrier must pay the called party's carrier for "terminating" a call depending on how far away the call *originated* (i.e., whether it is "local" or "long distance"), even though the *costs* of call termination normally have nothing to do with the call's place of origin. The result is that carriers have incentives to reconfigure traffic patterns inefficiently so that "long distance" traffic appears "local" to the carrier (usually an incumbent local exchange carrier) that completes the call. Those arbitrage incentives made front-page headlines in 2003, as some carriers stood accused of "laundering" long distance traffic through collaborating "local" carriers in the called party's area en route to the different local carrier that actually served the called party. And, as we shall see, the FCC has likewise warped market incentives by leaving it unclear what difference it makes, for access charge purposes, whether a given long distance call is transmitted over the "public switched network" or, instead, by means of VoIP technologies over the "Internet."

In each case, the regulatory distinction that the FCC wishes to enforce is collapsing under the weight of a basic economic reality: like services need to be regulated alike, except where there is some compelling *economic* reason for treating them differently. Otherwise, regulating them differently will produce inefficiency and a great deal of expensive regulatory commotion. At some point, policymakers will need to face up to this reality not just in their treatment of network element combinations, as discussed in this chapter, but also by reforming today's unworkably balkanized scheme of "intercarrier compensation" for apportioning the costs of calls traversing different networks. That is the topic of chapter 9.

* * *

The regulatory controversies we have covered in this chapter, while undoubtedly significant in the short run to the bottom lines of the companies involved, may well diminish in importance over the long term. As we explain in the next several chapters, the most lasting competition in the telecommunications industry will probably come not from wireline competitors to wireline incumbents, but from non-wireline providers of alternative information platforms. If, by 2010, you wish to cut the cord to the ILEC, you are less likely to defect to a CLEC lessee of traditional telephone facilities than to a wireless carrier or to the provider of a VoIP service that you can run on top of your broadband Internet connection. The consequence of these developments, as we will explain in chapter 6, is to strain the basic framework of the Communications Act to the breaking point.

4

A Primer on Internet Technology

The previous two chapters focused on "wireline" competition issues that, for the most part, originated before the Internet began fundamentally reordering the telecommunications industry. Many of these issues will remain with us for years. In the long term, however, they will become increasingly less important than the competition policy challenges raised by the Internet's complete transformation of the telecommunications landscape. Chapters 5 and 6 examine those challenges in detail. This chapter sets the stage by explaining, on a technological level, what "the Internet" is and what competitive issues it presents.

I. The Basics

Our technological discussion in chapter 2 focused on the physical characteristics of telecommunications networks: copper wires, switches, fiber-optic transport pipes, and so forth. What defines a network, however, is not only its physical infrastructure, but also the logic embedded within the streams of 1s and 0s flitting across it. To understand the distinction between those two "layers" of a network, and thus to understand the nature of the Internet, it is first necessary to elaborate on the nature of digital technology.

A. From analog to digital

When Alexander Graham Bell spoke into the first telephone in the 1870s, the sound came out of his mouth in continuous pressure waves of air particles. The transmitter's role in that telephone was to convert those waves into analogous variations of electrical current. Once that electrical current reached the receiver (i.e., Mr. Watson's handset), they were converted back into continuous pressure waves of air particles in the form of audible sounds. The common denominator in each of these steps was the use of continuous waves (of air particles or electrical current) to convey information. The term "analog" describes the various methods of transmitting information in such continuous waveforms.

The term "digital," in contrast, describes the quite different way in which computers operate and communicate. The silicon chip at the heart of your personal computer is an intricate network of microscopic transistors whose basic function is to open and close circuits. At the most elemental level, each circuit has two possible states: "on" and "off." The 1s and 0s in a digital transmission—known as *bits*, short for "binary digits"—correspond to those two states, and can be used as a mathematical shorthand for describing anything, from the sound of a voice to the image of a child to a thousand-page document. Digital technology came of age in the computer world in the 1950s and 1960s. Once computers entered the telephone network in the 1970s and 1980s, this technology swept through the telecommunications world, transforming it forever.

A digital communication often begins with an analog signal, such as the human voice. A device on the speaker's end mathematically "samples" the properties of that voice at regular intervals, many times a second. These samples are represented as a particular configuration of 1s and 0s, which collectively describe the sounds the voice makes in roughly the same way that the topography of a mountain range can be described by a series of numbers reflecting longitude, latitude, and altitude. If enough samples are taken in rapid succession, the resulting bitstream can convey a complex enough mathematical representation to capture all the important nuances of the human voice—or any other sound or image.

In a digital transmission, what gets sent is this abstract mathematical representation, not (as in an analog transmission) a direct and continuous representation of the wave characteristics of the sound itself. The device at the receiving end then "decodes" the stream of 1s and 0s and translates them back into a continuous analog sound. How does the receiving device "know" how to decode the 1s and 0s? It "knows" because it and the transmitting device share an agreed-upon *protocol* for the exchange of encoded information, much as telegraph operators can encode and decode otherwise inscrutable messages because they have both learned the Morse Code. We discuss the question of protocols below.[1]

Why do telecommunications engineers go to the trouble of converting analog signals into digital form and back again? One important efficiency made possible by digital technology is *compression*, a means of conserving bandwidth when transmitting information. Consider an evening news broadcast in which the background image behind the anchorman remains constant for extended periods. In a conventional analog transmission, the same information about that background image must be wastefully transmitted anew many times a second, even though the information is unchanged each time. In a digital transmission, the information need be transmitted only once, along with short subsequent placeholders indicating to the receiving device that the background image has not changed and should continue to be shown in its original form. Other compression techniques use sophisticated algorithms to represent, say, repeating patterns in a music file.

An additional benefit of digital technology is also one of the most obvious: greater signal clarity. If you remember placing long distance telephone calls before the mid-1980s, you probably recall that the voice on the other end sounded more distant and less distinct than the voice of your neighbor on the other end of a local call. That was an unfortunate side effect of analog technology. On conventional telephone facilities, signals tended to fade over distances. The only way to transmit an ordinary voice call from New York to Los Angeles through analog technology is to "amplify" the continuous wave signal transmitted over the telephone network, imperfections and all. The result is background static and some distortion. Digital technology avoids that problem. Because a digital signal is just a mathematical representation of an underlying analog signal, its constituent 1s and 0s can be "repeated" from one device to the next with no resulting loss of signal fidelity and no increase in background noise. The difference between analog and digital technology is illustrated by the difference in quality between the tenth successive photocopy of a document (much fuzzier than the first) and the tenth successive e-mail exchange of a document (exactly the same as the first). This is the primary reason why long distance calls today, unlike those placed in the 1970s, sound just as good as local calls.

The distinction between analog and digital technology is relevant to, but different from, the distinction (discussed in chapter 2) between *circuit-switched* and *packet-switched* networks. To review, ordinary telephone networks have traditionally been circuit-switched, which means that, when a call is placed between two points, a fixed increment of transmission capacity (the "circuit") is held open for the duration of the call on a static, predetermined path, regardless of whether any information is passing through the circuit. In contrast, a packet-switched network does not dedicate fixed capacity to a given communication, generally relying instead on a system known as *dynamic routing*. That system economizes on transmission capacity by subdividing the information contained in the communication into millions of packets and sending them off in different increments over whatever paths might be most efficient at any given instant. When these packets reach their ultimate destination, they are then reassembled from start to finish and decoded.

Packet-switched networks, by definition, *must* be digital. Circuit-switched networks can be *either* analog *or* digital. In the old days, the "circuit" that was held open for the duration of a telephone call was used exclusively for the transmission of analog signals. Today, the circuit is still held open, but now it is host to long streams of 1s and 0s. Put more concretely, when you now place an ordinary telephone call, your voice may travel down a copper wire in the form of continuous (analog) electrical impulses, but those impulses will have been converted into digital bits by the time they pass through the first computerized switch that will help direct the call to its ultimate destination.

B. Modularity and layering

To explain what "the Internet" is, we begin with the related concepts of *modularity* and *layering*, which have spurred tremendous entry and innovation in the markets for Internet-related products and services. Modularity is a means of managing complexity by enabling different products to work together through well understood sets of rules.[2] Think of a Chinese menu that allows one choice from column A, one from column B, one from column C, and one from column D. A more restrictive menu would contain a pre-combined list of offerings that could not be ordered separately from one another. Like the Chinese menu, modularity allows mixing and matching among different technologies in adjacent markets. And, in the Internet sphere, what gets mixed and matched are the data technologies at different "layers" of Internet communications.

We'll introduce the layering concept with an example from the nineteenth century: a Union Army telegraph transmission from Gettysburg to Washington in 1863. There are four basic levels on which we can describe this transmission. *First*, we could describe the physical properties of the medium over which the signal was sent. In this case, it was a copper wire—as opposed to, say, a fiber-optic cable or the airwaves. *Second*, we could describe the shared code, or "protocol," that enabled the sender and receiver to know what words were being sent over that copper wire. In our example, the protocol was the Morse Code: dot-dash, dash-dot-dot-dot, etc. Both the message's sender and the immediate recipient needed to agree on that protocol (or some other shared protocol), or else no message could be effectively transmitted. *Third*, we could describe the telegraph operator, who possessed the relevant "intelligence" to understand that dot-dash signifies "a," dash-dot-dot-dot signifies "b," and so on. If the operator at either the sending or the receiving end lacked proficiency in the Morse Code, the message would get garbled. *Fourth*, we could describe the content of the message itself, as translated by the telegraph operator on the receiving end. In our example, the message (at the end of Day 3) would have been: "Confederates retreat after disastrous charge up hill."

Each of these four attributes of the "call" from Gettysburg to Washington describes a "layer" of the transmission: a physical layer (the copper wire), a logical layer (the Morse Code), an applications layer (the telegraph operators), and a content layer (the message about the Confederate retreat). The important point to grasp for now is that each layer is largely independent of the others, meaning that, for the most part, we could vary one element without varying the others. For example, if Guglielmo Marconi had invented the radio in 1862 rather than 1895, the same message, in the same Morse Code format, could have been sent over the airwaves rather than through a copper wire. In other words, one could vary the physical medium of delivery in our hypothetical transmission but leave the logical, application, and content layers untouched. Second, if Samuel Morse had not developed his system and some other protocol had been developed to convert letters into simpler elements (like the dots and dashes of a Morse Code transmission) understandable to a trained operator of a telegraph machine, the same Union Army message could have been sent through the same physical medium (the copper wire) and interpreted by the same people. Third, the same message could be delivered if another set of operators were at the helm and were also proficient in the Morse Code or another relevant protocol. Finally, our Civil War combatants could have used the same physical medium (copper wire), the same logical protocol (Morse Code), and the same application (the telegraph operators) to transmit a different message content altogether if the battle had gone differently: "Confederates take hill, begin unimpeded march towards Washington."

To summarize now, and move our discussion into the digital era, there are several mutually independent layers in any Internet communication. For the sake of simplicity, we will identify just four.[3] At the bottom is the physical layer. This denotes the physical characteristics—copper wires, fiber-optic cable, or the airwaves—of the medium over which the information is transmitted. Next up is the logical layer. This includes the basic protocols for a transmission: the digital signal formats that enable the electronic devices on each end to cooperate in transmitting information successfully. On top of this is the applications layer, which includes, among a great many other things, Web browser software such as Internet Explorer and the corresponding server software used by websites. And on the very top is the content layer, which describes the actual words in an e-mail, the music played by a media player, or the images and text contained in a webpage.

This division of technology into self-contained, mutually independent layers makes the Internet environment highly modular. This means that, at least in theory, firms can compete independently at each layer without worrying about entering the market for services at other layers. For example, it enables a website like eBay, or an applications software company like RealNetworks, to provide service to anyone on the Internet without becoming an Internet service provider in its own right and without incurring the prohibitive expense of building a physical network.[4]

Without the Internet's careful separation of layers, consumers today, like Prodigy or CompuServe subscribers in the 1980s, would be at the mercy of their service provider for their on-line content. As discussed below in more detail, the Internet is not only modular but *open*,[5] in the sense that no one owns the core protocols at the logical layer and anyone can develop complementary products at the adjacent physical and applications layers. This tradition of modularity and openness provides much of the explanation for the Internet's phenomenal success in generating consumer value. By stimulating entry and disaggregated competition at each layer, and by allowing end users to mix and match the best technologies at each layer, the Internet is a uniquely suitable platform for innovation of all kinds.

C. The logic of the Internet

At the *physical* layer, discussed later in this chapter, the Internet includes millions of networked computers and smart devices joined together by fiber-optic pipes and other transmission media into a world-wide "network of networks." At the *logical* layer, the Internet consists of a common computer "addressing" scheme and a set of protocols for the accurate and efficient transmission of packet-switched data across different computer networks. Those protocols—known collectively as the "TCP/IP suite" (for "transmission control protocol" and "Internet protocol")—enable each packet in a transmission to "tell" the packet switches it encounters where it is headed and enables the computers on each end to confirm that the message has been accurately transmitted and received.[6] "The Internet" is defined as the combination of these characteristics—the IP-based addressing system and the interconnected network of networks that rely on TCP/IP as a common logical layer standard.[7]

Together, these elements of the Internet enable a computer in one corner of the world to find a different computer in another corner of the world and exchange information that can be "understood" by the applications software loaded onto the computers at each end of the transmission. Indeed, the two computers (or smart devices) may use entirely different hardware and operating systems. One might be a powerful server running on the UNIX operating system, and the other might be an IBM-compatible personal computer running Windows XP or an Apple Macintosh running its own operating system. The critical point is that all computers connected to the Internet speak the same logical layer language: TCP/IP. As noted, this language is used by all in the Internet world and, like English, is owned by no one.

We will make this point more concrete with a simplified example. Suppose that you wish to download a particular webpage—that is, load it into your computer's memory and call it up on your screen. To do that, you type in the webpage's *domain name*, such as "www.amazon.com." This domain name is just a user-friendly shorthand for the real information needed to reach the website: the *IP address* of the computer hosting that site. The IP address—four numerical sequences separated by dots (in this case, 207.171.163.30)—performs much the same function as the number you dial in an ordinary phone call: it designates the computer you are trying to reach. Like the number assigned to a mobile phone, an IP address is not location-specific. It can be accessed from anywhere and it could be located anywhere.

In our simplified example, your computer finds the IP address for the website by transmitting the domain name to a special type of computer on the Internet called a *domain name server*, whose job it is to keep track of which domain names correspond to which IP addresses. (Domain names— valuable commodities in the world of e-commerce—are allocated by private companies such as Verisign under the general supervision of a non-profit entity known as the Internet Corporation for Assigned Names and Numbers, or "ICANN."[8]) The message transmitted in your Web inquiry is broken down into discrete packets—strings of 1s and 0s—which may fly off individually in several directions in search of the fastest, least congested route to the computer running that website. Messages are compartmentalized this way for the sake of efficiency. By analogy, as John Naughton explains in his masterful history of the Internet:

[Nobody] would contemplate moving a large house in one piece from New York to San Francisco. The obvious way to do it is to disassemble the structure, load segments on to trucks and then dispatch them over the interstate highway network. The trucks may go by different routes—some through the Deep South, perhaps, others via Kansas or Chicago. But eventually, barring accidents, they will all end up at the appointed address in San Francisco. They may not arrive in the order in which they departed, but provided all the components are clearly labelled the various parts of the house can be collected together and reassembled.[9]

In an Internet packet, the labeling function is performed by an address *header*—the 1s and 0s that appear in preassigned slots near the beginning of each packet and convey information about the packet's destination. Ideally, the related packets in a message will end up in the right place in short order because various packet switches throughout the Internet's telecommunications infrastructure—the *routers*—are constantly exchanging information about the most efficient way to reach a particular destination. Additional pre-assigned slots within an Internet packet contain other standard information, such as where the packet originated, how many bits it contains, and how it relates to the other packets within the same transmission. The "TCP/IP protocol suite" is, in essence, the set of rules governing which slots within a packet will contain what information about a packet's destination, source, length, and so forth. Together, those rules enable the computers on each end to ensure the efficient transmission of the data "cargo"—the substance of the transmission—across the Internet. The "TCP" in TCP/IP governs the assembly and reassembly of the packets at each end (including checking for errors such as missing packets), while the "IP" is responsible for moving packets of data from one node to another.[10]

The high capacity computer hosting the website you contact could be in the same city or halfway across the globe; you do not know, and it often makes no difference to you. When it receives your inquiry, that computer, known as a *server* (in that it "serves" you, the "client"), sends a burst of digital packets back to you. Again, the 1s and 0s in the header of each packet contain addressing information to ensure that the return message reaches your computer. Other 1s and 0s identify the content of the webpage using protocols specific to the World Wide Web. Your computer is able to translate those 1s and 0s into pictures and words only because it is outfitted with client software (a *browser* such as Netscape Navigator or Internet Explorer) designed to "understand" the meaning of 1s and 0s transmitted from distant websites. This is a critical point: the telecommunications facilities of the Internet itself—and, more generally, the Internet's physical and logical layers—do not "know" what those 1s and 0s mean; they simply send the 1s and 0s your way and let your computer software figure out the rest.

The Internet's effectiveness depends on universal agreement on the non-proprietary protocols to be used to translate information into 1s and 0s and back again. As discussed below, this agreement is the legacy of the government's early sponsorship of the Internet's antecedents combined with the power of network effects once the Internet assumed public stature. The important point for now is that, because the Internet's core logical layer standards are not owned by any firm, any operator of a data network can connect to the Internet. Similarly, because the intelligence of the Internet is provided primarily by the devices connected to it, and not by centralized switches, any developer of an "application," such as a file sharing program like Napster, is free to make her work available via the Internet and give all Internet users access to it. Consequently, the creator of new media content, such as a short film, can rely on the Internet to distribute her work, thereby displacing such traditional intermediaries as movie theaters or television networks. To summarize, these two related features of the Internet's open architecture—the openness of its protocols and the ability of anyone to develop applications and content for it—help explain the Internet's spectacular growth.

The Internet's generally open architecture is no accident. The engineers who developed the basic protocols for the Internet self-consciously promoted an *end-to-end* design principle that gave maximal control to end users and minimized the intelligence necessary to operate the Internet itself.[11] When applied faithfully, this principle means that packets are delivered on a first come, first served basis without regard to their content, origin, or destination, and are free from any intermediate error checking or filtering. This end-to-end feature makes TCP/IP a quintessential form of common carriage. But it also means that, as originally conceived, the Internet was an imperfect medium for real-time applications such as voice conversations and video-conferencing because it provided no assurance that bits would arrive in time for such applications to work with the requisite quality of service.

Because of the characteristics just described, the Internet is sometimes described as the circuit-switched telephone network "turned inside out." The intelligence in a telephone network resides in centralized switches, which tightly control the range of permissible applications and the quality of service for each application. Telephone company engineers conserve switching and transport capacity by limiting the bandwidth available to those making telephone calls. In the Internet world, by contrast, the principal limit on bandwidth—if no one else is using the network—is the overall capacity of the routers and pipes between point A and point B. If these facilities are congested, you don't get an "all circuits busy" signal as you might when placing a telephone call at peak calling hours on Mother's Day. Rather, you simply face delay and the potential degradation of whatever application you are trying to run.

As noted in chapter 2, ISPs and network service providers have begun deviating from the end-to-end principle by, for example, filtering out unwanted traffic and assigning priority within their IP networks to packets (identified by special headers) associated with certain real-time applications. At a high level of abstraction, they have effectively made these networks function somewhat more like traditional telephone networks.

These steps are designed both to improve service quality for voice and video-conferencing applications and to cope with the proliferation of spam and threats to network security. In this respect, some of the interconnected networks that make up the Internet are becoming "smarter" and have thus reduced the need for the use of inefficiently duplicative circuit-switched networks for voice services. But they have done so only by compromising, to some extent, the end user's traditional control over her Internet experience and raising a set of policy concerns addressed in chapter 5.[12]

D. E-mail and the World Wide Web

To launch a successful network standard, one must persuade a critical mass of users to adopt it. In the case of the Internet, the advent of digital technology and digital networks, which businesses had previously adopted for their own purposes, provided an important building block that made adopting Internet technologies easier. But the question remained: why would anyone *want* to use the Internet? The answer lay in two "killer applications"—e-mail and the World Wide Web—that led the total number of Internet users to double each year through the late 1990s.

The basic protocols that facilitate e-mail were developed in the 1970s and early 1980s on a non-proprietary basis. The Simple Mail Transfer Protocol (SMTP) provided an effective means for delivering e-mail messages and is still used today, although it is often supplemented by various complementary protocols.[13] While the original e-mail systems were somewhat difficult for non-specialists to use, ordinary consumers began exchanging e-mails in increasing numbers in the 1990s with the development of user-friendly software programs like Qualcomm's Eudora, Microsoft's Outlook, and Lotus Notes. Thus, whereas very few business cards in 1990 contained a line for an e-mail address, very few business cards in 2000 *lacked* such a line.

The driving force behind e-mail's explosive popularity during that decade was the familiar phenomenon of network effects. The technology quickly reached a tipping point: because more and more people began to use e-mail, it became correspondingly more valuable to each user, and the *absence* of an e-mail address became a serious liability, at least within many professions. Another reason for e-mail's quick adoption cycle was its use of an open standard. Users did not worry about being locked into a proprietary standard, and businesses (such as Microsoft and others) could enhance e-mail's appeal by easily developing extensions for the open standard.

The Internet's second mass market application, the World Wide Web, was conceived by Tim Berners-Lee at a Swiss particle research laboratory in 1989.[14] Like e-mail, the Web relies on a set of non-proprietary protocols for formatting webpages on computer screens ("hypertext mark-up language," or HTML), establishing transmission procedures between a Web server and its clients ("hypertext transport protocol," or HTTP), and identifying the server address and file location where a particular webpage can be found (the "uniform resource locator," or URL). The Web's defining characteristic, a core feature of the HTML protocol, is the use of hyperlinks. These are the embedded codes in a webpage (often associated with underscored words) that, when clicked, tell your computer to retrieve another webpage, either from the same website or another one, thereby enabling users to move quickly from one webpage to the next.

The best way to think of the World Wide Web is as a particular application that rides on top of the Internet's lower layer TCP/IP protocols and uses its own higher layer protocols for exchanging information. Many people, including some federal judges, confuse the Internet with the Web,[15] but this is a bit like confusing the Windows operating system with the Microsoft Word program that runs on top of it. That the Internet itself and the Web operate at independent layers explains why you can use your computer to run applications other than the Web over the Internet (such as an instant messaging program or a media player), and why you can use Web-oriented software for functions unrelated to the Internet (such as searching the contents of your computer hard drive).

Like e-mail, the Web was not an immediate popular success. To view "websites"—collections of files posted on Web servers—a user needs a browser that translates her requests into code that those servers can understand and then translates the code sent back by those servers into sights, words, and sounds she can understand. The first browsers were text-based, pictureless, and non-intuitive, at least from a layperson's perspective, and their audience was largely limited to university settings. That changed in 1993 when Marc Andreessen and Eric Bina, then working at the National Center for Supercomputing Applications at the University of Illinois, released to the public (for free) the first multimedia browser with a point-and-click graphical user interface, which they called Mosaic. Along with

Jim Clark, Andreessen then founded Netscape. There he improved upon Mosaic to produce the more popular "Navigator" browser and became an overnight Internet tycoon by taking Netscape public in 1995.[16] The spectacular success of Netscape's initial public offering helped awaken the general public to the Internet's transformative significance for the economy at large. In retrospect, it also marked the beginning of the Internet gold rush, which largely ended with the NASDAQ crash five years later.

The development of user-friendly browsers in the early 1990s coincided with the federal government's decision to privatize the Internet and allow it to support electronic commerce (more on that later). By 1996, the Web had entered the popular consciousness and began a period of explosive growth. Why did executives, in a relatively short period, turn from asking "what is a website?" to "when can we get our business's website up and running?" As with e-mail, the short answer lies in the network effects phenomenon.

In the early years of the Web, ordinary consumers had no real incentive to devote the time and resources needed to use it because too few of their peers were using it and no one had developed user-friendly software to exploit its commercial potential. The tipping point arrived with the invention of Mosaic and Navigator, which made the Web easy for the masses to surf. As John Naughton explains, the Web presented the same "chicken and egg story" as the slow initial growth of the telephone—but with one key difference: "[W]hereas the spread of the telephone depended on massive investment in physical infrastructure—trunk lines, connections to homes, exchanges, operators, engineers and so forth—the Web simply piggybacked on an infrastructure (the Internet) which was already in place. By the time Mosaic appeared, desktop PCs were ubiquitous in business and increasingly common in homes. . . . The world, in other words, was waiting for Mosaic."[17]

Once the Internet reached critical mass, it could rely on the network effects phenomenon to keep it—and its most successful applications, such as e-mail and the Web—from fragmenting into mutually unintelligible systems, even though no governmental authority enforces the uniformity of their respective protocols. In that respect, the development of the Internet, e-mail, and the Web is somewhat like the development of spoken languages—which, indeed, are the most fundamental of all "standards." As words change meaning and new words come into use, individuals adjust their own linguistic practices to ensure that they are understood by others. The language changes, but it remains mutually intelligible to everyone within a single linguistic community.

The same is true of the protocols that constitute the Internet itself, e-mail, the Web, and other Internet applications. As the standards change, individuals follow because that is the only way they can continue exploiting the Internet's prodigious network effects. But whereas language normally evolves without much guidance from any recognized decisionmaking body,[18] the same is not true of the Internet. Instead, since 1986, the key standards associated with the Internet have evolved largely under the close supervision of the Internet Engineering Task Force (IETF)—which, in its own words, is an open and "loosely self-organized group of people who contribute to the engineering and evolution of Internet technologies."[19] And the World Wide Web Consortium (W3C) performs a similar standard-setting function for Web-oriented protocols.

Significantly, the IETF and the W3C have no formal regulatory authority of any kind. Thus, once the IETF introduces a new standard—say, an upgrade to the Internet's core TCP/IP protocol (called IPv6), which, among other things, provides for more Internet addresses—it has no means, beyond its powers of persuasion, of ensuring that firms employ this upgrade. In many cases, and potentially this one, the self-interest of firms will coincide with the collective interest of the entire Internet community, and firms will voluntarily adopt the new standard. But where those interests are not aligned, the IETF cannot enforce compliance with its official standards. As we discuss in chapter 12, a standard-setting body will sometimes need to work hand-in-hand with government agencies when policymakers conclude that a single recognized authority *needs* to prescribe a standard and that the standard-setting body is the proper institution to develop it.

II. The Internet's Physical Infrastructure

To this point, we have focused mostly on the Internet's logical layer characteristics. Now we shift our focus to the physical layer, which is the site of most, though by no means all, Internet-related telecommunications policy disputes.

A. Beginnings

A brief synopsis of the Internet's origins helps explain its close relationship to the traditional telecommunications infrastructure. In the usual telling, the Internet is described as the brainchild of the same military-industrial complex that brought us the theory of Mutually Assured Destruction. In the 1960s, at the height of the Cold War, some of America's brightest minds were fixated on a macabre question: If the Soviet Union wiped out much of the United States in a preemptive nuclear strike, how could the president convey a "launch" order to America's own assembled nuclear forces? For Paul Baran, then a technologist at Rand, the answer to this telecommunications problem seemed obvious: build a network with a series of broadly interconnected *nodes* (routers) so that no one node is critical to the functioning of the network as a whole.

The problem was that the military's long distance communications infrastructure was largely contained within AT&T's circuit-switched network. As we discussed in chapter 2, an efficient circuit-switched voice network conserves on switching capacity by economizing on the number of switches that need to be occupied for the duration of a voice call. This requires a highly centralized network with a rigid hierarchy of switches. The efficiency of that hierarchical arrangement, however, is also its greatest military vulnerability. Precisely because it was centralized and hierarchical, AT&T's circuit-switched network was exceptionally susceptible to destruction. If the Soviets could hit just a few central switches, they might have been able to prevent Washington from sending messages to missile silos in Nebraska, Arizona, and Montana. The solution was a digital and "distributed" (decentralized) network developed by a taxpayer-supported think tank within the Defense Department known as the Advanced Research Projects Agency, or "ARPA."

Like the nodes in Baran's imagined distributed network, each of the nodes in the ARPANet was linked to several other nodes in a generally non-hierarchical way that maximized the number of routes a signal could take from Point A to Point B. One node would hand off a message to another with the destination information attached, the next node would hand it off to yet a third node with the same destination information, and so on down the line until the destination was reached. If one node along the way was out of commission, the message could be rerouted to another, still-active node. Thus, even though the ARPANet still leased its transport links from AT&T, it was much less vulnerable than AT&T's own circuit-switched network. Just as Baran had envisioned, if half of the ARPANet had been wiped out in an attack, signals still would have arrived at missile silos or any other critical governmental location, albeit in a more round-about way.

For the ARPANet to work, however, the messages had to be transmitted in digital form, in part because that is the only feasible way of preserving the clarity and integrity of messages after frequent repetition at many nodes. And the network could operate efficiently only if it was packet-switched, for, as we have explained, packet-switching technology enables the portions of a "call" (or "session") to hop through a large number of nodes in small packets without needlessly tying up capacity on each of those nodes in the form of dedicated "circuits."

The ARPANet also accomplished a number of relatively mundane objectives, such as linking together government-supported labs for purposes of aggregating the processing power of the mainframe computers in each lab. Indeed, some observers submit that the government funded the ARPANet project more to achieve such conventional objectives than, as in Baran's vision, to preserve communications in the event of a catastrophic attack.[20] Nonetheless, the distributed and digital character of this network, conceived amid the Cold War paranoia of the 1960s, forms the basis for the current Internet.

To be sure, today's Internet differs from the original ARPANet in several important respects. The ARPANet started out as a single unified network overseen by the government and affiliated research institutions. The main applications from the 1970s through the birth of the modern Internet in the early 1990s were file exchanges (employing the now outdated but still used File Transfer Protocol), TELNET (a means of logging on remotely to a mainframe computer), newsgroups, and e-mail.[21] The most influential users were academics who relied on government funding to develop the basic protocols on which the Internet still relies. And the federal government's sponsorship was critical throughout these early years. ARPA funded a Berkeley program to incorporate TCP/IP into the UNIX operating system; the Defense Department required its contractors to adopt TCP/IP; and the National Science Foundation provided grants to the IETF and invested more than $200 million to support "NSFNet," a TCP/IP network that linked the networks of various universities.[22]

This official sponsorship finally ended in the early 1990s, when the federal government proposed to privatize the NSFNet and, for the first time, open it up to commercial uses.[23] The government thereby sought to enlist "the enthusiasm of private sector interests to build upon the government funded developments to expand the Internet and make it available to the general public," as two Internet pioneers have observed.[24]

The result of this privatization decision is the wildly successful modern Internet. On the physical and logical layers, it is a decentralized network of dissimilar networks with otherwise incompatible computers and other smart devices joined together by their common use of the TCP/IP set of protocols. On the higher layers, it is an engine for economic growth and an unrivaled resource for electronic applications and content, whose variety is bounded only by the limits of the human imagination. By 1997, it had become conventional wisdom that, in the words of Bill Clinton and Al Gore, "[t]he private sector should lead" the Internet's continued growth and that, although the government had played a critical role in the Internet's development, "its expansion has been driven primarily by the private sector."[25]

B. The Internet backbone

Like any physical network, the Internet consists of pipes ("links") and switches ("nodes" or "routers"). The pipes used in Internet communications, like those in the telephone network, fall into two general categories. *Transport* facilities, also known as Internet *backbone* facilities, connect one network node to another and one network to another. *Access* facilities, addressed later in this chapter, are "last mile" pipes that connect an end user's computers to a network node and thence to the Internet.

As noted in chapter 2, there is enormous overlap between long distance telephone networks and Internet backbone networks. For example, the fiber strands that carry Internet backbone traffic often coexist along the same intercity routes as the fiber strands that carry conventional long distance traffic. It is thus no coincidence that the largest voice long distance carriers, such as AT&T, MCI, Sprint, and Qwest, own some of the largest Internet backbone networks. These backbone providers sell transport services to the Internet's major players, including Internet service providers (ISPs). ISPs serve as a kind of liaison between end users and the broader

Internet. For example, when you dial into the Internet over a regular telephone connection, your ISP performs (among other things) the "protocol conversion" functions that allow your analog computer modem to talk to distant computers on the Internet. Most of the key backbone providers, such as MCI's UUNet, are vertically integrated with ISPs and sell Internet-related services directly to end users—particularly large businesses—and to content providers such as websites. Virtually all backbone providers sell transport services to unaffiliated ISPs as well.

When you use the Internet, whether at home or at work, you expect your ISP to provide access to the entire Internet, including all public websites and e-mail addresses. But there are many different ISPs and many different networks that provide backbone transport services to those ISPs. Your ISP will therefore want to do business only with a backbone provider that can arrange for your signals to reach any destination on the Internet. This means that the ISP's backbone provider must arrange for interconnection with a number of other backbone providers. Particularly in the Internet's early days, many backbone providers exchanged traffic at government-sponsored Network Access Points (NAPs)—the Internet's equivalent to public airports, where the routes of many different carriers converge. (When the government privatized the Internet, it transferred control of these points to commercial providers.) Internet backbone providers now increasingly rely on privately arranged points of interconnection, largely because of congestion at the NAPs.

As a business matter, backbone-to-backbone interconnection agreements take two basic forms: *peering* and *transit*. As the name suggests, peering agreements are usually signed by two backbone providers of roughly equivalent market stature. Each "peer" arranges to hand off its Internet traffic to the other peer for ultimate delivery to the latter's customers, such as ISPs. The hand-off normally occurs at the point of interconnection closest to the point of origination—a convention known as "hot potato routing." Because no money changes hands in the process, such peering arrangements are a form of "bill-and-keep," a concept further discussed in chapter 9.

Transit agreements, in contrast, normally involve backbone providers of unequal market presence. As observed in one prominent FCC white paper, "[t]ransit and peering are differentiated in two main ways. First, in a transit arrangement, one backbone pays another backbone for interconnection, and therefore becomes a wholesale customer of the other backbone. Second, unlike in a peering relationship, with transit, the backbone selling the transit services will route traffic from the transit customer to its peering partners."[26] The very largest providers, such as AT&T, MCI, and Sprint, have global networks of such comprehensive reach that they never need to purchase transit services from other backbones. These are known as "top tier" (or Tier I) backbones.

These peering and transit arrangements are completely unregulated. Neither the FCC nor any other governmental authority regulates the prices that a larger backbone network may charge a smaller one for transit services or mandates that backbone providers interconnect at all. This deregulatory approach has worked so far because no backbone provider has grown large enough to dominate the market and charge inefficiently high prices for transit. By most accounts, a competitive equilibrium prevails today in this market, where the larger backbones "compete for the transit business of smaller backbones in order to increase their revenues," and that competition keeps transit prices down.[27]

To be sure, if a given backbone provider were to surpass a given threshold of market share, it might obtain both the inclination and the ability to dominate the backbone market and force rivals to pay supracompetitive rates for transit—thereby driving up retail prices, depressing Internet usage, and undermining the efficiencies of the Internet as a whole.[28] Such an anticompetitive dynamic could arise because smaller backbone providers, with their lower numbers of websites and other users, value interconnection with the dominant provider more than that larger provider values interconnection with them. In theory, a dominant provider, simply by leaving current interconnection agreements in place and not upgrading them to meet increased demand, could ensure that its connections with rivals become increasingly congested, leading to latency and packet loss problems between the two networks. For the dominant provider's customers, such problems, which would lead to delays in interacting with users or websites on the smaller firm's backbone, would be a minor annoyance; for the smaller provider's customers, however, this degraded access could cause enormous frustration and thus lead customers to defect en masse to the dominant provider.[29]

The antitrust authorities have taken such concerns seriously and have acted to ensure that no provider grows large enough to occupy a dominant share of the backbone market. For example, when WorldCom acquired MCI in 1998, the Justice Department and the European Union compelled them, as a condition of their merger, to divest MCI's backbone affiliate (InternetMCI)—which, at the time, was second only to WorldCom's UUNet in market share. But for this divestiture, the combined company would have controlled 50% of the total Internet backbone market, thereby presenting a risk "that it would attempt to tip the market by charging existing peers for interconnection or by degrading the quality of interconnections."[30] For similar reasons, together with concerns about excessive concentration in the voice long distance market, the Justice Department and the European Union effectively blocked the proposed merger of MCI-WorldCom and Sprint in 2000.[31] To date, these antitrust measures constitute the most significant governmental response to fears of anticompetitive conduct in the Internet backbone market. For its part, the FCC has decided not even to monitor the competitive aspects of Internet backbone interconnection relationships—for example, through disclosure of peering agreements or reporting obligations for market share—so long as the market continues to function well without regulation.[32] It remains to be seen whether some form of self-regulation or FCC oversight will ultimately be necessary to ensure reliable interconnection in this increasingly critical market.[33]

C. The last mile: from narrowband to broadband

The chicken-and-egg problem

In contrast to the prevailing free-market approach to the Internet's backbone facilities, the government has historically regulated the pipes—or, as we discuss in the next chapter, some of the pipes—connecting ISPs to individual end users. These access facilities are often ordinary loops provided by local telephone companies. Indeed, until the late 1990s, virtually everyone who logged on to the Internet from home did so by means of a dial-up connection.

As shown in Figure 5, dial-up connections involve the use of a computer modem to place a regular telephone call through an ordinary circuit-switched network to the local access number obtained by an ISP. The ISP converts these analog signals into a digitized IP format and places them onto a packet-switched network en route to the broader Internet. During the duration of the end user's dial-up Internet connection, the telephone company keeps a dedicated circuit open between the end user and the ISP.[34] The traditional design of telephone company networks limits such dial-up Internet access to narrow bandwidths, traditionally capping out at around 56 kilobits per second. This speed limitation places severe constraints on the kinds of Internet applications that end users can run over their dial-up connections—and thus limits the inherent value to them of the Internet itself.

In contrast, by connecting an end user directly to a packet-switched network, without any intermediate stop at a circuit switch, a *broadband* connection permits much faster interaction with the Internet. Typical examples in the residential market include *cable modem* service, which provides Internet access over the same cables that pipe television signals into the home, and *digital subscriber line* service (DSL), which, as discussed below, dedicates certain frequencies on a copper telephone line to data transmission. The FCC currently defines as "high speed" (i.e., broadband)

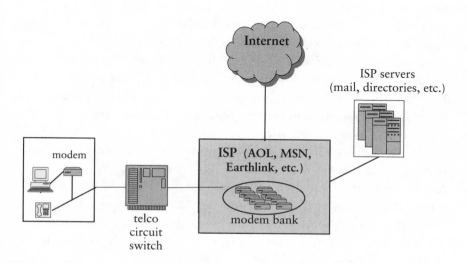

Figure 5. Dial-up Internet architecture

any connection with data speeds above 200 kilobits per second.[35] Over time, this definition is bound to change, as consumers demand faster connection speeds to accommodate their increasing appetite for bandwidth-intensive Internet applications. Indeed, even today, many cable modem connections provide download speeds of up to 3.0 megabits per second, 15 times the FCC's current standard for broadband.

The speed differential between broadband and dial-up connections produces a qualitative as well as quantitative distinction in one's experience of the Internet. Broadband not only makes Web browsing much easier and more enjoyable, but also allows users to run particular applications unavailable over dial-up connections. For example, you can watch a high resolution streaming music video over a broadband connection, play a graphics-intensive video game in real time against somebody three thousand miles away, and—as explained in chapter 6—place a crystal-clear voice-over-IP (VoIP) call to anyone with a telephone anywhere in the world. You cannot do any of those things over a traditional dial-up connection. A broadband connection makes the Internet more attractive in a second way as well: it is "always on" and thus frees you from the time-consuming hassle of waiting while your modem dials up an ISP and establishes a connection. This inconvenience is another reason why people with dial-up connections are less likely to use the Internet for commercial and other purposes than are people with broadband connections.[36]

Consumers in the United States have made the transition from dial-up to broadband more slowly than some policymakers had hoped. The reason relates to the same chicken-and-egg problem that afflicts many new technologies in any network industry. Until a critical mass of consumers has broadband access at home, content providers will not invest heavily in high value applications that can be run only over broadband connections. On the other hand, until those providers *do* invest in such "killer applications," too few consumers will perceive enough extra value in a broadband connection to pay the somewhat higher rates for one. As the *Wall Street Journal* reported in late 2003, this challenge has economy-wide implications: "Rising rates of high speed Internet access are expected to trigger everything from increased sales of new computers to a massive rise in worker productivity as employees are able to more easily and efficiently telecommute or work from home after business hours. A 2003 study from the Brookings Institution asserted that universal broadband access could add $300 billion a year to the U.S. economy. Conversely, forgoing a major broadband rollout may hinder economic growth and worsen an already bleak picture for battered telecommunications and high tech industries."[37] The "big question," as one analyst frames it, "is whether the marketplace can deliver it on its own or whether the government steps in, as it has in other nations."[38]

Estimates of the exact levels of residential broadband usage vary, but they all suggest that the United States is at or near the point when more households use broadband connections than dial-up ones.[39] Although this is a far cry from the broadband adoption rate of several other nations— such as South Korea, where 75% of households already had a broadband Internet connection by 2003—it is a promising sign that market forces are bringing high speed Internet access to most parts of the United States. Indeed, consumers have adopted broadband technology more quickly than most other popular technologies, such as cellphones and VCRs, during analogous periods in their introduction to the market.[40] Moreover, as VoIP technology—which relies on broadband connections—grows in popularity, it may well drive adoption of broadband connections because the combined price of a broadband service plus a VoIP subscription is often lower than the combined price of local and long distance calling over a conventional telephone line and a dial-up ISP account (particularly by means of a second line).[41]

Nonetheless, many technology companies and consumer groups, impatient with the pace of broadband deployment, have urged the government to intervene more actively. Discussions about the role of the government in accelerating broadband deployment often center on either the "demand side" or the "supply side" of the issue. On the demand side, the largest question is whether there is more that government can do to encourage the development of killer applications that will stimulate consumers' demand for broadband connections. Music file sharing seemed poised to serve as such an application before the courts began suppressing it because of its widespread use as a tool for copyright infringement.[42] Policy discussions on this issue often concern proposals to encourage copyright holders to make their content available in digital form on-line for a fee, an issue that relates to the "digital rights management" questions we will discuss in chapter 12 in connection with the digital television transition.

There are two major questions on the supply side of the issue. The first is whether the federal government should provide significant tax incentives or other inducements to encourage providers to invest in the infrastructure needed to bring broadband access to residential addresses in less populous areas, with their significantly lower economies of density. The second is whether the government should do more to facilitate broadband adoption in the inner cities and other poverty-stricken areas, where the prospect of a *digital divide*—between "digital haves" and "digital have nots"—stems more from considerations of income and affordability than from any scarcity of the necessary infrastructure. In chapter 10, we discuss this digital divide and its relation to the 1996 Act's treatment of universal service goals.

We now turn to the specific technologies for providing broadband Internet access to end users. Our discussion tracks the two major markets at stake: the market for connecting large (enterprise) and mid-sized business customers to the Internet, and the separate market for bridging the last mile to residential customers and small businesses.

The business market for broadband technology

Many Americans got their first taste of high speed Internet access at the office. Most businesses of any size have "local area networks" (LANs)—private packet-switched data networks that link the various computers within an office. Larger businesses also lease high capacity telephone lines to link their various offices together, so that (for example) a manager at a bank's branch office can instantaneously check the records stored in a computer at the bank's corporate headquarters. Such networks have long employed high capacity lines that use various packet-switched protocols, including the now-obsolescent X.25 (first introduced in the 1970s), "frame relay," "asynchronous transfer mode" (ATM), and the new "Gigabit Ethernet" protocol.[43] As the Web became an increasingly central part of life during the 1990s, companies began using these high capacity lines to connect their corporate data networks to the broader Internet. Indeed, the very prevalence of these packet-switched data networks throughout the business world greatly facilitated the growth of the Internet. In return, the Internet contributed to the unusual productivity increases that many businesses enjoyed in the late 1990s.

Today, as discussed in chapter 3, the market leaders for the provision of these comprehensive network services to the largest (enterprise) business customers remain the independent long distance companies such as AT&T and MCI, which were never subject to the Bell companies' restrictions (since lifted) on transmitting data between a company's far-flung branch offices. The Bells and other ILECs, however, occupy a larger share of the market for providing high speed Internet access to smaller businesses, traditionally through high capacity loops known as "T-1 lines" and more recently through the various flavors of DSL technology as well.

Until recently, almost all businesses have used separate networks for voice telephony and data communications. The result has been an inefficient duplication of both infrastructure and labor. But IP technology is finally poised to eliminate these costly redundancies at their source. New technologies such as *multiprotocol label switching* (MPLS)—which assigns priority to some packets (such as those for voice) over others (such as those for data)—make it feasible for businesses to run voice, data, and video applications over a single IP platform, with at least the same quality of voice service as provided by traditional circuit-switched telephony. Figure 6 illustrates the architecture of a converged network capable of handing voice and data.

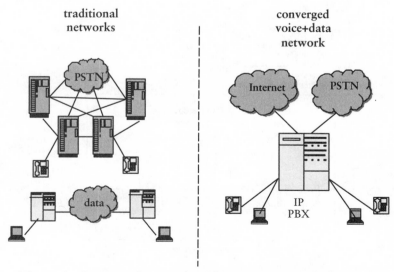

Figure 6. Converged network within an enterprise business
("PSTN" = "public switched telephone network")

The benefits of such integration extend well beyond the enormous cost savings of consolidating voice and data. IP technologies also offer customers an integrated suite of innovative communications services beyond the capabilities of today's balkanized voice and data networks. Just to scratch the surface, integrated IP networks allow a voicemail to appear as an audio file in a user's e-mail inbox so that it can be effortlessly forwarded to coworkers without once touching a telephone keypad. And these networks allow business travelers to plug IP telephones into laptops, enabling them to call from, and be reached at, a single telephone number anywhere in the world (see chapter 6).

The mass market

Only since the late 1990s have U.S. consumers begun ordering broadband service to their homes. As of this writing, there are two primary types of residential broadband service, each of which can provide connections ten to twenty times faster than the speediest dial-up connection. The first,

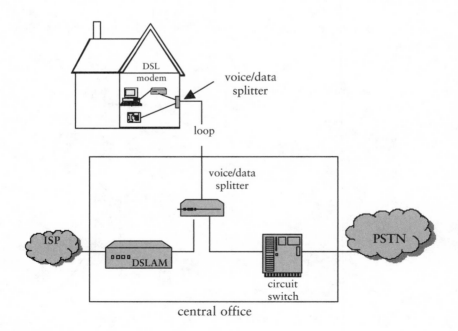

Figure 7. DSL architecture

offered by wireline telephone companies, is a type of DSL service known as *asymmetric DSL* (ADSL). This technology divides the bandwidth of a copper telephone line into "high" and "low" frequencies, dedicating the former to the transmission of high speed data traffic while reserving the latter for conventional voice calls. At each end of the copper line, these voice and data channels are split apart. On the customer's side, the voice channel plugs into a telephone and the data channel into a computer or home network. On the telephone company's side—either at the central office or at an intermediate "remote terminal"—the voice channel plugs into the circuit switch as before. The higher frequency data signals, however, are routed *around* the circuit switch, aggregated with other customers' data signals in a device called a "DSLAM" (for "DSL access multiplexer"), and sent off to the Internet. Figure 7 illustrates the basics of DSL.

The asymmetrical characteristic that gives ADSL its name is the reservation of greater bandwidth on the "downstream" path of the data channel *to* the customer from the Internet than on the "upstream" path *from* the customer to the Internet. That asymmetry suits most residential customers, who download webpages and other files from the Internet much more than they send bulky files to others on the Internet. And because the frequencies assigned to voice and data can be used simultaneously, this technology spares those customers the need to order costly second lines if they wish to conduct ordinary telephone conversations while using the Internet.

The other major type of residential broadband access is cable modem service, provided over the same facilities that deliver cable television signals into people's homes. Cable companies assign Internet data to discrete "channels" (frequency blocks) within their cables in the same way that they assign television stations to such channels. Just as DSL providers split data from voice, cable modem providers split data from conventional television signals, and in two places: at the customer's home and typically at the *headend*, which is the cable company's counterpart to a telephone company central office (and where the company collects television programming signals from fiber-optic and satellite links). At the headend, a "cable modem termination system" (or CMTS) performs a role similar to the DSLAM in a DSL system: it aggregates the incoming data traffic and transports it to an ISP, usually affiliated with the cable company itself, en route

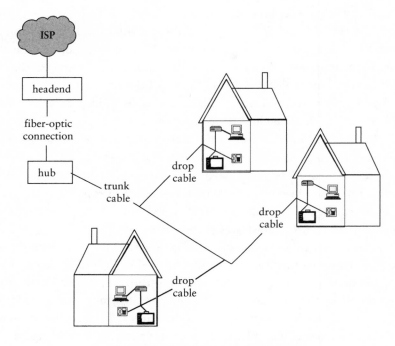

Figure 8. Cable system architecture

to the Internet. Figure 8 shows the basic configuration of a cable system designed to offer both video programming and broadband Internet access.

Cable modem and DSL technologies differ significantly in the way they segregate "downstream" Internet data among individual end users in the last mile to the home. With DSL, the mechanism is relatively straightforward. In a telephone company's network, each end user typically has a dedicated loop, which carries only that end user's Internet traffic just as it carries only that end user's voice conversations. Cable television systems, in contrast, were never designed to provide a separate physical connection to each end user. Because such systems traditionally "broadcast" the same television content to all subscribers, it was much more efficient to configure a network that sent exactly the same signals past everyone's home, enabling each subscriber to tap into any of the television signals streaming by. Obviously, this network architecture requires some adjustment before it can be used for Internet access. Among other concerns, you do not want your neighbors to view the e-mails you read and the websites you visit, and you presumably aren't interested in viewing their Internet transactions either. Cable modem providers address this challenge in part by employing a system similar to the "Ethernet" technology long used to connect computers within a corporate LAN: downstream packets are tagged for individual users, and, because of various system controls such as encryption technology, only those users will be able to pull them off the common network and read them.[44]

These two rival broadband platforms (DSL and cable modem) differ in the physical medium of the last mile transmission facilities they use, but this difference is eroding as both cable companies and telephone companies have begun making extensive use of fiber-optic lines in their respective networks. Traditionally, cable companies provided service entirely over coaxial cables. Over time, however, cable companies began installing increasing amounts of fiber throughout their networks and deep into individual neighborhoods. This trend reflects both an effort to comply with the edicts of local franchising authorities and, more significantly, a response to market developments, such as the competitive threat posed by direct-to-home satellite broadcasters and consumer demand for greater bandwidth in the form of more TV channels, video-on-demand services, and faster Internet connections. In some cases, the only coaxial cable left in these networks occupies the last hundred feet connecting a subscriber's home with the fiber-optic lines in the street.

Although these upgrades are still underway, the cable companies are generally far ahead of their telephone company rivals in the deployment of high capacity fiber-optic facilities in residential neighborhoods throughout the United States. That is in part because most phone companies—which have long specialized in the provision of quintessentially narrowband voice services—had no analogous incentive until recently to invest in an exponential expansion of their network capacity. It may also be in part because telephone companies profited from the growth of dial-up Internet access, which caused many customers to order high-priced second lines to avoid tying up their primary voice lines while surfing the Net. Only when the cable companies began rolling out cable modem service as an alternative to dial-up—thereby giving customers faster Internet access and, as part of the bargain, freedom from any need to order second telephone lines—did most phone companies confront any pressing need to roll out services that, like DSL, tended to "cannibalize" their more lucrative second-line offerings.[45]

From a technological perspective, the deployment of fiber presents a somewhat different set of challenges for the telephone company providers of DSL service than for the cable company providers of cable modem service. DSL can be provided *only* over copper facilities, and DSL speeds vary inversely with the length of a copper line until, at around 18,000 feet, DSL can no longer be effectively provided at all. By pushing fiber more deeply into individual neighborhoods, telephone companies can decrease the portion of a loop that is copper and can therefore both raise the number of DSL-eligible customers and dramatically increase the bandwidth of the DSL service provided over those customers' lines. Doing so, however, requires telephone companies to invest billions of dollars in tearing up the streets to lay new fiber pipes. It also requires them to install DSLAMs and other sophisticated electronic equipment not just in central offices, but also in large numbers of intermediate residential locations. DSL technology ends wherever the copper portion of the loop ends, and that is thus the point at which a DSL provider must split voice from data services and route them over segregated fiber facilities to their respective circuit-switched and packet-switched networks.

One lively topic of debate today is whether DSL will turn out to be just a stop-gap technology for the major telephone companies while they deploy, over the next several years, pervasively fiber-based and packet-switched technology throughout their networks for the joint provision of voice, data, and video applications. The conventional wisdom is that residential consumers will increasingly wish to purchase, from a single provider, the fabled "triple play" of communications services: (i) dependable voice service, (ii) broadband Internet access, and (iii) high quality video programming. Like much conventional wisdom, this might turn out to be right or wrong, but the market takes it seriously for now. So do the major telephone companies, some of which have vowed, to a still-skeptical financial community, that they will meet this challenge by devoting many billions of dollars over the next several years to the construction of sprawling all-fiber networks to the home.[46]

Cable television companies have long led the market for video services, although they face significant competition from direct-to-home satellite providers. Cable companies quickly assumed a two-to-one advantage over the telephone companies in the U.S. residential broadband market, although (with aggressive pricing policies) the telephone companies may be narrowing the gap somewhat. While cable companies have a weaker broadband presence in the business market—mostly because they never built out their networks to provide *television* service to most business districts—they are expected to challenge the telephone companies in that market over the next several years as they expand their footprints to exploit the new revenue opportunities presented by broadband.[47] Finally, cable companies are accelerating plans to introduce residential phone service over their facilities, increasingly in the form of high quality VoIP services offered at low incremental cost on top of cable modem connections.[48]

Telephone companies believe that, to ensure their relevance in the residential market, they may need to invest billions of dollars to bring fiber closer to the home in neighborhoods throughout the United States—either "to the curb" or "to the premises," in the industry jargon. This indeed may be the only way for them to match the bandwidth of cable pipes in that market. The required multi-billion dollar investment is a huge gamble for these companies.[49] But it may ultimately be a commercial imperative as they struggle to avoid the fate of Western Union, itself once a monopoly provider of electronic communications until the disruptive technology of the telephone itself eroded demand for its services. In the next chapter, we discuss the controversy surrounding the FCC's 2003 decision largely to exempt the telephone companies from any obligation to lease these next-generation facilities to competitors at prescribed rates.

Our discussion of last-mile broadband technologies has focused almost entirely on services provided by telephone and cable companies because, as of this writing, those technologies account for the great majority of the residential broadband market and because it remains uncertain whether and when alternative technologies will succeed on a similar scale.[50] A few of those alternatives warrant brief mention, however. First, consumers can obtain broadband Internet access via satellite, but the service is typically both slower and more expensive than either cable modem or DSL, and the high orbits used by the satellites produce enough transmission delay to degrade real-time applications such as voice. For these reasons, satellite Internet access is purchased largely by consumers—many of them in rural areas—whose cable and telephone companies have not yet rolled out broadband products of their own. Nonetheless, some firms continue to look for ways to make satellite Internet access more successful in the mass market.[51]

Second, electric utilities have begun developing ways of providing broadband access over the power lines into people's homes. There are still significant technical obstacles to this service, but the FCC's Chief Engineer claims that the technology is "ready for prime time," and power company Cinergy in Cincinnati began rolling out the service on a commercial basis in 2004.[52] The regulatory status of this new technology, however, is still very much up in the air. The FCC opened a proceeding in 2004 to address concerns about the potential for interference with wireless transmissions.[53] To nurture this fledgling technology, however, the Commission deferred for now an entire set of important issues ranging, in the words of one frustrated FCC commissioner, from "disabilities access, E911, pole attachments, competition protections, and, critically here, how to handle the potential for cross-subsidization between regulated power businesses and unregulated communications businesses."[54]

The final two candidates for mass market broadband alternatives to cable modem and DSL involve different forms of terrestrial (as opposed to satellite) wireless technology, addressed in greater detail in chapters 7 and 8. The first of these, *Wi-Fi,* is popular in home and office networking and in public "hot spots" such as coffee shops and airports. But because current Wi-Fi technology can carry signals only several hundred feet, it cannot yet serve as a direct substitute for broadband connections to the home. A next-generation variant of Wi-Fi with somewhat better prospects is *WiMAX,* a technology that promises speeds between 300 kilobits per second and 2 megabits per second over a range of 30 miles.[55] Finally, some industry analysts believe that the true future of wireless broadband lies not in Wi-Fi or WiMAX, but in *3G* (for "third generation") mobile wireless services, as described in chapter 8. Indeed, Verizon Wireless and others have already begun offering broadband wireless services using the same spectrum and physical infrastructure now used for conventional cellular telephony. At this point, however, such services are priced well above DSL and cable modem services and are marketed primarily to businesses, not consumers. And it remains unclear whether any provider will be able to offer either 3G or WiMAX services at very large volumes in the near future, given the scarcity of the spectrum the FCC has made available for them—a government-created shortage that we address in chapter 7.

* * *

Some commentators have argued that, while only advanced fiber-optic technology to the home can deliver the prodigious bandwidth needed to satisfy consumer demand over the long term, this technology may never be deployed in a competitive environment, in which recovery of the enormous costs is uncertain. These commentators thus conclude that fiber-to-the-home technology, much like the copper loop of a century ago, should be treated as a natural monopoly.[56] Following this logic, some foreign governments have sponsored the deployment of fiber-optic networks of this type and have prevented private firms from offering competitive alternatives.[57]

The ethic of competition is now so deeply engrained in U.S. telecommunications policy, however, that such government intervention is unlikely to arise on a broad scale in this country. American policymakers seem inclined to conclude that broadband competition, whatever its shortcomings, will best sort the technological wheat from the chaff. And, ever since MCI built its first city-to-city microwave relay links to challenge AT&T Long Lines, they have grown increasingly skeptical of assumptions that any portion of the telecommunications market is, or should be treated as, a "natural monopoly."[58] The commitment of U.S. policymakers to competition—and their skepticism of the traditional natural monopoly model—gives rise to the complex policy issues discussed in the next chapter.

5

Monopoly Leveraging Concerns and the Internet

Until very recently, all telecommunications services were joined hip to hip with the particular facilities on which they were provided. When AT&T was split up in 1984, for example, few people expected telephone networks to offer widespread video programming or cable television networks to carry voice calls. The Internet, however, upsets this established order. Every single form of content ever conveyed over any electronic communications system—voice (telephony), audio (radio), video (television), documents (faxes), and so forth—can be instantly converted into 1s and 0s and transmitted as the cargo in digital packets flying over the Internet, no matter what the underlying physical medium.

Telecommunications engineers are now radically transforming the telecommunications industry by using the Internet's layered architecture, together with the power of broadband platforms, to uncouple particular *services* from the physical *networks* over which they have traditionally been provided. As we have explained, this phenomenon of convergence is attributable to the Internet's openness and modularity—its compartmentalization of computer-enhanced communications into separate physical, logical, applications, and content layers. Competition and product diversity have flourished on the Internet's higher layers because the universality of the Internet's core protocols liberates applications and content providers (like RealNetworks and eBay) from any need to become Internet service providers (like AOL or Earthlink) or "last mile" transmission providers (like Comcast or BellSouth).

Nothing guarantees, however, that market forces alone will indefinitely preserve this traditional compartmentalization of the Internet into distinct layers. The basic policy challenge, familiar to antitrust lawyers, is how best to prevent any dominant provider of physical layer transmission services from exploiting its control of bottleneck facilities to stifle competition in the adjacent markets for applications and content in ways that reduce overall consumer welfare. Of course, this type of challenge is not unique to the telecommunications field. There are a number of industries in which vertically integrated firms are said to leverage (or preserve) their monopoly in one market by thwarting competition in others. And when disputes arise about what, if anything, the government should do about that concern, they are usually resolved by antitrust law. In general, antitrust law evaluates such disputes by defining the relevant markets and then evaluating whether the firm in question is dominant in one of those markets, whether it has both the incentive and the ability to exploit (or protect) that dominance by harming competition in adjacent markets, whether the costs of any antidiscrimination remedy outweigh the benefits, and so forth.[1] And as communications platforms converge and compete, policymakers should look to technology-neutral antitrust principles as a replacement for the technology-specific quirks and artifices of the legacy regulatory regime.[2] In chapter 6, we discuss how, as a legal matter, they can try to achieve this outcome within the existing framework of telecommunications law.

In this chapter, we examine the complex economic merits of concerns that broadband transmission providers will leverage their putative market power at the physical layer to harm competition on the higher layers, and we analyze three basic and non-exclusive types of regulatory proposals for dealing with these monopoly leveraging concerns. The first proposal would compel broadband access providers to give their end users a choice of independent Internet service providers (ISPs) in the hope that those ISPs will perform in the broadband world the same competition-preserving function they have traditionally played in the narrowband dial-up world: buffering applications and content providers against competitive encroachment by vertically integrated firms with market power at the physical layer. The second proposal, associated with the term "Net neutrality," seeks to protect competition at the higher layers more directly by forcing broadband access providers to justify their failure to support particular applications or to carry particular content. The third set of proposals involves promoting greater competition at the physical layer itself, thereby removing any transmission-related "monopoly" that could be leveraged in the first place.

Before we address these present-day policy issues, however, we must start at the beginning: with the FCC's *Computer Inquiries* and the questions about their continuing relevance in a broadband age.

I. The History and Economics of Monopoly Leveraging Concerns in the Internet Marketplace

A. The *Computer Inquiries*

The *Computer Inquiries* were a series of orders the FCC adopted in the 1970s and 1980s to govern the relationship between traditional "common carriers" (telephone companies) and the emerging data processing industry. For present purposes, *Computer I* now has only historical significance; the main legacy of the *Computer Inquiries* derives instead from the set of orders called *Computer II,* finished in 1981, and the later set of orders known as *Computer III,* completed in the decade before the 1996 Act.[3]

The rules adopted in these various orders were designed to control the physical layer monopoly power that AT&T's Bell System and its progeny then exercised in providing the links over which distant computers could "talk" to each other. As we shall see, it was a more straightforward matter in that era than in today's emerging broadband world to keep market dominance at the physical layer from blurring the lines between layers and threatening competition at the higher layers. For example, in a dial-up setting, customers can "call" one of several ISPs over the public switched telephone network just as they can call another person. The telephone company may not tell you which ISP to call because it is expected to operate the network as a common carrier. Just as it cannot keep you from calling your next-door neighbor, it cannot keep you from calling the ISP of your choice.

In *Computer II,*[4] the FCC expanded on traditional common carrier concepts to foster the growth of independent providers of "enhanced" services, whose ranks included the forerunners of today's ISPs. The Commission began by distinguishing between (i) *basic* (transmission) services, defined to include a "pure transmission capability over a communications path that is virtually transparent in terms of its interaction with customer supplied information,"[5] and (ii) *enhanced* services, defined to include "services, offered over common carrier transmission facilities used in interstate communications, which employ computer processing applications that act on the format, content, code, protocol or similar aspects of the subscriber's transmitted information; provide the subscriber additional, different, or restructured information; or involve subscriber interaction with stored information."[6]

The "basic" vs. "enhanced" distinction, while technical and legalistic, is central to today's regulatory debates about the Internet. In a nutshell, a carrier providing a basic service delivers voice or data signals to their intended destination in the same format in which it picked them up at the point of origination. The category of basic services covers everything from ordinary voice telephone calls to a telephone company's lease of private lines to large business customers, even when these businesses use their own equipment to perform a variety of data processing functions over those lines. A basic service offered to the public at large is a "common carriage" service. An enhanced service provider, in contrast, sells content or data processing services to the public by means of underlying transmission facilities. Early examples included "dial-a-joke," voicemail providers, Lexis-Nexis, and Westlaw; more recent ones include the full range of Internet service providers. At the risk of some oversimplification, a basic service, from the end user's perspective, operates primarily at the physical layer, whereas an enhanced service involves significant provision or manipulation of data at the higher layers as well.

As discussed below, the 1996 Act codifies the distinction between basic and enhanced services with different but essentially synonymous terms. For all relevant purposes, *telecommunications* means basic service; *telecommunications service* means a basic service offered at common carriage; and *information service* means enhanced service.[7] For the most part, we use these more recent terms in discussing the distinction. It is important to keep two points in mind for now. First, what ISPs like AOL or Earthlink provide their end users are generally viewed as "information services," not "telecommunications services." Second, a "telecommunications service," as we noted in chapter 3, is subject to traditional common carriage obligations under Title II of the Communications Act. In contrast, an "information service" is *not* subject to those obligations and is generally subject to regulation only under Title I of the Act, which gives the FCC catch-all jurisdiction over interstate communications but contains few rules of any kind.

The origins of the government's deregulatory approach to "information services" go back to the *Computer Inquiries*. In *Computer II*, the FCC reaffirmed its policy of encouraging the growth of long distance data processing applications—the precursors of today's Internet—by shielding information service providers from common carriage regulation under Title II. In a similarly deregulatory vein, the Commission recognized that telephone companies—and specifically AT&T's still-integrated Bell System, with its prodigious resources—could play a valuable role in developing such applications. Originally, the FCC excluded telephone companies altogether from the market for enhanced services. In *Computer II*, however, the FCC authorized telephone companies to enter that market subject to two critical conditions. First, it imposed a regime of "structural separation," under which the largest telephone companies (Bell and GTE) could provide enhanced services only through a formally separate corporate affiliate. Second, it directed each telephone company to separate out (unbundle) the raw transmission functions (such as high speed circuits) underlying any information service from higher layer enhancements (such as Web hosting); tariff those transmission functions as a stand-alone "telecommunications service"; purchase that service for its own use from that tariff; and sell the same telecommunications service on a non-discriminatory basis to all unaffiliated information service providers that request it. (This requirement is sometimes known as the *Computer II* "unbundling" rule,[8] which should not be confused with the *facilities* unbundling obligations of the 1996 Act.[9]) Together, these requirements were intended to prevent the telephone company from discriminating in favor of, or cross-subsidizing, its own information service operations.

Even now, in the broadband era, the *Computer II* unbundling obligation governs the wireline telephone companies regulated as common carriers under Title II of the Communications Act. For example, if a telephone company wishes to sell end users a broadband service that bundles Internet access with DSL transmission, it must strip out the DSL transmission component of that service, tariff it, and offer it on non-discriminatory terms as a telecommunications service to unaffiliated ISPs. Characterizing the bundled service as a unitary information service does not exempt the ILEC from that obligation; indeed, it *triggers* that obligation. As discussed below, however, the FCC has declined to extend this unbundling obligation to *non*-telephone company providers of bundled high speed Internet access, such as the cable companies that now occupy the largest share of the residential broadband market. Although the Commission has sought public comment on whether to relax or eliminate the *Computer II* unbundling requirement generally, even as applied to telephone companies, it has not yet taken significant steps towards that end.

Before we address those issues, we briefly summarize the set of orders known as *Computer III*, in which the FCC simultaneously relaxed some

Computer II restrictions and expanded others. First, the *Computer III* rules eliminated the "structural separation" requirement and substituted a more flexible scheme of "non-structural" safeguards against discrimination and cross-subsidization. The short life of the structural separation requirement reflected both the deregulatory climate of the mid-1980s and, more generally, an abiding ambivalence about how to balance the efficiencies of vertical integration against the potential dangers. In the end, the FCC concluded that those efficiencies were great enough to allow telephone companies into the market for information services, such as voicemail, so long as various non-structural safeguards provided some protection against monopoly abuses.[10]

Second, at the same time that it eliminated the structural separation requirements, the *Computer III* rules retained the *Computer II* unbundling obligation and expanded on it, at least in theory. Specifically, the "non-structural" safeguards imposed on the major carriers included a new set of affirmative non-discrimination obligations known by the names "comparably efficient interconnection" (CEI) and "open network architecture" (ONA). These obligations bear a distant family resemblance to, and were a source of inspiration for, the facilities-unbundling rules of the 1996 Act. Although the details of these new *Computer III* obligations generated much controversy at the time,[11] those details have limited competitive significance today. Perhaps the most enduring legacy of *Computer III* is the FCC's decision to maintain federal jurisdiction over enhanced services under Title I of the Communications Act and preempt state regulation of most such services to ensure a deregulatory environment for the fledgling Internet industry.[12] This jurisdictional legacy is discussed in the next chapter.

Congress left the *Computer Inquiry* rules essentially untouched when it overhauled the Communications Act in 1996. The various non-discrimination requirements of *Computer II* and *Computer III* thus continued to ensure that telephone companies could not leverage their then-clear dominance in the market for last mile transmission services to preclude robust competition in the adjacent market for Internet services. Since consumers had a choice of ISPs, each ISP had obvious incentives to permit non-discriminatory access to any application or content provider on the Internet; otherwise, their disappointed subscribers could and would look elsewhere for service. To be sure, a few of the larger ISPs—most notably AOL—tried to encourage their subscribers to stay within "walled gardens" of affiliated sites. Indeed, AOL spent the 1980s and early 1990s as a closed "on-line service provider" of proprietary content. But as the World Wide Web captured the public's attention in the 1990s, even AOL was careful to permit unbridled access to the Internet as a whole.

B. Monopoly leveraging concerns in a broadband world

The *Computer Inquiries* were designed to govern competition in a narrowband world in which Internet access was provided almost exclusively by common carrier telephone companies. The economics of monopoly leveraging within the Internet sphere has become significantly more complicated now that broadband technology has begun supplanting dial-up as the Internet access mechanism of choice for consumers. The ascendancy of broadband is significant here for four reasons.

First, it dramatically increases the competitive stakes for the communications industry as a whole. Widespread use of broadband connections makes industry-wide technological convergence less of a theoretical possibility and more of an imminent, transformative reality. Suddenly, the company that efficiently controls the highest quality pipes to end user premises could theoretically dominate not just one communications service, but *all* communications services: voice, data, and video programming.

Second, broadband access threatens to marginalize the ISP intermediaries that, in the narrowband environment, act as competitive buffers between the monopoly provider of last mile access and the Internet at large. An ISP necessarily plays a less central role in a user's broadband experience than it plays in the traditional dial-up setting. In the latter context, the end user scarcely notices the telephone company's involvement in her relationship to the Internet because the call she places to her ISP appears much the same as any other "local" call, the telephone company charges nothing extra for it, and the ISP performs all protocol conversion functions. In contrast, and for technical reasons discussed below, the broadband consumer is inevitably aware that the existence, quality, and price of her Internet connection depends largely on her cable or telephone company or other platform provider. That remains the case whether or not her ISP is affiliated with that company—as it usually is.

These first two factors could be cited as reasons why the arrival of broadband technology warrants greater government intervention to prevent monopoly leveraging by providers of last mile transmission services. The third and fourth considerations, however, cut in the opposite direction.

The third relates to cross-platform competition. Whereas dial-up Internet access has traditionally required the use of a single company's circuit-switched telephone network, today's Internet access market is subject to competition among rival broadband platforms. Opponents of government intervention say that robust platform competition will safeguard the interests of consumers better than regulation ever could, avoiding any of the investment disincentives and unintended consequences that regulation is often thought to produce. They thus argue that, so long as consumers can choose among a range of broadband providers, the resulting competition will force each provider to ensure nondiscriminatory use of the Internet; otherwise, consumers will retaliate by moving to another platform.

Of course, the prospect of cross-platform competition can protect against anticompetitive practices only to the extent that consumers may easily drop one broadband service and subscribe to another. Several factors can complicate this competitive dynamic. Although consumers in many densely populated markets today have a choice of two or more broadband providers (cable, DSL, and perhaps wireless), consumers in less densely populated areas may have no realistic choice of providers at all; indeed, they may be lucky even to have one. Even if they have two, a duopoly is unlikely to produce optimal output and pricing decisions over the long term, although it is surely better than a monopoly.[13] Also, consumer choice can provide a check on a dominant provider's market power only to the extent that these platforms are close market substitutes. For example, if consumers perceive that cable modem service is significantly faster for the money than DSL—as, in fact, it often is—they may tolerate some discrimination by their cable modem provider against certain applications or content providers before canceling their accounts and calling the telephone company. Likewise, if consumers invest heavily in the platform they initially adopt—say, by making extensive use of an e-mail address specific to that platform—they may hesitate before incurring the costs necessary to switch to an alternative platform. But the central point remains: over time, consumers can expect increasing choices in the broadband marketplace, and those choices will tend to weaken a firm's incentives to engage in significant monopoly leveraging.

The final factor that may reduce the need for heavy preemptive safe-guards against such leveraging relates to a firm's *internalization of complementary externalities*. This economic phenomenon, which we will call the "complementary externalities" principle for short, is closely related to the "one monopoly profit" principle we addressed in chapter 1. Recall that the total profits a monopolist can earn if it seeks to leverage its monopoly in one market (here, the market for physical-layer broadband access) by dominating a complementary market (here, the applications and content markets) are theoretically no greater than the extra profits it could earn in an unregulated environment simply by charging more for the monopoly product itself. This fact gives the monopoly platform provider a powerful incentive to enhance its platform's attractiveness to consumers so that more of them will pay a higher price for it. Accordingly, the monopolist can normally be expected to take whatever steps are necessary, including steps to promote competition in the applications market, to spur the creation of complementary products that will drive demand for its platform.

This complementary externalities principle is subject to several exceptions, the best known of which, as mentioned in chapter 1, is called "Baxter's law" in honor of the Justice Department antitrust official who invoked it in breaking up AT&T in the early 1980s. As applied here, Baxter's law holds that a platform monopolist does have strong incentives to monopolize a largely unregulated applications market if the platform market itself is subject to rate regulation.[14] This exception had great significance for Internet access in the pre-broadband world because regulators have long capped the price that telephone companies may charge consumers for use of the circuit-switched telephone network that served as the monopoly platform for Internet access for many years. Because these companies were barred from extracting monopoly profits from the use of that platform itself, they had an incentive to extract such profits instead by charging supracompetitive rates for Internet access and other information services—an objective that would necessarily require discriminating against rival providers that could offer subscribers lower, cost-based rates for the same services. The regulatory response, as discussed above, was the set of non-discrimination requirements adopted in the *Computer Inquiries*.

As a practical matter, however, Baxter's law does not apply—and the complementary externalities principle arguably *does* apply—in the broadband world because regulators have not capped the rates that providers may charge their customers for broadband Internet access. This fact removes a key incentive for even a dominant broadband provider to discriminate against unaffiliated applications and content providers, for such discrimination cannot increase the provider's overall profits and could possibly lower them if it degraded consumers' perceptions of the platform as a whole.

We do not, however, wish to overemphasize this last point, for the complementary externalities principle is subject to several additional exceptions beyond Baxter's law. To take a few examples, a dominant broadband firm might have incentives to discriminate against unaffiliated content or applications providers if it views them as potential rivals in the platform market itself; or if the applications market is to some extent independent of the platform market and is itself subject to scale economies or network effects; or if the dominant firm is simply irrational and misperceives how its interests are affected by the "one monopoly profit" rule.[15] Our essential point is this: if they enjoy significant market power at the physical layer, non-price-regulated broadband providers might, but do not inevitably, have incentives to discriminate against unaffiliated content and applications providers. The complex economics of that point often get lost in the rhetoric about whether to force last mile broadband providers to open up their networks to unaffiliated ISPs or to provide non-discriminatory access to content and applications providers.

II. Three Proposals for Addressing Monopoly Leveraging Concerns

Some policymakers view the steady mass migration to broadband Internet access with mixed emotions. On the one hand, they recognize that the cable and telephone providers of these new broadband services are adding enormous value to the economy, both by making electronic communications much more versatile and efficient and by exponentially expanding the range of communications-related services available to ordinary consumers. They also acknowledge that, to an extent, these broadband companies need adequate incentives—i.e., the prospect of significant profits—to continue investing billions of dollars in the construction of broadband facilities to ever greater numbers of consumers, including those who live in "high cost," less densely populated regions.

On the other hand, some observers worry that these companies, if inadequately regulated, will carve up the country into broadband monopolies or duopolies and, after getting consumers hooked on this new technology, will discriminate against unaffiliated firms at the applications and content layers. For example, they speculate, once Time Warner's cable system dominates the market for broadband access in particular areas, it will have incentives to discriminate subtly in favor of Warner Brothers' content and against the content of corporate rivals like Disney. Advancing this type of argument, Stanford professor Lawrence Lessig claims that broadband providers, disdainful of the Internet's traditionally non-proprietary openness, can and will "use the architecture [of their networks] to regain strategic control" of the Internet as a medium for communication. In particular, Lessig suggests: "'Everyone knows that the broadband era will breed a new generation of online services, but this is only half the story. Like any innovation, broadband will inflict major changes on its environment. *It will destroy, once and for all, the egalitarian vision of the Internet.*'"[16]

The monopoly leveraging concerns raised by Lessig and others have spawned three general categories of proposed policy responses, each of which is distinguished from the others by the layers of the Internet on which it focuses. The first would entitle an end user to gain nondiscriminatory access to the ISP of her choice, no matter who her broadband transmission provider might be. This approach, sometimes known as *open access*—or, as the FCC calls it, *multiple ISP access*—seeks to preserve in the broadband environment the role of independent ISPs as competition-protecting intermediaries operating at the logical layer. The second proposal, often accompanied by the catchphrase "Net neutrality," would limit the ability of any broadband provider to deny end users access to particular applications or content over its system. The third aims to stimulate greater competition at the *physical* layer, and thus limit monopoly leveraging concerns at the higher layers, through the creation or elimination of leasing obligations for the broadband-specific facilities of wireline telephone companies. We address each of these policy responses in turn.

A. Multiple ISP access

As noted, the *Computer II* unbundling rule has long required telephone companies to strip out the underlying transmission function from any

Internet access services they sell consumers, tariff it, and sell it on equal terms to unaffiliated ISPs. This assures "open access" to wireline broadband platforms such as DSL. Not until the late 1990s did anyone think that cable television pipes, originally designed to carry the same TV signals past everyone's house, could provide the same range of information services as telephone networks with their dedicated, customer-specific loops. But the cable modem providers, wasting no time in proving the skeptics wrong, secured an early head start in the race for the residential broadband market, leaving their rivals to play catch-up ever since. Unlike the telephone companies, these cable companies have never had any *Computer II* obligation to "unbundle" the transmission component of their broadband Internet access and sell it to unaffiliated ISPs. Instead, they typically offer their customers Internet access through an affiliated ISP: subscribers to Comcast's cable modem service, for example, are served by Comcast.net.

The upshot was that, by the turn of the millennium, many industry observers expected these largely unregulated cable networks to replace telephone networks as bottleneck last mile facilities for residential Internet access and put much of the historically independent ISP industry out of business. This concern spurred an incongruous coalition of telephone companies, ISPs, and consumer advocates to lobby local, state, and federal authorities to require cable systems to provide "open access" to unaffiliated ISPs.

In a nutshell, advocates of "multiple ISP access," as the FCC now calls it, want the government to ensure that consumers of cable modem service have a choice among ISPs and enjoy the same sort of independent relationship with their chosen ISPs that consumers have traditionally enjoyed in the dial-up context. They hope that these unaffiliated ISPs can serve as logical layer buffers between the Internet's physical layer on the one hand and its applications and content layers on the other, frustrating any effort by the cable companies to leverage their presumed dominance in the broadband transmission market to discriminate against unaffiliated providers of content and applications. As one AOL proponent of multiple ISP access described the debate to the New York Times in August 1999, "I'm in awe of the magnitude and money involved . . . . But at its core this is really about an important principle. This involves a lot more than whose garage the Mercedes will be parked in, as the saying goes about big money cases. It involves who will control the Internet."[17] AOL's own advocacy for open access was notoriously short-lived: in early 2000, after announcing its proposed merger with cable giant Time Warner, it wavered in its commitment to the cause. But others have carried it on to the present day.

Proponents are often vague about the technical details of their "multiple ISP access" proposals, and that lack of specificity makes it difficult to analyze the precise merits of those proposals. From an engineering perspective, there are several different ways to ensure an ISP's "access" to end users over a cable modem system. Some methods are more meaningful than others. For example, multiple ISP access would mean very little if it signified only that cable companies must allow each end user to select the website of her chosen ISP as her default home page when she opens her Web browser. That would essentially equate ISPs with Web "portals" like Yahoo! and Excite. End users are unlikely to attribute enough independent value to such portals to send them monthly paychecks for access to their directories and content (with the primary exception of AOL), particularly if they are already subscribing to the default ISP service bundled with cable modem service.

"Opening" a cable network to independent ISPs becomes somewhat more complicated if access means more than merely allowing them to serve as a user's default home page. The basic challenge lies in the fact that— unlike telephone networks, with their dedicated loops to each end user— cable networks employ an Ethernet-type (or "bus") configuration similar to that used in office LANs (see chapter 4). This means that many end users with separate ISPs must share a given "loop," which in turn means that some mechanism must be devised to allocate bandwidth on that shared loop among the ISPs, either at the cable headend or elsewhere in the cable operator's packet network. Most cable "multiple ISP access" arrangements thus leave much of the physical "traffic cop" control of the system as a whole in the hands of the cable modem operator. This does not itself preclude robust forms of multiple ISP access, but it does significantly complicate their implementation.

Indeed, there is some evidence that, even when given the opportunity to minimize their reliance on the cable company's packet network, independent ISPs opt against it. Consider, for example, how the parties have implemented the ISP access condition the FTC imposed in 2000 as a condition for approving the Time Warner merger.[18] Christopher Yoo contends that, "[c]ontrary to the original expectations of the FTC, the unaffiliated

ISPs that have obtained access to AOL-Time Warner's cable modem systems under the FTC's merger clearance order have not placed their own packet network and backbone access facilities within AOL-Time Warner's headends. Instead, traffic bound for these unaffiliated ISPs exits the head-end via AOL-Time Warner's backbone and is handed off to the unaffiliated ISP at some external location."[19] And, he concludes, "[t]he fact that these unaffiliated ISPs have found it more economical to share AOL Time Warner's existing ISP facilities rather than build their own strongly suggests that integrating ISP and last-mile operations does in fact yield real efficiencies."[20] Although it would be a mistake to draw industry-wide conclusions from this one example, the Time Warner experience does point out the complexities and limitations of the "multiple ISP access" model for addressing monopoly leveraging concerns.

Such limitations have led some industry observers to conclude that, if the government wishes to intervene in the Internet marketplace to protect the independence of applications and content providers, it should do so more directly, by forcing physical layer transmission providers to justify any deviation from the Internet's end-to-end principle. We address such "Net neutrality" proposals later in this chapter. For now, however, we focus on the tortuous regulatory history of multiple ISP access proposals, which remain alive and relevant to this day.

The first regulators to require cable companies to provide multiple ISP access were local franchising authorities, the city and county agencies that allow cable companies to use public rights-of-way to provide cable television service, traditionally on a monopoly basis, in exchange for the payment of franchise fees and various other concessions. Cable operators went to court to challenge these new ISP access requirements, and the ensuing litigation ultimately turned on questions about the proper statutory frame of reference for determining whether and how cable modem service should be regulated.

As discussed in chapters 1 and 6, the industry-governing Communications Act of 1934—as it has developed over the decades, both before and after its substantial revision by the 1996 Act—remains divided into several substantive "Titles" that prescribe distinct regulatory schemes for different types of end-user services. Although the Internet places great strains on these distinctions, they remain a critical part of U.S. telecommunications law. Here, the facilities underlying cable modem service are clearly cable networks, which are otherwise subject to regulation under Title VI of the Act.[21] The service itself, however, is a chameleon: it supports higher layer *applications* that often resemble traditional services regulated under various titles of the Act.[22] For example, cable modem service supports high quality VoIP applications, which resemble voice telephone services traditionally regulated under Title II of the Act. Cable modem service also supports streaming video, which resembles video programming traditionally regulated under Titles III and VI.

But these are voice and video "services" with a twist. The "intelligence" that makes them possible can, and often does, reside not in the cable infrastructure as such, but in server software maintained by non-carrier applications providers and in client software controlled by end users. There are, however, important exceptions to this rule. For example, cable operators have begun selling applications-layer VoIP services to end users over physical layer cable modem connections. And, like other IP network operators, they may well prioritize the packets associated with such latency-sensitive applications by assigning them special headers that move them to the front of the queue in the event of congestion in the network's routers. For the most part, however, the layered nature of Internet traffic means that a physical network is indifferent to the applications-related cargo of the packets streaming across it, and those packets are themselves indifferent to the physical layer characteristics of the network so long as they can move across it quickly enough for their associated applications to run properly.

In essence, there are now two principal contenders in the debate about how to characterize cable modem service within the legacy framework of the Communications Act of 1934. Opponents of heavy regulation for that service, such as the cable companies, tend to characterize it solely as an interstate "information service." This description would place cable modem service within the FCC's long tradition of exempting enhanced service providers—from Lexis/Nexis to full-blown ISPs like Earthlink—from common carrier regulation under Title II and from any state telecommunications regulation at all. So characterized, cable modem service would be subject to presumptively minimalist regulation under the FCC's "ancillary" Title I authority, which we discuss in the next chapter.

In contrast, proponents of multiple ISP access rules characterize cable modem service as a combination of (i) an information service at the logical and higher layers and (ii) an interstate telecommunications service at the physical layer.[23] Paradoxically, characterizing cable modem service as (in part) a telecommunications service has the effect of precluding *local franchising authorities* from imposing any multiple ISP access requirement: the Act generally prohibits them from "requir[ing] a cable operator to provide any telecommunications service or facilities . . . as a condition of" any cable franchise.[24] But the silver lining for multiple ISP access advocates is that, under this approach, cable modem service would be presumptively subject to the full complement of federal common carrier regulation under Title II, including (they argue) obligations to provide unaffiliated ISPs with nondiscriminatory access to the cable network.

The Ninth Circuit did much to encourage this way of thinking in a pair of decisions issued in 2000 and 2003. In the first of these cases, the court invalidated the City of Portland's multiple ISP access requirement on the theory that cable modem service does indeed contain a telecommunications service component: "Like other ISPs, [a cable modem service] consists of two elements: a 'pipeline' (cable broadband instead of telephone lines), and the Internet service transmitted through that pipeline. However, unlike other ISPs, [the cable broadband provider] controls all of the transmission facilities between its subscribers and the Internet. To the extent [a cable broadband provider] is a conventional ISP, its activities are one of an information service. However, to the extent that [a cable operator] provides its subscribers Internet transmission over its cable broadband facility, it is providing a telecommunications service as defined in the Communications Act."[25] In so ruling, the court stripped the *localities* within its jurisdiction of any power to require multiple ISP access and simultaneously embraced a characterization of cable modem service that, if followed in other contexts, would subject that service to federal common carrier regulation under Title II.

During the course of the controversy, the FCC took no meaningful steps to resolve these issues because, given the perceived enormity of the stakes, opposing political pressures had kept the Commission in a state of near-paralysis for several years. As a result, the Commission stood by and watched as the courts took the lead in defining national telecommunications policy. Indeed, the Ninth Circuit began its *Portland* opinion by noting that the "FCC has declined, both in its regulatory capacity and as amicus curiae, to address the issue" before the court.[26]

In March 2002, the FCC finally issued its long-awaited *Cable Modem Order*, which declined to impose any "multiple ISP access" regime for cable modem service and, in the process, sought to clear up the confusion about the proper legal characterization of that service.[27] The Commission began with the fairly uncontroversial observation that cable modem service embodies at least an information service "regardless of whether subscribers use all of the functions provided as part of the service, such as e-mail or web-hosting, and regardless of whether every . . . service provider offers each function that could be included in the service."[28]

The FCC next reaffirmed prior suggestions that the categories of "information service" and "telecommunications service" are, by statutory definition, "mutually exclusive." The term "telecommunications service," it observed, is defined as "the offering of telecommunications for a fee directly to the public . . . regardless of the facilities used," and "telecommunications" in turn is defined as "the transmission . . . of information of the user's choosing, without change in the form or content of the information as sent and received."[29] The Commission reasoned that end users who purchase an "information service" cannot simultaneously receive "transmission . . . *without* change in the form or content of the information as sent and received." After all, the very definition of information service, which closely tracks the FCC's earlier definition of "enhanced service," is "the offering of a capability for generating, acquiring, storing, transforming, processing, retrieving, utilizing, or making available information via telecommunications[.]"[30]

The Commission, which had not been a party to the *Portland* litigation and did not view itself as bound by the Ninth Circuit's decision, thus rejected that court's conclusion that, in selling cable modem service to end users, a cable company sells them a "telecommunications service" subject to Title II common carrier obligations in addition to a Title I "information service."[31] And the FCC reaffirmed that cable modem providers would remain exempt from any *Computer II* obligation to unbundle the transmission component of their service and sell it on a wholesale basis to unaffiliated ISPs. As the FCC explained, "for more than twenty years, *Computer II* obligations have been applied exclusively to traditional wireline services and facilities"—i.e., to telephone companies, not cable companies.[32] The Commission refused to extend the *Computer Inquiry* rules outside that industry context or, more broadly, "to find a telecommunications service inside every information service, extract it, and make it a stand-alone offering to be regulated under Title II of the Act."[33]

The FCC's *Cable Modem Order* was appealed in several circuits and, in a stroke of bad luck for the Commission, ended up back in the Ninth Circuit. In *Brand X Internet Servs. v. FCC*,[34] the Ninth Circuit invalidated the Commission's belated characterization of cable modem service as solely an "information service" and, following the precedent of the *Portland* decision, concluded that this broadband product contains a Title II "telecommunications service" as well. This decision, which the Supreme Court agreed to review as this book went to press, reflects a quirk of administrative law. Whereas reviewing courts are normally required to defer to an agency's interpretation of ambiguous statutory language in the first instance, the FCC's earlier *failure* to interpret the Act on this point before the *Portland* case was decided led the *Brand X* court, in the words of a concurring judge, to "aggrandize, rather than limit [its] power over an admittedly complicated and highly technical area of telecommunications law."[35]

The Ninth Circuit's decision immediately complicated the FCC's initiative to develop a new regulatory model for broadband services. As chapter 6 explains, Title I, which contains no substantive rules of its own, begins with the premise that regulation is unwarranted and permits policymakers to add rules only as the need for them is demonstrated. Title II, by contrast, begins with the premise that regulation is justified and allows policymakers to lift particular regulations only upon showing that there is *no* need for them. If ultimately adopted by the Supreme Court, the Ninth Circuit's approach would presumably require the FCC to take the Title II route.

Despite the rhetoric from the critics of the Ninth Circuit's decision, however, the outcome of this battle of competing characterizations may ultimately have limited significance for the cable industry. It is by no means clear what sorts of "multiple ISP access" obligations, if any, follow from the mere characterization of the transmission component of cable modem service as a "telecommunications service." And the FCC has hedged all bets by proposing to exercise its broad statutory authority (discussed in the next chapter) to "forbear" from the application of any Title II common carriage requirements that any court, including the Ninth Circuit, might deem applicable to cable modem service—a proposal the Ninth Circuit itself seemed to endorse.[36] In so doing, the FCC promised to address in a separate proceeding the concern that this selective non-regulation of cable modem service imposes a serious competitive disadvantage on the telephone company providers of competing DSL services, to which common carriage obligations remain applicable.[37] But so far it has taken no concrete measures in that direction.

In another passage of the *Cable Modem Order* left undisturbed by the Ninth Circuit, the FCC took one further step in shielding cable companies from any obligation to open their networks to unaffiliated ISPs. Some parties had claimed that certain cable modem providers were already, in effect, providing raw transmission services to ISPs, which in turn incorporated these services into the finished information services that they sold to the public. These parties hoped that the FCC would thus characterize these cable companies as "telecommunications service" providers from the perspective of the ISPs (as opposed to end users) and require them to provide similar telecommunications services to other ISPs on a common carrier basis. The FCC rejected this argument. It first found that the issue does not generally arise because cable companies, not ISPs, retain the primary commercial relationship with end users in the provision of cable modem service, such that the ISP cannot be meaningfully characterized as a "purchaser" of any transmission service. The Commission acknowledged a single possible exception to this general rule, arising from the FTC merger condition that forced AOL-Time Warner to negotiate the terms on which unaffiliated ISPs can gain access to its broadband platform. Although the Commission expressed uncertainty that these ISPs actually purchase anything that could be called a stand-alone transmission service from Time Warner, it concluded that, even if they do, Time Warner should be free to sell that service to them on a private carriage basis under Title I rather than as a common carriage "telecommunications service" under Title II.[38]

This treatment of cable modem service perpetuates a competitively significant asymmetry in the way that cable and telephone companies are regulated when they provide broadband services. Telephone companies commonly wish to sell bulk DSL transmission services to chosen ISP partners and other large business customers without incurring any obligation to provide those same services more generally on a common carrier basis. For example, a telephone company might enter into a joint venture with an unaffiliated ISP like MSN or AOL to provide a bundled DSL and Internet access service to end users. Under such an arrangement, the ISP might act as the primary retail provider of that bundled service to end users and would purchase the DSL transmission input from the telephone company at a volume discount. (In effect, the telephone company would provide DSL transmission over each end user's line as though it were providing the service to the end user directly, but it would sell that transmission service to the ISP on a discounted wholesale basis instead and leave it to the ISP to combine this wholesale transmission input with Internet access.) Such an arrangement might make sense to both sides as a business matter, however, only if they can flexibly negotiate a special contractual relationship without thereby entitling all similarly placed ISPs to opt into the same contractual terms with the telephone company. There can be no such flexibility, at least as a formal matter, if the telephone company must act in this context as a common carrier, publicize the details of the deal in a filed tariff, and sell the same transmission services to other ISPs on the same terms.

Since, in these circumstances, the incumbent telephone company is selling the ISP a pure transmission service, it cannot argue for exemption from Title II common carriage obligations on the ground that it is providing only an information service. Instead, such companies have petitioned the FCC to allow them, like cable companies, to sell bulk transmission services to ISPs on a private carriage basis.[39] As discussed in the next chapter, permitting a wireline service to be offered at private carriage is one of two established statutory mechanisms (the other being the "information service" classification) for removing the service from the scope of legacy regulation under Title II and placing it fully within the FCC's "ancillary" Title I jurisdiction, under which deregulation is the rule. The FCC has sought comment on whether to allow wireline ILECs to sell bulk DSL services to ISPs at private carriage, but here too it has taken no concrete steps in that direction.

B. "Net neutrality" and the end-to-end principle

The debate continues about whether the government should impose multiple ISP access obligations on cable modem and DSL providers. This controversy obviously has enormous implications for the nation's many independent ISPs, which are struggling to define their role in an increasingly broadband-oriented industry. But even advocates of greater government intervention in this market wonder whether such access obligations are the best response to concerns about monopoly leveraging.

First, relying on ISPs to address those concerns seems a bit retrograde because, as discussed, there is no straightforward way to ensure in the broadband context—and specifically in the cable modem context—the same clear distinction that prevails in the dial-up setting between an end user's last mile transmission provider and her ISP. This, however, does not mean that an end user's choice of ISPs is completely irrelevant. ISPs can differentiate themselves through features like distinctive privacy policies, proprietary content, creative e-mail options, and opportunities to filter out spam and other unwanted content. And, at a minimum, giving end users a choice of ISPs introduces a separate brand and a new commercial relationship into their Internet experience. As Tim Wu observes, however, "[c]ompetition among ISPs does not necessarily mean that broadband operators will simply retreat to acting as passive carriers in the last mile."[40]

Second, requiring broadband access providers to accommodate novel forms of multiple ISP access—much like requiring incumbent telephone companies to "unbundle" the "elements" of their networks to CLECs—can present significant regulatory costs. Particularly in the cable modem context, where such access remains technologically experimental, such obligations require intrusive and ongoing oversight by regulators. Wu points out that these obligations could also hobble the developing market for high-quality voice and other real-time services over IP networks. To provide such services, network operators must give priority to packets associated with real-time applications. "To the extent open access regulation prevents broadband operators from architectural cooperation with ISPs for the purpose of providing [such real-time] applications," Wu notes, "it could hurt the cause of network neutrality" by "discriminat[ing] in favor of data applications" that are less sensitive to delay.[41]

Over the past several years, such concerns have led an increasing number of commentators to call for a more direct alternative: voluntary adherence to—and, if necessary, regulatory enforcement of—an anti-discrimination principle that its proponents sometimes call "Net neutrality." Although it can be used in combination with either of the other two forms of regulatory intervention discussed in this chapter, the Net neutrality principle does not itself try to promote greater competition at either the physical or the logical layer. Instead, it assumes imperfect competition at both of these layers and responds by directly regulating the ability of any physical transmission provider to compromise consumer choice at the applications and content layers. Understanding the purpose of Net neutrality proposals requires a review of the *end-to-end* principle of the Internet, first articulated in a famous paper by network architects Jerome Saltzer, David Clark, and David Reed.[42]

One key difference between the Internet and the telephone network, as discussed in the previous chapter, is where the "intelligence" is said to lie. In the telephone network, the intelligence resides in centralized circuit switches, which run the software needed for caller identification, call-forwarding, and other smart features. In the Internet environment, the intelligence traditionally resides at the "edges" of the network, in end user devices and in the servers of various applications providers. The network itself is "dumb"; it notes the destination of individual packets and sends them on their way, but it is indifferent to the nature of the applications those packets will run within the computers on either end.

Lawrence Lessig, perhaps the best-known advocate of Net neutrality principles, views this end-to-end characteristic as the defining principle of the Internet, with three critical benefits:

First, because applications run on computers at the edge of the network, innovators with new applications need only connect their computers to the network to let their applications run. . . . Second, because the design is not optimized for any particular existing application, the network is open to innovation not originally imagined . . . Third, because the design effects a neutral platform—neutral in the sense that the network owner can't discriminate against some packets while favoring others—the network *can't* discriminate against a new innovator's design. If a new application threatens a dominant application, there's nothing the network can do about that.[43]

Lessig, Wu, and others believe that the broadband revolution threatens to compromise this end-to-end principle by placing Internet access in the hands of companies that, like cable modem providers, inherently favor "control" over "freedom." "If the cable companies prefer some content over others, that's the natural image of a cable provider. If your provider declines to show certain stations, that's the sort of freedom we imagine it should have. Discrimination and choice are at the core of what a cable monopoly does; neutrality here seems silly."[44] And that, in a nutshell, is what troubles Lessig about the trajectory of the modern Internet. Internet access was traditionally provided for many years on the networks of common carrier telephone companies that have long been subject to the *Computer II* unbundling rule and various other regulatory obligations of neutrality, and those obligations kept the Internet free and open to all. But "[a]s the Internet moves from the telephone wires to cable," Lessig asks rhetorically, "which model should govern? . . . Freedom or control?"[45]

Lessig has called for whatever government intervention might be needed to ensure the ultimate triumph of "freedom." And, like Wu, he suggests that the optimal way to achieve this outcome might be a less structural solution than multiple ISP access to cable systems and a more direct requirement of network neutrality: "If the concern at stake is that network providers will leverage control over the network into some control over content—if the concern is that they will have an incentive to compromise the principle of end-to-end—then rather than requiring unbundling of services, the government could adopt a more direct regulatory strategy: if you provide Internet services, then you must provide them consistent with the principle of end-to-end."[46]

To assess this "Net neutrality" proposal, we must move from theory to practice and ask two critical sets of questions. First, what is the harm to be avoided? Second, how would any regulatory remedy for that harm be enforced, and would it present costs that outweigh the benefits?

The asserted need for Net neutrality rules

Let's begin with identification of the harm to be avoided. The literature abounds with pessimistic scenarios in which broadband providers—typically cable companies—achieve monopolies in the Internet access market and then begin overtly discriminating against unaffiliated providers of applications and content. Jerome Saltzer fears that cable modem providers will curtail consumers' ability to run streaming video over their broadband connections because these providers "have a conflict of interest—they are restricting a service that will someday directly compete with cable TV."[47] Lessig likewise fears that the same technology that facilitates high quality VoIP—identifying the packets associated with voice and other real-time applications and moving them to the front of the queue—will enable broadband providers "to slow down a competitor's offerings while speeding up [the provider's] own—like a television set with built-in static for ABC but a clear channel for CBS."[48]

There is no strong empirical basis for these concerns, at least so far.[49] There is certainly no evidence that cable companies have yet engaged in the sort of overtly anticompetitive conduct that Lessig fears. There may be several reasons for this. First, such conduct would subject cable companies at least to the risk of antitrust sanctions—a topic we explore at greater length in chapter 13. To be sure, antitrust is an imperfect remedy, and monopolists have many means at their disposal to discriminate subtly against rivals without crossing any explicit lines. And, as the *Microsoft* litigation revealed, such discrimination in high tech markets may be easier to preempt prospectively than to remedy retrospectively.[50] In particular, once a monopolist in a network industry chooses a particular architecture—say, one that facilitates certain applications only for a limited set of preferred providers—network effects may cause the market as a whole to become dependent on that architecture, even if it turns out to have inseverable anticompetitive characteristics. Even so, the threat of treble liability or structural remedies under the Sherman Act may well keep most monopolists fairly honest most of the time, and some observers argue that it is unnecessary to supplement this threat with prescriptive Net neutrality regulation.[51]

Second, the industry trend is away from, not towards, monopoly in any event. In an increasing number of markets, consumers have a choice of at least two broadband providers. Such cross-platform competition itself provides an additional check at least against flagrant discrimination, although some fear that a duopolistic market structure, where it persists, will do a poor job of safeguarding consumer interests.

Third, even in the absence of cross-platform competition, a platform monopolist's *incentives* to discriminate against unaffiliated applications providers are both more qualified and less straightforward than many commentators assume. This often unappreciated complexity relates to the "complementary externalities" principle discussed earlier in this chapter. Consider, for example, Saltzer's fear that cable companies would block streaming video over cable modem connections to preserve their cable television revenues. The pipe into the home that supports cable modem service is the same pipe that supports conventional cable television service. If this pipe were to give the cable company a monopoly in the provision of high bandwidth services (data and video), the company could theoretically maximize its overall revenues by charging monopoly profits for use of the pipe to transmit signals or bits of any kind, irrespective of the higher layer services provided on top of it. Indeed, limiting those services might degrade the value of the pipe to end users and reduce the monopoly rates they are willing to pay for it.

In the early years of cable modem service, however, some providers *did* in fact block streaming video applications from their systems, a practice they have since discontinued in the face of consumer outcry. Indeed, Dan Somers, the former CEO of AT&T Broadband, fueled the concerns of consumer advocates by declaring that "AT&T did not spend $56 billion to get into the cable business 'to have the blood sucked out of our veins.'"[52] How, though, can Somers' sentiment be squared with the complementary externalities principle? Remember that this principle is subject to several exceptions. For example, allowing unrestrained video streaming might restrict a cable company's ability to engage in retail price discrimination in the sale of video programming, such as the opportunity to impose different charges for distinct tiers of service. Or a vertically integrated cable company might discriminate against rivals whose content appears on non-cable platforms as well and who, absent such discrimination, would benefit overall from greater network effects or scale economies. Or the cable company might simply overlook the economic logic of the complementary externalities principle and engage in irrational discrimination for its own sake.[53]

Whatever the reason, the more important practical point is that cable companies, responding to market pressures, no longer restrict streaming video applications. And, to date at least, cable companies have generally limited any other "discrimination" to restrictive policies that particular consumers may find inconvenient but that policymakers should not generally find alarming.[54] For example, cable companies have included clauses in subscribership agreements that preclude ordinary end users from hosting servers on the network; if particular users want to host websites, they must pay more. Here, though, the cable companies appear to be acting appropriately as "traffic cops," setting the price signals needed to ensure efficient conservation of bandwidth on a shared network. Sometimes cable companies have also blocked the use of *virtual private networks* (VPNs), which include secure but bandwidth-intensive "work at home" applications. Although this policy too was justified as a means of bandwidth conservation, the linkage between the policy and objective was weaker, and the largest cable companies have now generally opened their networks to VPN applications. Finally, a number of cable companies sought to engage in routine retail price discrimination by prohibiting subscribers from connecting more than one computer to a single cable modem connection. But the growing popularity of wireless home networks, together with the availability of DSL as an alternative, has caused most of these companies to rescind that prohibition as well.

In short, there is little evidence so far of comprehensive plans by the major broadband providers to leverage their market power at the physical layer to crush competition at the higher layers.[55] This is not to rule out the possibility that they may someday pursue such plans, nor is it a reason for regulators to fall into complacency. At this point, it is still far from clear what will drive the conduct of the cable companies in this market: the complementary externalities principle or its numerous exceptions. Thus, unlike many proponents (or opponents) of government-imposed Net neutrality rules, we do not assume uncritically that vertically integrated broadband providers will (or will not) engage in reflexive discrimination at the applications and content layers. At this point, however, the dearth of genuine abuses gives regulators good reason to hesitate before preemptively regulating how broadband providers run their networks.

The potential costs of Net neutrality rules

We now turn to the second set of questions raised by the Net neutrality debate: how exactly would a "neutrality" principle work, and what sorts of costs might accompany the benefits? To get a sense of the potential answers, we turn to an analogy often favored by Net neutrality advocates: the electric power grid. "The Internet," Lessig explains, "isn't the only network to follow an end-to-end design, though it is the first large-scale computer network to choose that principle at its birth. The electricity grid is an end-to-end grid; as long as my equipment complies with the rules for the grid, I get to plug it in."[56] Lessig and others cite the grid as a model of a successful, egalitarian, and quintessentially *dumb* network, whose example can and should be followed in the Internet world as well, through moral suasion if possible and regulatory compulsion if necessary. But the analogy to the grid is flawed in at least two critical respects, each of which instructively points out the costs that such compulsion might entail.

First, when pressed, few people seriously advocate the enforced maintenance of *completely* dumb broadband networks in strict adherence to the end-to-end principle—i.e., networks that can draw no distinction among packets on the basis of their associated applications. As an initial matter, network providers and their associated ISPs increasingly offer—and consumers are happy to accept—standard "filtering" features to protect against spam, viruses, and other unwanted content or applications. Although these features require providers to violate the strong form of the end-to-end principle by blocking some of the packets moving across the network on the basis of their "cargo," few people would suggest that doing so is inherently problematic from a public policy perspective. If carried to an extreme, the end-to-end imperative for keeping intelligence at the edges of a network would also undermine the feasibility of running real-time applications.[57] To provide quality of service for VoIP, for example, a network often must identify (by means of special headers) the packets associated with such latency-sensitive applications and give those packets priority over others.

The essential challenge presented by Net neutrality proposals, then, is not how to prevent deviations from the end-to-end principle, for they are inevitable and often desirable, but how to distinguish "good" deviations from "bad" ones. This task is often phrased in terms of requiring broadband providers to justify, as a form of neutral network management, any "discrimination" they enforce against particular applications.[58] But that is an inherently subjective and context-specific task, and assigning it to the government would embroil regulators in the day-to-day specifics of particular network use policies. This, by itself, is not a reason to avoid the inquiry altogether, but it is a reason to be wary of the regulatory transaction costs and rent-seeking it would inevitably generate.

The second flaw in the analogy to the neutrality of the electric power grid relates to the trade-off that reappears in various forms throughout this chapter: how best to balance the public's interest in preserving a *neutral* broadband network with its interest in encouraging private companies to *create* such networks in the first place. Much like the legacy telephone network itself, the electric power grid was built either by government agencies or (more commonly) by regulated monopolists who, in exchange for building out their facilities to underserved areas, were guaranteed an opportunity to earn a reasonable rate of return for their services. No one is guaranteeing cable companies any particular return on the multi-billion dollar network upgrades required to provide cable modem service to the public. Nor can telephone companies assume that they will earn a return on the billions they may invest in next generation fiber networks to serve mass market customers. Nor is anyone likely to guarantee such returns to any of the other would-be competitors to the first-in broadband providers, such as wireless companies or, for that matter, the electric power companies themselves (which are experimenting with "broadband over power-line" technology). For its part, the government has shown little inclination to underwrite the broadband buildout, except to the extent that it has assessed special fees on telecommunications providers to help subsidize broadband connections for schools and libraries, as noted in chapter 10.

These considerations present a dilemma. Outside the regulated monopoly setting, rational firms do not generally choose to incur huge sunk costs to provide a product that, by regulatory design, must be largely indistinguishable from all other such products. That is because the potential downside of the investment (non-recovery on the enormous sunk costs) remains as catastrophic as before, but now the potential upside is limited by the customarily modest margins earned by even successful providers of products that have very close market substitutes. For the same reason that investors do not buy bonds with high risks and low yields, potential broadband competitors might be deterred from building out networks in a regulatory environment intent on keeping networks "neutral." This is not necessarily because they wish to integrate vertically and then discriminate against rival applications providers, but rather because they rightly fear that they would be unable to distinguish their products in the market or take advantage of the ability to engage in efficient price discrimination. Put differently, they worry that the risks they incur in making enormous infrastructure investments are insufficiently balanced by the potential reward.

These last points warrant elaboration. Before investing in risky propositions like building out broadband infrastructure, firms will ensure that they will be able to reap high profit margins (sometimes called "rents") from their investments. At least in the short term, firms can earn higher margins on products that occupy market niches that similar firms cannot immediately fill, and they are therefore more likely to build the necessary infrastructure if they believe that they will be allowed to earn those margins. This dynamic, which characterizes many markets lying somewhere between states of natural monopoly and perfect competition, is good for consumer welfare: although some resources are suboptimally allocated, society is better off because the market benefits from *dynamic innovation* (i.e., the introduction of new products).[59]

Broadband providers also seek to extract extra profits from their investments through efficient price discrimination. Such "discrimination," despite the ominous name, often advances consumer welfare in the course of enabling producers to maximize profits by segmenting the relevant market among classes of customers.[60] In the broadband marketplace, providers can engage in price discrimination by offering different tiers of service, charging more to certain users and less to others—ideally to users who would not otherwise adopt the service. This method of "versioning" products is by no means the only method of price discrimination available to broadband providers, nor is it necessarily the most effective one. But, by providing complementary services (such as e-commerce opportunities) on an exclusive or preferred basis, or by tailoring their services for particular applications, the broadband platform provider may well be able to identify with greater confidence those customers who are willing to pay more (or insist on paying less) and thereby find ways to extract greater profits from them (or give them special discounts).[61] At the same time, these profit-maximizing practices can both spur innovation and ameliorate the "misallocative effects of monopoly" by limiting the likelihood that the search for monopoly rents will lead some consumers to be inefficiently priced out of the market.[62] Thus, to the extent that an excessively strict application of the Net neutrality principle may limit a provider's ability to engage in effective price discrimination, it could subtly harm consumers by undermining investment incentives or leading to higher prices overall.

Christopher Yoo cites similar considerations as reasons for opposing government-enforced Net neutrality rules. In his view, allowing broadband providers to differentiate their product offerings through customer-specific deviations from the end-to-end principle will ultimately help promote last mile investment and prevent the broadband access market "from devolving into [a] natural monopol[y]."[63] One method of slicing the onion more finely to accommodate this concern might be to treat dominant providers of broadband services differently from the upstarts and free the latter from any Net neutrality requirements. But, like its more universally restrictive counterpart, that approach also would generate regulatory costs in the form of disincentives to innovation by dominant providers as well as indeterminate disputes about who is "dominant" and how the relevant markets should be defined. Perhaps these costs are worth incurring, but advocates of Net neutrality have not yet demonstrated—at least through convincing empirical evidence—that they are.[64]

Given the minimal evidence of genuine monopoly leveraging abuses, regulators have stopped short of imposing actual Net neutrality rules on broadband providers, preferring instead to *threaten* regulation in the hope that doing so will make *actual* regulation unnecessary. In February 2004, FCC Chairman Michael Powell engaged in precisely such "jawboning" when he "challenge[d] the broadband network industry" to honor four "Internet Freedoms" for consumers. These "Freedoms" are: (i) "access to their choice of legal content," subject to "reasonable limits . . . placed in service contracts"; (ii) a right "to run applications of their choice," except where "they exceed service plan limitations or harm the provider's network"; (iii) the right "to attach any devices they choose to the connection in their homes," so long as "the devices operate within service plan limitations and do not harm the provider's network or enable theft of service"; and (iv) access to "meaningful information regarding their service plans."[65]

Except for the last, each of these "freedoms," as articulated by Powell, comes with a significant and open-ended exception designed to accommodate the concerns of network providers. The very indeterminacy of these exceptions ("reasonable limits," "exceed service plan limitations," and "operate within service plan limitations") underscores the difficulty policymakers would face if they were ever to enforce these "Freedoms" with actual rules. Powell himself appeared to recognize as much when he added that, "[b]ased on what we currently know, the case for government imposed regulations regarding the use or provision of broadband content, applications and devices is unconvincing and speculative. Government regulation of the terms and conditions of private contracts is the most fundamental intrusion on free markets and potentially destructive, particularly where innovation and experimentation are hallmarks of an emerging market. Such interference should be undertaken only where there is weighty and extensive evidence of abuse"—which, Powell indicated, there is not now.[66]

Although they are understandably hesitant to impose formal common carriage-like rules on this incipient market, policymakers have begun considering less restrictive regulatory permutations on the Net neutrality theme. At present, there are two notable such candidates. First, along the lines of the FTC's approach to Internet privacy, the FCC could require companies to post their policies and then enforce adherence to them.[67] Second, the FCC could adopt an antitrust-like model of regulation, which would forgo prescriptive regulation in favor of investigating discriminatory practices on a case-by-case basis.[68] The latter approach would move the FCC in the direction of acting more like an enforcement agency and thus would raise questions about whether such inquiries should be committed instead to antitrust courts—a question to which we return in chapter 13.

C. Wireline broadband unbundling rules

To this point, we have covered two of the three major types of proposals for protecting the competitive integrity of the Internet against the threat of monopoly leveraging by firms that may have market power in the provision of last mile transmission services: multiple ISP access and Net neutrality. We now turn to the third set of proposals: those designed to address the monopoly leveraging concern at its physical layer source by promoting greater competition in the market for last mile broadband transmission services. Of course, this set of proposals aims to spur competition in this market not just to protect competition at the applications and content layers, but also to provide consumers with higher quality and lower priced broadband services for their own sake. But since they serve the parallel purpose of safeguarding against monopoly leveraging, we will discuss them here.

The terms of debate

It may seem a bit counterintuitive to lump together, for discussion purposes, all proposals to foster greater broadband competition, since the proposals within this class are often mutually antagonistic. The debate concerns whether new entrants in the wireline telecommunications market (CLECs) should have regulatory entitlements to lease capacity on the broadband-specific network elements owned by incumbent local telephone companies (ILECs) such as the Bell companies. ILECs argue that the best way to promote broadband competition in the last mile is to free them from any obligation to lease ("unbundle") such capacity to their rivals. Such unbundling obligations, they claim, would depress the incentives of ILECs and CLECs alike to invest in costly facilities that could be used to challenge the cable companies, which took a substantial early lead over the telephone companies in the residential broadband access market.[69]

CLECs, in contrast, claim that *unless* regulators give them expansive rights of access to these wireline broadband facilities, the mass market for broadband services will indefinitely remain a duopoly shared between

ILECs and cable companies. In that environment, CLECs argue, each of the duopolists could raise prices above efficient levels, reduce output, stifle innovation, and discriminate in favor of their higher layer affiliates in the provision of applications and content to mass market consumers—precisely the monopoly leveraging concerns that have preoccupied policymakers since the emergence of "enhanced services" at the dawn of the digital era. The ILECs respond that widespread cuts in the retail price of DSL services belie any claim that the industry bears the hallmarks of an entrenched duopoly today. Invoking the Schumpeterian perspective, they further maintain that the additional broadband platforms discussed at the end of the previous chapter (powerline, satellite, and various fixed and mobile wireless services) will destabilize any duopoly over the long term. The ILECs add that it would be perverse in any event to subject the second-place telephone companies to disproportionately invasive "unbundling" obligations as they build out the next generation networks needed to catch up to the cable companies, which are subject to no such requirements.

This debate also involves several fiercely disputed questions of market definition. First, taking their cue from definitions employed by the FCC itself in the *Triennial Review Order*,[70] discussed in chapter 3, ILECs tend to view the broadband access world as divided into two relevant markets: one for large "enterprise" business customers and one for "mass market" customers. The latter market they define to include both residential consumers and small businesses, including the many home offices in residential neighborhoods served by cable providers. This dichotomy permits ILECs to argue that they are trailing in both relevant markets: behind the cable companies in the mass market and behind the established long distance companies (AT&T, MCI, and Sprint) in the enterprise market. On that ground, ILECs have sought relief not just from facilities unbundling obligations, but also from a range of other obligations, such as tariff filing requirements, in the provision of broadband transmission services.[71] CLECs, in contrast, tend to analyze the relevant markets on a more segmented basis. They argue, among other things, that ILECs continue to lead all competitors in the market for small-to-mid-sized businesses, particularly those with between 20 and 99 employees, although cable companies have begun making inroads in that market as well.[72]

Second, CLECs define an independent market for *wholesale* broadband transmission services—e.g., services that can be purchased by ISPs and, in turn, bundled into those ISPs' own retail Internet access services.

ILECs indisputably "lead" in the provision of these wholesale services, if only because, under *Computer II*, they alone are subject to any enforceable industry-wide obligation to provide them. CLECs thus argue that broadband unbundling obligations are necessary to break the "monopoly" that ILECs could otherwise exploit in this putative wholesale market. As evidence of such monopoly abuses, CLECs and others claim that ILECs subject ISPs to anticompetitive "price squeezes" in the form of wholesale rates for DSL transmission services that are often only slightly lower, even at discounted levels, than the retail rates that those same ILECs charge end users for bundled DSL Internet access.[73] ILECs respond that defining a separate wholesale market is inappropriate because, among other considerations, retail competition from vertically integrated broadband Internet access providers, such as cable companies, deters ILECs from trying to extract monopoly profits from wholesale customers.[74] They also claim that the small margin between their retail prices and their wholesale transmission rates is the unremarkable product of their need to slash retail prices to compete effectively with these vertically integrated competitors.

As a legal matter, this set of facilities-leasing disputes is governed by the same "impairment" standard applicable to all network elements. As we discussed in chapter 3, section 251(d)(2) directs the FCC, when deciding which network elements should be subject to any unbundling obligation under section 251(c)(3), to "consider, at a minimum, whether . . . the failure to provide access to such network elements would impair the ability of the [CLEC] seeking access to provide the services that it seeks to offer." For present purposes, there are two major categories of broadband elements subject to this standard: those relating to "line sharing," and those relating to "next generation networks." We address each in turn below.

In considering the unbundling rules related to broadband networks, keep the following point in mind: the obligations we are about to discuss relate to the *facilities* that ILECs must lease to *CLECs*, not the *services* that ILECs must provide to unaffiliated *ISPs*. Like the facilities-leasing rights discussed in chapter 3, these are circumscribed not just by section 251(d)(2), but also by the clause of section 251(c)(3) restricting the class of lessors to "telecommunications carrier[s] for the provision of . . . telecommunications service[s]." Because ISPs are generally deemed to fall outside this class, they benefit from any section 251 leasing rights only indirectly, by purchasing telecommunications services from CLECs that exercise those rights directly.

Line sharing

As discussed in the previous chapter, ADSL services involve dividing up a copper loop into a "low frequency" band dedicated to voice telephone services and a "high frequency" portion dedicated to broadband Internet access. At your house, a special adapter splits the loop into a voice line leading into your telephone and a data line leading into your computer or home network. At the telephone company central office—or, in some cases, at a "remote terminal" between your house and the central office—a separate splitter likewise divides the loop into a voice line leading into a circuit switch and a data line leading into a packet-switched network en route to the Internet. The splitter performs the latter task in combination with a digital multiplexer known as a DSLAM.

In 1999, the FCC—following earlier state initiatives—defined the "high frequency portion of the loop" as a separate network element and ordered ILECs to provide it on a stand-alone basis to specialized CLECs.* An ILEC normally continues providing voice service over these lines and charges end users the standard retail rates. This arrangement, in which an ILEC provides voice service and a CLEC provides DSL over a single copper loop, is known as *line sharing*. Occasionally, under a distinct arrangement known as *line splitting*, the ILEC leases the voice portion of the loop to one CLEC, usually at the standard rate for the loop as a whole, and the data portion to another CLEC.[75]

Under either scenario, regulators often (though not invariably) construed the applicable cost-allocation principles to preclude the ILEC from charging anything to the CLEC that leased the high frequency portion of the loop. They reasoned that loop costs as a whole were already being recovered either through retail rates, in circumstances where the ILEC kept the customer for voice services, or through the TELRIC-based wholesale rate for the loop in its entirety, where the ILEC ceded the voice service to a CLEC. Moreover, when the incumbents were asked, for cost-recovery purposes, what costs they had allocated in their accounting books specifically for the high frequency portion of the loop, they generally replied that

---

* These data-centric providers are sometimes known as "data LECs," or "DLECs," because they provide only data services and do not wish to lease the *entire* loop to provide voice as well as data services to the end user.

they had allocated none and had allocated all loop costs instead to the voice service. The FCC and the state commissions concluded that CLECs deserved access on the same terms, which effectively enabled CLECs to receive the DSL functionality of the loop for free. Of course, this functionality did not present the only network expense for a CLEC seeking to provide competing DSL services; the CLEC was normally required to provide its own splitter and DSLAM at the central office and, in combination with an ISP, obtain transport to an Internet backbone provider.

In its 2002 decision in *USTA I*, which we discussed in chapter 3, the D.C. Circuit vacated the FCC's line-sharing rules on the ground that the FCC had inadequately considered the market leadership of cable modem service when finding that the high frequency portion of the loop met the "impairment" standard.[76] The court reasoned that "mandatory unbundling comes at a cost, including disincentives to research and development by both ILECs and CLECs and the tangled management inherent in shared use of a common resource. . . . [N]othing in the Act appears a license to the Commission to inflict on the economy the[se] sort[s] of costs . . . under conditions where it had no reason to think doing so would bring on a significant enhancement of competition. The Commission's naked disregard of the competitive context risks exactly that result."[77]

As a legal matter, this reasoning raises more questions than it answers. At least on its face, the threshold "impairment" inquiry asks whether CLECs need access to the ILEC's network in order to compete, not whether ILECs themselves face cross-platform competition. And the court expressed no qualms about the Commission's determination that line sharing met that threshold "impairment" standard. Nonetheless, in the *Triennial Review Order* issued the following year, the FCC eliminated ILEC line-sharing obligations, albeit at the conclusion of a multi-year transition period designed to cushion the blow for CLECs.[78]

In a bizarre twist, four of the five members of the Commission—all but Commissioner Kevin Martin—expressed substantive disagreement with this decision to phase out line sharing. As Chairman Michael Powell explained, "[l]ine sharing rides on the old copper infrastructure, not on the new advanced fiber networks that we are attempting to push to deployment. Indeed, the continued availability of line sharing and the competition that flowed from it likely would have pressured incumbents to deploy more advanced networks in order to move from the negative regulatory pole to the positive regulatory pole, by deploying more fiber infrastructure."[79] In a similar vein, Alfred Kahn explained that the sunk nature of the copper loop infrastructure "would seem to [present] the archetypal case for mandatory sharing—a heritage of [the ILECs'] franchised monopolies, the sharing of which would therefore not seem to involve any discouragement of future risk-taking investment."[80] The Commission's two Democratic members nonetheless reluctantly agreed to end line sharing anyway as part of a package deal with the Republican Martin to keep the UNE platform available to CLECs in the narrowband voice world (see chapter 3). As expected, the D.C. Circuit upheld the gradual elimination of line sharing in its subsequent decision in *USTA II.*[81] In August 2004, in a fittingly surreal postscript to this story, Chairman Powell sought to enlist the aid of these two Democratic commissioners to resurrect some version of the very line-sharing obligations whose elimination the D.C. Circuit had just affirmed. That effort remains pending as this book goes to press. Evidently because of internal FCC politics, however, no revived line-sharing obligations appeared in the interim rules the Commission adopted on remand from the D.C. Circuit's invalidation of other aspects of the *Triennial Review Order.*[82]

Significantly, any absence of line-sharing rights would not itself keep CLECs from providing DSL over an ILEC's copper loops. A CLEC remains entitled to lease the whole loop, albeit at the usual TELRIC-based rate. If it does, the ILEC will no longer serve as the retail provider of circuit-switched voice service over the line. If the customer demands that service, the CLEC must lease the UNE platform from the ILEC (where available), pair up with another CLEC that leases the platform ("line splitting"), or partner with a CLEC able to route the voice portion of the ILEC loop to its own circuit switch. Over time, such expensive complications may subside as end users become more comfortable using their DSL broadband connection for packet-switched VoIP services.

Next generation networks

In chapter 3, we addressed the portions of the *Triennial Review Order* that have sparked the greatest public controversy: the FCC's 3-2 decision, vacated by the D.C. Circuit, to maintain the right of CLECs to lease the circuit switching element—and thus the UNE platform—at TELRIC-based rates in most areas throughout the country. In some ways, though, that was yesterday's fight, despite the amount of money at stake in the short term. The circuit-switched telephone platform, designed for voice, is gradually giving way to packet-switched broadband platforms that can support IP-based applications of all kinds, including voice. In the long term, the regulatory game between ILECs and CLECs in the mass market lies in access to an ILEC's broadband-enabled pipes to homes and small businesses, not in access to an ILEC's increasingly obsolescent circuit switches. And, in the *Triennial Review Order*, a different 3-2 majority awarded the ILECs an important victory on that issue.

Very roughly speaking, this portion of the *Order* distinguishes between the "legacy" facilities in the ILEC network—i.e., the facilities the ILECs have built as legacy providers of circuit-switched voice telephone service—and the next generation fiber-oriented facilities the ILECs are building or will build as providers of broadband services for mass market customers.[83] The FCC largely exempted these fiber-oriented facilities from unbundling obligations under section 251 because, in a nutshell, it feared that imposing them would deter ILECs from building these facilities in the first place and would likewise deter CLECs from building alternative broadband networks of their own. The Commission thus eliminated section 251 unbundling obligations altogether for packet switches themselves and sharply curtailed such obligations for fiber pipes leading all the way from an ILEC's central office to the premises of mass market customers—so-called *fiber-to-the-premises* (FTTP) loops. In "overbuild" situations, where an ILEC replaces existing copper loops with all-fiber loops, the ILEC retains an obligation either to keep the copper loops in service for leasing to CLECs or to lease narrowband voice-grade circuits to requesting CLECs over the new fiber loops. In "green field" situations, where the ILECs build these all-fiber loops out to new developments, it owes no unbundling obligations to CLECs at all. In October 2004, the FCC extended these rules to *fiber-to-the-curb* (FTTC) loops, in which the fiber portion extends deep into given neighborhoods but not all the way to particular homes.[84]

In the short term, only a limited number of ILEC loops will qualify for this exceptionally deregulatory treatment because building fiber facilities even to within a few hundred feet of customers' premises will take time and enormous capital investments. Instead, ILECs will focus on providing DSL over existing loops, which now consist partially or entirely of copper. This is where several technical features of DSL become highly relevant to the portions of the *Triennial Review Order* relating to unbundling obligations for so-called *hybrid* loops—which, as of this writing, consist of loops that contain some fiber but not enough to qualify as FTTP or FTTC loops.

First, recall that many (though by no means all) "legacy" loops built for the traditional telephone network consist of a hybrid of copper and fiber technologies. As we explained in chapter 2, this means that the copper distribution lines running from individual homes and businesses converge at road-side metal boxes known as "remote terminals," where the signals on those lines are multiplexed and connected to fiber-optic feeder links leading to the telephone company central office. Second, as noted in the previous chapter, DSL as such can be provided *only* over the copper portion of a loop. Thus, if a telephone company wishes to provide DSL to a customer served by means of a hybrid copper-fiber loop, it must install special electronics (splitters and DSLAMs) at the remote terminals themselves. Although these electronics multiplex the data signals for transmission over the fiber feeder lines back to the central office, this is done by means of a packet-switched technology—not by means of the circuit-switched ("time-division multiplexing") technology used by different equipment at the same remote terminals for the conventional telephone network (see chapter 2). As we shall see, the FCC has based much of its broadband unbundling policy on the distinction between these two different uses of a hybrid loop.

Finally, the shorter the copper portion of the loop is, the faster will be the DSL connection that the ILEC can provide over that portion. Customers with all-copper loops extending more than about 18,000 feet to the central office cannot receive genuine DSL service at all. Customers with copper links less than a few thousand feet long can receive a very high bandwidth form of DSL known as *VDSL* (for "very high bit-rate DSL"), which can support, among other things, high quality video services. For this reason, ILECs often perceive significant advantages to deploying more fiber feeder links and pushing them more deeply into individual neighborhoods. That enables ILECs to provide DSL to many customers who would otherwise have been unable to receive it at all (because their homes are too far from the central office to receive DSL over all-copper loops) and to provide faster VDSL connections to customers that would otherwise be eligible only for slower ADSL connections.

In the *Triennial Review Order*, the Commission wished to encourage ILECs both to build more fiber into their networks for these purposes and to install the requisite electronics at the remote terminals. To that end, the Commission exempted ILECs from any obligation under section 251 to share the *broadband functionality* of hybrid copper-fiber loops with

CLECs. The upshot is that CLECs may continue leasing an ILEC's hybrid loops to provide circuit-switched voice services, but they must generally make significant investments in loop facilities of their own if they wish to provide packet-switched broadband services to their customers.[85]

Of course, as a legal matter, the Commission had to justify all of these policy decisions within the statutory framework of section 251(d)(2). To that end, it first found that denying CLECs the right to lease capacity on an ILEC's fiber-to-the-premises loops would not "impair" their ability to provide broadband services, reasoning (controversially) that ILECs had no special advantages in the deployment of such loops. The Commission faced a more complex legal challenge in justifying its Solomonic disposition of the unbundling obligations related to hybrid loops, for it acknowledged that denying access to the broadband functionality of those loops *could* somewhat impair a CLEC's ability to provide broadband services.[86]

The Commission first qualified that impairment finding by noting that CLECs retain competitive alternatives: for example, they can theoretically build their own fiber links out to remote terminals and lease the copper distribution lines ("subloops") from the ILEC for individual customers.[87] Then, taking a page from the D.C. Circuit's rationale for eliminating line sharing, the Commission emphasized that impairment of CLEC business plans is not the end of the statutory inquiry in any event. Instead, the Commission observed, section 251(d)(2) requires it to "consider" such impairment "at a minimum," and thus allows it to consider other factors as well. These include the overarching objective of section 706(a) of the 1996 Act to remove regulatory "obstacles to infrastructure investment."[88] Here, recognizing the "state of competition for broadband service," the Commission determined that imposing an obligation to unbundle the broadband capabilities of hybrid loops "would blunt the deployment of advanced telecommunications infrastructure by incumbent LECs and the incentive for competitive LECs to invest in their own facilities."[89] In concluding that "the costs associated with unbundling these packet-based facilities outweigh the potential benefits," the Commission predicted that "[t]he end result" of removing those unbundling obligations will be "that consumers will benefit from this race to build next generation networks and the increased competition in the delivery of broadband services."[90] And, the Commission added, any concerns about the accuracy of this prediction were "obviated to some degree by the existence of a broadband service competitor with a leading position in the marketplace"—namely, cable modem service.[91]

On review, the D.C. Circuit expressed skepticism about some of the FCC's predicate factual findings,[92] but it ultimately upheld the Commission's decision to eliminate the relevant unbundling obligations for next generation broadband elements. In its core legal holding, the court rejected CLEC arguments that the Commission's "impairment" finding for hybrid loops compelled it to grant CLECs access to the broadband functionality of those loops. While "'impairment' [i]s the 'touchstone'" of the section 251(d)(2) analysis, the court held, the Act nonetheless compels the Commission to look beyond impairment to "consideration of factors such as an unbundling order's impact on investment."[93] The court also found it relevant that "robust *intermodal* competition from cable providers . . . means that even if all CLECs were driven from the broadband market, mass market consumers will still have the benefits of competition between cable providers and ILECs."[94] In sum, the court concluded, the Commission's decision "not to unbundle" hybrid loops and fiber-to-the-home loops "was reasonable, even in the face of some CLEC impairment, in light of evidence that unbundling would skew investment incentives in undesirable ways and that intermodal competition from cable ensures the persistence of substantial competition in broadband."[95]

One final dimension of these broadband unbundling controversies warrants discussion here. Recall from chapter 3 that section 271 requires the Bell companies, as a condition of providing long distance service, to meet a fourteen-point checklist, many of whose terms track the basic unbundling obligations the FCC has separately imposed under section 251. In the *Triennial Review Order*, the FCC reaffirmed earlier suggestions that these checklist requirements still apply even after a Bell company wins section 271 authorization; that whatever unbundling obligations the checklist imposes are independent of section 251 requirements; and that these section 271 obligations persist even after the Commission has determined that particular broadband elements no longer meet the unbundling standards of section 251(d)(2).[96] Although the *Order's* treatment of these issues focuses on narrowband elements such as circuit switches, it was widely read to apply to broadband elements as well, including broadband loop transmission.

This reading means that, even after *Triennial* and *USTA II*, the Bell companies were still required to provide wholesale transmission to CLECs over the next generation loops that the FCC had insulated from section 251 unbundling obligations. At the same time, however, the FCC has made clear that such checklist unbundling obligations are less demanding than their section 251 counterparts. For example, as noted in chapter 3, the price a CLEC must pay when invoking a right to unbundled switching under the checklist is governed by the amorphous "just and reasonable" standard of section 201, which is generally understood to permit higher rates than the TELRIC standard applicable to section 251 unbundling obligations.[97] Nonetheless, citing the investment uncertainty caused by these vaguely defined section 271 obligations, the Bell companies asked the FCC to exercise its general "forbearance" authority (discussed in the next chapter) to eliminate those obligations altogether when the Commission has found that particular broadband elements do not meet the unbundling criteria of section 251(d)(2). At press time, the Commission granted that forbearance request and, subject as always to the prospect of judicial review, removed section 271 as a source of independent unbundling obligations for next generation broadband elements.[98]

* * *

The debate about whether and how to regulate broadband requires regulators to make a high stakes bet on how the market will evolve. Most observers agree that, in a world of robust competition at the physical layer, consumers will enjoy high quality, cost-based broadband services at that layer and will enjoy full access to the Internet's applications and content layers free from monopoly leveraging. The policy challenge arises in devising a regulatory strategy when the prospects for physical layer competition are unclear.

Those favoring greater government intervention tend to view broadband access as a relatively static market prone to monopoly or duopoly over the long term. On that view, the government *should* risk creating some disincentives for facilities investment at the margins if that is the only means of ensuring that at least one of the two main broadband platforms remains open to a range of complementary higher layer providers who might otherwise be shut out of the market. These proponents of a greater government role also express great skepticism that regulation actually does deter any provider from building facilities when it is efficient to do so.[99]

By contrast, those favoring less intervention tend to view the heavy hand of regulation as both unnecessary and affirmatively harmful. First, they view the broadband market as dynamic in the Schumpeterian sense—i.e., subject to the emergence of new broadband platforms that, without regulatory prodding, will undermine any market dominance of the established players. Second, they believe that, particularly in a technologically uncertain environment, the *costs* of regulation—as illustrated by past regulatory failures—should create a presumption against aggressive government intervention. Regulation, they say, is at best a gratuitous source of transaction costs and rent-seeking and at worst a gravely misconceived brake on the broadband roll-out and, by extension, on the U.S. economy as a whole.

Who is right? At this point, the answer is as philosophical as it is empirical, and it will become clear only in hindsight, if at all. In a sense, the broadband market confronts the FCC with the same theoretical question as the *Computer Inquiries:* how to chart a sensible regulatory course in an uncertain technological environment. Two differences between now and then are that (i) no single provider has a monopoly on transmission services in most markets and (ii) Baxter's Law (the most prominent exception to the complementary externalities principle) no longer applies because broadband services are not generally subject to rate caps. Each of those factors tends to cut against the need for heavy regulation at the physical layer. Perhaps for these reasons, the FCC appears inclined to watch the market develop—and to take stock of the facts on the ground—before it initiates any bold new form of regulatory intervention. And the same is true not just of these physical layer platforms, but also of a particularly disruptive new applications-layer service—VoIP, to which we now turn.

6

VoIP and Proposals for "Horizontal" Regulation

Although Joseph Schumpeter was writing in 1942 when he described the dynamics of "creative destruction," his analysis presciently captures the Internet's transformation of the global economy:

> The opening up of new markets, foreign or domestic, and the organizational development from the craft shop and factory to such concerns as U.S. Steel illustrate the same process of industrial mutation—if I may use that biological term—that incessantly revolutionizes the economic structure *from within*, incessantly destroying the old one, incessantly creating a new one. This process of Creative Destruction is the essential fact about capitalism. . . . [I]n capitalist reality as distinguished from its textbook picture, it is not [competition within a rigid pattern of invariant conditions] which counts but the competition from the new commodity, the new technology, the new source of supply, the new type of organization (the largest-scale unit of control for instance)—competition which commands a decisive cost or quality advantage and which strikes not at the margins of the profits and the outputs of the existing firms but at their foundations and their very lives. This kind of competition is as much more effective than the other as a bombardment is in comparison with forcing a door.[1]

"Voice over Internet protocol," known by its increasingly monosyllabic acronym VoIP ("voyp"), is a textbook model of such creative destruction. And, in a few short years, this technology may well uproot the foundations of traditional telephone regulation.

I. Introduction to VoIP

"VoIP" denotes a diverse family of voice applications that, on one or both ends of a "call," ride on top of the Internet protocol, whether over the public Internet itself or on private ("managed") IP networks. People have plugged microphones into their computers and placed "telephone calls" over the Internet since before the 1990s. But such real-time voice applications do not work particularly well for users with dial-up connections. As explained in chapters 2 and 4, packet-switched networks are more efficient than their circuit-switched counterparts for most data applications, but the price they pay for this efficiency is latency—i.e., difficulty in delivering all of the packets in a real-time voice "call" to their destination predictably and on time. Running voice applications over narrowband Internet connections thus produced, in the words of one trade publication, "some of the most garbled, inaudible conversations since tin can met string."[2]

Broadband technology changes all that. The more bits per second that can be processed at a given end of an Internet call, the higher the call quality, and the greater the number of innovative features that VoIP providers can include. In the early years of the 21st century, as a critical mass of American consumers ordered broadband connections, new service providers and software developers began specializing in VoIP products that rivaled conventional circuit-switched telephone service in call quality. The result is a tremendous boon for consumers—and a potential catastrophe for the traditional telephone industry.

VoIP technology enables end users to treat voice telephone calls and their accompanying features as just another set of applications they can run over any broadband connection at the edge of diverse packet-switched networks. VoIP thus frees such applications from the control of telephone company software locked in centralized circuit switches. In this respect, VoIP invites end-user innovation for voice services in the same way that the Internet facilitates such innovation for communications in general: it turns the circuit-switched telephone network "inside out." To accomplish this feat, VoIP providers have made ever greater use of an open signaling standard known as the Session Initiation Protocol (SIP).[3] As one analyst puts it, with only mild overstatement, "SIP means that telecom players, which controlled the physical network and leveraged its value commercially via applications in the past, won't be able to do so anymore."[4]

There are two basic categories of VoIP services: those that do, and those that do not, permit their end users to reach subscribers on the public switched telephone network (PSTN), an industry term for the sum of all of the mutually interconnected circuit-switched telephone networks. A VoIP service that does not interconnect with the PSTN—such as the Pulver service discussed below, or one form of the service offered by Skype—allows its subscribers to reach one another through SIP-enabled "peer-to-peer" communications. VoIP services that do interconnect with the PSTN—such as those offered by Vonage, AT&T, and a growing number of cable and local telephone companies—use "softswitches" to mediate between the protocols used by the two types of networks: SIP on the VoIP side, and the traditional SS7 signaling protocol (see chapter 12) on the PSTN side.

Later in this chapter, we will discuss the mechanics of how a voice call travels from the Internet to the PSTN and vice versa. The central point for now is that, in many contexts, VoIP technology permits significant cost savings as compared to traditional circuit-switched telephony;[5] it yields increasingly comparable, and someday greater, call quality; and it shifts significant control over voice applications from network providers to end users.

In the long run, VoIP will likely become the industry norm for voice services, used wherever there are broadband connections, and circuit-switched telephony will become an increasingly anachronistic rarity. The transition is likely to come faster in some markets than others. In the enterprise business market, the transition is already well underway.[6] Although businesses are not abandoning their circuit-switched PBXs overnight, they will gradually phase them out. Among other advantages, VoIP allows a company to slash costs by consolidating its traditionally separate voice and data networks into a single packet-switched network over which voice rides as one application among many. And it permits a range of attractive new features, as noted in chapter 4. Voicemails, for example, can be made to appear as audio files in e-mail in-boxes, and each end user can take her handset along with her on business trips, plug it into her laptop, and seem to be calling from the office wherever in the world she might be.

The transition to VoIP will come more slowly in the residential market, but it will pick up pace with the proliferation of broadband. One reason is price. Because VoIP runs as an application over any broadband platform, a residential consumer who already has a broadband connection can purchase VoIP services at an incremental cost far below what conventional telephone companies charge for voice service on a stand-alone circuit-switched platform. Indeed, vertically integrated broadband access providers will increasingly include VoIP services "for free" with the sale of their other services, as Cablevision has already done (see below).

In the near term, however, many mass market consumers will remain skeptical of this new technology. First, VoIP is only as reliable as the broadband connection it rides on top of, and DSL or cable modem connections tend to fail more often than dial tone on an ordinary telephone line. Also, VoIP requires customers to take greater responsibility for much of the functionality traditionally provided by the telephone companies. End users generally need to take extra steps to ensure that a 911 call will reach the right emergency response team, as discussed below, and they must protect themselves against viruses, spam, and other risks intrinsic to the Internet.[7] Nonetheless, industry analysts expect one million households to sign up for VoIP by the beginning of 2005 and perhaps tens of millions by 2010.[8]

All told, the VoIP revolution threatens to knock the legs out from under the traditional telephone industry. First, consumers who subscribe to VoIP services over broadband connections are unusually apt to curtail their use of circuit-switched telephone service or cancel it altogether. After all, since a broadband connection permits a user to talk and surf the Web at the same time, why have two voice-capable lines in the same home, particularly if there are one or two mobile wireless phones waiting in reserve in the event the broadband connection gives out? "Line loss" of this type is potentially devastating for local telephone companies, particularly those that have not diversified their operations by aggressively introducing wireless services and broadband offerings of their own or by developing their own VoIP products to win the business of customers in the traditional service regions of other local telephone companies. Some on Wall Street thus view the emergence of VoIP services, particularly over cable modem connections, as "the largest risk to Bell fundamentals over the next 5 years."[9]

As VoIP becomes widespread, any local telephone company will have to work hard to persuade its customers, once they cancel their circuit-switched telephone service, to keep their traffic on its network in some form by purchasing DSL (or one of the telephone company's other broadband services) as the platform over which their VoIP services will ride. To be sure, that commercial imperative may seem difficult to square with the conduct of some telephone companies to date. Several such companies have refused to provide DSL service to customers who do not also subscribe to conventional circuit-switched telephone service over the same loop (where, for example, those customers have signed up with CLECs for voice service). But that may be an unsustainable strategy over the long term.[10] A customer wishing to avoid a redundant voice service may cut the cord to the telephone company central office altogether and run VoIP applications over a cable modem connection instead, unless she lives in one of the dwindling number of neighborhoods where DSL but not cable modem service is available. In early 2004, that prospect led Qwest, the nation's fourth-largest local telephone company, to offer its customers the option of purchasing "naked DSL"—DSL without conventional circuit-switched telephone service. As VoIP becomes widespread, other telephone companies will almost certainly have to follow suit. Given the choice between keeping their customers on less favorable terms (by selling them a lower margin broadband service that cannibalizes their sometimes higher margin circuit-switched telephony) and losing them outright, economic necessity will ultimately force these telephone companies to choose the first option.

In the shorter term as well, telephone companies have much to lose from the advent of VoIP. First, even when customers are unwilling to cancel their traditional telephone service outright, they will increasingly rely on separate VoIP services for the types of calls that tend to generate the greatest telephone company revenues. Such services are attractive to consumers in part because they offer large "buckets" of long distance and international minutes at minimal or no extra cost. A customer placing long distance calls over a broadband connection will, by definition, not be using her conventional circuit-switched telephone service to place those calls, and the telephone company therefore will not be receiving the often above-cost access or toll charges it otherwise would receive (see chapter 2). And, for complex reasons discussed below, a VoIP customer *receiving* long distance calls from the PSTN will sometimes deprive the *calling* party's local telephone company of the access charges it might otherwise have received for originating the call. Telephone companies thus fear a massive shortfall in the revenues that, in the aggregate, traditionally helped underwrite inexpensive telephone service to everyone within a particular geographic region. Such concerns have spawned a complex set of regulatory disputes about whether particular VoIP services should be subject to access charges to the extent that they enable subscribers to call not just each other, but the hundreds of millions of people connected to the PSTN. We will defer a full treatment of those access charge issues until chapter 9, which addresses intercarrier compensation generally.

If traditional telephone companies have the most to lose from the VoIP revolution in the consumer mass market, cable companies may have the most to gain. VoIP enables cable companies, at a fairly low cost, to complete the "triple play" of voice, data, and video products over a single cable into the home. Telephone companies are much farther from that goal, as discussed in the previous two chapters, and their threats to reach it by building fiber-optic cables deep into residential neighborhoods leave the cable companies unfazed. As Comcast Cable President Steve Burke observes: "Whereas a phone company has to go out and spend tens of billions of dollars to put in place an infrastructure that can deliver video in addition to voice and data, we've already made the investment. So for us to sell a Verizon customer phone service costs us under $300. For Verizon to offer a customer fiber to the home costs in the thousands."[11]

In June 2004, Cablevision announced that it would make good on that advantage by offering, for $90 a month, a bundle of cable modem service, digital TV, and unlimited local and long distance calling. As the *Wall Street Journal* observed, "[m]any consumers already pay $90 a month just for their cable television and high-speed Internet access bills, meaning Cablevision is effectively giving away phone service."[12] In the long run, the race for mass market customers will be won by the provider with the fattest and most cost-efficient pipes for delivering torrents of bits into the home, as we observed in chapter 4. Some analysts predict that cable companies, given their head start and strong current position in the broadband market, will take a very substantial share of the voice telephony market in territories where they offer the "triple play." Indeed, Time Warner's telephone push in Portland, Maine reportedly attracted one out of eight telephone subscribers in one year alone.[13]

One final feature of the emerging VoIP marketplace is worth noting here at the outset of our discussion. Although it is too early to make confident predictions, the VoIP market is unlikely to remain dominated, as it was in 2003-04, by VoIP companies (like Vonage) that are unaffiliated with physical layer broadband providers. Although such companies have won disproportionate attention from regulators as vanguards in the fight for VoIP deregulation and are likely to remain active, particularly in niche markets, the long run profitability of specializing in mass market VoIP services is questionable. First, particularly as VoIP becomes more widespread commercially and cuts away at the price umbrella currently provided by higher cost circuit-switched telephony, many customers will be more inclined to purchase VoIP services from established providers than from unfamiliar upstarts.[14] Second, all else held equal, customers would rather deal with one service provider than two. They will thus be inclined to purchase VoIP on a bundled basis from their broadband access provider, such as the cable company, which may offer VoIP services either by itself or by teaming up with another name-brand provider like AT&T. Some industry observers also believe that these vertically integrated broadband firms, which increasingly provide VoIP entirely over managed IP networks rather than the public Internet, will exploit their ownership of the physical transmission platform to provide higher quality or (through bundling) lower prices for their own VoIP services than their non-integrated rivals could match using the same platform.[15] Whether or not this is a valid concern, it underscores the likelihood that the "Net neutrality" issues discussed in chapter 5 will assume increasing prominence within the field of telecommunications regulation.

* * *

The remainder of this chapter is divided into two main sections. The first explores the different types of VoIP services, focusing on the pivotal role that PSTN-interconnecting VoIP services in particular will play in the transition to an IP-centered world. The second then turns to a central policy question of the Internet age: whether, and to what extent, regulators can and should apply traditional telephone company regulation to voice services that are detached from any underlying bottleneck transmission facilities and ride merely as applications on top of interchangeable broadband platforms.

II. The Regulatory Treatment of VoIP Services

In 1996, in section 230(b)(2) of the Communications Act, Congress broadly affirmed "the policy of the United States . . . to preserve the vibrant and competitive free market that presently exists for the Internet and other interactive computer services, unfettered by Federal or State regulation."[16] This language is often cited as a mandate for keeping VoIP services unregulated. But it paints with too broad a brush to help regulators distinguish between IP-related voice services that should be viewed as bound up with "the Internet" and those that should be viewed instead as the functional and legal equivalent of ordinary telephone calls. To illustrate this point, we begin by describing two types of voice services that purport to use "the Internet" but are polar opposites in their dependence on the PSTN and have, accordingly, received sharply divergent treatment from the FCC. We then turn to the more ambiguous but highly significant *IP-to-PSTN* voice services that fall between these two poles, in that they enable people to use their broadband connections to call, and be called by, people connected to the PSTN.

A. IP-to-IP services

Consider, first, the "Free World Dialup" (FWD) service offered by pulver.com (Pulver), founded by industry maverick Jeff Pulver. Offered free of charge, this service facilitates voice "calls" over the Internet in somewhat the same way that AOL uses its "names and presence directory" to permit its subscribers to communicate through instant messaging (see chapter 1). Pulver "acts as a type of directory service, informing its members when fellow members are online or 'present'" and "at what IP address a member may be reached[.]"[17] Having performed those functions, Pulver then leaves it to the subscribers to proceed with their call independently on a "peer-to-peer" basis, roughly as file-sharers used the pre-injunction Napster to locate others with whom they could exchange music files over the Internet for free.[18] Pulver provides no transmission functionality itself; instead, subscribers must "bring their own broadband" to the table. Significantly, moreover, FWD subscribers can call only one another; they cannot use this service to call ordinary telephone numbers on the PSTN. Nor do Pulver subscribers receive telephone numbers of their own at which they can be reached by people calling from the PSTN. We will call this an "IP-to-IP" service to signify that both ends of a call must run on top of an IP broadband platform.

In early 2004, in the first of its orders addressing VoIP "characterization" issues, the FCC ruled that, because Pulver provides no transmission service, what it offers end users is neither a Title II "telecommunications service" nor even "telecommunications," but a pure Title I information service, in the form of various "computing capabilities" that enable subscribers to find one another on-line and set up their own calls.[19] From a technological perspective, Pulver's service is indeed less like circuit-switched telephone service than like a Yahoo!-sponsored on-line gaming service, which no one would seriously consider a "telecommunications service." The consequence of this finding was, among other things, to exempt Pulver from any Title II obligations to serve the public as a common carrier or, under the current rules, to contribute to the universal service fund (see chapter 10).

The FCC then took its deregulatory analysis one step further, asserting exclusive federal jurisdiction over Pulver's service and insulating it from virtually any state-level regulation as well. Reaffirming the broadly pre-emptive policies it had embraced in *Computer III*, the FCC decided that, because FWD "is an unregulated information service[,] . . . any state regulations that seek to treat FWD as a telecommunications service or otherwise subject it to public-utility type regulation would almost certainly pose a conflict with our policy of nonregulation."[20]

The FCC reasoned that, even though a subscriber can use Pulver's service to call people both within the state and outside it, there is no meaningful respect in which that service can be divided up into distinct "interstate" and "intrastate" components. No matter where in the world she travels, a subscriber can gain access to Pulver's server, and that server, the FCC found, has no way of identifying her geographic location when she does. Thus, the Commission concluded, "even if the members' locations were somehow relevant to their use of FWD, FWD's portable nature without fixed geographic origination or termination points means that no one but the members themselves know where the end points are. Attempting to require Pulver to locate its members for the purpose of adhering to a regulatory analysis that served another network [i.e., the PSTN] would be forcing changes on this service for the sake of regulation itself, rather than for any particular policy purpose."[21]

For that matter, even if the FCC wanted to regulate FWD (or the similar services of Skype or SIPphone), it would find the task difficult precisely because the service is not location-specific, does not use telephone numbers, and is virtually indistinguishable from other Internet applications that use SIP. To be sure, the end point of the network, where the user gains access to the Internet, might "know" in some sense approximately where that user is located. But that information is often not passed along to higher layer VoIP application providers, which have no need to know it. In any event, the FCC concluded that any effort to subject Pulver to traditional common carrier regulation would subvert Congress's endorsement, in section 230 of the Act, of "the vibrant and competitive free market that presently exists for the Internet and other interactive computer services, unfettered by Federal or State regulation."

B. PSTN-to-PSTN services

Now contrast Pulver's service with the so-called "phone-to-phone" service that AT&T offered around the turn of the 21st century.* (This service should not be confused with AT&T's newer IP-to-PSTN service, "CallVantage," which more closely resembles the Vonage service discussed below.) From the perspective of calling and called parties alike, the calls placed by means of this service are just like any other long distance calls placed over the PSTN. No broadband connection is needed; the customer just picks up an ordinary telephone, connected to an ordinary wall jack, and dials "1" plus the area code plus the number. The call is routed through the local telephone company's circuit switch and is directed to AT&T's network, just like all other long distance calls placed by AT&T's subscribers. Only once the signals reach its network do they get converted into IP packets and sent on their way along AT&T's Internet backbone, where they are given priority over routine data packets to ensure quality of service. On the terminating end of the call, the same thing happens in reverse. AT&T converts the packets back into the traditional format used by circuit-switched networks and hands the call off to the called party's local telephone company. That company then completes the call by routing it through a circuit switch en route to the called party. Thus, whereas Pulver's subscribers do not (and cannot) gain access to the PSTN on *either* end of a call, AT&T's service necessarily uses the PSTN on *both* ends of a call. And AT&T's subscribers generally have no idea that their voice signals spend any part of their journey on the "Internet."

AT&T nonetheless asked the FCC to rule that, because its service makes use of the Internet in this quite limited sense, it qualifies as an "information service" and, as such, should be exempt from any obligation to pay access charges to the local telephone companies on each end of the call. AT&T argued that it owed those companies, at most, the lower busi-

---

* The terms "phone-to-phone," "computer-to-phone," and "computer-to-computer" are holdovers from the FCC's first major discussion of VoIP issues in a 1998 Report to Congress on universal service issues. *See* Report to Congress, *Federal-State Joint Board on Universal Service*, 13 FCC Rcd 11,501, ¶¶ 87-88 (1998). Those terms, however, are obsolescent. For example, an end user no longer needs a normal "computer" to place voice calls over an IP broadband platform and thereby avoid the PSTN. We thus use the more technology-neutral terms "IP" for "computer" and "PSTN" for "phone."

ness-line rate that an ordinary ISP would pay for a connection to the local telephone network under the so-called "ESP exemption," which, where applicable, shields information service providers from an obligation to pay access charges to local telephone companies (see chapter 9).

In April 2004, the FCC rejected that argument, reaffirming a tentative suggestion in 1998 that such "phone-to-phone" (PSTN-to-PSTN) VoIP offerings should be classified as telecommunications services subject to access charge obligations.[22] It reasoned that "[u]sers of AT&T's specific service obtain only voice transmission with no net protocol conversion" and, indeed, "do not order a different service, pay different rates, or place and receive calls any differently than they do through AT&T's traditional circuit-switched long distance service."[23] Accordingly, the Commission concluded, AT&T's service remains an ordinary "telecommunications service," not an "information service"; it is subject to regular federal and state regulation as a common carrier service; and AT&T must therefore pay interstate and intrastate access charges.

The Commission deferred for another proceeding AT&T's argument that access charges are inflated well above "cost" and that it is economically irrational as a general matter for carriers to pay local telephone companies different rates for performing the exact same function—the completion of calls—depending on whether the calls are "local" or "long distance." (We return to these issues in chapter 9.) In so doing, however, the Commission was just buying itself some time. The true threat to the access charge regime lies in the creatively destructive class of IP-to-PSTN services on which VoIP provider Vonage focused the Commission's attention in 2003.

C. IP-to-PSTN services: the basics

Unlike the AT&T service just described, an IP-to-PSTN service requires a subscriber to obtain a broadband connection on her own and to place her VoIP calls over it. But, unlike Pulver's IP-to-IP service, an IP-to-PSTN service makes use of ordinary telephone numbers and enables a subscriber to reach anyone, and *be* reached *by* anyone, who is served by any ordinary telephone network anywhere in the world. Precisely because it is interconnected with all other telephone networks in this manner, the provider of such services benefits from the same network effects as any circuit-switched telephone company. Such IP-to-PSTN products thus provide consumers, for the first time, a realistic substitute for conventional circuit-switched telephony. For this reason, Vonage and its technological kin—including vertically integrated broadband transmission providers—may transform both the voice telephone market and its regulatory structure almost beyond recognition within the next several years.

Some technical background is needed for a full understanding of these commercial and regulatory implications. We will use Vonage's own service for purposes of illustration—not because Vonage is at all likely to dominate this market, but only because it filed the FCC petition that has brought VoIP-related regulatory issues to center stage.

A Vonage subscriber originates a voice call over the Internet by plugging an ordinary telephone into a special Vonage-provided adapter, which is associated with an IP address. The subscriber connects that adapter, in turn, not to a telephone jack, but to whatever broadband connection he has separately purchased from, say, a cable modem or DSL provider. Once connected, the adapter communicates with Vonage's server. If the called party is herself a subscriber, the server plays a role analogous to that played by Pulver's server. But if the called party is (like most people today) a subscriber to the PSTN, Vonage, in partnership with various telecommunications wholesalers, arranges to drop the call off on the PSTN after first converting it from IP packets into the standard format understood by circuit-switched networks. Similarly, Vonage (through its wholesale partners) obtains telephone numbers managed by the North American Numbering Plan Administrator—a federal authority that works closely with the FCC—and assigns specific numbers to its subscribers so that they can be called by subscribers to the PSTN. Vonage explains: "When someone calls you, they dial your number. Behind the scenes, your number looks very much like an e-mail address. This number instructs the call to travel over the Internet and through our network to the phone adapter we sent you free, your phone rings, and all you have to do is pick up and answer it."[24]

Because a Vonage subscriber's telephone number is, from Vonage's perspective, just a proxy for the IP address associated with the adapter, it liberates the subscriber from the geographical constraints usually associated with landline telephone numbers. Suppose, for example, that a subscriber resides in Washington, D.C. and thus obtains from Vonage a number with the 202 area code, yet often commutes to New York City during the workweek.[25] When he travels to New York, he plugs his adapter into a broadband connection there—say, in his hotel room. When a Verizon wireline subscriber back in D.C. calls him, she can reach him through Verizon's ordinary circuit-switched network by making a local call to his 202 number without incurring toll charges. One of Vonage's telecommunications wholesalers has made this possible by establishing a physical point of presence in the D.C. area and associating Vonage's 202 numbers with it. A shared database tells all telecommunications carriers, including Verizon, to drop off calls to Vonage's 202 numbers at that point. From there, each call is sent on its way, ultimately in the form of IP packets, to the subscriber's adapter, wherever on the Internet it might be plugged in. What seems to the friend back in D.C. as a local call is in fact a long distance call with a local stop at an Internet gateway. It is a bit like visiting a distant Web server through a dial-up Internet connection, except that the call is processed seamlessly to the called party without any discernible set-up delay, and the digital application being run is a voice conversation rather than a session of Web browsing.

So far, our description of the numbering flexibility offered by Vonage might seem similar to what cellular telephone companies offer; after all, when you travel with your cellphone, your friends back home can reach you by placing a "local" call. But VoIP, like the Internet generally, takes geographical flexibility to a new level. Suppose that our Vonage subscriber wishes to enable friends in both New York and D.C. to reach him for free over the PSTN by placing "local" calls to him no matter which of those cities he is in. He need only ask Vonage to "associate" a second number to his account—this time, a number with a 718 (New York) area code. Since both the 202 and 718 numbers are proxies for the adapter's IP address, a "local" call over the PSTN to either number will direct the caller to the Vonage subscriber.[26]

This service is functionally indistinguishable from the "FX lines" we discussed in chapter 2. The main difference is that, at $5.00 a month, Vonage's Internet-based service costs a mere fraction of what one would pay a conventional circuit-switched telephone company for a private line. Such arrangements, of course, alarm many such companies. One concern is that the stocks of unassigned telephone number numbers are finite, and assigning multiple telephone numbers to a single VoIP account could accelerate their depletion. Regulators cannot simply make more such numbers—say, by adding an extra digit—without inflicting enormous new costs on the industry in the form of telephone infrastructure upgrades.

Telephone companies also argue that, by allowing users of the PSTN to call distant VoIP subscribers without placing conventional long distance calls replete with access charges, these sorts of arrangements will drain billions of dollars of implicit cross-subsidies from telephone company coffers. In the end, though, the "fault" here lies in the reliance of policymakers on such cross-subsidies, not with the VoIP providers themselves. They are simply heralds of the news that such cross-subsidies are irrational and ripe for elimination, as discussed in chapters 9 and 10.

D. IP-to-PSTN services: classification and jurisdiction

Recall from chapter 2 that retail telephone service—particularly local service—is heavily regulated at both the state and federal levels. Telephone companies usually must file tariffs; they must adhere to the ethic of "common carriage"; they are subject to various complaint procedures before regulatory bodies; they must provide access to local emergency services through "enhanced" 911 dialing; and so forth. This tradition raises two related questions about the proper regulatory treatment of IP-to-PSTN services. The first is whether, as with Pulver's IP-to-IP service, the FCC should assert *exclusive* federal jurisdiction over any IP-to-PSTN service on the ground that it would be infeasible to bifurcate the service, as traditional telephone services are bifurcated (see chapter 2), into separate "interstate" and "intrastate" components and permit the states to regulate the latter. The second is whether, on the federal level, such services should be treated, like conventional telephony, as "telecommunications services" subject to common carrier regulation under Title II, or instead as "information services" generally exempt from such regulation.

These questions became particularly pressing in 2003, when the Minnesota Public Utilities Commission ordered Vonage, among other things, to obtain state certification as a telephone company, file a tariff, and ensure that its service provides the same dependable 911 calling functionality offered by regular telephone companies. In a widely publicized decision, a federal district court stayed the Minnesota commission's order on the grounds that Vonage was providing an "information service" rather than a "telecommunications service," that "[w]hat Vonage provides is essentially the enhanced functionality on top of the underlying network, which the FCC has explained should be left alone," and that "State regulation would effectively decimate Congress's mandate that the Internet remain unfettered by regulation."[27] When the Minnesota PUC appealed that decision to the Eighth Circuit, the FCC sprang into action, having learned from experience in the *Brand X* case the price it pays when it stays silent on such issues and permits courts to fill the regulatory void (see chapter 5). In November 2004, the FCC ruled that Vonage's IP-to-PSTN service, like Pulver's IP-to-IP service, is indivisibly interstate. And it preempted traditional state public utility regulation of that and similar services offered by any VoIP provider, including vertically integrated cable and telephone companies. The Commission nonetheless deferred any formal finding that these services are Title I "information services" and folded that "statutory characterization" issue into its broader (and slower paced) inquiry into the regulatory treatment of "IP-enabled services" generally.[28]

The two legal questions posed here—concerning jurisdiction and statutory characterization—are distinct in theory, as the FCC's *Vonage Order* shows, but closely related in practice. The FCC almost reflexively asserts federal jurisdiction over, and preempts most state regulation of, any genuinely Internet-based offering, and it typically characterizes such offerings as "information services" as well.[29] The FCC recites arcane legal formulas to justify these assertions of exclusive federal jurisdiction, always careful to stress the predominantly "interstate" (and international) nature of the Internet.[30] To be sure, a given Internet-related service might have "intrastate components"—for example, an ISP offers its subscribers access to servers within the same state as well as outside it, and any VoIP service, including Pulver's, permits someone to call her next-door neighbor. But the Commission normally concludes that any given Internet-related service is "indivisibly" interstate in the sense that it would be analytically and practically infeasible to divide the service up, like conventional telephone services, into distinct "interstate" and "intrastate" jurisdictional spheres.[31]

Beneath this jargon is a critical policy judgment. Balkanizing Internet-related services into 50 different schemes of state-level common carrier regulation would be deeply inconsistent with several of the Internet's defining characteristics. Among these characteristics are the geographical indeterminacy of Internet transmissions, including the portability of IP addresses; the Internet's traditional freedom from regulatory intrusion; and, more generally, the Internet's celebrated tendency to obliterate political boundaries of all kinds. This is the same judgment that Congress embraced when, in 1996, it codified "the policy of the United States . . . to preserve the vibrant and competitive free market that presently exists for the Internet and other interactive computer services, unfettered by Federal or State regulation."[32]

To say that a service "uses the Internet," however, does not by itself resolve the regulatory issues posed here, for not all such services are plausibly distinct enough from conventional telephony to justify different regulatory treatment. For example, the AT&T phone-to-phone service discussed above "uses the Internet" in the sense that the IP functionality "in the middle" is said to run over pipes that AT&T has also devoted to public Internet backbone traffic. But, as noted, the FCC attached no regulatory significance to that fact; it deemed AT&T's service a telecommunications service and kept intact the traditional division of authority between the federal government and the states over interstate and intrastate calls, respectively. This resolution left open whether an IP-to-PSTN service should also be treated as a "telecommunications service" and whether it should be subject to the same traditional scheme of dual jurisdiction. Not surprisingly, providers of that service have pressed the position that their VoIP offerings are indivisibly interstate "information services" subject, like Pulver's FWD service, to immunity from common carrier regulation on the state level and presumptively on the federal level as well.

Although it addressed only the jurisdictional side of the issue, the FCC's November 2004 *Vonage Order* appears highly sympathetic to that position. As an original matter, however, there are no straightforward answers to these questions of regulatory classification and jurisdiction. On the one hand, an IP-to-PSTN service like Vonage's indisputably uses "the Internet" in the fullest sense of the word. It relies on the Internet's IP addressing scheme, and at least one party to each call bypasses the PSTN altogether by transmitting signals over a broadband connection in the form of IP packets. The providers of such services also use softswitches to perform net protocol conversion in exchanging calls between the packet-switched Internet and the circuit-switched PSTN. The FCC has commonly cited such protocol conversion as a key criterion for distinguishing information services from telecommunications services, even though the relevant statutory definitions do not explicitly mention it.[33]

On the other hand, stripped to its essential retail features, an IP-to-PSTN service may seem to an end user very much like regular telephone service. Again, take Vonage's product as an example. Any regular telephone will work on Vonage's network; when plugged into Vonage's adapter (rather than a wall socket), the phone produces a dial tone; and the service can be used to place or receive what seem like ordinary telephone calls to or from anywhere in the world. Vonage has designed its product with these reassuringly familiar features precisely to underscore its substitutability with conventional telephony. As for "net protocol conversion," it is unclear why, as a policy matter, immense regulatory consequences should follow from Vonage's rote translation of user-provided content from one format to another when connecting calls to or from the PSTN. Finally, although Vonage contracts out to independent telecommunications carriers to provide the transmission platform for its service, that fact cannot be dispositive of whether Vonage provides a telecommunications service. After all, resellers of conventional long distance service are still classified as telecommunications carriers, and are subject to Title II regulation, even if they have no facilities of their own.*

In the long term, however, these are quibbles. VoIP services delivered over a broadband Internet platform, like most other Internet services, will almost inevitably mutate into more sophisticated and interactive offerings that indisputably meet the criteria of information services. This technological evolution should proceed without artificial regulatory influences. A finding that standard VoIP services today are "telecommunications services" would just induce a provider to attach additional bells and whistles to its products—say, real-time translation into another language, conversion into text messaging, "play-back" functionality, and so forth—to expedite a

---

*The fact that Vonage is not a facilities-based provider probably does, however, spare it from the precedential effect of the Ninth Circuit's *Brand X* decision, discussed in the previous chapter. There, the court reasoned that, "unlike other ISPs, [a cable modem provider] controls all of the transmission facilities between its subscribers and the Internet. . . . [T]o the extent that [a cable operator] provides its subscribers Internet transmission over its cable broadband facility, it is providing a telecom service." *Brand X Internet Servs. v. FCC*, 345 F.3d 1120, 1129 (9th Cir. 2003), *cert. granted*, Nos. 04-281 et al. (Dec. 3, 2004). The plain implication is that if an information services provider does not control such facilities, it cannot also be a telecommunications carrier. This distinction is problematic. A long distance company qualifies no less as a "telecommunications carrier" than does a local telephone company simply because the latter, but not the former, "controls all of the transmission facilities between its subscribers" and the relevant long distance network. For that reason and others, the Ninth Circuit's approach, if it stands, may erect questionable distinctions in the regulatory treatment of VoIP services, even if they qualify as information services, on the basis of whether the company providing such services is the same as (or perhaps affiliated with) the company that owns the underlying transmission facilities.

finding that those products fit the statutory definition of "information service": "the offering of a capability for . . . storing . . . processing, retrieving, utilizing, or making available information."[34] Where the Internet is involved, drawing fine metaphysical lines between "telecommunications services" and "information services" is as futile in the long term as it is litigation-inviting and destabilizing in the short term.[35]

Finally, whether or not Vonage-type IP-to-PSTN servicess are properly deemed information services, the FCC was on solid ground in following the *jurisdictional* precedent of the *Pulver Order* and declaring such services off-limits to *state-level* common carrier regulation. If, as the FCC concluded in the *Pulver Order*, it would be infeasible to carve out an intrastate component of IP-enabled services that (like Pulver's) always have both legs in the Internet, it would also be difficult to carve out an intrastate component from VoIP services that, like Vonage's, leave one leg in the Internet even while interconnecting with the PSTN.[36] It is no less true of Vonage's service than of Pulver's that, given the inherent geographic anonymity of IP addressing schemes, "[a]ttempting to require [the provider] to locate its members for the purpose of adhering to a regulatory analysis that served [the legacy PSTN] would be forcing changes on this service for the sake of regulation itself, rather than for any particular policy purpose. . . . [I]mposing this substantial burden would make little sense and would almost certainly be significant and negative for the development of new and innovative IP services and applications."[37]

The FCC's assertion of exclusive interstate jurisdiction over VoIP services ensures national consistency in VoIP policy, but it does not necessarily exclude the states from playing any part in effectuating that policy, as the Commission suggested in the *Vonage Order*. By analogy, the FCC's local competition regulations are supreme in the field of local competition regulation, but section 252 gives the states an essential role in applying those regulations to specific factual circumstances (see chapter 3). And the FCC has delegated authority to the states to implement federal programs specifically relevant to VoIP, including the administration of telephone numbers under the North American Numbering Plan.[38] On the other hand, the D.C. Circuit's broad-brush anti-delegation holding in *USTA II*, discussed in chapter 3, casts a shadow over the legality of any non-statutory delegation of open-ended federal authority to the states. There is also significant political resistance to giving states any role in regulating "the Internet," lest a few of them exploit that role as an opening wedge to over-regulate this traditionally unregulated sphere.

In 2004, Congress began considering legislation designed to nip in the bud the escalating controversy about the proper characterization and jurisdictional treatment of VoIP services.[39] Rather than forge a quick consensus that would eclipse the FCC's incipient inquiry, the House and Senate produced bills that diverged sharply in philosophy. There are some similarities: for example, as of this writing, the Senate bill and the leading House bill both would place VoIP within the primary jurisdiction of the FCC, and both would permit local telephone companies to recover compensation from a VoIP provider for the use of the PSTN. But the House bill is more aggressively deregulatory than the Senate bill. It would entirely deprive the states of authority to regulate VoIP or any other IP-enabled service; would strip the FCC itself of any power to subject these services to common carrier regulation; and, for good measure, would largely detach such services from most existing regulatory schemes by excluding them from the statutory categories of "telecommunications service" and "information service." The Senate bill is vaguer about any deregulatory objective and would permit the states to subject VoIP to intrastate access charges, 911 dialing requirements, and various universal service regulations.[40] Congress has much work to do before either of these bills, or anything like them, becomes law. But industry observers view these dueling legislative proposals as significant opening moves in an ongoing congressional debate that may reshape telecommunications regulation.

III. VoIP, "Horizontal" Regulation, and Title I

As Congress was contemplating these bills, the FCC was asking for comment on whether, in the absence of such legislation, it already had the statutory authority to adopt the same type of qualified deregulatory regime for VoIP services on its own. We now turn to this and related issues about the FCC's regulatory flexibility in a convergent and increasingly IP-centric age.

A. Calls for a layers-oriented model of regulation

In this chapter and the previous one, our analysis of Internet policy veered into discussions of scholastic complexity about the proper way to "characterize" particular services, such as cable modem service and the varieties of VoIP, for purposes of classifying them within the obsolescent framework of the Communications Act of 1934. If we could turn back the clock and design a regulatory regime from scratch, there would be no need for discussion of such issues. These issues arise only because the Act, written mostly in a pre-convergent era, assumes that particular types of facilities will always be closely associated with particular services, which should be individually classified and regulated pursuant to mutually distinct statutory regimes. Wireline telephone companies are subject to "common carrier" regulation under Title II, and their retail services are subject to the traditional division of regulatory authority between the FCC and the states (see chapter 2). Use of the airwaves, such as for over-the-air broadcasting or cellular telephone service, is regulated in whole or in part under Title III, which, among other things, preempts most forms of state regulation (see chapter 8). And "cable services" are regulated under Title VI, which essentially divides regulatory responsibility between the FCC and local franchising authorities (see chapter 5). In revising the Act in 1996, Congress left intact each of these three statutory "silos," as they are disparagingly known, along with the markedly different rules contained in each for governing the corresponding physical layer platform.

As we have seen, the Internet holds such rigid service-specific distinctions in contempt. Each of these three physical layer media—the wireline telephone network, the airwaves, and cable company infrastructure—is capable of providing Internet access, and the Internet in turn can serve as a platform for any communications service imaginable: voice telephony, Web surfing, audio and video entertainment, and so forth. Indeed, these "services" are often properly viewed as higher layer "applications" in much the same way that Excel spreadsheet software is an application that rides on top of an operating system platform. In each case, ultimate control of the product's use may reside largely with end users and the applications providers, not with the provider of any underlying transmission platform.

Given the Internet's modular structure, a number of commentators have urged policymakers to replace the Act's legacy regulatory approach with a more antitrust-oriented "horizontal" approach that focuses on the critical role of layering in modern telecommunications.[41] They argue that the only rational way to regulate the Internet industry is to draw lines within the layering hierarchy to distinguish between (i) those layers (if any) that should be subject to continued economic regulation because there is insufficient competition within them and (ii) those layers that should not be subject to such regulation because they are presumptively competitive. Most of these commentators would regulate economic activity relating to the Internet only to the extent that a dominant firm threatens to undermine consumer welfare by abusing market power at a particular layer. And they would free the rest of the communications industry from legacy public utility regulation at all levels, state and federal.

Although the FCC has not always drawn clear lines of this sort, it has indicated that they are appropriate and ultimately necessary. As it explained in 1998, "[c]ommunications networks function as overlapping layers, with multiple providers often leveraging a common infrastructure. As long as the underlying market for provision of transmission facilities is competitive or is subject to sufficient pro-competitive safeguards, we see no need to regulate the enhanced functionalities that can be built on top of those facilities."[42] Under this approach, VoIP services, as applications riding on top of physical layer platforms, would not be subject to public utility regulation of the sort imposed by Title II because there are no extraordinary barriers to the entry of new VoIP providers into the market. The physical layer platforms themselves may or may not be subject to such regulation, depending on the economic considerations canvassed in the previous chapter. Those include (i) whether particular providers can be said to dominate the provision of broadband transmission services in a given market, (ii) whether those providers have the incentive and ability to abuse their monopoly power in various respects, such as by leveraging it to suppress competition in the applications and content layers, and (iii) whether, in particular circumstances, that threat of monopoly abuses is outweighed by the efficiencies of vertical integration.

Skepticism that regulators would answer such questions correctly has led some industry analysts to oppose any layers-oriented regime altogether in favor of general deregulation. Libertarian George Gilder cautions that any layering approach, by seeking to preserve the Internet in its current modular form, "ignore[s] ever changing trade-offs between integration and modularization," slights the importance of innovation within the "core" of the network as well as at the edge, and inappropriately "assume[s] there is one network, that it is sufficient and timeless, [and] that no new networks are possible or needed."[43] "The real threat to monopolize and paralyze the Internet," he concludes, "is not the communications industry and its suppliers, but the premature modularizers and commoditizers, the propo-

nents of the dream of some final government solution for the uncer-
tainties of all life and commerce."[44] Similarly, a coalition of industry advocates warned the FCC in July 2004 that, even though engineers view the
Internet in terms of layers, regulators should not design competition policy in those terms as well.[45] The coalition directed its critique at a much-
discussed MCI white paper that argued not just for a layers-oriented
regulatory model in the abstract, but for a more substantive conclusion
that the physical layer—the market for wholesale transmission services—is
dominated by ILECs and should be heavily regulated as such.[46]

Despite these concerns, it makes abundant sense to reorient telecommunications policy from the current approach, characterized by now-arbi-
trary legacy classifications, to a more technology-neutral approach that
reflects the new independence of services from the transmission networks
over which they were traditionally provided. Such an approach must
account for the modular, layered structure of modern communications.
Taking that structure into account, however, should be only the beginning,
and not the end, of serious policy analysis. For example, any inquiry into
whether a particular broadband provider should be regulated as a dominant carrier at the physical layer—and whether, if so, it should be permitted to integrate vertically—must consider the complex economic
considerations discussed in the previous chapter and also the differences in
competitive conditions from one market to another.[47] Policymakers must
also continue to weigh the costs of regulation against the hoped-for benefits. These costs include not just the administrative burdens policymakers
can anticipate, but also the unintended and often unpredictable inefficiencies that regulation of any kind can inflict on a market. In designing a layers-oriented regime, policymakers must also accommodate differing views
about how to define particular layers and must take extreme care not to let
their own definitions distort the efficient evolution of communications
technologies.[48] And they should be careful not to misconstrue the *formal
structure* of a layers-oriented analysis as a *substantive presumption* against
the use of vertically integrated, "managed" IP networks that ensure quality of service for particular applications, such as voice and video.

Suppose, then, that policymakers decide that some form of "horizontal," layers-oriented regime is appropriate for the industry. One of the critical questions they confront is whether it is legally possible to get from here
to there within the existing structure of the Communications Act.
Although, as discussed, Congress began holding hearings in early 2004 on
the need to bring the Act up to date, it is notoriously slow to take bold
action in the telecommunications arena, in part because the political fallout of doing little or nothing is milder than the political fallout of choos-

ing between the opposing interests of powerful industry segments. The issue in the intermediate term is what the FCC can do in the absence of major statutory revisions to break free of the Act's service-oriented categories and adopt a more unified, antitrust-like approach to the regulation of Internet-related communications generally.

This issue can be subdivided into two major questions. First, to what extent can the FCC ensure greater regulatory parity in this convergent industry by relieving firms of the vestigial "legacy" obligations to which they would otherwise be subject only because of their regulatory pedigree? Second, to what extent can the FCC, once it has generally removed such obligations, impose whatever regulatory requirements (such as effective 911 dialing or amenability to wiretapping) it nonetheless deems appropriate for all providers of a particular type of service, no matter what the state of competition in the industry? We address each of these questions in turn.

B. Title I, Title II, and forbearance

Most of the regulatory classification issues discussed in the past two chapters have involved questions about whether particular services at the physical layer (such as cable modem service) or the applications layer (such as VoIP) should be regulated "under Title I" or, alternatively, "under Title II." This distinction has become so central to today's policy debates that industry participants often use "Title I" (as in a "Title I service") as a shorthand for "deregulated" and "Title II" as a shorthand for "regulated." But the choice is a bit more nuanced than that.

We begin with a refresher on some basic terminology. Recall from chapter 3 that the FCC and the courts have essentially equated the term "telecommunications service," as used in the 1996 Act, with the older term "common carrier service."[49] If it seeks deregulation, a provider of "telecommunications" can try to avoid the "telecommunications service" characterization, and thus regulation within the framework of Title II, in one of two basic ways. First, in limited circumstances, it can request permission to operate only as a Title I private carrier, selling transmission lines or services on a purely contractual basis, at least to sophisticated business customers.[50] Examples of such private carriers include the Internet backbone operators, which provide long distance transmission services to each other and to ISPs without ongoing regulatory oversight. Second, a provider of "telecommunications" may seek to avoid the "telecommunications service" characterization by bundling transmission together with an information service, such as Internet access via cable modem service, but only if it can escape the independent *Computer II* obligation to strip out that transmission component and sell it on an unbundled basis to all takers. As noted in the previous chapter, however, the Ninth Circuit's *Brand X* decision, if it stands, complicates this latter regulatory strategy, at least for providers that "control[] all of the transmission facilities between its subscribers and the Internet."[51]

Significant consequences turn on these definitional judgments. As the FCC recently reiterated, only providers that qualify as Title II "common carriers" are subject to "[v]arious regulatory obligations and entitlements set forth in the [Communications Act of 1934]—including a prohibition on unjust or unreasonable discrimination among similarly situated customers and the requirement that all charges, practices, classifications, and regulations applied to common carrier service be 'just and reasonable.'"[52] And various other rights and duties—"including, for example, the entitlement to access an incumbent's unbundled network elements for local service[,] . . . attach only to entities providing 'telecommunications service.'"[53] These characterization issues also matter for purposes of allocating the burden of supporting federal universal service programs, discussed in chapter 10. Section 254(d) requires "[e]very telecommunications carrier that provides interstate telecommunications services" to pay considerable sums into the federal universal service fund. As of this writing, any such wireline carrier is required to contribute nearly 10% of its interstate retail revenues—in effect, a government-mandated tithe—to support low telephone rates in rural areas, broadband connections for schools and libraries, and other such objectives. In contrast, "[a]ny other provider of interstate telecommunications"—such as a private carrier or a facilities-based information service provider—need contribute to the universal service fund only if and when the FCC decides that "the public interest so requires."[54]

At the same time, a service can be highly deregulated on the retail level even if it is formally classified as a "telecommunications service" and is therefore subject, in some sense, to regulation "under Title II." For example, carriers deemed "nondominant" in their respective markets have long enjoyed more regulatory flexibility than their "dominant" counterparts in such matters as the timing of their tariff filings.[55] And, in highly competitive markets, the FCC has eliminated tariffing obligations altogether. For example, the FCC has not only permitted but compelled carriers in the con-

sumer long distance business to "detariff" their services and deal on a purely contractual basis with their individual customers.[56] To be sure, even
such highly deregulated carriers remain subject, at least in the abstract, to
the non-discrimination requirements of sections 201 and 202, to FCC complaint procedures under section 208, and to the various market entry and
exit regulations imposed under section 214. As a practical matter, however, the retail obligations of these carriers are often only marginally different from what they would be if their services were formally excluded from
the scope of Title II altogether.

The FCC's current freedom to deregulate services within the framework of Title II is a fairly recent development. In a string of decisions spanning the decade from 1985 to 1994, the D.C. Circuit, ultimately upheld by
the Supreme Court, invalidated the FCC's various efforts to detariff long
distance services offered by non-dominant providers (a class that now
includes all domestic long distance carriers).[57] As those courts found, section 203 of the Communications Act effectively compels telecommunications carriers to file tariffs even after rigorous competition has emerged and
continued enforcement of tariffing requirements would frustrate the public's interest in a well-functioning, non-collusive free market.

In the 1996 Act, Congress dealt with this type of problem by dramatically expanding the FCC's power, previously authorized only in the cellular telephone context, to "forbear from applying" outdated regulatory
requirements.[58] With astonishing breadth, Congress directed the
Commission to nullify "any regulation or any provision" of the
Communications Act of 1934, including the provisions added by the 1996
Act itself, to any "class of telecommunications carriers or telecommunications services" once the Commission finds (i) that the requirement in question is "not necessary" to ensure just and reasonable terms of service, (ii)
that it is "not necessary for the protection of consumers," and (iii) that
"forbearance . . . is consistent with the public interest."[59] The lone quali-
fication to this sweeping authority concerns the core local competition and
Bell entry provisions: "the Commission may not forbear from applying the
requirements of section 251(c) or 271 . . . until it determines that those
requirements have been fully implemented."[60] But this standard is itself so
vague that it permits a great deal of interpretive play in the joints.

In sum, the FCC has several tools at its disposal for deregulating
providers when it concludes that the relevant market is competitive. The
first is the Commission's power to resolve close "statutory characteriza-

tion" questions by deciding that a given service falls within the scope of its Title I jurisdiction over interstate communications, and therefore within the Commission's authority to preempt state economic regulation, but outside the scope of Title II regulation of "telecommunications services." In particular, it can try to exclude a service from Title II by finding either (i) that the service is an "information service" or (ii) that, even if it would otherwise qualify as a "telecommunications service," the provider should be entitled to offer it on a private carriage basis. Or the FCC can "forbear" from some or all Title II requirements as it deems appropriate (with limited and hazy exceptions), in which case the service at issue will remain within the scope of the Commission's preemptive Title I "ancillary" jurisdiction. Finally, these various tools are not mutually exclusive; the FCC sometimes uses them in tandem when pursuing a deregulatory strategy. In the *Cable Modem Order*, for example, the Commission simultaneously deemed cable modem service a Title I information service without a telecommunications service component and then, to confront the risk that the Ninth Circuit might disagree (as it ultimately did), tentatively concluded that forbearance from any Title II obligation would be appropriate.[61]

Of course, the FCC's strategies for freeing Internet-related services from unnecessary federal requirements would accomplish very little if the states could simply reimpose the same requirements under state law that the Commission has deemed counterproductive as a matter of federal policy. Recall, moreover, that the Commission can normally preempt state-level retail regulation only if it establishes that the service in question should always be viewed as "indivisibly interstate" rather than (like ordinary telephone services) either interstate or intrastate depending on the physical locations of the calling and called parties. As discussed above, the Commission almost invariably finds that Internet-related information services are indivisibly interstate in nature, reasoning that most Internet transmissions cross state boundaries and that tracking the divergent paths of different IP packets across the backbone would be so difficult, and so inimical to the boundary-shattering ethic of the Internet, as to be categorically inappropriate.

C. The contours of the FCC's ancillary jurisdiction

So far we have discussed how the FCC may *free* carriers from federal and state regulatory obligations that it deems inappropriate. Now we discuss how the FCC may *impose* other obligations on them to the extent it succeeds in removing their services from the framework of Title II common carriage regulation. Suppose, for example, that the Commission concludes that all Vonage-type IP-to-PSTN VoIP services should be classified as "information services" and exempted from such regulation. To what extent may the Commission invoke its so-called "ancillary" authority under Title I to impose, through the back door, various discrete requirements that Title II imposes on providers of any conventional "telecommunications service," such as obligations to "ensure that the service is accessible to and usable by individuals with disabilities" (section 255(c)) or to cooperate with the wire-tapping needs of law enforcement authorities (section 229)? The answer to this question is as unclear as it is consequential.

We first note an important but often overlooked wrinkle in the analysis. Although the provisions of Title II are limited mostly to the regulation of "common carriers" and (what are the same) "telecommunications service" providers, Title II contains a few provisions that are not so limited. For example, section 251(e)(1) grants the FCC or its delegate "exclusive jurisdiction over those portions of the North American Numbering Plan that pertain to the United States." (The FCC has, in turn, delegated much of its authority over number administration to the state commissions.) And section 251(e)(3) directs the FCC to "designate 9-1-1 as the universal emergency telephone number within the United States for reporting an emergency to appropriate authorities and requesting assistance," and the FCC's authority under this provision extends "to both wireline and wireless telephone service." In each case, the FCC may exercise its specific statutory authority under these provisions to define the rights and obligations of all service providers, including those that are otherwise exempt from Title II regulation altogether. The precise question we address here, therefore, is the scope of the Commission's residual authority under Title I to regulate such non-Title II providers with respect to matters that Title II itself addresses only to providers of "telecommunications services."

On its face, Title I is unremarkable. It contains very little beyond general pronouncements about the purpose of the FCC, the scope of the Communications Act, assorted statutory definitions, and the "forbearance" provision itself. The first two provisions of Title I—sections 1 and 2 respectively of the Communications Act—establish the FCC "[f]or the purpose of regulating interstate and foreign commerce in communications by wire and radio" and recite that "[t]he provisions of this [Act] shall apply to," among other things, "all interstate and foreign communications by wire or radio."[62] And section 4(i), sometimes called the FCC's "necessary and proper" clause,[63] authorizes the Commission to "perform any and all acts, make such rules and regulations, and issue such orders, not inconsistent with this [Act], as may be necessary in the execution of its functions."[64] But it does not specify the permissible scope of those "functions."

Together, these three rather bland provisions constitute the sum total of what people are talking about when they propose regulating Internet-related services "under Title I." To say that a given communications technology—cable modem service, DSL, or higher-layer applications such as VoIP or instant messaging[65]—should be regulated under Title I is to embrace two conclusions. The first is that the service in question slips through the cracks of the substantive titles of the Communications Act (II, III, and VI), and is thus immune from the industry-specific regulations contained in those titles. The second is that the FCC has broad discretion to regulate or deregulate the service as it sees fit and (just as important) to preempt states and localities in many circumstances from regulating it on their own.

Although the provisions of Title I may seem a slender basis for substantive FCC regulatory authority, it is difficult to imagine how the FCC could function properly without such authority in an industry that, like this one, spawns new technologies and thus new regulatory issues more quickly than Congress can legislate to address them.[66] When the cable television industry arose in the 1960s, for example, the FCC promptly exercised its Title I authority to protect the local advertising revenues of the nation's over-the-air broadcasters by, for example, limiting the ability of cable operators to transmit the signals of distant television stations (see chapter 11). In its 1968 decision in *United States v. Southwestern Cable*, the Supreme Court upheld those regulations as ancillary to the Commission's undisputed responsibility to preserve the broadcasting industry, even though Congress had never formally authorized the FCC to regulate the previously non-existent cable industry.[67] Indeed, as the Court later remarked, not to give the FCC latitude in meeting such new regulatory problems "would place an intolerable regulatory burden on the Congress—one which it sought to escape by delegating administrative functions to the Commission."[68]

At the same time, the FCC lacks unbounded authority to impose under Title I whatever regulations it likes on anyone involved in the interstate or international transmission of electronic communications. Instead, the

FCC's Title I authority is confined to regulations that are "reasonably ancillary to the effective performance of,"[69] or "necessary to ensure the achievement of,"[70] the Commission's responsibilities under the other, substantive titles of the Act. The scope of such "ancillary" jurisdiction is a bit murky. Several years after its initial decision in *Southwestern Cable*, the Supreme Court upheld the Commission's adoption of more adventurous regulations for the cable industry, including a new obligation for cable operators to serve their communities by transmitting programming of their own in addition to the signals independently aired by broadcasters.[71] This time, however, the Commission prevailed only by the narrowest of margins, and Chief Justice Burger, who cast the tie-breaking vote, observed that the Commission had "strain[ed] the outer limits" of its ancillary jurisdiction.[72]

The Supreme Court finally delineated those limits when, in its 1979 decision in *FCC v. Midwest Video Corp.* ("*Midwest Video II*"),[73] it balked at the Commission's assertion of Title I jurisdiction to require cable operators to provide (among other things) public access channels on their systems. The Court based its decision on what it perceived as a tension between the Commission's jurisdictional theory and the substance of its regulations. The basic problem was that, although the Commission had predicated jurisdiction on its underlying Title III authority to regulate broadcasters in the same video programming industry, it had exercised that jurisdiction by imposing, in the form of these public access channels, the very form of common carrier regulation that the Act would prohibit if the regulated parties had been broadcasters rather than cable companies.[74] More recently, the D.C. Circuit invalidated, as an unauthorized and constitutionally problematic regulation of programming "content," the Commission's invocation of its Title I authority to require television broadcasters to include "video descriptions" in their shows—that is, aural descriptions of the show's visual content for the benefit of the visually impaired.[75] But the court limited its holding to the particular concerns presented in that case, including its desire to "avoid potential First Amendment issues" and the fact that, "[a]fter originally entertaining the possibility of providing the FCC with authority to adopt video description rules, Congress declined to do so."[76]

The upshot is that there are important limits on the Commission's Title I authority to create rules from whole cloth, but so far the courts have enforced them mostly when those rules are in tension with other legal principles codified elsewhere. The case law is still too sparse for confident predictions about which Title I regulations will survive judicial scrutiny and which will not. But the courts seem more solicitous of the FCC's efforts to use Title I as a mechanism for dealing sensibly with emerging and congressionally unanticipated technologies than for supplementing the established statutory schemes applicable to the more established communications media. *Southwestern Cable* is one case in point; another is the D.C. Circuit's 1982 decision to uphold the Commission's use of its ancillary authority in *Computer II* to regulate the provision of Title I enhanced services by Title II telecommunications carriers.[77] Ultimately, however, the "test" for a permissible exercise of the FCC's ancillary authority is a bit like Justice Stewart's test for "obscenity" under the First Amendment: one knows it only when one sees it, and all bets are off until a court actually rules.[78]

The precise dimensions of the FCC's ancillary authority will assume increasing importance as the Commission folds within the deregulatory scope of Title I the growing number of applications-layer IP products that resemble the services that have traditionally been regulated under one of the Act's substantive titles—Title II in particular. For example, whether or not (as the Ninth Circuit has held) cable modem service is ultimately deemed to contain a "telecommunications service," its transmission functionality is at least a close market substitute for the more traditional telecommunications services that are provided by telephone companies and regulated by the Commission under Title II. A reviewing court is thus likely to uphold Title I regulations reasonably designed to ensure, among other things, some degree of competitive neutrality between these two competing broadband platforms, despite their different regulatory pedigrees. Indeed, broadband platforms are, almost by definition, substitutes for all of the more conventional communications media regulated under the Communications Act because they can support any "service" of the types traditionally regulated under Titles II (voice), III (radio and television broadcasting), and VI (video).[79]

Similarly, if Congress fails to legislate a solution to the VoIP policy crisis in the near future, the FCC will likely succeed in asserting its ancillary Title I authority to regulate VoIP services as needed to ensure an orderly coexistence between them and the more traditional circuit-switched telephone services for which they are fast becoming market substitutes. This does not mean that the FCC must or even should subject VoIP providers to the full gamut of common carrier obligations under Title II, such as quality-of-service rules, entry and exit regulation, tariff filing requirements, and rate regulation. Historically speaking, the very point of placing a service within Title I has been to free it from such legacy public utility regulation; indeed, the "information service" classification is often cited as a paradigm of regulatory restraint.[80] And, beneath all the labels, insulating VoIP providers from traditional public utility regulation makes abundant sense as a policy matter. Such regulation is designed to protect consumers in monopolistic markets with formidable barriers to entry. It has no clear place in competitive markets that, like this one, have relatively low entry barriers and thus built-in consumer protections.

If the result of such "unregulation" of VoIP providers is to place their traditional telephone company rivals at a competitive disadvantage, the solution is to relax common carrier obligations on the latter as competition makes them unnecessary, not to impose such regulations on the former. So far, the FCC appears to agree with this instinct and has erred on the side of exempting emerging technologies like VoIP from unnecessary public utility regulation.[81] This inclination reflects several basic cautionary lessons. First, the FCC recalls the public choice pressures that distorted its regulation of other emerging technologies (such as cable television, discussed in chapter 11) and the axiom that "new entrants are regulated because incumbents want it that way." Second, the FCC understands that it is often easier to add regulations than to rescind them. Third, as we saw in the previous chapter, the FCC worries, often with good reason, that the costs of regulation may thwart a firm's incentives to develop new technologies. Finally, the FCC appreciates that the best guardian of consumer welfare is not a government agency, but a well-functioning market.[82]

For these reasons, most of the debates about the proper scope of the Commission's Title I authority will concern its power to impose regulatory obligations designed to serve other policy goals that are to some extent unrelated to the level of competition in a particular market. In the VoIP context, these include, among other things, susceptibility of communications to interception by law enforcement officials, various privacy safeguards, accommodation of the needs of the disabled, and consistency with universal service goals (see chapter 10). The FCC should have quite plausible arguments for imposing such rules under its residual Title I authority in cases where the rules have direct counterparts in Title II.[83] Establishing such rules for the new class of IP-related services is arguably the best way to ensure fidelity to congressional objectives in the translation from a Title

II world to a fully competitive Title I world.[84] In that respect, these rules are the very opposite of those invalidated in *Midwest Video II*, where, as noted, the FCC had invoked Title I to impose obligations that it could not impose on parties directly regulated under the corresponding substantive Title (Title III).

Even in adopting these "social policy" rules, the FCC is likely to regulate VoIP providers more flexibly than their circuit-switched rivals, and often with sound justification. Take, for example, the case of emergency access to 911 services. For technical reasons, requiring VoIP providers to facilitate access to emergency services on the exact same terms as a traditional provider—and through the same technology—would subject these upstarts to enormous burdens.[85] The FCC has thus chosen to rely on industry initiatives to address 911 challenges in the VoIP context. In all likelihood, the solutions to these challenges will follow a staged approach analogous to the path followed by cellular telephony providers, which face 911 dialing challenges of their own (see chapter 8). At present, for example, Vonage encourages its customers to register each of their locations as they travel, and it routes their 911 calls to the local public safety answering point—although often the number reached belongs to an administrative office rather than the emergency personnel who would normally answer a 911 call. Over time, however, the FCC might well add more requirements, mandating increased sophistication in 911 functionality as technology evolves and VoIP services become more popular.

VoIP services present similarly nettlesome challenges for law enforcement officials that have long relied on wiretapping voice conversations as a means of solving and preventing crimes. It is difficult enough to wiretap VoIP conversations when the VoIP providers themselves often have no idea where their customers are located. Those challenges grow exponentially when customers use software that encrypts these digitized voice conversations.

The Communications Assistance in Law Enforcement Act of 1994 (CALEA) establishes technical requirements that must be built into all telecommunications equipment in order to facilitate access to "call-identifying information," and it authorizes the FCC to prescribe the necessary implementing regulations.[86] The service providers that CALEA subjects to these obligations, however, are limited to "common carriers" and "telecommunications carriers."[87] Concerned that VoIP network architectures make effective wiretapping difficult, the FCC tentatively concluded in mid-2004 that broadband Internet access and most VoIP services should be subject to CALEA's requirements.[88] In so doing, it concluded that VoIP providers should be classified, if only for purposes of the specialized definition set forth in CALEA, as "telecommunications carriers."[89] At the same time, the FCC tentatively exempted from CALEA's scope "non-managed" VoIP applications (such as Pulver.com's peer-to-peer service) and instant messaging "chat" applications. A broad coalition of Internet interests opposed extending CALEA's requirements to such applications, raising concerns about their effect on the Internet's development and whether they could be enforced effectively in any event. As of this writing, it is difficult to tell how the FCC will respond to these competing concerns, whether the courts will allow it to classify a given VoIP service as an "information service" under the Communications Act and as a "telecommunications service" under CALEA, and whether additional legislation might be needed to balance the needs of law enforcement against the traditionally unregulated character of Internet services.

* * *

As of this writing, we remain in the earliest stages of the VoIP revolution. Only 27% of Internet users, and just 17% of all Americans, had even heard of VoIP technology by mid-2004, and only a tiny fraction contemplated signing up for a VoIP service.[90] Before long, however, this obscure technology will transform the telecommunications industry.

The same could have been said of wireless telephony 20 years ago. Today, placing a call on one's cellphone is so routine that we forget how much the wireless revolution has enhanced our lives, now that we can speak to someone whenever we wish without first driving home or waiting in line to use a public phone booth. That revolution in personal communications habits has been accompanied by an equally significant revolution in the way the federal government manages rights to use the radio spectrum. That revolution, which remains a work in progress, is the subject of the next two chapters.

7

The Spectrum

In addressing the physical layer of telecommunications, this book has focused so far on the electronic delivery of information through wires and cables, whether copper, coaxial, or fiber optic. But wires and cables are only part of the telecommunications story, as anyone with a cellphone or a wireless-enabled laptop computer—or, for that matter, a radio—can attest. And this brings us to the wireless side of the industry.

If this book had been written in 1980, our discussion of the "airwaves" would have focused almost entirely on the regulation of radio and television broadcasting because that was the most significant commercial use to which the electromagnetic spectrum was then put. Engrained tradition had made it seem natural that telephone service involved running wires into people's homes and that television signals should be transmitted through the air (except in less populous areas, where cable companies had stepped in to compensate for the dearth of nearby transmission towers). But, as we now know, technological change has up-ended this tradition. Many Americans rely more heavily on their wireless telephones than on their wired ones, and, as of 2003, fewer than 15% of households with televisions rely on terrestrial "over-the-air" broadcasting to receive their TV signals.*

---

* The FCC recently reported that, as of mid-2003, the percentage of U.S. television households subscribing to a "multichannel video programming distributor" (MVPD), such as a cable TV company or direct-to-home satellite provider, was just over 85%, falling slightly from the previous year's level of around 86.5%. *See* Tenth Annual Report, *Annual Assessment of the Status of Competition in the Market for the Delivery of Video Programming*, 19 FCC Rcd 1606, ¶ 7 (2004). The FCC found that approximately three-quarters of the households subscribing to a MVPD receive

This transformation in the means of delivering television and telephone services is one more illustration of convergence—i.e., the use of different technologies to provide similar services. In this case, moreover, the technologies used to provide these different services are not merely converging, but trading places to some extent. Because it is more feasible and useful to carry a telephone around than a television, and because the airwaves permit mobility whereas wires do not, the airwaves are in some respects a more natural medium than wires for telephony. And, as the prevalence of cable television has shown, wires provide greater bandwidth than the available airwaves for pumping high quality video programming into people's homes. This swapping of transmission media is often called the "Negroponte switch," a term named after MIT Media Lab founder Nicholas Negroponte and popularized by industry analyst George Gilder.[1] As in other contexts, however, technology changes much more quickly than regulation, so the policy response to this new reality is still very much a work in progress.

In this chapter, we address the question of "spectrum" at the highest policy levels, focusing on how, and how much, the government should get involved in apportioning the airwaves among different uses and users. We explain the technological and market forces pressing for reform of traditional spectrum regulation, the initial steps in that direction, and the reasons why fundamental regulatory change may be slow in coming. Those reasons, as we shall see, include a manifestation of the "public choice" theory discussed in chapter 1. In particular, today's spectrum incumbents—including broadcasters and the government itself—use their political clout to stifle competition by keeping a firm chokehold on large swaths of spectrum that could be put to more efficient uses, including by cellular telephone providers. In chapter 8, we turn to the competitive structure and regulatory oversight of such providers.

TV signals from a franchised cable company; most other such households receive those signals from satellite television companies. *Id.*, ¶ 6. Although the precise numbers are subject to debate, there is little doubt that only a small minority of viewers now receive their television signals from traditional "over-the-air" broadcasts.

I. Revolution in the Air

While other children were outside playing baseball, one of us spent the better part of his after-school hours in early 1978 breathing in the fumes of burnt solder while assembling, transistor by transistor, a shortwave radio from a build-it-yourself kit. After two or three months, the radio seemed complete, and a visit to the local hardware store produced enough copper wire to string a crude antenna from the side of the house to a tree in the yard. Finally, the radio was turned on: silence. A return visit to the grownups at the hardware store revealed that sloppy soldering had shorted out one of the main circuits, an embarrassing but fixable problem. The radio returned home several days later, and, the circuit having been repaired (at a cost of some $100), the sounds of several dozen countries came bursting into the room. It seemed vaguely occult, this discovery that radio signals are continuously flitting through our backyards like a swarm of bats in the night, unknown to us until we reach out to capture them with a copper wire, a properly soldered circuit board, and (at the end of the circuit) a speaker.

For many years, scientists believed that electromagnetic waves flowed through the "ether"—a hypothetical substance said to reside invisibly throughout space. In the late nineteenth century, Albert Michelson and Edward Morley conducted experiments that led them and others to abandon the "ether" construct, though the term lives on in colloquial usage. The modern concept of the radio spectrum, informed by a series of scientific advances in the late nineteenth and early twentieth century, was soon born. When asked to explain the underlying physical mechanics of the wireless spectrum—i.e., how electric and magnetic fields travel in waves that can be sent from point A and received at point B—Albert Einstein is reported to have remarked: "You see, wire telegraph is a kind of very, very long cat. You pull his tail in New York and his head is meowing in Los Angeles. Do you understand this? And radio operates exactly the same way: you send signals here, they receive them there. The only difference is that *there is no cat.*"[2] There are several critical points to be gleaned from this enigmatic remark.

As Einstein's metaphor suggests, wired and wireless communications have more in common than many people realize. In both cases, the waves that carry information are electromagnetic signals riding on discrete frequencies. To oversimplify matters a bit, traditional wireless communications involve three basic steps. At the transmitting end, a *carrier signal* with a given frequency—represented graphically as a simple sine curve—is "modulated" by the information to be transmitted, such as a text message or a song.* Second, an antenna launches this modulated signal into open space, where it eventually reaches the recipient's antenna. This antenna feeds into a receiver which, when properly tuned, is designed to accept signals at the specified frequency and to disregard the rest. Finally, the receiver decodes the information by retrieving it from the carrier signal in a process called "demodulation." Thus, when you tune your radio or television to a particular station, you are directing the receiver to translate, into sounds or images, one frequency range of electromagnetic signals to the exclusion of all others.

The signals flowing over wires and cables are manipulated in much the same way as radio signals transmitted through the airwaves. An ADSL line (see chapter 4) is simply a copper wire divided into frequency ranges, some of which are used for voice transmissions and others for data. Coaxial television cables are themselves divided into dozens or hundreds of "channels," each spanning a slice of frequency six megahertz wide. Some of these channels correspond to individual television channels and others to cable modem bitstreams. And a strand of optical fiber is, as Thomas Hazlett put it, "spectrum in a tube."[3] As we explained in chapter 2, the capacity of fiber-optic cables expanded dramatically in the 1990s as engineers found ways to transmit different signals simultaneously over a single strand by means of different "colors" (light frequencies). In this respect, wires and cables are very much like the airwaves: telecommunications engineers can

---

* The "frequency" of an electromagnetic signal is measured by its number of "cycles" per second—i.e., the number of times it moves from crest to trough back to crest during the course of a second. A signal's frequency is inversely proportional to its "wavelength": the distance from crest to crest or from trough to trough. Thus, a "microwave" has a much higher frequency than a conventional AM (or FM) radio signal, with its much longer waves. Specific frequency bands are identified by their "hertz," or cycles per second, named in honor of the nineteenth century physicist Heinrich Hertz. A "kilohertz" (kHz) is a frequency of a thousand cycles per second, a "megahertz" (MHz) is a million cycles per second, and a "gigahertz" (GHz) is a billion cycles per second.

exploit the division of electromagnetic signals into frequencies to expand the information-carrying capacity of any medium, including empty space itself.

Despite these similarities, the absence of Einstein's "cat"—of a tangible transmission medium like a wire or cable—carries important consequences for telecommunications policy. We know who owns a wire or cable and, at least as a legal matter, that firm or person generally has the right to control how it is used. In contrast, there is no obvious "owner" of the airwaves. Also, a wire or cable is usually wrapped in shielding material and is thus reasonably well protected from interference by external signals. Not so with the airwaves: there is no natural "shielding" in the air that can keep two signals from interfering with each other if they use the same frequency in the same place at the same time. The result of such interference is that ordinary receivers cannot decode the separate information carried by each signal. And, in a world dominated by ordinary receivers, this portion of the spectrum is "wasted."

The twin peculiarities of over-the-air transmissions—an absence of obvious property rights in the medium and the prevalent threat of interference—are at the root of today's spectrum policy. As this chapter explains, the federal government has heavily regulated who may transmit signals over the air and has rigidly prescribed the services that may be provided over defined frequency bands. Since the 1920s, the government has justified such regulation on the grounds that the "airwaves," like the Grand Canyon, are a "public resource" belonging to the whole American polity; that this resource would be quickly exhausted by the unregulated demand for it; and that unpoliced private use of this resource would lead to its despoliation through widespread interference. Taken together, the government's rationales for regulating the spectrum coalesce around the assumption that it is "scarce"—that there is less of it than an unregulated public could use without causing serious interference problems. The Supreme Court first embraced this rationale in 1944 when it denied First Amendment and other challenges to the FCC's authority to regulate access to the spectrum. In so doing, it concluded not just that the FCC can serve as the traffic cop of the airwaves, but that it can "determin[e] the composition of th[e] traffic" permitted on particular slices of the spectrum.[4]

Without the scarcity rationale, the government's justification for playing its traditional spectrum-management role would largely evaporate.

Consider your household cordless phone or garage door opener, each of which is a transmitter of electromagnetic signals. In part because they emit so little energy, such devices pose little threat of interfering with whatever uses your neighbors might be making of the spectrum. You would therefore probably object if the government proposed to make you pay for the "right" to use these off-the-shelf devices to perform the routine functions of talking on the phone or opening your garage door. After all, you already paid a sales tax at the store—why another tax on top of that?

Now imagine that the entire electromagnetic spectrum were so inexhaustibly vast that anyone could easily use any device—including a 100,000 watt radio transmitter—to transmit information of any kind, for any purpose, without worrying about interfering with anybody else's use of the spectrum. In *that* world, for the same reason that the government could not justify charging a 50-cent fee in *this* world every time someone uses a remote device to open a garage door, the government would be hard-pressed to justify charging for any use of the spectrum. And the government would likewise find it difficult to justify "licensing" portions of spectrum to designated parties to the exclusion of everyone else. Indeed, just as the First Amendment bars the government from limiting who can own a printing press, it might well bar the government from restricting access to the airwaves as a medium of communication in the hypothesized world of super-abundant spectrum.[5]

Of course, this hypothesized world is not our world, at least not yet. The range of frequencies usable for particular telecommunications services is large but finite. And the spectrum within that range *is* arguably scarce in the sense that, if the government just opened it up for a free-for-all tomorrow morning with no transition, significant interference problems would likely impair people's ability to decode the signals sent by radio stations, cellular telephone providers, and ambulance dispatchers.

Under traditional spectrum regulation, however, it is the mere *possibility* of interference, not the reality of it, that governs when, where, and what devices can be used. Therein lies the problem. Today, the interference concerns that underlie traditional government control of the airwaves are increasingly detached from engineering realities. This disconnect is largely the result of advances in microchip technology. By building microprocessing capacity into receivers, the emerging "smart" wireless technologies can isolate the signals one *does* wish to receive from all the other signals in the same frequency range one does *not* wish to receive. We discuss such technologies in more detail below. The important point to appreciate for now is that current spectrum policy largely ignores the potential of such technologies to avoid interference without government oversight. And, more generally, current policy often errs too much on the side of constraining efficient private uses of spectrum in the name of stamping out the remotest possibility of interference.

There is a broad consensus that the government's traditional command-and-control licensing regime, which we describe in the first half of this chapter, should give way to a nimbler and more decentralized approach to spectrum management. At the highest level of generality, there are two basic proposals for such an approach, which are known by the catch-phrases *property rights* and *commons*. Under the former approach, which Congress and the FCC have only partially embraced over the past dozen years, the government would assign alienable property rights in different portions of the spectrum to private parties and then allow those rights to be freely bought and sold in a secondary market, much as real property is bought and sold today. Under the latter approach, the government would establish much of the spectrum as a public "commons" and rely on different users to avoid interference problems cooperatively by means of "smart" wireless technology, with the FCC (or some other institution) playing the role of traffic cop to ensure that users actually cooperate. We discuss each of these two approaches, as well as proposed middle-ground alternatives, in the second half of this chapter.

II. The Basics of Traditional Spectrum Regulation

When Guglielmo Marconi first made use of the airwaves to transmit information in the 1890s, he envisioned the primary use of spectrum as ship-to-shore communications. During the ensuing 50 years, wireless technology produced the telegraph-like services that Marconi developed, amateur ("ham") radio, and radio broadcasting, which was born in the early twentieth century and gained widespread popularity by the early 1920s. The amateur operators back then, however, included what we might call "hackers" today. Their numbers included some whom, in 1910, the United States Navy called "[m]ischevious and irresponsible" in that they took "great delight in impersonating other stations and in sending out false calls."[6]

Whatever the extent of this practice or the merits of the Navy's call for tighter control of "amateurs," the era of spectrum non-regulation in this country ended in the wake of the Titanic disaster in 1912, when "chaos in the spectrum" was said to have confused a potential rescue ship "so it missed the calls of help from the sinking luxury liner."[7] The result was the Radio Act of 1912, which authorized the Secretary of Commerce to license users of equipment that communicated via the spectrum.

Secretary of Commerce Herbert Hoover used his administrative authority under the Act to preclude interference by restricting access to the spectrum. But when the courts balked at Hoover's assertion of authority to regulate use of the airwaves on the basis of a license applicant's merits, Congress responded with the Radio Act of 1927, which established a Federal Radio Commission and gave it broad jurisdiction to regulate access to the spectrum under a general "public interest" standard.[8] The Act further established the regulatory premise that persists to this day: that the spectrum belongs to the public and that, at least as a formal matter, licensees have no property right to continue using it.[9] When it passed the Communications Act of 1934, Congress kept this model of regulation intact but transferred the functions of the Federal Radio Commission to the newly established Federal Communications Commission.

The resulting model of regulation generally involves careful administrative oversight of the spectrum to avoid "harmful interference" between competing uses and users. "Harmful interference," as defined by the FCC, is "unwanted energy" that "endangers the functioning of a radionavigation service or of other safety services or seriously degrades, obstructs, or repeatedly interrupts a radiocommunication service operating in accordance with [international] Radio Regulations."[10] But the federal government has carried its regulation of the airwaves much farther than needed simply to police against interference. The government has seized upon spectrum "scarcity" as a basis for asserting a comprehensive stewardship of the airwaves, exercising broad authority to determine how particular bands of spectrum shall be used (such as for television or FM radio or cellular telephony) and precisely who may use them and subject to what restrictions. Here we will focus on the two most critical aspects of the FCC's traditional spectrum management regime: "allocation" of particular spectrum bands for prescribed uses and "assignment" of spectrum within those bands to particular licensees.

A. Allocation

The FCC "allocates" the spectrum by dividing it up into different frequency bands and specifying the uses to which the frequencies within each band may be used. Under the FCC's "band plan," the Commission "zones" spectrum by, for example, reserving the spectrum between 300 and 535 kilohertz (kHz) for aeronautical and maritime communications and the spectrum between 535 and 1605 kHz for AM radio. This allocation function parallels how a zoning authority decides that some land should be designated for residential uses, other land for commercial uses, and so forth. Overall, the FCC has divided the spectrum into scores of different uses, each of which is associated with a particular band (or bands). The current allocation of spectrum is displayed in a full-color chart at www.ntia.doc.gov/osmhome/allochrt.pdf.

Significantly, not all segments of the spectrum can be used for the same purposes, for the physical characteristics of signal propagation vary with the frequency. A high frequency "microwave" signal, for example, behaves in some respects like visible light: it can carry information successfully only if there is a "line of sight" path between the sender and the receiver. In contrast, signals at the lower frequencies (i.e., the ones with longer wavelengths) can pass more easily through walls or trees, and they are not subject to "rain fade." This is one reason why the spectrum reserved for television broadcasters is described as "beachfront property." The spectrum the FCC entitles them to occupy—much of the expanse between 470 and 800 MHz—is not only immense in *quantity*, but also nearly incomparable in *quality*, at least for the most lucrative commercial applications.

The FCC's allocation decisions are complicated by a key institutional consideration: the Commission is authorized to regulate access to the spectrum only for private uses and for state and local governmental uses. Under a presidential delegation of authority, it is the job of the National Telecommunications and Information Administration (NTIA), a subagency of the Commerce Department, to allocate spectrum for use by the federal government, including the military. This is no small point, as the federal government controls outright nearly 14% of all allocated spectrum bands and shares 56% of all bands with other users.[11] This arrangement thus requires the FCC to coordinate with NTIA when re-allocating spectrum initially allocated to the federal government. To make matters even more complicated, both the FCC and NTIA must confer with the State Department to develop a unified position for the United States to present at the International Telecommunications Union (ITU), an arm of the United Nations.[12] At regularly scheduled World Radio Conferences, the ITU develops international spectrum policy on such issues as the reservation of certain frequencies for broad categories of usage around the world. Because the ITU's decisions have the force of binding treaty obligations, the FCC must accommodate them in developing domestic spectrum allocation policies.

Within the United States, the division of authority between the FCC and NTIA in managing spectrum allocation complicates prospects for comprehensive reform of spectrum policy. NTIA currently lacks adequate tools to prod federal agencies to use spectrum more efficiently—and, even if it had such tools, it would lack the resources to conduct careful audits of the more than 270,000 frequency assignments to federal agencies. For their part, those agencies have no particular incentive to abdicate to others whatever portions of their assigned spectrum they do not need. It is thus quite likely that many of the assigned frequencies are barely used and that others are used inefficiently.[13] If federal agencies were required, for example, to pay even a nominal spectrum usage fee, they might evaluate their spectrum needs more carefully. The absence of any such measures to induce efficient spectrum usage has led the General Accounting Office to recommend that the federal government charter a commission like the one used to decide what military bases should be closed after the end of the Cold War.[14] Moreover, a presidential task force commissioned in June 2003 has also developed a series of recommendations for how the federal government can use its spectrum more efficiently.[15] So far, however, suggested reform measures are longer on gestures than results, and federal agencies, like other incumbents, are growing increasingly adept at exempting their spectrum from re-allocation to other uses.

After allocating the spectrum into bands, the FCC sometimes moves further to determine how much spectrum to *allot* to particular licensees within a given band (if use of the spectrum in that band is subject to licensing). If, for example, the FCC allocates the spectrum between 535 and 1605 kHz for AM radio, it must decide how to allot individual licenses within that overall allocation (e.g., in blocks of 10 kHz), and it must likewise decide how wide of a "guard band" of unused frequency to interpose between different stations within the same geographic area to avoid mutual interference. These licenses are generally saddled with additional restrictions that vary from band to band, such as duration of the license, limits on transferability, maximum power levels, requirements to adhere to certain technical standards, and build-out obligations. Like so much of spectrum policy generally, some of these "service rules" seek to limit interference between users.

The amount of spectrum allotted to a given licensee is a function of whatever *bandwidth* the FCC concludes is needed for the service in question. All else held constant, the greater the frequency range over which signals are transmitted, the more information they can carry—and thus the higher in quality will be the radio signal, television picture, or cellular telephone call. In the traditional world populated by "dumb" receivers—i.e., those without advanced microchips—policymakers have assumed that the only feasible way to increase bandwidth is to enlarge the allotment of contiguous spectrum a given licensee is entitled to occupy. Only recently, as we discuss at the end of the chapter, has the FCC begun to recognize that the development of "smart" wireless technologies is making that assumption somewhat obsolescent. Accordingly, an increasing number of spectrum allocations are not subdivided into allotments at all.

B. Assignment

For the most commercially important uses of the spectrum—television, radio, and cellular telephony—the FCC follows up its allocation and allotment decisions with exclusive *assignments* of spectrum to particular licensees. We should make clear at the outset that not all spectrum is divvied up this way. In some cases, the FCC does not assign licenses to any exclusive user, but allows any qualified user to obtain a license, as with the spectrum reserved for amateur radio operators. In other cases, as with the spectrum designated for "citizens' band" ("CB") radio, the public may use the spectrum without even obtaining a license (as it is "licensed by rule"). And in its so-called "Part 15" rules, discussed later in this chapter, the FCC allows such wireless devices as garage door openers and remote controls to operate in unlicensed bands of spectrum, or even in bands of licensed spectrum, provided they do so at low power levels.

For now, however, we focus on the FCC's traditional regime for licensing the bulk of prime spectrum for the exclusive use of designated private parties. For most of its history, the FCC relied on "comparative hearings" for this purpose: drawn-out affairs designed to evaluate the relative worthiness of rival applicants for a free spectrum license. In theory, this procedure discharged the FCC's statutory obligation to serve the "public interest" by assigning the use of the airwaves to the "most qualified" users. In practice, however, it tended to favor entrenched incumbents and those with political ties. In one noteworthy example, the FCC awarded radio and television broadcasting licenses to then-Congressman (and later President) Johnson's wife.[16] And, in another widely re-told finding, not a single newspaper that endorsed Adlai Stevenson over Eisenhower in the 1952 presidential election received a TV license in a contested proceeding.[17]

Even apart from the appearance of favoritism to political insiders, the comparative hearing process was inevitably expensive and time-consuming. Unless only one application was filed for an available license, the FCC had to hold a "beauty contest," and the loser was entitled to appeal.[18] Because there was no procedure for resolving a "tie" between the two applicants, and because the stakes involved were huge, such litigation invariably prolonged and complicated the assignment process. The FCC nonetheless used comparative hearings until the 1980s as its exclusive method of assigning licenses for any commercial use of the spectrum. The FCC had little choice in the matter: the Communications Act of 1934 guaranteed license applicants a right to a hearing and did not provide an alternative assignment mechanism.

The pressure to devise new models for assigning spectrum licenses ultimately grew, particularly when, after many years of delay, the FCC finally allocated blocks of spectrum for cellular telephony in the 1970s and assigned them to specific providers in the early 1980s.[19] The FCC recognized that comparative hearings, originally designed to judge which of several applicants would air television or radio programming in the "public interest," were poorly tailored for determining who should provide common carrier telephone service. And, more generally, such hearings had fallen into well-deserved disrepute for the costs, delays, and arbitrariness they inevitably imposed on the process.

In 1984, Congress first authorized lotteries as a replacement for comparative hearings for cellular telephone licenses.[20] As the name implies, a "lottery" is a mechanism for assigning licenses among competing applicants for free and, to a large extent, randomly. Within a few years, however, it became clear that lotteries were not quite the solution that either Congress or the FCC was looking for. First, the prospect of obtaining a free but commercially valuable license generated so many applications—hundreds of thousands of them—that they caused the partial collapse of the FCC facility used to contain them.[21] And, because the FCC prescreened these applicants to ensure that they met the minimum qualifications for operating a cellular telephone business, the process turned out to be burdensome for the FCC to administer and costly for the parties involved.

But lotteries suffered from an even greater shortcoming, more political than economic. Those who "won" the lottery were under no obligation to keep the licenses themselves; they were generally able to sell them to others on the secondary market so long as the buyers honored all of the initial license restrictions and thus agreed to use the relevant spectrum bands only for their allocated use—cellular telephony. Thus, although the ultimate users of the spectrum often paid enormous sums for the right to do so, they paid those sums to the randomly selected private individuals who had won the lotteries rather than to the public treasury. For both fairness and public finance reasons, this struck both Congress and the FCC as wrong. Finally, the front end delays attributed to the lottery process may well have deprived consumers of prompt access to valued wireless services.

In the early 1990s, to cut down on such delays and raise revenue in the process, Congress authorized government-sponsored spectrum auctions for various types of licenses, including cellular telephony licenses.[22] To design its auction process, the FCC consulted the branch of mathematics and economics devoted to game theory and its close cousin, auction theory. In some respects, the proto-architect of the FCC's auction process was the now-famous Nobel Laureate John Nash, who developed many of the applicable principles of game theory several years before he was overcome by paranoid schizophrenia. Indeed, Sylvia Nasar devotes several pages of *A Beautiful Mind,* her biography of Nash, to the FCC's auction process in the 1990s and credits him with its apparent success.[23] But the branch of game theory invented by Nash did not definitively resolve such basic questions as whether all goods should be auctioned at once, whether bids should be sealed, and how collusion between firms can best be prevented.[24] The answers to such questions would determine whether the FCC's auctions would succeed—both in terms of generating prodigious sums for the public fisc and in terms of assigning licenses to firms that would make the best use of them for the public benefit.

In conducting its first set of auctions in 1994, the FCC sold the right to use large "blocks" of spectrum in one fell swoop. This approach ensured that a bidder putting together mutually dependent spectrum assets—say, licenses in a tri-state area like New York, New Jersey, and Connecticut— could decide whether to buy any of the relevant spectrum licenses at once. The FCC also modified the traditional English bidding model used at art auctions, in which potential buyers openly bid against one another. The Commission decided instead to announce the high bid after each round, but otherwise to keep the terms of the bids closed. In so doing, the FCC sought to limit the use of inefficient strategic behavior such as retaliation or collusion. The FCC further adopted a set of anti-collusion rules that, among other things, limited communications among competing bidders.

Juxtaposed against the comparative hearing tradition, at least, the FCC's use of auctions has been a reasonably effective means of assigning spectrum licenses to those best able to put them to productive use. From 1993 to 1997 alone, the FCC granted 4,300 licenses via auction, for which the winners bid a total of $23 billion (not all of which was ultimately collected, as noted below). Happy with the results, and particularly with the new revenues, Congress required auctions for most types of initial spectrum licenses in section 309(j) of the Communications Act.[25] Notable exceptions to the auction requirement include public safety agencies and incumbent television broadcasters, whom Congress granted free licenses to operate in new spectrum allocated for digital television (see chapter 12). Also, even where applicable, the auction requirement extends only to the assignment of *initial* licenses, not to applications for renewals or modification (such as those filed by the original cellular licensees who obtained their licenses via comparative hearings or lottery).

Auctions are no panacea, however. Much like technology stocks over the past decade, slices of spectrum are subject to wild swings in market valuation. In Europe, speculative zeal and a poor auction design helped push up the bids for broadband spectrum rights so high in 2000 that the process eventually bankrupted some of the auction winners and sent the European wireless industry into a tailspin.[26]

Similar problems have beset the U.S. auction experience as well. One notable example is the NextWave debacle, which illustrates the precarious relationship between telecommunications policy and U.S. bankruptcy law.

In auctions reserved for small businesses, the FCC allowed the winners to pay off the bids for their licensees in a series of installments. But several successful bidders—including NextWave Communications (which bid approximately $4.74 billion for its licenses)—had trouble financing the build-out of their networks and petitioned the FCC to restructure their payments. Invoking the need to protect the integrity of the auction process, the FCC refused to defer these payment obligations. When NextWave declared bankruptcy and defaulted on those obligations, the FCC moved to take back its licenses. After several years of litigation, during which this portion of the spectrum went unused, the Supreme Court finally ruled in 2003 that the FCC had to stand in line like any other creditor; it could not simply reach into NextWave's estate, pluck out the company's greatest assets (its spectrum licenses), and sell them to someone else.[27] This ruling, while reflecting established bankruptcy law principles, complicated the task of designing auctions to convey spectrum licenses quickly into the hands of the firms that will actually use them to provide valuable services to the public.

III. Beyond Command-and-Control

Although auctions are a more market-oriented mechanism for assigning licenses than comparative hearings, the FCC's spectrum management regime remains an exemplar of "command and control" regulation. The government continues to allocate spectrum into bands, prescribe the services for which most of these bands may be used, and supervise the process of assigning exclusive usage rights to particular licensees. The result, as discussed at the beginning of the chapter, is under-utilized spectrum, business plans restricted by excessive regulatory control, and depressed incentives to innovate. As FCC Chairman Michael Powell put it in 2002, innovation in wireless technologies is "inhibited by the 'mother may I' phenomenon—businesses must go to the FCC for permission before they can modify their spectrum plans to respond to consumer demand."[28]

Among neutral observers, there is little dispute that, for these reasons, the current spectrum regime requires a comprehensive overhaul. In recent years, commentators have offered two different visions for reform: a "property rights" model, which would treat the spectrum much as the government now treats private land, and a "commons" model, which would treat the spectrum much as the government now treats a city park. Yet these reform models are not necessarily mutually exclusive. At least over the long term, the FCC is likely to pursue each to some degree, as we discuss below.

The effort to reform spectrum policy in either of these directions, however, must confront the lobbying prowess of the entrenched spectrum-holders. In the public sector, these include the military, whose historic claim to prodigious swaths of spectrum for national defense has become even more difficult to challenge after September 11, 2001. In the private sector, there are few political forces more potent on Capitol Hill—and at the FCC, which must answer to Capitol Hill—than the local broadcasters' lobby, whose news coverage can make or break political careers.

To appreciate the political clout of the incumbent broadcasters, one need only examine the FCC's star-crossed "low power FM" initiative (although there are numerous other examples as well). In 1999, then-FCC Chairman William Kennard embraced what, in the larger scheme of things, seemed a fairly modest initiative: granting new licenses to "low power" stations for the right to broadcast locally in the unused interstices ("guard bands") between existing FM radio stations.[29] This step, he hoped, would give rise to a proliferation of stations devoted to community programming. And the costs would be minimal: the FCC's engineers had determined that, because of stringent caps on the transmission power of these "microradio" stations, their broadcasts would not interfere with existing FM stations to an unacceptable degree.

"Interference," however, is an elusive concept. For the incumbent broadcasters, interference poses an unacceptable risk to a conventional station if, because of a low power transmission, a single listener cannot hear a broadcast that she could otherwise hear—even if scores of other listeners would enjoy listening to the low power transmission. Also, in judging whether that single listener faces any interference, the broadcasters presume that she owns the lowest quality receiver on the market, which is unusually incapable of distinguishing signals in one frequency from those in adjacent frequencies. The broadcasters further assume that she is also incapable of moving slightly or reorienting her radio in order to minimize interference that can be corrected rather easily. In short, by focusing on the interests of this lone, immobile listener with a low quality radio, an incumbent broadcaster can almost always play the interference card to oppose the entry of potential rivals seeking to use adjacent spectrum.

The National Association of Broadcasters played this card to quash the low power radio initiative, circulating on Capitol Hill a compact disc purporting to replicate the type of interference that low power transmissions would cause to neighboring broadcasts on the FM dial. The *New York Times* reported: "Although government engineers say the [simulation] is downright fraudulent and cannot be replicated at the [FCC's] radio lab, the compact disk has had a substantial impact on the debate in Congress and has repeatedly been cited by lawmakers as evidence of the need to block the low-power radio program."[30]

This battle for the hearts and minds of Congress was not a fair fight. Members of Congress fear local broadcasters—who regularly endorse candidates and are often pillars of the community—more than virtually any other lobbying force, and there was no political constituency of comparable significance on the other side of this debate. When Kennard moved forward with his initiative despite the broadcasters' fervent opposition, Congress responded with an alacrity rarely seen on Capitol Hill. Billy Tauzin, who chaired the House Telecommunications Subcommittee, exclaimed that the FCC "is an agency out of control that demands congressional action to straighten it out."[31] And he demanded a criminal investigation of FCC staffers who had sent talking points in favor of low power FM to their congressional counterparts, supposedly in violation of obscure restrictions on "lobbying" activities by federal employees.[32] Ultimately, underscoring the broadcasters' influence, Congress overrode the FCC's initiative through legislation that radically reduced the number of low power stations that could be licensed on the FM band.[33]

There is some small hope for a happy ending to this story. In 2004, Senators McCain and Leahy proposed a bill that would repeal Congress's previous override of Kennard's initiative on the strength of an independent engineering study that, in the bill's words, revealed the broadcasters' interference arguments to be "unsubstantiated."[34] The proposed legislation would further find that the multi-year delay in licensing low power FM stations "prevented millions of Americans from having a locally operated, community based radio station in their neighborhood."[35]

The introduction of the McCain-Leahy bill is an important first step in righting the wrong of four years before, although such politically sensitive legislation stood little chance of enactment in an election year and will remain controversial thereafter. For as long as the government has regulated access to the airwaves, spectrum incumbents have invoked "interference" concerns as a rallying cry against new entry, and unassailable engineering conclusions rarely end the debate. The only real surprise, as Lawrence Lessig observes, "is how blatantly this protectionism continues."[36] For our purposes, the low power FM story serves as a sobering reminder of the political moat that lies between today's command-and-control regime and the more efficient theoretical alternatives we are about to discuss.

A. Property rights

Nobel Laureate Ronald Coase observed in 1959 that the FCC's traditional model of regulation unnecessarily limited the possible uses of the airwaves and that the free market offered a more logical system of allocating the spectrum and assigning licenses to use it.[37] As Coase explained, the FCC's traditional rationale—"scarcity" and the ever-present threat of interference—could not by itself justify adherence to a command-and-control regime. After all, most other valuable resources (such as land, metal, etc.) are "scarce" in some sense, and the government nonetheless relies on the free market to regulate their use.[38] Similarly, while the stories of "chaos" among early users of the airwaves may support an argument for *defining* property rights clearly and providing for their effective enforcement, they do not justify perpetuating the government's micro-management of the spectrum's possible uses.

In practice, a property rights model would function in much the same way as the law governing private transactions for the purchase and sale of land. Spectrum owners—acting as "band managers"—would freely sell or lease patches of spectrum in a robustly competitive secondary market. The role of the government would be to define the relevant property rights and enforce contractual agreements. It would *not* be to allocate spectrum for particular uses on "public interest" grounds. For example, a television station could sell or lease its spectrum license to a wireless telephone company, and regulators would play no role in second-guessing whether the public is better served by having one more wireless company and one fewer broadcast television station.

Coase's advocacy for a private property-like regime of spectrum management rested on his more general proposition—now known as the *Coase theorem*—that, with well-defined property rights, the free market will generally allocate resources to their most efficient use so long as transaction costs are low. For example, a firm using assigned spectrum for its own internal communications would be free to sell its licenses to a wireless telephone carrier and purchase capacity on a fiber-optic network instead. In this example, the spectrum would be more valuable to the buyer than the seller, both parties would be better off if they made the trade, and so would the wireless carrier's many subscribers. Coase criticized the FCC's command-and-control model of regulation for precluding just this type of efficient market-based outcome, except perhaps after a time-consuming and costly FCC inquiry into its economic merits.

The Easter Bunny wins the Preakness

In the 45 years since Coase's critique, parties have entered into all sorts of private transactions even under the current regime, but these transactions bear only a distant resemblance to those that would be permitted under a genuine property rights model. With FCC approval, one company may purchase another company along with the spectrum licenses that it holds, but the buyer generally must continue to use the spectrum to provide the same service specified in the license. That model thus "locks in" existing uses of spectrum either by precluding efficient transactions altogether or by reducing their likelihood by interposing substantial transaction costs in the form of bureaucratic hurdles. The command-and-control model thus forecloses alternative, and more socially valuable, uses of spectrum that would be available under a market-based system.

The traditional system of spectrum management principally benefits the incumbent license-holders, who typically favor regulatory barriers to the entry of others into the markets they dominate. Indeed, Thomas Hazlett suggests that the origins of the command-and-control regime lie largely in a desire to protect incumbents, and he has catalogued the government's long and troubling history of enabling those incumbents to keep competition at bay through various pretexts dressed up as "public interest" concerns.[39] Of course, the FCC does not view its congressionally assigned role in this pejorative light; instead, it has traditionally subscribed to the "wise man theory of regulation," under which it is deemed "capable of deciding what [uses of spectrum are] best for the public."[40] These separate but complementary interests of incumbents and regulators helped confine Coase's views to the classroom for many years. Indeed, almost twenty years after the publication of his article, two Commissioners colorfully remarked that the odds of using auctions or some other market-based system for assigning spectrum licenses were "about the same as those on the Easter Bunny in the Preakness."[41]

In the late 1980s and early 1990s, the FCC finally took a few steps in a market-based direction, but more by happenstance than by design. In one instructive story, Morgan O'Brien, the founder of the wireless company now known as Nextel, parlayed his nine years experience as an FCC lawyer into creating a competitor to the existing cellular providers. O'Brien's insight was that the spectrum allocated to "specialized mobile radio," a wireless dispatch service for taxis and other service vehicles, could just as easily be used for cellular telephone service. The main difference between the licenses for these two services was that the dispatch licenses came with various restrictions designed to keep them from becoming a source of competition for cellular telephone providers. Those restrictions, as Hazlett recounts, produced an enormous discrepancy in the value of the two types of licenses in the secondary market: "the same amount of spectrum sold for just $100,000 with a dispatch license and $2 million with a cellular license."[42]

For O'Brien, the discrepancy in cost between the two licenses presented a striking arbitrage opportunity. He acquired dispatch licenses and—knowing from his FCC experience that "he could not succeed in a straight-up rule making to re-allocate SMR bands to cellular"—devised a "below-the-radar-screen approach" that sought various waivers from the FCC's restrictions on those licenses, emphasizing the need to "upgrade dispatch service, not compete with cellular."[43] After much time and effort, he eventually succeeded in freeing up this spectrum for the wireless telephony services that would create the greatest consumer value (although the regulatory controversies associated with Nextel's spectrum strategy resurfaced in the early 2000's, as discussed below). While this first chapter in Nextel's founding has a happy ending,[44] the convoluted path that O'Brien had to take, and the fact that this regulatory discrepancy existed in the first place, underscore the gross inefficiencies of the government's traditional spectrum policy.[45]

Over the past decade or so, the FCC has taken somewhat more deliberate steps towards a market-based model. One example of this trend, discussed above, is the use of auctions rather than comparative hearings for the assignment of many licenses. A second example is the FCC's allocation of several bands to "personal communications service" (PCS) licenses, which the holder may use to provide "any mobile communications service," as well as "fixed services" if provided in combination with mobile ones (but not broadcasting services under any circumstances).[46] For the most part, carriers have used PCS licenses to provide cellular telephone and paging services. Unlike almost all other licenses, however, the PCS licenses are like private property in that, generally speaking, they neither restrict allowable uses nor dictate a particular technology. Even these licenses, however, could not be treated like real property; for example, they were initially encumbered by a longstanding FCC rule against leasing spectrum licenses to third parties.[47]

A third example of the FCC's market-oriented reforms is its *Secondary Markets Order*, which in 2003 reversed that anti-leasing rule, at least for certain bands, and relaxed the standards for approval of certain spectrum license transfers.[48] This move, while long overdue, was still controversial (and opposed by one Commissioner) because it departed from the traditional conception of public interest regulation by leaving certain spectrum licensees with free rein.[49] In the same *Order,* the FCC also suggested its willingness to consider a variety of additional reforms, including policies that would encourage the development of efficient spectrum-leasing mechanisms. Although the reforms adopted in the *Secondary Markets Order*, as well as the further reforms the FCC adopted in a follow-up order in 2004,[50] are considered watersheds in spectrum policy, they stop short of the privately ordered regime that Coase envisioned. Under a true Coasian model, firms could freely exchange spectrum rights in a genuinely private market and then use their licenses to provide whatever services meet consumer demand, subject only to the most minimal "traffic cop" and "zoning" role by the government.

Controversy in the transition

Much of the reluctance to take more aggressive steps towards a market-based regime stems from an essentially political objection—namely, that any incumbent licensee that did not pay "the public" for its spectrum at auction should be denied the "windfall" it would receive if it were permitted to sell its license for millions of dollars on the newly privatized market.[51] Despite its intuitive appeal, this objection suffers from two basic conceptual flaws. First, as Eli Noam explains, the public's claim to "ownership" of the spectrum, such that it "deserves" compensation for its use by private actors, is arguably no stronger than the claim (which no one makes) that the public deserves special compensation from the airlines for the right to fly planes through lanes in the public airspace.[52] Policymakers, however, sometimes forget that auctions are properly justified not as mechanisms for compensating the public for the use of "its" airwaves, but as a means of assigning spectrum rights as quickly as possible to those who would make the most efficient use of them.

Second, from a consumer welfare perspective, granting incumbents this "windfall"—if that is the only quick way to free up the spectrum at issue for more efficient uses—is usually superior to letting the incumbents tie up that spectrum in perpetuity with the less efficient uses specified in their licenses. To place this issue in perspective, consider that the U.S. cellular industry today uses little more than half of the radio spectrum used by its counterpart in the European Union.[53] The reason for this discrepancy is not that the U.S. cellular industry is incapable of putting that spectrum to equally valuable uses, but that so much of the spectrum in this country is occupied by longstanding incumbents that have no intention of giving up their licenses without a commensurate payoff. This problem has been greatly compounded by Congress's 1996 decision, discussed in chapter 12, to double the amount of "free" spectrum in the hands of television broadcasters as part of what has turned out to be a lengthy transition to digital technology in television broadcasting.

In short, if policymakers delay a transition to a market-based system out of concern that incumbents would be unjustly enriched in the process, they will deprive the incumbents of any incentive to move off the currently underutilized bands and encourage them to frustrate the "band-clearing" efforts needed to free that spectrum for more valuable uses. As participants in one recent Aspen Institute Conference concluded, incumbents "often feel threatened by proposals to require them to shift or share frequencies. Proposals for reform therefore tend to run into stiff political and legal resistance, and this fact means discussions of spectrum policy must devise realistic means of ensuring or compensating incumbents. Decision criteria must take pragmatic note of the fact that incumbent licensees have political and economic clout that they can use to delay or prevent entry of new spectrum occupants."[54]

One example of these transitional difficulties involves the FCC's plan for re-allocating parts of the broadcast spectrum. In the late 1990s and early 2000s, the FCC began to clear much of the "upper 700 MHz" band, the traditional home of television stations in channels 60-69 of the UHF range, for other uses. (The FCC has pursued distinct initiatives on a different track for clearing the spectrum occupied by channels 52-59.) Although the upper 700 MHz band is valuable spectrum for bandwidth-deprived providers of, among other things, cellular telephone service and Internet access, the incumbency of UHF television licensees greatly complicated the process of reallocating this band for such applications. That was unfortunate from the public's larger perspective—not just because most of those who watch programming on channels 60-69 do so through landline cables rather than the airwaves anyway, but also because, like other conventional television broadcasters, these stations are all but locked in to the use of older and less efficient technologies. In 2001, the FCC prudently relaxed regulatory impediments to market-oriented solutions to this problem and enabled these entrants to engage in "private transactions" with the incumbents to induce them to clear out of this band voluntarily before the expiration of their licenses.[55]

This process of clearing the upper 700 MHz band, which is still underway, marks an initial step in the much larger task of dealing with the problem of incumbency during any transition from a command-and-control model to a more rational, market-based approach. To enact any genuinely fundamental reforms, the FCC will need to develop a much more ambitious plan for managing that transition across the board by addressing a far greater number of spectrum licenses. To that end, FCC staffers Evan Kwerel and John Williams have proposed that the Commission "facilitate the rapid transition from administrative allocation of spectrum to market allocation by (1) reallocating a large amount of presently restricted spectrum to flexible use; (2) conducting large-scale, two-sided 'band restructuring' auctions of spectrum voluntarily offered by incumbents together with any unassigned spectrum held by the FCC; and (3) providing incumbents with incentives to participate in such auctions, by immediately granting participants flexibility and allowing them to keep the auction proceeds from the sale of their spectrum."[56] Although, under this proposal, incumbents opting out of the process could still operate under the terms of their current licenses and would receive full flexibility after five years, they would nonetheless:

have strong incentives to participate voluntarily and to allow their spectrum to move quickly to higher valued uses. By doing so they would share in the gains from immediate flexibility as well as from the rapid and efficient combining and restructuring of their spectrum together with highly complementary spectrum assigned to other incumbents and held by the FCC. Incumbents would not have to sell their spectrum to gain flexibility as long as they participate in the auction. Even if a license is not sold, a useful purpose will have been served by inducing the incumbent to participate thereby making the opportunity cost of holding a license more apparent. By ensuring that most interdependent spectrum is up for sale at the same time, this proposal would facilitate a rapid and efficient restructuring of spectrum rights and use.[57]

In advancing this proposal, Kwerel and Williams spoke only for themselves. To date, the FCC itself has taken no steps in the direction of implementing this or any similarly ambitious transition plan, and its hesitation is understandable. If it did attempt to facilitate such a transition, it would confront considerable congressional pressure not to allow a "spectrum giveaway." And the Commission would almost certainly be hauled into court, as there are serious questions about the Commission's authority to implement such a plan without significant revisions to the Communications Act.

Perhaps the most controversial of the FCC's recent initiatives in this area is its effort to resolve interference problems by relocating Nextel's operations from one set of frequency bands to another. Recall that Nextel's founder purchased inexpensive "dispatch" spectrum on the secondary market and then quietly won enough regulatory flexibility in the use of this spectrum, most of it in the 800 MHz band, to provide cellular telephone service. A dozen years later, Nextel's well-subscribed cellular operations had created widespread interference with the transmissions of hundreds of public safety authorities that still used adjoining frequencies within the 800 MHz band for traditional dispatch operations. After years of mutual discord, Nextel and public safety leaders forged a deal, which they called the "Consensus Plan," under which Nextel would vacate some of its existing spectrum assignments in exchange for others in the 1.9 GHz band and would underwrite the considerable costs to the public safety authorities of modifying their equipment to operate in different frequencies. The only catch, of course, was that the FCC would have to approve the deal and grant Nextel the new 1.9 GHz spectrum it wanted—without an auction.[58]

In July 2004, after several years of intense lobbying, the FCC finally announced its approval of a modified version of Nextel's plan.[59] Although the FCC traditionally has enjoyed wide latitude in managing the spectrum, the movement towards an auction-based property rights model greatly complicated the legal picture, making the Nextel proceeding "by far one of the most complex matters" that Chairman Michael Powell had faced at the FCC.[60] The FCC's ultimate disposition is complicated, but its basic terms require Nextel to relinquish its spectrum in the 800 MHz band and pay (1) the transition costs incurred by the public safety agencies in modifying their equipment to operate on new frequencies; and (2) several billion dollars to the federal treasury as an "anti-windfall payment" to substitute for revenues the FCC estimated would have been captured in an auction for the 1.9 GHz spectrum. Opponents of the plan claimed that this resolution violated section 309(j), which (as discussed) requires auctions for most new spectrum assignments. Verizon Wireless, for example, argued that it would have outbid Nextel in any auction and would have placed the 1.9 GHz spectrum to better use. Verizon then leveled additional arguments against the plan just days before the FCC approved it, warning that "proceeding on this course would place *the Commission's members themselves* in direct violation of federal laws governing the *personal* accountability of federal officials for the disposition of federal resources[,] . . . some of which are criminal in nature."[61] Unfazed by this extraordinary warning, the FCC unanimously approved the plan nonetheless.

One final set of transitional issues warrants discussion here. For much the same reason that spectrum policy should be largely indifferent to whatever "windfalls" incumbents win as the result of efficient band-clearing, policymakers should be circumspect in weighing claims that it would be "unfair" if—because of changes or anomalies in the government's assignment regime—some but not all providers within a given market had to pay for their spectrum rights at auction. Such "fairness" concerns recently arose, for example, when certain satellite-based mobile telephony providers sought the FCC's permission to use their satellite-specific licenses, for which they did not pay at auction, to compete with terrestrial mobile telephony providers, which have collectively spent many billions of dollars for their own licenses.[62] In this and other settings, policymakers cannot focus single-mindedly on fairness concerns without disserving the public's more general interest in the efficient use of the spectrum.

In competitive industries, firms set prices on the basis of their *opportunity costs*—the cost of forgoing alternatives—not on the basis of their historical costs, which are "sunk" (generally unrecoverable) and thus irrelevant to their current business decisions. For example, if you put your house on the market today, the ultimate sales price would not depend on whether you inherited the house from your parents or bought it at the top of the market five years ago, just before the market crashed; you wouldn't charge less than the market rate if you inherited the house, and you wouldn't be able to charge more if your own purchase price exceeded the current valuation. But despite the cold market realities, many individuals don't act rationally in such cases, instead indulging the "sunk cost fallacy"—i.e., a belief that it is sensible to compromise one's present and future self-interest because of past economic decisions.

On occasion, the FCC itself has fallen prey to this fallacy. The D.C. Circuit once invalidated an FCC order because, in justifying the disparate treatment of two different classes of spectrum licensees, the Commission had presumed that carriers that obtained their spectrum at auction would have incentives to return a profit on that spectrum more quickly than carriers that obtained it for free. As the court observed, with an intemperate bluntness characteristic of its recent treatment of many FCC orders: "This is a foolish notion that should not be entertained by anyone who has had even a single undergraduate course in economics. Failing that advantage, a moment's reflection would bring one to the realization that the use to which an asset is put is based not upon the historical price paid for it, but upon what it will return to its owner in the future. Would anyone be less interested in earning a return on money he had inherited than on money he had worked for? Of course not! Are radio licensees not as alert as inheritors?"[63]

Several years later, in a different context, a chastened FCC recognized the "sunk cost fallacy" for what it is and rejected claims that liberalizing the uses of spectrum by providers that had obtained it outside the auction process would give them an anticompetitive advantage in competing with providers that had paid at auction: "[T]he telecommunications experience in the U.S. has . . . been consistent with the theory that historic costs don't alter pricing. For example, within a given market, the prices charged by cellular operators who obtained their licenses via comparative hearings [or] lotteries are not lower than the prices of those firms that purchased their cellular licenses in the secondary market, or firms that obtained PCS licenses in an auction. Similarly, where a U.S. cellular license has been bought at a significant cost from a party that obtained it at no cost, we have not observed any increase in consumer prices."[64] These observations, the FCC concluded, confirm what economic theory suggests: "[L]icensees do not have an incentive to forgo recovery of the value of spectrum and price below competitive levels merely because the spectrum was obtained without an auction. Pricing that does not include recovery of the market value of an asset such as spectrum represents a loss (compared to the price that could be sustained in the marketplace) that [these] operators would have to bear regardless of how much, if anything, they spent on acquiring the asset initially."[65]

B. Commons: Einstein's cat in the age of the mouse

In today's spectrum policy debates, the major alternative to Coase's property rights model is the so-called *commons* model. In its purest form, that model would dispense with any scheme for licensing exclusive rights to private entities across very broad swaths of spectrum. Everyone operating devices within those swaths would be free to exploit that spectrum simultaneously for any number of uses, just as everyone is free to exploit Central Park simultaneously for any number of uses, subject in each case only to the most basic nuisance-type prohibitions.

The technological premise of this approach is that we have now entered the age of "smart" transmitters and receivers with advanced microchip technology. Those devices, the commons advocates maintain, are capable of avoiding mutual interference by transmitting at low power over wide expanses of spectrum and exploiting the intelligence of next generation receivers to identify and decode the transmitted signals. Commons advocates then take the "smart device" argument one step further, calling not just for more unlicensed spectrum, but also for rights of unlicensed users to operate these smart devices in *licensed* bands of spectrum as well. As discussed below, these proposed unlicensed uses in licensed spectrum would take two primary forms: *underlay* transmissions, which operate at such low power levels as to pose a theoretically low threat of interference with the primary uses of the relevant frequency bands; and higher power transmissions that fill the *white spaces* (unused frequencies) within spectrum that is allocated for some other use and is sometimes even assigned to a particular licensee.[66] Sometimes these white spaces fluctuate from frequency to frequency at any given moment, and sometimes they are relatively fixed, as in the portions of the UHF spectrum that remain unused at all times (because, for example, they serve as "guard bands" designed to prevent interference between adjacent television channels).

This "commons" approach has always been the exception rather than the rule in the FCC's spectrum management regime, but it is not quite as novel as it might sound. First, the FCC has long set aside patches of spectrum for common use by a class of defined users. Familiar examples are the frequencies set aside for pilot-to-ground communications, amateur radio, and CB radio, a trucker's medium that briefly developed a faddish popularity with the general public in the mid-1970s. The FCC requires some of these users to obtain licenses, as in the case of amateur radio, and sometimes it dispenses with licensing requirements altogether, as in the case of CB radio, where the maximum allowable transmission power level is lower and all users are "licensed by rule." But the common denominator is that, in all of these bands, users must share the spectrum and find ways to cooperate to avoid interference.[67]

The "commons" concept appears in traditional regulation in a second sense as well. Under its Part 15 rules the FCC allows certain wireless devices—such as cordless phones, TV remote controls, and garage door openers—to use unlicensed blocks of spectrum, or licensed spectrum at very low power levels, without prior authorization and without any restrictions on use.[68] But operators of these "Part 15 devices" have no guarantee against interference by others and bear responsibility for avoiding interference with licensed users. Moreover, the FCC has long required that all Part 15 devices be "certified" as compliant with certain technical standards—such as low transmission power levels—that ensure a low probability of interference with other users of the spectrum.[69]

At present, the frequencies made available for unlicensed uses are narrow and increasingly congested, as exemplified by widespread interference in the 2.4 GHz band used by both cordless phones and Wi-Fi computer networking devices. Such crowding has forced service providers and device manufacturers to find ways to exploit spectrum more efficiently. The first step in the modern wireless revolution was the deployment of *spread spectrum* technology, first authorized for commercial use in unlicensed bands in the late 1980s.[70] This technology enables paired devices, such as a cordless telephone and its accompanying base station, to exchange signals over a range of frequencies within a band rather than over a single frequency. Apart from cordless phones, the best-known spread spectrum applications are Wi-Fi devices, which, as noted in chapter 4, are used in home and business networks and in public "hot spots" (such as airports and coffee shops) to allow cordless Internet access over short distances. The Wi-Fi market is growing rapidly, at a rate of 40% in 2003 with $2.5 billion in sales, and Wi-Fi transmission has filled up much of the unlicensed spectrum that the FCC once regarded as its "garbage bands."[71] Since the mid-1990s, spread spectrum technology has also proliferated in licensed bands, as illustrated by the success of Qualcomm's proprietary "CDMA" technology, used widely in cellular telephone service (see chapter 8).

Like spread spectrum technology, *cognitive radio* devices (including the so-called "software defined radios") use advanced microchip technologies to "sniff out" and opportunistically exploit underutilized spectrum within a given band. For example, a transmitter and receiver, acting in tandem, might hop dynamically from frequency to frequency during the course of a call or data session, avoiding frequencies along the way that, at given instants, are occupied by unrelated signals or excessive noise. By "intelligently" filling in the gaps of unused spectrum within a given band, such devices can use available spectrum much more efficiently than can traditional "dumb" devices, and each device can thus occupy more bandwidth without causing mutual interference. Also like spread spectrum, cognitive radio technology can be used not just in unlicensed bands, but also in licensed ones, where they can facilitate shared access to spectrum through (for example) secondary market arrangements.

A related example of an innovative technology that is just now moving from theory to application is *ultra-wideband*, a logical extension of spread spectrum technology. Understanding ultra-wideband requires some familiarity with a principle of information theory known as Shannon's Law.

In 1948, Bell Labs engineer Claude Shannon observed, in mathematically precise detail, that the information-carrying capacity of a communications channel increases in direct relation to the breadth of the frequencies employed and the "signal-to-noise" ratio.[72] That ratio reflects the power of the transmission as compared to the background electromagnetic radiation, whether emitted by other wireless devices, by "unintentional radiators" such as car motors, computers, and hairdryers, or by natural sources of noise such as lightning, cosmic radiation, and so forth. Because no wireless channel is free of such noise, conventional transmissions must use significant wattage to enable receivers to identify and decode the relevant signal, just as you must raise your voice over the "noise floor" of a crowd-ed restaurant to be heard.

Shannon's Law largely explains why television broadcasters consume such vast tracts of spectrum. Such broadcasters transmit enormous amounts of information, in the form of high quality real-time video, to tel-evision sets on static, pre-assigned frequencies. The conventional way to convey all that information to such "dumb" receivers is to allow broadcast-ers to blare their signals at enormous wattage over broad swaths of spec-trum. That arrangement works out well for the television station and its passive viewers, but only at the expense of crowding out many other wire-less applications for dozens of miles in every direction—regardless of whether the channels are being watched or even used (as they are not late at night, for example). The immense signal strength of these transmissions also reflects a perversely self-perpetuating fact of broadcasting life. As noted, FCC policy has protected the ability of broadcasters to reach even the poorest quality receivers, which can work well only if the signals are transmitted with great bandwidth, ample guard bands, and overwhelming power. For that reason, the market for more discriminating receivers has not developed as quickly as it otherwise might—and thus the broadcasters can credibly go on claiming that they need all this spectrum and all that wattage to reach their audiences.

"Wideband" technologies exploit the innovations of the information age to avoid the trade-off between power levels and the bandwidth of a transmission. As Yochai Benkler explains: "The implication of [Shannon's Law] is that if a communication is sent using a sufficiently wide band of frequencies, the power of its signal need not be more powerful than the power of other sources of radiation. This implication was not practically usable for wireless communications until substantial computation became cheap enough to locate in receivers and transmitters, but it is now the basis of most advanced mobile phone standards [such as the CDMA standards discussed in the next chapter], as well as the basic [Wi-Fi] standards and other wireless systems."[73]

The ultimate extension of this insight is "ultra-wideband" technology. Imprinting information either on many different carrier signals or in mil-lions of short pulses of radiation, ultra-wideband devices transmit signals over such an enormous expanse of spectrum that they can operate at power levels so low as to fall beneath the "noise floor" for conventional uses of the affected spectrum. Theoretically, therefore, they can avoid interfering with existing devices that use licensed spectrum, although some of the licensees that use those devices express skepticism on that point.[74] Like the other technologies mentioned above, ultra-wideband systems rely on an intelligent receiver that translates the signals by listening for a familiar pattern sent by the transmitter.

In February 2002, after several years of delay, the FCC finally permitted the use of ultra-wideband devices under exceptionally restrictive conditions.[75] As always, these steps towards liberalizing the use of the airwaves were accompanied by much hand-wringing about the interference concerns of various incumbents. One commissioner explained that the FCC had adopted an "ultra-conservative" policy "to reduce the interference risks associated with the technology to levels far, far below those placed on technologies that place energy into narrower portions of the spectrum. These limits are intentionally at the extreme end of what FCC engineers—the best spectrum engineers in the country—believe necessary."[76]

Some analysts, however, view the FCC's order as a significant precedent nonetheless. Describing ultra-wideband as "a highly disruptive new wireless technology," the Precursor Group predicted: "[I]nitial authorization of UWB is the proverbial regulatory camel's nose under the investment tent. Although the initial uses will be circumscribed by 'technical' issues, e.g., in-building, the potential for a broad array of wireless applications—devices and services—is huge."[77] Unfortunately, regulatory approval of the technology is only the first step. The industry must also develop common standards before the technology can gain widespread adoption, and they have not yet emerged. By contrast, Wi-Fi technologies have succeeded in the marketplace precisely because the industry has coalesced around common standards—the 802.11 family of protocols forged by the Institute of Electrical and Electronics Engineers (IEEE), a private engineering association that operates as a standard-setting authority.

Benkler has cited ultra-wideband technologies as well as the popularity of Wi-Fi as harbingers of what he predicts will be the next revolution in telecommunications technology: a widespread alternative to "carriers" as providers of last mile access. If end users are allowed to treat spectrum as a commons, he claims, they will create "open wireless network[s] that no one owns," that are "[b]uilt entirely of end use devices," and that can be set up "simply by using equipment that cooperates, without need for a network provider to set up its owned infrastructure as a precondition to effective communication."[78] These devices, Benkler speculates, would spontaneously converge into "mesh" networks, repeating one another's signals as needed from origin to destination while avoiding interference by observing constraints on the power of their respective transmissions. In such an environment, telecommunications regulators would shift their focus from regulating *service providers* to regulating *equipment providers* to ensure cooperation among devices in the commons.[79] And local governments might begin to provide wireless hot spots throughout town as a public service akin to the lighting of the streets—as Philadelphia is now considering doing.[80] But commons model advocates like Benkler emphasize that developments like these will not reach their potential unless the government first frees up large swaths of spectrum for unlicensed uses.

For the commons model to work as advertised, however, it must overcome the fabled "tragedy of the commons." The problem lies in the temptation for users of resources held in common—whether those resources are something tangible like a grazing field or intangible like the electromagnetic spectrum—to spoil them through overuse or neglect.[81] On Stuart Benjamin's view, for example, that temptation would be overwhelming if large portions of the spectrum were opened up to individuals to exploit as they choose. In that event, each user would have strong incentives to "cheat" by, for example, employing high power devices that would interfere with the devices of other users—and those other users would then have escalating incentives to raise *their* power levels to make themselves heard over the increasing din, and so forth.[82] Such problems could be controlled by regulation, but Benjamin contends that "the level of regulation involved [would be] significant."[83] Indeed, commons advocates often acknowledge the need for such regulation in one form or another, but devote little explanation to exactly how it would work. To be sure, many property rights advocates have likewise provided scant explanation of who would define the boundaries of (and enforce) property rights under their model. But the role of the government in that model would likely be more predictable than under a commons approach, less complicated, and closer to the FCC's traditional role in spectrum management.[84]

Critics of the commons approach argue that the advantages of observing private property rights in spectrum management are similar to the advantages of observing those rights throughout the rest of the economy: the purchase and sale of such rights permit efficient private ordering through the mechanism of price signals. Those price signals would be largely absent in a "commons" world *without* enforceable property rights.[85] The commons advocates respond by downplaying that concern and by noting a countervailing flaw in markets where transaction costs are high. Lawrence Lessig, for example, suggests that the Achilles heel of the property rights model consists of "the costs imposed on the market by the need to negotiate and secure rights to access. . . . [I]f the ability to 'share' spectrum becomes central to efficient spectrum management, then the costs of securing this right to 'share' through private contract could become quite prohibitive"[86]—and the commons model becomes commensurately advantageous. Kevin Werbach adds: "Coase's proposed solution"—a property-rights approach to spectrum—"was based on the contemporary view of interference when he proposed it. Interference was still thought to necessitate exclusivity in spectrum. The less we think of interference as a high and rigid barrier, and the more we see it as a phenomenon that technology is gradually conquering, the more the transaction cost ledger favors commons."[87] Of course, a property-rights regime also provides compelling incentives for firms to develop interference-reducing technologies; the question, Lessig and Werbach suggest, is whether it generates such high transaction costs that a commons approach is more efficient, at least in particular contexts.

C. From theory to practice

The academic back-and-forth between opposing theorists obscures a central point: few people advocate either a pure "property" or a pure "commons" approach to spectrum policy.[88] "Commons" advocate Lessig argues that, in the face of technological uncertainty, "[t]he ideal mix in the short term would be a regime that had both a commons and a property component . . . . There would be broad swaths of spectrum left in the commons; there would be broad swaths that would be sold[.]"[89] And "property rights" advocates Gerald Faulhaber and David Farber would likewise accommodate transaction cost concerns by recognizing low power "easements" in otherwise "private" spectrum.[90] And, while there are many ideological differences between the two camps, they both agree that the government should begin by abandoning the current command-and-control approach as promptly as possible.

To its credit, the FCC has begun to take that advice seriously, at least in principle. In November 2002, the FCC's Spectrum Policy Task Force—a team of high-level FCC staffers—issued a well-publicized report that critically analyzes spectrum policy and offers significant suggestions for reform. Very few of the basic ideas in the report are novel; most of them cover the same ground already addressed by the existing commentary. What *is* new is that, in this report, the FCC has produced for the first time an official (albeit completely non-binding) document acknowledging that the existing "spectrum drought" is more the product of dubious regulatory restrictions than inherent technological limitations.

Although the Task Force self-consciously advocates a "balance" among the competing regulatory models, it leans strongly towards the property-rights camp over the commons camp on most important theoretical issues. First, it shies away from recommending any major commitment of new spectrum to a commons regime, with the exception of frequencies above 50 GHz, whose "propagation characteristics . . . preclude many of the applications that are possible in lower bands (e.g., mobile telephone service, broadcasting), and instead favor short-distance line-of-sight operation using narrow transmission beams."[91] Second, it expresses skepticism about claims that a commons approach, rather than a property-rights approach, would be appropriate for the use of cognitive radios and other "opportunistic" devices designed to fill in the "white spaces" of spectrum in bands primarily occupied by others. The report noted the concerns of some incumbents that "(1) 'non-interfering' operation tends to work better in theory than in practice, and (2) even where spectrum is otherwise not being used by the licensee, creating easements for third party access without the licensee's consent could lead to squatter's rights problems."[92] And the report speculated that, "[i]n most cases of potential opportunistic use of spectrum, efficient secondary market mechanisms can be developed that would allow negotiated access at reasonable transactions costs."[93] Nonetheless, it is at least symbolically significant that the report identified the commons model as a peer of the property-rights model, since earlier FCC pronouncements focused exclusively on the virtues of the latter.[94]

The report further endorses the position that "underlay" devices—those transmitting at power levels below the electromagnetic noise floor—should generally be free to operate outside the scope of any property rights regime. To implement this principle, the report introduces the key concept of *interference temperature*.[95] If implemented, even in part, this concept would transform spectrum policy by giving spectrum licensees incentives to ensure, in some cases for the first time, that receivers designed for the licensee's services are developed with enough sensitivity that they can tune out the permitted level of background noise.

Under the current system, as we have noted, the FCC uses a subjective and poorly defined standard that largely accepts as given a spectrum licensee's subjective claims about how much spectrum it needs to guard against interference. Recall, for example, the FM radio receiver that the incumbents had in mind when invoking "interference" concerns to suppress low power FM broadcasts. They focused on the very cheapest and dumbest of the "lone, stupid receiver[s]"[96] whose needs have long preoccupied spectrum policy. As Thomas Hazlett has emphasized, when the government declines to allow new entry on the ground that it would disturb such receivers, "[i]nterference becomes a self-fulfilling regulatory prophecy," since "radio sets need not upgrade performance" (to conserve on their use of spectrum) and, worse yet, "there is no demand for equipment to receive additional signals (which fail to be licensed by the FCC)."[97]

Under the "interference temperature" approach, in contrast, the FCC would define an objective level of tolerable radiation on particular frequencies in a particular geographic area and would assure the licensees for those frequencies that they will not face interference above that "temperature." In effect, this approach would define the property rights conferred on spectrum "owners" and recognize that some level of interference is unavoidable. In so doing, it would give the industry new and powerful incentives to design receivers capable of accommodating certain interference levels by, for example, exploiting advances in microchip technology.

The interference temperature proposal has sparked enormous controversy within the industry. Cellular telephone companies, for example, argue that they have already taken extraordinary technological steps to squeeze all available bandwidth out of the sharply limited spectrum the government has assigned them. And, they say, permitting additional uses within the same bands would simply degrade the quality of their service without creating any corresponding consumer benefits. It may be that the interference temperature concept has more utility in bands, like those now reserved for television broadcasting, in which service providers have no extraordinary incentives to ensure efficient spectrum usage—and in which end user devices (such as televisions) are manufactured by independent companies with no such incentives at all. In any event, it remains to be seen whether the Commission will experiment with this approach in a couple of bands now used for fixed satellite uplinks and fixed terrestrial services (i.e., the 6525-6700 MHz and 12.75-13.25 GHz bands),[98] whether it will look for an alternative means of spurring improvements in receiver standards,[99] or whether it will continue to avoid addressing the issue.[100]

* * *

Simply coming up with the "right" theoretical answers to spectrum policy is complex and contentious enough. As we have noted, however, it is only one challenge among several that policymakers must meet if there is to be true reform in this area. To begin with, policymakers must fill in the practical details of whatever regime they choose, defining (for example) the "interference temperatures" applicable in various contexts, identifying new opportunities for unlicensed uses, facilitating market-based flexibility for licensed spectrum, and implementing a resource-intensive enforcement scheme to administer those reforms.[101] They must further devise a comprehensive transition plan that overcomes the political and legal obstacles that incumbent license holders will lay in the path of liberalization. And they must confront formidable coordination problems among the many different governmental authorities involved, including not just the state and local authorities who use spectrum for important public safety functions, but also the Defense Department and other federal agencies that do not answer to the FCC and have few incentives today to part with their allotted spectrum, no matter how inefficiently they may use it. Taken together, these factors conspire to make genuine spectrum reform as contentious as it is important.

8

Mobile Wireless Services

Although "the spectrum" is used for many commercial purposes, the one that has most pervasively transformed person-to-person communications over the past quarter century has been the family of mobile voice and data services characterized by the use of "cellular" technology, described below. By all accounts, the development of these services has been a nearly unrivaled boon for consumers. In 1982, virtually no one in the general public owned a cellular telephone, and trips to a telephone booth were time-wasting detours of necessity for anyone who needed to stay in touch while away from home or the office. Just over twenty years later, at the close of 2003, the U.S. market had 160.6 million cellphone users and a nationwide penetration rate of roughly 54%.[1] Competition in this market is fierce: the overwhelming majority of the population lives in a county served by at least four alternative providers of wireless services; customers can and do switch from one carrier to another; the quality and diversity of wireless services continue to improve; and prices have fallen precipitously since 1990, often to levels competitive with wireline service.[2]

The mobile wireless industry has achieved this level of success without the intrusive regulation that characterizes the wireline telephone industry. This divergence in treatment is the product of the different economic characteristics of these two industries. In many wireline markets, as we have seen, the sheer expense of digging up the streets to install physical cables from the central office to each home and business in a given serving area creates what regulators have traditionally viewed as natural monopoly conditions in the "last mile," which are only now beginning to subside with the rise of VoIP and cross-platform broadband competition. The last mile connections between a wireless carrier's transmission sites and its subscribers, however, consist of signals sent at different frequencies through the air. The main limits on the availability of the spectrum to multiple wireless providers are regulatory, not economic. There was a time, as discussed below, when the FCC enforced an artificial duopoly, allotting spectrum rights to just two mobile telephony firms in each geographic market—the incumbent telephony company and one independent carrier. By the 1990s, however, the FCC had set aside additional frequency bands for wireless services, and this more liberal spectrum policy, combined with the proliferation of digital technology, produced the intensely competitive wireless services market that prevails today.

There is a broad consensus that this competition has made pervasive regulation of the wireless market unnecessary. Regulators have hewed closely to an appropriately deregulatory policy since the mid-1990s, and, when they have deviated from it, they have generally recognized and corrected their error. Advocates of deregulation point to this approach as a model for how to treat the telecommunications world in general once cross-platform competition removes the last vestiges of natural monopoly from the wired telecommunications market as well.

But the triumph of competition does not mean that policymakers can just wish the wireless industry well and leave it alone entirely. First, although that industry does not have natural monopoly characteristics, it remains a *network* industry, with the associated interconnection and standard-setting challenges. Many of those challenges—but not all—can be resolved through market dynamics without government intervention. Second, as consumers come to view unregulated wireless services not just as a *supplement* to more regulated wireline services, but increasingly as a *substitute* for them, the convergence of these competing platforms gives rise to important issues of regulatory neutrality. Both of these issues are discussed below. We begin, however, with a basic overview of how wireless telephone service works and how it traditionally has been regulated.

I. The Basics of Cellular Technology

A mobile telephone is a sophisticated two-way radio that relies on a network of transmission antennas operated by a wireless carrier. In some cases, particularly in rural areas or along highways, these antennas are attached to towers specially built for radio communications. In other cases, wireless carriers attach their antennas to rooftops, utility poles, or other preexisting structures.[3] For the most part, only the link between the cell-phone and the nearest transmission site—the analogue to the "loop" in a wireline network—is "wireless." Once the signals reach that site, they are normally routed through a wireline connection to one of the carrier's centralized switches and then through more wireline connections en route to their ultimate destination. Of course, if you are calling someone else on her cellphone, the last link of the transmission on her end will be wireless as well, but most of the transmission in between will be channeled through wireline connections.

The key to mobile telephony today is the division of a wireless service area into many small geographic "cells," each of which is served by a single transmission site. This "cellular" approach is best introduced by contrasting it to the quite different method used for ordinary radio broadcasting. When you turn on your car radio, select a station, and drive twenty miles down the highway, you will generally receive the station's signals from the same transmission site during the entire trip. The station's transmitter, placed atop a tall tower, hill, or skyscraper, blasts out signals at enormous wattage to reach everywhere in a metropolitan or multi-county area. Until the final decades of the twentieth century, this was essentially the same technological model on which most mobile person-to-person telecommunications services were provided as well. Taxi companies, the police, and others used (and still use) their assigned slices of spectrum for radio "dispatch" services, in which signals are transmitted over wide geographic areas from centrally located antennas (sometimes with the aid of repeaters that boost the signal strength in areas far away from the transmission site).

This centralized transmission approach worked well enough so long as the airwaves were used mostly for "one-to-many" transmissions such as radio broadcasts to large audiences or generalized alerts from police dispatchers ("calling all cars"). But it is ill-suited for one-to-one voice calls on a mobile telephone network. Precisely because a conventional radio transmitter pumps out signals at high power to reach listeners throughout a broad geographic area, it tends to crowd out different uses of the same spectrum. This same approach would be immensely wasteful if the high-powered transmitter were tying up a given frequency throughout an entire metropolitan area *not* to broadcast radio signals to hundreds of thousands of passive listeners, but simply to send voice signals to a single mobile telephony subscriber.

Cellular technology helps avoid such waste by dividing a broad geographic area into small discrete cells, each of which is (generally speaking) a few miles wide. These cells are often portrayed on a map in a honeycomb arrangement. The transmission antenna serving each cell emits relatively low power signals that soon fade out once they pass beyond the cell's boundaries. As a result, wireless carriers can use the same set of frequencies for calls in one cell that they are simultaneously using for other calls in geographically distant cells. "Reusing" these frequencies in this manner enables these carriers to exploit their assigned spectrum much more efficiently than if they used a single high-powered transmitter for the entire area. Because cellphones require commensurately lower power to communicate with these nearby transmission sites, they can operate for several hours on smaller batteries than they would need if they had to transmit to a single tower much farther away. Small batteries, along with advances in micro-engineering, allow for very small cellphones. That fact helps explain the rapid growth of the wireless industry, for consumers are more likely to carry a cellphone that slips inconspicuously into a pocket than one that, like the earliest cellular phones, has the size and weight of a brick.*

These efficiency advantages, however, come with two basic trade-offs. Cellular telephony requires both (i) deployment of an extensive and sometimes aesthetically controversial network infrastructure and (ii) investment in extremely sophisticated technology to keep track of, and handle the calls of, millions of mobile customers.

First, a wireless carrier must incur the costs of establishing transmission sites and installing all of the antennas that compose a cellular network.

---

* This was one of the lessons learned too late by a company called Iridium that, in the 1990s, launched a fleet of satellites into orbit to provide wireless telephony to areas of the earth not yet served by terrestrial cellular systems. Iridium's handsets were bulky and heavy; they did not work well indoors; and the service was exorbitantly expensive when compared to ordinary wireless telephony. Iridium declared bankruptcy after only eight months in operation upon discovering, to its investors' dismay, that few people wished to order this service. *See* David Barboza, *For Iridium, A Quick Trip Back to Earth*, N.Y. TIMES, Aug. 14, 1999, at C1.

Even apart from the considerable expense of this infrastructure, the need for many antennas can also present significant bureaucratic obstacles to the build-out of a cellular network, since many localities exercise their traditional zoning authority to limit the placement of unsightly towers. Section 332(c)(7)(B) of the Communications Act, added in 1996, balances the interests of zoning authorities with those of wireless carriers by limiting the substantive bases on which localities can exclude transmission facilities from particular areas and permitting aggrieved parties to seek review in either federal or state court.[4] This provision requires localities to base any denial of a siting request on "substantial evidence," an amorphous standard that, as one court explains, "requires balancing two considerations. The first is the contribution that the antenna will make to the availability of cellphone service. The second is the aesthetic or other harm that the antenna will cause. The unsightliness of the antenna and the adverse effect on property values that is caused by its unsightliness are the most common concerns . . . . But adverse environmental effects are properly considered also, and even safety effects: fear of adverse health effects from electromagnetic radiation is excluded as a factor, but not, for example, concern that the antenna might obstruct vision or topple over in a strong wind."[5]

The second basic trade-off presented by the efficiencies of cellular technology is the need to invest in considerable "intelligence" within the network both to identify where a subscriber is at any given moment and to hand calls off seamlessly from one cell site to the next as she changes location. The intelligence of today's cellular systems resides in the "base station" equipment at the bottom of each antenna, in a carrier's centralized switches, and, to an increasing extent, in the mobile phone itself.

When you turn your cellphone on, it "listens" for a signal announcing the presence of your wireless carrier, constantly transmitted by each base station in the form of a carrier-specific "system identification code." In turn, your phone transmits two bits of information about itself: a ten-digit telephone number your carrier has assigned you, plus a secret 32-bit number, called an "electronic serial number," that was installed in the phone at the time of manufacture. So long as you keep your phone turned on, it will stay in contact with the cellular network. If someone calls you, the network will already know where you are, it will instantaneously send the call (via a microwave or wireline connection) to the appropriate cell site, and it will transmit the call to you from there, whether that site is in the same city as your home address or on the other side of the continent. Now suppose that, when you turn your cellphone on, it hears only the signal of some *other* carrier's base station because you are out of the range of your own carrier's network. Your phone will still send its identifying information to that other carrier, which will check to see whether it has a "roaming" agreement with your carrier (discussed below). If it does, the other carrier will stand in for your carrier and process your calls through its own network upon receiving confirmation from your carrier that you are a current subscriber.

The easiest way to understand how a wireless network hands calls off from one cell to the other as you drive through them is to consider what happens in systems using analog or "time-slicing" digital technology, even though the details are different in certain digital systems (specifically, in the "CDMA" networks described below). When you place or receive a call, the network assigns your phone a pair of channels among the several dozen it has devoted to the cell you are in; you transmit in one channel and receive in the other. During the call, the telephone and the base station adjust their power levels to maintain a certain level of quality, and when the telephone moves to the edge of a cell, the power level reaches the maximum allowed. When the ratio of signal strength to background noise falls below a predetermined level, a new pair of channels is assigned in a neighboring cell. Once the system determines that you will receive better reception using the channels in the new cell, it tells both your phone and the new base station to resume the transmission using the new channel. These handoffs are sometimes fumbled because, for example, all channels in the adjacent cell are in use or because there is no adjacent cell at all—i.e., there is a "hole" in the coverage area. This leads to the familiar phenomenon of the dropped call.

Given the explosive popularity of wireless services, particularly in metropolitan areas, each carrier must struggle to squeeze enough bandwidth out of its limited spectrum to serve the anticipated demands of its customers. Dividing up service areas into small cells, thereby using the same channels in one cell that might be used in a different cell 20 miles away, is only part of the solution. Carriers must also find ways to use the same frequencies for the transmission of multiple calls in the *same* cell. To do this, they use one of the several time- or "code"-based multiplexing mechanisms discussed later in this chapter. Carriers similarly use various digital "compression" techniques that, as discussed in chapter 4, reduce the amount of total information that needs to be transmitted in order to convey a reasonably accurate representation of a sound or image.

II. The Regulatory Landscape

A. Categories of wireless telephony licenses

"Mobile" wireless services fall into two major statutory categories: "commercial" and "private." The term "commercial mobile services"—often known by the acronym "CMRS" (with the added "R" standing for "radio")—encompasses "any mobile service . . . that is provided for profit," is "interconnected with the public switched network," and is provided "to the public or . . . to such classes of eligible users as to be effectively available to a substantial portion of the public."[6] It includes the full range of wireless telephony services addressed in this chapter, as well as commercial paging and various other services. In contrast, "private mobile services" are, for the most part, dispatch-oriented services that are not interconnected with the public switched network: i.e., a taxi driver cannot call home on his car radio.[7] Unlike these private services, commercial mobile services are subject to basic common carriage requirements—albeit only in the most skeletal form, as discussed below.

The FCC grants three main types of spectrum licenses for mobile voice services: "cellular," "personal communications service" (PCS), and "specialized mobile radio" (SMR). These names are a bit confusing because all three types of licenses can be and are used extensively in the provision of "cellular" service as we have described it. Indeed, the distinctions among these three subcategories of licenses can usually be ignored in thinking about big picture policy issues, for they are a dwindling vestige of regulatory history.[8] But that history is itself instructive, and so we briefly canvass it here.

Cellular technology was conceived in the 1940s, but it stood in line for several decades while policymakers debated whether this quixotic new technology warranted the allocation of any spectrum that could otherwise be devoted to more conventional uses like broadcasting.[9] Although estimates vary, some say that this delay cost the U.S. economy some $86 billion (measured in 1990 dollars).[10] Finally, after monitoring an experimental system in Chicago and satisfying itself that consumers would actually order cellular telephone service, the FCC allocated 50 megahertz of spectrum in the 800 MHz band for that purpose throughout the United States in the early 1980s.[11]

The FCC initially conceptualized the service areas of cellular providers as "local," perhaps by analogy to local radio stations, and it doled out "cellular" licenses to each of 734 "cellular market areas." Fifty megahertz was not enough spectrum to support full-blown competition within each of these markets, but it was enough to support two rival carriers. The FCC thus created an official duopoly in each market, ultimately assigning one license (for a frequency band 25 megahertz wide) to the incumbent LEC and another to an independent provider chosen, for the most part, by lottery.[12] This remained the state of wireless competition for the next dozen years, and cellphone service remained spotty and expensive.[13] Of course, the FCC could have expedited the transition to robust competition by freeing up more spectrum for additional providers. As discussed in the previous chapter, however, the FCC had compiled an unimpressive track record for the efficient allocation of spectrum under its traditional command-and-control regime.

In the mid-1990s, the Commission finally recognized that duopolies are a pale substitute for true competition, and it exercised its newly granted auction authority to assign PCS mobile telephony licenses covering an additional 120 megahertz of spectrum. This PCS spectrum was divided into a number of frequency "blocks," some of which were 30 megahertz wide, and some 10 megahertz wide. These licenses were originally assigned on a local or regional basis, and they remain so today; two of the blocks are assigned to (relatively large) "major trading areas," and the rest are assigned to (smaller) "basic trading areas."[14] Unlike their "cellular" competitors, which had built all-analog networks in the 1980s, these new PCS carriers built out their networks from the ground up with digital technology. That technology enabled them to provide higher quality service and to squeeze more calls into the available spectrum, in part through digital compression techniques. Today, all major "cellular" licensees have bridged this technical divide by offering digital service to their customers. And, despite a popular misconception to the contrary, PCS carriers use cellular technology every bit as much as the original "cellular" licensees do, although PCS cells tend to be smaller because the transmissions are at a higher frequency.

The final class of mobile telephony providers consists of "specialized mobile radio" licensees, of which the best known is Nextel. As discussed in chapter 7, Nextel has exploited its founder's regulatory acumen to transform itself from a provider of private dispatch services to a provider of wireless services of all types. These include service plans that offer a given customer, using a single phone, both mobile telephony over an ordinary cellular network and a "push-to-talk" walkie-talkie feature over Nextel's distinct dispatch-oriented network (traditionally characterized by much larger "cells"). A similar push-to-talk feature is now offered by conventional "cellular" and PCS licensees as well.

In sum, the mobile telephony services offered by "cellular," "PCS," and "SMR" licensees are generally market substitutes, despite the differences in name and origin. For the most part, the FCC has conformed its rules to this market reality, recognizing that differential treatment on the basis of regulatory pedigree can lead only to inefficient competitive distortions. But there have been some notable lapses on the road to parity. For example, in the early 1990s, the FCC continued subjecting ILECs with cellular licenses to longstanding "structural separation" requirements, but exempted ILECs with new PCS licenses from those same requirements. These rules, much like their counterparts in the enhanced services context (see chapter 5), directed ILECs to place their relatively unregulated wireless operations in a formally separate affiliate to guard against cross-subsidization and discrimination in interconnection with the wireline network. This differential treatment made no sense: for all practical purposes, these licensees all provide the same service, and any cross-subsidization and discrimination concerns that might justify the structural separation requirements should apply, or not apply, to cellular and PCS services equally. After the Sixth Circuit invalidated the FCC's rules in 1995 on essentially that ground,[15] the FCC steered a middle course, retaining but somewhat relaxing the structural separation requirement, applying it equally to all ILECs with wireless telephony licenses of any kind, and "sunsetting" the requirement altogether on January 1, 2002, once the relevant interconnection arrangements had become well established.[16]

B. The general deregulation of wireless telephony

In the decade after assignment of the first cellular licenses, the FCC imposed common carriage obligations on wireless providers by cobbling together various sources of authority both under Title II, which had long governed wireline "common carriers," and under Title III, which covers "radio" (which, in this context, means the electromagnetic spectrum in general rather than broadcast radio services in particular). In 1993, Congress revamped section 332 of the Communications Act to formalize the basic substance of this approach and to harmonize the regulatory treatment of the different classes of wireless telephony services.

Congress began with the presumption that such services would be subject to common carriage regulation under Title II. But foreshadowing its broader, industry-wide grant of "forbearance" authority three years later,[17] Congress authorized the FCC to *exempt* wireless carriers from any Title II requirements that the Commission deems unnecessary, except for the skeletal nondiscrimination and similar obligations of sections 201 and 202 and the FCC complaint procedure of section 208.[18] In 1994, the FCC exempted wireless carriers from the tariffing obligations of section 203 and the market entry and exit regulations of section 214, reasoning that competition made most forms of traditional common carrier regulation superfluous at best and counterproductive at worst.[19] The practical upshot of the detariffing determination is that, although section 202 still theoretically prohibits a narrow category of "unjust and unreasonable discrimination in charges and service," wireless carriers are generally free to strike dissimilar bargains with similarly situated customers.[20]

Two similar FCC policies illustrate the deregulatory trajectory of wireless policy in this age of robust competition. First, as anyone who has purchased a discounted cellphone with a one-year service contract is aware, the FCC has exempted wireless carriers from generally applicable restrictions on a common carrier's right to sell customers bundles of services and equipment on more favorable terms than if it sold the two separately. As discussed in chapters 2 and 5, such restrictions, which derive from the *Computer Inquiries*, sometimes make economic sense when the discounted bundle includes the products of a dominant firm in a monopolistic market, particularly (given Baxter's Law) one that is subject to price regulation.[21]

The firm may have both the incentive and the ability to leverage its monopoly in that market by discriminating against competitors in adjacent markets and, when subject to traditional rate-of-return regulation, by engaging in anticompetitive cross-subsidization as well.

But such restrictions make little sense when, as in the wireless sector, the markets for both the service and the equipment are competitive; in that context, bundling is both commonplace and pro-consumer.[22] In the early 1990s, the FCC agreed with this general conclusion (after first coming out the other way) and excluded wireless carriers from the scope of its general bundling prohibition.[23] This is plainly the right policy call. Consider the consumer who is unwilling to pay $200 up front for a cellphone, but is willing to commit to paying $40 each month for service for the next two years. Wireless companies routinely accommodate such customers by waiving or reducing the charges for the cellphone in return for such a commitment. As a general matter, few would preclude wireless companies and their customers from entering into such agreements. Widespread competition in the markets for both wireless service and cellphones, together with the absence of price regulation for either, leaves firms with neither the incentive nor the ability to engage in anticompetitive abuses (as opposed to the run-of-the-mill sharp dealing found in any industry).

The FCC took a similarly deregulatory approach to the subject of wireless resale. Suppose that a facilities-based wireless carrier charges individual subscribers $40 a month for a particular wireless service but gives a 20% volume discount to any large business that purchases that service in bulk for at least 100 people—say, a sales force that needs to stay in constant contact with the home office and with clients. A non-facilities-based reseller might then seek the same 20% volume discount for 100 different wireless accounts, which it would in turn sell, at a slightly less discounted rate, to individual subscribers. The facilities-based carrier might well reject that request if it believed that a large number of those 100 subscribers would otherwise pay full price by subscribing directly to it. During the early years of the industry, the FCC generally prohibited wireless carriers from imposing such restrictions on resellers, just as it had required AT&T to accommodate resellers like MCI in the early days of long distance competition.[24]

The difference, however, was that AT&T was a monopolist in the wireline long distance market, whereas competition was beginning to blossom in the wireless telephony market. In 1996, the FCC found that, as the new PCS licensees built out their networks and gave consumers a fuller choice of facilities-based providers, there would be progressively less consumer welfare justification for the government to intervene in the market to preserve resale opportunities. First, as competition in a market increases, efficient resale opportunities tend to arise through market dynamics. In our example, the facilities-based carrier in a reasonably competitive market might well have strong incentives to sell those 100 accounts to the reseller at the discounted rate because otherwise it would have no assurance of selling those accounts at all. Also, government prohibitions on resale restrictions can impose significant costs of their own. Even apart from the administrative costs of enforcement, which can be considerable, such prohibitions may operate as an economically inefficient flat ban on all price discrimination among classes of consumers.[25] In its 1996 order, the FCC decided to "sunset" its wireless resale rules by 2001 on the basis of its expectation that, by then, facilities-based competition would be robust enough that the costs of government intervention in this area would outweigh the dwindling need for it.[26]

More recently, the FCC has likewise taken a more market-oriented approach to spectrum management, as discussed in the previous chapter. Mobile telephony licenses are no exception to this general trend. The FCC initially precluded any single firm from holding licenses accounting for more than 45 MHz of spectrum—whether in the cellular, SMR, or PCS bands—in any metropolitan area.[27] At the time, the Commission viewed this cap as an important safeguard against excessive consolidation during the initial development of competition in wireless telephone service. In 2001, however, the FCC concluded that the emergence of six national wireless networks—now five, with the 2004 merger of Cingular and AT&T Wireless—made any rigid cap unnecessary. It thus decided to adopt a case-by-case approach (used for the first time in approving that merger) for reviewing future mergers and acquisitions—a task it shares, somewhat redundantly, with the Department of Justice (see chapter 13).[28] Along similar lines, the FCC now permits all mobile telephony providers to "disaggregate" their licenses (i.e., divide up their allotted spectrum) or "partition" them (i.e., divide up a license's geographic area) and, after jumping through some bureaucratic hoops, sell the reconfigured licenses to other providers. And the FCC's recent facilitation in the *Secondary Markets* proceeding (see chapter 7) of spectrum leasing arrangements will also help ensure more efficient use of this spectrum.

Up to this point, we have addressed the minimalistic approach of *federal* wireless regulation in the wake of Congress's amendment of section 332 in 1993. In a similar deregulatory vein, Congress sought to insulate the industry from unnecessary regulation of all kinds by preempting most *state* efforts "to regulate the entry of or the rates charged by any commercial mobile service."[29] This preemption provision comes with assorted qualifications, all set forth in section 332(c)(3)(A). First, states may "regulat[e] the other terms and conditions of commercial mobile services." Second, "where such services are a substitute for land line telephone exchange service for a substantial portion of the communications within such State," the state may subject them to the requirements it imposes "on all providers of telecommunications services necessary to ensure the universal availability of telecommunications service at affordable rates."[30] And the state is free to "petition the Commission for authority to regulate the rates for any commercial mobile service" when (among other things) "market conditions . . . fail to protect subscribers adequately from unjust and unreasonable rates"—an authority that is rarely sought and even more rarely (if ever) granted.[31]

Unsurprisingly, lawyers have argued at length about what these preemption and "savings clauses" mean. One widely litigated issue concerns how to draw the statutory line between (preempted) "entry" and "rate" regulation and (unpreempted) regulation of "the other terms and conditions" of service. For example, may disgruntled customers sue wireless carriers under state tort, contract, or consumer protection law for false advertising, misleading billing practices, or simply allowing too many dropped calls after promising to provide seamless coverage throughout a given area?[32] In 2000, amid widespread disagreement in the courts, the FCC stepped in and opined that such state law claims generally may proceed. It added, however, that "this is not to say that such awards can never amount to rate or entry regulation"; instead, whether a particular remedy constitutes "rate or entry regulation prohibited by Section 332(c)(3) would depend on all facts and circumstances of the case."[33]

Running parallel to these litigation-oriented disputes are similar controversies about the proper role of state consumer protection laws designed specifically to ensure the high quality of wireless services. Led by California, a number of state commissions have enacted prophylactic "wireless bill of rights" initiatives despite concerns that such market intervention is unnecessary in a competitive industry subject to generally enforced rules of contract and tort law.[34] Whatever the ultimate fate of such initiatives, the industry's trade association, the Cellular Telecommunications and Internet Association, has tried to address the underlying discontent by instituting a consumer code for wireless services, to which individual companies have voluntarily committed themselves.[35]

III. Interoperability Among Wireless Networks

In chapter 1, we explained that the telecommunications industry is more regulated than most because it hosts an unusual confluence of three basic types of economic phenomena: network effects, immense scale economies, and widespread monopoly leveraging opportunities. All three of these phenomena remain highly relevant to policy debates about the non-wireless side of the industry. Scale economies and monopoly leveraging concerns are responsible for the lion's share of disputes concerning both local wireline competition, as discussed in chapters 3, and preservation of the Internet's "end-to-end" ethic, as discussed in chapter 5.

There are no similar economic conditions that could warrant pervasive regulation on the wireless side of the industry. As a general matter, there are no wireless monopolies to worry about, "natural" or otherwise, and thus no anticompetitive "leveraging" opportunities. There are, to be sure, nontrivial fixed costs and scale economies in the wireless market. To serve even a few customers, wireless firms must invest large sums both to acquire spectrum rights, either at auction or in a secondary market, and then to build out an infrastructure of transmission antennas, base stations, and switches. Within a given metropolitan area, the average cost per customer of those investments is obviously much lower for the millionth customer than for the first. But that fact does not make wireless telephony a natural monopoly market, just as the high fixed costs and low unit costs of the automobile industry do not make car manufacturing such a market. A wireless firm's long run average costs do not decline "over the entire extent of the market"[36] with every increase in output, as the persistence of successful competition in this industry has shown. Of course, competition can thrive only to the extent that the government makes enough spectrum available for multiple wireless firms to conduct their business. But, as we have seen, the FCC has now freed up enough spectrum for use in this market to alleviate what had been, in the era of government-sanctioned duopolies, an *artificial* restriction on entry.

In the previous section, we explained that policymakers have cited widespread competition as their basis for liberating wireless carriers from most forms of public-utility-type regulation. Even though wireless telephony lacks natural monopoly characteristics, however, it remains very much a network industry and, as such, is highly subject to the first of our three phenomena: *network effects*. Like any network, a wireless network is only as valuable to any subscriber as the number of other people she can reach through that network. This fact gives rise to a rich assortment of issues concerning whether and when the government should intervene in the wireless market to force cooperation among different networks.

Some of these are familiar issues of *interconnection*: the terms on which one network must cooperate with another to enable its subscribers to call, or be called by, the other network's subscribers. Wireless telephony could never have developed without rights of interconnection with wireline networks. A wireless subscription would be worth much less to a subscriber if she could call only other subscribers to the same wireless network and not, for example, her colleagues at the office or her family at home. But few doubted that wireline ILECs would be required to interconnect with wireless carriers on *some* terms. In the *Carterfone* decision, discussed in chapter 2, the FCC required such interconnection with mobile radio networks even before the dawn of cellular telephony, albeit on less than favorable terms.[37] When the FCC first authorized cellular service in the early 1980s, it took the interconnection requirement to the next logical step, conditioning an ILEC's own cellular licenses on its commitment to provide nondiscriminatory interconnection with unaffiliated cellular operators on a carrier-to-carrier basis.[38]

In the wireless industry, the enduring interconnection disputes between wireless carriers and their wireline counterparts have generally involved the compensation that such carriers owe, or are owed, when they handle part of a call that originates or terminates on some other network, including ordinary wireline telephone networks. That compensation issue can be enormously complicated, in part because a wireless carrier often interconnects *directly* only with a large regional ILEC such as a Bell company. When it handles calls to or from the subscriber of some other carrier—such as a wireline CLEC, a small rural ILEC, or another wireless carrier—it typically interconnects *indirectly* with that carrier by relying on the Bell company to play the intermediary, routing calls between the other two carriers' networks over its ubiquitous transport pipes. The rates that the Bells may charge terminating carriers for that so-called *transiting* service, and the rates that the terminating carriers may in turn charge the originating ones, are matters of intense controversy. We defer that set of issues until the next chapter, which addresses questions of "intercarrier compensation" generally.

Here in this section we address the proper scope of government involvement in promoting interoperability among wireless networks: the ability of one carrier's subscribers to use their cellphones when traveling through geographic regions covered only by other carriers' wireless networks. Let's start at the beginning. Although there are half a dozen national wireless networks in operation today, there were none at all in the early days of wireless telephony. That is because, as we have seen, the FCC assigned the first "cellular" licenses on a strictly local basis. Although the FCC subsequently allowed different carriers to consolidate these geographically disparate networks, the local character of the initial license assignments gave rise to hundreds of millions of dollars in transaction costs, such as the legal fees needed to file the necessary applications. In the interim, it also created an acute need to ensure that a subscriber could still use her cellphone when she traveled away from her own carrier's geographically limited network and into the territory of unaffiliated wireless carriers, for otherwise cellular service would have been much less valuable to her and all other subscribers and the wireless industry might never have gotten off the ground. A consumer can enjoy such interoperability, however, only if (i) those other carriers agree to let her use their wireless networks and (ii) her cellphone is compatible with those networks.

Carriers address the first of these issues through *roaming agreements*. The most common of these are agreements between wireless carriers to allow the mutual use of each carrier's network by the other carrier's subscribers. Each carrier pays the other for the privilege and passes the costs on to its own subscribers, either directly in the form of per-minute roaming fees or as part of a flat monthly rate for a national calling plan. Because there are so many wireless carriers and thus so many permutations of carrier-to-carrier agreements, third-party clearinghouses, rather than the parties themselves, often negotiate them. The FCC has generally declined to regulate the terms of these carrier-to-carrier roaming agreements, observing that, because no carrier dominates the wireless industry, most carriers perceive much to gain and little to lose from negotiating efficient roaming arrangements on behalf of their subscribers.[39] As a backstop, however, the Commission does require all carriers to provide "manual roaming" on a pay-per-use basis to individual cellphone users in the absence of a carrier-to-carrier agreement, usually by means of a credit card.[40]

Of course, two carriers cannot enter into a meaningful roaming agreement if they have built out their networks with incompatible technology. From the advent of cellular service, the FCC specified a single analog standard—Advanced Mobile Phone System (AMPS)—to ensure interoperability among geographically disparate cellular systems throughout the country. This uniformity provided the technological basis for all customers to use the same cellphones when roaming in parts of the country not served by their own wireless carriers.

When PCS carriers received their first licenses in the mid-1990s, however, they began building out "second generation" (2G) networks that, from the beginning, used purely digital technology—an advance that allowed them to provide better signal quality than their "first generation" analog rivals and more voice conversations per increment of spectrum. But the FCC did not require all of them to use, and they did not in fact use, the same *type* of digital technology. Instead, they employed different and incompatible standards for squeezing additional bandwidth out of available spectrum by using the same frequencies for more than one call at a time. These standards fall into two general families: those that allocate bandwidth on the basis of *time slicing*, and those that use "spread spectrum" technology (see chapter 7) to allocate bandwidth on the basis of a sophisticated *code*. We address each approach in turn, and then turn to the arguments for and against government intervention to ensure national uniformity in digital standards.

The time-slicing family of standards is analogous to the time division multiplexing techniques we discussed in chapter 2 when surveying the technology of wireline networks. This approach aggregates, within the same frequency, the signals associated with several different calls. It "samples" each call's signals many times a second and transmits those samples—e.g., digital representations of the sounds of your voice—within precisely calibrated time slots. If the samples are taken often enough, the system can convey an accurate representation of the sounds coming out of your mouth. Of course, like wireline telephony companies, any wireless carrier saves bandwidth by disregarding many of the natural frequencies associated with the human voice, so the transmitted signal will never approximate what you would sound like if the listener were sitting next to you.

There are several different standards within this family of time-slicing techniques. These include TDMA (for "time division multiple access"), which is the original standard of this type in the United States; GSM (for "Global System for Mobile"), which is the industry standard in Europe; and iDEN (for "Integrated Digital Enhanced Network"), which is used by Nextel. As discussed below, European regulators have long required that carriers use GSM for conventional wireless telephony. In the United States, the major carriers that had been using TDMA, such as Cingular, have replaced that standard with GSM or are in the process of doing so. Significantly, despite their use of similar multiplexing techniques, all of the standards mentioned here are mutually incompatible. You cannot use a TDMA-only phone in a GSM network or vice versa, nor can you use an iDEN-only phone in a TDMA or GSM network.

The second major family of digital access standards is called "code division multiple access," or "CDMA." In the 1980s, building on military applications developed during World War II, Qualcomm's Irwin Jacobs pioneered CDMA for commercial uses, and it now is used by such carriers as Verizon Wireless and Sprint PCS in the United States. CDMA relies on spread spectrum technology to disperse the signals associated with each call over many different frequencies. Some have likened CDMA to permitting ten pairs of people to converse simultaneously across a dinner table in ten different languages and counting on each pair to pick out and focus on the language they understand. To perform this feat, a CDMA system exploits advances in digital processing technology to attain the almost unfathomable intelligence needed for the devices on each end of a transmission to understand which signals belong to which calls and decode them for end users.

While CDMA is more efficient than the time-slicing standards at squeezing more bandwidth out of available spectrum, its equipment (because of the necessary intelligence in it) is more sophisticated and expensive. Nonetheless, it is winning many converts throughout the industry, for reasons that are instructive about the trends in high technology markets more generally. As *The Economist* reported in June 2003: "Perhaps the greatest lesson from the story of CDMA is that what seems impossibly complex today may well seem simple tomorrow—thanks to the relentless advance of Moore's law," which "states, roughly, that the cost of a given amount of computing power halves every 18 months. . . . Without it, Dr Jacobs admits, CDMA handsets would have been too large, and the base-stations would have been too expensive. 'Our argument was that Moore's law will take care of cost, size and power for us,' he says"[41]—and he was right.

At first blush, one might think that the proliferation of all these mutually incompatible digital standards would preclude any given carrier's customers from using their cellphones as they travel through the United States. But market forces, combined with minimal regulation as a backstop, have generally kept that from happening. First, there are now a number of "national" wireless networks; although no carrier has built a ubiquitous digital network covering every part of the country, each can offer coverage in most major metropolitan areas and along most major highways from coast to coast, either through its own network or through mutual arrangements with other facilities-based carriers that use the same standard. Second, the original "cellular" licensees are obligated until February 2008 to provide service by means of the analog AMPS standard (in addition to the digital service these major cellular carriers now provide to their own customers). The FCC reasoned that keeping the analog standard in place for this long period would facilitate roaming agreements among carriers with incompatible digital standards, would accommodate hearing-impaired individuals whose hearing aids may be incompatible with digital telephones, and would enable rural providers that still rely on an analog system to offer a service usable by subscribers to a national digital service.[42]

Of course, to ensure that they can receive service when they drive into less populous areas, customers must have "dual mode" phones capable of transmitting and receiving in analog mode in addition to whatever digital standard their wireless carrier has chosen for its own network. Some carriers also offer "tri-mode" phones, which, depending on the model, offer a choice of two digital standards (such as GSM and TDMA) plus analog mode. Increasingly, however, consumers are buying handsets that operate *only* in digital mode, with a resulting lack of service in some rural areas.[43] Taking a page from "software defined radio" technology, the cellphones of the future may obviate many compatibility issues through versatile software capable of switching back and forth among many different standards in roughly the same way that a single operating system can run multiple applications. The problem is that chips capable of such versatility are expensive and tend to be gluttons for battery power. Moore's Law will likely solve that problem too, but only over time.[44]

While U.S. regulators have let these digital access standards proliferate, European regulators—not known for their faith in wholly unregulated markets—have taken the opposite course.[45] In the late 1980s, anticipating the transition from the first (analog) to the second (digital) generation of wireless services, they adopted a single digital standard, GSM, and required all European providers to adopt it. This decision was widely hailed as a principal reason why Europe jumped ahead of the United States in the 1990s in overall cellphone penetration. A European consumer could invest in a cellphone and expect compatible digital service from any transmission site she passed, no matter where in Europe she traveled. For their part, manufacturers were assured of a giant market for digital cellphones of a particular type. Precisely because more phones could be designed for a single standard, manufacturers and consumers both benefited from scale economies that were unavailable where, as in the United States, the proliferation of incompatible standards has balkanized the cellphone market.

European regulators sought to replicate this success by centrally managing the transition to the third generation of wireless services (3G), which offer advanced data applications in addition to plain vanilla mobile telephony. In particular, they required every auction winner of a 3G license to provide service using a spread spectrum standard known as "Universal Mobile Telephone System" (UMTS)—or, more commonly now, "W-CDMA." This time, however, the transition has gone less smoothly. First, fanciful speculation about the rapid growth of 3G markets led key European carriers to pay such extravagant sums for their licenses that, in some cases, they could no longer secure financing to build out their networks on schedule. Second, a lack of coordination caused manufacturers to produce mutually incompatible equipment; for example, some handsets did not function properly when used with cellular transmission facilities produced by a different manufacturer, despite their theoretical conformity to a single standard. Finally, as of this writing, W-CDMA remains commercially unproven. In head-to-head competition outside of Europe, W-CDMA-based services have reportedly fared less well than services based on Qualcomm's competing CDMA2000 standard.[46]

Although Verizon Wireless and others already use their existing spectrum to offer broadband mobile services, primarily to business customers, the planning continues for the widespread introduction of 3G networks in the United States, with auctions for additional spectrum tentatively set for 2005.[47] Following its earlier model, the FCC will likely let the market choose the standards that ultimately will be used. There are, to be sure, drawbacks to this laissez-faire philosophy. Uncertainty about standards makes it riskier for manufacturers to develop products designed for any particular standard. And, as noted, heterogeneity among the standards that reach the market raises the unit costs for products designed for any particular standard and reduces the number of transmission sites that any given consumer's handset can communicate with.

On the other hand, if U.S. regulators had followed the lead of their European counterparts in the late 1980s and adopted GSM as the universal standard, the world might well be a worse place overall. In particular, if the FCC had reduced or eliminated any U.S. market for CDMA products, it would have deprived consumers of this technology's benefits, undermined the progress in spread spectrum technologies more generally, and set back the development of CDMA-oriented 3G services—both in the United States and in Europe. And in the long run, the carriers that chose CDMA technologies from the beginning may well be rewarded for doing so, not only in the form of more efficient spectrum usage, but also in the sense that 2G CDMA networks enjoy an easier transition path to 3G than their GSM counterparts do.[48] This is one of many contexts in which government intervention in standard-setting presents difficult trade-offs between short term market growth and long term innovation. We examine such trade-offs more fully in chapter 12.

IV. Wireless-Wireline Competition and Regulatory Parity Questions

In chapter 6, we discussed the prospect that VoIP applications, riding on top of non-wireline broadband platforms such as cable modem service, would provide the long-awaited facilities-based alternative to traditional telephone networks for mass market voice services. In fact, however, the wireless industry has already been quietly playing that role for several years. As FCC Chairman Michael Powell told Congress in 2003, "much of the most significant competition in voice . . . has come from wireless phone service."[49] Most policymakers, however, are still unused to thinking of wireless carriers as new entrants into traditional local exchange markets. Indeed, Congress self-consciously excluded providers of "commercial mobile service" from the definition of "local exchange carrier," and thus from the ranks of CLECs, even though wireless carriers indisputably provide "telephone exchange service."[50] This approach reflects the public's traditional view that wireless and wireline services are just market complements rather than substitutes.

That traditional perception of wireless service, however, is beginning to change. The change is most obviously revealed in the decisions of approximately 6% of American households to "cut the cord" to their wireline telephone company altogether and subscribe *only* to a wireless service.[51] So far, of course, most wireless subscribers have kept their landline connections. But many of them, too, use wireless as a substitute for wireline service in at least two important respects. First, a customer with a cellphone is less likely to purchase a second landline connection into the home, and this is a key reason why, "[s]ince 2000, we have seen for the first time a decrease in the number of retail access lines served by the incumbent LECs."[52] Second, wireless customers are also likely to pay a flat fee for large buckets of "anytime/anywhere" minutes and use those minutes to make many of their long distance calls. They thereby avoid paying minute-of-use fees to place long distance calls over conventional wireline networks. Wireline telephone companies thus earn lower revenues in the form of direct toll charges to end users and access charges to independent long distance companies.

Worse yet for the wireline incumbents, the main reasons that wireless subscribers keep circuit-switched wireline connections at all—greater reliability and call quality—will subside with time as more spectrum is allocated for this purpose and wireless carriers overcome obstacles to filling in the gaps in their networks with new transmission sites. Of course, wireless service also offers something that, by definition, wireline service never can: mobility. These considerations have led some market analysts to predict that within several years, "[m]obile phones will dominate personal calling and severely cannibalize landline minutes of use," with dramatic industry-wide consequences.[53]

This prospect raises familiar issues of regulatory parity. For the most part, the emergence of the wireless platform as a facilities-based replacement for the traditional wireline voice platform should affect regulation of the latter more than it affects regulation of the former. After all, the sensible policy response to new competition in a regulated industry is to relax regulation of the incumbents, not to increase regulation of the largely deregulated upstarts. But regulatory inertia will inevitably cause state and federal policymakers to move slowly in adjusting legacy regulation to reflect the declining dominance of wireline telephone companies in the voice market. The result, during the transition, will be a messy but perhaps unavoidable regulatory asymmetry between these competing platforms. To illustrate the types of regulatory challenges presented by the convergence of these platforms, we examine two case studies: number portability and requirements for enhanced 911 functionality.

A. Number portability

A standard ten-digit telephone number is "portable" if a customer can take it with her when she cancels service with one provider and orders service from another. On a technological level, such portability requires each carrier to cooperate with national databases that peg any given number to a particular carrier and instruct all other carriers processing calls destined for that number to send them to that carrier's network.[54]

Under section 251(b)(2) of the Communications Act, as revised in 1996, all local exchange carriers must provide number portability for their subscribers. Although wireless carriers are not formally classified as LECs, the FCC exercised independent authority in 1996 to compel all wireless carriers to ensure number portability among themselves within several years.[55] The Commission's policy objective, as in the wireline context, is to reduce the *switching costs* that customers incur—in the form of printing out new business cards, or telling friends about a new telephone number—when they move from one carrier to the next in the hope of better service. Portability rules can ameliorate such switching costs, but usually with a trade-off: providers can comply only by incurring extra engineering and administrative costs.[56] Here the FCC reasoned that imposing those extra costs on the industry was necessary because, without number portability, some consumers would be locked in to their existing service, no matter how mediocre, and would be unable to benefit from competition on the merits from superior services.[57] That would be bad not just for them individually, but for wireless consumers generally: the more captive a wireless carrier's customer base is, the more complacent that carrier will be in seeking to meet its customers' needs.

The wireless industry fiercely resisted the Commission's wireless-to-wireless number portability requirement for many years, arguing that customer turnover was great enough already, that portability rules would add only marginally to the already intense competition among carriers for existing wireless customers, and that the significant implementation costs would outweigh the benefits. Industry opposition delayed, but did not derail, the eventual imposition of these wireless-to-wireless number portability obligations. In June 2003, the D.C. Circuit rebuffed the final legal challenges to the Commission's rules.[58] The industry's entreaties for a legislative override fell flat when Verizon Wireless, breaking ranks with its fellow carriers, announced its support for number portability upon realizing that, with its general reputation as the most reliable wireless network, it stood to gain more than to lose from greater customer churn. Thus, in November 2003, the FCC's portability rules finally took effect.[59] Technical problems made the initial mechanics of "porting" a wireless customer's number (i.e., reassigning it from one carrier to another) more problematic than the FCC had hoped. The industry is slowly resolving those problems, however, and implementation of the number portability mandate ranks among the best-known of Michael Powell's accomplishments during his tenure as FCC chairman.

Despite its deep divisions on wireless-to-wireless portability, the wireless industry stood united behind a related and ultimately successful proposal: if that industry had to implement such portability for itself, the *wireline* industry should also have to accommodate a cord-cutting customer's request to port her conventional wireline telephone number to her new *wireless* carrier. Theoretically, the obligation would run both ways: another customer could cancel her existing *wireless* account and take the number with her when signing up with a *wireline* carrier. But everyone knew that wireline-wireless number portability would operate to the net benefit of the wireless industry, since customers increasingly view mobile wireless phones as a potential replacement for stationary landline phones, and not vice versa.

That consideration itself, of course, does not make such "intermodal number portability," as the FCC calls it, competitively problematic. To the contrary, so long as the implementation costs are manageable, these requirements increase allocative efficiency by facilitating consumer choice. In execution, however, there is one respect in which wireline-wireless portability can be competitively skewed, at least in the short term. The reason lies in the importance to wireline carriers, and the unimportance to wireless carriers, of associating particular telephone numbers with particular *rate centers*.

Traditionally, ILECs assigned telephone numbers to customers on the basis of the central office switch (the "exchange") that handled their calls, and those numbers themselves specified for carriers throughout the country exactly where a call bound for those customers should be directed. ILECs remain dependent on this geographic pairing of particular numbers to particular places, in part because that is how they have designed their call-routing systems, and in part because they have configured their billing systems to assess toll charges (or not) on the basis of the geographic rate center to which given numbers are assigned. If you live in Denver and place a call over Qwest's network to someone with a number associated with the rate center that includes Boulder, the network knows from that number not to impose toll charges on you, for state regulators have deemed the call "local." But if you place a call to a Qwest customer in Colorado Springs, the network knows from that customer's number that this is a non-local toll call, and Qwest bills you accordingly.

To an ILEC's systems, the precise digits in those numbers decide whether or not the ILEC will receive millions of dollars in toll revenues. These, of course, are just legacy conventions. For example, the economic cost to the ILEC of placing the "long distance" call to Colorado Springs is little different from the economic cost of placing the "local" call to Boulder. But the extra toll charges assessed for the call to Colorado Springs are part of the vast web of implicit cross-subsidies that have traditionally supported cheap telephone service for residential subscribers. Both ILECs and state regulators, moreover, are loath to ignore rate-center boundaries in the name of greater regulatory rationality, for that would immediately cut off the source of those cross-subsidies.

The problem for ILECs is that wireless carriers are unbound by these conventions. Precisely because wireless service is characterized by mobility, a wireless number cannot indicate to all carriers where a given customer is located, and it is not designed to do so. Instead, it indicates to them only which wireless carrier serves that customer. Once a call is handed off to the proper carrier's network on the basis of that information, the customer's telephone number has, of itself, no direct geographic significance to the carrier. Instead, it serves as a proxy for the customer's handset, which, if it is turned on, is tracked down through the electronic mechanisms discussed at the beginning of this chapter. For that reason, and because wireless service plans often make no distinction between "local" and "long distance" minutes anyway, the rate-center approach to the assignment of telephone numbers is quite alien to the wireless industry. Wireless carriers do not even bother to obtain blocks of assignable numbers from the North American Numbering Plan Administrator for every ILEC rate center in which they provide service. Instead, a wireless carrier obtains blocks of numbers for only a fraction of rate centers within its service territories and assigns them to subscribers without regard to which rate centers their billing addresses are in.

It is thus comparatively easy for a wireless carrier to take on a telephone number previously assigned to a wireline customer because the carrier is largely indifferent to the precise digits in the number. But it may be difficult for a wireline ILEC to take on a telephone number previously assigned to a wireless customer because the odds are small that her number happens to belong to the exact rate center in which she requests telephone service. ILECs claim that they cannot resolve this problem overnight by eliminating legacy rate-center boundaries because doing so would both require enormous expenditures in system overhauls and, as noted, would threaten millions of dollars in toll revenues. As a result, legacy regulatory choices artificially magnify the extent to which natural market forces already make wireless carriers the net winners under intermodal number portability rules. The major wireline carriers, with the notable exception of Verizon, thus opposed such rules as inimical to principles of competitive neutrality.

In November 2003, the FCC weighed those concerns against the consumer benefits of portability and came out decisively in favor of the latter. "In our view," it said, "it would not be appropriate to prevent wireline customers from taking advantage of the mobility or the larger local calling areas associated with wireless service simply because wireline carriers cannot currently accommodate all potential requests from customers with wireless service to port their numbers to a wireline service provider. . . . To the extent that wireline carriers may have fewer opportunities to win customers through porting, this disparity results from the wireline network architecture and state regulatory requirements, rather than Commission rules."[60] Although the phrasing is inartful, the meaning is clear: the FCC will tolerate some lack of competitive neutrality when it is an unavoidable by-product of popular initiatives to promote cross-platform competition—particularly if, as in this case, the non-neutrality results from legacy practices that the Commission believes the aggrieved parties should be working to eliminate in any event.

B. "Enhanced 911" mandates

Number portability is not the only area in which the very mobility that defines wireless service gives rise to inevitable asymmetries in the regulation of that service and wireline telephony. Consider, for example, the FCC's regulations requiring effective 911 dialing. When you dial 911 from your *wireline* telephone, not only is your call automatically routed to the emergency calling center appropriate to your location—a functionality known as "basic 911"—but the telephone company gives that calling center your call-back number and tells it exactly where you are: namely, the fixed location of the telephone from which you have placed the call. This location information can be a life-saving necessity if you are in such distress that you cannot tell the person answering the 911 call where to send help.

This information, however, is much more difficult for wireless carriers to provide precisely because the service is mobile: the caller could be anywhere. That is a matter of some concern because 150,000 calls are placed each day to 911 from wireless phones.[61] To be sure, after upgrading its systems, a wireless carrier can pass along to emergency personnel what cell site the caller is transmitting to. But the cell itself could be up to several miles wide—hardly enough information to permit a timely rescue mission. To provide this more exact information, wireless carriers rely on one of two principal means of pinpointing a caller's location within a cell. First, they can install in their cellphones global positioning system (GPS) devices that rely on satellite communication to identify the cellphone's exact position in much the same way that new cars employ GPS devices in their on-board navigation systems. Second, providers can install sophisticated electronic gadgetry within the network to "triangulate" a cellphone's signal by measuring it from several different transmission sites. Either way, building such "enhanced 911" (E911) functionality into wireless networks can be quite expensive.

Like number portability, the E911 question raises difficult issues for policymakers. Should they require wireless carriers simply to provide "basic 911" functionality—the routing of calls to the appropriate calling center—given the extra costs that must be incurred before wireless carriers, unlike their wireline counterparts, can provide accurate customer locations? Or should they require wireless carriers to provide exactly the same enhanced functionality, no matter what the extra costs? Such questions require complex and ultimately subjective judgments about the importance of E911, the need for this functionality in the wireless environment, and what role considerations of "regulatory parity" should play in contexts where, as here, it is technologically much easier to implement a given regulatory obligation on one telecommunications platform than another. Ensuring regulatory parity between rival telecommunications platforms is more an exercise in practical judgment than in formal equality of treatment.

The FCC ultimately required wireless carriers to provide the same E911 functionality as their wireline counterparts,[62] but the road to implementing this mandate has been long and winding. As an interim ("Phase I") measure, the FCC has largely succeeded in requiring carriers to pass along the relevant cell site to 911 call centers as well as a call-back number. But the FCC has struggled to complete Phase II of this initiative: ensuring that carriers upgrade their networks to provide pinpoint location information. Indeed, by early 2003, only around 5% of all 911 call centers were receiving such information.[63] Former FCC Chief Engineer Dale Hatfield, whom the FCC commissioned to study the problem, reported that the slow implementation of Phase II stemmed from inadequate funding and poor coordination by different stakeholders—wireless carriers, wireline incumbents, public safety authorities, the FCC, and state governments, among others.[64] Over the past two years, Congress and the FCC have redoubled efforts to finish the job by prodding these interested parties to cooperate.[65] Nonetheless, a recent report by the General Accounting Office concluded that the implementation of wireless E911 is still several years away, again emphasizing how funding and coordination problems have complicated this effort.[66]

* * *

Outright competition between wireless and wireline telephony services will only accelerate in the years ahead. Over time, this cross-platform rivalry will require adjustments to the rules governing each platform. On the one hand, competition from wireless carriers (as well as VoIP providers) will justify a lighter touch in the traditional economic regulation of wireline ILECs. On the other hand, as consumers rely increasingly on mobile telephony, both federal and state regulators will be inclined to subject wireless carriers, much like VoIP providers, to the gamut of "non-economic" regulation to which wireline ILECs have long been subject, of which E911 has been perhaps the most prominent example to date. In so doing, however, policymakers must resist the temptation to achieve superficial regulatory parity by senselessly subjecting wireless carriers in a robustly competitive market to forms of regulation that are appropriate only for dominant carriers, such as rate regulation[67] or obligations to provide "equal access" to unaffiliated long distance carriers.[68]

Of all the legacy regimes that will need to be adjusted to account for the rise of such cross-platform competition, however, perhaps the most complex is the set of rules addressing intercarrier compensation—i.e., the terms on which one carrier completes calls originated on another carrier's network. We turn now to that topic.

9

Intercarrier Compensation

There are many telecommunications networks in the world, and each day millions of voice or data "calls" cross from one network to another. Suppose, for example, that you turn on your Nextel wireless phone and call your mother a few miles away, who has been a loyal wireline customer of BellSouth for many years. Nextel *originates* the call and hands it off to BellSouth at a point of interconnection. BellSouth then *terminates* (or "completes") the call by routing it to the switch nearest your mother and dedicating network capacity to the call for as long as it lasts. Viewed in isolation, this particular call to your mother is easily accommodated by existing network capacity. But the cumulative effect of all such calls placed during peak traffic periods is to impose enormous demands on the networks involved. Each carrier must respond to those demands by investing in enough switching and transport capacity to process all of this traffic in the aggregate.

Now assume, simply for the sake of illustration, that the majority of calls exchanged between these two networks are placed *by* Nextel's customers *to* BellSouth's customers—say, because many Nextel customers leave their phones turned off when not in use. This means that, in meeting its regulatory duty to interconnect with Nextel's network, BellSouth incurs extra network costs of its own that are attributable to calls originated on Nextel's network by Nextel's customers, with whom BellSouth may have no contractual relationship of any kind. In particular, BellSouth must purchase, on the margin, larger switches and fatter transport pipes to accommodate the extra incoming telecommunications traffic. In contrast, Nextel incurs proportionately lower incremental costs to accommodate the calls that are placed by BellSouth's customers and bound for Nextel's customers.

This example introduces the basic threshold question in "intercarrier compensation" policy: who should pay for the additional network costs that a carrier incurs because of its duty to terminate calls originated on *other* telecommunications networks by callers with whom the carrier may have no direct relationship?[*] There are two basic answers. One, known as *bill-and-keep*, would require each such carrier to absorb these extra costs itself and pass them on to its own subscribers in the form of higher retail rates. The other solution would require the *calling* party's carrier, whose customers originate the calls that "cause" these extra costs, to compensate the terminating carrier that incurs the costs. This latter approach, known as *calling-party's-network-pays* (CPNP), has been the traditional rule in the telecommunications industry for many years. For simplicity, we will refer to it simply as "calling-network-pays."

The choice between these two approaches, which we examine in parts II and III of this chapter, may seem at first blush like a fairly narrow issue, but in fact it has broad structural implications for the telecommunications market. As noted in chapter 2, the current flow of intercarrier compensation payments—which some estimate at $14 billion per year[1]—reflects basic regulatory choices made around the time of the AT&T breakup and then in the passage of the 1996 Act. Under the dichotomous system in place today, a long distance carrier pays *access charges* to the local carriers on each end of a long distance call; and a local exchange carrier typically pays lower *reciprocal compensation* rates whenever it hands off local calls to be terminated on another carrier's network. Each of these two schemes follows basic calling-network-pays principles, albeit in quite different ways. As explained below, competition and technological innovation have made a mockery of the local/long distance distinction underlying these two schemes and, more generally, have drawn into doubt the long run utility of the calling-network-pays approach. Dissatisfaction with that approach has

---

[*] There are many contexts in which telecommunications carriers owe compensation to one another. For example, a CLEC must pay an ILEC for the right to lease its network elements, and one wireless carrier must pay another to give its customers roaming privileges on that other's network. The term "intercarrier compensation," however, is misleadingly broad in that it does *not* refer to the carrier-to-carrier payments made in those contexts. Instead, in the telecommunications world, that term is used to describe arrangements governing who owes what to whom when two or more carriers cooperate to complete a call between subscribers to different networks.

sparked considerable interest in the bill-and-keep alternative, which presents policy and legal questions of its own.

I. The Crazy-Quilt of Intercarrier Compensation Schemes

To show the importance of devising a coherent set of rules for intercarrier compensation, we begin by focusing on what happens when regulators settle instead for an incoherent patchwork of mutually inconsistent intercarrier compensation schemes, each of which applies only to an arbitrarily compartmentalized class of calls or carriers. The result is arbitrage and competitive distortion, as we demonstrate through four case studies.

A. Access charge arbitrage scandals—and their origin in regulatory artificiality

In the summer of 2003, the debt-ridden, scandal-wracked company once known as WorldCom, since renamed MCI, was poised to come out of bankruptcy with a new lease on life. On a Sunday morning in late July, however, the *New York Times* ran an ominous if somewhat obscure front-page story about a scandal that threatened (but ultimately failed) "to derail the company's plan to reorganize and emerge from the bankruptcy proceedings."[2] The story reported that MCI, "the nation's second-largest long distance carrier," may have "defrauded other telephone companies of at least hundreds of millions of dollars over nearly a decade. . . . The central element of MCI's scheme, people involved in the inquiry said, consisted of disguising long distance calls as local calls[.]"[3] The particular allegations against MCI may or may not be true; MCI denied them, and, as of this writing, they remain unproven.[4] Our objective here is not to assess the factual legitimacy of those allegations, but to explain why any carrier might have an incentive to engage in such arbitrage, and why such schemes expose radically unstable fault lines at the core of the government's traditional intercarrier compensation regime.

Suppose that a long distance company wishes to place a voice or data transmission from its customer in Los Angeles to a called party in New York served by Verizon's wireline network. The long distance company would save money if, instead of delivering the call directly to Verizon, it sent the call instead to a CLEC accomplice in the New York area, which in turn would deliver the call to Verizon. Why would the long distance company add this seemingly unnecessary middleman to an otherwise uncomplicated call from Los Angeles to New York? The answer has to do with regulatory arbitrage. Verizon—the "terminating carrier"—is entitled to charge much higher rates for completing "long distance" calls than "local" calls. As a result, the long distance company would do better if it reimbursed the CLEC for paying Verizon the lower "local" call termination rate than if it paid Verizon the higher rate for a completed long distance call to the same destination, even if that company also had to pay the CLEC additional consideration (beyond simple reimbursement) for its trouble.[5] For this scheme to work, of course, the CLEC accomplice would need to strip off the signaling information that identifies Los Angeles as the origination point for the call; by doing so, it can trick Verizon's switch into perceiving the incoming transmission as a "local" call originated by the CLEC rather than a "long distance" call originated by the long distance company. That, in a nutshell, is what some carriers allege that WorldCom and other long distance companies, together with their CLEC business partners, have done to evade access charges.

From a theoretical perspective, the most interesting thing about these allegations is that such arbitrage opportunities arise in the first place. Why, in particular, is there this tempting discrepancy in Verizon's call termination rates? After all, the cost of completing the call—of routing it through Verizon's own switch en route to the called party—is the same no matter where the call originally came from. Indeed, that is why Verizon can be so easily fooled into thinking that these long distance calls are local. Technologically speaking, Verizon's network is indifferent as to whether the caller is sitting in Los Angeles or in Manhattan. Why, then, does Verizon's compensation for completing the calls vary so much depending on that apparently irrelevant detail?

The answer is rooted in decades of calcified regulatory tradition. As discussed in chapter 2, regulators have traditionally viewed access charges—the fees that carriers impose for originating and terminating long distance calls—as a critical source of implicit subsidies for local telephone incumbents. As a result, the access charges collected by the local carrier at each end of a long distance call have traditionally exceeded any rigorous measure of the costs such carriers incur in handling those calls. That is particularly true of "intrastate" access charges set by state commissions: the fees that long distance carriers pay local carriers for handling calls that stay within a given state's boundaries. To a lesser extent, it may also be true of "interstate" access charges set by the FCC for long distance calls that do cross state lines, although the FCC has taken measures to lower such charges closer to cost and replace the lost implicit subsidies with explicit funding mechanisms under the universal service provision of section 254, as discussed in the next chapter.

In 1996, Congress took no immediate steps to stem this uneconomic money flow; indeed, in the grandfathering provision of section 251(g), it expressly authorized the FCC to conduct business as usual in its regulation of access charges for long distance calls. But there was never any analogous subsidy flow—and thus no irrational regulation to protect—in the carrier-to-carrier exchange of local traffic.[6] And permitting ILECs to charge similarly above-cost rates for terminating calls originated by their new local exchange rivals would obviously raise a host of competitive concerns. In sections 251(b)(5) and 252(d)(2), therefore, Congress prescribed a "reciprocal compensation" regime that permits each terminating carrier to charge each originating carrier only for the "additional costs" of completing a call, and no more.[7] Although the statutory language of these provisions seems to anticipate that money will flow from one carrier to another, Congress added that it did not mean "to preclude arrangements that afford the mutual recovery of costs through the offsetting of reciprocal obligations, including arrangements that waive mutual recovery (such as bill-and-keep arrangements)."[8] We return to that beguiling caveat later in this chapter.

In the 1996 *Local Competition Order*, the FCC interpreted this obscure collection of provisions to require, for the most part, a calling-network-pays regime for "local" calls.[9] Under this approach, the calling party's carrier reimburses the called party's carrier for the latter's costs in (i) transporting a call from the point of hand-off between the two carriers to the switch directly serving the called party and then (ii) terminating the call through that switch en route to the called party.[*] For purposes of measuring these costs, the FCC chose, and the individual states must apply,

---

[*] For ease of exposition, we will use the word "termination" to encompass both of these functions except where we explicitly distinguish between them. *Cf.* 47 C.F.R. § 51.701(c), (d) (setting forth formal FCC definitions of "transport" and "termination").

the same TELRIC cost methodology that governs what CLECs traditionally paid ILECs when leasing these same usage-sensitive transport and switching functions as constituent elements of the "UNE platform" (see chapter 3). Although the resulting TELRIC-based cost estimates vary wildly from state to state, they all produce "reciprocal compensation" rates for CLECs far below the access charges that ILECs receive for terminating long distance calls, even though the functions involved are often exactly the same.

This brief synopsis brings us back to the arbitrage scheme described at the beginning of the chapter. If you were a long distance carrier looking to cut costs on the substantial terminating access charges you must pay to the called party's local carrier, you might look with some envy on the much lower rates that CLECs are paying that same carrier for the termination of local calls. You might be so envious, in fact, that you would try to disguise your long distance calls as local calls. Indeed, some industry analysts estimate that as much as 20% of all calls terminated on the public switched network fall within the category of "phantom traffic"—i.e., traffic whose origin is unidentified and thus cannot be accurately billed.[10]

Whatever their morality or legality, such arbitrage opportunities inevitably arise whenever regulators treat like services differently. No matter how hard regulators try to close the loopholes, such distinctions induce a thousand ways of cheating, and cheating creates not just market distortions but significant enforcement costs. As one former Bell company executive put it, the current situation "begs the participants to try to game . . . the system to reduce costs."[11] In the scenario outlined above, as in the EELs controversy described in chapter 3, the arbitrary distinction between "local" and "long distance" calls is what invites gaming. If this distinction sounds unsustainable over the long term, the following case study—which adds the Internet into the mix—should put to rest any doubt about that point.

B. The ISP reciprocal compensation controversy

In the 1990s, a peculiar type of "call" suddenly became popular: "dial-up" connections to the Internet over the public switched telephone network.[12] As we saw in chapter 4, such a call begins like any other telephone call except that the caller uses a computer modem rather than a telephone handset to dial a local number on the telephone network. The called party that answers is another computer modem—this one belonging to an Internet service provider such as AOL or Earthlink—rather than a human being. For the duration of this data "call," the telephone company's circuit switch establishes a fixed connection between the calling party and the ISP, and the ISP translates the analog signals exchanged by the two modems into digital signals and connects the calling party to the websites of her choice.

For jurisdictional purposes, the FCC has long viewed this transaction as a single long distance call—from the end user to the website—rather than a local call to the ISP.[13] Indeed, as discussed in chapter 5, that is how the FCC has justified regulating such calls as part of its traditional jurisdiction over "interstate" services—and preempting state efforts to regulate the terms of Internet access. As a purely technical matter, this jurisdictional characterization makes abundant sense. Although it may seem at first blush to be something else, an ISP is a kind of long distance carrier. It enters into a direct relationship with an end user to receive his calls, via his local carrier, and transport them over a long distance network—either its own Internet backbone or that of another provider—to a distant called party (the computer server hosting the website). To be sure, the ISP uses packet-switching technology and performs higher layer "protocol conversion" services not traditionally provided by circuit-switched long distance providers. But those logical layer services are independent of the raw transmission functions performed by the ISP (or its backbone subcontractor) on the physical layer.

So, given the essential similarity between ISPs and conventional long distance carriers—both in terms of the network role they play and in their independent relationship with their own fee-paying end users—one would expect ISPs to pay the same per-minute access charges that conventional long distance carriers pay ILECs. But they do not. For more than twenty years, the FCC has exempted ISPs and other information ("enhanced") service providers from federal or state access charges. It has entitled them instead to pay the ILEC whatever flat monthly fee is paid by the banks, department stores, and other ordinary, non-carrier customers that purchase local "business lines" of comparable capacity.[14] This longstanding FCC policy is known as the *ESP access charge exemption.*[*]

When people laud the FCC's storied decision not to "regulate the Internet," what they usually mean (whether or not they think about it this way) is that, through this exemption, the government has adopted a kind of industrial policy encouraging the growth of information services by insulating providers of those services from the obligations imposed on similarly situated non-Internet long distance carriers. And, as with any agenda-laden regulatory distinction, this asymmetry in treatment creates incentives for information service providers to take advantage of their privileged position by emphasizing services that, because of access charges, can be provided by conventional long distance carriers only at higher retail prices. A primary example of this, discussed in chapter 6, is the Internet telephony application known as "voice over Internet protocol," or VoIP. Partly because they can avoid paying access charges in whole or in part, VoIP providers can undersell regular circuit-switched carriers for domestic and, to an even greater extent, international long distance calls.[15] We will discuss the access charge issues raised by VoIP services later in this chapter.

In the late 1990s, increasing numbers of dial-up ISPs realized that they could avoid paying an ILEC anything at all, including business-line rates, by choosing CLECs as their local service providers. What does it mean for a CLEC to step in as the "local" service provider for an ISP? One curious feature of Internet-bound traffic over the public switched network is that it is essentially all one-way: an ISP's subscribers place calls to the ISP's modem bank (and thence to the distant websites, with which the subscribers can carry on protracted "conversations"), but the ISP's modem bank originates no calls back to those subscribers. A CLEC serves the ISP by interconnecting with the ILEC's network (the network that the ISP's subscribers are typically calling in from), receiving the incoming Internet-bound calls, routing them through a switch specially designed to terminate such calls to an ISP's modem bank, and then conveying them to that modem bank through high capacity loops.

---

[*] The distinction between telecommunications services and information services is discussed in chapters 5 and 6. The terms "information service provider" and "enhanced service provider" (ESP) are synonyms for all present purposes; "Internet service providers" (i.e., ISPs) are one subclass within that larger category of providers.

These tasks of "transporting "and "terminating"Internet-bound calls to an ISP impose costs on the CLEC, at least in the aggregate. Those are costs that the CLEC is taking off the shoulders of the ILEC, which would otherwise be performing these tasks for the ISPs and charging them business-line rates. Under the traditional "reciprocal compensation" regime for local calls, the ILEC in this arrangement must cover the total costs of the call all the way to the ISP, which means compensating the CLEC for its share of those costs. As noted, and for reasons explained below, the FCC's rules provide that the rates the ILEC pays the CLEC for these call-termination functions are the same TELRIC-derived rates that CLECs have traditionally paid the ILEC when leasing usage-sensitive switching and transport capacity on the ILEC 's network as part of the UNE-P arrangement (where available).[16] *In theory*, this payment system would give no carrier any artificial advantages or incentives if regulators accurately calculated the underlying costs of that capacity, arranged for the CLEC to recover those costs from the ILEC in a rational way, and allowed the ILEC, in turn, to pass those costs through to the end users that place these ISP-bound calls.

This basic theoretical point often gets lost in all the rhetoric about the "arbitrage" opportunity that ultimately developed. The devil, however, is in the details. Suppose that regulators get the "termination" rate wrong and set it far above the cost of obtaining and maintaining a switch to serve an ISP modem bank. Carriers would then have an artificial incentive to specialize in the termination of calls in order to receive, in effect, a regulatory subsidy for each minute of overstated costs for which they can bill the carrier that hands calls off to them. Indeed, as Internet usage increased, the subsidies would become so huge that CLECs would compete for them by offering to charge ISPs little or nothing for call termination services—or, in some cases, offering to pay them money outright for the privilege of serving them. Unlike the economically efficient arbitrage opportunity presented by the ESP access charge exemption itself, which frees market forces to drive supracompetitive access charges closer to cost, the self-sustaining subsidies produced by above-cost reciprocal compensation rates are economically inefficient in that they would detach prices from cost without the possibility of a market-based correction.

This is precisely what happened in the immediate aftermath of the 1996 Act. Most state commissions set the per-minute rate for the "switching element"—and thus for the termination of traffic—above forward-looking cost. At the time, ILECs were sanguine about this arrangement for two reasons: first, they benefited from high network element rates whenever CLECs leased capacity on ILEC switches as part of the UNE platform; and, second, they expected to be net recipients, rather than net originators, of traffic exchanged with other carriers, such that they would benefit from high call-termination rates as well. To appreciate the latter point, recall that in the days preceding the Internet boom, much of the traffic handed off between networks was between wireline ILECs and wireless carriers, whose subscribers tended to place more calls than they received.* In advocating higher rates for switching, the ILECs did not foresee that such rates would help create an enormous, regulation-driven windfall for the growing numbers of CLECs that specialized in terminating traffic to ISPs.[17]

From an ILEC's perspective, the large sums paid to ISP-serving CLECs as "reciprocal compensation" might still be tolerable if the ILEC could recoup those sums from its own individual residential customers to the extent they are placing these ISP-bound calls to begin with. But that approach was always politically out of the question. First, most state public utility commissions require ILECs to charge flat-rated monthly fees for

---

* The reason is that wireless subscribers often kept (and to some extent still keep) their cellphones turned off when not in use, in part to conserve battery power and in part to avoid paying the per-minute charges they would otherwise incur when answering unwanted calls. The retail plans of wireless carriers differ from those of most wireline carriers in that (i) local calls are typically charged by the minute and (ii) customers are charged for the calls they receive as well as the calls they place. It is important, however, not to confuse such retail practices with the wholesale carrier-to-carrier compensation rules discussed in this chapter. For example, even though wireless customers pay wireless carriers for taking calls originated on some other carrier's network, the wireless carrier does not itself compensate that other carrier for receiving those calls.

Occasionally, the FCC turns its attention to the retail side of these issues. In the late 1990s, for example, the Commission considered adopting a regulatory scheme that would have made it easier for wireless carriers to offer "calling-party-pays" plans to subscribers, under which retail fees for incoming calls would be charged not to the called party, but directly to the calling party upon some form of notification at the beginning of the call—much as calling parties pay for "900 number" calls. *See* Declaratory Ruling and Notice of Proposed Rulemaking, *Calling-Party-Pays Service Offering in the Commercial Mobil Radio Services*, 14 FCC Rcd 10,861 (1999). The FCC quietly scrapped this initiative later after determining, among other things, that the administrative costs of that regulatory scheme would outweigh the consumer benefits.

local service, not usage-sensitive rates, and most Americans have come to think of "local" calls as "free." Second, no state commission would entitle ILECs to charge more to households placing high volumes of calls to ISPs, much less to CLEC-served ISPs. That would be viewed—by political actors with only a partial understanding of the regulatory picture—as "taxing" the Internet.[18]

The state commissions arguably could have alleviated the arbitrage problem created by ISP-bound traffic simply by lowering call termination rates to levels that would reflect a CLEC's actual costs of termination and provide for recovery of those costs as they are incurred. But that process would have taken too long, and few ILECs trusted regulators to get those rates "right." Instead, for a multi-year period beginning in 2001, the FCC all but exempted ISP-bound traffic from the calling-network-pays principle that had governed intercarrier compensation for decades, devastating the business plans of CLECs whose corporate earnings depended on the continued receipt of above-cost compensation from ILECs for the termination of calls to ISPs.

Specifically, the FCC steadily reduced termination rates for ISP-bound traffic over the course of three years and capped the total "minutes" for which each CLEC could receive any compensation for such traffic at all.[19] This three-year program appeared to set the stage for a "transition towards a complete bill-and-keep recovery mechanism,"[20] under which no money would change hands. Under such a regime, each provider—the ILEC, the CLEC, and the ISP—would look to its own subscribers, rather than each other, to cover its costs. The ILEC would look to its end users, the CLEC would look to the ISP, and the ISP would look in turn to its own customers. And ISP subscription charges might increase (because CLEC providers would now have to charge ISPs rather than ILECs for termination costs), but less dramatically than if the ISP access charge exemption were eliminated outright (which would mean dramatically increased costs to ISPs). The FCC subjected the ILECs to one proviso: to benefit from this new regime, they had to agree to a similar transition towards bill-and-keep for all calls "subject to section 251(b)(5)"—roughly speaking, all local calls. That proviso included the local wireless traffic that remains unbalanced in that the number of wireless-to-wireline calls still exceeds the number of wireline-to-wireless calls, although somewhat less so than in 1996.

To this point, we have addressed the "ISP reciprocal compensation" controversy purely from a policy perspective; the debate became even more obscure whenever it reached the courts. Recall that, for jurisdictional purposes, the Commission viewed a "call" to an ISP and thence to a distant website as a single, unitary connection between the end user and the website, not as two separate calls—a local call from the end user to the ISP and then a long distance transmission from the ISP to the website. Before the FCC, and in two rounds of appeals in the D.C. Circuit, ILECs and CLECs argued about whether, for compensation purposes, dial-up Internet traffic should be viewed from a "one call" or "two calls" perspective. Through various legal theories, the FCC tried to use the one-call construct to exclude such traffic from the reciprocal compensation provision of section 251(b)(5). The FCC's basic argument each time was that these purportedly unitary "calls" to distant websites are properly analogized to conventional long distance calls to which the reciprocal compensation rule of section 251(b)(5) is currently inapplicable, not to the local calls to which that rule applies.* The FCC focused almost single-mindedly on this battle of analogies because, as discussed below, it had previously construed the 1996 Act to bar bill-and-keep for any traffic within the scope of that provision whenever the traffic is "unbalanced"—i.e., where, as in this setting, one carrier sends more calls to the other than it receives.

The D.C. Circuit twice rejected these efforts to remove dial-up Internet traffic from the scope of section 251(b)(5),[21] and it expressed skepticism about the FCC's analogy between surfing the Web and placing a seamless long distance call to a distant subscriber.[22] But it nonetheless left intact the FCC's three-year ramp-down to bill-and-keep, at least pending further proceedings on remand (which, as we completed work on this book, remained in progress). The court reasoned that—contrary to the FCC's narrow view of its own ability to impose bill-and-keep—"there is plainly a non-trivial likelihood that the Commission has authority to elect such a system," even for unbalanced traffic falling within section 251(b)(5), under the bill-and-

---

* Carrying this analogy (i.e., between Internet-bound traffic and ordinary long distance calls) to its logical conclusion in a calling-network-pays regime would mean (i) abandoning the ESP access charge exemption, (ii) stopping the money flow from the ILEC to any ISP-serving CLEC, and (iii) replacing it with an access charge-type money flow from the ISP to the ILEC, at least to the extent that the ILEC handles some portion (or all) of the end user's call to the ISP. In reality, however, no one has suggested carrying the one-call theory to this logical conclusion.

keep savings clause of section 252(d)(2)(B)(i).[23] We return to that legal determination—which may be critical to the FCC's ability to impose bill-and-keep as the intercarrier compensation rule for telecommunications traffic generally—at the conclusion of this chapter.

C. Intercarrier compensation and VoIP

The rise of VoIP as an alternative to circuit-switched telephony has thrown one more monkey wrench into the traditional intercarrier compensation regime. This time the wrench may break the whole machine.

As discussed in chapter 6, there are, for regulatory purposes, three basic categories of VoIP calls. In "IP-to-IP" calls (sometimes called "computer-to-computer" calls), both parties connect to an IP network via a broadband service. In "PSTN-to-PSTN" calls, both parties connect to the public (circuit-) switched network using ordinary telephones, but the long distance provider has routed their signals over an intermediate IP transport network. And in "IP-to-PSTN" calls, one party connects to an IP network via a broadband service and the other connects to the public switched network. The compensation rules for the first two categories are settled. Because IP-to-IP calls never leave the Internet and never touch the public switched network, any compensation arrangements between the firms involved—i.e., ISPs, Internet backbone providers, and the VoIP provider itself—are unregulated. And because the FCC has equated PSTN-to-PSTN calls with ordinary circuit-switched telephony for access charge purposes (see chapter 6), those calls are subject to the same intercarrier compensation rules that would apply if there were no IP transport link in the middle.

The third category—IP-to-PSTN calls—presents the hard case. Suppose that you use your broadband connection to place a long distance VoIP call to someone on the public switched network. The VoIP provider—in effect, your long distance carrier—has never owed access charges to any local provider for the origination of that call on your end, for the call does not pass through the public switched network there. To complete your call, however, the VoIP provider must arrange to have it converted from IP to a circuit-switched format and then dumped off at a point of interconnection with the local telephone company serving the called party. Since this is a long distance call, does the VoIP provider owe terminating access charges to that telephone company? Or is that provider, insofar as it is offering an "information service," covered by the ESP access charge exemption?[24]

There is no obvious answer to that question. Traditionally, the access charge exemption arose as an issue only where, as with dial-up calls to ISPs, the information ("enhanced") service provider needed to rely on the public switched network to establish a connection with one of its own subscribers. VoIP providers turn that traditional relationship between the Internet and the public switched network on its head. Rather than processing "calls" from its subscribers over the public switched network to the Internet, as a dial-up ISP does, IP-to-PSTN VoIP providers process calls from the Internet to the public switched network—and, in particular, to people on that network who are not their subscribers. Some ILECs argue that the access charge exemption, designed to foster the growth of the fledgling "enhanced services" industry in the 1980s, should be limited to its traditional role in facilitating connections between providers and their own subscribers and that access charges should thus apply on the PSTN end of IP-to-PSTN calls. VoIP providers and their allies disagree, contending that the access charge regime is itself an economically irrational relic of a pre-competitive age. In their view, so long as a VoIP provider (or its telecommunications partner) sets up a point of interconnection near the ILEC's network, any hand-off of traffic between the ILEC and that provider should be subject to lower reciprocal compensation rates, no matter how far away the VoIP party to the call might be. Each side claims a long pedigree for its position in FCC access charge doctrine dating back to the early 1980s,[25] and each argues that the other's position would pervert that doctrine.

The same legal question arises in a slightly different form when someone on the public switched network places a call to a distant VoIP subscriber who has acquired a telephone number in the same calling area as the calling party. As discussed in chapter 6, this "virtual FX" arrangement allows you, as a VoIP subscriber, to pay only a few dollars a month to obtain a telephone number in the city your parents live in, even if it is on the other side of the country, so that they can call you without incurring toll charges. When they place the call, their circuit-switched telephone company sees only the local number, which it recognizes as belonging to a customer of your VoIP provider's CLEC partner, and it drops the call off at a local point of interconnection associated with that CLEC. From there, unbeknownst to your parents' telephone company, the call is directed thousands of miles to you over the Internet or a managed IP network. In this setting, too, the party on the PSTN side of a long distance call has no contractual relationship with the provider of the information service that is said to trigger the ESP access charge exemption. The interested factions argue about the legal significance of that fact; some ILECs claim that such VoIP providers or their telecommunications partners owe them access charges, whereas those telecommunications partners argue that the ILECs owe them reciprocal compensation.

In each scenario, the stakes are enormous. As VoIP services become more popular, an increasing percentage of calls may contain at least one VoIP party, and many billions of dollars may turn on the outcome of this legal debate. But the debate is as indeterminate and pointless as it is obscure. Ultimately, there is no good reason to retain a schizophrenic intercarrier compensation regime that gives rise to such questions in the first place. The carriers on the PSTN side of the call, much like the ILEC "victims" of the alleged access charge "fraud" discussed at the beginning of this chapter, are performing the same call-processing functions no matter how the calls in question are characterized as a legal matter. And identical functions should be compensated identically. At least in the long term, they should not be compensated differently on the basis of distinctions rooted in yesterday's regulatory policy rather than today's technological or engineering reality.

This time, however, technology may simply force the issue and impose economic rationality on the industry whether regulators are ready or not. No matter how the PSTN end of a broadband-to-PSTN call is treated, the broadband side will be exempt from access charges, and of course no access charge liability will arise at all in broadband-to-broadband calls. These savings will allow VoIP providers to widen the price differential between themselves and circuit-switched telephony providers and will thereby accelerate the migration to VoIP services throughout the market. Access charges—to the extent they deviate from the economic cost of the underlying functions—will apply to a rapidly shrinking universe of circuit-switched calls. The upshot is that, wherever broadband connections are found, VoIP will undermine decades of finely wrought regulatory decisions about the price of "access" to the public switched network.

D. Intercarrier compensation rules for wireless and transiting carriers

Let's pause here to survey the hodgepodge of mutually inconsistent intercarrier compensation rules we have discussed so far. When a calling party's ILEC hands a call off to a conventional long distance carrier, the latter pays the former *originating access charges*. If the ILEC hands the call off to an ISP instead, the latter has paid the former the standard *retail rate* for a business line—the rate paid by customers rather than carriers. If the ILEC hands the call off to a CLEC that in turn serves the ISP, then, at least as of this writing, the ILEC pays the CLEC the *specialized low rate for ISP-bound traffic* so long as the ILEC has "opted into" the FCC's grand compromise and charges the same rate to complete incoming local calls from CLECs and others. If, in its discretion, the ILEC has *not* opted into that compromise, it must pay the CLEC the higher *reciprocal compensation* rate derived from TELRIC.[26] On the other hand, when a long distance carrier hands a call off to the called party's ILEC, it must pay a *terminating access charge* considerably higher than a TELRIC-based reciprocal compensation fee, even though the ILEC is performing essentially the same work as when it completes incoming calls from CLECs and wireless carriers. If that long distance carrier collaborates with a CLEC to disguise the long distance call as a local call when handing it off as to the ILEC—well, that might be a *crime*. If a telecommunications carrier pairs up with a VoIP provider, however, and if the two of them handle a call that either originates or terminates over a subscriber's broadband connection, *all bets are off*, at least for now, on what they and any circuit-switched LEC on the other end of the call might owe each other.

This list of mutually inconsistent compensation rules, moreover, describes only one dimension of the chaos. In most of the cases just mentioned, there are at least well-recognized state and federal procedures and practices (often, but not always, under the state arbitration provisions of section 252) for determining intercarrier compensation arrangements involving the major ILECs, even if the substance of the applicable rules is incoherent from a global perspective. But even those procedures are absent in many disputes among the classes of carriers that have assumed sudden prominence in the market since 1990—including, in particular, wireless carriers.

One intractable issue concerns whether wireless carriers, like LECs, are entitled to collect access charges when they terminate a long distance call handled by some other carrier's long distance network. In 1996, the FCC tentatively suggested that wireless providers should be entitled to collect such charges.[27] The FCC then let the matter fall into regulatory limbo for six years. In 2002, it found that, because wireless carriers are subject to mandatory detariffing (see chapter 8), they may impose terminating access charges only by contract, not by tariff—but it then pointedly declined to adopt prospective rules governing such contractual negotiations.[28] The Commission's indecision has triggered more strategic behavior and more litigation. Under one practice, a given wireless carrier, worried about its ability to collect access charges directly for the long distance calls it terminates, might arrange for such calls to be delivered to an intermediate CLEC, which, unlike the wireless carrier, can assess such charges by tariff. Once the long distance carrier pays the bill, the CLEC passes a portion of these access revenues back to the wireless carrier behind the scenes. If the long distance carrier in this arrangement finds out that a wireless carrier rather than the CLEC is in fact terminating these calls, it can refuse to make some portion of that payment, perhaps inciting litigation.[29]

Adding to the confusion is uncertainty about the legal rules applicable to *transiting* arrangements. A wireless carrier does not normally incur the expense of building its own transport facilities out to each of the other networks with which it exchanges calls, including networks operated by an array of CLECs, small rural LECs, and other wireless carriers. Instead, these different types of carriers often rely, for mutual interconnection, on the extensive transport network of a large regional ILEC. An ILEC (or other carrier) is said to perform transiting services when it bridges two other carriers' networks in this manner but has no independent relationship with either the calling or the called parties and thus can charge them nothing. Such arrangements raise two basic sets of issues: what the transiting carrier may charge the other carriers for these transiting services, and what, if anything, the terminating carrier may charge the carrier that originated the call. There is no clear answer to the first question and often no clear answer to the second.

On the first issue, the FCC has ruled that, whereas an originating carrier may not charge a terminating carrier for handing off its own subscribers' calls, a transiting carrier may charge the terminating carrier for handing off the calls originated by some other carrier.[30] Although the FCC has explained this rule as a simple application of "the cost causation principle of allocating the cost of delivering traffic to the carriers responsible for the traffic,"[31] ultimately that rationale is incoherent. As discussed below, the premise of the FCC's calling-network-pays regime is that the calling party "causes" all of the costs of a call and that her carrier should thus be required to cover them. If that principle is applied consistently, a transiting carrier should be required to pass the costs back to the originating carrier, not to the terminating carrier.

Of course, if the terminating carrier in such transiting arrangements can itself just pass those costs back to the originating carrier, the problem would be worked out in the wash—but only if the charges imposed genuinely reflect the "costs" incurred. Alas, there is no legal or market mechanism that consistently produces any efficient, cost-based exchange of compensation. First, there are no clear rules governing how much the transiting carrier in the middle may charge the terminating carrier—indeed, the FCC has never ruled that any carrier must provide transiting services in the first place.[32] Second, when the terminating carrier is a CLEC, a wireless carrier, or a rural ILEC exempt from the relevant 1996 Act obligations, there are no clear, generally applicable rules limiting the charges it may impose on an originating carrier.[33] The result is that, when they originate calls, wireless carriers and others sometimes face intercarrier price-gouging with no effective regulatory recourse. The FCC has sought comment on aspects of this problem,[34] but is unlikely to resolve them even prospectively until it has reformed intercarrier compensation more generally.

II. The Economics of Intercarrier Compensation Reform

Many of the questions addressed so far in this chapter remain the subject of intense controversy. Permitting such uncertainty to persist is no way to govern this already volatile industry. Who pays what to whom should turn on coherent economic principles applied equally to any exchange of traffic. The fee charged for terminating a call should not vary radically, as it does today, with technologically irrelevant details such as the call's geographic origin or the legacy regulatory classification of the originating carrier. And the direction and amount of the money flow should not turn on metaphysical questions about whether, for example, a dial-up Internet connection to a distant website is properly conceptualized as one "long distance" call or instead as one "local" call plus one "long distance" call. Such questions invite clever arbitrage schemes and lack any basis in technology or economics—sure signs that they should not be asked at all.

As we have seen, the basic problem is that most of the distinctions that regulators have drawn between carriers and services—such as those between "local" and "long distance" calls, and those between information service providers and long distance carriers—are unstable and ultimately unprincipled in a competitive world. Such distinctions may have made sense in the wake of the AT&T breakup in 1984, when there was no competition from CLECs, wireless carriers, or VoIP providers. Back then, tidy regulatory fences separated local telephone companies from each other geographically, and the distinction between a local and a long distance call was relatively straightforward. Consequently, for the decade or so following the AT&T consent decree, the access charge rules created only limited opportunities for arbitrage. But those days are long gone. The FCC now recognizes that the current intercarrier compensation regime is a sinking ship—with technology and competition creating new holes faster than regulatory responses can plug the old ones.

The FCC has thus proposed, in the sketchiest of terms, to formulate a new, "unified" regime for intercarrier compensation.[35] The ultimate objective of this multi-year, politically fraught project is to apply the same internally consistent set of compensation principles across the board for any hand-off of telecommunications traffic from one carrier to another, irrespective of the legacy classification of the carriers at issue or the technology used to deliver the call. For these purposes, the FCC has excluded as beyond the scope of its inquiry only the exchange of traffic between Internet backbone providers, in what are called "peering" and "transiting" arrangements. (We discussed those arrangements, and the rationales for keeping them unregulated, in chapter 4.)

There are two serious contenders for a "unified" intercarrier compensation regime in the long run. The first is a truly cost-based calling-network-pays approach that, unlike the current access charge regime, contains no implicit subsidies. The second is bill-and-keep. The choice between these two basic approaches presents one of the most complex and important debates in telecommunications policy today. Understanding it requires us first to examine the *terminating access monopoly*, a subtle economic phenomenon that is unique to certain network industries and lies at the root of today's intercarrier compensation controversies.

A. The economic logic of the "terminating access monopoly"

Consider the following thought experiment about how two carriers involved in the placement of a call (whether local or long distance) might treat each other in a world *wholly without intercarrier compensation rules*—i.e., without regulatory limits on access charges for "long distance" calls or on termination rates for "local" calls. No matter how competitively insignificant it may be in other respects, the terminating carrier normally owns the only line connecting the called party to the outside world. Other carriers' subscribers will wish to reach the called party, and that wish will not magically disappear if the terminating carrier acts on its obvious incentive to abuse its "terminating access monopoly" by charging above-cost rates for the privilege of completing their calls to her. Except in extreme cases, the calling party's carrier will typically acquiesce and pay those rates because its customers will expect it to connect them to everyone they wish to call. Otherwise, those customers might start looking elsewhere for service because, from their perspective, life is too short to sit in frustration when one needs to reach somebody, even if getting through means paying more for dependable service. Moreover, even if the originating carrier were able to pass these supracompetitive rates back to its own end users (say, in the form of higher per-minute rates for originating calls), that would not strongly deter the *called* party's carrier from charging those rates, for the called party often lacks incentives to protect the interests of the *calling* party.

For example, suppose that you live in New York and use AT&T to call an acquaintance served by a small—and, by our hypothesis, completely unregulated—CLEC in Los Angeles. That CLEC lacks full incentives to keep you or your long distance carrier happy by charging low, competitive rates for terminating the call. Instead, it has both the incentive and the opportunity to charge AT&T significantly above-cost rates for that task. If (contrary to current regulation) AT&T were able to pass those above-cost rates back to you in the form of higher per-minute long distance charges, what recourse would you have? Most of the time, you would not know about the higher rates until the bill arrived. Even then, you could not do much about them unless you took the trouble to complain to your acquaintance in Los Angeles. (Switching from AT&T to another long distance carrier would not help because that other carrier would presumably also be gouged by the terminating CLEC.) At some point, if the CLEC in Los Angeles hiked the termination rates to prohibitively high levels, your acquaintance might begin receiving fewer calls as people find out about the problem and stop calling him. But you and others are likely to keep calling him even if the rates are significantly above cost, so long as they are not absurdly so, because you might well still have a strong need to reach him even if it costs more than usual to do so. As a result, your acquaintance would have little incentive to fix the problem by complaining to the CLEC about the high termination charges or by switching to another local carrier.

Indeed, your acquaintance's own incentives might lead him to act against your interests—at least up to a point—because he may well be paying a very low monthly telephone bill precisely because the CLEC, his local service provider, extracts enormous subsidies from other carriers in the form of supracompetitive termination rates. This problem could soon spiral out of control. Each carrier competes for subscribers largely on the basis of low service rates. "Bad" carriers that extort above-cost termination charges from other carriers can afford to charge their subscribers lower rates than carriers that remain good corporate citizens by capping termination charges at cost. Thus, only "bad" carriers will survive. The inefficiency of this outcome, from an economic perspective, is obvious.

For these reasons, the terminating access monopoly would lead to inefficient outcomes for both local and long distance traffic even if non-terminating carriers were free to pass supracompetitive termination charges back to the calling party. In the real world, however, the problem is even more severe than in our hypothetical world of minimal regulation. In most settings, regulatory norms prohibit any carrier—local or long distance—from passing terminating access overcharges back to the calling party, thereby negating whatever incentive a calling party might have to hold terminating carriers in check by complaining to the called party. In the case of local calls, at least in the United States, customers are used to fixed monthly fees for basic wireline service, and most ILEC customers can rely on their state commissions to enforce that traditional expectation through regulatory mandate. In the case of long distance calls, Congress, led by senators from remote rural states, improvidently required all long distance carriers to charge nationally averaged rates to every subscriber of a given service, irrespective of the costs of completing any given subscriber's calls. This retrograde implicit subsidy arrangement, enacted in 1996 and codified in section 254(g), flies in the face of the universal service reform ordered at the local level (see chapter 10) in that it deliberately detaches the prices charged for services from the costs incurred in providing them. But it remains the law nonetheless. In each case, the practical effect of prohibiting a carrier from passing terminating access overcharges back to the calling party is that no end user has any real incentive to object to them because the ultimate burden of paying them is diffused among the thousands or millions of customers subscribing to the calling party's carrier.[*]

We have discussed the terminating access monopoly at such length because the need to hold it in check, one way or the other, underlies an enormous range of telecommunications policy issues—including those listed at the beginning of this chapter. Practitioners often lose sight of the centrality of this phenomenon within telecommunications regulation because they are inured to a world in which traditional mechanisms for capping termination fees—"access charges" for long distance calls and "reciprocal compensation" rates for local calls—seem like immutable facts of life. The terminating access monopoly comes into sharp focus only when a new class of calls falls through the cracks of those two schemes.

That is why, in our hypothetical, we used the example of a CLEC terminating a long distance call. For many years, no regulator had limited the

---

[*] Indeed, those same regulatory obstacles deprive a calling party of any incentive to object if her own (hypothetically unregulated) LEC imposes arbitrarily high originating access charges on any unaffiliated long distance carrier to which she also subscribes, for section 254(g) precludes any such carrier from charging her more as a result. Unlike the terminating access monopoly, however, that problem is a product of regulation (i.e., the long distance carrier's inability to pass back the extra charges), not of any intercarrier dynamic inherent in network industries.

charges that "non-dominant" carriers like CLECs could impose for terminating conventional long distance calls, and many CLECs were in fact charging radically above-cost rates. This led the FCC in 2001 to take the seemingly unprecedented step of exercising its "legacy" ratemaking authority under section 201 of the Communications Act to curb the interstate access charges imposed by these non-dominant carriers.[36] But the underlying economic phenomenon arises no matter who the terminating carrier is and whether the call is "local" or "long distance." Suppose that, in our example, both the calling and called parties lived in Los Angeles and had different local service providers. The called party's carrier would still want to charge the calling party's carrier above-cost rates—and, absent regulatory limits on "reciprocal compensation" rates, it would almost certainly succeed.

The premise underlying the FCC's drive towards a "unified" intercarrier compensation scheme is that the same regulatory solution should be used to deal with the terminating access monopoly in all the contexts in which it arises. In theory at least, there are three candidates for such a solution: one antiregulatory, one highly regulatory, and one only moderately regulatory. We briefly address the first of these—removal of interconnection obligations—before addressing the latter two: calling-network-pays and bill-and-keep, respectively.

B. The antiregulatory solution: freedom to deny interconnection

One rather risky way to try to hold the terminating access monopoly in check is to exclude the government altogether. The aim here would be to avoid any need for regulatory limits on access charges or local reciprocal compensation rates by freeing carriers from interconnection obligations in the hope that the ensuing brinksmanship between originating and terminating carriers would intimidate the latter into charging reasonable intercarrier rates. Suppose, in the example above, that AT&T announced to the world that it would henceforth refuse to place calls to individuals served by local carriers that charge more than one cent a minute for terminating access. The hope would be that this threat might chasten errant local carriers into lowering their rates to that level, lest their subscribers switch to another local carrier upon suddenly discovering that their friends and relatives cannot reach them.

From a policy perspective, this approach presents several basic short-comings. First, the extent to which this strategy would lead to economically efficient outcomes is uncertain and depends on the relative bargaining strength the two parties would bring to this game of chicken. Perhaps a leading national long distance carrier could succeed in intimidating small terminating CLECs into submission. But the strategy might well backfire on a smaller originating carrier in a competitive market, particularly if it tries to blackmail a large local carrier—say, a Bell company—with a sizable customer base. If the originating carrier's customers became frustrated at their inability to reach the people they need to call, they would cancel service and sign up with a more compliant carrier that promises completed calls ("dependable telephone service") at slightly higher rates.

More generally, there is often no reason to suppose that the equilibrium point in any given game of brinksmanship between an originating and a terminating carrier will lead to economically efficient, cost-based rates for termination. In most cases the equilibrium point is likely to end up above cost (for the reasons previously discussed); in rare cases, it could also end up below cost. For example, if AT&T could succeed in intimidating small CLECs into lowering their termination rates to cost, there is no reason in principle why AT&T would have to stop there. It could exploit its superior negotiating position by forcing rates still lower—or even, in theory, by forcing the CLEC to pay AT&T for the privilege of receiving calls from the latter's much larger customer base. Analogously, ILECs sometimes charged wireless carriers for terminating the ILECs' own traffic until the FCC put an end to that practice by, among other things, deeming it implicitly inconsistent with section 251(b)(5).[37] All this said, there is at least one notable telecommunications setting in which the absence of government-mandated interconnection rules arguably has produced an economically efficient equilibrium: the market for Internet backbone services, where the terms of intercarrier peering and transit arrangements are left purely to the dynamics of the free market. In chapter 4, we addressed that apparent equilibrium and discussed some of the ways in which the hand-off of traffic over the Internet backbone presents fewer "terminating access" concerns than the completion of telephone calls over the last mile to individual end users. But even there, we noted, some observers believe that the current competitive equilibrium is vulnerable to any substantial increase in market concentration.

Finally, removing interconnection obligations as a means of dealing with the terminating access monopoly is also as politically untenable as it is operationally risky. Most countries view dependable telecommunications service as a hallmark—indeed, a criterion—of normal industrial development. Few policymakers would place dependable service in jeopardy by replacing regulation, however imperfect, with service-interrupting tests of will between carriers.[38]

C. The highly regulatory solution: calling-network-pays

The second means of dealing with the terminating access monopoly is the calling-network-pays approach. Under that approach, the calling party is deemed to "cause" all the costs of any given call, and the called party's carrier may thus charge the calling party's carrier (a LEC for local calls, and a long distance carrier for long distance calls) a regulated rate for the costs of completing that call. For the most part, this has been the traditional intercarrier compensation scheme in the United States for many years. As discussed, however, regulators have devised two very different approaches to measuring those costs, one of which (reciprocal compensation) applies to "local" traffic, and the other of which (access charges) applies to "long distance" traffic.*

As we have explained, it is unsustainable over the long term to have two different cost inquiries, arising from an artificial regulatory distinction between "local" and "long distance" calls, for what amounts to the same transport and call-termination functions. There are, to be sure, powerful political reasons for preserving the higher access charges for long distance service because those have traditionally cross-subsidized low residential local service rates. Sooner or later, though, VoIP and the arbitrage opportunities discussed at the beginning of this chapter will crush this artificial distinction as service providers find more and more ways to avoid paying

---

* The access charge regime is properly conceptualized as an application of the calling-network-pays principle, even though long distance calls often involve three carriers rather than two. The calling party's principal carrier in such a call—the long distance company—is deemed responsible for the costs of the entire call and must therefore compensate the called party's local carrier for the costs of call completion. Of course, the long distance carrier also typically pays originating access charges to the calling party's local carrier, but that is consistent with the long distance carrier's overall obligation to cover all costs of the call.

access charges. Thus, if calling-network-pays is to serve as the regulatory answer to the terminating access monopoly, the first order of business will be to reconcile these two different schemes and establish a single, coherent means of measuring "cost" for purposes of terminating any call.

The next order of business will be to ensure that regulators get these costs "right" in the sense that ordered intercarrier rates neither overcompensate nor undercompensate the terminating carrier. If regulators could succeed in this task, a unified calling-network-pays regime for all kinds of calls would be a fully satisfactory means of dealing with the terminating access monopoly. If, however, they are unsuccessful, they will produce the types of economically inefficient regulatory distortions described above, such as the above-cost termination rates that induced a generation of CLECs to specialize in serving ISPs in part to capture a regulatory windfall. This has become a central dilemma for the industry because there may be no "right" way, even in theory, to measure call-termination costs. Moreover, even if there were such a way, regulators would face formidable challenges in applying theory to reality.

Several independent factors complicate the ability of regulators to "get the costs right" under any calling-network-pays approach. As with the pricing of unbundled network elements, a regulator's first task is to choose a basic cost methodology, and the complexities of that threshold inquiry are formidable, as discussed in appendix A. Here it is important to ensure consistency with whatever the rate-setting methodology happens to be for network elements, at least if switching and shared transport remain on the list of network elements that are sometimes subject to unbundling obligations. Recall that when a CLEC purchases "switching" and "shared transport" as part of the UNE platform, it obtains (among other things) the same usage-sensitive switching and transport capacity that it sells right back to the ILEC when it completes the ILEC's calls. As the FCC suggested in 1996, it would be problematic to make the ILEC pay that CLEC, for the use of those facilities, usage-sensitive rates for call termination that exceed the usage-sensitive rates the CLEC is paying the ILEC for that same use.[39] The usage-sensitive portions of these rates should ideally be the same—and should cancel each other out—because ultimately it is the ILEC, as owner of the facilities, that is bearing the costs. By contrast, higher termination rates could produce purely regulation-driven arbitrage opportunities.

Choosing a particular cost methodology for call-termination services—say, some variant of forward-looking cost—still leaves many basic questions for which there may be no theoretically satisfying answer.[40] First, should a regulator take into account the type of carrier whose forward-looking costs are at issue? There is much debate between wireless and wireline carriers, and between ILECs and CLECs, about the disparate costs of terminating traffic over different types of networks. Each carrier naturally wants regulators to raise their estimates of its call termination costs and lower their estimates of other carriers' termination costs. Should regulators compromise by making ILECs and wireless carriers pay each other the same rate for call termination, in which event that rate (as an average) may reflect no carrier's true network costs? Or should different carriers pay different rates that reflect the architectural differences in their respective networks, in which event regulators will stand accused of artificially favoring some technological choices over others? Nine years after passage of the 1996 Act, this question is still the topic of lively debate.[41]

Second, how should regulators apportion any given carrier's termination costs among the call-originating carriers that—under the basic premise of the calling-network-pays rule—are said to "cause" those costs? As a thought experiment, assume that a given carrier has installed a switch that does nothing except terminate traffic to a class of customers. Under the calling-network-pays rule, the carrier can expect to recover the entire cost of that switch, not from its own customers, but from the carriers that originate the calls that are then terminated through the switch. We know that the total costs to be recovered are those of the switch, that the period for recovering them is whatever regulators predict to be the useful life of the switch, and that those costs need to be recovered from other carriers (because, by hypothesis, the switch is used only to terminate other carriers' calls). But there is no one economically "correct" way of apportioning payment responsibility among the many different carriers that originate these calls because the short term marginal costs of actually terminating a call for the benefit of any given carrier, once the network is up and running, are effectively zero.[42] The terminating carrier incurs most of its costs before any call is placed at all: i.e., when it orders and installs the switch and transport facilities large enough to accommodate the unusually high call volumes present during "peak load" periods. To cover its high fixed costs, however, the terminating carrier in our example must recover rates of greater than zero from someone. Doing so means that rates will not be paid in close correspondence with how those costs are incurred.

As a practical matter, regulators typically order some variant of per-minute pricing because such pricing is the most feasible way to allocate responsibility for these costs among the many different carriers that deliver traffic to the facilities whose costs are being recovered. But per-minute pricing raises more questions than it answers. If regulators set the same rate for all hours of the day, they may produce what amounts to a cross-subsidy running from those who use the network mainly during off-peak hours to those who use it mainly during peak hours (since many network costs are incurred specifically to ensure enough capacity to handle calls during peak hours). For that reason, regulators sometimes impose higher per-minute rates for peak periods than for non-peak periods. But this can be only a partial solution to the cross-subsidy problem, since, as the FCC has noted, there may be no "right" mark-up for use of the network during peak periods, no "right" way to define when those peak periods occur, and more generally no economically satisfying way to use such premium rates to reflect the up-front, lumpy manner in which carriers incur the fixed costs of switching and transport.[43]

Finally, even if there *were* a "right" methodology for calculating and apportioning the call termination costs of the many different carriers in the world, regulators would still confront enormous subjectivity in the task of applying that methodology to produce actual rates. Take the two primary contexts in which regulators have set intercarrier compensation rates: the "reciprocal compensation" regime for local calls and the "access charge" regime for long distance calls. Until reformed by a now-expiring industry consensus plan (see chapter 10), the rates for interstate access were tied up in protracted litigation as carriers successfully attacked, as arbitrary and capricious, the FCC's "X-factor" formula (which, as discussed in chapter 2, reduces access charges over time by taking into account efficiency improvements in the industry as a whole).[44] As for local calls, "reciprocal compensation" rates can vary by more than 100% from state to state—presumably not because of any commensurate difference in the underlying "cost," but because state regulators disagree fundamentally about cost inputs—an issue we address in appendix A.

Given these multiple layers of theoretical indeterminacy, how can we reliably know when regulators have set intercarrier compensation rates at "correct" levels? We cannot. We can, however, hope for some measure of regulatory rough justice. And we can surmise in hindsight that rates have been set about right if they do not appear to have caused major competitive distortions. We also know in hindsight when the rates have been set wrong, as they were in the case of ISP-bound traffic, because then they cause major industry distortions. But we cannot know with accurate foresight that we will avoid such mistakes, so ratesetting of any kind—including reciprocal compensation—necessarily involves a constant process of readjustment. This continual imposition of administrative costs is one reason why calling-network-pays arrangements are problematic.

D. The moderately regulatory solution: bill-and-keep

All of the regulatory conundrums just discussed arise wherever regulators choose, as a threshold matter, to entitle carriers to recover their call termination costs from *other carriers*. Bill-and-keep represents a radically different threshold choice. Instead of making the calling party's carrier responsible for *all* of the costs of a call, bill-and-keep divides responsibility for those costs *between* the carriers serving the calling party and the called party. Specifically, it allocates (i) to the calling party's carrier responsibility for the costs of delivering the call to a (regulatorily defined) point of interconnection with the called party's carrier and (ii) to the called party's carrier the responsibility for the costs of transporting the call the rest of the way from that point, through the terminating switch, to the called party. For simplicity, our discussion focuses on the dynamics of bill-and-keep for calls involving only two carriers, but the same basic rules would apply to calls involving a third carrier—one that provides transport services in between "local" carriers on each end of a call.*

---

* Such three-carrier calls fall into two basic categories: those in which the intermediate transport provider has an independent relationship with the calling party (i.e., conventional long distance calls), and those in which it does not (the "transit" scenario discussed above). As to the first category, a bill-and-keep rule would require a calling party's LEC to hand off calls to that party's long distance ("transport") provider at a prescribed point without charge, and the LEC on the terminating end of the call would similarly be required to accept calls from that provider at a designated point without charge. The LECs at each end would thus have to recover from their own end users the costs previously recovered through access charges, with potentially radical effects on the end user rates charged by small rural LECs unless subsidy mechanisms are reformed accordingly. (See the final paragraph of this chapter.) The rule that bill-and-keep would prescribe for the second, "transit" scenario is a close variation on the general rule for two-carrier calls. The originating carrier would bear financial responsibility for getting the call to the terminating carrier's network, and that might well mean paying the transiting carrier for the use of its transport pipes. In a nutshell, the transiting carrier serves as a paid subcontractor to the originating carrier, helping it to meet its default responsibilities.

Thus, whereas the calling-network-pays rule imposes all "transport and termination" costs on the calling party's carrier, bill-and-keep imposes all "termination" costs, and at least some "transport" costs, on the called party's carrier.[45] How will that carrier recover those costs? By building them into the rates it charges its own end users. Of course, that does not necessarily mean that end user rates will go up, for each carrier is simultaneously freed of the responsibility to cover any costs attributable to the termination of other carriers' calls. Put differently, bill-and-keep addresses the problem of the "terminating access monopoly" not by regulating the intercarrier compensation that the first carrier must pay the second, as calling-network-pays does, but by eliminating intercarrier compensation altogether, at least in all cases where each carrier meets the other at a prescribed "point of interconnection" (on which more below).

In one special set of cases, bill-and-keep is uncontroversial and indeed dovetails with the calling-network-pays approach. In particular, all agree that bill-and-keep is appropriate where two comparable carriers have "balanced" traffic flows: i.e., where neither is, with respect to the other, a net "originator" or "terminator" of traffic. In those circumstances, their respective liabilities more or less cancel out, and the transaction costs of monitoring all the traffic to the last bit may exceed any net liability one carrier might be shown to have to the other. Our discussion thus does not focus on whether bill-and-keep is desirable in these circumstances, for it is undisputed that it is. Instead, we are addressing only the harder case in which the traffic flow between two carriers is "unbalanced" (or "asymmetric"). Such imbalances arise, for example, in the case of traffic (i) between ILECs and ISP-serving CLECs and (ii) between wireline LECs and wireless carriers, which have traditionally originated more calls than they have terminated.

Proponents of bill-and-keep argue that, over the long term, as the telecommunications industry becomes more competitive, bill-and-keep will produce less and less of a need for regulation of any kind. To see why this may be so, take the problem of excessive terminating access charges. As we saw above, the terminating access monopoly tends to allow any LEC—say, a non-dominant CLEC—to charge other carriers significantly more than cost for the privilege of completing a call to its customer. Now suppose that the CLEC has an obligation to terminate calls originated by another carrier but no power to charge that other carrier anything at all for performing the task, so long as the carrier delivers the call to the defined point of inter-connection. How would the CLEC recover these call-termination costs, if not from the originating carrier? Again, by passing them on to its own end users. And here is the crucial point: the CLEC must compete for those end users against various rivals in the local exchange market. What if the CLEC tried to charge those end users the same above-cost rates for call termina-tion it could get away with charging the long distance carrier (by virtue of the terminating access monopoly)? *It would lose them as its customers.* The fear of that outcome will cause the CLEC, at least in a competitive market, to lower its rates to cost.

This point is a central argument for bill-and-keep. One defining draw-back of the calling-network-pays approach is that regulators must remain involved in perpetuity to estimate the costs of call termination. That is because, as a result of the terminating access monopoly, market forces alone are often incapable of producing genuinely cost-based intercarrier compensation rates no matter how competitive the industry becomes. In contrast, regulators need not remain forever involved in the estimation of a carrier's costs if direct responsibility for paying them is shifted—as bill-and-keep prescribes—from other carriers to the terminating carrier's own end users. After all, a competitive market (by definition) will itself produce end user rates that reflect the underlying costs of providing service—and it will do so with greater accuracy, and far less controversy, than any regula-tory proceeding could ever do. And end users in the aggregate would be no worse off under this approach because (as discussed) each carrier would no longer pass along to its customers the call termination costs of other carri-ers. Indeed, end users may well be better off in the aggregate because the market as a whole would benefit from greater regulatory certainty and lower administrative costs.

To be sure, in the short to intermediate term, regulators would still need to regulate even the end user rates of "dominant" carriers in markets that are not yet fully competitive. A carrier that dominates the market for local exchange services—a carrier whose customers lack alternatives—may often get away with charging its customers above-cost rates for any num-ber of services, including the termination of other carriers' traffic to them. That, indeed, is the whole rationale for retail rate regulation, as discussed in chapter 2. Thus, in the near term, a key advantage of bill-and-keep over the calling-network-pays rule is the opportunity to deregulate CLECs and other non-dominant carriers—those whose customers have alternatives. In the long term, however, the advantage of bill-and-keep is that, as competition develops and fewer carriers remain "dominant," regulation of the telecommunications industry would become increasingly unnecessary because market forces (acting on end user rates) could perform the cost-estimation functions traditionally assumed by regulators. Over time, therefore, bill-and-keep may promise an end to much of the regulatory indeterminacy that has plagued the implementation of the calling-network-pays regime for many decades.

Bill-and-keep is nonetheless subject to a number of objections, which run the gamut from highly theoretical to highly pragmatic. We will address the theoretical objections first, which, as a general rule, are less substantial than the pragmatic ones.

Some critics contend that bill-and-keep defies the economic principle that costs should be allocated to the party that "causes" them because, they say, most of the costs of a call are attributable to the calling party and her carrier. That objection is somewhat overstated, however, because the called party can also be said to "cause" at least some of the costs of a call. In particular, those costs would never be incurred but for the called party's active cooperation in the form of deciding to be on the network and thus available to receive calls, and subsequently answering the telephone when it rings and engaging in conversation rather than hanging up immediately. To be sure, the calling party can be said to cause more of the costs than the called party for undesired calls that end quickly because the "call set-up costs" associated with the first second of a call on a circuit-switched network occupy a disproportionate percentage of that call's total costs. But the proponents of bill-and-keep do not argue that the calling and called parties each cause exactly 50% of the costs of a call. Instead, they argue that there can be no theoretically satisfying account of who "causes" what percentage of any call's costs—and thus no theoretically compelling reason to impose 100% of the costs of a call on the calling party's network.[46]

The opponents of bill-and-keep further argue that it would create perverse incentives for carriers to specialize in serving customers (such as telemarketers) that mostly originate calls, just as the calling-network-pays regime created perverse incentives for carriers to specialize in serving customers (such as ISPs) that mostly terminate calls. Indeed, the FCC itself expressed that concern in rejecting bill-and-keep for local traffic in 1996.[47] But this concern appears overstated as well. The main reason that the traditional calling-network-pays regime favored carriers that specialized in the termination of traffic is that regulators had set termination rates above cost, entitling those carriers to a mini-subsidy whenever they terminated a call. In a bill-and-keep world, each carrier would still incur the considerable costs of originating calls and transporting them much of the way to the called party's network, and they would have to recover those costs from end users, at rates those end users are willing to pay, rather than from other carriers at whatever rates a regulator might set. Those end users will be unwilling to pay rates above cost, and thus the market itself would foil an originating carrier's plans to derive supracompetitive revenues for its services.

The deeper controversies about bill-and-keep relate to more pragmatic questions. Recall that bill-and-keep requires regulators to pick a demarcation point between two networks that separates where the first carrier's financial obligations begin and the other's ends. It is not at all obvious how that point should be defined. From a competitive standpoint, moreover, much turns on that definition.

One of the earliest proposals—devised in 2000 by Patrick DeGraba, an economist then with the FCC—argued for setting the default point of interconnection at the central office used by the terminating carrier to serve the called party.[48] Thus, if Joe, served by Carrier X, places a call to Susan, served by Carrier Y, then Carrier X would bear financial responsibility for delivering the call to the central office that houses the Carrier Y switch that is directly connected to Susan's loop. One concern about this approach is that it could place CLECs at a competitive disadvantage as compared to ILECs. As discussed in chapter 2, a traditional ILEC network typically features many switches (and thus end offices), and modern CLEC networks tend to feature fewer switches and longer loops. Thus, whereas an ILEC would satisfy its financial obligations under DeGraba's approach by building lines to just a few CLEC central offices, the CLEC could satisfy its corresponding obligations only by building or leasing connections to a much larger number of ILEC central offices. More recent proposals therefore tend to advocate a default point of interconnection less deep in the terminating carrier's network: i.e., a point from which the terminating carrier will deliver calls to customers over a larger geographic area than just the one served by a single ILEC central office. As a limiting principle, almost all bill-and-keep proposals would retain the FCC's existing rule that any carrier serving customers in a given geographic region must establish at least one physical point of interconnection within that region where other carriers can hand off calls bound for those customers.[49] Thus, if the carrier connects those customers to a far-away switch outside the region, it cannot expect other carriers to bear financial responsibility for delivering calls all the way to that switch.

Significantly, establishing a "default" point of interconnection would not necessarily require any carrier to build its own facilities out to that point on pain of losing interconnection rights. At least under one approach to bill-and-keep, carriers would remain free to interconnect elsewhere on the terminating carrier's network as well; the default point would merely prescribe the division of financial responsibility for covering the costs of any given call in the absence of a negotiated agreement to the contrary.[50] In the simplest case, if the first carrier actually does drop the call off at the default point and the second takes it from there, the application of bill-and-keep is straightforward: no money changes hands, and the carriers recover their respective costs from their own end users. But what happens if either the first or the second carrier lacks the transport facilities needed to reach that point? The carrier must purchase transport capacity or services from some other carrier—often from the other carrier handling the call. If, as is increasingly the case, there is a competitive market for such transport services, no regulation is required; the carrier simply pays the market rate. If there is not a competitive market, the carrier would purchase transport at regulated rates from an ILEC, with its ubiquitous transport network; indeed, in many such cases, the ILEC would be serving one of the parties to the call. The prospect that bill-and-keep can work properly only if combined with continued regulation of ILEC transport rates, at least along some routes, is a further reminder that its greatest deregulatory benefits could be achieved only in the longer term, as competition takes hold throughout the telecommunications marketplace. But if, as the FCC suggests, its "unified regime" for intercarrier compensation should last for many decades, the longer term is an appropriate frame of reference.

III. Intercarrier Compensation Reform and the 1996 Act

We have discussed the choice between calling-network-pays and bill-and-keep in a legal vacuum, as though the FCC would be equally free under existing law to adopt either of those approaches in a "unified" intercarrier compensation regime. Alas, federal telecommunications law is never quite so straightforward. When Congress passed the 1996 Act, the calling-network-pays principle had governed telecommunications regulation for many decades, and proposals to use bill-and-keep in cases of unbalanced traffic (as, for example, between wireless carriers and ILECs) were controversial. If the FCC now wished to retain some version of calling-network-pays as the default principle for any hand-off of traffic on the public switched network, it would face few legal impediments to doing so (although the nature and extent of FCC jurisdiction over intercarrier compensation for non-local intrastate calls is questionable, as discussed below). The harder question is whether the FCC has legal authority to order *bill-and-keep* across the board for all categories of telephone traffic. The answer is entirely unclear, and depends on how the FCC, and ultimately the courts, interpret several profoundly ambiguous sentences in the 1996 Act.

The FCC has two explicit sources of authority for regulating intercarrier compensation: (i) its general authority under section 201 to regulate the terms and conditions of interstate and international services, and (ii) its more specific authority, under *Iowa Utilities Board*,[51] to issue rules implementing the "reciprocal compensation" provision of section 251(b)(5). For the reasons discussed below, the strength of the FCC's claim to reshape intercarrier compensation rules as it pleases varies with the kinds of telecommunications traffic at issue. For these purposes, there are three principal categories: (i) any traffic that might fall within the scope of section 201 but not section 251(b)(5); (ii) traffic that falls within the scope of section 251(b)(5), whether or not it also falls within the scope of section 201; and (iii) traffic that arguably falls outside the scope of both section 201 and section 251(b)(5). We address each in turn.

The FCC's discretion to enforce its policy preferences is greatest as to the first category of traffic: any interstate or international long distance calls within the scope of section 201 but not section 251(b)(5). Like the other provisions of the original 1934 Act, section 201 places few constraints on the substance of the FCC's rules beyond the general requirements of "reasonableness" and adequate explanation. Thus, if the Commission wished to abolish the traditional access charge regime for such calls in favor of some form of bill-and-keep, it would bear the important burden of persuading a court that such a fundamental change is warranted, but it would confront no specific substantive limits on its authority.

The picture becomes more complicated when we turn to the second category of traffic: "local" (and any other) calls that fall within the scope of section 251(b)(5). After *Iowa Utilities Board*, there is no question that the FCC has statutory jurisdiction to set intercarrier compensation rules for local traffic as part of its general authority to implement any substantive provision of the 1996 Act, even though the calls themselves are usually intrastate. The reason for the complexity is thus not jurisdictional, but substantive. The text of section 251(b)(5) itself requires "reciprocal compensation arrangements for the transport and termination of telecommunications." Section 252(d)(2) prescribes, in several paragraphs, a seemingly precise set of reciprocal compensation rules for all traffic covered by section 251(b)(5), at least "[f]or the purposes of compliance by an incumbent local exchange carrier with section 251(b)(5)." But, as the Supreme Court said about the 1996 Act generally, section 252(d)(2) is "in many important respects a model of ambiguity or indeed even self-contradiction."[52]

First, section 252(d)(2)(A) directs regulators (i) to "provide for the mutual and reciprocal recovery by each carrier of costs associated with the transport and termination on each carrier's network facilities of calls that originate on the network facilities of the other carrier," and (ii) to "determine such costs on the basis of a reasonable approximation of the additional costs of terminating such calls." At first blush, this seems to anticipate a calling-network-pays rule. But what, exactly, is "a reasonable approximation of the additional costs of terminating such calls?" Remember that the "costs" of termination are composed almost entirely of the fixed costs of building in enough network capacity to handle peak traffic loads, and the short term marginal cost of terminating any given call is therefore negligible. The term "additional costs" is not defined in the Act, and it might plausibly be defined in a number of different ways, including as the relevant TELRIC value for the switching and transport elements as a whole (the FCC's interpretation under the original calling-network-pays rule) or as zero (short term marginal cost). To prescribe a rate of zero for transport and termination is, in effect, to adopt a bill-and-keep regime; it would be a controversial interpretation of this language, but not a frivolous one.

The next subparagraph, section 252(d)(2)(B), compounds the uncertainty by providing that the statutory language just discussed "shall not be construed . . . to preclude arrangements that afford the mutual recovery of costs through the offsetting of reciprocal obligations, including arrangements that waive mutual recovery (such as bill-and-keep arrangements)." This "bill-and-keep savings clause" is amenable to several different interpretations. In its 1996 *Local Competition Order*, the FCC narrowly interpreted this provision as confined to "easy" cases where two carriers' reciprocal obligations are fully offset because the traffic flows from each carrier to the other are balanced.[53] But the savings clause might also be amenable to a broader interpretation as well, under which it would preserve the FCC's authority to order bill-and-keep even in the "hard" case in which traffic between two carriers is unbalanced. To be sure, taken in isolation, the first half of section 252(d)(2)(B)(i) suggests that this savings clause applies only where traffic is balanced, since it preserves "arrangements that afford the mutual recovery of costs through the *offsetting* of reciprocal obligations." But the second half of the same clause goes on to preserve bill-and-keep arrangements that "waive mutual recovery." Conceivably, that language authorizes the FCC to order bill-and-keep arrangements even for unbalanced traffic so long as carriers have adequate opportunities for "recovery of costs" from their own subscribers.

The D.C. Circuit seemed to endorse that interpretation when, in the 2002 decision discussed above, it cited the bill-and-keep savings clause for the proposition that "there is plainly a non-trivial likelihood that the Commission has authority to elect" bill-and-keep for unbalanced ISP-bound traffic.[54] For example, section 252(d)(2) might plausibly be read to permit a choice of either bill-and-keep or a truly cost-based calling-network-pays scheme. Under this approach, the statute would be read to tell regulators, "you may do X or Y, but not Z." And what is Z? This class of prohibited intercarrier compensation practices would include any scheme in which money changes hands for reasons unrelated to the actual costs of transport and termination. Thus, intercarrier compensation for traffic falling within the scope of sections 251(b)(5) and 252(d)(2) could not be inflated for the purpose of subsidizing universal service needs. And ILECs could not charge other carriers for the right to receive calls originated by the ILECs themselves, as they sometimes did in their dealings with wireless carriers before 1996—at least if they enter into interconnection agreements with them.[55]

Finally, the third category of traffic—"intrastate access traffic," consisting of toll calls that stay within state boundaries—is the one that the FCC may find hardest to bring within the fold of a nationally "unified" intercarrier compensation scheme. An example is a conventional circuit-switched long distance call from Los Angeles to San Francisco. Because the call is "intrastate," the access charges imposed on each end are regulated not by the FCC, but by the California Public Utilities Commission. Moreover, if section 251(b)(5) is assumed to apply only to "local" traffic, such intrastate access calls would also fall outside the scope of the Commission's general authority to implement the local competition provisions under *Iowa Utilities Board*. As such, they would arguably fall within the scope of the "intrastate" matters that section 2(b) still bars the FCC from regulating directly, sometimes even when such regulation is important to effectuating federal policies.[56]

Theoretically, the FCC could try to solve this problem, and assert jurisdiction over the intercarrier compensation rules for such calls, in one of several ways. First, it could reaffirm ambiguous suggestions it made in 2001 that, contrary to what it found in 1996, section 251(b)(5) encompasses not just "local" telecommunications, but all telecommunications.[57] The text of section 251(b)(5) does not expressly draw a distinction between "local" and "long distance" calls, which is arguably just a relic of an obsolescent regulatory paradigm in any event.[58] Also, although the provision imposes "reciprocal compensation" obligations only on "local exchange carriers," it "does not explicitly state to whom the LEC's obligation runs," and the FCC has found "that LECs have a duty to establish reciprocal compensation arrangements with respect to local traffic originated by or terminating to any telecommunications carriers," such as non-LEC wireless carriers.[59]

It is by no means clear, however, that the drafters of the 1996 Act meant to include "access" traffic within the scope of section 251(b)(5). First, a provision requiring "reciprocal" compensation for the "transport and termination" of calls seems focused on arrangements in which each of two carriers pays compensation to the other for terminating calls originated on that other's network. In 1996, most two-carrier calls were "local," whereas most long distance calls with different LECs on each end involved an independent third carrier—a long distance company—as a middleman. The language of section 251(b)(5) seems to have been written without these traditional three-carrier access calls in mind. Also, Congress almost certainly did not mean to trigger a multi-billion-dollar flash cut in intrastate access charges—a critical source of universal service subsidies—back when it enacted this provision in 1996. That, some say, might be the import of reading section 251(b)(5) to apply to all "telecommunications" because intrastate access charges in most states traditionally dwarfed the underlying "costs" of originating or terminating this traffic.*

If the FCC wishes to adopt a comprehensive bill-and-keep regime but nonetheless concludes that conventional intrastate access traffic falls outside the scope of section 251(b)(5), it might try to negotiate a national compact under which the states would agree to exercise their own jurisdiction in ways that are consistent with that regime.[60] If, however, it concludes that the states would resist that negotiated solution, the FCC might look for other ways to mandate their adherence to the federal bill-and-keep regime. For example, the FCC could invoke its mandate under section 254 to bring greater rationality to universal service funding by forcing the states to strip implicit subsidies from any intercarrier charges.[61] But even if the FCC could lawfully undertake that approach, it is quite unclear whether the FCC could require states not only to remove subsidies from intrastate access charges, but to abandon access charges altogether in favor of a bill-and-keep rule for intrastate access traffic. On the other hand, a state's dedication to a calling-network-pays approach, as opposed to bill-and-keep, may diminish rapidly if the Commission could force the state to strip out any implicit cross-subsidies from its intrastate access traffic.

Navigating the transition to a unified intercarrier compensation regime is treacherous in part because, in 1996, Congress did not fully "get" the long term unsustainability of the legal distinctions governing this area. Congress may thus need to wade back into this quagmire to facilitate a coherent federal solution. Barring such congressional action, regulators will need to perform legal handstands to accomplish the same result and then hope for the best in court. Time is running out, however, on the policymakers who find it politically easier just to keep muddling through. They can try to keep one step ahead of technology by designing regulations of

---

* This reading would not have a similarly revolutionary effect on interstate access charges, for the FCC could point to the grandfathering provision of section 251(g), noted earlier in this chapter, as a basis for maintaining the status quo for those charges. That provision grandfathers the "access" rules adopted by the FCC itself before 1996 or by the federal court administering the AT&T consent decree. Whether the provision likewise grandfathers intrastate access charges is subject to debate.

increasing complexity and arbitrariness. But, as discussed at the beginning of this chapter, technological ingenuity will almost always find ways to circumvent regulatory distinctions based on political considerations rather than deep-seated economic or technological ones.

* * *

Shortly after the FCC opened its global inquiry into intercarrier compensation in 2001, a group of diverse telecommunications carriers, many of whom are antagonistic on a range of issues, began meeting privately to work out a solution. This "Intercarrier Compensation Forum" (ICF), as it is called, built on the example of the "CALLS" coalition, which helped the FCC reach a consensus approach to reforming interstate access charges in 2000 (see chapter 10). The participating carriers sought to negotiate a unified but mutually acceptable intercarrier compensation regime (based largely on bill-and-keep principles), shepherd the proposal through the Commission, and present a common front to Congress in the event that any statutory amendments were deemed necessary to insulate the proposal from legal challenge.

In August 2004, the remaining carriers in the ICF—SBC, AT&T, MCI, Sprint, Level 3, and a few others—finally presented the details of their plan to the FCC. By then, however, the defection of several major carriers such as Verizon—together with widespread opposition by consumer groups and rural carriers and the submission of several competing plans—made the prospects for eventual adoption of the ICF plan uncertain. That uncertainty, in turn, placed the burden back on government policymakers themselves to design a unified and economically efficient regime for intercarrier compensation, even though any such regime will undoubtedly offend powerful interest groups.

The question is not whether these policymakers care about regulatory rationality and economic efficiency: they do. The real question is whether they have the political will to pursue those goals when doing so means redirecting huge money flows within the industry and disadvantaging some consumers and politically influential companies that benefit from the hidden web of cross-subsidies. For example, the small rural telephone companies and their customers depend heavily on above-cost access charges to subsidize low retail rates for their unusually high per-line costs. Under section 254(g), the long distance carriers paying such charges cannot pass them back to the specific rural customers that "cause" them; instead, they must include them within the nationally averaged long distance rates they charge their customers throughout the United States. Moving to bill-and-keep, however, would shift cost recovery from the access charges paid by long distance carriers to the local retail rates paid by end users, which lie outside the protective ambit of section 254(g). The result would be to place the full burden of covering the rural carriers' unusually high costs, for the first time, squarely on the shoulders of those carriers' particular customers.

Holding such rural companies and their customers harmless in the face of significant intercarrier compensation reforms—that is, shielding them from the monetary effects of regulatory reform—would thus require a dramatic expansion of the universal service fund. This is but one example of the deep connection between the FCC's pursuit of intercarrier compensation reform and its need to support universal service through more explicit, competitively neutral subsidy mechanisms and to nudge state agencies to move in the same direction. Whether the FCC can pull off this transition remains, as the next chapter explains, an unanswered question.

10

Universal Service in the Age of Competition

In the narrowest sense of the term, a "universal service" program is a government-sponsored subsidy scheme designed to add users to, or keep existing users on, the public switched telephone network through low rates. The principal economic justification for such government intervention lies in the "network externality" concept—a manifestation of the "network effects" phenomenon discussed in chapter 1. Simply put, the value of a network to any given user is directly proportional to the number of *other* users who can be reached on it, and no individual user internalizes the full extent of that value in making decisions about whether to join or drop off the network. Ubiquitous telephone subscribership, moreover, benefits not just individual consumers, but society as a whole by enhancing economic development, democratic participation, and public safety.

Although universal service subsidies might well have accelerated subscribership levels in the early years of telephone service, it is by no means clear that such subsidies are still necessary to keep those levels high. Because basic telephone service is so integral to contemporary life, most people above the poverty line would likely purchase it even if the government ended all existing subsidies and rates increased commensurately.[1] In its broader senses, the term "universal service" is commonly used to denote various subsidy programs that have very little to do, even as a conceptual matter, with keeping people on the network.

Today, the FCC's $6 billion "universal service fund," as revised in the wake of the 1996 Act, is composed of four disparate programs: (1) the federal Lifeline and Link-Up programs, which provide need-based subsidies for low-income households; (2) the *non*-need-based government mechanisms designed to keep telephone rates for "high cost" customers "affordable"—namely, below cost—even in the vast majority of cases in which letting rates rise to cost would not necessarily induce anyone to forgo service; (3) a program for funding broadband connections to the nation's schools and libraries; and (4) a similar program for funding such connections to rural health care facilities.[2] Of these programs, only the first, which is dwarfed in size by the second and third,[3] is specifically designed to subsidize telephone service for subscribers who might otherwise drop off the network.

In this chapter, we focus on the second of these four—the so-called "high cost" program, whose implementation presents the most vexing challenges to rational competition policy. As we shall see, that program reflects broad distributional equity goals that, depending on their execution, may be at odds with principles of economic efficiency.[4] At the end of the chapter, we turn to one of the central ironies of universal service policy in the Internet age: the fact that the government does *not* provide subsidies in the one market—residential broadband service—in which such subsidies might be justified today by network externality considerations.

I. The Political and Economic Dynamics of Universal Service

For policymakers, the term "universal service" denotes the whole gamut of explicit and implicit subsidies designed to keep telephone rates in "high cost" areas "affordable"—i.e., below cost—even for customers with sufficient means. If, for example, the estimated monthly cost of serving a given household in a rural town is $100, the state public utility commission may nonetheless cap monthly retail rates in that town at $25. That is true even if the rural town also happens to be a wealthy resort where raising the price to $100 per subscriber would actually induce very few residents to leave the network.

Who pays the extra $75 per month per line? As discussed in chapter 2, the traditional underwriters have included the customers whom the telephone company has charged above-cost rates to make up the difference. First, under the practice known as *geographic rate averaging*, customers in cities often pay roughly the same rates as customers in remote rural locations even though, because of economies of density (see chapter 1), the per-line cost of installing and maintaining a line in the city is a fraction of the cost of doing the same in the countryside. Second, local telephone companies have traditionally charged up to twice as much for a "business line" as for a "residential line," again without any cost-based justification. Third, as discussed in chapter 9, local telephone companies impose on long distance companies regulated "access charges" that, at least on the state level, often exceed any genuine measure of cost, and the difference is passed along to heavy users of conventional long distance services in the form of inflated per-minute rates. Fourth, "vertical services," such as call waiting, are also priced well above cost. In all of these cases, the people contributing to universal service often have no idea that they are doing so: that is why these types of subsidy are called "implicit."

For many decades, regulators developed a universal service policy dependent on a maze of such cross-subsidies. For two basic reasons, these cross-subsidies were economically problematic even before the age of competition. First, by detaching the rate charged for a service from its underlying cost, they defied basic principles of cost-causation, artificially inflating demand for some services and dampening demand for others, such as long distance. Second, such cross-subsidies transgress *Ramsey pricing* principles, which hold that, when there is no straightforward way to allocate costs among different services, the most efficient solution is to recover them through necessary services that consumers would be reluctant to drop (such as basic local service) and not through more elective services that customers would more easily forgo at the margins (such as long distance calls).[5] Because implicit cross-subsidies disregard these economic principles, they have cost billions of dollars in allocative inefficiencies over the past century by diverting social resources from their most productive uses.

The growth of local competition over the past dozen years has added an entirely new dimension to the problem. As we have stressed, high "business line" rates, geographic rate averaging, above-cost access charges levied on long distance calls, and other implicit subsidies are unsustainable in a competitive world. Those policies rely on the prevalence of captive customers who have no choice *but* to pay a telephone monopolist the above-cost rates for essential services that subsidize below-cost rates to certain subscribers, such as those living in rural areas. Once competition arises, the erstwhile monopolist—the ILEC—cannot get away with charging downtown business customers rates far above the cost of serving them, for those customers would then take their business to competitors who can and do charge much less. And if the ILEC continues imposing above-cost access charges that raise end users' long distance rates above cost, more and more end users will make long distance calls using their wireless phones or, as broadband adoption picks up, using VoIP services—thereby avoiding access charges altogether (at least on the originating end).

Unless policymakers are content to watch the ILEC fall slowly into financial distress, they will need to come up with a new type of subsidy scheme designed to function in a competitive environment. This is the avowed purpose of section 254 of the Communications Act, added in 1996.[6] In exceptionally vague language, section 254 envisions a transition from traditional implicit cross-subsidies to a system of "explicit" subsidies underwritten by competitively neutral assessments on telecommunications providers generally. The problem is that regulators, particularly on the state level, need considerable prodding to undertake that transition. Consumers often notice when they must pay tax-like fees that appear as line items on their telephone bills, and they look for someone to blame. But they typically do not know when they are simply paying rates that, in some abstract economic sense, exceed cost.

From the short term perspective of many regulators, the political costs of genuine universal service reform may outweigh the benefits. And the 1996 Act contains no specific time frame for the elimination of the old implicit subsidies, leaving most regulators content to confront this challenge gradually. In effect, these regulators hope that, at least until they have moved on to their next jobs, competition will progress slowly enough that carriers of last resort (the traditional incumbents) can stay financially healthy without any need for abrupt, politically controversial changes to the system. If this hope appeared tenable before the advent of VoIP, it now seems increasingly delusional.

This chapter explores how universal service programs work in practice and why they raise so many difficult problems. We begin, however, by making two general observations about universal service that, because of their political sensitivity, policymakers hesitate to articulate in public.

First, there is no uncontroversial policy reason to keep telephone rates below cost for people who can afford to pay cost-based rates. Prices for many goods and services, such as gasoline, often vary tremendously from one place to another, but the government usually perceives no need to equalize them. Such unremedied disparities extend to the very basics of life, such as housing. For example, a typical four-bedroom house in the middle class suburbs of the nation's capital may cost $500,000 more than a comparable house in the suburbs of Kansas City. But no one suggests that the government should make homeowners in Missouri pay more for their houses so that homeowners in suburban Maryland may pay less. Similarly, there is no clear reason why middle income families in Denver should pay more for telephone service so that high income residents of Aspen may receive such service on the cheap.

The controversial rationale for such programs is that telephone service—like postal delivery—is so fundamental to modern life that it should be insulated from market forces and extended, at comparable rates, to all Americans as a civil right. Whatever the merits of that position, the government's commitment to traditional, non-need-based "universal service" programs is unlikely to change. The reason can be traced to the grand compromise that produced the U.S. Constitution in 1789. Rural voters in the western states are disproportionately represented in Congress—Alaska, for example, has the same number of senators as New York—and they exploit that advantage to keep their telephone rates low. (Of course, the political influence of the rural states is even more dramatically apparent in other sectors of the economy: consider the case of farm subsidies.) For our purposes, therefore, we must take as given that, for the foreseeable future, the political process will preclude a more targeted, need-based approach to "universal service" in which those who cost more to serve pay commensurately higher rates unless, because of their limited means, they would otherwise be likely to drop off the network.

Second, to *whatever* extent policymakers subsidize telephone service—either for poor subscribers or those living in high cost areas—it remains questionable policy to pay for those subsidies through "contribution obligations" imposed on telecommunications providers, as section 254 requires, rather than through general taxes. Industry-specific excise taxes and similar assessments artificially depress demand for the taxed product or service and are therefore less economically efficient than general taxes.[7] And the telecommunications industry incurs not only the full burden of supporting universal service programs, but also a welter of regular federal, state, and local taxes—including the 3% federal excise tax that was initially adopted in 1898 to fund the Spanish-American War and that, despite calls for its repeal, remains stubbornly in place.[8] Indeed, one of the many issues raised by the transition to VoIP is the fact that all the taxes assessed on telecommunications services—approximately $9 billion per year on the state and local level alone—may be jeopardized as consumers sign up for VoIP services, which are arguably exempt from taxation and any direct assessment of universal service fees.[9]

Like much of universal service policy, the current reliance on industry-specific assessments is largely a function of politics. Politicians are loath to raise income taxes and are only too happy to adopt alternative funding mechanisms that, through their sheer complexity, obscure the extent to which ordinary American voters are indirectly paying taxes by another name. From a politician's perspective, implicit cross-subsidies are most appealing because they are the hardest for individual voters to perceive. But if the growth of competition—which is also popular among voters—makes such cross-subsidies unsustainable, complex universal service assessments are politically preferable to an ordinary tax hike, at least until consumers figure them out and complain. And even when consumers do complain, they may well get lost in the confusing array of fees and not know whether to blame politicians or service providers.[10] Unfortunately, by mandating such industry-specific assessments, Congress has needlessly compelled regulators to answer intractable questions about which types of providers should be required to bear what percentage of the contribution burden. As discussed below, those questions have no fully satisfying, competitively neutral answer.

Traditionally, universal service programs have exemplified what Richard Posner has called *taxation by regulation*—a means of compelling "members of the public to support a service that the market would provide at a reduced level, or not at all," while keeping them largely in the dark about the existence, extent, or purpose of the subsidies they must pay.[11] Of course, universal service programs are more transparent now than they were several decades ago, when virtually all subsidies were implicit and AT&T's Bell System routinely cited "universal service" to compliant regulators as a basis for opposing any competitive threat to its nationwide local and long distance monopoly.[12] But even today, as competition is taking hold in most telecommunications markets and the long transition from implicit to explicit subsidies has begun, regulators still cling nostalgically to non-transparent forms of universal service support.

Finally, it bears emphasis that universal service issues differ markedly from many of the other policy challenges discussed in this book. Most of those other challenges arise from the underlying economic characteristics of the telecommunications industry: a combination of high fixed and sunk costs, large scale economies, significant network effects, and rapid technological change. Many of the conundrums and economic distortions associated with universal service programs, by contrast, are the creatures of regulation itself.

With this background, we now turn to the actual mechanics of the emerging universal service support system. There are, in essence, three distinct questions. First, on the "disbursement" side, which providers are entitled to receive universal service funds, and what is the process for deciding how much they receive? Second, which providers must contribute to universal service funds, and in what amounts? Finally, as broadband Internet access becomes more widespread, what services *beyond* conventional telephony are likely to be subject to universal service support? We address each of these questions in turn.

II. Universal Service Funding Mechanisms

Two somewhat arbitrary distinctions, which date back to the early days of the Bell System monopoly, remain at the heart of universal service policy issues. First, the FCC and the states have divided up responsibility, for purposes of managing universal service subsidy mechanisms, into distinct "interstate" and "intrastate" spheres. Second, regulators at both levels treat the larger ILECs, such as the Bell companies, quite differently for universal service purposes from the smaller "rural" ILECs. While both distinctions (federal/state and non-rural/rural) are artificial, they will nonetheless drive universal service policy for the foreseeable future—as will a third arbitrary classification discussed later in this chapter: the distinction between "telecommunications services" and "information services."

A. The basics

Recall from chapter 2 that federal and state regulatory authorities "separate" the costs of the local loop into "interstate" (federal) and "intrastate" (state) jurisdictions so that, among other things, courts can evaluate the merits of a "takings" claim (alleging confiscatory regulation) against either one.[13] Under this system, the FCC, after consulting with the states, splits an incumbent LEC's "costs" into two arbitrary categories: "interstate" costs, whose recovery the FCC superintends, and "intrastate" costs, whose recovery is the responsibility of the states.[14] For example, under the federal-state separations process, 25% of a Bell company's loop costs are generally "allocated" to the interstate jurisdiction and 75% to the intrastate jurisdiction. Once the FCC makes that separation, each jurisdiction must decide how to enable the incumbent to recover the relevant costs.[15]

In general, the federal government enables incumbents to recover the costs on the interstate side of the ledger through (mostly) prescribed per-minute interstate access charges imposed on long distance carriers and flat-rated "subscriber line charges" imposed directly on end users. To some extent, this regime still follows the framework adopted in the wake of the AT&T breakup, although the amounts of the different charges have changed dramatically.[16] The states separately enable incumbents to recover their intrastate costs through (among other things) intrastate access charges, various toll charges, fees for "vertical features" like call waiting and caller ID, and monthly rates for basic local service.

Taken together, the array of authorized charges imposed on high cost customers may fall far short of the cost of serving those customers. In a monopoly environment, such shortfalls could be addressed through cross-subsidies that enable the incumbent's books to come out even in the end anyway. In a competitive environment, they do not, for new entrants will "cherry-pick" the customers that would otherwise pay above-cost rates, as noted above. There would be no problem, of course, if the incumbents could simply drop their high cost customers or raise their rates to cost. But incumbents are almost invariably subject to state-law carrier-of-last-resort obligations that compel them to provide service to high cost customers and all others who request it—and to do so at low rates.[17]

In the 1996 Act, Congress included the highly ambiguous provisions of section 254 to address this concern. Under the prevailing interpretation,[18] section 254 instructs the FCC, after formally consulting with a "Federal-State Joint Board,"[19] to take steps to keep rates "affordable" and "comparable," both from place to place within each state and from state to state across the country. It also envisions that the FCC will accomplish that goal, in cooperation with the states, by phasing out the unsustainable implicit cross-subsidies that characterized universal service policy before 1996. In their place, section 254 sets up an explicit funding mechanism—known as the "high cost fund"—that is underwritten by "equitable and non-discriminatory contribution[s]" by all telecommunications carriers.[20] That fund pays out money to carriers that serve high cost customers.

The recipients of such subsidies are usually incumbents, since they are the ones with the carrier-of-last-resort obligations and thus the ones that normally serve these traditionally uncoveted customers. But these subsidies are also "portable" in the sense that they are available to any carrier that is willing to serve all customers within a defined geographic area and is designated (usually by the relevant state commission) as an *eligible telecommunications carrier* (ETC).[21] ETCs can include wireless carriers as well as wireline CLECs, and their receipt of universal service funds raises complex questions about the extent to which they must demonstrate their ability to meet the same carrier-of-last-resort expectations to which the corresponding ILECs have long been held.[22] In theory, these portable subsidies are supposed to be large enough to entice wireless carriers and CLECs to compete head-to-head against incumbents for high cost customers and, if successful, turn a profit.

In the aftermath of the 1996 Act, the FCC asked to what extent the federal fund should bear the burden of replacing *all* traditional subsidy mechanisms, including those that, like geographic rate averaging, have been managed mostly by the states. Conceivably, Congress could have instructed the states, through a process known as *rate rebalancing*, to eliminate implicit cross-subsidies altogether by lowering the above-cost rates charged to business customers, residential customers in densely populated neighborhoods, and others. And Congress then could have made the incumbents whole for their sudden revenue shortfall by paying them, through the federal high cost fund, the complete difference between the cost of serving high cost customers and the retail rates they are allowed to charge them. That approach, however, would have required a radical enlargement of the federal fund by several billion dollars, and it thus would have imposed immense contribution burdens on telecommunications providers and, ultimately, telecommunications consumers nationwide.

Congress did not require that approach, and the FCC has never seriously considered it. Instead, the Commission has concluded that the federal high cost fund should replace (i) the use of the traditional cross-subsidies (such as above-cost access charges) on the *interstate* side of the cost ledger and (ii) a small portion of traditional cross-subsidies on the *intrastate* side of the cost ledger. The FCC typically addresses those discrete functions in separate proceedings. And, to make matters more complicated still, it addresses both of them differently depending on whether the geographic territories at issue are served by "non-rural" ILECs (the Bell companies and a few others) or the smaller "rural" ILECs. We address the former first.

As to non-rural carriers, the FCC's most significant reform efforts on the *interstate* side of the ledger came in a June 2000 order adopting the main components of an access charge reform program proposed by a broad-based industry alliance known as the "Coalition for Affordable Local and Long Distance Services" (CALLS). Roughly speaking, the FCC ordered significant reductions in the interstate access charges imposed by the largest ILECs and compensated them for the shortfall by increasing the size of the federal fund from which they may seek support as well as the flat-rated subscriber line charge imposed on end users.[23] Although not as large as the access charges assessed by rural ILECs, the resulting interstate access charges for the non-rural ILECs are still well above the rates set under the FCC's TELRIC methodology for the corresponding network functions when they are leased as network elements. The magnitude of that discrepancy has led some to claim that, even as reformed in the *CALLS* order, these charges remain in some sense above cost; others reject that conclusion on the ground that TELRIC itself understates costs (see appendix A). To reduce such controversies, as discussed in the previous chapter, policymakers are considering various proposals to eliminate access charges altogether in favor of higher flat-rate end user charges and, most likely, a further expansion of federal universal service funds for carriers of last resort in high cost areas. As of this writing, however, the prospects for such proposals remain highly speculative.

The FCC takes a much more limited view of the federal fund's role as a replacement for implicit subsidies on the *intrastate* side of the cost ledger. As to the areas served by the Bell companies and the other non-rural incumbents, the Commission has sought to limit its role to helping states with unusually high *average* costs (specifically, more than 135% of the national average) attain rates reasonably comparable to those of other states.[24]

To see how this works, consider a state that has (i) very high cost rural areas, (ii) very low cost urban areas, and (iii) a proportionate enough mix of the two that *statewide* average costs are reasonably close to the national norm.* Under the FCC's current policy, the federal high cost fund does not help compensate for the intrastate costs of serving any high cost area within the state. The FCC reasons that, unless statewide average costs are unusually high, the state's own funding mechanisms can serve to equalize rates within the state's borders so that each subscriber's rates are roughly comparable to those in most other states. In 2001, the Tenth Circuit rejected the FCC's treatment of this issue, expressing skepticism that the FCC had discharged its responsibility to "induce" the states to follow through on equalizing rates in this manner.[25] On remand, the FCC conducted a comprehensive rate review and tweaked the details of its rules a bit, but largely adhered to its prior policy. In so doing, it promised to study the need for additional federal action should it become necessary to ensure reasonable rate comparability across the nation. This most recent order has itself been appealed to the Tenth Circuit, where it remains pending at press time.[26]

The upshot of the FCC's universal service policies is that, at least with respect to the regions served by the major incumbents, the states are supposed to bear the lion's share of responsibility for ensuring sustainable high cost support programs as competition erodes the traditional sources of implicit cross-subsidies. In theory, this permits the states to experiment with different approaches to the problem and to learn from the innovations of their fellow states.[27] To date, however, only a few states have made serious efforts to replace implicit cross-subsidies with more durable support mechanisms analogous to the federal high cost fund. Instead, to avoid political controversy in the short term, most states continue to rely on geographic rate-averaging and other such devices in the apparent expectation that competition will progress slowly enough that immediate change is unnecessary. Only in hindsight will we know for certain if that judgment is as improvident as it now appears.

---

* Here we are using the term "rural" in its usual, vernacular sense, not in its specialized sense as an identification of regions served by small ILECs. To determine whether a particular state has unusually high average costs for purposes of allocating high cost support to non-rural ILECs, the FCC excludes from the calculus all areas of a state served by rural ILECs.

The FCC, too, has moved slowly in reforming the almost century-old system of cross-subsidies, mostly confining its efforts to reducing traditionally subsidy-laden interstate access charges closer to the underlying costs of the relevant services. Congress did not make the FCC's job any easier by enacting a statute that, while filled with vague aspirations to "affordable" service and "reasonably comparable" rates, is short on policy details for addressing politically difficult challenges such as replacing massive implicit subsidies with explicit ones.[28] And Congress compounded the problem, as discussed below, by leaving unclear the scope of the FCC's authority to cut through the traditional interstate/intrastate jurisdictional divide when doing so is necessary for genuine reform.[29] This regulatory impasse carries significant costs. For example, many residential markets have yet to see competitive wireline entry because telephone rates are held below economic cost by implicit cross-subsidies that remain non-portable to competing carriers.

B. The case of "rural" carriers

We have focused so far on the universal service support issues raised by the largest non-rural incumbents such as the Bell companies. In contrast, a "rural" carrier—defined by its small customer base rather than the rustic qualities of its territory—is typically subject to rate-of-return regulation rather than price caps and is eligible for more generous universal service support than is available to the Bell company serving an adjacent territory.[30] In line with its general solicitude for such carriers, the FCC has largely forestalled addressing how competition will affect them and, correlatively, how the universal service schemes that govern them will need to be changed. To be sure, the 1996 Act sought to insulate many of these carriers from the effects of competition and thus from any immediate need to reform implicit cross-subsidies. Section 251(f), for example, allows state commissions to keep these carriers exempt from unbundling requirements and certain other pro-competitive mandates of sections 251 and 252.[31] But, with the steady build-out of wireless and cable infrastructure into the countryside, the day of reckoning for rural carriers can only be postponed, not avoided entirely.

In the so-called *MAG* ("Multi-Association Group") proceeding in 2001, the Commission adopted interstate access charge reforms for rural carriers that were similar in spirit to, though much less far-reaching than, the reforms adopted for the Bell companies and other non-rural carriers in the *CALLS* proceeding.[32] On a conceptual level, the FCC's methodology for calculating rural support is little changed from before 1996: it allocates a larger portion of a rural carrier's loop cost recovery to the "interstate" jurisdiction to the extent the carrier's costs exceed various federal benchmarks.[33] And, until at least 2006, the FCC will continue to base support levels on those carriers' embedded costs rather than (as with the non-rural carriers) their forward-looking costs, thereby assuring a steady subsidy flow.[34] The FCC has justified this differential treatment on the grounds that, unlike the Bell companies, the rural incumbents have "higher operating and equipment costs, which are attributable to lower subscriber density, small exchanges, and a lack of economies of scale," and that these carriers need a degree of "stability and certainty" in confronting the development of competition.[35]

Nonetheless, even while deferring any dramatic universal service reforms, the FCC has sought to promote local competition in rural areas by providing, as the 1996 Act requires, "portable" and "competitively neutral" subsidies to any state-certified "eligible telecommunications carrier."[36] These efforts are on a collision course with the traditional efforts of both Congress and the FCC to protect the economic welfare of rural incumbents. That is because increases in competition effectively force the Commission to come up with more funds not just to subsidize the prevailing competitive ETC, but also to reimburse the ILECs for their revenue shortfall. As the FCC explains:

As an incumbent "loses" lines to a competitive eligible telecommunications carrier, the incumbent must recover its fixed costs from fewer lines, thus increasing its per-line costs. With higher per-line costs, the incumbent would receive greater per-line support, which would also be available to the competitive eligible telecommunications carrier for each of the lines that it serves. Thus, a substantial loss of an incumbent's lines to a competitive eligible telecommunications carrier could result in excessive fund growth.[37]

Exacerbating the burdens on the universal service program, state commissions are only too happy to certify new ETCs to get the benefits of competition without having to confront the hard questions about whether such entry undermines the viability of the incumbent carriers in the relevant service areas. Nonetheless, at least as of this writing, the FCC has taken no decisive action to deal with this problem before it becomes overwhelming.[38]

Further straining the existing subsidy mechanisms is the fact that, at present, carriers certified as ETCs can obtain federal support for providing more than one wireline or wireless connection to a given "high cost" customer. A wireless carrier, for example, can receive support from the high cost fund for serving a customer who already has a supported wireline connection. Enticed by this multiple subsidy opportunity, competitive ETCs have entered rural markets at a rapid clip. Whereas there were only two such ETCs in 1999, which together received about $500,000 in federal support, there were 109 in 2003, and they received approximately $131.5 million.[39] That figure constitutes a small but rapidly growing percentage of the high cost fund. As one state official observes, "[s]ince current [FCC] rules provide support to all lines of all ETCs, states have been faced with the perverse incentive of gaining more federal universal service support the more ETCs they approve," an incentive that "is especially strong in areas served by rural carriers since these areas generally receive higher levels of federal support."[40]

In early 2004, a sharply divided Federal-State Joint Board proposed controlling the growth of the high cost fund by, among other things, limiting subsidies to one consumer-designated "primary connection" per user.[41] FCC Commissioner Kathleen Abernathy, a member of the Board, explained that "the universal service fund can no longer subsidize an unlimited number of connections provided by an unlimited number of carriers. Nor do I believe that the Communications Act contemplates such a result. Section 254 at bottom requires a 'lifeline' connection to the [public switched telephone network]—in other words, reasonably priced access to the network that provides the core 'supported services' that make up universal service."[42] A number of other Board members dissented from this recommendation, reasoning that high cost support has never been limited to a single "lifeline" per customer; that limiting support in this manner would discourage carriers from deploying needed infrastructure in rural areas; that it would present significant administrative challenges (e.g., by raising questions about how to treat multiple people living at the same address); and that other means should be found to control the growth of the fund.[43] Whether the FCC will adopt the Joint Board's controversial recommendation, or find some other means of ensuring the fund's viability (such as by making it more difficult for carriers to become certified as ETCs), remains to be seen.

The proliferation of competitive ETCs poses another regulatory challenge as well, this one as theoretical as it is practical: what *level* of support should such an ETC receive if its cost structure is radically different from the incumbent's? Today, as noted, the support level for any ETC is based on the incumbent's costs: forward-looking costs in the case of non-rural ILECs, and historical costs in the case of rural ILECs. As the Joint Board observes, with some understatement, "funding a competitive ETC based on the incumbent LEC's embedded costs may not be the most economically rational method for calculating support"[44] because, among other things, those costs may bear little resemblance to the actual costs of the ETC. First, they may be far too high, as in the case of a rural ILEC that has operated inefficiently, or of a competitive ETC that wins customers located disproportionately in the lower cost areas of the rural ILEC's territory. In either event, basing subsidies on the ILEC's costs will confer a windfall on competitive ETCs.

On the other hand, as Commissioner Abernathy observes, "several parties have suggested that wireless carriers' per-line support would be *higher* than incumbents' if calculated based on their own network costs."[45] Entitling those carriers to subsidies based on their higher costs would not only "frustrate [the FCC's] goal of *restraining* growth in high cost funding,"[46] but also present vexing issues of regulatory neutrality among competing telecommunications platforms. To what extent should regulators give extra subsidies to carriers that have designed networks with higher cost structures but greater functionality, such as mobility in the case of wireless carriers? To what extent should regulators "penalize" competitive ETCs with particularly efficient network architectures by granting them lower subsidies than the rate-of-return rural carrier itself would receive? These sorts of questions pose essentially the same dilemma that regulators face when, under the prevailing "calling-network-pays" rule, they must decide whether to prescribe different reciprocal compensation rates to different carriers on the basis of differences in network technology and architecture. As we explained in chapter 9, there is no perfectly satisfying solution to that problem in the reciprocal compensation setting. For similar reasons, there is no such solution in the subsidy context either.

III. Universal Service Contribution Mechanisms

So far, we have discussed how the money in the federal high cost fund is spent; now we turn to who must contribute to the fund in the first place. Section 251(d) requires every carrier that provides "interstate telecommunications services" to contribute to the federal fund in a manner directed by the FCC. In the wake of the Act, the Commission tested the extent of its authority in this area by declaring that such carriers should contribute to the fund on the basis of their interstate retail revenues and, potentially, their intrastate revenues as well.[47] In 1999, however, the Fifth Circuit held that, despite the Supreme Court's expansive reading of the FCC's jurisdiction to implement the 1996 Act's competition-related provisions, the FCC lacked jurisdiction to base contribution obligations on the magnitude of a carrier's "intrastate" revenues—i.e., revenues attributable to the provision of intrastate telecommunications services.[48]

The upshot of this ruling was that the heaviest contribution burden fell on traditional long distance carriers such as AT&T and MCI, which specialized in the provision of "interstate" services. This was bad timing: the long distance market was beginning to implode as the fiber glut of the late 1990s pushed down long distance rates and as customers began using e-mail and wireless services as substitutes for conventional long distance calling.[49] The FCC has responded by continually raising the "contribution factor" that dictates the percentage of interstate revenues that a carrier must pay into the universal service fund to underwrite all the various federal programs. In 2004, the FCC's proposed contribution factor stood at about 9%.[50] Attentive consumers will recognize these fees as ever-increasing line items on their long distance bills.

This interstate revenue-based approach to contribution obligations is competitively skewed and ultimately unsustainable for several reasons. First, it artificially dampens demand for long distance and other interstate services, since federal contribution obligations are assessed solely on the basis of revenues derived from such services, and since the states generally assess no contribution obligation of comparable size on the basis of *intrastate* revenues. Second, as the FCC observed in 2002, the interstate/intrastate distinction is quickly becoming unsustainable in the face of marketing and technological developments:

[I]nterstate telecommunications revenues are becoming increasingly difficult to identify as customers migrate to bundled packages of interstate and intrastate telecommunications and non-telecommunications products and services. This has increased opportunities to mischaracterize revenues that should be counted for contribution purposes. Such mischaracterization may result in decreases in the assessable revenue base. Increased competition also is placing downward pressure on interstate rates and revenues, which also contributes to the decline in the contribution base. For example, traditional long-distance providers increasingly are entering local markets at the same time that competitive and incumbent local exchange carriers are increasingly providing long-distance services. Customers also are migrating to mobile wireless and Internet-based services. As we recently noted, these changes have led to fluctuations in the contribution base and rising contribution obligations.[51]

In line with this analysis, almost all observers agree that the current system is broken, although there is no consensus on how to fix it.

As of this writing, the FCC is considering a variety of proposals for contribution reform. One major candidate is a *connections-based* approach, which would assess contribution obligations on the basis of the physical layer connections that a carrier provides to any "public network," including a conventional telephone network or the Internet. A principal challenge presented by such an approach is that "connections" can take many different forms for which there is no universal standard of measurement. Different industry segments thus argue at length about how the FCC should "count" the number of connections provided by (i) various types of high capacity loops, (ii) wireless carriers, (iii) paging companies, and (iv) broadband providers.[52]

There are also a number of legal questions about how to configure such an approach to make it comport with section 254(d), which requires contributions from all carriers that provide interstate telecommunications services. A pure connections-based approach would partially exempt some of the carriers that currently bear the greatest burden for universal service support—specifically, the long distance providers—because, in many circumstances, those carriers rely on a LEC to provide the end user with the contribution-triggering direct connection to a public network. For that reason, the FCC has sought comment on whether to supplement any connections-based approach with a mandatory minimum assessment for any provider of interstate telecommunications services. And some carriers have proposed combining a connections-based approach with revenue-based assessments on stand-alone long distance companies—which, depending on the details and one's own industry perspective, may or may not be competitively neutral.[53]

As its name suggests, an alternative *numbers-based* approach would base contribution obligations largely on the volume of telephone numbers that a provider assigns to its customers, combined with connections-based assessments for special access and private lines. A principal virtue of this option is that, in many respects, it would be relatively easy to administer. It would also encourage conservation in the use of telphone numbers, which should appeal to policymakers focused on preserving the diminishing stock of unassigned ten-digit numbers. Critics respond that, even more than a connections-based scheme, a numbers-based approach would largely exempt certain long distance carriers and broadband providers from contribution obligations because they do not usually assign telephone numbers to their subscribers. On that and other grounds, these critics question the Commission's jurisdiction and substantive legal authority to base contributions on the use of telephone numbers as such, rather than more directly on the provision of interstate telecommunications.[54]

Up to now, we have addressed contribution-related policy conundrums that essentially originate from the artificial distinction that section 254 draws between "interstate" and "intrastate" services. Section 254 presents a separate layer of policy problems by distinguishing as well between providers of (interstate) "telecommunications services" and providers of mere (interstate) "telecommunications." Under section 254(d), the former providers are subject to compulsory contribution obligations; the latter are subject to such obligations only when, in its discretion, the FCC concludes that they should be. Although the FCC has exercised this discretion to impose contribution obligations on certain "private carriers,"[55] which by definition do not provide "telecommunications services" (a term defined as synonymous with "common carriage"), the Commission has yet to impose contribution obligations on providers of transmission services generally.

So long as it persists, the distinction between "telecommunications services" and mere "telecommunications" will produce significant competitive anomalies in the broadband arena. For example, as discussed in chapter 5, the FCC has concluded that a cable operator provides only an "information service," without any "telecommunications service" component, when it provides cable modem service to its end users. At the same time, a cable modem provider uses "telecommunications" as a part of this bundled product. If only the provision of "telecommunications services" (rather than "telecommunications") continues to trigger contribution obligations, then cable modem providers and facilities-based ISPs will enjoy an artificial regulatory advantage over wireline carriers that provide DSL transmission services to end users or ISPs, since such services undoubtedly qualify as "telecommunications services." Of course, this competitive asymmetry would not arise (at least in its current form) if the FCC were to exercise its discretionary authority to impose universal service fees on cable companies or information service providers to the extent they provide "telecommunications" to themselves or others. Nor would it arise if the Ninth Circuit is ultimately upheld in concluding, in its (independently problematic) *Brand X* decision, that cable modem service *does* contain a "telecommunications service" component (see chapter 5). In that case, the mandatory contribution obligation would necessarily apply to cable modem providers and facilities-based ISPs as well.

In either event, however, difficult issues would still arise about exactly how to identify the "telecommunications" (or "telecommunications service") component of an information service for purposes of assessing universal service contributions. For example, recall from chapter 6 that some VoIP providers, such as Pulver, have been found not to provide any "telecommunications" at all. But other VoIP providers, even those that are not vertically integrated with last mile broadband access providers, do build transmission components into their service, often by purchasing them from telecommunications carriers behind the scenes. To what extent should the contribution burden fall on the downstream VoIP providers in such arrangements, and to what extent should it fall on the upstream transmission wholesalers, which in turn can be expected to pass some of that burden through to the VoIP providers?[56]

The FCC could try to answer these sorts of questions by moving to a contribution methodology based, to some degree, on both telephone numbers and connections to a public network. Under that model, the primary burden would fall on last mile access providers, and VoIP providers would assume an increasing share of the burden to the extent they make use of the ten-digit telephone numbers associated with the public switched telephone network. But, as noted, such measures would be subject to legal challenge, and the ensuing litigation would prolong the current state of uncertainty. Again, that uncertainty, like the hornet's nest of contribution disputes more generally, is the inevitable by-product of the Act's maze of legal distinctions as well as Congress's regrettable decision to fund universal service programs out of fees specific to the telecommunications industry rather than tax revenues more generally.

IV. Universal Service in a Broadband World

As we explained at the beginning of this chapter, "universal service" policies, in the narrowest sense of the term, are defended as necessary to facilitate network externalities—i.e., to enhance the network's value to each subscriber by increasing the number of other subscribers. But the subsidies needed to keep subscribers on the telephone network are a fraction of the subsidies actually spent on "universal service" in the broader sense. Indeed, because the voice telephony market is mature and ubiquitous, and because virtually every user regards subscribership as an indispensable feature of modern life, very few of the people who benefit from universal service support would actually drop off the network in the absence of that support—though many people in rural areas would be understandably outraged at the resulting price hikes.

In its current incarnation, the universal service system subsidizes, for everyone regardless of wealth, low priced access to whatever communications services are deemed essential to participation in modern society. To date, policymakers have confined the universe of such services to voice-grade telephone connections, and they have resisted making subsidies available for broadband Internet access.[57] But as broadband becomes more widespread in the residential market, it will become more indispensable to ordinary people, and the FCC will likely face heightened pressure to subsidize broadband adoption on the ground that, like telephony, it is an essential service.[58] Indeed, the Act calls for universal service support at "an evolving level of telecommunications service that the [FCC] shall establish periodically . . . taking into account advances in telecommunications and information technologies and services."[59] Noting the increasing importance of broadband to society, Commissioner Michael Copps concluded in 2002 that "advanced services *are* essential. Indeed, they are becoming more so with each passing day."[60] Over time, others may well join him in that conclusion.

Ironically, if the network externality justification *were* the guiding light of universal service policy—as economic efficiency concerns suggest it should be—that policy would work in a manner almost exactly opposite to how it works today. At present, broadband is still an underdeployed technology that residential consumers do *not* yet view as indispensable. By subsidizing its development, as South Korea and other countries have done, the government would accelerate the "virtuous cycle" needed for widespread broadband deployment: a dynamic in which greater consumer demand (prompted by lower prices) spurs greater broadband investment, which in turn spurs more broadband "killer applications," which in turn spurs more consumer demand.[61] The benefits of this dynamic would extend beyond immediate consumer satisfaction to greater long term growth in the economy as a whole. In 2004, President Bush called for universal, affordable access to broadband by 2007, although he, like the FCC, stopped short of endorsing government subsidies as a means to that end.[62]

On the other hand, the pace of broadband adoption is equal to or faster than that for other major information technologies, and the case for massive government subsidies has not yet been proven.[63] From a purely fiscal perspective, moreover, the government's reticence to mount that subsidy initiative is understandable, for underwriting "affordable" broadband access to all residential customers would radically enlarge the revenue needs of the universal service program and thus the fees exacted to support it. So far, policymakers have confined themselves to the generally successful initiative to fund broadband access for local schools and libraries—to the tune of more than $2 billion per year.[64] And some state governments have helped bring broadband access to rural communities by building out fiber-optic networks for their own use and allowing citizens to tap into them. But the costs of ensuring affordable broadband connections for all residential customers, particularly in areas where providing broadband access would require enormous investment in new facilities, would dwarf the financial burdens imposed by these two programs.[65]

We are *not* contending, of course, that the government should never subsidize residential broadband access. To the contrary, there may well be a strong justification for genuinely need-based subsidies. As is often noted, urban and rural poverty threatens to create a "digital divide" that, unchecked, will worsen current economic inequalities by depriving low-income Americans of the opportunities the Internet presents for education and upward mobility.[66] But we *are* contending that whatever subsidies the government extends to the broadband rollout should not reflexively follow the traditional model of universal service programs. Among other considerations, insofar as the government subsidizes consumer access to this new technology, it should focus first on addressing inequalities of economic opportunity, perhaps through an extension of the Lifeline and Link-Up programs, and it should not confer extravagant benefits on people who would be willing to pay cost-based rates for the service in the first place.[67] And it should focus on lowering entry barriers as a means of promoting universal access—say, by driving down the costs of deployment (through its own actions as a purchaser, for example), facilitating access to rights-of-way, or supporting basic research into promising technologies. Finally, any new government initiatives in this area should be financed through general revenue mechanisms—not through massive additional outlays from an already strained subsidy program underwritten by telecommunications providers. On this last point, Congress has already begun to break away from the traditional universal service model by considering tax credits to spur broadband deployment.[68]

* * *

Economists often talk of "path dependence" to describe the surprising decisions that society sometimes makes because of decisions it made before. Few policymakers, for example, would design a health care system that looks like the one we currently have—in which the uninsured rely on emergency rooms for care (because there alone can they demand attention) and the insured are substantially insulated from the costs of their elective treatment choices.[69] But in a world of incremental policy decisions, reliance interests build up over time, old policies are hard to change, and the cumulative results are often deeply flawed. So it is with universal service policy.[70]

Part of the challenge for the FCC is that it lacks the expertise to manage what is, in effect, a complicated taxation system targeted at a dynamic industry. Like other taxation programs, moreover, this one inspires efforts by prospective payers and beneficiaries to game the system, and it thus requires constant vigilance by regulators. The FCC's challenge is multiplied, of course, by the overlay of state regulation, which often maintains artificial rate structures and stringent carrier-of-last-resort obligations even where competitors have made significant inroads on an incumbent's territory. Ideally, as competitive pressures increase, policymakers will rebalance rates and complete the transition to enforceable and economically efficient subsidy mechanisms. To get from here to there, however, policymakers at all levels will need to acknowledge that universal service programs impose tremendous costs as well as benefits and that they cannot be "deficit-financed" indefinitely at the expense of the incumbents.

11

Competition in the Delivery of Television Programming

To this point, we have examined the regulation of information platforms that deliver voice and data traffic from one point to another or, at most, to a discrete set of points. Such platforms include wireline and wireless telephone networks and the Internet. The FCC also plays a central role in regulating the delivery of television ("video") programming. For several decades after World War II, the FCC's television-related policies focused on conventional *broadcasting*—i.e., the transmission of over-the-air television signals by local TV stations to their surrounding communities. For the past quarter century, the Commission has focused as well on the complex policy issues raised by the emergence of two main types of *multichannel video program distribution* (MVPD) providers: cable television companies and direct-to-home satellite television providers.

All three of these "video distribution platforms"—local broadcasting, cable, and satellite—differ from the point-to-point telecommunications platforms discussed elsewhere in this book in that these video platforms generally transmit the same widely watched TV signals to very large numbers of viewers at the same time. In many contexts, this approach is the most efficient way to disseminate television programming to mass audiences. For example, when you watch the Super Bowl on cable television, you are "tapping," from a common video stream in the cable running along the street, the same signals that all your neighbors are simultaneously receiving. Given the widespread demand to watch the Super Bowl at the same time, and the prodigious bandwidth needed to transmit high-quality images of the action, this arrangement is much more efficient than transmitting separate and wastefully redundant video streams of the Super Bowl to each of the many subscribers that request them.

This chapter discusses the major types of *competition-oriented* regulation that Congress and the FCC have imposed on these video distribution platforms. There is much room for disagreement about whether this market exhibits the economic characteristics that warrant prescriptive competition-related oversight by the government. In particular, with the rise of satellite TV providers as competitors to cable companies, it is challenging to argue that any aspect of the market for video programming distribution remains a "natural monopoly." And some critics claim that, from an economic perspective, many of the regulatory policies relating to television are inefficient and unjustified.[1]

One answer to such critics is that, given the centrality of television to American life, these policies serve important *non*-efficiency-related purposes in addition to the narrower, antitrust-type goals that policymakers pursue in other telecommunications markets.[2] These purposes include promoting *localism* in programming content and preserving *free over-the-air television*, principally for the benefit of those who cannot afford to subscribe to cable or satellite television services. A third key objective of government intervention in the television market is to increase programming *diversity* for its own sake.* In many markets, of course, product diversity, like vigorous price competition, can be an important goal of antitrust policy itself. In the television programming context, however, Congress and the FCC have long intervened to generate greater diversity than could ever be justified strictly from the perspective of economic efficiency.[3]

This policy has generated a long-running debate about whether the government should take affirmative regulatory steps to promote such diversity or whether, as former FCC Chairman Mark Fowler provocatively suggested in 1981, the government should treat television instead as "just another appliance . . . a toaster with pictures."[4] Because this book primarily concerns competition policy, it is not our purpose to evaluate the

---

* The concept of "diversity" is hardly self-defining. In different contexts, it can mean several distinct things: diversity of sources for programming (source diversity); diversity of types of programs (output or programming diversity); diversity of ownership, in terms of numbers of different owners and full representation of different ethnic and racial backgrounds (input diversity); and, of course, diversity of views (viewpoint diversity). *See generally* FCC v. National Citizens Comm. for Broad., 436 U.S. 775, 796-97 (1978) ("[d]iversity and its effects are . . . elusive concepts, not easily defined let alone measured").

highly contested merits of the government's non-efficiency-related objectives in the television world, much less to weigh them against the costs that inevitably accompany regulatory intervention in any market. We have accordingly limited our discussion in this chapter to concise summaries, rather than full expositions, of the federal government's major competition-related TV policies.[*]

These policies fall into three major categories, which we discuss sequentially below, after a brief introduction to the structure of the television market. The first category consists of regulations that mediate the relationships *among* different video distribution platforms, entitling or obligating one such platform (a broadcast station, cable operator, or satellite carrier) to carry the programming of another. These regulations—which encompass compulsory copyright rules, retransmission consent requirements, "must carry" obligations, and "program access" rules—are designed to promote a number of objectives, ranging from "localism" in broadcast content to the preservation of "free" broadcast television and the development of alternative video distribution platforms.

The second category of competition-related policies consists of rules designed to promote greater programming diversity by mediating the *vertical* relationships between video distribution platforms and video programming suppliers. These rules include the now-defunct "finsyn" (financial and syndication) restrictions, once applicable to the broadcast networks, and the "channel occupancy" and horizontal ownership limits that the FCC has more recently sought to impose on cable television systems.

The third category of competition-related policies consists of limits on a given firm's ownership of multiple media outlets in particular geographic markets. These policies, too, are designed not just to curb potentially undue concentration in advertising and other local markets, but also to promote greater programming diversity by ensuring a multiplicity of voices within given communities, particularly on matters of local concern.

---

[*] We similarly do not address issues relating to wholly *non*-competition-oriented rules, such as the now-defunct "fairness doctrine," restrictions on "indecent" content, obligations to carry certain amounts of educational children's (or other public interest) programming, or the various regulations applicable to political advertising.

I. The Basics of Television Programming Delivery

Today, nearly every American household with a television receives the transmission of video programming signals in one of three ways: (i) by receiving over-the-air broadcasts from conventional television stations, or by subscribing to either (ii) a cable television service or (iii) a direct-to-home satellite TV service. As noted in chapter 7, only about 15% of television households now rely on terrestrial broadcasting to receive their television signals; of the remaining 85%, roughly three-quarters subscribe to a cable television service, and almost all of the rest to satellite. Perhaps within a few years the major telephone companies will offer widespread IP-based video services over next generation fiber-based facilities (see chapter 5). For now, however, those services remain in the planning stages, except in a few trial areas.[5]

The broadcasters dominated the television market until the 1980s and are still characterized today as "trustees" of their assigned blocks of spectrum, obligated to run programming "in the public interest."[6] In a typical urban market, the FCC has licensed a handful of television stations to broadcast in "VHF" frequency channels (channels 2-13), and a handful more to broadcast in the "UHF" channels, whose over-the-air signals tend to travel less far and reach fewer households. A VHF station is typically affiliated with—i.e., has obtained the rights to carry the programming distributed by—one of the major television networks. These networks include CBS (owned by Viacom), NBC (owned by General Electric), ABC (owned by Disney), and Fox (owned by News Corp.).

Each such network *owns and operates* a number of stations outright, which are known as "O&Os." As discussed below, however, FCC rules—designed to promote localism and programming diversity—effectively limit the number of such stations a network may own. The remaining network "affiliates" deal with the networks on an arm's length contractual basis and occasionally defect from one network to another, as happened in the mid-1990s when the new Fox network aggressively recruited affiliates.

The relationship between a television network and its affiliates is mostly, though not entirely, symbiotic.[7] The network contributes national programming for much of an affiliate's broadcast day, including its "prime time" schedule. An affiliate typically contracts for exclusive rights in a given geographic market to air the first broadcast of a network's programs, although the network is generally free to sell any other station in the same market the "syndication" rights to those programs (i.e., the right to show reruns in subsequent years), and the affiliate is likewise free to purchase syndicated programming that originally aired on other networks. With infrequent exceptions, however, the affiliate is contractually bound to air its own network's programming during prime time, and its revenues thus increase with the popularity of the network's shows, since advertisers will pay more to have their commercials run during shows with high ratings. From the network's perspective, the affiliates contribute, in the aggregate, the coast-to-coast viewership needed to generate the enormous national advertising revenues that in turn underwrite the network's programming expenses. The networks draw substantial revenues from national advertising aired during network programs, and the affiliates draw most of their revenues from their own advertising, aired during (or adjacent to) network programs and during non-network programs, such as the local news.

Policymakers often cite the essential role of local broadcasters—both network affiliates and the unaffiliated "independent" stations—in preserving America's longstanding system of "free" over-the-air television. We place the word "free" in quotes only because over-the-air television is *not* cost-free except in the narrow sense that viewers need pay no money to watch it. As noted in chapter 7, the opportunity costs of preserving the current regime are substantial: television broadcasts consume enormous swaths of spectrum that could arguably be put to more efficient uses, particularly now that the overwhelming majority of Americans do not use that spectrum to watch television. Even if access to television programming, like telephone service, were deemed a necessity of life, the government could provide need-based subsidies for those who might otherwise be unable to afford a cable or satellite TV subscription. There is, in short, no uncontroversial rationale for continuing to reserve immense blocks of spectrum for television broadcasting, particularly in the absence of any auction-based process to ensure their efficient use. This objection, however, is water under the bridge. As explained in chapter 12, Congress recently reaffirmed its commitment to the traditional regime, inefficient or not, in assigning additional spectrum to broadcasters for digital television.

Unlike broadcasters, cable and satellite companies supplement advertising revenues with subscription fees. Until the 1980s, cable television providers focused mostly on retransmitting the broadcasters' signals to areas where they otherwise might not come through strongly enough to provide clear pictures to viewers. Starting in the 1970s and 1980s, these providers looked for ways to increase their subscribership by offering programming available only on their cable platforms. The result was a proliferation of cable-only channels such as HBO, MTV, and ESPN. The programming on some of these channels is produced by major studios affiliated either with the cable companies themselves or with the major television networks. For example, Time Warner, the parent of Warner Brothers, owns CNN, TBS, and HBO; Disney owns ABC Family, the Disney Channel, and most of ESPN; and News Corp. owns the Fox News Channel. Particularly in the largest markets, cable systems are owned by national media companies such as Comcast, Cox, and Time Warner, known as "multiple cable system operators," or MSOs. As we shall see, Congress directed the FCC to limit the number of markets such MSOs may serve, principally to protect the viability of independent programmers.

Traditionally, cable television service was viewed as a natural monopoly (see chapter 1), and a single company would operate the sole cable system in a given geographic region, sometimes under a (now-banned) exclusive franchise agreement with local authorities.[8] Today, cable "overbuilders" have provided a "terrestrial" (non-satellite) source of competition for incumbent cable companies in the market for MVPD services. For example, RCN provides cable television in New York City, as well as bundles of voice, data, and video services. Such overbuilders have focused their operations on the most densely populated urban areas, however, and even in those areas they have had trouble covering their considerable costs.[9]

Although direct-to-home satellite providers first offered service in the 1980s, it was not until the 1990s that these providers assumed their current position as serious competitors to cable companies in the MVPD market. There are currently two major "direct broadcast satellite" (DBS) firms that beam television programming directly to American consumers: DirecTV and EchoStar. In 2004, a year after the FCC effectively blocked a proposed merger of these two companies,[10] it voted 3-2 to approve News Corp.'s bid to purchase a controlling interest in DirecTV.[11] EchoStar, which operates the Dish Network, remains independent.

The satellites operated by these companies occupy highly coveted orbital slots that are both "geostationary," in that they remain fixed in place above the earth, and located in positions from which the satellites can transmit signals to the entire continental United States. (These are thus known as "full CONUS" slots.) The FCC has assigned separate blocks of spectrum to these carriers, each of which uses digital compression technology to transmit hundreds of TV channels. Most subscribers now receive satellite signals via pizza-sized dish antennas affixed to their rooftops, whereas the earliest generation of subscribers, most of them in rural areas, relied on much larger antennas the size of compact cars.

II. Regulation of Relationships Among Video Distribution Platforms

Over the years, Congress and the FCC have devoted much time and energy to mediating the relationships among the three main video distribution platforms: broadcasting, cable, and satellite. The government's regulation of these three platforms has sought not merely to promote efficient cross-platform competition, but also to protect the interests of the broadcasters. From the mid-1960s to the late 1970s, for example, the FCC struggled to justify various burdens it had placed on the upstart cable television companies—including an obligation to originate their own local shows and a prohibition on charging extra for premium programming—to protect the interests of the incumbent broadcasters. One court later described such regulatory burdens as "hostile to the growth of the cable industry, as the FCC sought to protect, in the name of localism and program diversity, the position of the existing broadcasters, and particularly, the struggling UHF stations."[12] Today, Congress and the FCC are less obviously protectionist in their television policies. Nonetheless, much of the regulation in this area reflects an abiding solicitude for the continued existence and traditional prerogatives of the nation's local television broadcasters. Critics view this approach as symptomatic of the public choice pressures discussed throughout this book; proponents view it as an important part of a continuing effort to support the basic institutions of American democracy.[13]

A. Retransmission consent

In the early years of cable television, cable operators, known then as "community antenna television" ("CATV") providers, received the signals of local broadcasters off the public airwaves and retransmitted them over wires to households that would otherwise receive poor or no reception.

The broadcasters viewed such retransmission of their signals with mixed feelings. On the one hand, so long as the signals were retransmitted in their entirety to the same local communities, the broadcasters and their commercial sponsors benefited from the successful efforts of cable systems to increase the number of "eyeballs" watching the broadcasters' programming—and, in particular, the commercials accompanying that programming. On the other hand, the broadcasters feared, among other things, that cable companies would also pipe signals from distant broadcast stations into local broadcasting markets and would thereby dilute the share of the local viewership that any given local broadcaster could promise advertisers (a concern we discuss in more detail below).

In the late 1960s and early 1970s, the courts ruled in favor of the cable systems in the ensuing copyright litigation, reasoning that, as passive transmitters, such systems were more like "viewers" of the original programming than like infringing "performers" of it.[14] Congress then stepped in and, in the Copyright Act of 1976, struck a compromise. Congress deemed the cable systems "performers" for copyright purposes but, to obviate the enormous transaction costs of individualized negotiations between cable companies and each copyright holder, granted them a statutory license to retransmit broadcast programming.[15] The price of that copyright license is determined by a statutory formula implemented by the Library of Congress.[16] The result, as that institution recently described it, is an arrangement that is "technical, complex, and, many would say, antiquated."[17] Nonetheless, few people today advocate fundamentally altering this regime; indeed, some have cited it as a model for resolving copyright disputes relating to the availability of digital content on the Internet.[18]

This "compulsory license," however, addresses only *copyright* restrictions on the retransmission of programming content. In the Cable Act of 1992, Congress granted broadcasters a distinct property right by forbidding any cable system, with a few enumerated exceptions, from retransmitting broadcast signals without "the express authority of the originating station."[19] This *retransmission consent* provision operates to the financial benefit of many broadcasters. Although cable companies have resisted making substantial cash payments to broadcasters, they often agree to carry the broadcast networks' less prominent cable channels as consideration for the right to retransmit "must see" network programming to their subscribers.[20]

Occasionally, retransmission consent negotiations break down into high-profile games of chicken, as when Time Warner briefly responded to Disney's contractual demands by dropping ABC from some of its cable systems in 2000. Time Warner's timing could hardly have been worse: at the time, it was seeking regulatory approval of its controversial merger with AOL, and its apparent heavy-handedness enabled Disney to depict Time Warner as a ruthless monopolist worthy of intrusive government scrutiny. Time Warner soon resolved this embarrassing impasse. In a similar battle, EchoStar—which, along with DirecTV, is subject to the same retransmission consent obligation as the cable companies—pulled off the air all of Viacom's channels (CBS, MTV, and Nickelodeon, among others) in reaction to Viacom's "unreasonable demands" on behalf of its CBS stations, but it, too, quickly resolved the matter.[21]

Finally, under the FCC's *network non-duplication rule*, a cable company operating in an area served by a network affiliate is normally prohibited from carrying duplicative programming from some distant affiliate of the same network.[22] For example, a cable system in, say, Richmond may not strike a favorable deal with a broadcasting network's affiliate in, say, Nashville and pipe the Nashville affiliate's programming back to viewers in Richmond. The purpose of this prohibition is to protect the advertising revenues of the same network's Richmond affiliate insofar as it has bargained for exclusive rights to broadcast the network's programming in the Richmond area. That station's local advertising revenues would quickly evaporate if Richmond-area cable subscribers, who constitute most of the affiliate's viewers, began watching the Nashville station, with its own set of commercials, rather than the Richmond one. The network non-duplication rule is thus one of several key respects in which the FCC has intervened in the structure of the television market to protect the vitality of local broadcasters and their programming content.

B. Must carry

To this point, we have addressed the right of cable operators to carry broadcast programming they wish to carry; now we turn to their obligation to carry broadcast programming they do *not* wish to carry. If left to their own devices, cable companies would not retransmit, even for free, the signals of the least-watched stations, most of which broadcast in the UHF spectrum and are unaffiliated with the major networks.[23] Instead, cable operators would prefer to fill up their channel capacity with other types of programming and with their own commercial advertisers. That market-based outcome would arguably spell financial doom for many of these smaller television stations. Since most Americans watch television over cable, any broadcast station not carried by the local cable system would have few viewers and would be severely limited in what it could charge advertisers for commercial airtime. In 1992, to preserve these stations from this threat, Congress entitled any broadcaster that does not wish to engage in retransmission consent negotiations to rely instead on a statutory entitlement to have its programming carried on the local cable system, albeit without compensation.[24]

This *must carry* provision has been justified primarily as a necessary means of preserving a vibrant system of "free" and locality-based over-the-air television. In 1997, by a vote of 5-4, the Supreme Court relied mostly on that rationale to reject a First Amendment challenge to the must carry requirement.[25] Notably, the Court's decision settled only the constitutionality of must carry rights for *analog* broadcast channels. As discussed in the next chapter, the transition to digital television has raised new and difficult questions about the extent to which the government could constitutionally require cable companies to retransmit both analog and digital signals for a given broadcaster at the same time.

Even as confined to traditional analog signals, the must carry rules remain highly controversial as a policy matter. They are undeniably overbroad in that they benefit not just (or even primarily) stations with unusually meritorious "local" programming, but also the likes of home shopping stations, which typically are not well known for such programming and which obtained broadcasting licenses in part to guarantee themselves a free slot on the local cable line-ups.[26] More generally, as former FCC commissioner Glen Robinson has observed, the must carry regime and similar rules designed to protect "local" programming "assume[] that there is some plausible case to be made that the market will not assure local service sufficient to provide what the public needs in addition to what they want."[27] For now, however, that assumption remains engrained in U.S. television regulation.

C. Satellite retransmission of broadcast signals

The same traditional concerns about localism and the sustainability of non-subscription-based television underlie the rules governing the relationship between local broadcasters and the major satellite television providers. Because of their centralized national transmissions and limited spectrum, such providers historically found it infeasible to carry, at the same time, the signals of many different local affiliates of the same broadcast network (although, as we shall discuss, technological advances have recently begun easing the problem). The satellite companies thus long sought to retransmit the signals only of select network affiliates to everyone in the continental United States. This arrangement understandably concerned other network affiliates because, as in the Nashville-into-Richmond hypothetical posed above, it enabled viewers to watch the same network programming with commercials meant for distant communities and thus placed the non-carried affiliates' local advertising revenues in jeopardy. Similar concerns do not arise, of course, in rural areas where no terrestrial broadcasting signals can reach prospective viewers in the first place.

Balancing the interests of local broadcasters against those of television viewers in remote areas (for whom satellite television was, and still often is, the only means of delivering television signals), Congress enacted the Satellite Home Viewer Act of 1988 (SHVA, pronounced "SHIH vuh"). This legislation granted satellite providers a limited copyright license to retransmit the programming of distant broadcast stations only to households that would otherwise be "unserved" by (i.e., unable to receive clear signals from) a local network affiliate.[28] Congress delegated to the FCC much of the inquiry into whether particular areas should be deemed "unserved" for this purpose, and the FCC issued a set of highly specific technical criteria. The satellite providers nonetheless followed their own expansive interpretation of which households were "unserved," relying not on the FCC's objective criteria, but instead on viewers' subjective judgments about whether they received clear television signals from their local broadcasters. The broadcasters went to court and ultimately obtained injunctions banning this practice.[29] By the time the broadcasters prevailed, however, many consumers in technically "served" households were already receiving network programming over their satellite systems.

During this period, it became increasingly obvious that a satellite provider's inability to retransmit network programming to all of its subscribers placed it at a clear competitive disadvantage to the cable companies. In the early days of satellite television, the problem was as much technological as it was legal because, as noted, satellite providers lacked the transmission capacity to include a given subscriber's local stations in her programming package—i.e., so-called *local-into-local* retransmission. In contrast, because cable systems operate locally to begin with, they have always had the network capacity needed to retransmit the signals of a network affiliate to the affiliate's local viewers. Of course, satellite subscribers who lived in areas "served" by local broadcasters—and who were thus generally ineligible to receive network programming via satellite—could attach rabbit ears to their televisions, flick a switch, and receive such programming from those local broadcasters directly. But the picture quality would generally be worse than on the channels carried either on satellite systems or on cable TV systems. Moreover, market research revealed that "viewers want to be able to receive all of the television channels they watch from a single source" and that, in the words of one industry official, "most people who walk into a satellite dealer's showroom turn around and walk out because they can't get their local TV channels through [satellite]."[30]

By the late 1990s, satellite providers had overcome some of the *technological* hurdles needed to retransmit local-into-local programming in direct competition with the cable companies. First, advances in digital compression technology enabled them to squeeze more channel capacity from their allotted spectrum, and they could therefore beam a greater number of retransmitted broadcast signals than before. (Although the same signals might be beamed nationwide, the scrambler in a given subscriber's set-top box restricts the channels she can watch.) Second, satellite providers began developing "spot beam" technologies that could target particular signals to particular parts of the country, thereby reusing their assigned spectrum efficiently.[31]

Despite these technological advances, however, the satellite companies still lacked a statutory copyright license to broadcast network programming into areas adequately served by the signals of local broadcasters. This was a propitious time for the satellite companies to seek a legislative fix for this problem. During the 1990s, Congress had vacillated on how to deal with the dominance of the cable companies in the MVPD market. In the Cable Act of 1992, Congress directed the FCC to impose a scheme of retail rate regulation for cable television service.[32] Four years later, however, in the Telecommunications Act of 1996, Congress announced the repeal of that directive (effective in 1999) as applied to non-broadcast tiers of cable service.[33] The rationale for this deregulatory step was that free-market competition—principally from satellite providers, and potentially from cable overbuilders and telephone companies—would keep the incumbent cable companies' rates in check. By the late 1990s, however, such competition was slow to develop, and cable subscription fees had steadily increased during the intervening years (as, to be sure, had the cable companies' infrastructure investments). Amid a chorus of complaints, Congress concluded that more was needed to generate cross-platform competition in the MVPD market.

To that end, Congress passed the Satellite Home Viewer Improvement Act of 1999. SHVIA (pronounced "shuh VEE uh") grants satellite providers a conditional copyright license to make local-into-local retransmissions to all households in a given market, while holding those providers subject to the same retransmission consent obligation as cable companies (and retaining SHVA's prohibition on the transmission of one network affiliate's signals into a *distant* network affiliate's market).[34] This compulsory license is subject to a significant condition, which took effect in 2002. If a satellite provider invokes its right to retransmit some local broadcasting signals in a given geographic market, such as those of the network affiliates, it incurs an obligation (subject to several exceptions) to carry the signals of all other broadcasting stations in the same geographic market, including the less-watched UHF stations.[35] This *carry one, carry all* rule is the satellite industry's counterpart to the must carry rule in the cable industry. The satellite version is in one sense more voluntary than the cable version because satellite carriers remain free to avoid the must carry obligation altogether simply by declining to retransmit any local broadcaster's signals in a given market. For that reason, and relying on the Supreme Court's prior decision upholding the cable must carry rules, the courts rejected the satellite industry's First Amendment challenge to SHVIA.[36]

D. The program access rules

Our discussion so far has focused on the rights and obligations of cable and satellite providers to carry *broadcast* programming. Under the *pro-*

gram access rules added by the Cable Act of 1992, cable companies are themselves required in many contexts to make their *own* programming (including the programming of their corporate affiliates) available on reasonable terms to providers of rival MVPD platforms, such as cable overbuilders or satellite television providers.[37] For example, Time Warner, which owns both HBO and the local cable system in Manhattan, must allow cable overbuilders to purchase HBO programming on nondiscriminatory terms (as set forth in FCC rules) and provide it to their own Manhattan subscribers. The concern underlying this requirement is that, left to its own devices, Time Warner might withhold HBO programming from the overbuilders in the hope that HBO's programs are so indispensable to the television experience of many viewers that they will forgo the overbuilders' cable service in favor of Time Warner's service. This rule is often described as a ban on exclusive self-dealing by cable companies (even though it sweeps more broadly than that).[38]

In the 1992 Cable Act, Congress provided that this ban should remain in effect for only ten years unless, at that point, the FCC found that it remained "necessary to preserve and protect competition and diversity in the distribution of video programming."[39] In 2002, the FCC made that finding by a vote of 3-1 and kept the ban in effect at least through October 2007.[40] In dissent, Commissioner Kathleen Abernathy maintained that the relevant evidence "demonstrates that increased competition in both the video distribution and programming markets jointly render the ban on exclusive agreements no longer necessary."[41]

The program access rules might seem to resemble the traditional responses to monopoly leveraging concerns in the telecommunications industry, such as the AT&T divestiture (see chapter 2) or the *Computer Inquiry* rules (see chapter 5). In fact, however, they address quite different market dynamics. Rather than protecting suppliers of rival *applications* (programming) from a large firm's perceived strength in the *platform* (MVPD) market, these rules are designed to protect rival *platform* providers (cable overbuilders and satellite providers) from a large firm's perceived strength in the *applications* market—here, the market for "must see" TV channels. Examples of such channels include HBO, with widely watched programs such as *The Sopranos* and *Six Feet Under*.

The rationale behind the program access rules is controversial. On the one hand, as Commissioner Abernathy has observed, "[a] marketplace that pressures competitors to produce new original programming fosters diversity and competition; it certainly does not harm it."[42] Indeed, even before its 2004 merger with News Corp. (which owns Fox), DirecTV had developed original programming of its own, such as the highly successful "NFL Sunday Ticket." On the other hand, defenders of the rules claim that, somewhat like the facilities-leasing requirements of the 1996 Act (see chapter 3), program-sharing rights are necessary to lower the barriers to entry into the MVPD market. On this view, without a regulatory jump start in the programming market, prospective new entrants may be unable to develop a sufficient customer base quickly enough to justify the massive investments needed to enter the distribution market.

III. Regulation of Relationships Between TV Programming Producers and Distributors

The program access rules reflect a longstanding suspicion of vertical integration by large media companies in the separate markets for the production and distribution of television programming. From a strictly antitrust perspective, this suspicion is often difficult to substantiate.[43] Vertical integration between TV programming distributors and suppliers, at least in the abstract, poses few of the monopoly-leveraging threats that led to the AT&T divestiture or the *Computer Inquiry* rules. With the continuing success of satellite TV, few people strenuously maintain that any cable company is an entrenched monopolist in the market for either video production or distribution. And even if such a company were dominant in one of those markets, it would be unclear which, if any, of the several exceptions to the "complementary externalities" principle discussed in chapter 5 would lead the company to leverage that dominance to suppress competition in the other market. Until recently, however, regulators did not focus on such finer points of economic reasoning. Instead, the received wisdom was that all vertical integration, at least by large media companies, should be viewed with immense skepticism—such that the Hollywood studios, for example, could not be trusted with ownership interests in movie theaters.[44]

Carried too far, such suspicion not only exaggerates the anticompetitive potential of vertical integration, but ignores the efficiencies that such integration permits. In the 1970s, an influential academic movement known as "new institutional economics" drove this point home.[45] Building on the insights of Ronald Coase, this scholarship showed that, in the absence of market failure, ordinary market forces will generally induce a firm to integrate vertically when, and only when, doing so is economically efficient.[46] Specifically, a firm in a particular market will typically contract out for complementary goods or services when the transaction costs of doing so are low; conversely, when those transaction costs are high, it will vertically integrate rather than out-source. This scholarship explains how the strategic use of in-sourcing or out-sourcing by firms throughout the economy enables them to operate more efficiently and maximizes overall consumer welfare.

In the media context, when a single integrated firm both produces and distributes a given program, it economizes on transaction costs by streamlining the program development process, cutting out middlemen, and eliminating the concern that independent producers could extort supracompetitive prices during program renewal periods for the rights to continue airing long-running popular shows. At the same time, the major networks still sometimes contract out for programming to independent firms when that course is more efficient, as ABC recently did in turning to HBO for programming help.[47] Of course, any distributor might irrationally favor its own production affiliates because of managerial politics or corporate hubris, even when doing so results in fewer viewers, lower distribution revenues, and perhaps lower earnings for the corporate family as a whole.[48] Over time, however, competition in the video distribution market, along with the prospect that concerned corporate boards (or hostile corporate takeovers) will replace incompetent management, may well limit the extent and duration of such inefficient favoritism.

A. Broadcast networks

That policymakers remain categorically skeptical of vertical integration in media companies, despite the economic efficiency considerations just discussed, is a manifestation (at least in part) of a phenomenon we noted at the beginning of this chapter. Television regulation rests less on pure antitrust-type concerns about economic efficiency than on the more nebulous goals of localism and, of particular relevance here, programming "diversity"—i.e., the promotion of the "widest possible dissemination of information from diverse and antagonistic sources."[49]

The *finsyn* ("financial and syndication") rules, first adopted in 1970 and significantly revised in 1991, present the lead case study in the FCC's ill-fated efforts to promote programming diversity through restrictions on vertical integration. With complex exceptions irrelevant to our discussion, the finsyn rules largely precluded what were then the big three traditional television networks (CBS, NBC, and ABC) from, among other things, "syndicating" television programs—i.e., licensing individual stations to rebroadcast them after they are initially aired. The effect of that and the other finsyn restrictions was to sideline the three broadcast networks from much of the market for program production. The FCC justified these restrictions as necessary to promote greater diversity in television programming and to protect independent studios from the dominance of the networks by making it easier for such studios to earn the syndication revenues needed to subsidize their production operations.

By the 1990s, however, the growth of cable had diminished any "bottleneck" the broadcast networks may have once enjoyed in the market for programming distribution. And, as Judge Richard Posner observed for the Seventh Circuit in 1992, the finsyn rules "appear[ed] to harm rather than to help" their supposed beneficiaries—outside producers—because the restriction on the sale of syndication rights made it harder for them to market their programs to the networks, "a class of buyers that may be the high bidders for them. . . . Since syndication is the riskiest component of a producer's property right—for its value depends on the distinctly low-probability event that the program will be a smash hit on network television—restricting its sale [to the networks] bears most heavily on the smallest, the weakest, the newest, the most experimental producers, for they are likely to be the ones least able to bear risk."[50] That, Posner speculated, might well have been an animating purpose of these rules. "It becomes understandable why the existing producers support the [finsyn] rules: the rules protect these producers against new competition both from the networks . . . and from new producers. The ranks of the outside producers of prime-time programming have been thinned under the regime of financial interest and syndication rules. The survivors are the beneficiaries of the thinning. They do not want the forest restored to its pristine density. They consent to have their own right to sell syndication rights curtailed as the price of a like restriction on their potential competitors, on whom it is likely to bear more heavily."[51]

In the past, the Supreme Court had given considerable deference to the FCC's "predictive judgment" about the types of structural regulation needed to ensure programming diversity.[52] Posner, however, brushed off the FCC's invocation of that institutional expertise. He explained that, "while the word diversity appears with incantatory frequency [in the FCC's order], it is never defined," and, in all events, the FCC had made "no attempt to explain" how finsyn would increase diversity in the marketplace of ideas.[53] "Stripped of verbiage," he concluded, "the [FCC's] opinion, like a Persian cat with its fur shaved, is alarmingly pale and thin."[54]

In response to the Seventh Circuit's decision, the FCC abandoned the finsyn rules altogether and thereby dismantled what amounted to an artificial barrier to entry into both the network and programming markets. The result has been significant vertical integration—Viacom bought CBS, for example, and Disney bought ABC—but also far greater consumer choice among network programming lineups. Fox, which had previously provided only about ten hours of programming per week (and thus remained exempt from the finsyn rules) became a full-fledged major network. And Warner Brothers and Paramount created entirely new networks—the WB and UPN (though the latter is now owned by Viacom). Indeed, new broadcast networks have flourished in the past decade, and several of them—such as UPN, Univision, and PAX—have made their mark on popular culture by targeting their broadcast programming to previously underserved audiences.

Despite these developments, there remains considerable popular sentiment for vertical restrictions on the major media companies. A number of commentators, including media mogul Ted Turner, have proposed reinstituting the finsyn rules or some other type of limitation on vertical integration.[55] They claim, in essence, that a major media company is less innovative than smaller companies and typically refuses to deal with them. Commissioner Michael Copps has likewise championed "some sort of set-aside, like 25-35% of prime time hours, for independent creators and producers."[56] None of these proposals, however, is likely to take hold. The FCC in particular has expressed little interest in devising bold new ways of intervening in the market for conventional television programming in this generally deregulatory era.[57]

B. Cable television

If there is a counterpart to finsyn for the cable operators, it lies in the FCC's now-vacated rules implementing section 11(c) of the 1992 Cable Act.[58] In that provision, Congress ordered the FCC to develop rules designed, in different ways, to limit any undue influence by large cable companies in the market for video programming.[59] The FCC responded by imposing, as Congress directed, (i) a *horizontal* restriction on the number of subscribers a cable company or affiliated companies may reach nationwide and (ii) a separate *vertical* restriction on the number of channel slots on any given cable system that can be occupied by a programmer in which the system operator has an attributable interest.[60] Although the FCC's statutory responsibility to adopt both horizontal and vertical restrictions has never been in doubt, the cable industry has successfully challenged the specifics of the FCC's rules in the D.C. Circuit.

The vertical restriction was never particularly onerous. The FCC limited the number of affiliated channels to 40% of a system's channel capacity—but only up to 75 channels, beyond which the operator could include as much affiliated programming as it wished. As the FCC noted on appeal, no cable operator had ever actually complained that this rule seriously constrained its business decisions. Nonetheless, the D.C. Circuit invalidated the rule on the ground that, in the face of First Amendment concerns, the FCC had offered no analytically sound basis for concluding that a 40% limit was appropriate, particularly for cable operators subject to competition.[61] The matter remains before the FCC on remand, but is likely to have diminishing significance over time, as the deployment of digital technology expands the channel capacity of cable systems.

The FCC's horizontal rules were more commercially significant to the cable industry and thus more controversial, for they imposed clear limits on how large a cable operator could grow on a national level. The "monopsony" rationale for such limits requires a brief explanation.* Despite some inroads made by cable overbuilders, cable companies still compete infrequently with one another for customers. Notably, in most markets, there is only one cable system. Thus, even if a single cable company—say, Comcast—purchased all of the cable systems in the country, most consumers

---

* The term "monopsony" describes a firm's dominance as a *purchaser* (as opposed to a seller) in a given market.

would suffer no immediate loss of television delivery alternatives: they could still choose among Comcast, the two major satellite providers, all terrestrial broadcast stations within range, and any number of other possible niche offerings, such as streaming video over the Internet.[62] Nonetheless, Comcast's ability to expand horizontally by buying additional cable systems could raise a different type of competitive risk: that Comcast, acting either unilaterally or in collusion with other providers, might suppress competition in the *programming* market by favoring affiliated programmers in its purchasing decisions and disfavoring others. The principal concern is that an independent creator of programming cannot hope to recover its production expenses unless its shows reach a critical number of viewers—and could thus be doomed by the decision of a cable company not to carry those shows if that company owns many cable systems accounting for too large a share of the national audience.

The horizontal cable ownership rules, which the FCC adopted in the 1990s, were designed to preclude cable companies from growing large enough to exercise such monopsony power, principally through collusive favoritism for certain programming suppliers. Specifically, the FCC limited any single company (and all others in which the company had "an attributable interest") to ownership of cable systems that, in the aggregate, reached 30% of the MVPD market nationwide.[63] In 2001, the D.C. Circuit invalidated the 30% limit on two basic grounds. First, the court found that the limit rested on unsupported assumptions about the potential for collusion among cable companies in program-purchasing decisions. Second, it held that the FCC's analysis understated the extent to which satellite-based MVPD competition would force cable companies to purchase attractive programming, regardless of the originating studio, lest they lose their customers to these alternative video platform providers.[64]

The court's discussion of cross-platform competition was entirely theoretical, but in 2003, Cablevision conducted its own intriguing marketplace experiment on the extent to which such competition can enforce competitive norms in the programming market. In 2002, George Steinbrenner formed the YES Network to carry Yankees games after refusing to grant that privilege to Cablevision's MSG Network. Cablevision retaliated by refusing to carry the YES Network, which demanded a hefty license fee. This decision reportedly cost Cablevision tens of thousands of subscribers, many of them likely to DirecTV, which heavily promoted its own carriage of Yankees games.[65] Ultimately, the two sides settled the dispute, and the Yankees again appear on Cablevision's systems.[66] Although it is hazardous to extrapolate general principles from this isolated episode, it does tend to suggest that, as economic theory holds, cross-platform competition can have some disciplining effect on a cable operator's programming decisions.

One additional aspect of the D.C. Circuit's opinion warrants further attention, for it reveals an important ideological fault line in the regulation of the television media. In addition to the FCC's fairly tenuous antitrust-like arguments in support of its 30% horizontal limit, the Commission had also invoked its expertise to determine what steps were needed to ensure robust programming diversity. The court rejected this logic and expressed doubt, particularly in light of First Amendment concerns, that the FCC could adopt aggressive horizontal ownership limits solely to promote greater programming diversity in the absence of any showing of a genuine market failure in a rigorous economic sense.[67] Although the relevant statutes (and affected media outlets) are different, this holding stands in at least philosophical tension with the Third Circuit's subsequent decision in the broadcasting context (discussed in the next section). In the Third Circuit's view, the FCC not only can, but perhaps must, consider diversity values in addition to standard antitrust concerns in developing horizontal ownership limitations.[68] This subtle difference in perspective is likely to remain one of the key debates in media policy: the extent to which prescriptive FCC regulation remains necessary to promote greater programming diversity (and localism) than would be produced by an efficient and increasingly competitive video distribution market superintended by generalist antitrust authorities.[69]

The antitrust authorities have, in fact, sometimes intervened to protect the public against potential abuses of vertical integration in the mass media. For example, in 1994, the Federal Trade Commission imposed important conditions on the merger of Time Warner and Turner Broadcasting, including one that required Time Warner to carry a rival news network so that favoritism for Turner's CNN would not limit the entry of upstarts like the Fox News Network.[70] Similar concerns about vertical integration continue to arise today. For example, reacting to Comcast's now abandoned proposal to merge with Disney, one concerned screenwriter exclaimed that "[n]etworks not affiliated with the Comcast-Disney combination will be exiled to cable Siberia . . . there won't be any room for the

small, independent networks."[71] Whether or not these concerns are warranted, merger review authorities are likely to subject proposed media
combinations to unusually intense scrutiny.[72] So, too, will the FCC itself:
in 2004, for example, in approving News Corp.'s acquisition of a controlling interest in DirecTV, the Commission imposed special self-dealing
restrictions that are similar to, but go beyond, the program access rules discussed above.[73]

IV. Restrictions on Ownership of Television Broadcast Stations

We now turn to the set of issues that has generated perhaps the most political attention in the communications world, and certainly one of the most
prodigious letter-writing campaigns: horizontal restrictions on the ownership of television broadcast stations.

Until the final quarter of the twentieth century, many American cities
had only three major television stations; few homes subscribed to cable television; and (as is still the case) many cities had only one major newspaper.
To promote greater diversity, and to protect competition in advertising and
other markets, longstanding FCC rules precluded a single firm from owning more than one television or radio station in the same local market or
more than seven television stations nationwide.[74] In the mid-1970s, the
FCC also precluded any single firm from owning a full service TV station
and a daily newspaper in the same community.[75] In 1978, the Supreme
Court rejected a First Amendment challenge to this rule, reasoning that
most Americans got their news from television and newspapers and that
diverse ownership is necessary to ensure diverse viewpoints.[76]

In the 1980s, the FCC loosened a number of these ownership restrictions. In 1984, under the direction of Chairman Mark Fowler, a staunch
advocate of media deregulation, the FCC concluded that there should be
no restrictions on the number of local broadcasting stations that a single
corporate family could own nationwide.[77] Fowler's approach would have
dramatically increased the number of stations owned and operated by the
broadcast networks and decreased the number of network affiliates owned
by independent media companies. Amid the ensuing uproar, Congress
stepped in and authorized only the more modest step of increasing the
number of television stations a single firm could own nationwide, with the

proviso that any given firm's stations could reach no more than a combined total of 25% of the national viewing audience.[78] In 1988, the FCC took the more incremental step of providing for waivers of the television-radio cross-ownership restriction in particular circumstances.[79] But the FCC retained its flat ban on common ownership of two television stations, or of a television station and newspaper, in the same market.

In the Telecommunications Act of 1996, Congress set the stage for easing broadcast ownership restrictions more comprehensively. Among other measures, it relaxed the horizontal limit on ownership of TV stations nationwide by increasing from 25% to 35% the percentage of the national television audience that a single firm's stations may reach in the aggregate.[80] Congress also directed the FCC to open inquiries into whether it should further loosen that and the other TV-related ownership restrictions.[81] In response, the FCC revised its rules to permit a single firm, for the first time, to own two television stations in a market, subject to the restriction (among others) that both stations could not rank within the top four in that market.[82] Otherwise, however, the FCC decided to leave almost all of the existing rules in place, suggesting that it needed time to observe the effect of the changes Congress had already ordered.[83]

In *Fox Television Stations, Inc. v. FCC,* [84] the D.C. Circuit in 2002 rejected the FCC's "go slow" approach as too cautious, reasoning that the 1996 Act requires the FCC to lift ownership restrictions promptly unless it affirmatively finds that they should be retained. In particular, the court concluded that the 1996 Act's mandate for regular reviews of the broadcast ownership rules was closer to "Farragut's order at the battle of Mobile Bay ('Damn the torpedoes! Full speed ahead.') than to the wait-and-see attitude" adopted by the FCC.[85] Consequently, it directed the FCC to complete its inquiry into whether the 35% horizontal ownership cap should be further relaxed. And, in a striking display of judicial assertiveness, it ordered the FCC simply to abolish, as unnecessary for either competition or programming diversity, the Commission's 22-year-old ban on common ownership of a broadcast station and a cable system in the same community.

On remand, the FCC opened a new inquiry into the future of its broadcast ownership restrictions. The proceeding was one of the most contentious in the FCC's recent history. Advocates of deregulation argued that the existing restrictions are both inefficient, in that they artificially constrain economies of scale and scope, and unnecessary for viewpoint diversity, given the explosion of new media outlets such as cable systems and the Internet.[86] Those opposing further deregulation highlighted the increasing public unease with growing media concentration in the United States; observed (among other things) that neither the Internet nor cable systems feature much independent local news reporting; and concluded that permitting a single firm to own both a major television station and a major newspaper in a single community could leave the inhabitants without adequate diversity in the coverage of local politics and other matters of local interest.[87] In 2003, by a vote of 3-2, the FCC issued its *Media Ownership Decision*, which greatly relaxed a number of its horizontal broadcast ownership restrictions.[88]

First, the FCC responded to the *Fox* decision by loosening, once more, the restrictions on the number of local television broadcast stations any one firm (including a broadcast network) could own nationwide. Specifically, the FCC raised from 35% to 45% the total percentage of the national viewing audience that could be reached by commonly owned broadcast stations.[89] Many criticized this decision on the ground that independently owned network affiliates are more receptive to the needs of their local communities than are the stations owned and operated by the networks themselves. In reality, however, many such affiliates are themselves controlled by giant media companies like Sinclair and Hearst-Argyle, each of which owns or operates dozens of stations. Such companies have no greater claim than the networks to a keen understanding of the particular communities served by their stations. And the networks have similar (though not necessarily identical) economic incentives as these independent media companies to increase audience share in such communities by airing programs of local interest. Also, in contrast to the cable ownership limits, no national *broadcast* ownership limit can be persuasively justified as a necessary safeguard against monopsony power in the market for broadcast television programming. Unlike cable companies, which exercise enormous discretion in what types of programming to carry in scores of channel slots, any broadcast station affiliated with one of the major networks—whether it is owned by that network or not—almost invariably airs whatever programming the network has designated for prime time viewing.

When the issue is viewed in the cold light of economic analysis, there is thus no obvious reason why raising the national ownership cap from 35% to 45% should have alarmed anyone. Indeed, from a pure efficiency perspective, the real debate is whether such caps are needed at all. As we have discussed, however, media consolidation issues present an array of non-economic concerns that elude formal economic analysis. Much like Chairman Fowler's proposed elimination of a national cap in the 1980s, this new relaxation of that cap triggered such a popular furor that Congress immediately stepped back into the fray, setting a new statutory limit at 39% of the national audience instead of the FCC's 45% cap.[90] On the surface, this was a rebuke to the FCC. In reality, the 39% figure was gerrymandered to remain as low as possible while permitting the two largest broadcast station owners—Viacom (CBS) and News Corp. (Fox)—to hold on to all of their existing stations nationwide (including those authorized by previous waivers).[91]

The other set of controversies sparked by the *Media Ownership Decision* concerned the FCC's restrictions on common ownership of multiple media outlets within a given locality. In a nutshell, the FCC replaced its existing restrictions of this type with new ones that vary with the number of total media outlets in the community at issue. First, the FCC abolished all restrictions on a firm's cross-ownership of a television station with a newspaper or radio station in the largest markets (those with nine or more television stations), retained the preexisting restrictions for the smallest markets (those with three or fewer stations), and adopted a middle ground approach for all markets in between.[92] Second, it loosened its limits on common ownership of multiple TV stations in a single community, allowing a firm to own up to three stations in the largest markets and two in most others, so long as no more than one of the jointly owned stations ranks in the top four in the relevant market.[93] The FCC claimed that these new rules addressed the diversity concerns served by the old ownership restrictions but with "more precision and with greater deference to First Amendment interests."[94] The Commission further found that transformations in the media marketplace over the past 20 years, including the growth of the Internet, provide viewers with an unprecedented diversity of media outlets and justified a commensurate relaxation of the various ownership rules.

The FCC's analysis of diversity in particular markets was based on a modified version of the Herfindahl-Hirschmann Index ("HHI"), a standard economic measure of market concentration used by the Justice Department and Federal Trade Commission in assessing proposed mergers. The controversy surrounding the FCC's "diversity index," as it was called, lay in the details. Critics challenged the index's reliance on the Internet as an important source of independent local news, observing that the news-related content on the Internet tends to be either national or, if local, derivative of traditional media outlets (e.g., webpages duplicating print newspaper articles). The critics further assailed the FCC's across-the-board assumption that any two television stations (or any two newspapers) contribute equally to diversity of programming in local markets. As these critics pointed out, the resulting regime would anomalously allow the most popular television station in Tallahassee, Florida—the CBS affiliate with a 59% share for local news—to be owned by the same firm as the city's major newspaper (with 5 times the circulation of its alternative).[95]

Many parties sought review of the FCC's order in different courts. Unluckily for the Commission and the advocates of still greater deregulation, the appeal was assigned by lottery to the Third Circuit in Philadelphia rather than back to the D.C. Circuit. In June 2004, in *Prometheus Radio Project v. FCC,* a split panel of the Third Circuit invalidated much of the order.[96] In particular, the majority upheld the FCC's abolition of the flat ban on television-newspaper cross-ownership, but it agreed with the criticisms of the FCC's diversity index, including the objections that it overweights the Internet as a source of local content and irrationally assigns equal weight to all media outlets within a given category. The court thus remanded the matter to the Commission to conduct a more reasoned analysis and adopt a new set of cross-ownership rules for particular markets.[97] The majority further upheld in principle the Commission's decision to relax restrictions on ownership of multiple TV stations in a single market, agreeing that the efficiencies gained from consolidation can "translate[] into improved local news and public interest programming."[98] Here again, however, the majority invalidated the specifics of the FCC's new rules on the ground that they were tainted by the methodological flaws of its diversity index.[99] As this book goes to press, the FCC is considering an appeal to the Supreme Court, and its media ownership regime remains a work in progress.

* * *

The policy issues we have discussed in this chapter arise from a particular structure for the television industry: a system of checks and balances among broadcasters, cable companies, satellite providers, and content producers. That structure, however, derives from, and is heavily dependent on, a particular model of regulation. To appreciate this point, suppose that the government abolished all regulation specific to television, including the must carry rules, and allowed all broadcast stations to sell their existing spectrum rights on the secondary market to any willing buyer. In the short term, there would be turmoil; in the long term, the television market would reach an equilibrium that looks quite different from today's.

First, there would be many fewer broadcast television stations, and probably less local news coverage on television.[100] Many broadcasters would find it more profitable to sell their spectrum rights to non-television providers—such as the spectrum-starved wireless carriers—than to continue occupying vast expanses of spectrum that today are used to reach only 15% of television households. Second, the networks would act primarily as national providers of content to the cable and satellite companies, and they would become ever less distinguishable from their programming rivals occupying other cable or satellite channels—a process that is already underway.[101] Third, there might be even greater vertical integration than there is today between these cable and satellite providers, on the one hand, and content providers on the other. If policymakers relied solely on antitrust enforcement to limit media concentration, the precise degree of vertical integration would be determined by whatever net efficiencies such integration produces (see above), as well as such intangible factors as the subjective belief of corporate officers that even a producer of high quality content needs a formally affiliated distribution partner to guarantee a share of the viewing market.

On balance, this new industy structure might be more economically efficient than the current structure. The very prospect of this new television world, however, alarms the many policymakers and commentators who decry current levels of media concentration and who view traditional regulation as necessary to preserve localism and diversity in television as well as the long tradition of free over-the-air TV. It is thus quite unlikely that, within the foreseeable future, the government will make radical changes to the regulatory schemes described in this chapter. But technological advances have ways of undermining even the most venerable policy objectives. For example, TiVo and other digital recording devices may steadily erode the primary source of revenues underlying "free" broadcast television—advertising—by permitting viewers to avoid watching commercials. And as upgrades to last mile bandwidth make the pay-per-view option increasingly popular among viewers, the economic losers may include not just the neighborhood Blockbuster, but the broadcast networks and other content providers that specialize in slates of TV programs keyed to particular time slots.

The Internet may also transform television in much the same way that it has already transformed the music recording industry (think Napster and iPod) and promises to transform the voice telephone market (see chapter 6). Although it is far too early for confident predictions, the early evidence from abroad suggests that, with the proliferation of broadband, the Internet may ultimately reshape the markets for both video programming and distribution. For example, Yahoo! BB is offering Japanese consumers an Internet-based set-top box and 45 megabits per second of bandwidth to deliver a personalized television experience. In such a world, today's regulations would become not only obsolescent as a policy matter, but insusceptible to straightforward application in practice. For example, would Yahoo! or other providers of Internet-based streaming video services qualify as competing "MVPDs" eligible to invoke the program access rules against the cable incumbents? Would the IP-enabled video services offered by telephone companies over fiber-to-the-premises loops be properly characterized as Title VI "cable services," Title I "information services," or both? Such questions are today's classroom hypotheticals but will ultimately become, in some form, tomorrow's pressing policy challenges.

12

Telecommunications Standards, Technological Transitions, and Digital Television

By their nature, telecommunications networks rely on technological standards. Consider, for example, the standard for broadcast television. The reason you do not need two different television sets to watch the separate over-the-air broadcasts of channel 4 and channel 9 is that, as we shall see, a single industry-wide standard governs how traditional analog signals are transmitted and received by televisions sold in the United States.* Other industry-defining standards include the TCP/IP protocol suite used in the Internet; the standard specifications for equipment that connects to the public switched telephone network (PSTN); and the "signaling" standard behind the intelligent features of the PSTN, such as call forwarding and caller ID. In each case, the technology standard affects consumers, equipment suppliers, and service providers, all of whom must use the same specifications for the standard to be effective.

Policymakers must often make difficult decisions about how much to intervene in the development and selection of such standards. To oversimplify a bit, they can take one of three approaches, in order of decreasing government involvement. First, policymakers can intervene in the very process of standard-setting and help shape the details of the standards that emerge from it. Second, they can let private bodies or firms propose standards and then endorse one of them. Third, they can let dueling standards proliferate in the marketplace. Sometimes, but not always, such "standards wars" will be to the death, with one standard prevailing to the exclusion of others, much as the VHS format defeated its Betamax rival in the market

---

* We explain the nature of analog and digital technology, and the advantages of the latter, in chapter 4.

for video cassette recorders (VCRs) back in the 1980s. In other cases, such as the DVD standard that we discuss below, the relevant parties will avoid a standards battle by cooperating in the development of a consensus standard.

Choosing among these three levels of involvement is often an unenviable task, for regulators often cannot know beforehand how much government intervention is optimal.[1] The stakes, however, are enormous. If regulators intervene *too little* in resolving standard-setting impasses, the industry may become inefficiently balkanized or monopolized, and important new technologies may never take hold. For example, some have argued that the FCC's failure for many years to choose among warring standards for AM stereo explains why, with commercially insignificant exceptions, AM radio remains monophonic (i.e., each speaker connected to your receiver makes the same sounds when you are tuned in to an AM radio station).[2] Those favoring greater government involvement in standard-setting disputes likewise credit the FCC's early involvement in the development of the Part 68 rules—specifications of open interfaces for equipment that connects to the PSTN (see chapter 2)—with entry and innovation in the market for computer modems and ultimately with the growth of the Internet.

On the other hand, if policymakers intervene *too much* in the standard-setting process, they may force the industry to adopt a standard that turns out to be radically inferior to what the free market would have produced in the absence of such intervention. As we shall see, some have criticized the FCC's designation of television standards on this ground—both the original, short-lived standard it adopted for conventional color television in 1950 and, more recently, the 8VSB standard it prescribed for digital television in the 1990s. Similarly, advocates of government non-intervention in the standard-setting process laud the FCC's decision *not* to adopt a digital standard for second-generation wireless telephony. That decision, which contrasts sharply with Europe's adoption of GSM at the dawn of the 2G wireless era, is now credited with facilitating the rise of CDMA systems in particular and spread-spectrum technology more generally, as we saw in chapter 8.

One could fill an entire book with an analysis of standard-setting challenges in the information age and the proper extent of the government's role in resolving them. Our objective in this chapter is necessarily less ambitious. After first sketching the broad outlines of standard-setting institutions and economics, we give readers a flavor of the regulator's dilemma by presenting, as a case study, the FCC-managed transition from analog to digital television broadcasting in the United States. As we shall see, that ongoing transition is enormously important to the telecommunications world—not just because it affects the quality of television viewing, but also because it must be completed before the government will free up valuable swaths of the spectrum for more productive uses, such as wireless broadband and public safety. For the foreseeable future, this spectrum will be used for the redundant "simulcasting" of broadcast television programs in both digital and analog formats.

I. An Overview of Telecommunications Standards

A. The era of Bell and Sarnoff

For most of the twentieth century, AT&T's dominance in the telephone world largely freed the FCC from the role of overseeing the development of uniform telecommunications standards. Indeed, AT&T's famous motto—coined by its early leader, Theodore Vail—was "one system, one policy, universal service." Traditionally, the company's legendary Bell Labs developed the basic technologies for all aspects of telecommunications services, ranging from the infrastructure for emergency services (e.g., 911 calls) to the initial analog standard for wireless telephony. In the television world, the closest counterpart to AT&T was the Radio Corporation of America (RCA), which owned NBC and dominated television in the early years of its development almost as much as AT&T dominated telephony. Although CBS was a rival national network, it was not as vertically integrated as RCA into manufacturing and program production, nor did any aspect of its operations approach the prestige of RCA's Sarnoff Laboratories, which was television's counterpart to Bell Labs.

We begin first with Bell Labs, which may well be unparalleled—both in size and in marketplace impact—in the history of commercial research. AT&T authorized the legions of Bell Labs researchers to pursue wide-ranging scientific inquiries, some of which had very little direct impact on AT&T's immediate business. This was hardly irrational from AT&T's perspective. Under traditional rate-of-return regulation (see chapter 2), AT&T

had strong incentives to invest heavily in basic research because the associated costs expanded the rate base on which AT&T earned its returns. The research funded by this quirk of regulatory accounting produced much of the technology that defines the information industries today: the transistor, the UNIX operating system, cellular telephony, and the laser (now used in fiber optics), to name just a few. Moreover, some of the leading researchers in telecommunications—such as Claude Shannon, who invented information theory (see chapter 7)—found a home at Bell Labs.

Other countries as well looked to Bell Labs when developing telecommunications standards. In one notable example, the International Telecommunications Union (ITU), a branch of the United Nations, formalized an international telephone signaling standard based on AT&T's system of "Common Channel Interoffice Signaling" (CCIS). A traditional telephone call involves the transmission of two sets of signals—the signals representing the voices of the participants, and the signals that (among other things) instruct the telephone network how best to route the call. Before the advent of digital technology, the latter signals were transmitted in audible tones through the same pipes that connected the calling party to the network. In the early 1980s, building on Bell Labs' research, the ITU adopted the modern "Signaling System 7" (SS7) standard used widely today. This system employs "out-of-band signaling"—a separate packet-switched network that operates in tandem with the circuit-switched network still used to carry voice signals—to facilitate not just more efficient call routing, but also "advanced intelligent network" features, such as call forwarding, caller ID, and so forth. The standard's success depended on its broad adoption, which the Bell System pushed throughout the United States and the ITU promoted throughout the world.

In the 1950s and 1960s, the FCC turned to RCA for standard-setting guidance in the television industry in much the same way that it relied on Bell Labs for standards in the telephone industry. In 1950, the FCC improvidently endorsed a CBS-developed standard for color television that was not "backwards-compatible" with existing black-and-white systems; in other words, existing black-and-white television sets were incapable of displaying color programs transmitted in this new format even in black and white. This approach posed a serious problem because, at that time, there were hardly any color programs to watch on television, and few such programs would ever be developed so long as most consumers could not watch them on their existing sets. Seizing an opportunity to resolve this chicken-and-egg problem to his firm's advantage, David Sarnoff, the head of RCA, instructed his engineers to develop an alternative standard for color television that was backwards-compatible with the old black-and-white system. In 1953, RCA convinced the National Television Systems Committee to embrace its standard, and, with CBS's acquiescence, the FCC reversed its earlier decision and endorsed what has become known as the NTSC standard.[3]

RCA then turned to the more difficult task of goading the market itself into making the transition from black-and-white to color television. RCA took the lead in manufacturing color TV sets, developing color programming (including NBC's "killer application," *Walt Disney's Wonderful World of Color*), and pushing its affiliated broadcasters to upgrade their transmission systems to carry the signals in a color format. For ten years after the new standard's adoption, however, few other broadcasters aired any television shows in color. For their part, consumers did not begin buying color television sets en masse until the mid-1960s, and, until the early 1970s, there were more black-and-white sets in use than color ones.[4] Despite this long adoption period, however, most industry observers now agree that the NTSC standard improved the quality of television enormously, and that formal adoption by the FCC was necessary to ensure that the standard took hold.

B. Current standard-setting institutions

Many engineers remain nostalgic for the era of Bell and Sarnoff, when they could conduct basic research on technological standards free from the pressures of identifying an immediate revenue justification for their work. The flip side of that freedom was that the companies sponsoring such research sometimes failed to put the ensuing inventions to use, either because they threatened to undermine current revenue streams or because management did not appreciate the inventions' potential in the marketplace. As noted in chapter 8, for example, Bell Labs essentially invented the basics of cellular telephony in the 1940s, but neither AT&T nor the FCC saw much use for this alternative to wireline telephone service until decades later. Likewise, researchers in Xerox's Palo Alto Research Center (PARC) facility—not Apple, as is popularly believed—invented the computer mouse and the point-and-click graphical user interface in the 1970s, but Xerox itself never saw fit to convert that technology into a product of its own.[5]

Today, both Bell Labs (now owned by Lucent) and Sarnoff Labs exist in name, but they have become mere shadows of their former selves, leaving the telecommunications industry and the FCC without the technological leadership they once provided. A more fragmented equipment manufacturing industry—with a less robust research and development budget—is thus now struggling to forge a new model of standards development. In some cases, the government funds standard-setting activity directly, as the Defense Department did for the TCP/IP family of protocols (see chapter 4). More commonly, however, standard-setting is coordinated by formal organizations accredited by the American National Standards Institute (ANSI). These organizations operate with a high degree of formality and adhere to "due process"-type guidelines to achieve consensus on important points. The standards they endorse—such as the 802.11 Wi-Fi standards developed by the Institute of Electrical and Electronics Engineers (IEEE) (see chapter 7)—are known as *de jure* standards. In contrast, *de facto* standards, such as Microsoft Windows, are developed by individual companies or consortia, as discussed below. Whereas *de jure* standards benefit from sponsorship by governmental agencies or official standard-setting bodies, *de facto* standards rely on market dissemination driven by an individual firm (or collection of firms) and, in many cases, provide significant proprietary rewards to the firms that own the relevant technology.

The Internet Engineering Task Force (the IETF) and similar quasi-official organizations facilitate cooperation among firms in the development of *de jure* standards in the Internet world. For example, the IETF has superintended the continuing evolution of TCP/IP, the creation in particular of a next generation Internet addressing scheme (IPv6), and the development of the preeminent signaling standard for VoIP—the Session Initiation Protocol described in chapter 6. Like other such bodies, the IETF enjoys neither legal authority nor commercial dominance in the marketplace. Instead, to ensure that its approved standards are implemented in an effective and uniform manner, it must rely on moral suasion and on the enlightened self-interest of its members.

Even without formal authority, such organizations enjoy considerable stature within the industry. Indeed, the FCC itself often relies on their expertise when it ventures into the world of standard-setting. One example is the FCC's decision to out-source the administration of the process for certifying that equipment complies with the Part 68 rules. When the FCC first adopted those rules in 1977, it assumed this role for itself.[6] In 2000, however, the FCC delegated much of the Part 68 regime to alternative institutions that had emerged in the meantime.[7] In so doing, the FCC followed its general practice of delegating such authority only to standard-setting bodies accredited by ANSI, which insists on compliance with certain procedural safeguards.[8]

If an individual firm seeks to develop a product quickly, control its development, or reap more economic rewards than allowed by the relevant standards body, it may well grow frustrated with the formal, quasi-official procedures of established standard-setting institutions. To keep such firms in the standard-setting fold, these institutions—which traditionally embraced only open, non-proprietary standards such as TCP/IP—now commonly endorse standards containing patented, proprietary technologies, provided that any such technology is made available on "reasonable and non-discriminatory" terms.[9] This approach is often necessary to keep industry leaders on board, forge an industry consensus behind an official standard, and increase the likelihood that the standard will be adopted widely. At the same time, however, the prospect of proprietary rewards raises the stakes for individual participants and can lead to a more partisan developmental process. The basic problem is that official standard-setting bodies are necessarily less effective when mediating among conflicting proprietary interests than when developing common standards that do not implicate such interests.[10]

In the early days of the Internet, for example, the regular participants in the IETF all knew one another and worked cooperatively and expeditiously in developing the TCP/IP standard and its associated protocols. But once the Internet became commercialized in the early 1990s, scores of commercial participants began to participate in IETF initiatives. Because many of them had proprietary interests in the outcome, their involvement slowed the development of new standards and sometimes suffused the proceedings with strategic behavior. With enormous sums of money at stake in battles about the evolution of Internet technology, self-interest has often led participants to promote or contest standards based on their commercial impact.[11] In some cases, the resulting gridlock may justify either regulatory involvement or, as discussed below, the complete abandonment of con-sensus-building efforts in favor of letting proprietary standards battle it out in the marketplace.

If different firms within an industry need to ensure the interoperability of complementary products, and if they do not wish to make use of an offi-cial body like the IETF, they can charter an ad hoc consortium of compa-nies to coordinate the standard-setting process. One such consortium is the Moving Pictures Expert Group Licensing Administrator (MPEG-LA), to which various firms contributed their intellectual property (in the form of a "patent pool") so that they could coordinate the development of applica-tions for MPEG-2, the official standard for digital media. After receiving antitrust clearance for this venture,[12] some members of this consortium developed the standard for DVDs without the oversight of a formal stan-dard-setting body like the IETF or a federal agency like the FCC.[13]

Finally, a firm confident that its product can "win" a standards war can go it alone by seeking to make its own proprietary technology a *de facto* standard through market forces.[14] In the market for video cassette recorders, for example, Sony made a high stakes bet in the 1970s on its Betamax standard, which succumbed to the rival VHS standard in the 1980s. By contrast, the proprietary Windows and CDMA standards thrived in their respective markets (operating systems and wireless telecom-munications), reaping great rewards for Microsoft and Qualcomm respec-tively. Successful proprietary standards are similar to *de jure* standards in one respect: they provide some degree of stability in the terms of access to an information platform. Unlike *de jure* standards, however, they come with fewer checks and balances on how the technology's sponsor may con-trol the standards' technological evolution or manipulate the terms of use.

C. The economics of standard-setting and the role of the FCC

The FCC ventures into the standard-setting arena not just to coordinate technological transitions, but also to facilitate competition and the efficient use of public resources—as it has done in developing the Part 68 Rules for equipment connecting to the PSTN and the interference-minimizing Part 15 Rules for equipment that uses unlicensed spectrum (see chapter 7). Before discussing the FCC's role in standard-setting, however, we first outline some of the economics of standard-setting and explain why government intervention in this area is sometimes inevitable.

When Claude Shannon developed information theory, neither he nor anyone else envisioned its application to ultra-wideband devices. The subsequent creation of such devices was thus a dividend paid on his earlier, pathbreaking work. In general, the basic scientific research that must precede such inventions is aptly characterized as a *public good*. As economists define the term, a true public good is both "non-excludable" and "non-rivalrous" in that multiple firms can benefit from the technological advance (say, the insights of information theory) at the same time without reducing its value.[15] The question of how to finance public goods raises a basic conundrum: without any government-created incentive, few firms would invest in the development of such goods in the first place because rival firms would quickly exploit them without paying for them.[16] Thus, in competitive industries, the government must either take responsibility itself for subsidizing basic research, as in the case of TCP/IP, or—more commonly—give private parties research incentives by creating and enforcing intellectual property rights, such as patents and the associated right to charge licensing fees.

In the world of telecommunications standards, however, spurring invention is only half the battle, for a fundamental collective action problem remains. As we have seen, an "information platform"—i.e., any communications or data-processing technology on which higher level applications can ride—typically relies on the "network effects" phenomenon: its value increases with the number of users. Of course, users will be inclined to adopt the platform only after firms have developed killer applications for it; but those firms will themselves be reluctant to invest in developing such applications until after a large number of users have already signaled that they will adopt the underlying platform. This chicken-and-egg problem means that even a superb technology platform backed by patent protection can fail in the marketplace if providers of complementary applications ultimately abandon it or never support it in the first place.[17] Betamax, for example, was by some accounts superior to its VHS rival. But when a critical mass of application providers for the Betamax platform— i.e., the firms creating and distributing compatible rental tapes—defected to VHS, the VCR market tipped, and Betamax became a historical curiosity. Importantly, however, not all information platform technologies will tip to a single standard, as evidenced by the continued platform competition in cellphone standards and videogame consoles.

The fear of becoming the next Betamax, combined with the hope of becoming the next Microsoft, drives many business strategies in information platform markets. A platform provider committed to a proprietary strategy will have strong incentives, as discussed in chapter 5, to encourage the development of killer applications. To that end, it may rely on independent application developers, its own vertically integrated operations, or both. Sega, for example, challenged the dominant Nintendo videogame console system not only by inviting outside developers to create new games, but also by heavily promoting its own killer application: "Sonic the Hedgehog." If, in contrast, a firm is wary of fighting for control of an entire market, it will often push for the use of consortia or standard-setting bodies to set the relevant standards, as Sony (the loser in the VCR war of the 1980s) and others did in developing the DVD standard. Sometimes, however, such firms will go further and seek the government's formal imprimatur on whatever standard develops.

The classic claim by advocates for substantial regulatory intervention in the standard-setting process is that government endorsement of a single standard at the outset is necessary to spare consumers and companies from the costly standards wars that, under the worst case scenario, may prevent the industry from making any successful transition to a new technology.[18] The economic justification for government intervention is keenest when no standard can emerge without the mutual cooperation of different industry segments with radically divergent interests.

Regulatory minimalists, on the other hand, respond that government intervention in the standard-setting process is dangerous on a number of levels. First, they say, regulators may lack the needed technical expertise even to make proper decisions. Second, the regulatory minimalists contend, any standard selected even by technically proficient regulators might well be inferior to the standard that would otherwise emerge after robust marketplace experimentation. Finally, they observe, regulators may be swayed by politics and, for that reason alone, might side with established interests or favored upstarts.[19]

Neither approach—pervasive government intervention in, or complete detachment from, the standard-setting process—is categorically appropriate for all standard-setting challenges, as each such choice presents its own peculiar array of regulatory trade-offs. As a general matter, the government probably regulates best in this area when it focuses on setting generalized "performance" standards rather than more technical and specific "design" standards.[20] To the extent it must select a particular design standard, the government is usually wise to set broad boundaries for the standard's content, delegate formulation of the details to established standard-setting bodies, and thereafter confine its role to the ratification of the standard that emerges.[21]

But even these observations are subject to exceptions. Ultimately, there are no neat formulas for divining when, and how much, the government should involve itself in the resolution of particular standard-setting challenges.[22] To illustrate the nature of this conundrum, we present, as a case study, the FCC's role in the transition to digital television (DTV), which ranks as one of the most complex technological transitions of the present era.

II. The Digital Television Case Study

As noted, even a superlative new technology platform may succumb to the chicken-and-egg problem presented by the need to convince firms and consumers alike to incur the costs needed to upgrade from a more established platform. In many cases, only "early adopters" will seek out a new technology unless and until the price comes down to a point at which consumers will adopt it in droves. For example, several interrelated trends aligned to drive the mass adoption of DVD technology: higher picture quality than videocasettes could provide; a growing number of DVDs for consumers to watch; and aggressive marketing by retail outlets.

Success in the transition to digital television will require an alignment of factors similar to those that are driving the successful transition to DVDs: consumers must perceive DTV's superiority to conventional analog television; the market must produce television sets capable of displaying this higher quality; the cost of those sets must come down; and content producers must make programs available in digital format. In this respect, the transition will depend on widespread consumer awareness of how digital television differs from conventional television and why it is worth investing in a new TV set capable of receiving and displaying signals in digital format. The expected killer application for digital television, though not its only use, is *high definition television* (HDTV): a picture quality comparable to that of movies seen in theaters. What follows is an overview of the FCC's strenuous, multidimensional efforts—a combination of admonition and explicit regulation—to facilitate consumer adoption of digital television.

A. The development effort

In the 1980s, Congress and others looked with alarm at the development of high definition television in Japan and worried that the United States had fallen dangerously behind its Asian economic rival in this critical industry. The television broadcasters capitalized on this fear by calling on the FCC to dedicate unused UHF spectrum, which the Commission was otherwise poised to make available for public safety and wireless telephony services, for the *simulcasting* of first generation NTSC transmissions alongside high definition over-the-air broadcasts during what promised to be a long transitional period.[23]

In 1987, the FCC agreed to chart the development of a next generation color TV standard. To that end, it reserved large swaths of spectrum for the new service and set up the Advanced Television Services Committee (ATSC) as an official federal advisory committee to the FCC. It appointed former FCC Chairman Richard Wiley to chair the Committee and spearhead the development of the technical standard for a new transmission format.[24] The FCC proceeded on three main premises: (i) that the new technical standard would permit high definition viewing, which promised for home television sets the same picture resolution as is found in high-quality photographs; (ii) that transmissions using the new standard would be delivered by conventional broadcasting stations over the air (and not just by cable television systems); and (iii) that such transmissions would be simulcast along with transmissions employing the existing NTSC standard because the new standard would likely not be "backwards compatible" with the old.[25]

The Advisory Committee sponsored a competition for designing a new TV standard within these three constraints. This front-end competition promised great rewards (in the form of licensing fees) to the victor and thus spurred the entry of a number of alternative systems, including one sponsored by Sarnoff Laboratories.[26] Ultimately, however, the last minute entry of an "all digital" system developed by General Instruments up-ended the previous assumption—followed to that point in both Europe and Japan—that high definition television would use analog technology.[27] Recognizing the promise of digital technology in an era of ever increasing processing power, the Committee sponsored a "Grand Alliance" approach to the development of a digital television standard.

Although HDTV remains its most touted application, the digital television platform permits a range of other uses as well. Digital technologies can be used, for example, not just to broadcast a high definition signal within the standard six-megahertz-wide band the FCC allots to each analog television channel, but also to "multicast" half a dozen TV channels at standard picture resolutions within that same band. Digital technology also permits a much more efficient use of spectrum than analog technology for reasons relating mostly to digital compression. As described in chapters 4 and 8, such compression is a family of techniques for economizing on the bits that must be transmitted to convey a faithful representation of an image or sound.

During debates on the 1996 Act, Senators Bob Dole and John McCain challenged one of the key premises of the FCC's digital transition plan: the entitlement of broadcasters to free "digital spectrum" (i.e., spectrum allocated for digital broadcasts) in addition to the "analog spectrum" they would continue to occupy for simulcasting purposes.[28] Dole and McCain were particularly outraged at what they characterized as a $70 billion "giveaway" to the broadcasters, a figure they derived from FCC estimates of the total amount that bidders would pay at auction for the rights to this spectrum. Ultimately, Congress gave the broadcasters their second set of free spectrum licenses, but provided that they must return their analog spectrum for other uses by the end of 2006.[29]

This ten-year timetable, however, is subject to several gaping loopholes. The best known of these provides that broadcasters need *not* vacate their analog spectrum in a given market until at least 85% of all television households in that market either (i) can receive digital broadcast transmissions over the air (through television equipment designed for that purpose) or (ii) subscribe to a cable or satellite TV provider "that carries one of the digital television service programming channels of each of the television stations broadcasting such a channel in such market."[30] Few markets will even approach this 85% threshold by 2006. For the foreseeable future, therefore, broadcasters will continue to occupy enormous expanses of spectrum even though, in the age of cable and satellite TV subscriptions, only about 15% of U.S. households continue to receive broadcasters' television signals through *any* of that spectrum (see chapter 7).*

In 1996, the FCC sought to expedite this lagging digital transition by officially embracing the Committee's recommended 8VSB ("8-level vestigial sideband modulation") transmission standard.31 The FCC recognized the perils of government involvement in standard-setting, including the potential for capture by particular industry groups, but concluded that the challenges of digital television were unique and warranted an active regulatory role.32 The FCC soon found itself on the defensive, however, in responding to private tests purporting to show that the 8VSB standard was inferior to its new European counterpart. The FCC nonetheless determined, based on its own series of tests, that the costs of changing standards at that advanced stage in their development clearly outweighed any benefits from using the European alternative. In February 2000, the FCC thus declined to change approaches or even to sanction the European standard as an alternative, instead encouraging the industry to work on improving the 8VSB standard from within.33

B. The deployment effort

Once the FCC settled on the 8VSB standard, it could have concluded that the affected companies (i.e., broadcasters, cable providers, programmers, and equipment vendors) now bore the burden to ensure, on their own timetables, that the digital television transition proceeded successfully. But this option would have played into the hands of the broadcasters, who were ambivalent about the new technology because it required both small and larger market stations to make expensive upgrades to their transmitters with no prospects for commensurately greater revenues. The FCC was thus concerned that many broadcasters would "slow roll" the transition. As put colorfully by the Chief of the FCC Media Bureau, these broadcasters "would rather eat their children than give up their spectrum."34

---

* The statutory 85% standard should not be confused with the empirical (and entirely coincidental) fact that, as of this writing, approximately 85% of American television households receive their television signals from sources other than conventional terrestrial broadcasting.

Initially, the FCC addressed this concern by requiring the broadcasters to undertake the necessary build-out schedule to make digital television available via broadcasting within a few years. In 1997, it set a construction schedule for digital transmission facilities, requiring the top 120 stations to build their new facilities by 1999, the other commercial broadcasters to do so by mid-2002, and the non-commercial ones by mid-2003.[35] The actual schedule lagged somewhat behind this plan, as approximately 20% of all broadcasters remained unequipped to broadcast digital signals by the fall of 2003. To enforce the required transition, the FCC thus provided that broadcasters would forfeit the licenses to broadcast in digital format if they missed their deadlines without obtaining an extension, which the FCC announced that it would grant only on a showing of factors (such as antenna siting issues) beyond the broadcasters' control.[36] The FCC declined, however, to require any specific amount of high definition television programming.[37]

Despite these steps, the digital transition, as viewed from a consumer's perspective, has proceeded at a snail's pace. By January 2001, roughly 600,000 Americans had purchased television sets capable of receiving over-the-air digital signals at an average cost of about $2,200 per set.[38] Indeed, by the fall of 2002, 40% of the American public had never heard of the digital TV transition, another 43% were "somewhat aware," and less than 20% were "very aware."[39] Before imposing compulsory regulations, however, FCC Chairman Michael Powell admonished each affected industry segment—the broadcasters, the cable and satellite providers, and the equipment developers—to do their part to drive the transition.[40] He asked the top four networks, along with HBO and Showtime, to provide "value-added DTV programming"—which could include high definition, innovative multicasting, or interactive services—for 50% of their prime time schedules. He asked the top ten cable providers and the satellite TV providers to carry, at no cost, the signals of up to five digital broadcast or other digital programming services during 50% of prime time. He asked the equipment manufacturers to reach agreement with the cable industry to meet the demand for a digital cable-ready product (see below) and to include digital inputs on all HDTV-capable television sets so that they could play DVDs as well in high definition format. And he asked the manufacturers to ensure that all TV sets sold after January 1, 2004, could receive digital over-the-air broadcast signals.

Ultimately, the only group to balk at these requests was the consumer electronics industry. The FCC responded by subjecting consumer electronics manufacturers to a formal regulatory mandate to outfit new TVs with "digital tuners" used to receive over-the-air digital signals.[41] As the FCC saw it, the slow pace of digital television sales—by the end of 2004, only 10 million such TVs were expected to be in use (as opposed to 250 million analog televisions)—threatened to strand many consumers who rely on over-the-air signals once the broadcasters stop transmitting in an analog format. The logic behind the mandate, however, discounted the fact that 85% of all television households receive their TV signals from either cable or satellite providers. For such viewers, the set-top box, which is capable of receiving signals delivered in digital form and converting them for viewing on an analog television, represents the critical piece of equipment for determining what programs are available. Thus, for cable and satellite viewers who might not care to purchase a television capable of displaying terrestrial over-the-air digital broadcasts, the digital tuner mandate effectively forces them to subsidize the needs of the 15% of U.S. households that continue to receive television signals through such broadcasts. Put differently, by forcing the cable and satellite viewers to purchase televisions with a digital tuner functionality they do not need, this mandate brings down the cost of such televisions (because of scale economies) for those who do receive conventional broadcasts over the air.

The consumer electronics firms—whom this cross-subsidy injures by raising overall prices and thus depressing total sales—took the FCC to court. The D.C. Circuit upheld the FCC's mandate, however, concluding that the Commission has ample authority to balance public benefits against private burdens—i.e., those imposed on the manufacturers and the cable and satellite subscribers. The court observed, moreover, that cable and satellite viewers can theoretically avoid any unnecessary expense by purchasing a less expensive video monitor without any inherent receiving capabilities at all.[42]

C. Digital must carry and the statutory 85% threshold

Approximately two-thirds of U.S. households with televisions subscribe to a cable TV service. Cable providers will thus play a critical role in delivering digital signals to the great majority of the 85% of subscribers who, under the statutory scheme discussed above, must be reached before the analog spectrum can be returned to more efficient uses. There is no small irony here, for the federal government has nominally focused its regulatory efforts on the transition to *digital over-the-air broadcasting*. Cable providers face no regulatory mandate comparable to the broadcasters' obligation to upgrade their transmission facilities to deliver digital programs. No such mandate is likely to be needed, however, because competition from digital satellite TV service, among other factors, has induced cable companies to make those upgrades on their own.

The major unsolved controversy concerning the cable industry's role in the digital transition involves the application of the "must carry" rules to the digital environment. As discussed in chapter 11, these rules—designed primarily to preserve the viability of minor UHF stations—require a cable company to devote channel space to all TV stations broadcasting in a given local area, no matter how obscure or unwatched their programming may be. Cable providers and broadcasters disagree about whether, during the lengthy transition in which television stations will be simulcasting in both analog and digital formats, cable companies should be forced to reserve channel capacity not just for one set of signals (digital or analog), but for both. The FCC has long delayed answering this question—and has tentatively concluded that requiring cable operators to carry both sets of signals may violate the First Amendment because it would place unnecessarily broad burdens on their editorial rights in selecting programming for their systems.[43]

Hoping to resolve this problem without direct regulation, the FCC has encouraged broadcasters and cable operators to reach privately negotiated resolutions.[44] But the parties seem to be at loggerheads. In 2004, FCC Media Bureau Chief Ken Ferree proposed a resolution under which, by October 2008, broadcasters could invoke must carry rights only for whatever signals they are transmitting digitally, and cable companies would then decide whether to deliver those signals in digital form (via a set-top box or a digital cable-ready television) or to "down-convert" them at the cable provider's headend, where the signals are received, to lower-grade analog signals so that viewers could still watch the programming at issue on their old television sets. At that point, the Ferree plan would count *all* households with cable television service towards the 85% statutory threshold for the return of the analog spectrum, even if many of those households end up receiving downgraded analog signals from cable operators choosing that option.[45]

The Ferree plan—which, some argue, would require a statutory amendment to be implemented—ignited enormous criticism both from the broadcasters and from Congress.[46] Opponents argued that, by accepting a goal short of widespread DTV deployment, the plan would undermine the goal of improving the overall technology of the television system. They also expressed concern that, upon the return of the analog spectrum, the plan would deny television service to viewers who both lack a digital television set and do not subscribe to satellite or cable television.

These criticisms underscore the continuing lack of any consensus on what overarching objectives should guide the ongoing transition to digital television. The Ferree plan is eminently sensible if the principal objectives of the transition are to ensure that at least 85% of Americans continue to receive locally broadcast programs through one medium or another and that the spectrum now devoted to analog broadcasting is moved into more valued uses as soon as possible. But the plan is less sensible if judged for its ability to extend the benefits of digital television to all consumers. In all events, Congress seems unlikely to adopt either the Ferree plan or any of the several other alternatives that, while quite plausible as a policy matter, tend to alienate one industry faction or another.[47] Consequently, as Chairman Powell put it in September 2004, "we [currently] have no clear idea when the transition will be over in any particular market and not even a clear idea how we are supposed to count TV households toward the 85 percent threshold."[48]

D. Content providers and digital rights management

All the transitional steps we have discussed so far will produce little of value for the public if, at the end of the road, there is insufficient digital programming available for consumers to watch on television. So far, moreover, the major studios have produced less television-specific digital content than policymakers had hoped. That is largely because content providers fear that transmission of their programs in unencrypted digital form will expose them to massive "Napsterization"—i.e., widespread, illegal copying and retransmission over the Internet.[49] Indeed, Chairman

Powell has suggested that the current paucity of television-specific digital content—and the associated intellectual property concerns—represent the Achilles' heel of the digital transition.[50]

This piracy problem arises from some of the very characteristics of digital technology that make it superior to conventional analog technology. In the analog world, each subsequent copy of a movie, for example, degraded the quality of the image, and producing such copies took a fair amount of time as well. As a result, piracy did not significantly harm the movie industry's revenues. In the digital world, however, consumers can make and distribute identical copies of programming very quickly. Before agreeing to release video programming in digital form, therefore, content providers have insisted on the development of comprehensive "digital rights management" (DRM) systems, which limit the extent to which viewers can copy and redistribute digital content. Such systems cannot be truly effective, however, without the cooperation of equipment manufacturers, whose own interests may depart sharply from those of the content providers. This divergence of interests has led the FCC to undertake two principal DRM initiatives to break the digital content logjam.

The first of the initiatives relates to new *plug-and-play* TV sets—those ready-made to receive digital signals from cable television providers. Traditional TV sets can unscramble digital signals only by means of a set-top box supplied by the cable or satellite provider, and that box typically provides whatever types of copy protections the provider deems necessary. Plug-and-play sets avoid the need for such a box and thus deprive cable companies of their traditional end-to-end role in safeguarding digital content from piracy. In the early 2000s, under the threat of explicit regulation, the FCC induced the cable and consumer electronics industries to enter into a privately negotiated agreement under which new plug-and-play sets will accommodate different types of encoding rules ("copy never," "copy once," etc.) included within the cable companies' digital transmissions. In 2003, the FCC then ratified that agreement and imposed it on the industry as a whole after dismissing various procedural objections.[51]

The second major FCC DRM initiative relates to the so-called *broadcast flag* rules, which are designed to allay the concerns of content providers that *over-the-air* broadcasts of digital programming will facilitate easy copying and mass redistribution of copyrighted content. These concerns arise because, unlike cable and satellite providers, broadcasters do not encrypt the programming they air to the public at large. Indeed, any proposal to encrypt broadcast transmissions at their source would be a non-starter, not just because it would seem inconsistent with the tradition of freely available over-the-air television, but also because broadcasters have already begun broadcasting in digital format without encryption and consumers have purchased expensive television sets that would not be able to display encrypted programming.[52] On the other hand, "free over-the-air TV" may be just as threatened if content producers restrict the transmission of their programs to subscription-based cable or satellite channels for fear that any shows aired on broadcast television will be instantaneously redistributed on the Internet. Such redistribution would deprive the producers of subsequent revenue sources such as packaged DVD sets and the later syndication of first-run programming.

To solve this problem, the broadcast networks in particular and the entertainment industry in general proposed the "broadcast flag" system.[53] Under that system, television stations encode a digital broadcast with data bits (the "flag") identifying the broadcast as subject to restrictions on redistribution, and any digital consumer electronics equipment that is used to view that broadcast must be configured to honor those restrictions. In 2003, the FCC endorsed the use of this broadcast flag regime. It recognized, however, that this approach cannot altogether block illegal copying by sophisticated hackers. Nonetheless, the FCC concluded that the broadcast flag will at least raise a "speed bump" sufficient to frustrate copyright infringement efforts by most ordinary users.[54] The Commission rejected proposals to give the content industry a key role in selecting particular DRM technologies, and it instead assumed responsibility for evaluating whether consumer electronic devices that work in conjunction with digital televisions use DRM technology that is robust enough to foil routine attempts at unlawful copying.[55] This choice, however, only postponed the more difficult judgment calls the Commission will need to make about the merits of particular DRM technologies that purport to limit the ability of users to copy television programs and share them freely with others.[56]

The FCC's broadcast flag initiatives raise difficult and novel legal issues about the scope of its current authority under the Communications Act.[57] The FCC enjoys no express authority to regulate consumer electronics manufacturers to ensure their compliance with broadcast flag restrictions.

Indeed, in concluding that it possesses "ancillary jurisdiction" to enforce such compliance under Title I of the Communications Act (see chapter 6), the FCC recognized that all of its previous regulations governing the production of television equipment, unlike this one, have rested on specific statutory authorizations.[58] But like the FCC's earlier regulation of equipment used in connection with the telephone network, the FCC concluded that its Title I ancillary jurisdiction broadly covers all "instrumentalities, facilities, apparatus, and services" used in connection with radio communications.[59] Critics of the broadcast flag rules have appealed the FCC's assertion of such ancillary jurisdiction, and those appeals remain pending as this book goes to press.[60]

* * *

The digital television story exemplifies the trade-offs the government faces when deciding how much to intervene in an industry's transition to a new technology. One factor that makes the digital television transition in particular so problematic is the sheer scope of the collective action problem involved. Before digital television can become a reality for American consumers, many industry factions with divergent interests—including broadcasters, cable operators, equipment manufacturers, and content providers—must unite behind a common plan and its myriad constituent elements. If the FCC had played no role in uniting these different industry factions through moral suasion and, as necessary, outright regulation, an industry-wide digital television transition might not be underway at all—at least for the 15% of Americans who still rely on conventional over-the-air broadcasts, rather than cable or satellite, as their means of receiving television signals. On the other hand, Congress's solicitude for the needs of that 15% is responsible for much, though by no means all, of the complexity involved in this transition. Were it not for the government's tenacious commitment to the preservation of "free over-the-air television," a digital transition confined to cable and satellite platforms would have proceeded much more efficiently and with far less regulatory oversight.[61]

Direct government intervention in the standard-setting process is also risky in that it can easily produce imperfect technological outcomes. In particular, such intervention can lock the industry into technological choices inferior to those the free market would eventually make if given adequate time—as revealed by the FCC's aborted adoption of the CBS standard for color television in the 1950s and perhaps by its endorsement of the 8VSB standard for digital television. On the other hand, as the Part 68 Rules and the AM stereo experience arguably demonstrate, the government can sometimes undermine a technological transition altogether by *failing* to intervene in a standards battle. The FCC's need to exercise sound judgment in the face of such conundrums is but one of several respects in which the future health of the telecommunications industry will depend both on the Commission's technical expertise and on its humility in the face of its institutional limitations.

13

The Future of Telecommunications Policy

In 1977, President Carter selected Alfred Kahn, the noted regulatory economist, to head the now-defunct Civil Aeronautics Board. The Board was responsible for comprehensive regulation of the commercial airline industry: it awarded routes to airlines, limited carriers' entry into and exit from particular markets, and regulated passenger fares.[1] This system, which had been in place since the New Deal, was ready for a complete overhaul, as few informed observers believed that any part of the airline industry was a "natural monopoly" in need of such pervasive economic oversight by the government.[2] And Kahn concluded that such oversight was not just unnecessary, but affirmatively harmful, in that it produced flights with few passengers, barred potential competitors from entering the market, and created significant consumer welfare losses.[3] A year later, armed with Kahn's criticisms and broad political support, Congress passed the Airline Deregulation Act of 1978.[4] This legislation banished all of the classic command-and-control tools previously used by the agency—it ended price regulation, tariffs, and limits on market entry and exit. After a period of transition, the Board shut its doors for good in 1985.

When Congress passed the Telecommunications Act of 1996, some hoped that it would "deregulate" the telecommunications industry in much the same way that the 1978 legislation deregulated the airline industry. After all, the 1996 Act advertised itself as the "most deregulatory [law] in history."[5] Anyone who believed that characterization at the time, however, was quickly disillusioned. The Act is not at all deregulatory in the straightforward sense of "tending to abolish regulation." To the contrary, it adds an entirely new *dimension* to pre-1996 regulation by creating a broad new set of wholesale rules, including the unbundling obligations discussed in chapter 3, to the existing edifice of retail regulation.[6]

This regulatory expansion is not itself, of course, a basis for criticizing the Act. It seemed entirely plausible in 1996 that significant governmental intervention would be needed in the near term to jump start entry into local telephone markets and set the stage for deregulated facilities-based competition in the long term. Nine years later, however, that fully competitive, deregulated industry remains only an abstract future possibility.

There are many theories about where the blame lies for the current dysfunctionality of telecommunications regulation, and each industry faction tends to blame its adversaries. But Kahn, now a professor emeritus at Cornell University and an occasional consultant to the Bell companies, assigns culpability to the regulators themselves. He observes that "[t]he continued responsibility of public utility regulatory commissions to ensure access by challengers to essential network facilities at reasonable rates presents them with a temptation . . . to micromanage the process of deregulation itself."[7] The FCC, he claims, has succumbed to that temptation, much to the detriment of consumer welfare: "[T]here is every difference between regulatory interventions establishing the conditions under which competition may be relied on to determine the outcome and interventions intended, whether consciously or unconsciously, to *dictate* that outcome."[8]

Put differently, regulatory micromanagement, while integral to the oversight of an enduring monopoly, is anathema to the long run development of efficient competition. Stephen Breyer voiced similar concerns in 1987, long before his appointment to the Supreme Court. He warned that "regulators or antitrust enforcers confuse means with ends by thinking that the object of the law is to protect individual firms from business risks rather than to bring consumers the price and production benefits that typically arise from the competitive process. Where deregulation is at issue, the consequence of misdirecting protection is to threaten to deprive the consumer of the very benefits deregulation seeks."[9] Since joining the Court, Breyer has now twice expressed the more institution-specific concern—unshared by his more deferential colleagues—that the FCC systematically thwarts the cause of *competition*, at least in wireline regulation, by focusing too heavily on the needs of individual *competitors*.[10]

In this final chapter, we turn our focus to the FCC as an institution for managing telecommunications competition policy. Some critics, such as Peter Huber, contend that the FCC is culturally incapable of letting go of the industry's reins, now or ever. That concern has led Huber to propose abolishing the FCC, much like the Civil Aeronautics Board before it, and letting disinterested, non-bureaucratic antitrust courts remedy any anticompetitive practices in the industry.[11] Below, we explain why we disagree with such proposals and why the FCC will remain, for better or worse, the least problematic institution to oversee the development of competition in telecommunications markets, at least for the foreseeable future. Because the choice among potential regulators depends on the nature of the market to be regulated, however, we first review the state of the telecommunications industry.

I. Digital Juggernaut

The current telecommunications marketplace bears little resemblance to the one envisioned in the 1996 Act, mostly because Congress did not anticipate the full consequences of the Internet. The Internet has fostered entry and innovation precisely because it has traditionally operated as a "dumb network" that rewards the creativity of individuals and small firms at the edge of the network. As Andrew Odlyzko observes, moreover, "[i]n spite of many attempts, the established service providers and their suppliers have an abysmal record in innovation in user services . . . . The real 'killer apps,' such as email, the Web, browsers, search engines, [instant messaging], and Napster, have all come from users."[12] Significantly, many of the emerging Internet innovations, such as VoIP, depend on widespread adoption of broadband Internet access—a platform that did not yet exist in the mass market when Congress enacted the 1996 Act.

At least at present, the last mile for broadband transmission to homes and most businesses remains the province of established service providers. As discussed in chapters 4 and 5, the great hope for broadband competition is that wireless or powerline technology (or both) will provide a competitive check on the cable and telephone companies that, as of 2004, still share an overwhelming percentage of this market. As FCC Chairman Michael Powell explained, in stressing the importance of broadband rivalry, "[m]agical things happen in competitive markets when there are at least three viable, facilities-based competitors."[13] Much of the current dispute about broadband policy reduces to different empirical predictions about how quickly a third such competitor will arise to play a decisive role in the broadband market. Even here, however, the question for most consumers is not so much *if* that third competitor will arrive as *when*.

The flip side of accelerated entry, increased innovation, and greater consumer choice is a precarious economic environment for telecommunications firms. This environment now includes a long distance market in freefall, a continuing decline in wireline telephone connections (at a rate of about 7% per year), and the recent obliteration of $1.7 trillion in stock market capitalization.[14] As Qwest CEO Richard Notebaert put it, "[t]he voice industry—whether long distance, local, or wireless—finds itself in a commodity market with deflationary pricing. Volumes will rise, but prices will fall even faster."[15] Qwest and the other Bell companies have only accelerated this trend by rolling out their own VoIP services to businesses and consumers throughout the United States—services that can be run over any type of broadband Internet connection, including cable modem connections. By offering these VoIP products, the Bells are beginning to compete not just with each other, largely for the first time, but with their own traditional voice services.[16]

The Internet's revolutionary impact on the broader communications marketplace is just becoming apparent. In the wireless sector, for example, analysts have begun speculating about the competitive significance of a new breed of "dual mode" phone that runs VoIP and data applications over unlicensed Wi-Fi networks where available and over licensed cellular spectrum only where such networks are unavailable. This development could ease demand for licensed spectrum, with uncertain effects on the valuation of existing wireless telephony licenses.[17] Similarly, the advent of video-over-IP technology—which, like VoIP, can theoretically operate on any broadband platform—could eventually pose a challenge to the established cable and satellite television providers, although its competitive impact remains uncertain as well.[18]

When it drafted the 1996 Act, Congress did not account for these or the many other respects in which the Internet would subsequently destabilize the existing order in the communications industry. Although Congress anticipated some degree of convergence between different technology platforms, it focused almost exclusively on the prospect that cable companies would offer circuit-switched telephony and that telephone companies would offer video programming. Congress did not anticipate that voice, video, and data would someday be reduced to streams of bits running on top of a single and universal logical layer platform, the Internet protocol, which itself can be used on virtually any physical layer transmission medium.[19]

As IP technology engulfs the telecommunications world, policymakers will eventually have to abandon the arbitrary service-oriented distinctions of the Communications Act. Instead, as discussed in chapter 6, they should move towards a more functional model of regulation that takes greater account of the Internet's established layers: physical, logical, applications, and content. Under this approach, much of telecommunications policy would collapse into the familiar antitrust objective of keeping any genuinely dominant provider in one market—specifically the physical layer—from limiting competitive entry into that market or exerting undue influence on the adjacent markets for applications and content. As we have explained, the transition to a layers-oriented regulatory model would not necessarily inject any substantive bias into the resolution of particular policy problems. It certainly would not justify any *a priori* presumption that physical layer providers should be heavily regulated, nor would it supply a sufficient basis for opposing vertical integration of complementary services on different layers. It would, however, reinforce the importance of existing efforts to rationalize the regulation of different transmission platforms. And, by providing the starting point for defining the Internet's interrelated markets, it would create a useful analytical framework for addressing traditional monopoly leveraging concerns.

II. First Principles of Institutional Reform

At the highest level of generality, this "horizontal" model of regulation would reaffirm that, as a *substantive* matter, the first principles of telecommunications competition policy in the Internet age should merge with the first principles of antitrust. Answering that substantive question, however, begs a distinct *institutional* question: if we could remake current institutional arrangements from scratch, would we commit this antitrust-oriented project to the FCC or, as Huber and others have suggested, to generalist antitrust courts?

A. Four values for managing competition policy

One's answer to the foregoing question depends, of course, on how one judges the success of a given institutional arrangement for managing competition policy. In our view, such arrangements should be judged by their consistency with four basic values: determinacy, expertise, neutrality, and humility. The first two of these values are straightforward; the third and fourth less so.

We begin with *determinacy*. A regulatory regime is determinate if its governing institutions—Congress, regulatory agencies, and the courts—work together smoothly and expeditiously enough that the industry knows as quickly as possible what the ground rules for competition policy will be and can predict with reasonable precision how those rules will be applied. The more determinate these ground rules are, the more comfortable investors will be in placing bets on the future of this industry, and the more likely it is that innovators will obtain financing to put their ideas to work for the public good. Particularly in a dynamic industry like telecommunications, it is often "more important," as Justice Brandeis once put it, "that the applicable rule of law be settled than that it be settled right."[20]

Expertise, our second value, means that primary decisionmaking authority should be committed to institutions that understand, or can easily learn, the esoteric technology of telecommunications, the structure of the industry, and the complex economic and regulatory issues that have defined this field for many years.

The third value that an ideal institutional arrangement should promote is analytically rigorous *neutrality* in the resolution of controversial policy issues. This concept is subtler than the first two. By "neutrality," we mean that whoever writes the rules for competition policy should think of problems by reference to first principles about how to maximize consumer welfare—principles that, for the most part, are informed by antitrust analysis. And, when considering proposals for regulatory reform, policymakers should begin by asking "why have we done it this way?" rather than "why should we incur the political costs of changing our longstanding policy on this issue?"

Our fourth value, and admittedly the vaguest, is *humility*. We use the term to describe the attitude of a policymaker who, with every important decision, remembers the many times in which other policymakers have been flatly wrong in their predictions of how the telecommunications market would take shape and in their assessments of the regulatory measures needed to enhance consumer welfare within that evolving market. Humility also reminds policymakers that, over the long term, the unintended, undesired consequences of regulation can dwarf the intended, desired outcomes. That fact is not a reason for doing nothing when action is needed to correct genuine market failures. But it is a reason for policymakers to respect the market's ability to enhance consumer welfare and, as they evaluate the predicted benefits of their own regulatory involvement, to give due regard to the unpredictable course of technological and economic change.

Now that we have defined our objectives, we examine how best to structure the relationship among the principal institutional actors in this field—Congress, agencies, and the courts—to advance these four values in the aggregate to the greatest extent possible. We first evaluate the strengths and weaknesses of these institutions as creators and enforcers of telecommunications policy.

B. Judging Congress

Arguably, much of the indeterminacy that has plagued telecommunications policy for the past nine years could have been avoided if Congress had simply spoken more clearly in 1996. To take one example, consider the fate of the FCC's TELRIC pricing rules for unbundled network elements, discussed in chapter 3 and appendix A. Those rules lingered in a state of suspended animation for six years after they were first adopted, having been vacated twice by the Eighth Circuit and reinstated twice by the Supreme Court, the second time in 2002. Congress could have avoided those six years of investment-chilling uncertainty both by making it explicit from the outset that, contrary to the Eighth Circuit's initial reading of the 1996 Act, the FCC has the authority to issue pricing rules for network elements and by giving the Commission greater guidance on the appropriate content of those rules.

We should not be surprised, however, that Congress spoke as vaguely as it did. The 1996 Act was effectively written by warring interest groups that believed they were playing a zero-sum game. In these circumstances, it is always easier for a legislator to vote for an ambiguous provision—thereby punting hard issues to regulators and the courts—than to vote for a provision that decides important controversies clearly and directly. The latter course, while better for industry stability and the public interest, is sure to alienate one powerful interest group or another. Ambiguity, by contrast, enables politicians to waffle about what they really meant when they cast their votes, and to blame someone else if their votes are later construed by a court or agency against the interests of a particular constituency.

The Act's origins in interest group politics explain why so much of it seems written as though for a law school moot court: the opposing positions coexist in such perfect equipoise that no side enjoys any advantage over the others, and each side can litigate decisions with which it disagrees in a state of almost perfect interpretive competition. On the other hand, we do not want to overstate Congress' irresponsibility in enacting such a deliberately ambiguous statute, for the reality is that no significant legislation would have been enacted in the first place if it had addressed such highly consequential issues too clearly.

In all events, Congress is institutionally incapable of resolving on its own many of the policy challenges that divide this industry. Even if Congress had the political will to legislate with great clarity, it surely lacks the substantive expertise and institutional facility needed to enact the precise solution for a given problem in a reasonable timeframe, and then to react flexibly and promptly once circumstances warrant a different solution.[21] Unfortunately, in enacting the 1996 Act, Congress addressed some issues with language that superficially appears specific and definitive but, on closer inspection, turns out to be riddled with ambiguities.[22] This approach generated far greater litigation and uncertainty than would have arisen if Congress had simply granted broad authority to the FCC to address the relevant competition issues.

Given Congress' limitations in addressing the details of complex regulatory issues, there is a broad consensus that Congress has no choice but to delegate competition policymaking authority to some other institution. Here we reach a fork in the road. As an original matter, Congress could have delegated the lion's share of such authority to *courts*, in their role as generalist enforcers of the antitrust laws; or to a specialized *agency* such as the FCC, which can act as a prescriptive regulator and, to a lesser extent, as an enforcement agency as well. We address each possibility in turn.

C. The antitrust alternative

Arguably, generalist courts, largely immune from interest group politics and from entrenched assumptions about how the world must work, are better equipped than specialized agencies to resolve competition policy issues on their economic merits. With no lobbyists to appease and no bureaucracies to keep busy, antitrust courts, at least in theory, should do a better job than the FCC or other specialized agencies in resolving such issues with analytically rigorous neutrality. Perhaps the purest endorsement of courts over agencies as guardians of telecommunications competition policy appears in the scholarship of Peter Huber. In his view, the FCC and its "army of federal employees hanging around indefinitely to meddle and mess up" should be abolished altogether in favor of minimalist, case-by-case antitrust enforcement.[23]

Of course, antitrust courts are only as neutral as the judges who sit on them, and not all judges are exemplars of neutrality. A district judge selected to decide a critical antitrust case might do quite a bit worse than Judge Harold Greene, who administered the twelve-year antitrust regime spawned by the AT&T consent decree (see chapter 2) and, in that capacity, made a number of controversial policy judgments about the trajectory of competition within the industry.[24] The risks of vesting such enormous power in a single generalist district court judge are compounded by forum-shopping opportunities that sometimes enable an industry faction to choose, for the resolution of critical industry-wide controversies, whatever court the faction considers unusually sympathetic to its cause. In one well-known example, two Bell companies brought their constitutional challenge to section 271 (see chapter 3) in the remote Wichita Falls Division of a federal district court in Texas, where their desired judge, Joe Kendall, obliged them by invalidating that provision and several others on New Year's Eve in 1997.[25] Although Kendall's decision was eventually reversed, it symbolizes the dangers of letting individual judges play too significant a role in shaping the future of this uniquely volatile industry.

Huber is nonetheless correct that the FCC, like any entrenched bureaucracy, has developed a self-sustaining bias in favor of keeping itself important by intervening heavily in the industry it regulates. That bias indulges rent-seeking behavior and invites overregulation, with all of its attendant inefficiencies. Whenever an industry requires broad oversight, however, similar bureaucracies tend to arise spontaneously no matter what institution is formally charged with conducting the oversight. For example, the AT&T consent decree regime produced its own small "army of federal employees" in the Department of Justice who devoted a dozen years of their careers to the zealous enforcement of the decree's manifold restrictions. That group of lawyers and economists was not necessarily less disposed to government intervention in the telecommunications market than the FCC is today. Ultimately, Huber's *institutional* preference for antitrust courts over regulatory agencies could eliminate such bureaucracies only when he and his fellow libertarians are granted their *substantive* wish for a negligible government role of any kind in the oversight of telecommunications competition. That wish, however, is likely to be—and should be—granted only in the long term, once the market for last mile transmission becomes more robustly competitive than it now is.

The more basic problem with relying on antitrust courts to superintend the telecommunications industry is that the judicial process is deficient in the areas of determinacy and expertise. Consider determinacy first. Companies with market power are better off knowing now, not at the end of a multi-year antitrust suit, whether the aggressive business strategy they are contemplating will be deemed anticompetitive and will subject them to enormous liability.[26] The need for such predictability will be a special concern in the telecommunications industry for many years to come, given the prevalence of claims—many of them plausible—that certain firms still dominate particular markets despite the inexorable growth of cross-platform competition. Likewise, the absence of a regulatory agency to develop and enforce pre-set rules would make it more difficult for industry pioneers to compete with a dominant firm, particularly if they lack the money or endurance to prosecute an antitrust suit. In short, prescriptive regulation should theoretically do a better job than after-the-fact antitrust enforcement in providing all industry actors with greater certainty sooner rather than later—although, as we will discuss, reality does not always match that theory.

Generalist courts also lack the technical expertise needed to make fully informed judgments about the market consequences of any substantive remedies they order. As Frank Easterbrook observes, "[j]udges are the regulators with the broadest portfolios, and thus are the least competent."[27] In theory, this shortcoming could be alleviated either by relegating telecommunications competition issues to specialized courts (much as Congress has assigned all patent law appeals to the Federal Circuit) or by permitting judges to retain experts who can explain the industry to them. But these measures present considerable challenges of their own.[28] Indeed, ever careful to preserve the appearance of judicial self-sufficiency, the courts have sometimes expressed outright hostility to the use of retained experts to help resolve technically complex litigation on the merits, as illustrated by the D.C. Circuit's 1998 order barring Judge Thomas Penfield Jackson from using Lawrence Lessig as a special master in one phase of the Microsoft antitrust case.[29] Just as important, generalist judges lack both the resources and the technical proficiency to resolve the thousands of day-to-day disputes, on pricing and other issues, that must be decided under any local competition regime that involves even minimal leasing and interconnection rights.[30] Aware of these limitations, the judiciary has generally shown great solicitude for the greater expertise of regulatory agencies within the scope of their substantive authority.[31]

These institutional concerns form the backdrop to the Supreme Court's 2004 decision in *Verizon Communications, Inc. v. Law Offices of Curtis V. Trinko,*[32] which concluded that antitrust courts are generally inappropriate forums for the ongoing management of telecommunications competition policy, at least so long as the industry remains subject to pervasive regulation. Our discussion of *Trinko* first requires a brief review of the historical intersection between antitrust law and prescriptive telecommunications regulation.

Before 1996, as we have noted, much of telecommunications competition policy was managed by a single judge: Harold Greene. In 1982, AT&T agreed to the consent decree that ultimately spun off the Bell companies only after Greene rejected the company's argument that the FCC's comprehensive oversight of the industry precluded any role for antitrust enforcement. Greene found that argument unpersuasive because, as demonstrated by years of regulatory indecision, "the Commission is not and never has been capable of effective enforcement of the laws governing AT&T's behavior."[33] When it called for the termination of that consent decree in 1996, Congress directed the FCC and its state counterparts to implement wireline competition provisions that, as discussed in chapter 3, go far beyond the FCC's traditional mandate to require interconnection among carriers on just and reasonable terms. At the same time, however, Congress included an antitrust "savings clause" providing that "nothing in the Act or in the amendments made by this Act shall be construed to modify, impair or supercede the applicability of any antitrust laws."[34]

Like so many other provisions of the 1996 Act, this one led to widespread disagreement. Some argued that, despite the savings clause, antitrust courts should generally defer to regulators in deciding whether particular conduct is genuinely anticompetitive and, if so, what sorts of enforcement mechanisms would be appropriate for addressing it.[35] But others contended that the savings clause preserves antitrust remedies as a backstop for the protection of competitors whenever prescriptive regulation proves ineffective in keeping incumbents from exploiting any market power they might have.[36] Advocates of this position further maintained that, as in the AT&T antitrust litigation, defendants should have to bear the burden of proving that, as a factual matter, regulatory mechanisms are sufficiently effective to make antitrust intervention unnecessary. The major theories of liability expounded by these proponents of continued antitrust enforcement included the controversial "essential facilities" doctrine, under which some lower courts have forced monopolists to cooperate with their rivals' market entry plans by selling them access to bottleneck facilities.[37]

In *Trinko*, the Supreme Court resolved this debate with a resounding victory for telecommunications antitrust defendants in general and the Bell companies in particular. The Court began by explaining that, although the antitrust savings clause "preserves claims that satisfy existing antitrust standards, it does not create new claims that go beyond existing antitrust standards."[38] Then, in setting forth those existing standards, the Court sharply limited the circumstances in which courts may impose antitrust remedies—under the essential facilities doctrine or any other—for a monopolist's refusal to help rivals compete with it. Such remedies often do more harm than good, the Court reasoned, "because of the uncertain virtue of forced sharing and the difficulty of identifying and remedying anticompetitive conduct by a single firm," and because "[m]istaken inferences and the resulting false condemnations are especially costly" in that "they chill the very conduct the antitrust laws are designed to protect" by "lessen[ing] the incentive for the monopolist, the rival, or both to invest in . . . economically beneficial facilities."[39]

Moving from substantive to institutional concerns, the court added that "[e]nforced sharing also requires antitrust courts to act as central planners, identifying the proper price, quantity, and other terms of dealing—a role for which they are ill-suited."[40] Finally, the Court concluded, "[t]he 1996 Act's extensive provision for access" to an incumbent's facilities and services on regulated terms makes it as unnecessary as it is potentially harmful "to impose a judicial doctrine of forced access."[41]

In sum, whatever the right institutional arrangement might have been as an original matter, specialized regulatory agencies, led by the FCC, will play the dominant role in setting telecommunications competition policy for the foreseeable future—although, to be sure, the post-*Trinko* fate of antitrust claims unrelated to the essential facilities doctrine remains unclear.[42] We now turn to the FCC's performance in that role and the prospects for improving upon it.

III. The FCC in Transition

As Winston Churchill remarked in 1947: "Many forms of Government have been tried, and will be tried in this world of sin and woe. . . . No one pretends that democracy is perfect or all-wise. Indeed, it has been said that democracy is the worst form of Government except all those other forms that have been tried from time to time."[43] Continued reliance on the FCC is likewise the worst way to superintend competition policy in the telecommunications industry—except for the alternatives. The problem lies not in expertise, for the FCC has plenty of that. The problem lies instead in the FCC's ability to serve the other three values we have identified: determinacy, neutrality, and humility.

A. Determinacy

In theory, Congress delegates legislative rulemaking authority to administrative agencies not just because they are expert in their designated fields, but also because they, unlike Congress, have the institutional agility needed to adjust the rules promptly to accommodate changes in market conditions. In reality, the FCC has long displayed a regrettable tendency to string out its decisions on important matters, despite the D.C. Circuit's exasperated admonition to it more than half a century ago that "[a]gency inaction can be as harmful as wrong action."[44]

Congress has sometimes addressed this problem, with great effect, by giving the FCC strict statutory deadlines for the resolution of particularly time-sensitive issues. For example, the FCC completed its work on the initial implementation of sections 251 and 252 within the specified 180-day period after passage of the 1996 Act,[45] and, at least on paper, met the separate 90-day deadline under section 271 for deciding each Bell application to enter the long distance market in a particular state.[46] Sometimes, however, the FCC manages to elude congressionally mandated deadlines, as illustrated by its October 2003 decision to defer any resolution on the merits of a petition seeking forbearance from residual broadband unbundling obligations (see chapter 5).[47] And a great many of the Commission's most significant rulemaking proceedings have dragged on for many years because they are subject to no statutory deadline at all.

Such delays stem in part from the elaborate behind-the-scenes deal-making needed to reach consensus among the Commission's five members. Like cabinet officials, those members are appointed by the president and confirmed by Congress; unlike cabinet officials, however, no more than three of them may belong to the same political party, and, once confirmed, they may be removed during their five-year terms only for cause.[48] The result is that members other than the chairman, even those who belong to the chairman's (and president's) party, may worry more about pleasing their separate constituencies within Congress or the industry than about pleasing the White House. This is a recipe for internecine intrigue and deliberative inefficiency.

Some have cited these concerns as a reason to place the FCC more firmly within the Executive Branch, eliminate the current five-member structure, and vest plenary authority in a single decisionmaker at the top of the FCC's organizational chart, much as Congress has organized the Food and Drug Administration and the Environmental Protection Agency.[49] That proposal has much to commend it. Given the unprecedented pace of change that the Internet has brought to the telecommunications industry, the dilatory costs of the FCC's multi-member structure may now outweigh whatever benefits it was once thought to present in the form of internal checks and balances.[50] Any such reform, however, would face severe political obstacles in Congress, where legislators have exploited the FCC's instability at the top and its partial detachment from the White House as bases for exerting more direct influence over it than over more traditional Executive Branch agencies.

In all events, any reform of the FCC's own processes could serve as no more than a first step in bringing greater regulatory determinacy to this industry. Equally in need of reform are the FCC's relationships with other institutional players: with the courts that review the FCC's policy choices, with the state commissions that implement those choices, and with sister agencies on the federal level—the Justice Department and the Federal Trade Commission (FTC)—that share the FCC's responsibility to review proposed mergers between telecommunications companies. We address each of these institutional relationships in turn.

Relations with reviewing courts

Any final order of the FCC is subject to judicial review in a federal court of appeals.[51] The availability of such review contributes to the indeterminacy of telecommunications regulation, particularly when undertaken by activist generalist courts that consider themselves equally equipped as specialist agencies to understand the complexities of this industry.

Under the doctrine of judicial deference formalized in *Chevron U.S.A. v. National Resources Defense Council*,[52] a reviewing court may not act as a policymaker in its own right. Instead, it may serve only as a backstop against agency action that is patently irrational, inconsistent with a clear statutory (or constitutional) mandate, or inadequately justified in the written document that accompanies the agency's order.[53] A court that finds fault with an agency's decision is expected to remand the matter back to the agency itself for further deliberation within broad bounds.[54] Traditionally, the reason given for such deference is that agencies have greater topical expertise than judges and are subject to continuing congressional oversight as a check.[55] But an equally important rationale, particularly in the telecommunications field, is the value of regulatory determinacy.

Every time a court invalidates an FCC rule, it injects uncertainty into the industry that may distort economically efficient behavior for many years. The problem with such judicial second-guessing, which has become quite common, is not just that it delays the ultimate resolution of important policy issues, but also that courts can misunderstand those issues or their industry context and thus adopt rules that, on close inspection, make little policy sense. One recent example of this phenomenon was the Ninth Circuit's stubborn reaffirmation in 2003 of its misinformed conclusion in 2000 that cable modem service contains a "telecommunications service" component and is presumptively subject to traditional common carrier regulation (see chapter 5).[56] Each such instance of judicial hubris can throw the industry into long periods of investment uncertainty, even when the FCC succeeds in persuading the resource-constrained Supreme Court to intervene.

This is no way to run a major sector of the economy. If, alternatively, the courts stand down when faced with close questions about the lawfulness of agency decisions, the worst that can happen is that we as a society will get what we allow our politically accountable institutions—Congress and its administrative delegates—to give us. We are not suggesting that courts should play no role in reviewing the FCC's decisions. Sometimes the FCC does act irrationally, as illustrated by its differential regulatory treatment of "cellular" and "PCS" providers (see chapter 8), and sometimes it ignores clear statutory directives, as shown by its complete disregard in 1996 of the Act's "impairment" standard for leasing network elements (see chapter 3). Such abuses of delegated authority warrant judicial intervention. Reviewing courts should nonetheless pick their fights and remedies carefully, generally deferring to the FCC's greater expertise and, just as important, to the industry's need for regulatory predictability.

Relations with the states

As discussed in chapter 3, the 1996 Act largely displaced the traditional model of dual jurisdiction, which divides the *subject matter* of telecommunications regulations into mutually exclusive federal and state spheres, with a new model of cooperative federalism in which the FCC and the states often work together in complementary roles on the same subject matter. For Congress, this new model was the only feasible choice for regulating telecommunications competition. The need to hammer out the innumerable details of carrier-to-carrier relations under the 1996 Act presents an immense bureaucratic challenge. Congress was not about to create a series of FCC branch offices or increase the FCC's staff many times over, and the state commissions provided a ready source of labor for the task at hand.[57]

Delegating such responsibility to the states, however, unavoidably gives all of them substantial discretion, as sovereign actors, in deciding how federal law will be implemented. This carries both benefits and costs. As one of us has argued, the states' discretion in competition matters allows them to tailor regulatory approaches to local conditions, encourage public participation in the policymaking process, experiment with acceptable alternatives, and compete with one another to develop an optimal scheme of regulation.[58] As the other of us has noted, however, these benefits can come at a high cost, in the form of delay and confusion as well as massive lawyering and lobbying expenses.[59] The more complicated and multi-dimensional the regulatory scheme is, the more investment-chilling indeterminacy there will be about the rules of the road.

The debates about state participation in telecommunications policy are only just beginning, as demonstrated by the incipient controversy over the states' authority to regulate VoIP services. For as long as there is telecommunications regulation, there will be controversy about the proper role of the states in its implementation. Nonetheless, as the entire industry gradually coalesces around the Internet protocol, traditional state public utility regulation will quite likely succumb to two of the Internet's most cherished characteristics: its federally enforced freedom from state regulation and its tendency to efface political boundaries of all kinds. As noted in chapter 6, however, the states may yet preserve a critical role in managing non-competition-related public policy priorities, such as ensuring 911 functionality in VoIP services and designing subsidy mechanisms for affordable telephone service in rural areas.

Relations with coordinate merger review authorities

The FCC shares decisionmaking authority not just vertically, with the states, but also horizontally, with other federal agencies. As discussed in chapter 7, for example, the FCC's efforts to reform spectrum policy are inevitably complicated by NTIA's independent jurisdiction over spectrum allocated to the government itself. Here we discuss the similar bureaucratic challenges caused by the FCC's sharing of merger-review authority with the Justice Department and occasionally the FTC.[60]

The procedural hurdles for obtaining merger clearance may assume great prominence in the near future. Citing widespread competitive pressures and the erosion of pricing power, some analysts predict a "systematic wave of consolidation in the communications industry."[61] Such speculation intensified when, in the wake of *USTA II* (see chapter 3), AT&T announced that it could no longer afford to focus on the mass market for conventional voice telephony. As the *New York Times* reported, "AT&T, by retreating from the residential market, might face fewer regulatory hurdles for consolidation" with a Bell company because its pullback would alleviate "concern[s] about a union between a Bell and one of its chief competitors in the local and long-distance markets."[62] Any such merger proposal would nonetheless face considerable controversy. As recently as 1997, FCC Chairman Reed Hundt deemed a Bell-AT&T merger "unthinkable."[63] Five years later, however, once the telecom bubble had burst, new Chairman Michael Powell all but repudiated Hundt's assessment, observing that "[t]here are plenty of doctrines in antitrust and competition policy that would take into consideration the duress and state of the market . . . . If a Bell company brought a deal to us, that would certainly be part of the consideration."[64]

The Justice Department and FTC normally conduct their own merger reviews under section 7 of the Clayton Act, which requires an inquiry into whether the effect of a proposed merger "may be substantially to lessen competition, or to tend to create a monopoly."[65] This standard makes it much more difficult for two companies to merge if they *already* compete with one another than if they only *might* do so in the future. In 2000, for example, the Justice Department and the European Commission effectively blocked the proposed merger of MCI-WorldCom and Sprint on the ground that they were already competitors in the consumer long distance and Internet backbone markets.[66] In contrast, the Justice Department has permitted several mergers between Bell companies because, as former antitrust chief Joel Klein explained, these geographically separated local telephone carriers have generally not "invaded [one] another's territory."[67] Some have criticized this policy on the ground that the Bell companies are at least *potential* competitors in one another's markets and that inter-Bell mergers foreclose such competition. Under the Clayton Act standard, however, antitrust authorities may block mergers to protect "potential" competition only in the narrowest of circumstances.[68]

Once two communications firms persuade the Justice Department or the FTC to clear their merger, however, their task is only half-finished. They must also persuade the FCC to approve the transfer of lines or wireless licenses from the merging parties to the merged entity. (In part for comity reasons, and in part because it is easier to go second, the FCC often performs the bulk of its statutory review after the Justice Department or the FTC has completed its own review.) In deciding whether to approve such transfers, the FCC is officially unconstrained by the Clayton Act standard or, for that matter, by any standard more determinate than whether, in the FCC's view, the merger would advance the "public interest, convenience and necessity."[69]

The FCC has exploited this statutory freedom to great effect. For example, unlike the Justice Department, the Commission may inquire broadly into whether a merger would foreclose merely potential competition between the merging parties.[70] The procedures for obtaining clearance are also decidedly different, at least in form. Whereas the Justice Department must seek judicial intervention to block a proposed merger,[71] the FCC may unilaterally quash any merger simply by declining to approve the necessary license transfers. Similarly, whereas the Justice Department bears the burden of proving that a merger would violate the Clayton Act standard, the FCC takes the position that the burden falls on the merging parties to prove that their combination would affirmatively advance the public interest.[72]

In short, the FCC has virtually unfettered discretion in the merger process—and thus enormous power to extract concessions from the merging carriers. After meeting informally with the FCC's members and staff, such carriers typically end up making a range of "voluntary" commitments to persuade the FCC that, in some amorphous sense, the public interest benefits of the merger will outweigh the harms.[73] Sometimes these commitments, which might bear only a tenuous relationship to any concerns raised specifically by the merger itself, have created ongoing obligations that the FCC could not lawfully impose on the parties through its ordinary rulemaking authority.[74] But because the parties have agreed to them "voluntarily," such obligations are effectively immune from judicial scrutiny.

Many have questioned the legitimacy of this merger-review process. In 1999, before he was elevated from Commissioner to Chairman, Michael Powell expressed discomfort with the open-endedness of the Commission's inquiry, which "places harms on one side of a scale and then collects and places any hodgepodge of conditions—no matter how ill-suited to remedying the identified infirmities—on the other side of the scale."[75] As he explained, "the process of obtaining 'voluntary' conditions inevitably involves bilateral negotiations with the parties that leave the integrity of the Commission's process vulnerable to criticism," particularly when "we pursue conditions that do not go simply to the harms occasioned by the merger, but reach further into the [more general] rights and concerns of other parties."[76] Although the FCC now purports to have curbed this latter practice,[77] there is still no real check on the Commission's power to extract broad promises only loosely designed to alleviate any merger-specific concerns. Other commentators have likewise condemned these aspects of the FCC's merger review process as well as the Commission's speculative inquiries into potential, rather than actual, competition between the merging parties.[78]

Whatever the merit of these criticisms, there can be no doubt that the FCC's independent review of any merger adds months of delay and uncertainty to the merger-approval process. To compound the problem, many states view mergers as opportunities for imposing their own wish lists on the merging parties as preconditions for obtaining any necessary state-level approvals.[79] It is debatable whether the public interest demands these additional, largely unchecked layers of regulatory intervention beyond the basic inquiries already conducted by the Justice Department or FTC—inquiries that are considered more than adequate for other industries. Also, Congress itself is entirely capable of prescribing more specific and stringent standards for particular categories of mergers thought to present special competitive concerns, as it has done for proposed combinations of cable and telephone companies operating in the same region.[80]

To be sure, the Justice Department and FTC review only the strictly economic costs and benefits of mergers, and mergers between media companies may raise various *non*-economic concerns about society's need for a diversity of voices on television and radio (see chapter 11). Whatever the merit of those concerns, however, they can play no role when the merging parties are, for the most part, providers of transmission services rather than content. In that case, the inefficiencies of redundant merger review by the FCC may well outweigh whatever benefits such redundancy is thought to promote. If the FCC abuses its merger review authority too conspicuously, Congress might finally follow through on threats to impose radical constraints on the Commission's exercise of that authority, at least for certain types of mergers.[81]

B. Neutrality

As anyone who has watched the FCC in action is aware, the Commission often seems more adroit at jury-rigging intellectually sloppy deals to appease industry factions in the short term than at making the analytically sound but politically difficult policy choices needed to promote long term economic efficiency. Judge Richard Posner memorably described one

FCC regulatory scheme (the "finsyn rules" discussed in chapter 11) as a set of "unprincipled compromises of Rube Goldberg complexity among contending interest groups viewed merely as clamoring suppliants who have somehow to be conciliated."[82] Such dealmaking is particularly common in regulatory areas in which the FCC's decisions have immediate and quantifiable effects on consumer bills or on the bottom lines of the regulated parties. In chapters 9 and 10, for example, we documented the FCC's chronic preference for short term patches over long term solutions in the fields of intercarrier compensation and universal service.

There is no straightforward institutional reform that would force the FCC to stand up to political pressures and chart a course of analytically rigorous neutrality. One obvious priority is to staff the FCC with principled leaders who have demonstrated as much of an appetite for getting policy answers right on the merits as for appeasing political constituencies. And, so long as the person at the top meets that description, vesting ultimate authority in one decisionmaker rather than five would, as discussed, reduce much of the horse-trading that not only delays resolution of important issues, but compromises their analytical integrity when they are finally issued.

Another impediment to the FCC's neutrality comes from the formal arrangement of its staff into "bureaus" and "offices" corresponding to the obsolescent regulatory categories drawn by the Communications Act of 1934 and thus to arbitrarily defined industry segments. This organizational structure invites parochialism and occasionally outright protectionism. Spectrum policy reform, for example, is sometimes distorted by the differing perspectives of the Wireless Bureau, which takes special care to protect the incumbent cellular operators; the Office of Engineering and Technology, which looks after unlicensed uses; and the International Bureau, which oversees the spectrum used by satellite providers. A similarly arbitrary division of authority has also complicated the evolution of broadband policy. For example, the Wireline Competition Bureau, which oversees the battles between ILECs and CLECs, tends to focus disproportionately on the significance of traditional wireline platforms offered by telephone companies, as those are the only ones it regulates. Replacing this legacy structure with a regulatory orientation more in tune with industry realities would alleviate these institutional concerns at the same time it resolves the more substantive broadband policy anomalies discussed in chapters 5 and 6.

C. Humility

The FCC was created during the New Deal for two basic missions: micromanagement of the radio spectrum and traditional command-and-control regulation of telephone monopolies. As we have explained, technological developments and regulatory reforms have largely made each of those missions obsolete. The FCC must now respond by redefining its own role in an industry characterized by increasing competition and a commensurate decrease in the need for regulatory oversight.[83] To make that transition, the FCC must embrace the elusive virtue of regulatory humility.

In Alfred Kahn's words, the FCC's basic challenge is to reorient its efforts towards "establishing the conditions under which competition may be relied on to determine the outcome" and away from policies "intended, whether consciously or unconsciously, to *dictate* that outcome."[84] In practice, this means that, in an increasing number of regulatory areas, the FCC should focus more on back-end enforcement of basic competition norms, remedying only clear acts of anticompetitive conduct, instead of developing front-end prophylactic safeguards designed to anticipate all possible scenarios.[85] To be sure, at least for the foreseeable future, there are innumerable areas—such as interconnection, number portability, and intercarrier compensation—in which pre-set rules will be essential to industry stability. And the FCC thus will need to develop and superintend such rules for years to come. On the margins, however, as competition develops and relieves the need for comprehensively prescriptive regulation, the Commission should embrace the more neutral, adjudicative approach of an enforcement agency like the FTC.

This institutional reorientation will force the FCC to check its traditional instinct to "plan in advance of foreseeable events, instead of waiting to react to them."[86] The basic problem with such preemptive intervention is that, as the history of regulation has shown, policymakers are often wrong both in their predictions of how the market will develop and in their judgments of what regulatory measures will best promote consumer welfare. As discussed in chapters 7 and 8, nowhere has such bureaucratic miscalculation harmed the public interest more than in the FCC's assumption of the "wise man" role in dictating how the airwaves should be used. In contrast, the FCC's legacy has been brighter when it has exercised the passive virtues while awaiting concrete evidence that the market actually needs regulatory intervention. For example, the Commission has laudably confined itself to noting the mere prospect for "Net neutrality" rules in the event they ever become necessary (see chapter 5), rather than actually designing such rules today and imposing them on the industry before a clear need for them has been established.

Of course, when particular economic conditions demonstrably lead to market failure, regulators should intervene sooner rather than later. Our point is that regulators should not blithely assume that a market will fail if it has not already done so, nor should they proceed on the assumption that, because they have regulatory authority, they should exercise it somehow or another. This is regulatory humility: knowing when one's judgments as a policymaker cannot do better, and might do much worse, than the collective judgments of competing firms and millions of self-interested consumers operating in a genuinely free market.

* * *

In retrospect, it should not be surprising that an institution initially designed to regulate monopolies in perpetuity is poorly designed to intervene in the market just enough to promote competition and then, as appropriate, stand out of the way.[87] That new mission, however, is the FCC's most important assignment. The ultimate end game in telecommunications regulation—which, to be sure, will take many years to reach—should be a deregulatory environment in which market forces, rather than FCC officials, dictate the most productive uses of the radio spectrum, create crossplatform competition in the last mile, and devise efficient solutions to the terminating access monopoly. Of course, even in that world, regulators will play an important vestigial role in managing social welfare priorities such as universal service and 911 dialing, and they may well need to exercise some continuing oversight of basic interconnection arrangements. For the most part, however, the FCC, like Alfred Kahn's Civil Aeronautics Board, should define success as creating the conditions necessary for phasing out its legacy regulatory functions.

Appendix A

The Pricing of Network Elements

A critical issue in wireline competition policy is what price a competitive local exchange carrier (CLEC) must pay the incumbent local exchange carrier (ILEC) for the right to lease its network elements. The complexities of this subject are obscure but important, and we have written this appendix for readers who would like further background in the application of the FCC's pricing methodology: "total element long run incremental cost," or TELRIC.

The basics

As with many important questions, the 1996 Act left the FCC with considerable discretion in defining the standard for wholesale leasing rates. The Act merely specifies that those rates must be (1) "based on the cost . . . of providing" the network elements at issue, (2) "just," "reasonable," and "nondiscriminatory," (3) "determined without reference to a rate-of-return or other rate-based proceeding," and, (4) at the apparent discretion of the regulator, calibrated to "include a reasonable profit."[1] These terms set very few clear limits on a regulator's choice of vastly different cost methodologies, as the Supreme Court ultimately made clear in its 2002 decision in *Verizon Communications, Inc. v. FCC*.[2]

In the early months after enactment of the 1996 Act, there emerged four contending methodologies for setting wholesale leasing rates: *forward-looking* cost, *historical* cost, *Ramsey pricing*, and the so-called *efficient component pricing rule*. As principles for implementing the Act's "cost" standard, the last two were never really in the running.[3] This left historical cost and forward-looking cost. Although the FCC repudiated the former in 1996 and adopted a particularly strong form of the latter (TELRIC), the battle between these two alternatives continued in the courts until, in the *Verizon* case, the Supreme Court upheld the FCC's choice of TELRIC.

Whereas an historical cost approach (discussed below) focuses on the actual past costs reflected in a firm's accounting books, "[a] forward-looking costing methodology considers what it would cost today to build and operate an efficient network (or to expand an existing network) that can provide the same services as the incumbent's existing network."[4] As explained by the FCC, the policy goal of a forward-looking approach is to "replicate[], to the extent possible, the conditions of a competitive market"[5] in order to give CLECs appropriate "price signals" about when it would be efficient for them to enter particular markets.

Roughly speaking, this means that, once regulators have decided that it normally makes sense to give entrants the opportunity to lease rather than duplicate a particular facility—i.e., once they have made the "impairment" finding under section 251(d)(2)—setting the lease rate at levels found in a competitive market should theoretically ensure that, if the entrant uses the facility in combination with its own assets, it will do so on an economically efficient basis. Economic efficiency in this context means that a firm should neither enjoy an arbitrary subsidy (as where the price is set too low and discourages productive investment) nor suffer an anticompetitive handicap (as where the price is set too high and discourages desirable entry). Put differently, the rates set for shared facilities should be simultaneously (i) low enough to encourage competitive entry that adds value for consumers over the long term in the form of lower prices and greater product diversity but (ii) high enough to preserve incentives for incumbents and entrants alike to continue investing in new facilities to the extent that such investment is also needed to serve those same long run consumer welfare goals.

For such "signaling" purposes, most, but not all, economists agree that some version of forward-looking cost is superior to historical cost. "One of the most important lessons of economics is that you should look at the marginal costs and marginal benefits of decisions and ignore past or sunk costs."[6] And in fully competitive markets, prices are set not by any firm's historical costs, but by an efficient firm's forward-looking costs. Thus, for example, the price on eBay for which you could sell a laptop computer purchased two years ago is a function not of what you paid for it then, but of what newer models are on the market, what extra features they have, and what they are selling for. Before addressing the mechanics of a forward-looking methodology, however, we first address the mechanics of an historical cost methodology. As we shall see, understanding historical cost is essential to understanding forward-looking cost in general and the current policy debates *among* forward-looking cost methodologies in particular.

Historical cost

"Historical cost" and "forward-looking cost" are both "cost of service" methodologies. As the name suggests, such methodologies aim to base rates on one measure or another of a public utility's "costs." On the most abstract level, such "costs" fall into three general categories: (i) operating costs, which consist of non-capital costs such as the labor associated with maintenance and overhead, (ii) "depreciation expense," which enables a firm to account for and recover the costs of capital investment over time; and (iii) the "cost of capital," which, as discussed below, denotes the return a firm must earn on its investment to remain a viable going concern.

A traditional "historical" (or "embedded") cost methodology—the industry norm for retail ratemaking until the emergence of price cap regulation in the early 1990s—focuses on giving the incumbent an opportunity to recover from its retail or wholesale customers costs that, as reflected on its accounting books, it actually and "prudently" paid in the past. As economist Alfred Kahn has explained, regulators applying such a methodology "need[] to make determinations about which costs they [a]re prepared to authorize for inclusion in the computed company cost-of-service; and of these, which could be charged directly as operating expenses and thus included in annual revenue requirements dollar for dollar, and which capitalized, thus entering the cost of service in the form of annual allowances for depreciation and return on the undepreciated portion of the investment."[7]

A highly simplified example cuts through the accounting terminology and helps illustrate roughly how historical cost methodologies work in practice. Suppose that an incumbent bought a specialized switch in 1995 for $1 million. When purchased, the incumbent expected to keep that switch in operation until 2005, at which point, it was predicted, the switch would need to be junked and replaced with the next generation of technology. (We are assuming that the switch would have no "salvage value" at that point.) This ten-year period is known as the switch's *depreciation life,* and the overall cost of the switch would be recorded on the company's books over the next ten years as "depreciation expense." Roughly speaking, to cover its investment, the incumbent would need to recover the costs of that switch over the course of this ten year period at a base rate of $100,000 per year on average.

Of course, given the time value of money, the incumbent has every right to expect more than $1 million in the bank at the end of this period. Indeed, recouping only $1 million would produce a net loss in real money terms, so long as the rate of inflation is positive. Thus, the incumbent will try to recover from its $1 million investment a profit margin similar to what it could have earned if it had just put that money in some unrelated investment portfolio of roughly equivalent risk. This margin—a "normal profit"—is called the incumbent's *cost of capital.* If that figure is estimated at 50% over the entire ten-year life of the switch, the incumbent can expect to recover $1.5 million over that period, for an average of $150,000 per year.

A central point of applying a "historical cost" methodology to network element pricing is to ensure the hypothetical incumbent an opportunity to recover the full $1.5 million (so long as it was all "prudently incurred") from either (i) the retail rates it collects from end users, if it keeps them as its customers or (ii) the "wholesale" network element rates it collects from other carriers, to the extent capacity on the switch is devoted to them rather than to the incumbent's own retail customers. Let's suppose that, for the first five years (1995-2000) of the switch's expected ten-year life, the incumbent continues to use it solely to provide retail service to its customers. In an exceedingly simplified sense, the $750,000 the incumbent needs in order to recoup its investment over that initial five-year period is built into the retail rates it receives from its end users.* Those rates also

---

* For analytical clarity, our hypothetical embodies a number of greatly simplifying assumptions. We have abstracted away, for example, "joint and common costs" (such as the cost of the company headquarters building and the CEO's salary) as well as the "operating expenses" needed to operate the facility over time, such as electricity, labor costs for repairs and maintenance, etc. Whether and when those costs can be capitalized as part of investment is a complicated and sometimes controversial accounting question. We are also assuming the use of "straight-line" depreciation, under which the facility is depreciated at a steady rate over the course of its life. See also endnote 8 on p. 637.

include, of course, retail-specific costs as well, such as those for customer service.[8]

Now suppose that, in the year 2000, all the customers the incumbent had been serving by means of this switch sign up with a single CLEC for service, and the CLEC decides to lease the entire capacity of the switch in the form of network elements.* Under an historical cost approach, this CLEC would pay, during the term of the "lease," a prorated portion of whatever "undepreciated" costs remain on the incumbent's books. This also amounts to $150,000 per year. Now, fast-forward to 2005, and assume that the CLEC is still leasing this facility from the incumbent. If the incumbent does not replace the switch as originally expected but keeps it in service, it will nonetheless have recovered all of its historical costs. Put in accounting terms, the switch will have been fully depreciated. Thus, under a pure historical cost approach, the CLEC will pay the incumbent nothing at all, except for maintenance and other expenses, for the use of the switch in 2006. The incumbent can hardly complain about that outcome, for it has already fully recovered its historical costs. Indeed, in hindsight, the incumbent was never entitled to a brief ten-year depreciation life for this facility, and it therefore should have recovered less per year for it than it already did. In reality, however, regulators are more likely to err on the side of unrealistically long, not short, depreciation lives because that is a way to keep prices low.

Forward-looking cost

As noted, the principal alternative to the historical cost approach we have discussed so far is forward-looking cost. A forward-looking methodology rests on a long line of economic thinking on the regulatory use of *long run incremental cost* (LRIC) pricing. The LRIC formulation, popularized by Alfred Kahn in the 1970s,[9] elaborates on the *marginal cost* concept. In a perfectly competitive market, the price of a widget should

---

* This too is obviously a simplifying assumption: in reality, a CLEC will lease only a fraction of the capacity of an incumbent's switch, and the incumbent will recover the costs of the switch in any given year from a combination of (i) retail customers and (ii) other carriers (namely, UNE-purchasing CLECs and access-purchasing long distance carriers).

equal the marginal cost of producing just one more widget from a factory already built for that purpose; or at least that is the ideally efficient outcome. In the telecommunications industry, this concept of *short run* marginal cost would measure the comparatively minuscule costs of providing, *over an already built network*, just one more unit of service or capacity, such as the accommodation of a CLEC's request for capacity on a preexisting switch that has more than enough capacity to go around. These short run marginal (or incremental) costs may approach zero for any given customer.[10] For example, the overwhelming majority of switching costs are "fixed": they are incurred when a firm purchases and installs a switch for all future users, not when it later makes capacity on that switch available to any particular user.

More generally, as we discussed in chapter 1, telecommunications firms have enormous fixed costs and often tiny short run incremental costs; indeed, that is one reason why the industry was traditionally considered a natural monopoly. As a result, such firms would never recover the vast majority of their costs if regulators limited them to the recovery of short run incremental costs. The response to this problem is the concept of "long run" incremental cost, which asks not how much it would cost a firm to provide one more increment of capacity today on a facility already built yesterday, but in essence how much it would cost on average to provide such capacity on an efficient facility that the firm has *not* already purchased and whose costs must be factored into the equation. (This approach is said to measure incremental costs over a sufficiently long time horizon that all of a firm's costs are "variable" or "avoidable.") Since 1996, the FCC has adhered to a particular forward-looking cost methodology it calls "*total element* long run incremental cost" (TELRIC), whose details we discuss below.[11]

For now, we will put the terminology to one side and focus more generally on how any forward-looking cost methodology operates in practice. To that end, consider the specialized switch that we discussed above in illustrating historical costs, but with the following twist. In year 2000, when the CLEC wins the customers and wishes to lease the entire switch for which the incumbent paid $1 million in 1995, the CLEC would not necessarily pay the $150,000 figure it would have paid if the incumbent had a right to the recovery of its historical costs. Indeed, the amount that the incumbent paid in 1995 is completely irrelevant, as is the

$750,000 figure that remains as the incumbent's undepreciated "book costs" after five years of depreciation. The relevant starting point instead is (1) what it would cost to buy whatever facility an efficient carrier would obtain in 2000 to provide the functions of the actual (and older) facility the CLEC wishes to lease and (2) what the depreciation life of that replacement facility would be in a competitive environment (i.e., how long it would be expected to remain in service until it, too, would need to be replaced by next generation technology).

This difference is important because technological innovation has lowered the replacement costs of many (but by no means all) telecommunications-related facilities far below their historical costs, sometimes quite unpredictably. In our hypothetical, any unexpected improvements in switching technology between 1995 and 2000 would leave the incumbent worse off, for cost recovery purposes, under a forward-looking cost methodology than under an historical one. But before we address that divergence, we first make a brief detour into the world of state-level "UNE cost studies"—the ratemaking proceedings in which state commissions determine the underlying costs of the network elements that CLECs lease from incumbents and thus the rates they must pay.

A forward-looking cost study has two basic elements: a *cost model* and a set of *inputs*. The cost model is a computer program that purports to map out how an efficient carrier would build a network today to serve the population centers in a given geographic area. The model itself is generally quite malleable; what matter most are the "inputs" fed into it. These inputs are simply assumptions about the costs of the hypothetical network, such as: "X miles of telephone cable are needed to serve this neighborhood," "the materials needed for all that cable will cost $Y," and "hiring contractors to lay all that cable under the ground will require $Z in labor costs." Taken together, these inputs, each of which is usually the topic of vigorous dispute between dueling experts, generate the cost model's "output": the estimated replacement costs of whatever network elements a CLEC might wish to lease.

A simplified example, based on the proprietary cost model developed by HAI Consulting and used by some CLECs, helps illustrate how the game works in practice, although other cost models work somewhat differently. Suppose that a CLEC wishes to lease a loop to serve a suburban business. Regulators do not even try to consider the "cost" of that loop in isolation. Instead, they feed into the model a set of assumptions about what it would cost a single efficient carrier today to deploy loop facilities to serve the whole geographic area at issue. Next they divide that "total investment" figure by the number of working lines in that area to produce an average investment per line. The regulators then adjust that number to account for such variables as projected maintenance costs over time and a reasonable allocation of joint and common costs. They take the ensuing "average loop cost" and partially "deaverage" it across different "zones," which are usually defined by the density of customer locations within a given area. (Thus, to account for differences in economies of density, the projected loop cost for customers in the high density zone representing downtown urban areas will be significantly lower than the corresponding loop cost for customers in the lower density zones representing suburban or rural areas.) Regulators then divide the relevant loop cost for a given zone into monthly increments spanning the loop's depreciation life. The resulting number forms a preliminary basis for the monthly fee the CLEC must pay the incumbent for use of the loop when serving a customer in the zone at issue.

Like the central inputs concerning depreciation lives and the cost of capital—which are necessarily quite subjective, whether the inquiry is based on forward-looking or historical cost—many other inputs in this equation are studies in regulatory indeterminacy. How, in this hypothetical network, should the loops be routed to serve the various population centers with optimal efficiency? How much spare capacity (e.g., how many extra lines) should be laid in the ground now to forestall the need to dig up the streets all over again to accommodate customer turnover, repair needs, growing demand for extra lines per household, and perhaps future population growth? What percentage of telephone lines should be hung in the air between telephone poles instead of buried underground? How much will it cost to hire the contractors to dig up the ground (or, in developed areas, pavement) to lay those lines?

The subjectivity of such hypothetical inquiries explains why cost studies normally take years to complete and why each side can always find something to complain about in the result. It also explains why regulators conducting this type of inquiry keep their eyes cast sidelong at the bottom-line network element rates their input decisions will generate—which, they hope, will be low enough to spark competitive entry but high enough to keep the incumbent investing in its network and protect it from serious financial trouble.

The network element rates we have discussed so far relate to what are known as *recurring costs*. These are the costs of long term capital investments (such as the loop or a switch), together with the associated maintenance and other expenses, that an incumbent recovers on a monthly basis over a long period of time, whether in the form of wholesale charges to CLECs or ordinary telephone bills sent to retail customers. The other major cost category for which CLECs are expected to reimburse incumbents are known as *non-recurring costs*. These are the one-time costs that an incumbent incurs in "processing" and "provisioning" a CLEC's order for network elements. Take, for example, the case of hot cuts, described in chapter 3. When a CLEC places an order for an unbundled loop, the incumbent must process the order; identify the loop to be cut over; and (most of the time) send a technician to the "main distribution frame" to unplug that loop from the incumbent's switch and connect it to a separate circuit leading ultimately to the CLEC's switch. The cutover must be done in close coordination with the CLEC, to ensure that the end user does not lose telephone service in the interim. These one-time functions impose costs on the incumbent, which it traditionally recovers from the CLEC in the form of an up-front, one-time charge in addition to whatever recurring monthly charge it may separately recover for the loop itself.

In arguing for UNE-P rights (see chapter 3), CLECs have sometimes claimed that the retail rates they could charge their mass market customers would be inadequate to cover the up-front charges they must pay incumbents for performing hot cuts (often around $50 per line) under a UNE-L strategy. That is so, the CLECs say, because of high "churn" rates in this market. Unlike larger business customers, residential and small business customers rarely commit to buying services from any given wireline CLEC for longer than a few months, and they frequently hop from carrier to carrier before they can pay substantial revenues to any one carrier. Each time they switch carriers, they force the incumbent—and ultimately the CLECs—to absorb the costs of sending technicians to the frame to unplug the loop from one carrier's switch and redirect it to another's. To this, the incumbents respond that "churn" is just another word for competition, that a CLEC's inability to cover the costs of churn indicates that its business plan is economically wasteful, and that a CLEC's insecurity about holding on to its end users is no reason for granting that CLEC even cheaper access to the incumbent's network.

Where forward-looking and historical costs diverge

Historical costs and forward-looking costs are likely to diverge sharply in any industry that, like telecommunications, is marked by unexpected technological innovation and unpredictably fluctuating facilities costs. Let's return to our original example above. Suppose that a revolutionary new technology had been invented in 1999 that rendered the 1995 switch unexpectedly obsolescent in the sense that, only four years into its projected life, it is suddenly much less efficient than the new cutting-edge switches now available on the market. As we noted earlier, if a new technology provides the same (or better) functions at much lower prices, the "forward-looking" cost of the obsolescent facility may be dramatically lower than its historical cost. Thus, in our example, if the cutting-edge replacement switch could provide the same functions as the old switch at only $500,000 (rather than the original $1 million purchase price), then—if we hold all other variables constant, including depreciation and cost of capital—the CLEC would pay the incumbent only $75,000 per year, rather than $150,000. Now, the incumbent may or may not choose to replace its 1995 switch with the newer, more efficient alternative. After all, it has already incurred the sunk costs of the 1995 facility, and it will receive the same forward-looking network element rates from the CLEC whether it buys a new switch or not. So, no matter when it replaces the old switch, the net result is that, by 2005, the incumbent will be left holding the bag for a sizable portion of its original outlay.

Note that, to some degree, this shortfall may be a function of the erroneously long ten-year depreciation life the regulatory agency assigned to the switch in 1995 when it failed to foresee the technological innovation that would occur in 1999. Let's say that the innovation actually causes the incumbent to replace its 1995 switch in 2002 rather than 2005. If it had been foreseeable in 1995 that the switch would be rendered obsolescent by 1999, the incumbent might have either (i) waited to replace its existing (pre-1995) switch until 1999, thereby incurring no new sunk costs until then, when the more efficient technology became available, or (ii) purchased the 1995 switch anyway but tried to persuade the regulator to set a shorter depreciation life for it: seven years rather than ten. Under any cost methodology, that shorter depreciation life would have entitled the incumbent to recover its 1995 investment more quickly. Also, technological obsolescence is not the only factor that can strand investments; others include drops in network demand due to, among other things, the unforeseen emergence of rival transmission platforms.

Much of the debate about the relative merits of forward-looking and historical cost methodologies relates to the concern that, because costs in the telecommunications industry tend to decline over time, any forward-looking cost methodology will necessarily entitle incumbents to lower cost recovery over time and inevitably "strand" (preclude recovery of) many of its sunk costs. But that concern, which led the Bell companies to crusade for an historical cost methodology until finally rebuffed by the Supreme Court in 2002, is overstated on several levels.

First, network costs do not invariably fall over time; although the costs of some elements (such as computerized switches) do predictably decrease, the costs of others do not. For example, the cost of loop facilities is largely a function of hiring the skilled labor forces needed to install and maintain them, and those labor costs often *increase* with time. What's more, the copper loop facilities that CLECs lease from incumbents might have been installed long ago, such that they are now fully depreciated after decades of cost recovery through retail rates. Under a pure historical cost approach, the incumbent would be entitled to charge little more for the use of these facilities beyond maintenance expenses and any non-recurring costs of making them available to the CLECs. In contrast, under a forward-looking approach, the incumbent would be entitled to recover the full costs of replacing those facilities, including not just the costs of the underlying materials (copper, fiber-optic cable, electronics, etc.), but also the costs of hiring the labor force needed to dig up the streets to install them. Significantly, many (though not all) state commissions have tended to reduce the price of all network elements over time, even though the underlying costs for some of those elements—such as the loop—might seem to be taking the opposite trajectory. ILECs cite this as evidence of growing state commission bias in favor of CLECs. CLECs cite it as evidence that state commissions have learned to discount ILEC advocacy, which, they say, succeeded in producing inflated network element rates in the 1990s.

Second, even with respect to network elements whose costs do decrease over time, such as switches, any divergence between historical and forward-looking cost methodologies is more likely to result from *unexpect-*

edly fast technological innovation and cross-platform competition than from the fact of fast technological innovation itself. After all, predictable innovation is theoretically factored into the depreciation lives under either approach, and causes costs to be recovered more quickly than otherwise. As in the example above, underrecovery arises mostly where the regulator or incumbent underestimates the pace of recovery and thus sets erroneously long depreciation lives.

To be sure, even if the rate of technological innovation and cross-platform competition is correctly predicted, an incumbent subject to a forward-looking cost methodology could be systematically deprived of any opportunity to recover its investment in a "declining cost" element if the forward-looking cost is recalibrated several times during the course of the element's life. Go back to our previous example of a switch that is purchased in 1995 for $1 million and is expected to remain in use for 10 years. If a regulator set rates for the facility in 1995 as though its forward-looking cost would *remain* at $1 million during that entire period, the incumbent would achieve satisfactory cost recovery only if the original rate remained in force until 2005. (In our example, which takes the cost of capital into account, the incumbent would expect an average yearly recovery of $150,000 for a total of $1.5 million by 2005.) But what if the regulator revisits network element pricing in 1998, and then again in 2002, and each time determines that the forward-looking cost of the element has declined—*exactly as expected?* The regulator will set a lower forward-looking cost for the element and (if all else is held equal) the same ten-year rate of depreciation. The result of such constant recalibration of an element's forward-looking cost is that, over time, the incumbent will recover less and less than $150,000 per year—and by 2005 will not remotely approach the hoped-for $1.5 million.

Although incumbents have cited this result as a basis for criticizing TELRIC as such, that criticism is properly directed at TELRIC's implementation rather than its underlying methodology. In this example, the regulator's mistake was to ignore, in 1995, the effect that future cost proceedings themselves would have on the incumbent's ability to recover its investment. The solution to that problem is to take those future cost proceedings into account from the outset, either by shortening or "accelerating" the depreciation lives of the facilities in question or by increasing the cost of capital to reflect the risks of regulation. In short, what appears as a big-picture objection to any forward-looking cost methodology as such is, in reality, just an objection to a particular mistake in the implementation of such a methodology.

Varieties of forward-looking cost methodologies

We have addressed the question of network element cost methodologies as though it presented a binary choice: historical cost vs. forward-looking cost. In fact, there are many different methodological species within each genus, and there are also hybrid methodologies that contain attributes of both historical and forward-looking costs. Because the regulatory consensus now favors use of *some* kind of forward-looking cost methodology, we now focus more closely on the differences *among* such methodologies.

As originally adopted by the FCC in 1996, TELRIC "takes as given" only two aspects of the existing network: the locations of existing "wire centers" (i.e., switches), and the use of wireline rather than wireless technology. In all other respects, state regulators applying TELRIC are free (and theoretically compelled) to base costs entirely on their best guess about what an efficient network, built from scratch today, would look like.

In September 2003, the FCC formally sought comment on whether it should revise TELRIC to root it "more firmly . . . in the real-world attributes of the existing network, rather than the speculative attributes of a purely hypothetical network."[12] Sometimes this line-drawing controversy is cast as a debate about how "long run" the FCC's "incremental cost" methodology should be (the "LR" and "IC" in "TELRIC"). This is a somewhat controversial characterization of the debate because, as noted, the term "long run" is normally used to signify that a cost methodology measures not just the "short run" marginal costs of accommodating a CLEC's needs on already-built network facilities, but also the fixed capital investment in the facilities themselves. For the most part, there is no serious dispute that an incumbent should recover the full forward-looking costs of its capital investments. The question instead concerns the extent to which the hypothetical replacement facilities, whose present-day costs are at issue, should resemble the network facilities currently in the ground, both in their engineering pedigree and in their geographical placement.

Perhaps the easiest way to understand this controversy is to consider three concrete examples of how taking (or not taking) attributes of the existing network "as given" can make a practical difference in the forward-looking costs of network elements:

Example 1. First, suppose that the incumbent would have configured its network much differently if only it had known from the outset where population centers would spring up and grow over a given geographic area; specifically, it would have placed its central offices in vastly different locations, closer to what turned out to be the major residential and business developments. Suppose also that the incumbent would have included *fewer* wire centers overall in its network, if only it had predicted that advances in fiber-optic transmission technology would make it more cost-efficient to design a network with longer loops and fewer switches. When a CLEC wishes to lease a real-world loop from such an incumbent, what should it pay: (i) the cost of replacing that loop between the customer's location and the location of the real-world central office or (ii) the cost, in a completely hypothetical network, of building a loop from the customer premises to wherever the incumbent would have placed the relevant central office if only it had enjoyed greater foresight several decades ago?

Example 2. Let's say that regulators have chosen answer (i) to the previous question. Now suppose that the incumbent has copper loops throughout its network, but another carrier building a state-of-the-art, "most efficient" network today might well make much greater use of fiber-optic facilities to connect customer locations to central offices. What should a CLEC leasing a real-world loop pay: (i) the cost of replacing purely copper loops (like those it is actually leasing), or (ii) the cost of the fiber-optic facilities that would be deployed in a hypothetical state-of-the-art network?

Example 3. Suppose that a substantial number of analog switches remain in an incumbent's network, but that all carriers in the world today are installing digital switches. (In fact, very few analog switches remain in any carrier's network, so this example was chosen simply for its illustrative value.) All else held constant, should the CLEC leasing capacity on one of these analog switches pay a share of the cost of replacing the analog switch with (i) another analog switch today, or (ii) a digital switch? Assume, for these purposes, that analog switches are so obsolete that *they could not even be purchased on the market today*—and that the cost of obtaining one with the proper functionality would thus be enormous, because a new factory would need to built for the purpose of manufacturing one.

The answers given to these three questions mark points along a spectrum of cost methodologies. On one end of the spectrum is what is known as a *green field* approach to forward-looking cost. This approach takes nothing at all for granted about the existing network, including the locations of the incumbent's central offices. Instead, the cost inquiry would give free reign to the imagination of regulators in formulating how an efficient carrier would design an entire network from scratch today—and would set replacement costs on that basis. In theory, regulators might not even be confined to imagining more efficient designs for a wireline network, since they would enjoy unbounded discretion to posit, for replacement cost purposes, a *wireless* network that performs most of the same functions just as well.

On the other end of the spectrum is a so-called *reproduction cost* approach, under which a regulator asks what it would cost to replicate the network in all of its physical particulars. In its pure form, that approach gives rise to extreme cost anomalies. For example, if a regulator were compelled to "take as given" the analog character of the existing switch in considering the costs of replacing it, the estimated costs—and network element rates—of switching would soar off the charts, for the reason identified above. Such anomalies explain why, 80 years ago, Justice Louis Brandeis denigrated any cost methodology that woodenly asks "what it would cost to reproduce the identical property" whose costs are at issue.[13]

Few people seriously advocate using either a pure "green field" or a "reproduction cost" approach in pricing network elements. Rather, the real area of disagreement lies in the answer to questions like the one posed in Example 2 above: questions concerning the extent to which the basic characteristics of the existing network should be taken for granted in calculating replacement costs. As a general matter, CLECs prefer pricing rules near the "green field" end of the methodological spectrum, while incumbents prefer a methodology closer to the "reproduction cost" approach. This is because the more that costs are based on hypothetical, more efficient alternatives to the incumbent's actual facilities, the lower the ensuing network element prices are likely to be. (Indeed, there are very few networks built today whose efficiency is invulnerable to extensive second-guessing.)

In general, the CLECs argue that taking anything as given about the existing network improperly combines aspects of a long run cost methodology with aspects of a short run methodology. In so doing, they observe that a long run approach permits recovery of capital investment (the lion's share of network element costs) only because it presupposes the variability of all assets and thus, the CLECs say, the replacement of those assets with more efficient present-day alternatives. The CLECs add that the incumbents' insistence on taking aspects of the existing network "as given" is consistent only with a short run cost methodology, which treats very little of a firm's asset base as variable, but with the consequence (the CLECs maintain) of precluding recovery of that underlying investment.

On a more practical level, the CLECs further argue, as discussed in chapter 3, that these leasing rates *need* to be low to enable new entrants to get a foothold in local markets and develop a sizable customer base before making capital investments in new network facilities of their own. This strategy of protecting new entrants—sometimes referred to as "infant industry" protectionism—is controversial as a policy matter because carried too far it can severely distort the growth of an industry. For example, to the extent that network element rates fall below "cost" (however defined), they not only favor CLECs over incumbents, but also favor some CLECs over others by subsidizing the operations of non-facilities-based entrants and allowing them to underprice facilities-based entrants. If regulators wish to induce carriers in a particular market to invest in network infrastructure, this is a counterproductive strategy, unless perhaps they make clear at the outset that this regulatory largesse will be limited in duration.

This general theme underlies the incumbents' primary policy argument for higher network element rates than TELRIC has produced so far. Low rates, they say, would give CLECs every incentive to avoid investment risks by renting from the incumbent on a monthly basis, often without any long term commitment, rather than build out their own networks. (In theory, the cost-of-capital input in the forward-looking cost calculus is supposed to reflect all relevant investment risks, but incumbents express skepticism that it does in practice.) The incumbents add that low rates would leave them with few incentives to invest in new facilities (or in maintaining or upgrading old ones) if, upon the first sign that particular facilities are a good investment, CLECs may instantly use them to serve customers of their own at unbeatably low retail rates that reflect none of the costs of the incumbents' *less* successful investments. As Judge Frank Easterbrook of the Seventh Circuit sums up these twin concerns: "Prices for unbundled elements affect not only the allocation of income among producers, but also new investment and innovation: if the price to rivals is too low, they won't build their own plant (why make capital investments when you can buy for less, one unbundled element at a time?), and the incumbents won't maintain or upgrade their facilities (why make costly capital investments if you have to sell local loops to rivals for less than it costs to produce them?)."[14]

Note the striking similarity between these arguments and the incumbents' various rationales, discussed in chapter 3, for excluding particular facilities from the list of network elements subject to mandatory leasing in the first place. These pricing arguments tend to have the greatest force when, in conducting the "impairment" inquiry, regulators have already erred on the side of keeping elements on that list in close cases—i.e., when they have arguably overstated the infeasibility of duplicating an incumbent's facilities.

In 1996, when the FCC first considered how many attributes of the existing network regulators should take as given in conducting a forward-looking cost analysis, the CLECs won in a rout. Indeed, in adopting TELRIC, the FCC came as close to the hypothetical "green field" approach as a regulator could feasibly come without actually adopting that approach itself. As noted, the FCC broadly concluded that the forward-looking replacement cost of network facilities should take as given *nothing* about the physical attributes of the existing network except for current switch locations (and the use of wireline technology). In all other respects, the replacement costs at issue are the costs of obtaining, installing, and maintaining the most efficient facilities currently available to perform the network functions at issue, even if those facilities bear little resemblance to the facilities that the CLEC will actually lease.[15]

TELRIC is sometimes called a *scorched node* approach to forward-looking cost because it imagines, in effect, that the entire network has been blown up, leaving nothing but the "nodes" (wire center locations) around which engineers will "reconstruct" a new, optimally efficient network. The hypothetical costs of that reconstructed network then produce the rates that CLECs will pay incumbents. Thus, if an efficient carrier would rebuild the network today with more fiber than copper, and would place its feeder and distribution cables in different places than they now appear, the costs of building *that* network, rather than the costs of rebuilding the existing network in its current configuration and with its current emphasis on copper facilities, are what ultimately determine what CLECs will pay for leasing facilities in that existing network.*

Prospects for revisions to TELRIC

In its 2002 decision in *Verizon*, the Supreme Court affirmed the FCC's decision not just to adopt forward-looking cost rather than historical cost as the network element pricing standard, but also, deferring broadly to the FCC's presumed expertise, to adopt TELRIC in its original form. As the Court explained, "[w]e cannot say whether the passage of time will show

---

* In theory, *non-recurring* charges under TELRIC are subject to the same near-green field cost principles, although there is considerable debate about what that means in practice. To understand the conundrum, consider the following example. Suppose that a CLEC wishes to provide DSL service to a customer over an incumbent's loop and directs the incumbent to remove 40-year-old "load coils" from that loop. These devices were initially designed to "tune" the line to pass voice signals more efficiently, but they do so at the expense of blocking out the high frequency ones used in DSL technology. Consequently, an efficient carrier building a new network today would not place these devices on any loop that could otherwise be used to provide DSL service. This fact raises the question: when the incumbent dispatches technicians to remove these devices from the loop at the CLEC's request, should it be able to recover the considerable labor costs of doing so (because it has unavoidably incurred them), or not (because these devices would not appear on a similar loop deployed today)? In 1999, the FCC seemed to answer this question in the affirmative, leading CLECs to criticize (and incumbents to laud) that ruling as inconsistent with TELRIC's general emphasis on taking almost nothing for granted about the existing network in estimating forward-looking costs. *See* Third Report and Order, *Implementation of the Local Competition Provisions of the Telecommunications Act of 1996*, 15 FCC Rcd 3696, ¶ 193 (1999); *but cf.* Report and Order and Order on Remand and Further Notice of Proposed Rulemaking, *Review of the Section 251 Unbundling Obligations of Incumbent Local Exchange Carriers*, 18 FCC Rcd 16,978, ¶ 641 (2003) (allowing state agencies some discretion in resolving issue pending further FCC action).

competition prompted by TELRIC to be an illusion, but TELRIC appears to be a reasonable policy for now[.]"[16] The FCC retains broad discretion to change its mind on its interpretation of the statutory "cost" requirement so long as it provides an adequate rationale.[17] And, in September 2003, just after it had issued its controversial order in the *Triennial Review* proceeding (see chapter 3), the FCC announced in a Notice of Proposed Rulemaking that it would revisit the methodological underpinnings of TELRIC. Specifically, it proposed to refocus the cost inquiry more on the documented present-day costs of incumbents as they build out their networks and less on the costs of a hypothetical "most efficient" carrier that is imagined to build a new network from the ground up.[18]

When it originally adopted TELRIC in 1996, the Commission indicated that it would "issue additional guidance" on its pricing rules "[i]n the aftermath of the [state] arbitrations and relying on the state experience" in using TELRIC to set actual rates.[19] After seven years of such experience, the Commission expressed concern that "the excessively hypothetical nature of the TELRIC inquiry" had produced, in many state proceedings, "a 'black box' from which a variety of possible rates may emerge," and the "variable results may not reflect genuine cost differences."[20] TELRIC's main opponents argue that state commissions have incentives to exercise their discretion under this highly open-ended cost methodology by systematically ratcheting network element rates down. That phenomenon, they claim, follows from any regulator's short term political incentives to emphasize, at least on the margins, a proposed policy's short term benefits (such as the rapid emergence of UNE-based competition) and to de-emphasize any associated long term costs (such as inefficient underinvestment in network infrastructure).[21]

On a more substantive level, the Commission separately sought comment on a "central internal tension[]" that it had recently perceived in the traditional formulation of TELRIC. That formulation, it explained, "purports to replicate the conditions of a competitive market by assuming that the latest technology is deployed throughout the hypothetical network, while at the same time assuming that this hypothetical network benefits from the economies of scale associated with serving all of the lines in a study area. In the real world, however, even in extremely competitive markets, firms do not instantaneously replace all of their facilities with every improvement in technology. Thus, even the most efficient carrier's network will reflect a mix of new and older technology at any given time"—a point that TELRIC, with its traditional emphasis on a hypothetical "most efficient" network, tends to ignore.[22]

Merely observing that any efficient firm has a mix of new and old assets is not a complete argument for changing TELRIC. The defenders of TELRIC point out that, in a perfectly competitive wholesale market, technological innovation would instantaneously reduce wholesale *prices* to cost even though no rational carrier would instantaneously replace its *assets* the moment some slightly improved version appears on the market. That is because, in this purely hypothetical market of perfect wholesale competition, many different facilities-based carriers would compete for the same customers; and even though no *one* carrier would have only the most efficient facilities *throughout* its network, *some* carrier would have the most efficient facilities needed for any *given* wholesale service. As a result, that carrier's lower costs for that service would set the price a wholesale customer would end up paying. TELRIC, the defenders say, merely replicates this dynamic of a fully competitive market.

In its Notice, the Commission suggested nonetheless that TELRIC may be internally *inconsistent* in its application of this "perfectly competitive market" construct. As previously discussed, TELRIC models do assume a highly competitive market for some purposes, as where they presuppose that technological innovations will instantaneously and comprehensively drive costs down throughout the network. But, for other purposes, those models assume a very different kind of market: one dominated by a single ubiquitous carrier. For example, the model represents all the customer locations in a given region, and then asks how much it would cost to serve all of them. As a result, the costs modeled are those incurred by a carrier that can expect to serve all the customers within a given geographic region. Such a carrier's economies of scale and density may be dramatically greater (and its per-customer costs correspondingly lower) than those of a carrier in a "perfectly efficient" market. Likewise, TELRIC models have traditionally asked what an *incumbent's* costs of capital are, or what the average capital costs are of companies in a range of normally competitive industries, not what the potentially exorbitant costs of capital would be for a carrier that seeks to build out an enormously expensive facilities-based network in a perfectly competitive market already populated by many other facilities-based carriers all competing for the same customers.

The Commission expressed concern that, by "[s]imultaneously assuming a market inhabited by multiple competitors and one with a ubiquitous carrier with a very large market share," TELRIC "may work to reduce estimates of forward-looking costs below the costs that would actually be found even in an extremely competitive market" and thereby "undermine the incentive for either competitive LECs or incumbent LECs to build new facilities, even when it is efficient for them to do so."[23] AT&T has responded to this concern about TELRIC's internal consistency by recasting that methodology as a mechanism for simulating the price-disciplining conditions not of a perfectly *competitive* market, with multiple carriers, but of a perfectly *contestable* market—i.e., a market that is occupied by only one carrier (with correspondingly large scale economies) but that is nonetheless susceptible to immediate competitive entry at all points.[24] The incumbents reply that this construct is just as theoretically unsound as the "perfect competition" model because, for example, it assumes away the entry and exit costs of the potential entrants in this hypothetically "contestable" market.[25] More generally, they say, the increasingly byzantine economic constructs offered to support the current formulation of TELRIC reveal the detachment of that formulation from economically meaningful phenomena.

As this book goes to press, the Commission has taken no further action on its 2003 proposal to resolve TELRIC's purported tension and alleviate some of its indeterminacy by "more firmly root[ing]" TELRIC "in the real-world attributes of the existing network, rather than the speculative attributes of a purely hypothetical network."[26] The Commission's apparent loss of appetite for methodological change probably stems from the complex theoretical and political relationship between these network element pricing issues on the one hand and, on the other, the continuing controversies about the extent to which incumbents must make their network elements available to CLECs in the first place. On a political level, some industry observers believe that the same narrow coalition that voted to sustain the UNE platform in the *Triennial Review Order* lost any inclination to ease the related regulatory obligations of the Bell companies once it became clear that the D.C. Circuit would agree with key elements of the Bells' challenges to that *Order*.

On a theoretical level, the *Triennial Review Order*, combined with the impending technological transformation of this industry, presents a complex new dimension to network element rate-setting that may ultimately overshadow in practical significance the sort of methodological fine-tuning that the Commission proposed in 2003. As discussed in chapters 4-6, the day will arrive before too long when many, if not most, Americans place VoIP calls over the same broadband connections that they use for access to the Internet. In part because cable companies lead telephone companies in deploying facilities for broadband access, the FCC decided, in the *Triennial Review Order*, to spur cross-platform broadband competition by removing certain next generation ("packetized") loops from the list of elements that incumbent telephone companies must lease to their rivals under section 251.

What this means for present purposes is that an incumbent's networks will consist increasingly of elements that CLECs cannot lease at TELRIC-based rates and that may diverge technologically from the elements that incumbents would be deploying if they were designing a network optimized for voice services alone. Since (as we discuss in chapter 5) the legacy elements that CLECs can lease share some of the same underlying physical infrastructure as the next generation elements that CLECs cannot lease, this development may eventually pose complex issues of cost allocation no matter how the FCC resolves the logically independent questions it has asked about what sorts of characteristics the cost inquiry should take as given about the incumbent's existing network.

A related aspect of the *Triennial Review Order* raises another difficult set of issues as well. As incumbents gradually replace legacy facilities that CLECs can lease, such as copper loops, with next generation facilities that CLECs cannot lease, such as "packetized" fiber-based loops, the *Triennial Review Order* requires in some circumstances that the incumbents keep the former in service to accommodate the needs of their rivals. How should access to these "grandfathered" facilities be priced? The answer is complicated. TELRIC is ostensibly designed to convey price signals about efficient duplication of existing facilities. By hypothesis, these facilities will be obsolescent—and thus presumptively irrational to duplicate in anything resembling their present form—once incumbents begin widespread deployment of next generation fiber facilities. The CLECs have argued that the concept of "price signals" is meaningless in such circumstances and that it would be economically wasteful for them to pay anything more for access to these facilities than the incumbent's ongoing maintenance costs. That argument may have particular resonance with policymakers to the extent that the incumbents' historical costs for these facilities have been fully depreciated, such that there can be no valid claim of regulatory confiscation. Indeed, some observers contend that the Commission has indefinitely delayed any serious reconsideration of TELRIC in part because it believes that there is a decreasing need to worry about getting price signals "right" when the only elements to which those price signals apply are legacy narrowband facilities in an increasingly broadband world.

The practical consequences of the FCC's inaction may be minimal because it is unclear how much real-world difference a formal change in methodology would make in any event. At the end of the day, even if it makes significant changes to TELRIC, the FCC is unlikely to paint with a fine enough brush that it divests the state commissions of their customary discretion to set rates within a fairly broad range.

Appendix B

Enforcement Mechanisms Under the 1996 Act

The FCC's enforcement apparatus

By longstanding tradition, the FCC conducts two basic types of enforcement proceedings. First, under section 207 of the Communications Act, anyone aggrieved by a carrier's unlawful conduct may file a complaint either in federal district court or with the FCC, using the procedure set out in section 208. Sections 206 and 207 promise that the complainant may recover the "full amount of any damages sustained," but not any additional damages (such as punitive damages).[1] Second, in addition to these privately initiated proceedings, the FCC has independent authority to investigate violations of the Act, its regulations, and filed tariffs. For run-of-the-mill violations, the FCC's fining authority is limited to $6,000 per offense, with an additional $300 for each day the action continues.[2] But where a common carrier "repeatedly" or "willfully" violates its legal obligations—terms the FCC has construed expansively to include most major transgressions—the Commission can assess a "forfeiture penalty" of as much as $120,000 per day for each offense, up to an inflation-adjusted cap of $1.325 million in 2004 for each action or failure to act.[3] The FCC formally initiates a forfeiture proceeding with the issuance of a so-called "Notice of Apparent Liability,"[4] although in practice the FCC often negotiates the terms of any remedy with the investigated party before the Notice is issued.

In the 1996 Act, Congress grafted a whole new model of regulation onto this preexisting statutory framework. Before 1996, and particularly before the rise of competition in the long distance and equipment manufacturing markets, the FCC's complaint procedures were generally invoked not by rival carriers, but by consumers aggrieved by a provider's failure to deliver on its promised services. Such complaints were generally tested against the tariff filed by the regulated service provider. Under the filed rate doctrine (discussed in chapter 2), the tariff creates a legal regime of its own, displacing all other sources of law and specifying, at least in some cases, what measure of damages is available.[5] Beginning in the 1970s, the FCC entertained complaints about *business-to-business* conduct from new entrants in the equipment manufacturing and long distance markets, but it was notably ineffective in remedying them.[6] That ineffectiveness, in fact, became an issue in the antitrust litigation that the government and private parties pursued against AT&T in the 1970s and 1980s, and it helped justify the post-divestiture line-of-business restrictions imposed on the newly independent Bell companies, as noted in chapter 13. Indeed, if the FCC had been able to confront the potential for monopoly leveraging directly through effective enforcement measures, those restrictions might have been unnecessary from the outset.[7] By introducing a host of new carrier-to-carrier obligations into the preexisting regulatory regime, the Act implicitly called on the FCC to focus its enforcement energies, for the first time, on disputes about the terms of cooperation between rival carriers.

The FCC's new mission under the 1996 Act is complicated by the fact that many of the enforceable legal obligations that one carrier owes another are derived not directly from the 1996 Act or the FCC's regulations, nor from any federally filed tariff, but from state-approved interconnection agreements. The state commissions themselves normally enforce those obligations, although some such enforcement is channeled to private arbitration. Although the Act does not expressly authorize the state commissions to enforce interconnection agreements, all appellate courts to consider the question have concluded that, under "a common sense reading of the statute," the express authority of state agencies to approve or reject interconnection agreements impliedly authorizes them to interpret and enforce those agreements.[8]

There is considerable uncertainty about the extent of the FCC's role in enforcing the obligations that are contained in interconnection agreements or, more generally, set forth in sections 251 and 252 themselves.[9] Regardless of the extent of that role, however, the FCC retains authority to enforce local competition obligations arising under other sources of federal law, ranging from section 271 checklist obligations to various pro-competitive conditions undertaken as part of a merger approval between telecommunications carriers.[10]

To the extent that the FCC enforces wholesale obligations on incumbent providers, it seeks to ensure that those obligations are "something [that] carriers take seriously, and not merely a cost of doing business."[11] To that end, Chairman William Kennard created a stand-alone Enforcement Bureau in 1999 as an important first step in reorienting the FCC's mission to implement the 1996 Act. In so doing, he announced "a new enforcement ethic, a fundamental change in the way we do enforcement at the FCC" that would be "central to our mission."[12] And his successor, Chairman Michael Powell, asked Congress in 2001 to raise the limits on the agency's fining authority, authorize it to assess punitive damages, and enable it to award attorney's fees to the prevailing party.[13] While Congress has yet to act on this request, the FCC has since tried to underscore its commitment to aggressive enforcement by making examples of errant Bell companies. In 2002, it fined SBC $6 million for purportedly violating a condition of its merger with Ameritech related to the provision of network elements to CLECs,[14] and in 2004 it penalized Qwest $9 million for failing to file various interconnection agreements with state commissions, as required by section 252(a).[15]

Given the FCC's limited experience in acting as an enforcement agency, it is far from clear how it arrives at the particular dollar amounts in its notices of apparent liability. In theory, the FCC has constrained its discretion on such questions by adopting a Forfeiture Policy Statement, which sets out a number of factors that dictate the appropriate fine.[16] But in practice, the FCC regularly ignores these factors and relies instead on three principal considerations: whether the action had a potentially competitively significant impact; whether the firm's conduct was undertaken in knowing disregard of the FCC's rules; and whether the fine is "excessive." In justifying the $9 million dollar figure against Qwest, for example, the FCC pointed to these considerations as well as the fact that a number of state agencies had already taken remedial action and others were considering doing so.[17] Ultimately, the FCC may well decide on a more formulaic approach, but for now, it retains considerable discretion to tailor the fines to particular circumstances and to leave the ultimate amount up to behind-the-scenes negotiations.[18] When the penalized carrier agrees to a particular dollar figure beforehand, of course, its agreement renders the enterprise of formally justifying that figure somewhat academic.

The FCC's capacities and experience as an enforcement agency remain relatively limited. Over time, the FCC may begin to regularize its processes and rely more extensively on the sorts of tools employed by the Federal Trade Commission, such as the issuance of administrative subpoenas on the front end and cease-and-desist orders on the back end. In that regard, one major challenge for the FCC is to act as an enforcement agency at the same time that it regularly engages in rulemaking and other negotiations with the entities that are the targets of enforcement efforts. As of this writing, the FCC's continued emphasis on its quasi-legislative functions continues to eclipse its prosecutorial and adjudicative functions. If, over time, the FCC's emphasis shifts from developing the rules of local competition to enforcing them, its institutional priorities may shift as well.

Enforcement of interconnection agreements

As noted, the 1996 Act created a new mechanism for regulating the relationship between the incumbent providers and new competitors—the "interconnection agreement." Such agreements are odd hybrid animals that reflect the Act's sharing of responsibility between state and federal authorities: they are conceived under federal law but implemented, for the most part, by state commissions formed under state law. Their purpose is to protect competitors from an incumbent's incentive to withhold its cooperation—an incentive that arises because, as one court put it, the incumbent "stands to gain financially if customers become dissatisfied with [the competitor's] local service,"[19] and thus switch back to the incumbent provider.

To date, the primary vehicles for enforcing interconnection agreements are schemes of self-executing penalties contained in so-called "performance assurance plans." These plans, to which the Bell companies "voluntarily" agreed in order to win state commission endorsement (and ultimately FCC approval) of their section 271 applications to enter the long distance market, measure various areas of wholesale performance and impose automatic penalties for non-compliance. In general, these plans are relatively crude mechanisms for guarding against anticompetitive conduct, may not stay in place for the long term, and may not change as the relevant wholesale performance issues evolve. Moreover, their future remains uncertain, as some reviewing courts have overruled attempts by state agencies to add new self-executing penalties, at least outside of the established process for devising interconnection agreements.[20] To be sure, such rulings do not preclude state commissions from imposing penalties on incumbents for violating interconnection agreements, but they do require those commissions to hold evidentiary proceedings on both liability and damages before doing so. To date, however, few such proceedings have taken place, leaving many important issues unresolved and the effectiveness of such proceedings an open question.[21] Indeed, it is not always clear whether the orders in such proceedings should be appealed to federal or state court.[22]

Statutory Addendum

Note to readers—The following are selected provisions of the Communications Act of 1934, as amended by the Telecommunications Act of 1996. Practitioners should consult the most recent version of the U.S. Code when using this Addendum.

47 U.S.C. § 151

Purposes of chapter; Federal Communications Commission created

For the purpose of regulating interstate and foreign commerce in communication by wire and radio so as to make available, so far as possible, to all the people of the United States, without discrimination on the basis of race, color, religion, national origin, or sex, a rapid, efficient, Nation-wide, and world-wide wire and radio communication service with adequate facilities at reasonable charges, for the purpose of the national defense, for the purpose of promoting safety of life and property through the use of wire and radio communications, and for the purpose of securing a more effective execution of this policy by centralizing authority heretofore granted by law to several agencies and by granting additional authority with respect to interstate and foreign commerce in wire and radio communication, there is created a commission to be known as the "Federal Communications Commission", which shall be constituted as hereinafter provided, and which shall execute and enforce the provisions of this chapter.

47 U.S.C. § 152

Application of chapter

(a) The provisions of this chapter shall apply to all interstate and foreign communication by wire or radio and all interstate and foreign transmission of energy by radio, which originates and/or is received within the United States, and to all persons engaged within the United States in such communication or such transmission of energy by radio, and to the licensing and regulating of all radio stations as hereinafter provided .... The provisions of this chapter shall apply with respect to cable service, to all persons engaged within the United States in providing such service, and to the facilities of cable operators which relate to such service, as provided in subchapter V-A.

(b) Exceptions to Federal Communications Commission jurisdiction

Except as provided in sections 223 through 227 of this title, inclusive, and section 332 of this title, and subject to the provisions of section 301 of this title and subchapter V-A of this chapter, nothing in this chapter shall be construed to apply or to give the Commission jurisdiction with respect to (1) charges, classifications, practices, services, facilities, or regulations for or in connection with intrastate communication service by wire or radio of any carrier . . . .

47 U.S.C. § 153

Definitions

* * *

(20) Information service

The term "information service" means the offering of a capability for generating, acquiring, storing, transforming, processing, retrieving, utilizing, or making available information via telecommunications, and includes electronic publishing, but does not include any use of any such capability for the management, control, or operation of a telecommunications system or the management of a telecommunications service.

* * *

(43) Telecommunications

The term "telecommunications" means the transmission, between or among points specified by the user, of information of the user's choosing, without change in the form or content of the information as sent and received.

* * *

(46) Telecommunications service

The term "telecommunications service" means the offering of telecommunications for a fee directly to the public, or to such classes of users as to be effectively available directly to the public, regardless of the facilities used.

47 U.S.C. § 160

Competition in provision of telecommunications service

(a) Regulatory flexibility

Notwithstanding section 332(c)(1)(A) of this title, the Commission shall forbear from applying any regulation or any provision of this chapter to a telecommunications carrier or telecommunications service, or class of telecommunications carriers or telecommunications services, in any or some of its or their geographic markets, if the Commission determines that—

(1) enforcement of such regulation or provision is not necessary to ensure that the charges, practices, classifications, or regulations by, for, or in connection with that

telecommunications carrier or telecommunications service are just and reasonable and are not unjustly or unreasonably discriminatory;

(2) enforcement of such regulation or provision is not necessary for the protection of consumers; and

(3) forbearance from applying such provision or regulation is consistent with the public interest.

(b) Competitive effect to be weighed

In making the determination under subsection (a)(3) of this section, the Commission shall consider whether forbearance from enforcing the provision or regulation will promote competitive market conditions, including the extent to which such forbearance will enhance competition among providers of telecommunications services. If the Commission determines that such forbearance will promote competition among providers of telecommunications services, that determination may be the basis for a Commission finding that forbearance is in the public interest.

(c) Petition for forbearance

Any telecommunications carrier, or class of telecommunications carriers, may submit a petition to the Commission requesting that the Commission exercise the authority granted under this section with respect to that carrier or those carriers, or any service offered by that carrier or carriers. Any such petition shall be deemed granted if the Commission does not deny the petition for failure to meet the requirements for forbearance under subsection (a) of this section within one year after the Commission receives it, unless the one-year period is extended by the Commission. The Commission may extend the initial one-year period by an additional 90 days if the Commission finds that an extension is necessary to meet the requirements of subsection (a) of this section. The Commission may grant or deny a petition in whole or in part and shall explain its decision in writing.

(d) Limitation

Except as provided in section 251(f) of this title, the Commission may not forbear from applying the requirements of section 251(c) or 271 of this title under subsection (a) of this section until it determines that those requirements have been fully implemented.

(e) State enforcement after commission forbearance

A State commission may not continue to apply or enforce any provision of this chapter that the Commission has determined to forbear from applying under subsection (a) of this section.

47 U.S.C. § 201

Service and charges

(a) It shall be the duty of every common carrier engaged in interstate or foreign communication by wire or radio to furnish such communication service upon reasonable request therefor; and, in accordance with the orders of the Commission, in cases where the Commission, after opportunity for hearing, finds such action necessary or desirable in the public interest, to establish physical connections with other carriers, to establish through routes and charges applicable thereto and the divisions of such charges, and to establish and provide facilities and regulations for operating such through routes.

(b) All charges, practices, classifications, and regulations for and in connection with such communication service, shall be just and reasonable, and any such charge, practice, classification, or regulation that is unjust or unreasonable is declared to be unlawful . . . . The Commission may prescribe such rules and regulations as may be necessary in the public interest to carry out the provisions of this chapter.

47 U.S.C. § 202

Discriminations and preferences

(a) Charges, services, etc.

It shall be unlawful for any common carrier to make any unjust or unreasonable discrimination in charges, practices, classifications, regulations, facilities, or services for or in connection with like communication service, directly or indirectly, by any means or device, or to make or give any undue or unreasonable preference or advantage to any particular person, class of persons, or locality, or to subject any particular person, class of persons, or locality to any undue or unreasonable prejudice or disadvantage.

(b) Charges or services included

Charges or services, whenever referred to in this chapter, include charges for, or services in connection with, the use of common carrier lines of communication, whether derived from wire or radio facilities, in chain broadcasting or incidental to radio communication of any kind.

(c) Penalty

Any carrier who knowingly violates the provisions of this section shall forfeit to the United States the sum of $6,000 for each such offense and $300 for each and every day of the continuance of such offense.

47 U.S.C. § 214

Extension of lines or discontinuance of service; certificate of public convenience and necessity

(a) Exceptions; temporary or emergency service or discontinuance of service; changes in plant, operation or equipment

No carrier shall undertake the construction of a new line or of an extension of any line, or shall acquire or operate any line, or extension thereof, or shall engage in transmission over or by means of such additional or extended line, unless and until there shall first have been obtained from the Commission a certificate that the present or future public convenience and necessity require or will require the construction, or operation, or construction and operation, of such additional or extended line . . . .

* * *

(e) Provision of universal service

(1) Eligible telecommunications carriers

A common carrier designated as an eligible telecommunications carrier under paragraph (2), (3), or (6) shall be eligible to receive universal service support in accordance with section 254 of this title and shall, throughout the service area for which the designation is received—

(A) offer the services that are supported by Federal universal service support mechanisms under section 254(c) of this title, either using its own facilities or a combination of its own facilities and resale of another carrier's services (including the services offered by another eligible telecommunications carrier); and

(B) advertise the availability of such services and the charges therefor using media of general distribution.

(2) Designation of eligible telecommunications carriers

A State commission shall upon its own motion or upon request designate a common carrier that meets the requirements of paragraph (1) as an eligible telecommunications carrier for a service area designated by the State commission. Upon request and consistent with the public interest, convenience, and necessity, the State commission may, in the case of an area served by a rural telephone company, and shall, in the case of all other areas, designate more than one common carrier as an eligible telecommunications carrier for a service area designated by the State commission, so long as each additional requesting carrier meets the requirements of paragraph (1). Before designating an additional eligible telecommunications carrier for an area served by a rural telephone company, the State commission shall find that the designation is in the public interest.

(3) Designation of eligible telecommunications carriers for unserved areas

If no common carrier will provide the services that are supported by Federal universal service support mechanisms under section 254(c) of this title to an unserved community or any portion thereof that requests such service, the Commission, with respect to interstate services or an area served by a common carrier to which paragraph (6) applies, or a State commission, with respect to intrastate services, shall determine which common carrier or carriers are best able to provide such service to the requesting unserved community or portion thereof and shall order such carrier or carriers to provide such service for that unserved community or portion thereof. Any carrier or carriers ordered to provide such service under this paragraph shall meet the requirements of paragraph (1) and shall be designated as an eligible telecommunications carrier for that community or portion thereof.

*   *   *

47 U.S.C. § 251

Interconnection

(a) General duty of telecommunications carriers

Each telecommunications carrier has the duty—

(1) to interconnect directly or indirectly with the facilities and equipment of other telecommunications carriers; and

(2) not to install network features, functions, or capabilities that do not comply with the guidelines and standards established pursuant to section 255 or 256 of this title.

(b) Obligations of all local exchange carriers

Each local exchange carrier has the following duties:

(1) Resale

The duty not to prohibit, and not to impose unreasonable or discriminatory conditions or limitations on, the resale of its telecommunications services.

(2) Number portability

The duty to provide, to the extent technically feasible, number portability in accordance with requirements prescribed by the Commission.

(3) Dialing parity

The duty to provide dialing parity to competing providers of telephone exchange service and telephone toll service, and the duty to permit all such providers to have nondiscriminatory access to telephone numbers, operator services, directory assistance, and directory listing, with no unreasonable dialing delays.

(4) Access to rights-of-way

The duty to afford access to the poles, ducts, conduits, and rights-of-way of such carrier to competing providers of telecommunications services on rates, terms, and conditions that are consistent with section 224 of this title.

(5) Reciprocal compensation

The duty to establish reciprocal compensation arrangements for the transport and termination of telecommunications.

(c) Additional obligations of incumbent local exchange carriers

In addition to the duties contained in subsection (b) of this section, each incumbent local exchange carrier has the following duties:

(1) Duty to negotiate

The duty to negotiate in good faith in accordance with section 252 of this title the particular terms and conditions of agreements to fulfill the duties described in paragraphs (1) through (5) of subsection (b) of this section and this subsection. The requesting telecommunications carrier also has the duty to negotiate in good faith the terms and conditions of such agreements.

(2) Interconnection

The duty to provide, for the facilities and equipment of any requesting telecommunications carrier, interconnection with the local exchange carrier's network—

(A) for the transmission and routing of telephone exchange service and exchange access;

(B) at any technically feasible point within the carrier's network;

(C) that is at least equal in quality to that provided by the local exchange carrier to itself or to any subsidiary, affiliate, or any other party to which the carrier provides interconnection; and

(D) on rates, terms, and conditions that are just, reasonable, and nondiscriminatory, in accordance with the terms and conditions of the agreement and the requirements of this section and section 252 of this title.

(3) **Unbundled access**

The duty to provide, to any requesting telecommunications carrier for the provision of a telecommunications service, nondiscriminatory access to network elements on an unbundled basis at any technically feasible point on rates, terms, and conditions that are just, reasonable, and nondiscriminatory in accordance with the terms and conditions of the agreement and the requirements of this section and section 252 of this title. An incumbent local exchange carrier shall provide such unbundled network elements in a manner that allows requesting carriers to combine such elements in order to provide such telecommunications service.

(4) **Resale**

The duty—

(A) to offer for resale at wholesale rates any telecommunications service that the carrier provides at retail to subscribers who are not telecommunications carriers; and

(B) not to prohibit, and not to impose unreasonable or discriminatory conditions or limitations on, the resale of such telecommunications service, except that a State commission may, consistent with regulations prescribed by the Commission under this section, prohibit a reseller that obtains at wholesale rates a telecommunications service that is available at retail only to a category of subscribers from offering such service to a different category of subscribers.

(5) **Notice of changes**

The duty to provide reasonable public notice of changes in the information necessary for the transmission and routing of services using that local exchange carrier's facilities or networks, as well as of any other changes that would affect the interoperability of those facilities and networks.

(6) **Collocation**

The duty to provide, on rates, terms, and conditions that are just, reasonable, and nondiscriminatory, for physical collocation of equipment necessary for interconnection or access to unbundled network elements at the premises of the local exchange carrier, except that the carrier may provide for virtual collocation if the local exchange carrier demonstrates to the State commission that physical collocation is not practical for technical reasons or because of space limitations.

(d) **Implementation**

(1) **In general**

Within 6 months after February 8, 1996, the Commission shall complete all actions necessary to establish regulations to implement the requirements of this section.

(2) **Access standards**

In determining what network elements should be made available for purposes of subsection (c)(3) of this section, the Commission shall consider, at a minimum, whether—

(A) access to such network elements as are proprietary in nature is necessary; and

(B) the failure to provide access to such network elements would impair the ability of the telecommunications carrier seeking access to provide the services that it seeks to offer.

(3) Preservation of State access regulations

In prescribing and enforcing regulations to implement the requirements of this section, the Commission shall not preclude the enforcement of any regulation, order, or policy of a State commission that—

(A) establishes access and interconnection obligations of local exchange carriers;

(B) is consistent with the requirements of this section; and

(C) does not substantially prevent implementation of the requirements of this section and the purposes of this part.

(e) Numbering administration

(1) Commission authority and jurisdiction

The Commission shall create or designate one or more impartial entities to administer telecommunications numbering and to make such numbers available on an equitable basis. The Commission shall have exclusive jurisdiction over those portions of the North American Numbering Plan that pertain to the United States. Nothing in this paragraph shall preclude the Commission from delegating to State commissions or other entities all or any portion of such jurisdiction.

(2) Costs

The cost of establishing telecommunications numbering administration arrangements and number portability shall be borne by all telecommunications carriers on a competitively neutral basis as determined by the Commission.

(3) Universal emergency telephone number

The Commission and any agency or entity to which the Commission has delegated authority under this subsection shall designate 9-1-1 as the universal emergency telephone number within the United States for reporting an emergency to appropriate authorities and requesting assistance. The designation shall apply to both wireline and wireless telephone service. In making the designation, the Commission (and any such agency or entity) shall provide appropriate transition periods for areas in which 9-1-1 is not in use as an emergency telephone number on October 26, 1999.

*   *   *

(h) Definition of incumbent local exchange carrier

(1) Definition

For purposes of this section, the term "incumbent local exchange carrier" means, with respect to an area, the local exchange carrier that—

(A) on February 8, 1996, provided telephone exchange service in such area; and

(B)(i) on February 8, 1996, was deemed to be a member of the exchange carrier association pursuant to section 69.601(b) of the Commission's regulations (47 C.F.R. 69.601(b)); or

(ii) is a person or entity that, on or after February 8, 1996, became a successor or assign of a member described in clause (i).

(2) Treatment of comparable carriers as incumbents

The Commission may, by rule, provide for the treatment of a local exchange carrier (or class or category thereof) as an incumbent local exchange carrier for purposes of this section if—

(A) such carrier occupies a position in the market for telephone exchange service within an area that is comparable to the position occupied by a carrier described in paragraph (1);

(B) such carrier has substantially replaced an incumbent local exchange carrier described in paragraph (1); and

(C) such treatment is consistent with the public interest, convenience, and necessity and the purposes of this section.

(i) Savings provision

Nothing in this section shall be construed to limit or otherwise affect the Commission's authority under section 201 of this title.

47 U.S.C. § 252

Procedures for negotiation, arbitration, and approval of agreements

(a) Agreements arrived at through negotiation

(1) Voluntary negotiations

Upon receiving a request for interconnection, services, or network elements pursuant to section 251 of this title, an incumbent local exchange carrier may negotiate and enter into a binding agreement with the requesting telecommunications carrier or carriers without regard to the standards set forth in subsections (b) and (c) of section 251 of this title. The agreement shall include a detailed schedule of itemized charges for interconnection and each service or network element included in the agreement. The agreement, including any interconnection agreement negotiated before February 8, 1996, shall be submitted to the State commission under subsection (e) of this section.

(2) Mediation

Any party negotiating an agreement under this section may, at any point in the negotiation, ask a State commission to participate in the negotiation and to mediate any differences arising in the course of the negotiation.

(b) Agreements arrived at through compulsory arbitration

(1) Arbitration

During the period from the 135th to the 160th day (inclusive) after the date on which an incumbent local exchange carrier receives a request for negotiation under this section, the carrier or any other party to the negotiation may petition a State commission to arbitrate any open issues.

(2) Duty of petitioner

(A) A party that petitions a State commission under paragraph (1) shall, at the same time as it submits the petition, provide the State commission all relevant documentation concerning—

(i) the unresolved issues;

(ii) the position of each of the parties with respect to those issues; and

(iii) any other issue discussed and resolved by the parties.

(B) A party petitioning a State commission under paragraph (1) shall provide a copy of the petition and any documentation to the other party or parties not later than the day on which the State commission receives the petition.

(3) Opportunity to respond

A non-petitioning party to a negotiation under this section may respond to the other party's petition and provide such additional information as it wishes within 25 days after the State commission receives the petition.

(4) Action by State commission

(A) The State commission shall limit its consideration of any petition under paragraph (1) (and any response thereto) to the issues set forth in the petition and in the response, if any, filed under paragraph (3).

(B) The State commission may require the petitioning party and the responding party to provide such information as may be necessary for the State commission to reach a decision on the unresolved issues. If any party refuses or fails unreasonably to respond on a timely basis to any reasonable request from the State commission, then the State commission may proceed on the basis of the best information available to it from whatever source derived.

(C) The State commission shall resolve each issue set forth in the petition and the response, if any, by imposing appropriate conditions as required to implement subsection (c) of this section upon the parties to the agreement, and shall conclude the resolution of any unresolved issues not later than 9 months after the date on which the local exchange carrier received the request under this section.

(5) Refusal to negotiate

The refusal of any other party to the negotiation to participate further in the negotiations, to cooperate with the State commission in carrying out its function as an arbitrator, or to continue to negotiate in good faith in the presence, or with the assistance, of the State commission shall be considered a failure to negotiate in good faith.

(c) Standards for arbitration

In resolving by arbitration under subsection (b) of this section any open issues and imposing conditions upon the parties to the agreement, a State commission shall—

(1) ensure that such resolution and conditions meet the requirements of section 251 of this title, including the regulations prescribed by the Commission pursuant to section 251 of this title;

(2) establish any rates for interconnection, services, or network elements according to subsection (d) of this section; and

(3) provide a schedule for implementation of the terms and conditions by the parties to the agreement.

(d) Pricing standards

(1) Interconnection and network element charges

Determinations by a State commission of the just and reasonable rate for the interconnection of facilities and equipment for purposes of subsection (c)(2) of section

251 of this title, and the just and reasonable rate for network elements for purposes of subsection (c)(3) of such section—

(A) shall be—

(i) based on the cost (determined without reference to a rate-of-return or other rate-based proceeding) of providing the interconnection or network element (whichever is applicable), and

(ii) nondiscriminatory, and

(B) may include a reasonable profit.

(2) Charges for transport and termination of traffic

(A) In general

For the purposes of compliance by an incumbent local exchange carrier with section 251(b)(5) of this title, a State commission shall not consider the terms and conditions for reciprocal compensation to be just and reasonable unless—

(i) such terms and conditions provide for the mutual and reciprocal recovery by each carrier of costs associated with the transport and termination on each carrier's network facilities of calls that originate on the network facilities of the other carrier; and

(ii) such terms and conditions determine such costs on the basis of a reasonable approximation of the additional costs of terminating such calls.

(B) Rules of construction

This paragraph shall not be construed—

(i) to preclude arrangements that afford the mutual recovery of costs through the offsetting of reciprocal obligations, including arrangements that waive mutual recovery (such as bill-and-keep arrangements); or

(ii) to authorize the Commission or any State commission to engage in any rate regulation proceeding to establish with particularity the additional costs of transporting or terminating calls, or to require carriers to maintain records with respect to the additional costs of such calls.

(3) Wholesale prices for telecommunications services

For the purposes of section 251(c)(4) of this title, a State commission shall determine wholesale rates on the basis of retail rates charged to subscribers for the telecommunications service requested, excluding the portion thereof attributable to any marketing, billing, collection, and other costs that will be avoided by the local exchange carrier.

(e) Approval by State commission

(1) Approval required

Any interconnection agreement adopted by negotiation or arbitration shall be submitted for approval to the State commission. A State commission to which an agreement is submitted shall approve or reject the agreement, with written findings as to any deficiencies.

(2) Grounds for rejection

The State commission may only reject

(A) an agreement (or any portion thereof) adopted by negotiation under subsection (a) of this section if it finds that—

(i) the agreement (or portion thereof) discriminates against a telecommunications carrier not a party to the agreement; or

(ii) the implementation of such agreement or portion is not consistent with the public interest, convenience, and necessity; or

(B) an agreement (or any portion thereof) adopted by arbitration under subsection (b) of this section if it finds that the agreement does not meet the requirements of section 251 of this title, including the regulations prescribed by the Commission pursuant to section 251 of this title, or the standards set forth in subsection (d) of this section.

(3) Preservation of authority

Notwithstanding paragraph (2), but subject to section 253 of this title, nothing in this section shall prohibit a State commission from establishing or enforcing other requirements of State law in its review of an agreement, including requiring compliance with intrastate telecommunications service quality standards or requirements.

(4) Schedule for decision

If the State commission does not act to approve or reject the agreement within 90 days after submission by the parties of an agreement adopted by negotiation under subsection (a) of this section, or within 30 days after submission by the parties of an agreement adopted by arbitration under subsection (b) of this section, the agreement shall be deemed approved. No State court shall have jurisdiction to review the action of a State commission in approving or rejecting an agreement under this section.

(5) Commission to act if State will not act

If a State commission fails to act to carry out its responsibility under this section in any proceeding or other matter under this section, then the Commission shall issue an order preempting the State commission's jurisdiction of that proceeding or matter within 90 days after being notified (or taking notice) of such failure, and shall assume the responsibility of the State commission under this section with respect to the proceeding or matter and act for the State commission.

(6) Review of State commission actions

In a case in which a State fails to act as described in paragraph (5), the proceeding by the Commission under such paragraph and any judicial review of the Commission's actions shall be the exclusive remedies for a State commission's failure to act. In any case in which a State commission makes a determination under this section, any party aggrieved by such determination may bring an action in an appropriate Federal district court to determine whether the agreement or statement meets the requirements of section 251 of this title and this section.
*   *   *

(i) Availability to other telecommunications carriers

A local exchange carrier shall make available any interconnection, service, or network element provided under an agreement approved under this section to which it is a party to any other requesting telecommunications carrier upon the same terms and conditions as those provided in the agreement.

(j) "Incumbent local exchange carrier" defined

For purposes of this section, the term "incumbent local exchange carrier" has the meaning provided in section 251(h) of this title.

47 U.S.C. § 253

Removal of barriers to entry

(a) In general

No State or local statute or regulation, or other State or local legal requirement, may prohibit or have the effect of prohibiting the ability of any entity to provide any interstate or intrastate telecommunications service.

(b) State regulatory authority

Nothing in this section shall affect the ability of a State to impose, on a competitively neutral basis and consistent with section 254 of this title, requirements necessary to preserve and advance universal service, protect the public safety and welfare, ensure the continued quality of telecommunications services, and safeguard the rights of consumers.

(c) State and local government authority

Nothing in this section affects the authority of a State or local government to manage the public rights-of-way or to require fair and reasonable compensation from telecommunications providers, on a competitively neutral and nondiscriminatory basis, for use of public rights-of-way on a nondiscriminatory basis, if the compensation required is publicly disclosed by such government.

(d) Preemption

If, after notice and an opportunity for public comment, the Commission determines that a State or local government has permitted or imposed any statute, regulation, or legal requirement that violates subsection (a) or (b) of this section, the Commission shall preempt the enforcement of such statute, regulation, or legal requirement to the extent necessary to correct such violation or inconsistency.

(e) Commercial mobile service providers

Nothing in this section shall affect the application of section 332(c)(3) of this title to commercial mobile service providers.

(f) Rural markets

It shall not be a violation of this section for a State to require a telecommunications carrier that seeks to provide telephone exchange service or exchange access in a service area served by a rural telephone company to meet the requirements in section 214(e)(1) of this title for designation as an eligible telecommunications carrier for that area before being permitted to provide such service. This subsection shall not apply—

(1) to a service area served by a rural telephone company that has obtained an exemption, suspension, or modification of section 251(c)(4) of this title that effec-

tively prevents a competitor from meeting the requirements of section 214(e)(1) of this title; and

(2) to a provider of commercial mobile services.

47 U.S.C. § 254

Universal service

(a) Procedures to review universal service requirements

(1) Federal-State Joint Board on universal service

Within one month after February 8, 1996, the Commission shall institute and refer to a Federal-State Joint Board under section 410(c) of this title a proceeding to recommend changes to any of its regulations in order to implement sections 214(e) of this title and this section, including the definition of the services that are supported by Federal universal service support mechanisms and a specific timetable for completion of such recommendations. In addition to the members of the Joint Board required under section 410(c) of this title, one member of such Joint Board shall be a State-appointed utility consumer advocate nominated by a national organization of State utility consumer advocates. The Joint Board shall, after notice and opportunity for public comment, make its recommendations to the Commission 9 months after February 8, 1996.

(2) Commission action

The Commission shall initiate a single proceeding to implement the recommendations from the Joint Board required by paragraph (1) and shall complete such proceeding within 15 months after February 8, 1996. The rules established by such proceeding shall include a definition of the services that are supported by Federal universal service support mechanisms and a specific timetable for implementation. Thereafter, the Commission shall complete any proceeding to implement subsequent recommendations from any Joint Board on universal service within one year after receiving such recommendations.

(b) Universal service principles

The Joint Board and the Commission shall base policies for the preservation and advancement of universal service on the following principles:

(1) Quality and rates

Quality services should be available at just, reasonable, and affordable rates.

(2) Access to advanced services

Access to advanced telecommunications and information services should be provided in all regions of the Nation.

(3) Access in rural and high cost areas

Consumers in all regions of the Nation, including low-income consumers and those in rural, insular, and high cost areas, should have access to telecommunications and information services, including interexchange services and advanced telecommunications and information services, that are reasonably comparable to those services provided in urban areas and that are available at rates that are reasonably comparable to rates charged for similar services in urban areas.

(4) Equitable and nondiscriminatory contributions

All providers of telecommunications services should make an equitable and nondiscriminatory contribution to the preservation and advancement of universal service.

(5) Specific and predictable support mechanisms

There should be specific, predictable and sufficient Federal and State mechanisms to preserve and advance universal service.

(6) Access to advanced telecommunications services for schools, health care, and libraries

Elementary and secondary schools and classrooms, health care providers, and libraries should have access to advanced telecommunications services as described in subsection (h) of this section.

(7) Additional principles

Such other principles as the Joint Board and the Commission determine are necessary and appropriate for the protection of the public interest, convenience, and necessity and are consistent with this chapter.

(c) Definition

(1) In general

Universal service is an evolving level of telecommunications services that the Commission shall establish periodically under this section, taking into account advances in telecommunications and information technologies and services. The Joint Board in recommending, and the Commission in establishing, the definition of the services that are supported by Federal universal service support mechanisms shall consider the extent to which such telecommunications services—

(A) are essential to education, public health, or public safety;

(B) have, through the operation of market choices by customers, been subscribed to by a substantial majority of residential customers;

(C) are being deployed in public telecommunications networks by telecommunications carriers; and

(D) are consistent with the public interest, convenience, and necessity.

(2) Alterations and modifications

The Joint Board may, from time to time, recommend to the Commission modifications in the definition of the services that are supported by Federal universal service support mechanisms.

(3) Special services

In addition to the services included in the definition of universal service under paragraph (1), the Commission may designate additional services for such support mechanisms for schools, libraries, and health care providers for the purposes of subsection (h) of this section.

(d) Telecommunications carrier contribution

Every telecommunications carrier that provides interstate telecommunications services shall contribute, on an equitable and nondiscriminatory basis, to the specific, predictable, and sufficient mechanisms established by the Commission to preserve and advance universal service. The Commission may exempt a carrier or class of carriers from this requirement if the carrier's telecommunications activities are limited to such an extent that the level of such carrier's contribution to the preservation and advancement of universal service would be de minimis. Any other provider of interstate telecommunications may be required to contribute to the preservation and advancement of universal service if the public interest so requires.

(e) Universal service support

After the date on which Commission regulations implementing this section take effect, only an eligible telecommunications carrier designated under section 214(e) of this title shall be eligible to receive specific Federal universal service support. A carrier that receives such support shall use that support only for the provision, maintenance, and upgrading of facilities and services for which the support is intended. Any such support should be explicit and sufficient to achieve the purposes of this section.

(f) State authority

A State may adopt regulations not inconsistent with the Commission's rules to preserve and advance universal service. Every telecommunications carrier that provides intrastate telecommunications services shall contribute, on an equitable and nondiscriminatory basis, in a manner determined by the State to the preservation and advancement of universal service in that State. A State may adopt regulations to provide for additional definitions and standards to preserve and advance universal service within that State only to the extent that such regulations adopt additional specific, predictable, and sufficient mechanisms to support such definitions or standards that do not rely on or burden Federal universal service support mechanisms.

(g) Interexchange and interstate services

Within 6 months after February 8, 1996, the Commission shall adopt rules to require that the rates charged by providers of interexchange telecommunications services to subscribers in rural and high cost areas shall be no higher than the rates charged by each such provider to its subscribers in urban areas. Such rules shall also require that a provider of interstate interexchange telecommunications services shall provide such services to its subscribers in each State at rates no higher than the rates charged to its subscribers in any other State.

(h) Telecommunications services for certain providers

(1) In general

(A) Health care providers for rural areas

A telecommunications carrier shall, upon receiving a bona fide request, provide telecommunications services which are necessary for the provision of health care services in a State, including instruction relating to such services, to any public or nonprofit health care provider that serves persons who reside in rural areas in that State at rates that are reasonably comparable to rates charged for similar services in urban areas in that State. A telecommunications carrier providing service under this paragraph shall be entitled to have an amount equal to the difference, if any, between the rates for services provided to health care providers for rural areas in a State and the rates for similar services provided to other customers in comparable rural areas in that State treated as a service obligation as a part of its obligation to participate in the mechanisms to preserve and advance universal service.

(B) Educational providers and libraries

All telecommunications carriers serving a geographic area shall, upon a bona fide request for any of its services that are within the definition of universal service under subsection (c)(3) of this section, provide such services to elementary schools, secondary schools, and libraries for educational purposes at rates less than the amounts charged for similar services to other parties. The discount shall be an amount that the Commission, with respect to interstate services, and the States, with respect to intrastate services, determine is appropriate and necessary to ensure affordable access to and use of such services by such entities. A telecommunications carrier providing service under this paragraph shall—

(i) have an amount equal to the amount of the discount treated as an offset to its obligation to contribute to the mechanisms to preserve and advance universal service, or

(ii) notwithstanding the provisions of subsection (e) of this section, receive reimbursement utilizing the support mechanisms to preserve and advance universal service.

* * *

47 U.S.C. § 271

Bell operating company entry into interLATA services

(a) General limitation

Neither a Bell operating company, nor any affiliate of a Bell operating company, may provide interLATA services except as provided in this section.

(b) InterLATA services to which this section applies

(1) In-region services

A Bell operating company, or any affiliate of that Bell operating company, may provide interLATA services originating in any of its in-region States (as defined in subsection (i) of this section) if the Commission approves the application of such company for such State under subsection (d)(3) of this section.

(2) Out-of-region services

A Bell operating company, or any affiliate of that Bell operating company, may provide interLATA services originating outside its in-region States after February 8, 1996, subject to subsection (j) of this section.

(3) Incidental interLATA services

A Bell operating company, or any affiliate of a Bell operating company, may provide incidental interLATA services (as defined in subsection (g) of this section) originating in any State after February 8, 1996.

(4) Termination

Nothing in this section prohibits a Bell operating company or any of its affiliates from providing termination for interLATA services, subject to subsection (j) of this section.

(c) Requirements for providing certain in-region interLATA services

(1) Agreement or statement

A Bell operating company meets the requirements of this paragraph if it meets the requirements of subparagraph (A) or subparagraph (B) of this paragraph for each State for which the authorization is sought.

(A) Presence of a facilities-based competitor

A Bell operating company meets the requirements of this subparagraph if it has entered into one or more binding agreements that have been approved under section 252 of this title specifying the terms and conditions under which the Bell operating company is providing access and interconnection to its network facilities for the network facilities of one or more unaffiliated competing providers of telephone exchange service (as defined in section 153(47)(A) of this title, but excluding exchange access) to residential and business subscribers. For the purpose of this subparagraph, such telephone exchange service may be offered by such competing providers either exclusively over their own telephone exchange service facilities or predominantly over their own telephone exchange service facilities in combination with the resale of the telecommunications services of another carrier. . . .

(B) Failure to request access

A Bell operating company meets the requirements of this subparagraph if, after 10 months after February 8, 1996, no such provider has requested the access and interconnection described in subparagraph (A) before the date which is 3 months before the date the company makes its application under subsection (d)(1) of this section, and a statement of the terms and conditions that the company generally offers to provide such access and interconnection has been approved or permitted to take effect by the State commission under section 252(f) of this title. . . .

(2) Specific interconnection requirements

(A) Agreement required

A Bell operating company meets the requirements of this paragraph if, within the State for which the authorization is sought—

(i)(I) such company is providing access and interconnection pursuant to one or more agreements described in paragraph (1)(A), or

(II) such company is generally offering access and interconnection pursuant to a statement described in paragraph (1)(B), and

(ii) such access and interconnection meets the requirements of subparagraph (B) of this paragraph.

(B) Competitive checklist

Access or interconnection provided or generally offered by a Bell operating company to other telecommunications carriers meets the requirements of this subparagraph if such access and interconnection includes each of the following:

(i) Interconnection in accordance with the requirements of sections 251(c)(2) and 252(d)(1) of this title.

(ii) Nondiscriminatory access to network elements in accordance with the requirements of sections 251(c)(3) and 252(d)(1) of this title.

(iii) Nondiscriminatory access to the poles, ducts, conduits, and rights-of-way owned or controlled by the Bell operating company at just and reasonable rates in accordance with the requirements of section 224 of this title.

(iv) Local loop transmission from the central office to the customer's premises, unbundled from local switching or other services.

(v) Local transport from the trunk side of a wireline local exchange carrier switch unbundled from switching or other services.

(vi) Local switching unbundled from transport, local loop transmission, or other services.

(vii) Nondiscriminatory access to—

(I) 911 and E911 services;

(II) directory assistance services to allow the other carrier's customers to obtain telephone numbers; and

(III) operator call completion services.

(viii) White pages directory listings for customers of the other carrier's telephone exchange service.

(ix) Until the date by which telecommunications numbering administration guidelines, plan, or rules are established, nondiscriminatory access to telephone numbers for assignment to the other carrier's telephone exchange service customers. After that date, compliance with such guidelines, plan, or rules.

(x) Nondiscriminatory access to databases and associated signaling necessary for call routing and completion.

(xi) Until the date by which the Commission issues regulations pursuant to section 251 of this title to require number portability, interim telecommunications number portability through remote call forwarding, direct inward dialing trunks, or other comparable arrangements, with as little impairment of functioning, quality, reliability, and convenience as possible. After that date, full compliance with such regulations.

(xii) Nondiscriminatory access to such services or information as are necessary to allow the requesting carrier to implement local dialing parity in accordance with the requirements of section 251(b)(3) of this title.

(xiii) Reciprocal compensation arrangements in accordance with the requirements of section 252(d)(2) of this title.

(xiv) Telecommunications services are available for resale in accordance with the requirements of sections 251(c)(4) and 252(d)(3) of this title.

(d) Administrative provisions

(1) Application to Commission

On and after February 8, 1996, a Bell operating company or its affiliate may apply to the Commission for authorization to provide interLATA services originating in any in-region State. The application shall identify each State for which the authorization is sought.

(2) Consultation

(A) Consultation with the Attorney General

The Commission shall notify the Attorney General promptly of any application under paragraph (1). Before making any determination under this subsection, the

Commission shall consult with the Attorney General, and if the Attorney General submits any comments in writing, such comments shall be included in the record of the Commission's decision. In consulting with and submitting comments to the Commission under this paragraph, the Attorney General shall provide to the Commission an evaluation of the application using any standard the Attorney General considers appropriate. The Commission shall give substantial weight to the Attorney General's evaluation, but such evaluation shall not have any preclusive effect on any Commission decision under paragraph (3).

(B) Consultation with State commissions

Before making any determination under this subsection, the Commission shall consult with the State commission of any State that is the subject of the application in order to verify the compliance of the Bell operating company with the requirements of subsection (c) of this section.

(3) Determination

Not later than 90 days after receiving an application under paragraph (1), the Commission shall issue a written determination approving or denying the authorization requested in the application for each State. The Commission shall not approve the authorization requested in an application submitted under paragraph (1) unless it finds that—

(A) the petitioning Bell operating company has met the requirements of subsection (c)(1) of this section and—

(i) with respect to access and interconnection provided pursuant to subsection (c)(1)(A) of this section, has fully implemented the competitive checklist in subsection (c)(2)(B) of this section; or

(ii) with respect to access and interconnection generally offered pursuant to a statement under subsection (c)(1)(B) of this section, such statement offers all of the items included in the competitive checklist in subsection (c)(2)(B) of this section;

(B) the requested authorization will be carried out in accordance with the requirements of section 272 of this title; and

(C) the requested authorization is consistent with the public interest, convenience, and necessity.

The Commission shall state the basis for its approval or denial of the application.

(4) Limitation on Commission

The Commission may not, by rule or otherwise, limit or extend the terms used in the competitive checklist set forth in subsection (c)(2)(B) of this section.

* * *

(6) Enforcement of conditions

(A) Commission authority

If at any time after the approval of an application under paragraph (3), the Commission determines that a Bell operating company has ceased to meet any of the conditions required for such approval, the Commission may, after notice and opportunity for a hearing—

(i) issue an order to such company to correct the deficiency;

(ii) impose a penalty on such company pursuant to subchapter V of this chapter; or

(iii) suspend or revoke such approval.

(B) Receipt and review of complaints

The Commission shall establish procedures for the review of complaints concerning failures by Bell operating companies to meet conditions required for approval under paragraph (3). Unless the parties otherwise agree, the Commission shall act on such complaint within 90 days.

* * *

47 U.S.C. § 303

Powers and duties of Commission

Except as otherwise provided in this chapter, the Commission from time to time, as public convenience, interest, or necessity requires, shall—

(a) Classify radio stations;

(b) Prescribe the nature of the service to be rendered by each class of licensed stations and each station within any class;

(c) Assign bands of frequencies to the various classes of stations, and assign frequencies for each individual station and determine the power which each station shall use and the time during which it may operate;

(d) Determine the location of classes of stations or individual stations;

(e) Regulate the kind of apparatus to be used with respect to its external effects and the purity and sharpness of the emissions from each station and from the apparatus therein;

(f) Make such regulations not inconsistent with law as it may deem necessary to prevent interference between stations and to carry out the provisions of this chapter: Provided, however, That changes in the frequencies, authorized power, or in the times of operation of any station, shall not be made without the consent of the station licensee unless the Commission shall determine that such changes will promote public convenience or interest or will serve public necessity, or the provisions of this chapter will be more fully complied with;

(g) Study new uses for radio, provide for experimental uses of frequencies, and generally encourage the larger and more effective use of radio in the public interest;

(h) Have authority to establish areas or zones to be served by any station;

(i) Have authority to make special regulations applicable to radio stations engaged in chain broadcasting;

(j) Have authority to make general rules and regulations requiring stations to keep such records of programs, transmissions of energy, communications, or signals as it may deem desirable;

* * *

(r) Make such rules and regulations and prescribe such restrictions and conditions, not inconsistent with law, as may be necessary to carry out the provisions of this chapter, or any international radio or wire communications treaty or convention, or regulations annexed thereto, including any treaty or convention insofar as it relates to the use of radio, to which the United States is or may hereafter become a party.

482   *Statutory Addendum*

(y) Have authority to allocate electromagnetic spectrum so as to provide flexibility of use, if—

(1) such use is consistent with international agreements to which the United States is a party; and

(2) the Commission finds, after notice and an opportunity for public comment, that—

(A) such an allocation would be in the public interest;

(B) such use would not deter investment in communications services and systems, or technology development; and

(C) such use would not result in harmful interference among users.

47 U.S.C. § 309

Application for license

a) Considerations in granting application

Subject to the provisions of this section, the Commission shall determine, in the case of each application filed with it to which section 308 of this title applies, whether the public interest, convenience, and necessity will be served by the granting of such application, and, if the Commission, upon examination of such application and upon consideration of such other matters as the Commission may officially notice, shall find that public interest, convenience, and necessity would be served by the granting thereof, it shall grant such application.

* * *

(e) Hearings; intervention; evidence; burden of proof

If, in the case of any application to which subsection (a) of this section applies, a substantial and material question of fact is presented or the Commission for any reason is unable to make the finding specified in such subsection, it shall formally designate the application for hearing on the ground or reasons then obtaining and shall forthwith notify the applicant and all other known parties in interest of such action and the grounds and reasons therefor, specifying with particularity the matters and things in issue but not including issues or requirements phrased generally. When the Commission has so designated an application for hearing the parties in interest, if any, who are not notified by the Commission of such action may acquire the status of a party to the proceeding thereon by filing a petition for intervention showing the basis for their interest not more than thirty days after publication of the hearing issues or any substantial amendment thereto in the Federal Register. Any hearing subsequently held upon such application shall be a full hearing in which the applicant and all other parties in interest shall be permitted to participate. The burden of proceeding with the introduction of evidence and the burden of proof shall be upon the applicant, except that with respect to any issue presented by a petition to deny or a petition to enlarge the issues, such burdens shall be as determined by the Commission.

* * *

(i) Random selection

* * *

(5) Termination of authority

(A) Except as provided in subparagraph (B), the Commission shall not issue any license or permit using a system of random selection under this subsection after July 1, 1997.

(B) Subparagraph (A) of this paragraph shall not apply with respect to licenses or permits for stations described in section 397(6) of this title.

(j) Use of competitive bidding

(1) General authority

If, consistent with the obligations described in paragraph (6)(E), mutually exclusive applications are accepted for any initial license or construction permit, then, except as provided in paragraph (2), the Commission shall grant the license or permit to a qualified applicant through a system of competitive bidding that meets the requirements of this subsection.

(2) Exemptions

The competitive bidding authority granted by this subsection shall not apply to licenses or construction permits issued by the Commission—

(A) for public safety radio services, including private internal radio services used by State and local governments and non-government entities and including emergency road services provided by not-for-profit organizations, that—

(i) are used to protect the safety of life, health, or property; and

(ii) are not made commercially available to the public;

(B) for initial licenses or construction permits for digital television service given to existing terrestrial broadcast licensees to replace their analog television service licenses; or

(C) for stations described in section 397(6) of this title.

(3) Design of systems of competitive bidding

For each class of licenses or permits that the Commission grants through the use of a competitive bidding system, the Commission shall, by regulation, establish a competitive bidding methodology. The Commission shall seek to design and test multiple alternative methodologies under appropriate circumstances. The Commission shall, directly or by contract, provide for the design and conduct (for purposes of testing) of competitive bidding using a contingent combinatorial bidding system that permits prospective bidders to bid on combinations or groups of licenses in a single bid and to enter multiple alternative bids within a single bidding round. In identifying classes of licenses and permits to be issued by competitive bidding, in specifying eligibility and other characteristics of such licenses and permits, and in designing the methodologies for use under this subsection, the Commission shall include safeguards to protect the public interest in the use of the spectrum and shall seek to promote the purposes specified in section 151 of this title and the following objectives:

(A) the development and rapid deployment of new technologies, products, and services for the benefit of the public, including those residing in rural areas, without administrative or judicial delays;

(B) promoting economic opportunity and competition and ensuring that new and innovative technologies are readily accessible to the American people by avoiding excessive concentration of licenses and by disseminating licenses among a wide variety of applicants, including small businesses, rural telephone companies, and businesses owned by members of minority groups and women;

(C) recovery for the public of a portion of the value of the public spectrum resource made available for commercial use and avoidance of unjust enrichment through the methods employed to award uses of that resource;

(D) efficient and intensive use of the electromagnetic spectrum; and

(E) ensure that, in the scheduling of any competitive bidding under this subsection, an adequate period is allowed—

(i) before issuance of bidding rules, to permit notice and comment on proposed auction procedures; and

(ii) after issuance of bidding rules, to ensure that interested parties have a sufficient time to develop business plans, assess market conditions, and evaluate the availability of equipment for the relevant services.

*   *   *

(7) Consideration of revenues in public interest determinations

(A) Consideration prohibited

In making a decision pursuant to section 303(c) of this title to assign a band of frequencies to a use for which licenses or permits will be issued pursuant to this subsection, and in prescribing regulations pursuant to paragraph (4)(C) of this subsection, the Commission may not base a finding of public interest, convenience, and necessity on the expectation of Federal revenues from the use of a system of competitive bidding under this subsection.

(B) Consideration limited

In prescribing regulations pursuant to paragraph (4)(A) of this subsection, the Commission may not base a finding of public interest, convenience, and necessity solely or predominantly on the expectation of Federal revenues from the use of a system of competitive bidding under this subsection.

(C) Consideration of demand for spectrum not affected

Nothing in this paragraph shall be construed to prevent the Commission from continuing to consider consumer demand for spectrum-based services.

*   *   *

(11) Termination

The authority of the Commission to grant a license or permit under this subsection shall expire September 30, 2007.

*   *   *

(14) Auction of recaptured broadcast television spectrum

(A) Limitations on terms of terrestrial television broadcast licenses

A television broadcast license that authorizes analog television service may not be renewed to authorize such service for a period that extends beyond December 31, 2006.

(B) Extension

The Commission shall extend the date described in subparagraph (A) for any station that requests such extension in any television market if the Commission finds that—

(i) one or more of the stations in such market that are licensed to or affiliated with one of the four largest national television networks are not broadcasting a digital television service signal, and the Commission finds that each such station has exercised due diligence and satisfies the conditions for an extension of the Commission's applicable construction deadlines for digital television service in that market;

(ii) digital-to-analog converter technology is not generally available in such market; or

(iii) in any market in which an extension is not available under clause (i) or (ii), 15 percent or more of the television households in such market—

(I) do not subscribe to a multichannel video programming distributor (as defined in section 522 of this title) that carries one of the digital television service programming channels of each of the television stations broadcasting such a channel in such market; and

(II) do not have either—

(a) at least one television receiver capable of receiving the digital television service signals of the television stations licensed in such market; or

(b) at least one television receiver of analog television service signals equipped with digital-to-analog converter technology capable of receiving the digital television service signals of the television stations licensed in such market.

(C) Spectrum reversion and resale

(i) The Commission shall—

(I) ensure that, as licenses for analog television service expire pursuant to subparagraph (A) or (B), each licensee shall cease using electromagnetic spectrum assigned to such service according to the Commission's direction; and

(II) reclaim and organize the electromagnetic spectrum in a manner consistent with the objectives described in paragraph (3) of this subsection.

(ii) Licensees for new services occupying spectrum reclaimed pursuant to clause (i) shall be assigned in accordance with this subsection.

* * *

47 U.S.C. § 332

Mobile services

(a) Factors which Commission must consider

In taking actions to manage the spectrum to be made available for use by the private mobile services, the Commission shall consider, consistent with section 151 of this title, whether such actions will—

(1) promote the safety of life and property;

(2) improve the efficiency of spectrum use and reduce the regulatory burden upon spectrum users, based upon sound engineering principles, user operational requirements, and marketplace demands;

(3) encourage competition and provide services to the largest feasible number of users; or

(4) increase interservice sharing opportunities between private mobile services and other services.

* * *

(c) Regulatory treatment of mobile services

(1) Common carrier treatment of commercial mobile services

(A) A person engaged in the provision of a service that is a commercial mobile service shall, insofar as such person is so engaged, be treated as a common carrier for purposes of this chapter, except for such provisions of subchapter II of this chapter as the Commission may specify by regulation as inapplicable to that service or person. In prescribing or amending any such regulation, the Commission may not specify any provision of section 201, 202, or 208 of this title, and may specify any other provision only if the Commission determines that—

(i) enforcement of such provision is not necessary in order to ensure that the charges, practices, classifications, or regulations for or in connection with that service are just and reasonable and are not unjustly or unreasonably discriminatory;

(ii) enforcement of such provision is not necessary for the protection of consumers; and

(iii) specifying such provision is consistent with the public interest.

(B) Upon reasonable request of any person providing commercial mobile service, the Commission shall order a common carrier to establish physical connections with such service pursuant to the provisions of section 201 of this title. Except to the extent that the Commission is required to respond to such a request, this subparagraph shall not be construed as a limitation or expansion of the Commission's authority to order interconnection pursuant to this chapter.

* * *

(2) Non-common carrier treatment of private mobile services

A person engaged in the provision of a service that is a private mobile service shall not, insofar as such person is so engaged, be treated as a common carrier for any purpose under this chapter. A common carrier (other than a person that was treated as a provider of a private land mobile service prior to August 10, 1993) shall not provide any dispatch service on any frequency allocated for common carrier service, except to the extent such dispatch service is provided on stations licensed in the domestic public land mobile radio service before January 1, 1982. The Commission may by regulation terminate, in whole or in part, the prohibition contained in the preceding sentence if the Commission determines that such termination will serve the public interest.

(3) State preemption

(A) Notwithstanding sections 152(b) and 221(b) of this title, no State or local government shall have any authority to regulate the entry of or the rates charged by any commercial mobile service or any private mobile service, except that this paragraph shall not prohibit a State from regulating the other terms and conditions of commercial mobile services. Nothing in this subparagraph shall exempt providers of commercial mobile services (where such services are a substitute for land line telephone exchange service for a substantial portion of the communications within such State) from requirements imposed by a State commission on all providers of telecommunications services necessary to ensure the universal availability of telecommunications service at affordable rates. Notwithstanding the first sentence of this subparagraph, a State may petition the Commission for authority to regulate the rates for any commercial mobile service and the Commission shall grant such petition if such State demonstrates that—

(i) market conditions with respect to such services fail to protect subscribers adequately from unjust and unreasonable rates or rates that are unjustly or unreasonably discriminatory; or

(ii) such market conditions exist and such service is a replacement for land line telephone exchange service for a substantial portion of the telephone land line exchange service within such State.

The Commission shall provide reasonable opportunity for public comment in response to such petition, and shall, within 9 months after the date of its submission, grant or deny such petition. If the Commission grants such petition, the Commission shall authorize the State to exercise under State law such authority over rates, for such periods of time, as the Commission deems necessary to ensure that such rates are just and reasonable and not unjustly or unreasonably discriminatory.

* * *

(7) Preservation of local zoning authority

(A) General authority

Except as provided in this paragraph, nothing in this chapter shall limit or affect the authority of a State or local government or instrumentality thereof over decisions regarding the placement, construction, and modification of personal wireless service facilities.

(B) Limitations

(i) The regulation of the placement, construction, and modification of personal wireless service facilities by any State or local government or instrumentality thereof—

(I) shall not unreasonably discriminate among providers of functionally equivalent services; and

(II) shall not prohibit or have the effect of prohibiting the provision of personal wireless services.

(ii) A State or local government or instrumentality thereof shall act on any request for authorization to place, construct, or modify personal wireless service facilities within a reasonable period of time after the request is duly filed with such government or instrumentality, taking into account the nature and scope of such request.

(iii) Any decision by a State or local government or instrumentality thereof to deny a request to place, construct, or modify personal wireless service facilities shall be in writing and supported by substantial evidence contained in a written record.

(iv) No State or local government or instrumentality thereof may regulate the placement, construction, and modification of personal wireless service facilities on the basis of the environmental effects of radio frequency emissions to the extent that such facilities comply with the Commission's regulations concerning such emissions.

(v) Any person adversely affected by any final action or failure to act by a State or local government or any instrumentality thereof that is inconsistent with this subparagraph may, within 30 days after such action or failure to act, commence an action in any court of competent jurisdiction. The court shall hear and decide such action on an expedited basis. Any person adversely affected by an act or failure to act by a State or local government or any instrumentality thereof that is inconsistent with clause (iv) may petition the Commission for relief.

* * *

(d) Definitions

For purposes of this section—

(1) the term "commercial mobile service" means any mobile service (as defined in section 153 of this title) that is provided for profit and makes interconnected service available (A) to the public or (B) to such classes of eligible users as to be effectively available to a substantial portion of the public, as specified by regulation by the Commission;

(2) the term "interconnected service" means service that is interconnected with the public switched network (as such terms are defined by regulation by the Commission) or service for which a request for interconnection is pending pursuant to subsection (c)(1)(B) of this section; and

(3) the term "private mobile service" means any mobile service (as defined in section 153 of this title) that is not a commercial mobile service or the functional equivalent of a commercial mobile service, as specified by regulation by the Commission.

47 U.S.C. § 521

Purposes

The purposes of this subchapter are to—

(1) establish a national policy concerning cable communications;

(2) establish franchise procedures and standards which encourage the growth and development of cable systems and which assure that cable systems are responsive to the needs and interests of the local community;

(3) establish guidelines for the exercise of Federal, State, and local authority with respect to the regulation of cable systems;

(4) assure that cable communications provide and are encouraged to provide the widest possible diversity of information sources and services to the public;

(5) establish an orderly process for franchise renewal which protects cable operators against unfair denials of renewal where the operator's past performance and proposal for future performance meet the standards established by this subchapter; and

(6) promote competition in cable communications and minimize unnecessary regulation that would impose an undue economic burden on cable systems.

47 U.S.C. § 533

Ownership restrictions

(a) Cable operator holding license for multichannel distribution or offering satellite service

It shall be unlawful for a cable operator to hold a license for multichannel multipoint distribution service, or to offer satellite master antenna television service separate and apart from any franchised cable service, in any portion of the franchise area served by that cable operator's cable system. The Commission—

(1) shall waive the requirements of this paragraph for all existing multichannel multipoint distribution services and satellite master antenna television services which are owned by a cable operator on October 5, 1992;

(2) may waive the requirements of this paragraph to the extent the Commission determines is necessary to ensure that all significant portions of a franchise area are able to obtain video programming; and

(3) shall not apply the requirements of this subsection to any cable operator

in any franchise area in which a cable operator is subject to effective competition as determined under section 543(l) of this title.

* * *

(c) Promulgation of rules

The Commission may prescribe rules with respect to the ownership or control of cable systems by persons who own or control other media of mass communications which serve the same community served by a cable system.

* * *

(f) Enhancement of effective competition

(1) In order to enhance effective competition, the Commission shall, within one year after October 5, 1992, conduct a proceeding—

(A) to prescribe rules and regulations establishing reasonable limits on the number of cable subscribers a person is authorized to reach through cable systems owned by such person, or in which such person has an attributable interest;

(B) to prescribe rules and regulations establishing reasonable limits on the number of channels on a cable system that can be occupied by a video programmer in which a cable operator has an attributable interest; and

(C) to consider the necessity and appropriateness of imposing limitations on the degree to which multichannel video programming distributors may engage in the creation or production of video programming.

(2) In prescribing rules and regulations under paragraph (1), the Commission shall, among other public interest objectives—

(A) ensure that no cable operator or group of cable operators can unfairly impede, either because of the size of any individual operator or because of joint actions by a group of operators of sufficient size, the flow of video programming from the video programmer to the consumer;

(B) ensure that cable operators affiliated with video programmers do not favor such programmers in determining carriage on their cable systems or do not unreasonably restrict the flow of the video programming of such programmers to other video distributors;

(C) take particular account of the market structure, ownership patterns, and other relationships of the cable television industry, including the nature and market power of the local franchise, the joint ownership of cable systems and video programmers, and the various types of non-equity controlling interests;

(D) account for any efficiencies and other benefits that might be gained through increased ownership or control;

(E) make such rules and regulations reflect the dynamic nature of the communications marketplace;

(F) not impose limitations which would bar cable operators from serving previously unserved rural areas; and

(G) not impose limitations which would impair the development of diverse and high quality video programming.

* * *

47 USC. § 534

Carriage of local commercial television signals

(a) Carriage obligations

Each cable operator shall carry, on the cable system of that operator, the signals of local commercial television stations and qualified low power stations as provided by this section. Carriage of additional broadcast television signals on such system shall be at the discretion of such operator, subject to section 325(b) of this title.

(b) Signals required

(1) In general

(A) A cable operator of a cable system with 12 or fewer usable activated channels shall carry the signals of at least three local commercial television stations, except that if such a system has 300 or fewer subscribers, it shall not be subject to any requirements under this section so long as such system does not delete from carriage by that system any signal of a broadcast television station.

(B) A cable operator of a cable system with more than 12 usable activated channels shall carry the signals of local commercial television stations, up to one-third of the aggregate number of usable activated channels of such system.

(2) Selection of signals

Whenever the number of local commercial television stations exceeds the maximum number of signals a cable system is required to carry under paragraph (1), the cable operator shall have discretion in selecting which such stations shall be carried on its cable system, except that—

(A) under no circumstances shall a cable operator carry a qualified low power station in lieu of a local commercial television station; and

(B) if the cable operator elects to carry an affiliate of a broadcast network (as such term is defined by the Commission by regulation), such cable operator shall carry the affiliate of such broadcast network whose city of license reference point, as defined in section 76.53 of title 47, Code of Federal Regulations (in effect on January 1, 1991), or any successor regulation thereto, is closest to the principal headend of the cable system.

* * *

47 U.S.C. § 548

Development of competition and diversity in video programming distribution

(a) Purpose

The purpose of this section is to promote the public interest, convenience, and necessity by increasing competition and diversity in the multichannel video programming market, to increase the availability of satellite cable programming and satellite broadcast programming to persons in rural and other areas not currently able to receive such programming, and to spur the development of communications technologies.

(b) Prohibition

It shall be unlawful for a cable operator, a satellite cable programming vendor in which a cable operator has an attributable interest, or a satellite broadcast programming vendor to engage in unfair methods of competition or unfair or deceptive acts or practices, the purpose or effect of which is to hinder significantly or to prevent any multichannel video programming distributor from providing satellite cable programming or satellite broadcast programming to subscribers or consumers.

* * *

47 U.S.C. § 157 Note [Pub.L. 104-104, Title VII, § 706, Feb. 8, 1996, 110 Stat. 153]

Advanced Telecommunications Incentives

(a) **In general.** The Commission and each State commission with regulatory jurisdiction over telecommunications services shall encourage the deployment on a reasonable and timely basis of advanced telecommunications capability to all Americans (including, in particular, elementary and secondary schools and classrooms) by utilizing, in a manner consistent with the public interest, convenience, and necessity, price cap regulation, regulatory forbearance, measures that promote competition in the local telecommunications market, or other regulating methods that remove barriers to infrastructure investment.

(b) **Inquiry.** The Commission shall, within 30 months after the date of enactment of this Act [Feb. 8, 1996], and regularly thereafter, initiate a notice of inquiry concerning the availability of advanced telecommunications capability to all Americans (including, in particular, elementary and secondary schools and classrooms) and shall complete the inquiry within 180 days after its initiation. In the inquiry, the Commission shall determine whether advanced telecommunications capability is being deployed to all Americans in a reasonable and timely fashion. If the Commission's determination is negative, it shall take immediate action to accelerate deployment of such capability by removing barriers to infrastructure investment and by promoting competition in the telecommunications market.

(c) **Definitions.**—For purposes of this subsection:

(1) **Advanced telecommunications capability.** The term "advanced telecommunications capability" is defined, without regard to any transmission media or technology, as high-speed, switched, broadband telecommunications capability that enables users to originate and receive high-quality voice, data, graphics, and video telecommunications using any technology.

*   *   *

List of Notable Commentaries

Abbate, Janet, INVENTING THE INTERNET (MIT Press, 1999).

Abernathy, Kathleen Q., The Nascent Services Doctrine, Remarks Before the Federal Communications Bar Association (July 11, 2002) (http://www.fcc.gov/Speeches/Abernathy/2002/spkqa217.html).

Areeda, Phillip, *Essential Facilities: An Epithet in Need of Limiting Principles*, 58 ANTITRUST L.J. 841 (1989).

Areeda, Phillip E. & Herbert Hovenkamp, ANTITRUST LAW (Aspen, 2002).

Auletta, Ken, WORLD WAR 3.0: MICROSOFT AND ITS ENEMIES (Random House, 2001).

Baker, C. Edwin, *Media Concentration: Giving up on Democracy*, 54 FLA. L. REV. 839 (2002).

Baker, C. Edwin, MEDIA, MARKETS, AND DEMOCRACY (Cambridge Univ. Press, 2002).

Bakos, Yannis & Erik Brynjolfsson, *Bundling Information Goods in Pricing, Profits, and Efficiency*, 45 MGMT. SCI. 1613 (1999).

Baldwin, Carliss Y. & Kim B. Clark. DESIGN RULES (MIT Press, 2000).

Bamberger, Kenneth A., *Provisional Precedent: Protecting Flexibility in Administrative Policymaking*, 77 N.Y.U. L. REV. 1272 (2002).

Barkow Rachel E. & Peter W. Huber, *A Tale of Two Agencies: A Comparative Analysis of FCC and DOJ Review of Telecommunications Mergers*, 2000 U. CHI. LEGAL F. 29 (2000).

Barnouw, Erik, A TOWER IN BABEL: A HISTORY OF BROADCASTING IN THE UNITED STATES (Oxford Univ. Press, 1966).

Baumol, William J., *Predation and the Logic of the Average Variable Cost Test*, 39 J.L. & ECON. 49 (1996).

Baumol, William J., THE FREE-MARKET INNOVATION MACHINE: ANALYZING THE GROWTH MIRACLE OF CAPITALISM (Princeton Univ. Press, 2002).

Baumol, William J. et al., CONTESTABLE MARKETS AND THE THEORY OF INDUSTRY STRUCTURE (Harcourt, 1988).

Baumol, William J. & J. Gregory Sidak, TOWARD COMPETITION IN LOCAL TELEPHONY (MIT Press, 1994).

Beard, T. Randolph et al., *Why Adco? Why Now? An Economic Exploration into the Future Structure for the "Last Mile" in Local Telecommunications Markets*, 54 FED. COMM. L.J. 421 (2002).

Benjamin, Stuart, *Proactive Legislation and the First Amendment*, 99 MICH. L. REV. 281 (2000).

Benjamin, Stuart, *Spectrum Abundance and the Choice Between Private and Public Control*, 78 N.Y.U. L. REV. 2007 (2003).

Benjamin, Stuart M., *The Logic of Scarcity: Idle Spectrum as a First Amendment Violation*, 52 DUKE L.J. 1 (2002).

Benjamin, Stuart M. et al., TELECOMMUNICATIONS LAW AND POLICY (Carolina Academic Press, 2001)

Benkler, Yochai, *From Consumers to Users: Shifting the Deeper Structures of Regulation Toward Sustainable Commons and User Access*, 52 FED. COMM. L.J. 561 (2000).

Benkler, Yochai, *Overcoming Agoraphobia: Building the Commons of the Digitally Networked Environment*, 11 HARV. J.L. & TECH. 287 (1998).

Benkler, Yochai, *Some Economics of Wireless Communications*, 16 HARV. J.L. & TECH. 25 (2002).

Berg, Sanford V., *Technical Standards as Public Goods: Demand Incentives for Cooperative Behavior*, 17 PUB. FIN. Q. 29 (1989).

Berners-Lee, Tim, WEAVING THE WEB (Harper Business Press, 1999).

Besen, Stanley M. et al., MISREGULATING TELEVISION: NETWORK DOMINANCE AND THE FCC (Univ. of Chicago Press, 1985).

Besen, Stanley M. & Robert Crandall, *The Deregulation of Cable Television*, 44 LAW & CONTEMP. PROB. 77 (1981).

Besen, Stanley M. et al., *Copyright Liability for Cable Television: Compulsory Licensing*, 21 J.L. & ECON. 67 (1978).

Blumenthal, Marjory S. & David D. Clark, *Rethinking the Design of the Internet: The End-to-End Arguments vs. the Brave New World, in* COMMUNICATIONS POLICY IN TRANSITION: THE INTERNET AND BEYOND (MIT Press, Benjamin M. Compaine & Shane Greenstein eds., 2001).

Bork, Robert H., THE ANTITRUST PARADOX (Basic Books, 1978).

Bradner, Scott, *The Internet Engineering Task Force, in* OPEN SOURCES: VOICES FROM THE OPEN SOURCE REVOLUTION (O'Reilly Books, Chris DiBona et al. eds., 1999).

Brenner, Daniel L. et al., CABLE TELEVISION AND OTHER NON-BROADCAST VIDEO: LAW AND POLICY (Clark Boardman Callaghan, 2003).

Bresnahan, Timothy F., *A Remedy that Falls Short of Restoring Competition*, ANTITRUST (Fall 2001).

Breyer, Stephen, ECONOMIC REASONING AND JUDICIAL REVIEW (American Enterprise Institute Press, 2004) (http://www.aei.brookings.org/admin/authorpdfs/page.php?id=840).
Breyer, Stephen, REGULATION AND ITS REFORM (Harv. Univ. Press, 1982).

Brinkley, Joel, DEFINING VISION: HOW BROADCASTERS LURED THE GOVERNMENT INTO INCITING A REVOLUTION IN TELEVISION (Harvest Books, 1998).

Brock, Gerald W., TELECOMMUNICATIONS POLICY FOR THE INFORMATION AGE (Harv. Univ. Press, 1994).

Brock, Gerald W., THE SECOND INFORMATION REVOLUTION (Harv. Univ. Press, 2003).

Brown, George, AND PART OF WHICH I WAS: RECOLLECTIONS OF A RESEARCH ENGINEER (Angus Cupar, 1979).

Cannon, Robert, *Where ISPs and Telephone Companies Compete: A Guide to the Computer Inquiries*, 9 COMMLAW CONSPECTUS 49 (2001).

Carlton, Dennis W., *A General Analysis of Exclusionary Conduct and Refusal to Deal—Why Aspen and Kodak Are Misguided*, 68 ANTITRUST L.J. 659 (2001).

Carter, Kenneth R. et al., *Unlicensed and Unshackled: A Joint OSP-OET White Paper on Unlicensed Devices and Their Regulatory Issues*, FCC OSP WORKING PAPER (May 2003) (http://hraunfoss.fcc.gov/edocs_public/attachmatch/DOC-234741A1.pdf).

Chen, Jim, *The Legal Process and Political Economy of Telecommunications Reform*, 97 COLUM. L. REV. 835 (1997).

Chen, Jim, *TELRIC in Turmoil, Telecommunications in Transition: A Note on the Iowa Utilities Board Litigation*, 33 WAKE FOREST L. REV. 51 (1998).

Chen, Jim, *Standing in the Shadows of Giants: The Role of Intergenerational Equity in Telecommunications Reform*, 71 U. COLO. L. REV. 921 (2000).

Christensen, Clayton, THE INNOVATOR'S DILEMMA (Harv. Bus. School Press, 1997).

Coase, Ronald, *The Federal Communications Commission*, 2 J. LAW & ECON. 1 (1959).

Coase, Ronald, THE FIRM, THE MARKET, AND THE LAW (Univ. of Chicago Press, 1990).

Coll, Steve, THE DEAL OF THE CENTURY: THE BREAKUP OF AT&T (Atheneum Books, 1986).

Committee on the Internet in the Evolving Information Infrastructure, THE INTERNET'S COMING OF AGE (National Academies Press, 2000).

Compaine, Benjamin M. & Douglas Gomery, WHO OWNS THE MEDIA? COMPETITION AND CONCENTRATION IN THE MASS MEDIA INDUSTRY (Lawrence Erlbaum Assoc., 3d ed. 2000).

Cooper, Mark, MEDIA OWNERSHIP AND DEMOCRACY IN THE DIGITAL INFORMATION AGE (Gillis Pub. Group, 2003) (http://cyberlaw.stanford.edu/blogs/cooper/archives/mediabooke.pdf).

Cornes, Richard & Todd Sandler, THE THEORY OF EXTERNALITIES, PUBLIC GOODS, AND CLUB GOODS (Cambridge Univ. Press, 2d ed. 1996).

Crandall, Robert W., *The Failure of Structural Remedies in Sherman Act Monopolization Cases*, 80 OR. L. REV. 109 (2001).

Crandall, Robert W. & J. Gregory Sidak, *Is Structural Separation of Incumbent Local Exchange Carriers Necessary for Competition?* 19 YALE J. REG. 335 (2002).

Crandall, Robert & Leonard Waverman, WHO PAYS FOR UNIVERSAL SERVICE? WHEN TELEPHONE SUBSIDIES BECOME TRANSPARENT (Brookings Inst. Press, 2000).

Crandall, Robert et al., *The Effects of Ubiquitous Broadband Adoption on Investment, Jobs and the U.S. Economy*, New Millenium Research (September 17, 2003), (http://www.newmilleniumresearch.org/archive/bbstudyreport_091703.pdf).

Cremer, Jacques et al., *Connectivity in the Commercial Internet*, 48 J. IND. ECON. 433 (2000).

Cudahy, Richard D., *Whither Deregulation: A Look at the Portents*, 58 N.Y.U. ANN. SURV. AM. L. 155 (2001).

DeGraba, Patrick, *Bill and Keep at the Central Office as the Efficient Interconnection Regime*, OPP WORKING PAPER SERIES NO. 33 (FCC Dec. 2000) (http://www.fcc.gov/Bureaus/OPP/working_papers/oppwp33.pdf).

Department of Commerce, *Spectrum Policy for the Twenty-First Century— The President's Spectrum Policy Initiative* (June 2004) (http://www.ntia.doc.gov/reports/specpolini/presspecpolini_report1_0 6242004.pdf).

Duffy, John F., *Administrative Common Law in Judicial Review*, 77 TEX. L. REV. 113 (1998).

Duffy, John F., *The FCC and the Patent System: Progressive Ideals, Jacksonian Realism, and the Technology of Regulation*, 71 U. COLO. L. REV. 1071 (2000).

Easterbrook, Frank H., *When Does Competition Improve Regulation?* 52 EMORY L. REV. 1297 (2003).

Entman, Robert M., SPECTRUM AND NETWORK POLICY FOR NEXT GENERATION TELECOMMUNICATIONS: A REPORT ON THE EIGHTEENTH ANNUAL ASPEN INSTITUTE CONFERENCE ON TELECOMMUNICATIONS POLICY (Aspen Inst., 2004) (http://www.aspeninstitute.org/ AspenInstitute/files/CCLIBRARYFILES/FILENAME/0000000717/Tele com2003.pdf).

Esbin, Barbara S. & Gary S. Lutzker, *Poles, Holes, and Cable Open Access: Where the Global Information Superhighway Meets the Local Right-of-Way*, 10 COMMLAW CONSPECTUS 23 (2001).

Farber, Daniel A. & Philip P. Frickey, *The Jurisprudence of Public Choice*, 65 TEXAS L. REV. 873 (1987).

Farrell, Joseph, *Creating Local Competition*, 49 FED. COMM. L.J. 201 (1996).

Farrell, Joseph & Carl Shapiro, *Standard Setting in High Definition Television*, BROOKINGS PAPERS ON ECONOMIC ACTIVITY (Brookings Inst. Press, 1992).

Farrell, Joseph & Garth Saloner, *Installed Base and Compatibility: Innovation, Product Preannouncements, and Predation*, 76 AM. ECON. REV. 940 (1986).

Farrell, Joseph & Philip J. Weiser, *Modularity, Vertical Integration, and Open Access Policies: Towards a Convergence of Antitrust and Regulation in the Internet Age*, 17 HARV. J.L. TECH. 85 (2003).

Faulhaber, Gerald, TELECOMMUNICATIONS IN TURMOIL (Addison Wesley, 1987).

Faulhaber, Gerald R. & David Farber, *Spectrum Management: Property Rights, Markets, and the Commons* (2003) (http:// rider.wharton.upenn.edu/~faulhabe/SPECTRUM_MANAGEMENTv5 1.pdf).

Ferguson, Charles, THE BROADBAND PROBLEM: ANATOMY OF A MARKET FAILURE AND A POLICY DILEMMA (Brookings Inst. Press, 2004).

Fowler, Mark S. & Daniel L. Brenner, *A Marketplace Approach to Broadcast Regulation*, 60 TEX. L. REV. 207 (1982).

Freeman, Jody, *Private Parties, Public Functions, and the New*

Administrative Law, 52 ADMIN. L. REV. 813 (2000).

Freeman, Jody, *The Private Role in Public Governance*, 75 N.Y.U. L. REV. 543 (2000).

Frieden, Rob, *Adjusting the Horizontal and Vertical in Telecommunications Regulation: A Comparison of the Traditional and a New Layered Approach*, 55 FED. COMM. L.J. 207 (2003).

Froomkin, A. Michael, *Habermas@discourse.net: Toward a Critical Theory of Cyberspace*, 116 HARV. L. REV. 749 (2003).

Froomkin, A. Michael, *Wrong Turn in Cyberspace: Using ICANN to Route Around APA and the Constitution*, 50 DUKE L. J. 17 (2000).

Gabel, Richard, *The Early Competitive Era in Telephone Communications, 1893-1950*, 34 LAW & CONTEMP. PROBS. 340 (1969).

Gandal, Neil et al., *Standards in Wireless Telephone Networks*, 27 TELECOMM. POL'Y 325 (2003).

General Accounting Office, *Additional Federal Efforts Could Help Advance Digital Television Transition* (November 2002).

General Accounting Office, *Better Knowledge Needed to Take Advantage of Technologies that May Improve Specrum Efficiency* (2004).

General Accounting Office, *History and Current Issues Related to Radio Spectrum Management* (2002).

General Accounting Office, *Issues Related to Competition and Subscriber Rates in the Cable Television Industry* (2003).

General Accounting Office, *Subscriber Rates and Competition in the Cable Television Industry* (2004).

General Accounting Office, *Telecommunications: Characteristics and Competitiveness of the Internet Backbone Market* (2001).

General Accounting Office, *Uneven Implementation of Wireless Enhanced 911 Raises Prospect of Piecemeal Availability for Years to Come* (2003).

Gifford, Raymond L., *Regulatory Impressionism: What State Regulators Can and Cannot Do*, 4 REV. NETWORK ECON. 466 (2003).

Gilder, George, TELECOSM: THE WORLD AFTER BANDWIDTH ABUNDANCE (Free Press, 2000).

Goodman, Ellen P., *Digital Television and the Allure of Auctions: The Birth and Stillbirth of DTV Legislation*, 49 FED. COMM. L.J. 517 (1997).

Goodman, Ellen P., *Spectrum Rights in the Telecosm to Come*, 41 SAN DIEGO L. REV. 269 (2004).

Grove, Andrew S., ONLY THE PARANOID SURVIVE: HOW TO EXPLOIT THE CRISIS POINTS THAT CHALLENGE EVERY COMPANY (Doubleday, 1996).

Hafner, Katie & Matthew Lyon, WHERE WIZARDS STAY UP LATE: THE ORIGINS OF THE INTERNET (Simon & Schuster, 1996).

Hagel III, John & Marc Singer, *Unbundling the Corporation*, 3 MCKINSEY Q. 148 (2000).

Hatfield, Dale N., *A Report on Technical and Operational Issues Impacting the Provision of Wireless Enhanced 911 Services* (Oct. 15, 2002) (http://gullfoss2.fcc.gov/prod/ecfs/retrieve.cgi?native_or_pdf=pdf&id_document=6513296239).

Hatfield, Dale, *Architecture as Policy, in* THE STANDARDS EDGE: DYNAMIC TENSION (Bolin Communications, Sherrie Bolin ed., 2004).

Hatfield, Dale N., Challenges of Network Design in an Increasingly Deregulated, Competitive Market, Remarks at the IEEE International Symposium (March 27, 2003) (http://www.im2003.org/presentation%20files/RemarksDH_IM2003.doc).

Hausman, Jerry & Howard Shelanski, *Economic Welfare and Telecommunications Regulation: The E-Rate Policy for Universal-Service Subsidies*, 16 YALE J. REG. 19 (1999).

Hausman, Jerry & Jeffrey MacKie-Mason, *Price Discrimination and Patent Policy*, 19 RAND J. ECON. 253 (1988).

Hausman, Jerry A. & J. Gregory Sidak, *A Consumer-Welfare Approach to the Mandatory Unbundling of Telecommunications Networks*, 109 YALE L.J. 417 (1999).

Hazlett, Thomas W., *All Broadcast Regulation Politics Are Local: A*

Response to Christopher Yoo's Model of Broadcast Regulation, 53 EMORY L.J. 233 (2004).

Hazlett, Thomas W., *Digitizing "Must Carry" Under Turner Broadcasting v. FCC*, 8 SUP. CT. ECON. REV. 141 (2000).

Hazlett, Thomas W., *The Wireless Craze, the Unlimited Bandwidth Myth, the Spectrum Auction Faux Pas, and the Punchline to Ronald Coase's "Big Joke": An Essay on Airwave Allocation Policy*, 14 HARV. J.L. & TECH. 335 (2001).

Herzel, Leo, *"Public Interest" and the Market in Color Television Regulation*, 18 U. CHI. L. REV. 802 (1951).

Huber, Peter et al., FEDERAL TELECOMMUNICATIONS LAW (Aspen Pub., 2d ed. 1999).

Huber, Peter, LAW AND DISORDER IN CYBERSPACE: ABOLISH THE FCC AND LET COMMON LAW RULE THE TELECOSM (Oxford Univ. Press, 1997).

Hundt, Reed, E., YOU SAY YOU WANT A REVOLUTION: A STORY OF INFORMATION AGE POLITICS (Yale Univ. Press, 2000).

Hundt, Reed, E., *The Ineluctable Modality of Broadband*, 21 YALE J. REG. 239 (2004).

Hundt, Reed, E., Thinking About Why Some Communications Mergers Are Unthinkable, Address to the Brookings Institution (June 19, 1997) (http://www.fcc.gov/Speeches/Hundt/spreh735.html).

IEEE-USA, *Report from the Workshop* (March 2003) (http://afn.johnson.cornell.edu/publish/WSR/WSR.pdf).

Isenberg, David, The Rise of the Stupid Network (1998) (http://www.hyperorg.com/misc/stupidnet.html).

Joskow, Paul L. & Roger G. Noll, *The Bell Doctrine: Applications in Telecommunications, Electricity, and Other Network Industries*, 51 STAN. L. REV. 1249 (1999).

Kahn, Alfred, Regulatory Politics as Usual, AEI-Brookings Joint Center (March 3, 2003) (http://www.aei-brookings.org/policy/page.php?id=127).

Kahn, Alfred E., LETTING GO: DEREGULATING THE PROCESS OF DEREGULATION (Inst. of Pub. Utils. and Network Indus., 1998).

Kahn, Alfred E., THE ECONOMICS OF REGULATION: PRINCIPLES AND INSTITUTIONS (MIT Press, 1988).

Kahn, Alfred E., *The Theory and Application of Regulation*, 55 ANTITRUST L.J. 177 (1986).

Kahn, Robert E. & Vinton G. Cerf, *What Is the Internet? (And What Makes It Work)* (1999) (http://www.policyscience.net/cerf.pdf).

Katz, Michael L. & Carl Shapiro, *Systems Competition and Network Effects*, J. ECON. PERSP. (Spring 1994).

Katz, Michael & Carl Shapiro, *Technology Adoption in the Presence of Network Externalities*, 92 J. POL. ECON. 822 (1986).

Kearney, Joseph D., *From the Fall of the Bell System to the Telecommunications Act: Regulation of Telecommunications Under Judge Greene*, 50 HASTINGS L.J. 1395 (1999).

Kearney, Joseph D., *Twilight of the FCC?* 1 GREEN BAG 2D 327 (1998).

Kearney, Joseph D. & Thomas W. Merrill, *The Great Transformation of Regulated Industries Law*, 98 COLUM. L. REV. 1323 (1998).

Keating, Stephen, CUTTHROAT (Johnson Books, 1999).

Kende, Michael, *The Digital Handshake: Connecting Internet Backbones*, FCC OPP WORKING PAPER NO. 32 (2000) (www.fcc.gov/Bureaus/OPP/working_papers/oppwp32.pdf).

Kennard, William E., The FCC's New Enforcement Ethic, Remarks Before the Competitive Carrier Summit 2000 (January 19, 2000) (http://www.fcc.gov/Speeches/Kennard/2000/spwek003.html).

Kennedy, Leonard J. & Heather A. Purcell, *Wandering Along the Road to Competition and Convergence—The Changing CMRS Roadmap*, 56 FED. COMM. L.J. 489 (2004).

Kirkham, Christopher Wyeth, Note, *Busting the Administrative Trust: An Experimentalist Approach to Universal Service in Telecommunications*, 98 COLUM. L. REV. 620 (1998).

Klein, Joel, Making the Transition from Regulation to Competition: Thinking About Merger Policy During the Process of Electric Power Restructuring, Address to the Federal Energy Regulatory Commission (January 21, 1998) (http://www.usdoj.gov/atr/public/speeches/1332.htm).

Klemperer, Paul, *How (Not) to Run Auctions: The European 3G Telecom Auctions*, 46 EUR. ECON. REV. 829 (2002) (http://www.nuff.ox.ac.uk/users/klemperer/hownot.pdf).

Klopfenstein, Bruce C. & David Seidman, *Technical Standards and the Marketplace: The Case of AM Stereo*, 34 J. BROADCASTING & ELEC. MEDIA 171 (1990).

Krattenmaker, Thomas G. & A. Richard Metzger, Jr., *FCC Regulatory Authority over Commercial Television Networks: The Role of Ancillary Jurisdiction*, 77 NW. U. L. REV. 403 (1982).

Krattenmaker, Thomas G. & Lucas A. Powe, Jr., REGULATING BROADCAST PROGRAMMING (MIT Press, 1994).

Krattenmaker, Thomas G. & Steven C. Salop, *Anticompetitive Exclusion: Raising Rivals' Cost to Achieve Power over Price*, 96 YALE L.J. 209 (1986).

Kraus, Michael I., *Regulation vs. Markets in the Development of Standards*, 3 S. CAL. INTERDISC. L. J. 781 (1994).

Kwerel, Evan & John Williams, *A Proposal for a Rapid Transition to Market Allocation of Spectrum*, OPP WORKING PAPER Series No. 38 (2002) (http://hraunfoss.fcc.gov/edocs_public/attachmatch/DOC-228552A1.pdf).

Laffont, Jean-Jacques & Jean Tirole, COMPETITION IN TELECOMMUNICATIONS (MIT Press, 2000).

Langlois, Richard N., *Modularity in Technology and Organization*, 49 J. ECON. BEHAV. & ORG. 19 (2002).

Langlois, Richard N., *Technological Standards, Innovation, and Essential Facilities: Towards a Schumpeterian Post-Chicago Approach, in* DYNAMIC COMPETITION AND PUBLIC POLICY: TECHNOLOGY, INNOVATION, AND ANTITRUST ISSUES (Cambridge Univ. Press, Jerry Ellig ed., 2001).

Lavey, Warren, *The Public Policies that Changed the Telephone Industry into Regulated Monopolies: Lessons from Around 1915*, 39 FED. COMM. L.J. 171 (1987).

Lemley, Mark, *Intellectual Property Rights and Standard-Setting Organizations*, 90 CALIF. L. REV. 1889 (2002).

Lemley, Mark A., *Standardizing Government Standard Setting Policy for Electronic Commerce*, 14 BERKELEY TECH. L.J. 745 (1999).

Lemley, Mark A. & Lessig, Lawrence, *The End of End-to-End: Preserving the Architecture of the Internet in the Broadband Era*, 48 UCLA L. REV. 925, 934 (2001).

Lessig, Lawrence, CODE AND OTHER LAWS OF CYBERSPACE (Vintage Books, 2001).

Lessig, Lawrence, THE FUTURE OF IDEAS: THE FATE OF THE COMMONS IN A CONNECTED WORLD (Basic Books, 2001).

Lessig, Lawrence, FREE CULTURE: HOW BIG MEDIA USES TECHNOLOGY AND THE LAW TO LOCK DOWN CULTURE AND CONTROL CREATIVITY (Penguin Press, 2001).

Lewis, Michael, THE NEW NEW THING (Penguin Books, 1999).

Libicki, Martin et al., *Scaffolding the New Web: Standards and Standards Policy for the Digital Economy* (2000) (http://www.rand.org/publications/MR/MR1215).

Lichtman, Douglas & Randal C. Picker, *Entry Policy in Local Telecommunications: Iowa Utilities and Verizon*, 2002 SUP. CT. REV. 41 (2002).

Liebowitz, Stan & Stephen Margolis, WINNERS, LOSERS, AND MICROSOFT (Independent Institute, 1999).

Lubinsky, Charles, *Reconsidering Retransmission Consent: An Examination of the Retransmission Consent Provision (47 U.S.C. § 325(B)) of the 1992 Cable Act)*, 49 FED. COMM. L.J. 99 (1996).

MacAvoy, Paul, THE FAILURE OF ANTITRUST AND REGULATION TO ESTABLISH COMPETITION IN LONG-DISTANCE SERVICES (MIT Press, 1996).

Malik, Om, BROADBANDITS: INSIDE THE $750 BILLION TELECOM HEIST (John Wiley & Sons, 2003).

Margie, R. Paul, *Can You Hear Me Now?: Getting Better Reception From The FCC's Spectrum Policy*, 2003 STAN. TECH. L. REV. 5.

Marcus, Scott, *The Potential Relevance to the United States of the European Union's Newly Adopted Regulatory Framework for Telecommunications*, 2 J. TELECOMM. & HIGH TECH. L. 111 (2003).

McGuigan, Philip Palmer et al., *Cellular Mobile Radio Telecommunications: Regulating an Emerging Industry*, 1983 BYU L. REV. 305.

McMillan, John, REINVENTING THE BAZAAR (W.W. Norton & Co., 2003).

McTaggert, Craig, *A Layered Approach to Internet Legal Analysis*, 48 McGILL L.J. 571 (2003).

Minow, Newton N., *Television and the Public Interest*, 55 FED. COMM. L.J. 395 (2003).

Mueller, Milton, UNIVERSAL SERVICE: COMPETITION, INTERCONNECTION, AND MONOPOLY IN THE MAKING OF THE AMERICAN TELEPHONE SYSTEM (MIT Press, 1997).

Mullen, Megan, THE RISE OF CABLE PROGRAMMING IN THE UNITED STATES (Univ. of Texas Press, 2003)

Nadler, Jonathan Jacob, *Give Peace a Chance: FCC-State Relations After California III*, 47 FED. COMM. L.J. 457 (1995).

Nakahata, John T., *Regulating Information Platforms: The Challenges of Rewriting Communications Regulation from the Bottom Up*, 1 J. TELECOMM. & HIGH TECH. L. 95 (2002).

National Research Council, BROADBAND: BRINGING HOME THE BITS (National Academies Press, 2002).

Naughton, John, A BRIEF HISTORY OF THE FUTURE (Overlook Press, 1999).

Netanel, Neil Weinstock, *Impose a Noncommercial Levy to Allow Free Peer-to-Peer File Sharing*, 17 HARV. J. L & TECH. 1 (2003).

New Millenium Research Council, *Free Ride: Deficiencies of the MCI "Layers" Policy Model and the Need for Principles that Encourage Competition in the New IP World* (July 2004) (http://www.newmillenniumresearch.org/news/071304_report.pdf).

Newman, Stagg, *Broadband Access Platforms: An Assessment*, TPRC Working Paper (September 2003) (http://intel.si.umich.edu/tprc/papers/2003/254/BbandAccessPlatforms.pdf).

Noam, Eli, *Beyond Spectrum Auctions: Taking the Next Step to Open Spectrum Access*, 21 TELECOMM. POL'Y 461 (1997).

Noam, Eli, INTERCONNECTING THE NETWORK OF NETWORKS (MIT Press, 2001).

Noam, Eli, *Spectrum Auctions: Yesterday's Heresy, Today's Orthodoxy, Tomorrow's Anachronism*, 41 J.L. ECON. 765 (1998).

Noam, Eli M., *Will Universal Service and Common Carriage Survive the Telecommunications Act of 1996?* 97 COLUM. L. REV. 955 (1997).

Noll, Roger G., The FCC's New Television Ownership Rules, Stanford Institute For Economic Policy Research Policy Brief (June 2003) (http://siepr.stanford.edu/papers/briefs/policybrief_jun03.pdf).

Note, *Competition in the Telephone Equipment Industry: Beyond Telerent*, 86 YALE L.J. 538 (1977).

Note, *Federal Control of Radio Broadcasting*, 39 YALE L.J. 244 (1929).

Nuechterlein, Jonathan E., *Incentives to Speak Honestly About Incentives: The Need for Structural Reform of the Local Competition Debate*, 2 J. TELECOMM. & HIGH TECH. L. 399 (2003).

Odlyzko, Andrew, Telecom Dogma and Spectrum Allocations (June 20, 2004) (http://wirelessunleashed.com/papers/TelecomDogmas.pdf).

Odlyzko, Andrew, *The Many Paradoxes of Broadband*, 8 FIRST MONDAY 4 (September 2003) (http://firstmonday.org/issues/issue8_9/odlyzko/index.html).

Owen, Bruce M., *Regulatory Reform: The Telecommunications Act of 1996 and the FCC Media Ownership Rules*, 2003 MICH. ST. L. REV. 671 (2003).

Posner, Richard A., *Antitrust in the New Economy*, 68 ANTITRUST L.J. 925 (2001).

Posner, Richard A., ANTITRUST LAW (Univ. of Chicago Press, 2d ed., 2001).

Posner, Richard, *Taxation by Regulation*, 2 BELL J. ECON. & MGMT. SCI. 22 (1971).

Posner, Richard A., *The Chicago School of Antitrust Analysis*, 127 U. PA. L. REV. 925 (1979).

Powell, Michael K., *Preserving Internet Freedom: Guiding Principles for the Industry*, 3 J. TELECOMM. & HIGH TECH. L. 5 (2004).

Powell, Michael K., Broadband Migration III: New Directions in Wireless Policy, Remarks at the Silicon Flatirons Telecommunications Program (October 30, 2002) (http://www.fcc.gov/Speeches/Powell/2002/spmkp212.html).

Price, Monroe E. & John F. Duffy, *Technological Change and Doctrinal Persistence: Telecommunications Reform in Congress and the Court*, 97 COLUM. L. REV. 976 (1997).

Riordan, Michael & Steven Salop, *Evaluating Vertical Mergers: A Post-Chicago Approach*, 63 ANTITRUST L.J. 513 (1995).

Robinson, Constance K., Network Effects in Telecommunications Mergers—MCI Worldcom Merger: Protecting the Future of the Internet, Address Before the Practicing Law Institute (August 23, 1999) (http://www.usdoj.gov/atr/public/speeches/3889.htm).

Robinson, Glen O., *The Electronic First Amendment: An Essay for the New Age*, 47 DUKE L.J. 899 (1998).

Robinson, Glen O., *On Refusing to Deal with Rivals*, 87 CORNELL L. REV. 1177 (2002).

Robinson, Glen O., *The Federal Communications Act: An Essay on Origins and Regulatory Purposes*, *in* A LEGISLATIVE HISTORY OF THE COMMUNICATIONS ACT OF 1934 (Oxford Univ. Press, Max D. Paglin ed., 1989).

Robinson, Glen O., *The Titanic Remembered: AT&T and the Changing World of Telecommunications*, 5 YALE J. REG. 517 (1988).

Rohlfs, Jeffrey H., BANDWAGON EFFECTS IN HIGH-TECH INDUSTRIES (MIT Press, 2001).

Rohlfs, Jeffrey H. et al., *Estimate of Loss to the United States Caused by the FCC's Delay in Licensing Cellular Communications* (National Economic Research Associates, Nov. 8, 1991).

Rosenzweig, Roy, *Wizards, Bureaucrats, Warriors, and Hackers: Writing the History of the Internet*, 103 AMER. HIST. REV. 1530 (1998).

Rossi, Jim, *Lowering the Filed Tariff Shield: Judicial Enforcement for a Deregulatory Era*, 56 VAND. L. REV. 1591 (2003).

Rossi, Jim, *Participation Run Amok: The Costs of Mass Participation for Deliberative Agency Decisionmaking*, 92 NW. U. L. REV. 173 (1997).

Rubin, Edward L., *Computer Languages as Networks and Power Structures: Governing the Development of XML*, 53 SMU L. REV. 1447 (2000).

Rubinfeld, Daniel L. & Hal J. Singer, *Open Access to Broadband Networks: A Case Study of the AOL/Time Warner Merger*, 16 BERKELEY TECH. L.J. 631 (2001).

Russell, Donald J. & Sherri Lynn Wolson, *Dual Antitrust Review of Telecommunications Mergers by the Department of Justice and the Federal Communications Commission*, 11 GEO. MASON L. REV. 143 (2002).

Saltzer, Jerome H. et al., *End-to-End Arguments in System Design*, 2 ACM TRANSACTIONS ON COMPUTER SYSTEMS 277 (1984), *reprinted in* INNOVATIONS IN INTERNETWORKING 195 (Craig Partridge ed., 1988).

Schallop, Michael J., *The IPR Paradox: Leveraging Intellectual Property Rights to Encourage Interoperability in the Network Computing Age*, 28 AIPLA Q.J. 195 (2000).

Schmalensee, Richard, *Antitrust Issues in Schumpeterian Industries*, 90 AM. ECON. REV. 192 (2000).

Schumpeter, Joseph, CAPITALISM, SOCIALISM AND DEMOCRACY (Harper, 1975).

Schwartz, Marius, *The Economic Logic for Conditioning Bell Entry into Long Distance on the Prior Opening of Local Markets*, 18 J. REG. ECON. 247 (2000).

Scott, Ben, *The Politics and Policy of Media Ownership*, 53 AM. U. L. REV. 645 (2004).

Semeraro, Steven, *Speta on Antitrust and Local Competition Under the Telecommunications Act: A Comment Respecting the Accommodation of Antitrust and Telecom Regulation*, 71 ANTITRUST L.J. 147 (2003).

Shapiro, Carl, *Setting Compatibility Standards: Cooperation or Collusion?* in EXPANDING THE BOUNDARIES OF INTELLECTUAL PROPERTY (Rochelle Cooper Dreyfus et al. eds., 2001).

Shapiro, Carl & Hal R. Varian, INFORMATION RULES (Harv. Bus. School Press, 1999).

Shannon, Claude E., *A Mathematical Theory of Communications*, 27 BELL SYS. TECH. J. 379 (1948).

Sharkey, William, THE THEORY OF NATURAL MONOPOLY (Cambridge Univ. Press, 1982).

Shelanski, Howard A., *Competition and Deployment of New Technology in U.S. Telecommunications*, 2000 U. CHI. LEGAL F. 85.

Shelanski, Howard A., *Competition and Regulation in Broadband Communications, in* BROADBAND: SHOULD WE REGULATE HIGH-SPEED INTERNET ACCESS? 177 (Brookings Inst. Press, Robert W. Crandall & James H. Alleman eds., 2002).

Shelanski, Howard A., *The Bending Line Between Conventional "Broadcast" and Wireless "Carriage,"* 97 COLUM. L. REV. 1048 (1997).

Shelanski, Howard A. & J. Gregory Sidak., *Antitrust Divestiture in Network Industries*, 68 U. CHI. L. REV. 1 (2001).

Sicker, Douglas C. & Joshua L. Mindel, *Refinements of a Layered Model for Telecommunications Policy*, 1 J. TELECOMM. & HIGH TECH. L. 69 (2002).

Sidak, J. Gregory & Daniel L. Spulber, DEREGULATORY TAKINGS AND THE REGULATORY CONTRACT: THE COMPETITIVE TRANSFORMATION OF NETWORK INDUSTRIES IN THE UNITED STATES (Cambridge Univ. Press, 1998).

Speta, James B., *A Common Carrier Approach to Internet Interconnection*, 54 FED. COMM. L.J. 225 (2002).

Speta, James B., *A Vision of Internet Openness by Government Fiat*, 96 NW. L. REV. 1553 (2002).

Speta, James B., *Antitrust and Local Competition Under the Telecommunications Act*, 71 ANTITRUST L.J. 99 (2003).

Speta, James B., *Deregulating Telecommunications in Internet Time*, 61 WASH. & LEE L. REV. 1063 (2004).

Spitzer, Matthew L., *The Constitutionality of Licensing Broadcasters*, 64 N.Y.U. L. REV. 990 (1989).

Starr, Paul, THE CREATION OF THE MEDIA: POLITICAL ORIGINS OF MODERN COMMUNICATIONS (Basic Books, 2004).

Stefik, Mark, *Shifting the Possible: How Trusted Systems and Digital Property Challenge Us to Rethink Digital Publishing*, 12 BERKELEY TECH L.J. 137 (1997).

Tryniecki, Timothy J., *Cellular Tower Siting Jurisprudence Under the Telecommunications Act of 1996—The First Five Years*, 37 Real Prop. Prob. & Tr. J. 271 (2002).

U.S. Congress, Office of Technology Assessment, *Global Standards: Building Blocks for the Future* (1992).

Viscusi, W. Kip et al., ECONOMICS OF REGULATION AND ANTITRUST (MIT Press, 3d ed. 2000).

Wallman, Kathleen M. H., *The Role of Government in Telecommunications Standard-Setting*, 8 COMMLAW CONSPECTUS 235 (2000).

Webbink, Douglas W., *Frequency Spectrum Deregulation Alternatives*, FCC WORKING PAPER (1980) (http:/www.fcc.gov/Bureaus/ OPP/working_papers/oppwp2.pdf).

Weinberg, Jonathan, *ICANN and the Problem of Legitimacy*, 50 DUKE L.J. 187 (2000).

Weiser, Philip J., *Federal Common Law, Cooperative Federalism, and the Enforcement of the Telecom Act*, 76 N.Y.U. L. REV. 1692 (2001).

Weiser, Philip J., Goldwasser, *the Telecom Act, and Reflections on Antitrust Remedies*, 55 ADMIN. L. REV. 1 (2003).

Weiser, Philip J. *Internet Governance, Standard Setting, and Self-Regulation*, 28 N. KY. L. REV. 822 (2001).

Weiser, Philip J., *The Internet, Innovation, and Intellectual Property Policy*, 103 COLUM. L. REV. 534 (2003).

Weiser, Philip J., *Toward a Next Generation Regulatory Strategy*, 35 LOY. U. CHI. L.J. 41 (2003).

Weiss, James R. & Martin L. Stern, *Serving Two Masters: The Dual Jurisdiction of the FCC and the Justice Department over Telecommunications Transactions*, 6 COMMLAW CONSPECTUS 195 (1998).

Weller, Dennis, *Auctions for Universal Service Obligations*, 23 TELECOMM. POL'Y 645 (1999).

Werbach, Kevin, *A Layered Model for Internet Policy*, 1 J. TELECOMM. & HIGH TECH. L. 37 (2002).

Werbach, Kevin, *Supercommons: Toward a Unified Theory of Wireless Communication*, 82 TEX. L. REV. 863 (2004).

Werbach, Kevin, *Digital Tornado: The Internet and Telecommunications Policy*, FCC OFFICE OF PLANS & POLICY WORKING PAPER NO. 29 (1997).

Whitt, Richard S., *A Horizontal Leap Forward: Formulating a New Communications Policy Framework Based on the Network Layers Model*, 56 FED. COMM. L.J. (2004).

Wiley, Richard E., *The Challenge of Choice*, 47 FED. COMM. L.J. 401 (1994).

Williams, Mary Newcomer, *Comparative Analysis of Telecommunications Regulation: Pitfalls and Opportunities*, 56 FED. COMM. L.J. 269 (2003).

Williamson, Oliver, THE MECHANISMS OF GOVERNANCE (Oxford Univ. Press, 1996).

Winston, Clifford, *U.S. Industry Adjustment to Economic Deregulation*, J. ECON. PERSP. (Summer 1998).

Wu, Tim, *Copyright's Communications Policy*, __ MICH. L. REV. __ (2004).

Wu, Tim and Lessig, Lawrence, Ex Parte Letter, *In re: Inquiry Concerning High-Speed Access to the Internet Over Cable and Other Facilities* (2003) (http://faculty.virginia.edu/timwu/wu_lessig_fcc.pdf).

Wu, Tim, *Network Neutrality, Broadband Discrimination*, 2 J. TELECOMM. & HIGH TECH. L. 141 (2003).

Yoo, Christopher S., *Rethinking the Commitment to Free, Local Television*, 52 EMORY L.J. 1650 (2003).

Yoo, Christopher S., *The Rise and Demise of the Technology-Specific Approach to the First Amendment*, 91 GEO. L.J. 245 (2003).

Yoo, Christopher, *Vertical Integration and Media Regulation in the New Economy*, 19 YALE J. REG. 171 (2002).

Yoo, Christopher, *Would Mandating Broadband Network Neutrality Help or Hurt Competition? A Comment on the End-to-End Debate*, 3 J. TELECOMM. & HIGH TECH. L. 23 (2004).

Table of Authorities

Cases

Regulatory Decisions

2000 Biennial Regulatory Review Spectrum Aggregation Limits for Commercial Mobile Radio Services, Report and Order, 16 FCC Rcd 22,668 (2001). 591

1998 Biennial Regulatory Review-Review of the Commission's Broadcast Ownership Rules and Other Rules Adopted Pursuant to Section 202 of the Telecommunications Act of 1996, Report and Order, 15 FCC Rcd 11,058 (2003). 617

Aaron v. GTE Cal., Inc., Memorandum Opinion and Order, 10 FCC Rcd 11,519 (1995). 638

Access Charge Reform, Eighth Report and Order, CC Dkt. No. 96-262, FCC No. 04-110 (May 18, 2004). 599, 600

Access Charge Reform, Order on Remand, 18 FCC Rcd 14,976 (2003). 605

Access Charge Reform, Seventh Report and Order, 16 FCC Rcd 9923 (2001). 600

Access Charge Reform, Sixth Report and Order, 15 FCC Rcd 12,962 (2000). 605

Access Charge Reform, First Report and Order, 12 FCC Rcd 15,982 (1997). 577

Advanced Television Systems and their Impact upon the Existing Television Broadcast Service, Fifth Report and Order, 12 FCC Rcd 12,809 (1997). 623

Advanced Television Systems and Their Impact upon Existing Television Broadcast Service, Fifth Further Notice of Proposed Rulemaking, 11 FCC Rcd 6235 (1996). 622

Advanced Television Systems and Their Impact Upon Existing Television Broadcast Service, Fourth Report and Order, 11 FCC Rcd 17,771 (1996). 622

Advanced Television Systems and Their Impact on Existing Television Broadcast Service, Notice of Inquiry, 2 FCC Rcd 5125 (1987). 622

Amendment of the Commission's Rules to Allow the Selection from Among Mutually Exclusive Competing Cellular Applications, Report and Order, 98 F.C.C.2d 175 (1984). 580

Amendment of Part 2 of the Commission's Rules to Allocate Spectrum Below 3GHz, Second Report and Order, 17 FCC Rcd 23,193 (2002). 584

Amendment of Part 67 of the Commission's Rules and Establishment of a Joint Board, Decision and Order, 96 F.C.C.2d 781 (1984). 604

530   Table of Authorities

Notes

Note to readers—The Web addresses cited here are subject to change.

Chapter One

1 *See* Smithsonian Institution Libraries, *The Underwater Web: Cabling the Seas* (http://www.sil.si.edu/Exhibitions/Underwater-Web/uw-optic-02.htm).

2 Nicholas Lemann, *The Chairman*, THE NEW YORKER, Oct. 7, 2002, at 48.

3 *See generally* Neil Munro & Bara Vaida, *Free-Market Cheerleader*, NATIONAL JOURNAL, July 3, 2004 (2004 WL 84028182).

4 Lemann, *supra*, at 48.

5 *See, e.g.*, PETER W. HUBER, LAW AND DISORDER IN CYBERSPACE: ABOLISH THE FCC AND LET COMMON LAW RULE THE TELECOSM (Oxford Univ. Press, 1997).

6 *See, e.g.*, CHARLES FERGUSON, THE BROADBAND PROBLEM: ANATOMY OF A MARKET FAILURE AND A POLICY DILEMMA (Brookings Inst. Press, 2004).

7 One renowned study of these early years concludes that, before AT&T's Bell System cemented its lock on most major markets, the competition for market dominance prompted rival telephone companies to build out infrastructure throughout population centers as quickly as possible, with quite significant consumer benefits. *See* MILTON MUELLER, UNIVERSAL SERVICE: COMPETITION, INTERCONNECTION, AND MONOPOLY IN THE MAKING OF THE AMERICAN TELEPHONE SYSTEM (AEI Press, 1997). That may well be so, but there is broad consensus that, left to its own devices, such competition was bound in the end to produce a single dominant provider in any given market.

8 *See generally* GERALD W. BROCK, TELECOMMUNICATION POLICY FOR THE INFORMATION AGE 65-66 (Harv. Univ. Press, 1994).

9 David D. Kirkpatrick, *As Instant Messaging Comes of Age, AOL Says F.C.C. Rule Holds It Back*, N.Y. TIMES, May 26, 2003, at C1 (quoting Wharton professor Gerald Faulhaber).

10 Memorandum Opinion and Order, *Applications for Consent to the Transfer of Control of Licenses and Section 214 Authorizations by Time Warner Inc. and America Online, Inc., Transferors, to AOL Time Warner Inc., Transferee,* 16 FCC Rcd 6547, ¶¶ 191–200 (2001). For a critical evaluation of the decision, see Philip J. Weiser, *Internet Governance, Standard Setting, and Self-Regulation,* 28 N. KY. L. REV. 822, 844 (2001).

11 Memorandum Opinion and Order, *Time Warner Inc.,* 18 FCC Rcd 16,835 (2003) (lifting condition). The major IM providers have reportedly made progress on a negotiated solution to interoperability. *See* Jim Hu & David Becker, *IM Giants Drop Some Barriers to Peace,* CNET NEWS.COM (July 15, 2004) (http://news.com.com/2100-1032_3-5270067.html) (reporting on settlement of issue).

12 *See* United States v. Microsoft Corp., 84 F. Supp. 2d 9, 18–23 (D.D.C. 1999), *aff'd in relevant part,* 253 F.3d 34, 55-56 (D.C. Cir. 2001).

13 An analogous dynamic explains the victory of the VHS standard over Betamax in the market for video cassette recorders (VCRs). After a period of direct competition, the market tipped to VHS. At first glance, one might think that a Betamax user should have been indifferent to the choice of most other viewers to buy VHS recorders, so long as her own Betamax recorder continued to work. The problem was that her Betamax recorder was valuable to her largely to the extent that she could go to the store and rent videos to play in it. Once it became clear that the market was tipping, fewer firms manufactured Betamax videos and fewer retail outlets reserved shelf space for them. This process fed on itself, and users began switching in droves to VHS, which became the established standard in part because of these indirect network effects. For a classic exposition of such network effects phenomena throughout the economy, see CARL SHAPIRO & HAL VARIAN, INFORMATION RULES: A STRATEGIC GUIDE TO THE NETWORK ECONOMY 173-225 (Harv. Bus. School Press, 1998).

14 JOSEPH A. SCHUMPETER, CAPITALISM, SOCIALISM, AND DEMOCRACY 81–90 (Harper & Bros., 2d ed. 1947). For a discussion of the Schumpeterian perspective, see Philip J. Weiser, *The Internet, Innovation, and Intellectual Property Policy,* 103 COLUM. L. REV. 534, 576-583 (2003).

15 *See* Howard A. Shelanski & J. Gregory Sidak, *Antitrust Divestiture in Network Industries,* 68 U. CHI. L. REV. 1, 10–11 (2001).

16 *See* CLAYTON M. CHRISTENSEN, THE INNOVATOR'S DILEMMA (Harv. Bus. School Press, 1997) (discussing related concept of "disruptive technology").

17 *See, e.g.,* Richard Schmalensee, *Antitrust Issues in Schumpeterian Industries,* 90 AM. ECON. REV. 192, 194 (2000).

18 Richard A. Posner, *Antitrust in the New Economy,* 68 ANTITRUST L.J. 925, 930 (2001).

19 William Baumol explains the distinction:

There is considerable confusion in the literature about two pertinent concepts, fixed costs and sunk costs, which are really very different. . . . [F]ixed costs are costs that must be incurred in a lump in order for any output at all to be provided, and they do not vary when the magnitude of output changes. These costs are not variable either in the short or the long run. Any cost that is not fixed is defined to be variable. A sunk cost, however, is a cost that cannot be avoided for some limited period of time, but after that period it becomes avoidable or escapable. A cost that is fixed may or may not be sunk, and a cost that is sunk may not be fixed. For example, one cannot operate an airline between, say, New York and Milwaukee without investing in at least one airplane, an outlay whose amount does not vary with number of passengers until capacity is reached. Thus, this cost is fixed, and does not become variable even in the long run, because one cannot run an airline on the route with zero airplanes. In contrast, this cost is not sunk because, if traffic between New York and Milwaukee declines drastically, the plane can be shifted to serve another route.

William J. Baumol, *Predation and the Logic of the Average Variable Cost Test*, 39 J.L. & ECON. 49, 57 n.13 (1996).

20 *See generally* W. KIP VISCUSI ET AL., ECONOMICS OF REGULATION AND ANTITRUST 413-16 (MIT Press, 3d ed. 2000).

21 2 ALFRED E. KAHN, THE ECONOMICS OF REGULATION: PRINCIPLES AND INSTITUTIONS 119 (MIT Press, 1988).

22 *See generally* VISCUSI, *supra*, at 337-60.

23 Omega Satellite Prods. Co. v. City of Indianapolis, 694 F.2d 119, 126 (7th Cir. 1982).

24 *See, e.g.,* Warren G. Lavey, *The Public Policies that Changed the Telephone Industry into Regulated Monopolies: Lessons from Around 1915*, 39 FED. COMM. L.J. 171 (1987).

25 *See* Daniel A. Farber & Philip P. Frickey, *The Jurisprudence of Public Choice*, 65 TEXAS L. REV. 873 (1987); DENNIS C. MUELLER, PUBLIC CHOICE (Cambridge Univ. Press, 3d ed. 2003).

26 For a classic explanation of this point, see Richard Posner, *Taxation By Regulation*, 2 BELL J. ECON. & MGMT. SCI. 22 (1971).

27 To some extent, this was because regulators became more self-consciously familiar with public choice theory, which illustrates the many respects in which regulation can help individual industry participants but harm the consumers it is designed to serve. *See generally* Joseph D. Kearney & Thomas W. Merrill, *The Great Transformation of Regulated Industries Law*, 98 COLUM. L. REV. 1323, 1384, 1397 (1998).

28 *See* AUGUSTIN COURNOT, RESEARCHES INTO THE MATHEMATICAL PRINCIPLES OF THE THEORY OF WEALTH 103 (Macmillan, Nathaniel T. Bacon trans. 1927) (1838).

29 Hal R. Varian, *In Europe, G.E. and Honeywell Ran Afoul of 19th Century Thinking*, N.Y. TIMES, June 28, 2001 (http://www.sims.berkeley.edu/~hal/people/hal/NYTimes/2001-06-28.html). This phenomenon is often cited as a reason to per-

mit, rather than preclude, the merger of dominant firms in adjacent markets, for if "the copper and zinc producers merged, the merged entity would take into account that the price of copper affected the demand for zinc and set a lower price for both copper and zinc than independent producers would." *Id.*

30 Indeed, the reported ambition of Netscape chief technologist Marc Andreessen was to "reduce Windows to a set of poorly debugged device drivers." KEN AULETTA, WORLD WAR 3.0: MICROSOFT AND ITS ENEMIES 82 (Random House, 2001). Netscape CEO James Barksdale sounded a more nuanced tone at Microsoft's antitrust trial, acknowledging only that Netscape believed it could "substitute for some of the characteristics" of Windows. *Id.*

31 For a discussion of the complementary externality principle, its exceptions (as exemplified by the Microsoft case), and its application to telecommunications policy, see Joseph Farrell & Philip J. Weiser, *Modularity, Vertical Integration, and Open Access Policies: Towards a Convergence of Antitrust and Regulation in the Internet Age*, 17 HARV. J. L. & TECH. 85 (2003) (http://jolt.law.harvard.edu/articles/pdf/v17/17HarvJLTech085.pdf).

32 Because of similar concerns, the Federal Trade Commission conditioned the merger of Time Warner and Turner Broadcasting on the merged firm's commitment to carry at least one rival cable news network, thereby preventing Time Warner from discriminating in favor of CNN and against its upstart rivals. *See* Notice, *Time Warner, Inc.*, 61 FED. REG. 50,301 (1996).

33 The intermediate federal courts of appeals with jurisdiction to conduct direct review of FCC orders include the eleven "regional" circuits (such as the "Eighth Circuit," which sits in the midwest) plus the United States Court of Appeals for the District of Columbia Circuit. That court, known as the "D.C. Circuit," has at least concurrent jurisdiction with the regional circuits to review FCC orders, *see* 47 U.S.C. § 402(a), and exclusive jurisdiction to review certain categories of those orders, *see* 47 U.S.C. § 402(b). For that reason, and because of the expertise it gained in superintending the AT&T consent decree in the 1980s and 1990s, the D.C. Circuit plays an unusually central role in U.S. telecommunications policy.

34 Time Warner Entm't Co. v. FCC, 240 F.3d 1126, 1134 (D.C. Cir. 2001).

35 United States v. Southwestern Cable Co., 392 U.S. 157 (1968).

36 AT&T v. Iowa Utils. Bd., 525 U.S. 366, 430 (1999) (Breyer, J., concurring in part and dissenting in part).

Chapter Two

1 Fiber-to-the-Home Council, *Fiber-to-the-Home: Overview and Technical Tutorial* (Aug. 7, 2003) (http://www.fcc.gov/oet/tutorial/FTTH_Tutorial-8-7-03.ppt).

2 *See* New Paradigm Resources Group, *Dark Fiber: Means to a Network* 6 (Feb. 2002) (http://www.fibertech.com/docs/MeansToANetwork.pdf) (reporting that, as of 2002, "*95 percent* of [all] installed fiber is dark"); Stephen Lee & Jennifer Jones,

Shedding Light on Dark Fiber and the Lack Thereof, CNN.COM (July 31, 2001) (http://www.cnn.com/2001/TECH/internet/07/31/dark.fiber.debates.idg) (reporting that only 2% to 3% of fiber in backbone networks was being used in 2001).

3 *See Goodbye to the Video Store*, THE ECONOMIST, Sept. 19, 2002 (http://www.economist.com/displaystory.cfm?story_id=1324695).

4 Once these carriers realized that market prices were plummeting, some compensated by using accounting gimmicks to inflate reported revenues. For example, two carriers might "swap" fiber-optic facilities; each party to the swap would report the purchase of fiber capacity as a capital investment, whose costs would be reflected on the books only over the course of many years, but would simultaneously report all revenues associated with the *sale* of fiber capacity up front to include it in the current reporting period. Some of these accounting measures went beyond gimmicks to outright fraud. For a comprehensive account of the ensuing scandals, see OM MALIK, BROADBANDITS: INSIDE THE $750 BILLION TELECOM HEIST (Wiley, 2003).

5 *See, e.g.,* 47 U.S.C. §§ 153(21), (25), 271(a).

6 This figure is expressed as 4 followed by 16 zeros. Mathematically, if N is the number of subscribers, the number of lines needed to link each with every other equals $(N^2 - N)/2$.

7 That is true even of calls subject to time division multiplexing: even though the physical line itself is invariably host to a stream of signals, that line reserves dedicated time slots—i.e., capacity—for any given call for its entire duration, whether anyone is talking or not.

8 *See generally* JEAN-JACQUES LAFFONT & JEAN TIROLE, COMPETITION IN TELECOMMUNICATIONS 29-35 (MIT Press, 2000).

9 Verizon Communications Inc. v. FCC, 535 U.S. 467, 477 (2002) (citations omitted). In 1887, the Supreme Court upheld this system of regulation as consistent with the constitutional protection of property rights, including the protection against "takings" of property without just compensation, on the theory that the regulated entities were "affected with a public interest" and that "when private property is devoted to a public use, it is subject to public regulation." Munn v. Illinois, 94 U.S. 113, 130 (1876) (internal quotations omitted).

10 Duquesne Light Co. v. Barasch, 488 U.S. 299, 312 (1989).

11 *Verizon Communications, supra.*

12 47 U.S.C. § 152(b); *see* La. Pub. Serv. Comm'n v. FCC, 476 U.S. 355 (1986).

13 See Smith v. Ill. Bell Tel. Co., 282 U.S. 133, 148-149 (1930).

14 *See* GERALD W. BROCK, TELECOMMUNICATION POLICY FOR THE INFORMATION AGE 68, 190-91 (Harv. Univ. Press, 1994) (discussing "Ozark Plan" and subsequent separations regime).

15 *See generally* Tex. Office of Pub. Util. Counsel v. FCC, 265 F.3d 313 (5th Cir. 2001); Nat'l Ass'n of Reg. Util. Comm'rs v. FCC, 737 F.2d 1095 (D.C. Cir. 1984).

16 Brock, *supra*, at 139-45, 177-89.

17 *See* Decision and Order, *MTS and WATS Market Structure, Amendment of Part 36 of the Commission's Rules and Establishment of a Joint Board*, 4 FCC Rcd 5660 (1989); *see generally Qwest Corp. v. Scott*, 380 F.3d 367 (8th Cir. 2004).

18 *See generally* WorldCom, Inc. v. FCC, 238 F.3d 449 (D.C. Cir. 2001).

19 *See generally* Ill. Bell Tel. Co. v. FCC, 966 F.2d 1478 (D.C. Cir. 1992).

20 *See, e.g.*, Am. Tel. & Tel. Co. v. Cent. Office Tel., Inc., 524 U.S. 214 (1998).

21 *See* MCI WorldCom, Inc. v. FCC, 209 F.3d 760, 763-65 (D.C. Cir. 2000).

22 *See* United States Tel. Ass'n v. FCC, 188 F.3d 521 (D.C. Cir. 1999).

23 *See, e.g.*, W. Kip Viscusi, et al., Economics of Regulation and Antitrust 369-70 (MIT Press, 3d ed. 2000); Nat'l Rural Telecom. Ass'n v. FCC, 988 F.2d 174 (D.C. Cir. 1993).

24 *See United States Tel. Ass'n, supra* (invalidating FCC's rationales for imposing 6.0% X-factor).

25 The federal price cap regime contains a "low-end adjustment" mechanism that carriers may theoretically invoke to raise their rates if their rate of return falls below a prescribed level. *See* Southwestern Bell Tel. Co. v. FCC, 10 F.3d 892, 894-95 (D.C. Cir. 1993). That mechanism is unavailable, however, to price cap carriers that have availed themselves of the FCC's pricing flexibility rules. *See* 47 C.F.R. § 69.731.

26 In a few states, you may be paying even more: under "value of service" ratemaking, the rural customer pays less for his service, even though it costs much more to serve him, to compensate him for the fact that there are fewer people he can call "for free" in his local calling area.

27 And, as discussed in chapter 9, the "terminating access monopoly" would keep unregulated terminating access charges well above cost even if the local exchange market itself were fully competitive.

28 *See* chapter 10; *see generally* Viscusi, *supra*, at 352.

29 2 Alfred E. Kahn, The Economics of Regulation: Principles and Institutions 119 (MIT Press, 1989).

30 Steve Coll, The Deal of the Century: The Breakup of AT&T 105 (Atheneum, 1986).

31 *See* Note, *Competition in the Telephone Equipment Industry: Beyond Telerent*, 86 Yale L.J. 538, 552-53 (1977) (describing fears of states that competition in equipment markets would threaten a valued source of cross-subsidies).

32 *Hush-A-Phone Corp.*, 20 F.C.C. 391, 420 (1955).

33 *See* Hush-A-Phone Corp. v. United States, 238 F.2d 266, 269 (D.C. Cir. 1956).

34 Decision, *Use of the Carterfone Device in Message Toll Tel. Serv.*, 13 F.C.C.2d 420 (1968).

35 *See* 47 C.F.R. § 68.1 *et seq.* These and similar FCC rules, discussed in chapters 7 and 12, explain the certifications of compliance you may have noticed on many consumer electronic devices, particularly those that use either the telephone network or wireless spectrum.

36 *See, e.g.,* Litton Sys., Inc. v. Am. Tel. & Tel. Co., 700 F.2d 785 (2d Cir. 1983).

37 47 U.S.C. § 273.

38 COLL, *supra*, at 47-52; *see also* BROCK, *supra*, at 124-35.

39 *See* MCI Telecomm. Corp. v. FCC, 580 F.2d 590, 597 (D.C. Cir. 1978) (reaffirming an "expansive view of the scope of the interconnection obligations of AT&T," which the court attributed to prior FCC policies, in order "to allow carriers such as MCI to enter the market and compete with AT&T"); *see also* COLL, *supra*, at 83-91; BROCK, *supra*, at 135-39.

40 *See* Report and Order, *Resale and Shared Use of Common Carrier Domestic Public Switched Network Services*, 83 F.C.C.2d 167 (1980); Report and Order, *Resale and Shared Use of Common Carrier Services and Facilities*, 60 F.C.C.2d 261 (1976), *aff'd*, AT&T v. FCC, 572 F.2d 17 (2d Cir. 1978).

41 COLL, *supra*, at 52.

42 *See* United States v. Am. Tel. & Tel. Co., 552 F. Supp. 131 (D.D.C. 1982), *aff'd sub nom.* Maryland v. United States, 460 U.S. 1001 (1983); *see also* MCI Communications Corp. v. Am. Tel. & Tel. Co., 708 F.2d 1081 (7th Cir. 1983).

43 The Telecommunications Act of 1996 closed the loop on this issue by requiring dialing parity not just for all long distance calls crossing the decree's defined "local access and transport area" ("LATA") boundaries—calls that, under the decree, the Bells were forbidden to offer—but also for regional *intra*LATA "toll calls" that the Bell companies were still permitted to carry. 47 U.S.C. § 251(b)(3).

44 *See* United States v. Western Elec. Co., 993 F.2d 1572, 1580-81 (D.C. Cir. 1993); California v. FCC, 39 F.3d 919, 926-27 (9th Cir. 1994).

45 *See* Southwestern Bell Tel. Co. v. FCC, 153 F.3d 523, 548 (8th Cir. 1998) (dismissing "price squeeze" concerns); Supplemental Order Clarification, *Implementation of the Local Competition Provisions of the Telecommunications Act of 1996*, 15 FCC Rcd 9587, ¶¶ 19-20 (2000) (same), *aff'd,* CompTel v. FCC, 309 F.3d 8 (D.C. Cir. 2002).

46 *See* Marius Schwartz, *The Economic Logic for Conditioning Bell Entry into Long Distance on the Prior Opening of Local Markets*, 18 J. REG. ECON. 247, 286 (2000).

47 Access charges are keyed to particular links within the incumbent's network. To the extent that a long distance carrier arranges to circumvent one of those links, it avoids the obligation to pay the associated access charge to the incumbent. *See* Declaratory Ruling, *Implementation of the Local Competition Provisions in the*

Telecommunications Act of 1996, 14 FCC Rcd 3689, ¶ 9 (1999) ("When two carriers jointly provide interstate access (e.g., by delivering a call to an interexchange carrier (IXC)), the carriers will share access revenues received from the interstate service provider."), *vacated and remanded on other grounds,* Bell Atl. Tel. Cos. v. FCC, 206 F.3d 1 (D.C. Cir. 2000); *see also* Memorandum Opinion and Order, *Waiver of Access Billing Requirements and Investigation of Permanent Modifications,* 2 FCC Rcd 4518, ¶ 2 (1987).

48 *See* Report and Order and Notice of Proposed Rulemaking, *Expanded Interconnection with Local Telephone Company Facilities, Amendment of Part 69 Allocation of General Support Facility Costs,* 7 FCC Rcd 7369 (1992); Second Report and Order and Third Notice of Proposed Rulemaking, *Expanded Interconnection with Local Telephone Company Facilities, Amendment of Part 36 of the Commission's Rules and Establishment of a Joint Board,* 8 FCC Rcd 7374 (1993). The D.C. Circuit invalidated the "physical collocation" requirements of these orders in 1994, *see Bell Atl. Tel. Cos. v. FCC,* 24 F.3d 1441 (D.C. Cir. 1994), but that ruling was itself superseded by the 1996 Act, as discussed in the next chapter.

49 FCC regulations do require you to enable these guests to "dial around" the default long distance carrier to a different carrier of their choice, but put this complication to one side.

50 *See* Department of Justice Press Release, AG Unveils Plan to Allow Ameritech in Long Distance Market (Apr. 3, 1995) (http://www.usdoj.gov/opa/pr/Pre_96/April95/186.txt.html).

Chapter Three

1 Pub. L. No. 104-104, 110 Stat. 56 (1996) (codified as amended in scattered sections of 47 U.S.C.).

2 AT&T Corp. v. Iowa Utils. Bd., 525 U.S. 366, 397 (1999).

3 In characteristically turgid prose, the House-Senate Conference Committee called the Act a "procompetitive, de-regulatory national policy framework designed to accelerate rapidly private sector deployment of advanced telecommunications and information technologies and services to all Americans by opening all telecommunications markets to competition." H.R. Conf. Rep. No. 104-458, at 113 (1996), *reprinted in* 1996 U.S.C.C.A.N. 124. As we explain in chapter 13, not everyone agrees that the Act, at least as implemented, is "deregulatory." *See, e.g.,* ALFRED E. KAHN, LETTING GO: DEREGULATING THE PROCESS OF DEREGULATION (MSU Public Utilities, 1998).

4 1996 Act, Pub. L. 104-104, § 302(b)(1) (repealing 47 U.S.C. § 533(b)); *see* Chesapeake & Potomac Tel. Co. of Va. v. United States, 42 F.3d 181 (4th Cir. 1994) (invalidating section 533(b) as First Amendment violation), *vacated as moot,* 516 U.S. 415 (1996).

5 In June 2004, Qwest Corporation, a Bell company, sought forbearance from

dominant carrier regulation in Omaha on the ground that Cox Communications, a cable company, had long since captured an enormous share of the voice telephony market. *See Petition of Qwest Corp. for Forbearance Pursuant to 47 U.S.C. Sec. 160(c) in the Omaha Metropolitan Statistical Area*, WC No. 04-233 (filed June 21, 2004) (http://www.spri.com/pdf/reports/Qwest%20Nebraska/040621ForbPet FinalA.pdf).

6 *See, e.g.*, Duquesne Light Co. v. Barasch, 488 U.S. 299, 312 (1989); *see generally* Smith v. Ill. Bell Tel. Co., 282 U.S. 133 (1930).

7 Although the principle is clear, its application in particular contexts is often not. For example, courts have disagreed widely about the effect of section 253 on the sizable fees that localities often impose on carriers for the right to dig up the streets to lay telecommunications cable. Section 253(c) provides that "[n]othing in this section affects the authority of a State or local government to manage the public rights-of-way or to require fair and reasonable compensation from telecommunications providers, on a competitively neutral and nondiscriminatory basis, for use of public rights-of-way on a nondiscriminatory basis[.]" One unanswered question is whether, under sections 253(a) and 253(c), such fees may serve as affirmative sources of revenue for cash-strapped localities, as cable franchise fees long have been, or whether they must be capped at levels that make localities whole for any disruption caused by a telecommunications carrier's activities. For a sampling of this and other interpretive questions raised by the ambiguous text of section 253, see Qwest Communications, Inc. v. City of Santa Fe, 380 F.3d 1258 (10th Cir. 2004); TCG N.Y., Inc. v. White Plains, 305 F.3d 67 (2d Cir. 2002); BellSouth Telecomm., Inc. v. Palm Beach, 252 F.3d. 1169 (11th Cir. 2001); Auburn v. Qwest Corp., 260 F.3d 1160 (9th Cir. 2001); TCG Detroit v. Dearborn, 206 F.3d 618 (6th Cir. 2000); Cablevision v. Pub. Improvement Comm'n, 184 F.3d 88 (1st Cir. 1999). *See also* Nixon v. Mo. Mun. League, 124 S. Ct. 1555 (2004) (holding that section 253(a) does not bar state from prohibiting political subdivisions from providing services).

8 In addition to these specific substantive provisions, the 1996 Act also gives the FCC the fairly extraordinary power to *forbear* from (i.e., nullify) any provision of federal communications law that, in the Commission's considered view, is no longer necessary to protect competitors or consumers or to serve the public interest. *See* 47 U.S.C. § 160. The major exception is that the Commission may *not* "forbear" from enforcing the core substantive requirements of sections 251(c) and 271—i.e., the incumbent-specific requirements discussed below—until it finds that they "have been fully implemented." We discuss the FCC's forbearance authority further in chapters 5 and 6.

9 47 U.S.C. § 153(46) (defining "telecommunications service"); *see also* 47 U.S.C. § 153(43) (defining "telecommunications").

10 *See, e.g.*, Virgin Is. Tel. Corp. v. FCC, 198 F.3d 921 (D.C. 1999).

11 *See, e.g.*, Iowa v. FCC, 218 F.3d 756, 759 (D.C. Cir. 2000); Nat'l Ass'n of Reg. Util. Comm'rs v. FCC, 533 F.2d 601, 608-09 (D.C. Cir. 1976) (*NARUC II*).

12 FCC v. Midwest Video Corp., 440 U.S. 689, 701 (1979); *see, e.g.*, *Virgin Is. Tel.*, 198 F.3d at 925.

13 *See generally* Nat'l Ass'n of Reg. Util. Comm'rs v. FCC, 525 F.2d 630 (D.C. Cir. 1976) *("NARUC I"); *Declaratory Ruling, *NORLIGHT Request for a Declaratory Ruling,* 2 FCC Rcd 132, ¶¶19-21 (1987).

14 *See* 47 U.S.C. § 153(20) (defining "information service" as "the offering of a capability for generating, acquiring, storing, transforming, processing, retrieving, utilizing, or making available information via telecommunications").

15 Brand X Internet Servs. v. FCC, 345 F.3d 1120 (9th Cir. 2003), *cert. granted,* Nos. 04-281 et al. (Dec. 3, 2004).

16 47 U.S.C. § 153(26); *see also* 47 U.S.C. § 153(16), (47).

17 47 U.S.C. § 153(26), (44).

18 Technically, the RBOCs are the holding companies created as a result of the consent decree, each of which inherited a number of formally separate BOCs. *See generally* 47 U.S.C. § 153(4) (listing the "Bell operating companies"). Today, however, when people speak of "BOCs" or "Bell companies," they are generally referring to the holding companies.

19 *See* 47 U.S.C. § 251(f)(2).

20 *See* Verizon Tel. Cos. v. FCC, 292 F.3d 903, 906-07 (D.C. Cir. 2002).

21 *Iowa Utils. Bd.,* 525 U.S. at 394-95.

22 The "access" to network elements granted in this provision is distinct from the "access" that long distance companies receive from, and for which they pay "access charges" to, local exchange carriers on each end of a long distance call. The use of the same term in these two contexts often confuses newcomers to this field.

23 47 U.S.C. § 153(29) (defining "network element"); *see also Iowa Utils. Bd.,* 525 U.S. at 386-87.

24 The same provision imposes a somewhat higher hurdle (the so-called "necessary standard") to the imposition of unbundling obligations for "proprietary" elements—i.e., those that could not be shared without presenting a theoretical risk of compromising the ILEC's business secrets. Very few elements fall into this category, and the FCC's analysis under section 251(d)(2) almost always involves application of the "impairment" standard.

25 First Report and Order, *Implementation of the Local Competition Provisions of the Telecommunications Act of 1996,* 11 FCC Rcd 15,499 (1996) *("Local Competition Order").* We discuss the *Local Competition Order,* and its subsequent judicial history, later in this chapter.

26 *See* 47 C.F.R. § 51.505.

27 535 U.S. 467 (2002).

28 AT&T Communications of Ill., Inc. v. Ill. Bell Tel. Co., 349 F.3d 402, 404 (7th Cir. 2003).

29 Eli Noam, Interconnecting the Network of Networks 114 (MIT Press, 2001).

30 Raymond L. Gifford, *Regulatory Impressionism: What State Regulators Can and Cannot Do*, 4 REV. NETWORK ECON. 466, 474 (2003).

31 *See Resale and Shared Use of Common Carrier Domestic Public Switched Network Services*, 83 F.C.C.2d 167 (1980); *Resale and Shared Use of Common Carrier Services and Facilities*, 60 F.C.C.2d 261 (1976), *aff'd*, AT&T v. FCC, 572 F.2d 17 (2d Cir. 1978).

32 Iowa Utils. Bd. v. FCC, 219 F.3d 744, 754-56 (8th Cir. 2000), *rev'd in other respects,* Verizon Communications Inc. v. FCC, 535 U.S. 467 (2002).

33 Iowa Utils. Bd. v. FCC, 120 F.3d 753, 800 (8th Cir. 1997). For a description of the traditional dual jurisdiction regime, see La. Pub. Serv. Comm'n v. FCC, 476 U.S. 355, 360 (1986); Jonathan Jacob Nadler, *Give Peace A Chance: FCC-State Relations After* California III, 47 FED. COMM. L.J. 457, 462-88 (1995).

34 525 U.S. 366 (1999).

35 *Id.* at 378. In an oft-quoted footnote, the majority then dismissed the dissent's view that close questions about the FCC's preemptive jurisdiction should be resolved on the basis of federalism concerns in general and section 2(b) in particular:

[T]he question . . . is not whether the Federal Government has taken the regulation of local telecommunications competition away from the States. With regard to the matters addressed by the 1996 Act, it unquestionably has. The question is whether the state commissions' participation in the administration of the new *federal* regime is to be guided by federal-agency regulations. If there is any "presumption" applicable to this question, it should arise from the fact that a federal program administered by 50 independent state agencies is surpassing strange. The appeals by both Justice [Clarence] THOMAS and Justice [Stephen] BREYER to what might loosely be called "States' rights" are most peculiar, since there is no doubt, even under their view, that if the federal courts believe a state commission is not regulating in accordance with federal policy they may bring it to heel. This is, at bottom, a debate not about whether the States will be allowed to do their own thing, but about whether it will be the FCC or the federal courts that draw the lines to which they must hew. To be sure, the FCC's lines can be even more restrictive than those drawn by the courts—but it is hard to spark a passionate "States' rights" debate over that detail.

Id. at 378 n.6 (paragraph break omitted).

36 The traditional dual jurisdiction framework still applies, however, to "intrastate" matters *outside* the scope of the 1996 Act, such as retail rate regulation. *Id.* at 381 n.8 ("After the 1996 Act, § 152(b) may have less practical effect. But that is because Congress, by extending the Communications Act into local competition, has removed a significant area from the States' exclusive control. Insofar as Congress has remained silent, however, § 152(b) continues to function.").

37 *See* 47 U.S.C. § 252(e)(2)(A).

38 *See* 47 U.S.C. § 252(b), (c). Many of the important regulatory decisions under sections 251 and 252 are decided not in the context of a specific arbitration pro-

ceeding between two carriers, but in so-called "generic" rulemaking proceedings that address the obligations of incumbents to *all* competitors. For example, state commissions do not typically decide in specific arbitration proceedings the rates that a given competitor must pay the incumbent for leasing the latter's network facilities. Instead, most state commissions hold lengthy "cost proceedings" in which they decide, among other things, the rates that any carrier must pay for access to the incumbent's loops, switches, and transport facilities. The state commissions then include those rates as terms in any arbitrated interconnection agreement. Although the issue is not settled, litigants have asserted that federal district courts have jurisdiction over generic cost orders themselves, both under section 252(e)(6), even though that provision technically authorizes appeals from state arbitration decisions, and under the general "federal question" jurisdictional provision of 28 U.S.C. § 1331. *See generally* Verizon Md. Inc. v. Pub. Serv. Comm'n of Md., 535 U.S. 635 (2002).

39 *See* 47 U.S.C. § 252(e)(6). In *Verizon Maryland*, the Supreme Court rejected Eleventh Amendment challenges to the exercise of federal court jurisdiction against named state commissioners under the *Ex parte Young* doctrine. 535 U.S. at 645-48.

40 For an alternative view, see Douglas Lichtman & Randal C. Picker, *Entry Policy in Local Telecommunications: Iowa Utilities and Verizon*, 2002 SUP. CT. REV. 41, 58 (2002).

41 Second Report and Order, *Review of the Section 251 Unbundling Obligations of Incumbent Local Exchange Carriers*, 19 FCC Rcd 13,494, ¶1 (2004).

42 *Id.* Moreover, the FCC concluded that, because so many entrants opt into agreements in their entirety, the pick-and-choose rule's ability to prevent discrimination in practice was, contrary to the FCC's initial expectations, "superfluous." *Id.*, ¶ 18. It remains to be seen how the FCC's new rule will fare under judicial scrutiny, although the Ninth Circuit denied an emergency stay request in August 2004. *See* New Edge Networks, Inc. v. FCC, No. 04-73800 (9th Cir. Aug. 24, 2004). In upholding the original pick-and-choose rule in 1999, the Supreme Court had observed that, although an all-or-nothing approach "seems eminently fair" as a policy matter, the pick-and-choose rule "tracks the pertinent statutory language almost exactly" and "is the most readily apparent" interpretation of it. *Iowa Utils. Bd.*, 525 U.S. at 396.

43 There was not a corresponding bar on the Bell companies' authority to offer long distance service as part of a *wireless* plan, since the Bells have never dominated the wireless market. *See* 47 U.S.C. § 271(b)(3), (g)(3).

44 *See* 47 U.S.C. §§ 273-275.

45 *See, e.g.*, BellSouth Corp. v. FCC, 144 F.3d 58, 67 (D.C. Cir. 1998), *cert. denied*, 526 U.S. 1086 (1999).

46 *Id.*; BellSouth Corp. v. FCC, 162 F.3d 678 (D.C. Cir. 1998); SBC Communications, Inc. v. FCC, 154 F.3d 226 (5th Cir. 1998).

47 *SBC Communications*, 154 F.3d at 244.

48 The separate affiliate requirements are set forth in section 272. Most of those requirements "sunset" three years after a Bell company wins section 271 approval. *See* 47 U.S.C. § 272(f); *see also* AT&T Corp. v. FCC, 369 F.3d 554 (D.C. Cir. 2004) (per curiam). The one subsection that does *not* sunset is section 272(e), which, among other things, helps regulators detect and prevent any efforts by the Bell companies to manipulate their access charges to inflict anticompetitive price squeezes on unaffiliated long distance carriers. *See* 47 U.S.C. § 272(e)(3) (requiring Bell company to "charge the [section 272] affiliate . . . , or impute to itself (if using the access for its provision of its own services), an amount for access to its telephone exchange service and exchange access that is no less than the amount charged to any unaffiliated interexchange carriers for such service").

49 In the first several years after passage of the 1996 Act, the Bell companies filed half a dozen section 271 applications that, though they came with state commission backing, never had any serious chance of success at the FCC. The FCC rejected each of these before finally granting its first section 271 approval in late 1999—for Bell Atlantic (now Verizon) in New York. *See* AT&T Corp. v. FCC, 220 F.3d 607 (D.C. Cir. 2000).

50 47 U.S.C. § 271(d)(2).

51 47 U.S.C. § 271(d)(6).

52 *See generally* Verizon Communications Inc. v. Law Offices of Curtis V. Trinko LLP, 124 S. Ct. 872, 880-81 (2004) (noting, but neither endorsing nor repudiating, the essential facilities doctrine "crafted by some lower courts").

53 MCI Communications v. Am. Tel. & Tel., 708 F.2d 1081, 1132-33 (7th Cir. 1983).

54 *See Trinko*, 124 S. Ct. at 881-84.

55 United States Telecom Ass'n v. FCC, 290 F.3d 415, 428 n.4 (D.C. Cir. 2002) ("*USTA I*") (citing, for the first proposition, 3A PHILLIP AREEDA & HERBERT HOVENKAMP, ANTITRUST LAW ¶ 771c (1996)).

56 What this means, as a technical matter, is that competitors lease (i) a flat-rated "port" on the incumbent's switch corresponding to the loops they also lease from the incumbent; (ii) use of the switch's central processing unit (essentially a large computer) on a minutes-of-use basis, as needed by the customers using those loops and ports; and (iii) capacity on the incumbent's transport pipes not at fixed units of capacity, but, like the switch itself, on a minutes-of-use basis: i.e., only as needed to cover actual call volumes. This arrangement for usage-sensitive leasing of transport facilities (along with an associated "tandem switching" functionality) is known within the industry as "shared transport," as distinguished from the non-usage-sensitive "dedicated transport" links used in the UNE-L context.

57 In the early 2000s, Z-Tel specialized in providing high-end telephone service to mass market customers by means of UNE-P. Unlike most other UNE-P providers, it invested in separate network facilities that, through complex interaction with

ILEC switches, enabled its customers to receive calling features that the ILEC itself did not offer.

58 Section 251(c)(4) is expressly limited to local services that the incumbent "provides at retail to subscribers who are not telecommunications carriers." By definition, that category excludes carrier-to-carrier "access services"—the task of connecting long distance companies to their customers for the origination and termination of long distance calls. Thus, if a traditional long distance carrier becomes a CLEC and chooses the section 251(c)(4) resale option as a means of providing a complete package of local and long distance services, it will need to purchase both (i) the incumbent's local retail service at the "avoided cost discount" and (ii) "access" from the incumbent for the origination and termination of long distance calls, traditionally at rates above the "cost" of that service as measured by TELRIC. In contrast, if the carrier chooses the UNE-P option instead, it can lease, at TELRIC, the underlying facilities without service-related restrictions and use them to provide both local exchange services and access services. Thus, unlike the resale option, the UNE platform option both (i) removes any need to pay access charges to the incumbent for outgoing long distance calls and (ii) entitles the competitor to collect access charges of its own for incoming long distance calls delivered by unaffiliated carriers. Because access charges often exceed any rigorous measure of "cost," that factor tends to make the UNE platform option more attractive than the resale alternative, all else held constant.

In addition, the UNE-P option creates particularly lucrative arbitrage opportunities for small business customers and others whom the incumbent serves at retail rates exceeding cost (as part of an implicit cross-subsidy scheme, for example). Under the UNE pricing rules, a competitor can purchase the necessary elements at cost and can then exploit the incumbent's retail "price umbrella" to earn significant margins in serving these customers. Resale creates no similar arbitrage opportunity because the rates the competitor pays are keyed to the incumbent's retail rates and thus incorporate any implicit cross-subsidies. For the same reason, however, resale may be a more feasible entry strategy than UNE-P for entering markets in which incumbents serve customers at heavily subsidized, below-cost rates.

59 FCC News Release, *Federal Communications Commission Releases Data on Local Telephone Competition,* (December 22, 2003) (http://hraunfoss.fcc.gov/edocs_public/attachmatch/DOC-242397A1.doc).

60 *See, e.g.,* T. Randolph Beard et al., *Why Adco? Why Now? An Economic Exploration into the Future Structure for the "Last Mile" in Local Telecommunications Markets,* 54 FED. COMM. L.J. 421 (2002); CHARLES FERGUSON, THE BROADBAND PROBLEM: ANATOMY OF A MARKET FAILURE AND A POLICY DILEMMA (Brookings Inst. Press, 2004); *but see* Robert W. Crandall & J. Gregory Sidak, *Is Structural Separation of Incumbent Local Exchange Carriers Necessary For Competition?,* 19 YALE J. REG. 335 (2002) (arguing against the proposal). The closest that such a proposal ever came to fruition was an initial decision by the Pennsylvania Commission to mandate structural separation, *see* Bell Atl.-Penn., Inc. v. Pa. Pub. Util. Comm'n, 763 A.2d 440, 460-67 (Pa. Cmwlth. 2000), but the commission later retreated from that proposal. *See* Crandall & Sidak, *supra,* at 347-49.

61 John Hagel III & Marc Singer, *Unbundling the Corporation,* McKINSEY Q.,

2000, No. 3, at 148 (http://www.optimizemagazine.com/mckinsey/2002/ 0408.htm); *see also* Marguerite Reardon, *VoIP, Wireless Could Spur Baby Bell Negotiations*, CNET NEWS.COM (May 6, 2004) (http://news.com.com/2100-7352- 5207630.html) ("It's very short-sighted of [the incumbent local providers] to raise prices so high it puts the CLECs (competitive local exchange carriers) out of business, because they could potentially become a good source of revenue for them.") (quoting Jeff Kagan, an independent telecommunications analyst); Clifford Winston, *U.S. Industry Adjustment to Economic Deregulation*, J. ECON. PERSP., Summer 1998, at 89, 98 ("[M]anagers and employees of regulated firms settle into patterns of inefficient production and missed opportunities for technological advance and entry into new markets.").

62 *See, e.g.,* Jesse Drucker, *Sprint's Role as Wholesaler: "Arms Dealer" to the Industry*, WALL ST. J., May 21, 2004, at B1 ("Sprint has embarked on an aggressive strategy of reselling its telecommunications services at a deep discount to other companies, which then turn around and sell the service under their own brands – competing against Sprint.").

63 Anne Mario Squeo, *FCC's Powell Sits on Horns of Dilemma*, WALL ST. J., July 9, 2004, at A4 (quoting Jeffrey Bray, Managing Director of Babson Capital Management).

64 In particular, the incumbents also advanced failed challenges to (1) the FCC's determination that usage-sensitive "shared transport"—an indispensable component of the UNE platform, as discussed above—even qualifies as a "network element" under the statutory definition of that term; and (2) the FCC's "combinations" rule (47 C.F.R. § 51.315(b)), which requires incumbents to provide preexisting combinations of network elements to requesting carriers without disconnecting them first. *See* AT&T Corp. v. Iowa Utils. Bd., 525 U.S. 366, 392-95 (1999) (rejecting ILEC challenges to FCC's combinations rule and "all elements" policy); Southwestern Bell Tel. Co. v. FCC, 153 F.3d 597 (8th Cir. 1998) (affirming FCC's treatment of shared transport as a "network element" subject to unbundling).

65 47 U.S.C. § 251(d)(2).

66 *Iowa Utils. Bd.*, 525 U.S. at 391.

67 *Id.*

68 *Id.* at 389-90.

69 Third Report and Order, *Implementation of the Local Competition Provisions of the Telecommunications Act of 1996*, 15 FCC Rcd 3696 (1999) (*"UNE Remand Order"*).

70 *USTA I*, 290 F.3d 415.

71 *Id.* at 429.

72 *Id.* at 424.

73 *Id.* at 427 (emphasis added).

74 *Id.* (emphasis added).

75 Report and Order and Order on Remand and Further Notice of Proposed Rulemaking, *Review of the Section 251 Unbundling Obligations of Incumbent Local Exchange Carriers*, 18 FCC Rcd 16,978 (2003) (*"Triennial Review Order"*).

76 *Id.*, ¶ 84.

77 *Id.*, ¶ 459. The FCC separately decided that shared transport should be made available whenever switching is. *Id.*, ¶ 534.

78 Leasing an incumbent's loop unbundled from its switch means unplugging the loop from a circuit leading to that switch and redirecting it to a circuit leading to the competitor's switch. To avoid outages for the customer, the incumbent and competitor must coordinate the timing of the cutover; because the line ideally remains in service except for a moment, the "cut" is said to be "hot." A typical hot cut proceeds as follows. After the competitor asks to lease the loop, it and the incumbent work out when the incumbent's technician will unplug the loop from circuits leading to the incumbent's switch and reconnect it, via jumper cables, to circuits leading to the competitor's collocated facilities and thence to the competitor's switch. This procedure is typically conducted at a massive, intermediate switchboard for connecting loops with switches. If done properly, the hot cut is over almost instantaneously and causes no inconvenience to the customer. If done improperly, the customer may be left without service for hours at a time. Although either the incumbent or the competitor may be to blame, the customer, and anyone she talks to about the experience, may be reluctant ever to do business with the competitor again.

79 *Id.*, ¶ 465. One issue in this debate concerned the extent to which customer churn would preclude new entrants from recovering the up-front charges they must pay incumbents to perform these hot cuts, and whether such concerns warrant granting these entrants indefinite UNE-P rights so that they could avoid paying such charges in the first place. *See id.*, ¶¶ 470-71. For a discussion of that issue, see appendix A.

80 *Id.*, ¶ 461; *see id.*, ¶¶ 462-463 (summarizing "triggers" for findings of "no impairment").

81 United States Telecom Ass'n v. FCC, 359 F.3d 554 (D.C. Cir.) (*"USTA II"*), *cert. denied*, 2004 WL 2152860 (2004). Even the choice of the D.C. Circuit as the forum for this review was fiercely contested. The various review petitions (including the competitors') were assigned by lottery to the Eighth Circuit, where the competitors hoped to obtain a more sympathetic hearing, but the incumbents persuaded that court to transfer the case back to the D.C. Circuit on the ground that it was substantially related to *USTA I.*

82 *Id.* at 565.

83 *Id.* at 566.

84 *Id.* at 565.

85 *Id.* at 565-66.

86 *Id.* at 566.

87 *Id.* at 569.

88 *Id.* at 570.

89 535 U.S. 467 (2002) (discussed in appendix A). The D.C. Circuit issued its decision in USTA I shortly after the Supreme Court decided *Verizon.* The Supreme Court denied certiorari petitions filed by various private parties in *USTA I,* but the FCC had not sought the Court's review in that case, given the ongoing *Triennial Review* proceeding.

90 *See* Press Release, FCC Adopts New Rules for Network Unbundling Obligations of Incumbent Local Phone Carriers (Dec. 15, 2004) (*"TRO Remand Press Release"*). The text of the FCC's order was unavailable at press time. In October 2004, the D.C. Circuit held in abeyance a petition for mandamus filed by ILECs dissatisfied with the FCC's interim rules. Further briefing on the mandamus petition was set for January 2005.

91 See *Triennial Review Order,* ¶¶ 649–67; see *USTA II,* 359 F.3d at 589 ("The CLECs also claim that it was unreasonable for the Commission to apply a different pricing standard under § 271, but we see nothing unreasonable in the Commission's decision to confine TELRIC pricing to instances where it has found impairment.").The Bell companies could try to preclude access to the UNE platform as a practical matter by disconnecting the switch from the loop when a CLEC orders the two of them together. Significantly, the "combination" rule revived by the Supreme Court in *Iowa Utilities Board*—47 C.F.R.§ 51.315(b), mentioned in note 64, *supra*—is specific to unbundling requirements under section 251 and does not itself apply to any such requirements that may arise under section 271. It is unclear, however,whether disconnecting elements under these circumstances would violate the general non-discrimination requirement of section 202. *See USTA II,* 359 F.3d at 590 ("We agree with the Commission that none of the requirements of § 251(c)(3) applies to items four, five, six and ten on the § 271 competitive checklist. Of course,the independent unbundling under § 271 is presumably governed by the general nondiscrimination requirement of § 202. But as the only challenge the CLECs have presented to the FCC's § 271 combination rules is grounded in an erroneous claim of a cross-application of § 251, we do not pass on whether the § 271 combination rules satisfy the § 202 nondiscrimination requirement.").

92 City of New York v. FCC, 486 U.S. 57, 64 (1988). Under the Supremacy Clause of the U.S. Constitution, state law is "preempted" by (i.e., must yield to) federal law in a number of circumstances. Unless Congress directs otherwise, federal agencies have broad authority to preempt state law provisions. *See* Fid. Fed. Sav. & Loan Ass'n v. de la Cuesta, 458 U.S.141,154 (1982). And a federal agency's rules can preempt inconsistent state law whether or not the agency itself has spoken to the preemption issue. *See, e.g.,* Geier v. Am. Honda Motor Co., 529 U.S.861 (2000).

93 *See* 47 U.S.C. §§ 251(d)(3), 252(e)(3), 253(b), (c), 261(b), (c); 1996 Act, Pub.L. 104-104, Title VI, § 601(c)(1) (47 U.S.C. § 152 note).

94 *Triennial Review Order,* ¶ 192 ("If Congress intended to preempt the field, Congress would not have included section 251(d)(3) in the 1996 Act.").

95 The FCC has suggested, however, that the degree of inconsistency between state and federal law needed to trigger such preemption might be slightly higher under section 251(d)(3) than it would be under generally applicable conflict preemption principles. *Id.*, at ¶ 192 n.611.

96 *USTA I*, 290 F.3d at 427.

97 *Triennial Review Order*, ¶ 195.

98 See Press Statement of Commissioner Michael J. Copps, Feb. 20, 2003 (http://hraunfoss.fcc.gov/edocs_public/attachmatch/DOC-231344A5.doc) ("There are aspects of this Order that are certainly not my preferred approach, but which I have had to accept in order to reach compromise. In particular, there is the decision to eliminate access to only part of the frequencies of the loop as a network element. I would have preferred to maintain this access, also known as line sharing."); Separate Statement of Commissioner Jonathan S. Adelstein, Feb. 20, 2003 (http://hraunfoss.fcc.gov/edocs_public/attachmatch/DOC-231344A8.doc) ("There has been a great deal of compr[om]ise in this process. I am very comfortable with some of the decisions, while others quite frankly give me pause. This item does not reflect a perfect solution. But then this is neither a perfect world nor a perfect process. . . . The lights were burning brightly on the eighth floor late last night, and offices reached some agreements on major issues at the eleventh hour—and I mean that literally, around 11:00.") Both Copps and Adelstein later attributed their votes against line sharing to a conclusion that the D.C. Circuit had tied the Commission's hands on the issue in *USTA I*.

99 Alfred E. Kahn, *Regulatory Politics as Usual*, POL'Y MATTERS 03-3 (Mar. 2003) (http://www.aei.brookings.org/policy/page.php?id=127).

100 As one analyst concluded: "The real battle now is between circuit-switched networks and the Internet . . . [as] the Bells have to worry about how many customers they will lose to wireless, to cable operators, and to start-ups that provide voice over the Internet." Jon Van, *Phone Wars Ignore Industry Trends*, FORBES.COM (June 11, 2004) (http://www.forbes.com/technology/feeds/wireless/2004/06/11/wireless01086971085611-20040610-194508.html).

101 *Triennial Review Order*, ¶¶ 298–340 (high capacity loops), 359–418 (dedicated transport); *see also* p. 567 n. 73, *infra*. The FCC 's decision to delegate this issue to the states was somewhat curious because it had previously adopted national standards for deciding when there is enough competition in these same transport markets to justify granting the incumbents "pricing flexibility" in their special access charges. *See* WorldCom, Inc. v. FCC, 238 F.3d 449 (D.C.Cir.2001); *cf. Triennial Review Order*, ¶ 104 (distinguishing pricing flexibility analysis from impairment analysis).

102 USTA II, 359 F.3d at 573-77.

103 *See TRO Remand Press Release* (announcing new impairment-related determinations concerning, among other things, DS1 and DS3 loops and transport).

104 See 47 U.S.C. § 153(26); *see also* chapter 2, *supra* (defining switched and special access).

105 *See* Supplemental Order Clarification, *Implementation of the Local Competition Provisions of the Telecommunications Act of 1996*, 15 FCC Rcd 9587, ¶ 7 (2000) (*"Supplemental Order Clarification"*).

106 In particular, the FCC invoked the more demanding impairment standard to reason that, for purposes of section 251(d)(2), a given carrier's right to lease an element can turn not just on whether *some* carriers might need that element to compete in *some* market, but on whether *that* carrier needs the element to compete in the specific market that *it* seeks to enter. "The exchange access market," the Commission continued, "occupies a different legal category from the market for telephone exchange services; indeed, at the highest level of generality, Congress itself drew an explicit statutory distinction between those two markets." *Id.*, ¶ 14. Thus, "whether network elements should be made available for the sole or primary purpose of providing exchange access services" depends on "whether denying competitors access to that combination would in fact impair their ability to provide those services." *Id.*, ¶ 15. Lowering special access rates to cost, the Commission added, "could undercut the market position of"—i.e., remove the incumbents' price umbrella from—"many facilities-based competitive access providers. Competitive access, which originated in the mid-1980s, is a mature source of competition in telecommunications markets." *Id.*, ¶ 18. Finally, the Commission found that accounting and other safeguards would suffice to protect independent long distance carriers from the threat that incumbents could use putatively above-cost access charges (as opposed to TELRIC-based charges for the EEL) to subject independent long distance carriers to an anticompetitive "price squeeze" when the incumbents themselves provide long distance services. *Id.*, ¶¶ 19-20; *see, e.g.,* 47 U.S.C. § 272(e)(3).

107 CompTel v. FCC, 309 F.3d 8, 12-13 (D.C. Cir. 2002). Indeed, the court added, "it is far from obvious to us that the FCC has the power, without an impairment finding as to nonlocal services, to require that [incumbents] provide EELs for such services on an unbundled basis." *Id.* at 14. In the *Triennial Review Order*, the Commission tried to justify the same basic outcome by finding that, despite all appearances, long distance services do not qualify as "telecommunications services" for the provision of which carriers can assert unbundling rights under section 251(c)(3). On review, the D.C. Circuit rejected this new rationale as inconsistent with the Act's plain language and encouraged the Commission on remand to return to the market-specific impairment analysis that had worked the first time around. *USTA II*, 359 F.3d at 591-92.

108 Take, for example, the case of a telemarketing center. There may be many high capacity circuits leading out of that center for all the out-bound long distance calls; there are probably also a few ordinary telephone lines for the employees' everyday needs. Should AT&T be able to pay the lower "network element" rate for the high capacity outbound circuits, rather than the higher "special access" rate, so long as it agrees to provide "local" service on one or two of the ordinary telephone lines it has leased from the incumbent? And how would the incumbent, as the lessor of those facilities, ever know for certain what kinds of traffic they are actually being used for?

109 *Supplemental Order Clarification,* ¶¶ 21-23.

110 The Commission required CLECs to obtain at least one local telephone number for each circuit leased as an EEL and to follow "a variety of technical requirements aimed at preventing firms from gaming the system." *USTA II,* 359 F.3d at 591. On review, the D.C. Circuit deferred to the Commission's technical expertise and rejected the incumbents' claim that these new "architectural" requirements are too easily circumvented by carriers intending to provide mostly long distance voice or data services. *Id.* at 592-93.

Chapter Four

1 The federal government's on-line telecommunications glossary defines a "protocol" as the "formal set of procedures that are adopted to facilitate functional interoperation within the layered hierarchy" and a "code" as "a set of unambiguous rules specifying the manner in which data may be represented in a discrete form." *See* http://www.its.bldrdoc.gov/fs-1037/37search.htm. We use the term "protocol" in a broad, vernacular sense to encompass both of these distinct concepts.

2 As related to technology products, modularity involves "breaking up a complex system into discrete pieces — which can then communicate with one another only through standardized interfaces within a standardized architecture — [to] eliminate what would otherwise be an unmanageable spaghetti tangle of systemic interconnections." Richard N. Langlois, *Modularity in Technology and Organization,* 49 J. ECON. BEHAV. & ORG. 19, 19 (2002). "When a design becomes 'truly modular,' the options embedded in the design are simultaneously multiplied and decentralized. The multiplication occurs because changes in one module become independent of changes in other modules. Decentralization follows because, as long as designers adhere to the design rules, they are free to innovate (apply the modular operators) without reference to the original architects or any central planners of the design." CARLISS Y. BALDWIN & KIM B. CLARK, DESIGN RULES, VOL. 1: THE POWER OF MODULARITY 14 (MIT Press, 2000).

3 For simplicity, we have lumped into a single "logical" layer what telecommunications engineers would consider two different layers. In 1978, the International Standards Organization introduced a now-standard seven-layer "open systems interconnection" model for understanding layering hierarchies in digital environments. The TCP/IP protocols that define Internet communications appear on layers 3 and 4—"network" and "transport," respectively—of that "OSI stack." And, in any given transmission, those protocols often ride "on top of" a layer 2 "data link" protocol such as Ethernet, ATM, or frame relay. *See generally* Kevin Werbach, *A Layered Model for Internet Policy,* 1 J. TELECOM. & HIGH TECH. L. 37 (2002); Douglas C. Sicker & Joshua L. Mindel, *Refinements of A Layered Model for Telecommunications Policy,* 1 J. TELECOM. & HIGH TECH. L. 69 (2002). One way of conceptualizing the relationship between the traditional seven-layer OSI model and our simplified four-layer construct is presented in Figure A.

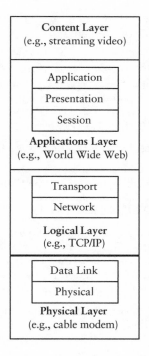

Figure A. Simplified four-layer model of the Internet

4 The Internet's modular structure is analogous to the current structure of the computer industry. In that industry, consumers who want to use the Microsoft Windows operating system do not have to buy computer hardware from a particular manufacturer—they can buy it from Dell, HP-Compaq, Gateway, IBM, and so on. And they can use WordPerfect rather than Microsoft Word as their word-processing software to run on top of Windows. But such modularity was by no means preordained. The first desktop computers that Apple produced in the early 1980s were tightly integrated machines: Apple produced the computer hardware, the operating system, and many of the software applications. Only after an open, IBM-compatible environment became dominant did the modern industry structure emerge. *See* ANDREW S. GROVE, ONLY THE PARANOID SURVIVE: HOW TO EXPLOIT THE CRISIS POINTS THAT CHALLENGE EVERY COMPANY 39–52 (Currency, 1996).

5 Like "protocol," the term "open" can mean different things in different contexts; here we use it simply to mean non-proprietary. Our use of the term does not mean that all relevant Internet standards are built on "open source" software (which has a different set of implications) or that they are open in name but proprietary to an individual firm, such as the Java standard pioneered by Sun Microsystems.

6 For a description of this standard, see T. Socolofsky & C. Kale, A TCP/IP Tutorial 2–8 (Network Working Group, Request for Comments No. 1180, 1991) (http://www.rfc-editor.org/rfc/rfc1180.txt).

7 *See* FNC Resolution: Definition of "Internet," October 24, 1995 (http://www.itrd.gov/fnc/Internet_res.html).

8 For a critical look at ICANN, see A. Michael Froomkin, *Wrong Turn in Cyberspace: Using ICANN to Route Around the APA and the Constitution*, 50 DUKE L.J. 17 (2000); Jonathan Weinberg, *ICANN and the Problem of Legitimacy*, 50 DUKE L.J. 187 (2000). For a discussion of its future, see Declan McCullagh, *Who Should Govern the Net?*, CNET NEWS.COM (March 26, 2004) (http://news.com.com/2100-1028-5180134.html).

9 JOHN NAUGHTON, A BRIEF HISTORY OF THE FUTURE 102 (Overlook Press, 2001).

10 Even the TCP/IP standard is modular in the sense that other protocols can govern the assembly and reassembly of data sent on IP networks. The User Datagram Protocol (UDP), for example, is an alternative to TCP that provides fewer error-checking services and is often used in voice over IP (VoIP) services.

11 Jerome H. Saltzer et al., *End-to-End Arguments in System Design*, 2 ACM TRANSACTIONS ON COMPUTER SYSTEMS 277 (1984), *reprinted in* INNOVATIONS IN INTERNETWORKING 195 (Artech House, Craig Partridge ed., 1988). For an explanation of some of the principle's implications, see David Isenberg, Rise of the Stupid Network (1997) (http://www.hyperorg.com/misc/stupidnet.html).

12 Marjory S. Blumenthal & David D. Clark, *Rethinking the Design of the Internet: The End-to-End Arguments vs. the Brave New World*, *in* COMMUNICATIONS POLICY IN TRANSITION: THE INTERNET AND BEYOND 91 (MIT Press, Benjamin M. Compaine & Shane Greenstein, eds., 2001).

13 The posting of the original specifications for SMTP can still be found at http://www.ietf.org/rfc/rfc0821.txt. For an explanation of its invention, see JANET ABBATE, INVENTING THE INTERNET 108–09 (MIT Press, 1999). Other (mostly proprietary) versions of e-mail existed before SMTP, but they failed to reach critical mass.

14 *See* TIM BERNERS-LEE, WEAVING THE WEB (Harper San Francisco, 1999).

15 *See, e.g.*, Sporty's Farm L.L.C. v. Sportsman's Market, Inc., 202 F.3d 489, 492 (2nd Cir. 2000) ("The Internet is a network of computers that allows a user to gain access to information stored on any other computer on the network. Information on the Internet is lodged on files called web pages[.]").

16 This was the first initial public offering of the Internet age. Ironically, the University of Illinois turned around and sold the Mosaic rights to Microsoft, which used Mosaic as the basis for the Internet Explorer browser that would soon eclipse Navigator and lead to the landmark Microsoft antitrust litigation, as discussed in chapter 1. For a telling of Netscape's rise and fall, see MICHAEL LEWIS, THE NEW NEW THING (W.W. Norton, 1999).

17 NAUGHTON, *supra*, at 246-47.

18 In some cases, dictionaries can play an unofficial gatekeeping role in a language's development, as the Oxford English Dictionary does for English. The French have taken the idea one step further, founding the *Académie Française* in

1635 and maintaining it ever since as the official organization for overseeing the development of their language. *See* http://www.academie-francaise.fr.

19 IETF, The Tao of IETF: A Novice's Guide to the Internet Engineering Task Force, RFC 3160, at 1 (August 2001) (http://www.ietf.org/tao.html). For other descriptions of the IETF, see Scott Bradner, *The Internet Engineering Task Force, in* OPEN SOURCES: VOICES FROM THE OPEN SOURCE REVOLUTION 47, 47–52 (O'Reilly, Chris DiBona et al. eds., 1999); COMMITTEE ON THE INTERNET IN THE EVOLVING INFORMATION INFRASTRUCTURE, THE INTERNET'S COMING OF AGE 124, 134–35 (2001); A. Michael Froomkin, *Habermas@discourse.net: Toward a Critical Theory of Cyberspace*, 116 HARV. L. REV. 749, 796–817 (2003).

20 *See* KATIE HAFNER & MATTHEW LYON, WHERE WIZARDS STAY UP LATE: THE ORIGINS OF THE INTERNET 10 (Simon & Schuster, 1996); *see also* Roy Rosenzweig, *Wizards, Bureaucrats, Warriors, and Hackers: Writing The History of the Internet,* 103 AMER. HIST. REV. 1530, 1532-33 (1998) (noting that Hafner & Lyon's telling of the Internet's history downplays Baran's role and its military origins).

21 Various "on-line" services, such as CompuServe and Prodigy, did achieve some commercial success in the 1980s and early 1990s, but these were not (at that time) genuine Internet service providers. Instead, an on-line service sold subscribers access to "walled gardens": proprietary content (news, stock quotes, and the like), sometimes with the ability to exchange e-mails with other subscribers to the same service, but without full-blown access to the Internet.

22 For a discussion of the government's role in developing the Internet, see Edward L. Rubin, *Computer Languages as Networks and Power Structures: Governing the Development of XML*, 53 SMU L. REV. 1447, 1449–52 (2000); ABBATE, *supra*, at 54–60.

23 *See* Scientific and Advanced Technology Act of 1992, Pub. L. No. 102-476, § 4, 106 Stat. 2300 (codified at 42 U.S.C. §1862(g)); ABBATE, *supra*, at 196–200 (explaining the change in government policy).

24 Robert E. Kahn & Vinton G. Cerf, What Is the Internet (And What Makes It Work) 5 (1999) (http://www.cnri.reston.va.us/what_is_internet.html); *see also* Notice of Proposed Rulemaking, *Appropriate Framework for Broadband Access to the Internet over Wireline Facilities*, 17 FCC Rcd 3019, ¶ 10 (2002) (noting that after a period of government support, "the Internet entered a commercial phase characterized by more widespread network interconnection, an explosion of applications and access to a growing universe of websites utilizing common, interoperable protocols").

25 PRESIDENT WILLIAM J. CLINTON & VICE PRESIDENT ALBERT GORE, JR., A FRAMEWORK FOR GLOBAL ELECTRONIC COMMERCE 4 (1997) (http://www.w3.org/TR/NOTE-framework-970706.html) (first principle of Internet policy).

26 MICHAEL KENDE, *The Digital Handshake: Connecting Internet Backbones,* FCC OPP WORKING PAPER NO. 32, at 7 (2000) (www.fcc.gov/Bureaus/OPP/working_papers/oppwp32.pdf).

27 *Id.* at 20; *see also* General Accounting Office, Telecommunications: Characteristics and Competitiveness of the Internet Backbone Market (Oct. 2001). The FCC white paper argues that another consideration, "unique to the Internet," also helps ensure competitive efficiency: "In negotiating peering, one important bargaining chip is the number of customers to which a backbone provides access; this includes the number of transit customers. Therefore, backbones will compete with each other to win transit customers to use as leverage when negotiating peering relationships with other backbones." Kende, *Digital Handshake*, at 22.

28 *See* Jacques Cremer et al., *Connectivity in the Commercial Internet*, 48 J. IND. ECON. 433, 458-460 (2000).

29 For an anecdotal account of this scenario, see Yuki Noguchi, *Peering Dispute With AOL Slows Cogent Customer Access*, WASH. POST, December 28, 2002, at E1 (http://www.washingtonpost.com/ac2/wp-dyn?pagename=article&node=& contentId=A45819-2002Dec27&notFound=true) (noting that withheld peering connections made content seven times slower to reach).

30 *See* Constance K. Robinson, Network Effects in Telecommunications Mergers; MCI Worldcom Merger: Protecting the Future of the Internet (August 23, 1999) (http://www.usdoj.gov/atr/public/speeches/3889.htm).

31 *See* Complaint, United States v. WorldCom, No. 00-CV-1526 (D.D.C. filed June 26, 2000) (http://www.usdoj.gov/atr/cases/f5000/5051.pdf).

32 Report, *Inquiry Concerning the Deployment of Advanced Telecommunications Capability to All Americans in a Reasonable and Timely Fashion*, 14 FCC Rcd 2398, ¶105 (1999).

33 For an argument that interconnection regulation in the Internet backbone market merits consideration, see James B. Speta, *A Common Carrier Approach to Internet Interconnection*, 54 FED. COMM. L.J. 225 (2002).

34 As we explain in chapter 9, retail rate conventions in the United States normally protect the end user from paying the telephone company anything for that service beyond the fixed monthly "local" service charge. And, under the "access charge exemption," the ISP pays the telephone company only if it leases its incoming lines—the ones leading into its modem bank—from the telephone company itself. Otherwise, if it leases those lines from a CLEC, it pays the ILEC nothing at all, even though the ILEC is still holding open a circuit for the duration of each "call" from one of its customers to the ISP (or, more precisely, to the CLEC serving the ISP).

35 Third Report, *Inquiry Concerning the Deployment of Advanced Telecommunications Capability to all Americans in a Reasonable and Timely Fashion*, 17 FCC Rcd 2844, ¶¶ 7, 9 (2002).

36 For a survey evaluating the state of broadband usage in early 2004, see John B. Horrigan, Pew Internet Project Data Memo (April 19, 2004) (http://www.pewinternet.org/pdfs/PIP_Broadband04.DataMemo.pdf).

37 Yochi Jo Dreazen, *What's Slowing Us Down?*, WALL ST. J., Oct. 13, 2003, at R4; *see also* Robert W. Crandall et al., *The Effects of Ubiquitous Broadband Adoption on Investment, Jobs and the U.S. Economy*, New Millennium Research (September 17, 2003) (www.newmillenniumresearch.org/archive/bbstudyreport_091703.pdf).

38 Dreazen, *supra* (quoting Scott Cleland of the Precursor Group).

39 *See* Jim Hu, *Study: Broadband Leaps Past Dial-up*, CNET NEWS.COM (August 18, 2004) (http://news.com.com/2102-1034_3-5314922.html) (reporting that, for the first time, broadband usage surpasses narrowband usage); Matt Richtel, *In a Fast-Moving Web World, Some Prefer the Dial-up Lane*, N.Y. TIMES, Apr. 19, 2004, at A1 (http://www.nytimes.com/2004/04/19/technology/19DIAL.html?ei+ 5012&en=1aaf47b7cb8) (reporting on lingering use of narrowband); Nielsen// NetRatings, Nearly 40 Million Internet Users Connect Via Broadband, Growing 49 Percent (June 17, 2003) (www.nielsennetratings.com/pr/pr_030618_us.pdf) (reporting on mid-2003 lead of narrowband, but clear direction of users toward broadband).

40 *See* Gerald R. Faulhaber, *Broadband Deployment: Is Policy In The Way?*, *in* BROADBAND: SHOULD WE REGULATE HIGH-SPEED INTERNET ACCESS? 226-27 (AEI-Brookings, Crandall & Alleman, eds., 2002).

41 In Japan, for example, the enormous success of "Yahoo! BB" relied largely on the ability of that service to offer broadband connections along with VoIP. *See* Benjamin Fulford, *Last Laugh*, FORBES (March 17, 2003) (http://www.forbes.com/billionaires/free_forbes/2003/0317/102.html) ("In the end, it was the ultracheap phone service that brought in customers in droves.").

42 *See* Lawrence Lessig, *Who's Holding Back Broadband?*, WASH. POST, Jan. 8, 2002, at A17 (http://www.lessig.org/content/columns/washpo.pdf).

43 These "physical" protocols, which are normally conceptualized as occupying Layer 2 ("data link") within the traditional seven-layer "OSI" model noted above, define how packets will be configured within a data network and assign particular roles to the individual bits or bytes (units of eight bits) within each packet. These protocols and TCP/IP are not mutually exclusive; the latter are "logical" protocols that occupy Layers 3 and 4 ("network" and "transport"), specialize in addressing and error-correction functions, and "ride on top of" Layer 2 physical protocols such as ATM.

44 Whereas dial-up users must rely on an ISP to translate their analog signals into a digitized IP format, DSL modems and cable modems modulate the digital content so as to facilitate their transmission over analog facilities such as loops. Also, in many cases, the DSL or cable modem connection is assigned a "static" (fixed) IP address and becomes in that sense a direct part of the Internet, whereas dial-up users are assigned a "dynamic" (temporary) IP address for each session and rely more on their individual ISPs as intermediaries.

45 Telephone companies did spend a fair amount of time and money in the early to mid-1990s deploying a service known as Integrated Services Digital Network, or "ISDN." Like DSL, a residential ISDN line enables customers to talk on the telephone and gain access to the Internet at the same time, but the data speeds, while faster than those of an ordinary dial-up connection, are much slower than DSL speeds. (Also, ISDN requires the use of two twisted pairs of copper wires, as opposed to DSL's one.) ISDN never became widely popular in residential markets, and the newer broadband technologies discussed in the text now overshadow it in any event.

46 *See* Scott Cleland, Why Bell Fiber Strategies Are a Profit "Pipe Dream," Precursor Research (June 23, 2004) (noting that the "Bells have hyped fiber deployments for years—but haven't delivered" and concluding that "Bell fiber announcements are much more about maintaining the *perception* of a better future than the *reality* of a better future").

47 *See* Yankee Group, Cable and DSL Battle for Broadband Dominance 4-5 (Feb. 2004).

48 *See* News Release, Time Warner Cable Partners with MCI and Sprint for Nationwide Rollout of Digital Phone (Dec. 8, 2003) (http://www.timewarnercable.com/InvestorRelations/PressReleases/TWCPressRele aseDetail.ashx?PRID=3&MarketID=0) (announcing plans to team up with MCI and Sprint in "aggressive" competition with Bell incumbents).

49 For a discussion of Verizon's decision to make that bet, see Steve Rosenbush et al., *Verizon's Gutsy Bet*, BUS. WK., Aug. 4, 2003, at 52 (pricing project between $20 to $40 billion, at a clip of $1,000 to $2,000 per line).

50 For an argument that other would-be broadband rivals will—on account of capital construction and customer acquisition costs—be unsuccessful in challenging the current incumbents, see Stagg Newman, Broadband Access Platforms for the Mass Market: An Assessment, TPRC Working Paper (September 2003) (http://tprc.org/papers/2003/254/BbandAccessPlatforms.pdf).

51 Jim Hu, *Satellite Seeks Broadband Re-Entry*, CNET NEWS.COM (March 11, 2004) (http://news.com.com/2100-1034-5172088.html).

52 Ken Brown, *The Web's New Outlet: Utilities Plan to Send Internet Service Over Electric Lines, Challenging Cable Modems and DSL*, WALL ST. J., Mar. 2, 2004, at B1 (http://online.wsj.com/article_print/0,,SB107818096941143377,00.html).

53 Report and Order, *Carrier Current Systems, Including Broadband over Power Line Systems*, ET Docket 04-37 (2004) (http://hraunfoss.fcc.gov/edocs_public/attachmatch/FCC-04-245A1.pdf) ("*Powerline Decision*").

54 Notice of Proposed Rulemaking, *Carrier Current Systems, Including Broadband over Power Line Systems*, 19 FCC Rcd 3335, 3370 (2004) (Commissioner Copps, dissenting in part and approving in part); *see also Powerline Decision, supra* (Joint Statement of Chairman Michael K. Powell and Commissioner Kathleen Q. Abernathy) ("Because BPL is a nascent technology and the broadband market has no dominant incumbent service provider, only minimal regulations are appropriate[.]").

55 Stephen Lawson, *When Will Wireless Hit Wi-Max Speeds?*, PC WORLD (June 17, 2004) (http://www.pcworld.com/news/article/0,aid,116545,00.asp); *Tomorrow's Wi-Fi*, THE ECONOMIST (May 24, 2004). In truth, no one knows what wireless technologies will prevail in the broadband access market. For a sampling of other such technologies, see www.navini.com and www.somanetworks.com.

56 For example, a workshop of the U.S. branch of the Institute of Electrical and Electronics Engineers (IEEE) concluded that advanced fiber networks are a natural monopoly and will replace the incumbent telephone (and cable) networks. It thus endorsed a "new paradigm" of end-user-owned telecommunications. *See* IEEE-

USA, Report From The Workshop (March 2003) (http://afn.johnson.cornell.edu/
publish/WSR/WSR.pdf); *see also* http://afn.johnson.cornell.edu/
referencedocuments.php. For additional arguments in favor of government sponsorship of the broadband build-out, see LAWRENCE LESSIG, THE FUTURE OF IDEAS
244-46 (2001); Reed Hundt, *The Ineluctable Modality of Broadband*, 21 YALE J.
REG. 239 (2004). On the other hand, some commentators suggest that, even though
fiber to the home may well be a natural monopoly, it is quite likely that consumers
will not need that much bandwidth and that last mile wireless technologies will
serve their needs just as well. *See, e.g.*, Andrew Odlyzko, *The Many Paradoxes of
Broadband*, 8 FIRST MONDAY 4 (September 2003)
(http://firstmonday.org/issues/issue8_9/ odlyzko/index.html); *see also id.* at 13-14
("Technological predictions have always been hard, of course, and much of what
broadband proponents say has to be treated cautiously.").

57 *See, e.g.*, Maria Hinas, *Wiring the Swedish Archipelago*, GOV'T TECH. INT'L
(Aug. 2002) (http://www.centerdigitalgov.com/international/story.php?docid=
21138); Rob Kirby, *Fiber—Can't Find Its Way Home?*, NETWORK MAG., Sept. 5,
2001 (http://www.networkmagazine.com/shared/article/showArticle.jhtml?
articleId=8703187&pgno=2). Similar reasoning has led a few municipalities to
consider similar initiatives, particularly in the absence of any commercial broadband option, although section 253 would preclude them from trying to ensure
recovery of their investment by barring subsequent competitive entry. Some high
profile efforts of this kind, such as the ambitious "Utopia project" initially envisioned for the Salt Lake City area, are facing increasing political resistance, as lawmakers reconsider whether such massive capital investment is worthwhile. *See*
Marguerite Reardon, *Quest for "Utopia" Hits a Roadblock*, CNET NEWS.COM
(April 19, 2004) (http://news.com.com/2100-1034-5193926.html).

58 *See, e.g.*, Howard A. Shelanski, *Competition and Regulation in Broadband
Communications, in* BROADBAND: SHOULD WE REGULATE HIGH-SPEED INTERNET
ACCESS?, *supra*, at 177 (emphasizing that facilities-based competition provides
opportunities for experimentation and facilitates independent innovation). For an
example of centralized planning gone awry, see our discussion of the digital television transition in chapter 12.

Chaper Five

1 *See generally* United States v. Microsoft Corp., 253 F.3d 34 (D.C. Cir. 2001) (setting forth standard for antitrust liability); Howard A. Shelanski & J. Gregory Sidak,
Antitrust Divestiture in Network Industries, 68 U. CHI. L. REV. 1, 19-20 (2001)
(discussing concerns about remedies).

2 Joseph Farrell & Philip J. Weiser, *Modularity, Vertical Integration, and Open
Access Policies: Towards a Convergence of Antitrust and Regulation in the Internet
Age*, 17 HARV. J.L. TECH. 85, 105-19 (2003) (http://jolt.law.harvard.edu/articles/
pdf/v17/17HarvJLTech085.pdf).

3 For a concise summary of the *Computer Inquiries*, see Robert Cannon, *Where
ISPs and Telephone Companies Compete: A Guide to the Computer Inquiries*, 9
COMMLAW CONSPECTUS 49 (2001).

4 *See* Tentative Decision and Further Notice of Inquiry and Rulemaking, *Amendment of Section 64.702 of the Commission's Rules and Regulations* (*"Computer II"*), 72 F.C.C.2d 358 (1979) (*"Tentative Decision"*), 77 F.C.C.2d 384 (1980) (*"Final Decision"*), 84 F.C.C.2d 50 (*"Reconsideration Order"*), 88 F.C.C.2d 512 (1981) (*"Further Reconsideration Order"*), *aff'd sub nom.* Computer and Communications Indus. Ass'n v. FCC, 693 F.2d 198 (D.C. Cir. 1982) (*"CCIA"*).

5 *Computer II Final Decision*, ¶¶ 93, 96.

6 47 C.F.R. § 64.702(a); *see Computer II Final Decision*, ¶ 120.

7 *See* 47 U.S.C. § 153(43), (46), (20); First Report and Order, *Implementation of the Non-Accounting Safeguards of Sections 271 and 272 of the Communications Act of 1934*, 11 FCC Rcd 21,905, ¶ 102 (1996) (*"Non-Accounting Safeguards Order"*), *modified,* 12 FCC Rcd 2297 (1997), 12 FCC Rcd 8653 (1997), *aff'd,* Bell Atl. Tel. Cos. v. FCC, 131 F.3d 1044 (1997); Report to Congress, *Federal-State Joint Board on Universal Service*, 13 FCC Rcd 11,501, ¶¶ 29-33 (1998) (*"1998 Report to Congress"*); *see also* chapter 3 (discussing statutory definitions). The *1998 Report to Congress* is sometimes known as the *"Stevens Report,"* after Sen. Ted Stevens of Alaska, who sponsored the legislation requesting it.

8 *See Computer II Final Decision*, ¶ 231; *see generally* Further Notice of Proposed Rulemaking, *Policy and Rules Governing the Interstate, Interexchange Marketplace*, 13 FCC Rcd 21,531, ¶ 33 (1998) ("In the *Computer II* proceeding, the Commission required common carriers that own transmission facilities and provide enhanced services to 'acquire transmission capacity pursuant to the same prices, terms, and conditions reflected in their tariffs when their own facilities are utilized.' This requirement has been interpreted in decisions since *Computer II* to mean that 'carriers that own common carrier transmission facilities and provide enhanced services must unbundle basic from enhanced services and offer transmission capacity to other enhanced service providers under the same tariffed terms and conditions under which they provide such services to their own enhanced service operations.'").

9 The *Computer II* unbundling requirement deals with obligations to provide transmission *services*; the facilities-unbundling requirements of the 1996 Act deal with obligations to lease *facilities* (or capacity on such facilities). At the margins, the two concepts merge, because leasing capacity on network facilities is often functionally equivalent to providing a transmission service over those facilities—as we saw in our discussion in chapter 3 about the relationship between "special access" services and the network element combination known as an "enhanced extended link." To make matters more complicated still, the *Computer II* rules separately imposed "unbundling" obligations on telephone companies to sell "customer premises equipment," such as telephones and computer modems, separately from telecommunications services, as discussed in chapter 2. *See CCIA, supra.*

10 *See* California v. FCC, 905 F.2d 1217, 1231-32 (9th Cir. 1990) (*"California I"*).

11 *See generally* California v. FCC, 39 F.3d 919 (9th Cir. 1994) (*"California III"*).

12 *See id.* at 931-33.

13 *See, e.g.,* United States Department of Justice/Federal Trade Commission, *Horizontal Merger Guidelines,* Section 2 (rev. April 8, 1997) (http:// www.usdoj.gov/atr/public/guidelines/horiz_book/hmg1.html).

14 *See* Farrell & Weiser, *supra,* at 105-07; *see also* Paul L. Joskow & Roger G. Noll, *The Bell Doctrine: Applications in Telecommunications, Electricity, and Other Network Industries,* 51 STAN. L. REV. 1249, 1249–50 (1999). To be fair, Baxter was not the first person to appreciate this point. *See, e.g.,* 1 ALFRED E. KAHN, THE ECONOMICS OF REGULATION: PRINCIPLES AND INSTITUTIONS 28 (Wiley, 1970) (discussing issue).

15 *See generally* Farrell & Weiser, *supra.*

16 LAWRENCE LESSIG, THE FUTURE OF IDEAS: THE FATE OF THE COMMONS IN A CONNECTED WORLD 176 (Vintage, 2001) (quoting Charles Platt, *The Future Will Be Fast but Not Free,* WIRED, May 2001 (http:/www.wired.com/wired/ archive/9.05/broadband_pr.html)) (emphasis added by Lessig).

17 Stephen Labaton, *Fight for Internet Access Creates Unusual Alliances,* N.Y. TIMES, Aug. 13, 1999, at A14.

18 Agreement Containing Consent Orders; Decision and Order, *America Online, Inc. and Time Warner, Inc.,* FTC Docket No. C-3989, 2000 WL 1843019 (proposed Dec. 14, 2000).

19 Christopher Yoo, *Would Mandating Broadband Network Neutrality Help or Hurt Competition? A Comment on the End-to-End Debate,* 3 J. TELECOMM. & HIGH TECH. L. 23, 55-56 (2004).

20 *Id.*

21 *See* 47 U.S.C. § 601 *et seq.*

22 One threshold step in the analysis is to identify the proper level of generality on which to characterize what an end user receives when she purchases cable modem service. Should we look at each higher layer application in isolation from the others, such that a cable modem subscriber might be using a Title II "telecommunications service" one minute and a Title VI "cable service" the next? Or should we base the answer on considered generalizations about the full range of applications to which end users can put the underlying broadband service? The FCC has consistently adopted the latter approach when addressing the statutory characterization of broadband platforms that, like cable modem or DSL service, are capable of supporting many different types of applications. A DSL or cable modem provider, it maintains, "do[es] not offer subscribers separate services — electronic mail, Web browsing, and others — that should be deemed to have separate legal status." *1998 Report to Congress,* ¶ 75.

23 Early advocates of multiple ISP access argued that cable modem service should be treated as a kind of "cable service" subject to regulation under Title VI. Because traditional cable services had long been subject to expansive regulation by local franchising authorities, these advocates hoped that, if cable modem service were treated as just another cable service, it too could be subject to broad regulation by

these local authorities, who were the first to impose multiple ISP access requirements. This argument soon foundered on an uncooperative statutory definition of "cable service," however, and little is heard of it today. Specifically, Title VI defines "cable service" as "(A) the one-way transmission to subscribers of (i) video programming, or (ii) other programming service, and (B) subscriber interaction, if any, which is required for the selection or use of such video programming or other programming service." 47 U.S.C. § 522(6). In turn, "video programming" means "programming provided by, or generally considered comparable to programming provided by, a television broadcast station," 47 U.S.C. § 522(20), and "other programming service" means "information that a cable operator makes available to all subscribers generally." 47 U.S.C. § 522(14). As the Ninth Circuit held in 2000, cable modem service provides a range of "interactive and individual" services, such as Web browsing and e-mail, that collectively defy this statutory definition, which appears designed more narrowly to encompass conventional television programming plus a rudimentary "interactive TV" service whose content is supplied by the cable company itself. *See* AT&T Corp. v. City of Portland, 216 F.3d 871, 873 (9th Cir. 2000) (*"Portland"*). Interestingly, the opposing parties in the Ninth Circuit case actually agreed (although the Ninth Circuit ultimately did not) that cable modem service is a Title VI "cable service," but disagreed about the implications of that characterization for the legality of open access regulations.

24 47 U.S.C. § 541(b)(3)(D); *see Portland*, 216 F.3d at 873.

25 *Portland*, 216 F.3d at 878.

26 *Id.* at 876. The FCC had filed an oddly inconclusive friend-of-the-court brief with the Ninth Circuit in the *Portland* case that touched on several of these issues, but it offered no clear guidance on any of them. Nor did it ask the court to refer the matter to it under the well-established doctrine of "primary jurisdiction," United States v. W. Pac. R.R. Co., 352 U.S. 59 (1956), for the Commission seemed more anxious to avoid this political hot potato than to help establish a coherent body of law on a nationwide basis. At the time, FCC Chairman William Kennard justified the policy of deliberate non-decision as an effort to "do no harm." William E. Kennard, *How to End the World Wide Wait*, WALL ST. J., Aug. 24, 1999, at A18; *see also* Barbara S. Esbin & Gary S. Lutzker, *Poles, Holes, and Cable Open Access: Where the Global Information Superhighway Meets the Local Right-of-Way*, 10 COMMLAW CONSPECTUS 23, 55 (2001) ("Ironically, had the FCC chosen to implement its 'hands off' policy through formal regulatory action, rather than through oblique pronouncements, it might have avoided the series of conflicting judicial open access decisions that eventually threatened the agency's ability to set broadband policy on a national basis."); Nat'l Cable & Telecomm. Ass'n, Inc. v. Gulf Power Co., 534 U.S. 327, 348 (2002) (Thomas, J., concurring in part and dissenting in part) (the FCC's responsibility to implement its regulatory statute "does not permit [it] to avoid this question").

27 Declaratory Ruling and Notice of Proposed Rulemaking, *Inquiry Concerning High-Speed Access to the Internet over Cable and Other Facilities*, 17 FCC Rcd 4798 (2002) (*"Cable Modem Order"*). The subsequent judicial history of this order is discussed later in this chapter.

28 *Cable Modem Order* ¶, 38; *see also 1998 Report to Congress*, ¶ 88.

29 47 U.S.C. §§ 153(43), (46).

30 47 U.S.C. § 153(20). Around the same time, the FCC likewise suggested that, when an incumbent local *telephone company* (an ILEC) bundles Internet access together with DSL transmission, the bundled product is an "information service" without a "telecommunications service" component. *See* Notice of Proposed Rulemaking, *Appropriate Framework for Broadband Access to the Internet Over Wireline Facilities*, 17 FCC Rcd 3019, ¶¶ 17-25 (2002) ("*Wireline Broadband NPRM*"). For the most part, so long as the *Computer II* rule remains in force, questions about how to characterize the bundled retail service sold to end users have only limited significance to the ILEC, for the ILEC must strip the underlying transmission component from that retail service and offer it separately at tariff. (As discussed in the text, the FCC has declined to extend that *Computer II* unbundling obligation to cable modem providers.) Nonetheless, the FCC's characterization of bundled DSL Internet access services does affect whether CLECs may invoke rights under section 251(c)(4) to obtain the retail-minus-avoided-cost discount for bundled DSL/ISP services offered directly to *end users*, because those rights are limited to "telecommunications services." And, as observed in note 39 below, CLECs have no corresponding rights to a wholesale discount on the bulk DSL services sold to *ISPs* (whether under *Computer II* or voluntarily), because those services are not provided at "retail."

Some ILECs claim that this statutory characterization issue also affects the separate issue of CLEC access to broadband-related network elements under section 251(c)(3). They observe that a facility can be a "network element" subject to the leasing obligation only if it is "used in the provision of a telecommunications service," 47 U.S.C. § 153(29), and they conclude that "used" in this definition means used by *the ILEC* for that purpose. FCC precedent, however, holds that the relevant question is whether the facility is "capable of being used" for that purpose. *See* Third Report and Order and Fourth Further Notice of Proposed Rulemaking, *Implementation of the Local Competition Provisions of the Telecommunications Act of 1996*, 15 FCC Rcd 3696, ¶ 329 (1999) ("*UNE Remand Order*") (interpreting "the term 'used' in the definition of a network element to mean '*capable of being used*' in the provision of a telecommunications service."); *see also Triennial Review Order*, ¶ 59. It seems unlikely that any court would second-guess that interpretation of the statutory language. At the same time, section 251(c)(3) itself separately limits a CLEC's leasing rights to the use of network elements for "the provision of a telecommunications service."

31 *See Cable Modem Order*, ¶¶ 31-41.

32 *Id.*, ¶ 43.

33 *Id.*

34 345 F.3d 1120 (9th Cir. 2003), *cert. granted*, Nos. 04-281 et al. (Dec. 3, 2004).

35 *Id.* at 1133 (O'Scannlain, J., concurring). The Ninth Circuit's resolution of this administrative law question is itself quite controversial. *See* Kenneth A. Bamberger, *Provisional Precedent: Protecting Flexibility in Administrative Policymaking*, 77 N.Y.U. L. REV. 1272 (2002).

36 *Cable Modem Order,* ¶ 95; *see Brand X,* 345 F.3d at 1138 (Thomas, J., concurring) ("Naturally, the FCC may choose to forbear from enforcing these regulations if it determines they are not necessary to promote competition or protect consumers."); *Portland,* 216 F.3d at 879-80 ("We note that the FCC has broad authority to forbear from enforcing the telecommunications provisions if it determines that such action is unnecessary to prevent discrimination and protect consumers, and is consistent with the public interest. *See* 47 U.S.C. § 160(a). Congress has reposed the details of telecommunications policy in the FCC, and we will not impinge on its authority over these matters.").

37 *See Wireline Broadband NPRM, supra.*

38 *Cable Modem Order,* ¶¶ 54-55.

39 *See Wireline Broadband NPRM,* ¶ 26. The ILECs won much more modest deregulatory relief in this context when they persuaded the FCC to rule that bulk DSL sales to ISPs do not qualify, for purposes of section 251(c)(4), as a "retail" service that a CLEC is entitled to purchase, for resale to ISP partners of its own, at the "retail minus avoided cost" wholesale discount discussed in chapter 3. *See* Ass'n of Communications Enterprises v. FCC, 253 F.3d 29 (D.C. Cir. 2001) (affirming FCC policy). Of course, that issue is separate from whether the ILEC must sell the transmission service on a common carrier basis to all willing purchasers *at the same price and on the same terms,* both to ISPs and to CLECs that might wish to resell that service to ISPs. *See* 47 U.S.C. § 251(b)(1). Resale on *those* terms, without the regulatorily prescribed mark-down, is of course a much less attractive option for CLECs, which, as intermediaries, normally hope for a substantial discount off the price that the ILEC charges ISPs so that they can mark the price back up and earn a profit.

40 Tim Wu, *Network Neutrality, Broadband Discrimination,* 2 J. TELECOMM. & HIGH TECH. L. 141, 149 (2003).

41 *Id.*

42 *See* J. H. Saltzer et al., *End-to-End Arguments in System Design,* 2 ACM TRANSACTIONS ON COMPUTER SYSTEMS 277 (1984), *reprinted in* INNOVATIONS IN INTERNETWORKING 195 (Artech House, Craig Partridge ed., 1988).

43 LESSIG, FUTURE OF IDEAS, at 36-37.

44 *Id.* at 167.

45 *Id.*

46 *Id.* at 248.

47 *See* http://web.mit.edu/Saltzer/www/publications/openaccess.html (quoted in LESSIG, FUTURE OF IDEAS, at 157).

48 LESSIG, FUTURE OF IDEAS, at 47; *see also* Ex Parte Letter of Professors Tim Wu and Lawrence Lessig, *Inquiry Concerning High-Speed Access to the Internet Over Cable and Other Facilities,* CS Dkt. 02-52 (Aug. 22, 2003) (http://faculty.virginia.edu/timwu/ wu_lessig_fcc.pdf) (outlining case for such regulations).

49 To date, most economic analyses have speculated about why anticompetitive practices might occur without documenting any actual such efforts. *See, e.g.,* Daniel L. Rubinfeld & Hal J. Singer, *Open Access to Broadband Networks: A Case Study of the AOL/Time Warner Merger,* 16 BERKELEY TECH. L.J. 631 (2001).

50 United States v. Microsoft Corp., 87 F. Supp. 2d 30, 38 (D.D.C. 2000), *aff'd in relevant part,* 253 F.3d 34 (D.C. Cir. 2001); *see also* Timothy F. Bresnahan, *A Remedy That Falls Short of Restoring Competition,* ANTITRUST, Fall 2001, at 67.

51 *See* Reinhardt Krause, *Big Companies Fight Over Online Content—Odd Alliances Formed,* INVESTOR'S BUS. DAILY, July 15, 2003 (quoting FCC Media Bureau Chief Ken Ferree as suggesting that Net neutrality proposals were moribund because of perception that antitrust enforcement alone is sufficient to address any anticompetitive abuses by dominant broadband providers).

52 David Lieberman, *Media Giants' Net Change: Major Companies Establish Strong Foothold Online,* USA TODAY, Dec. 14, 1999, at B3.

53 *See* Farrell & Weiser, *supra,* at 114-117.

54 For a fuller discussion of the examples in this paragraph, see the articles by Wu and Yoo, cited above.

55 Our point is not that there are no reported instances of discriminatory treatment, but that they are generally short-lived or limited in nature. For one example, see David Lazarus, *Lazarus At Large: SBC's Latest Twist,* SAN FRAN. CHRON. (April 23, 2003) (http://www.sfgate.com/cgi-bin/article.cgi?f=/c/a/2003/04/23/BU.DTL) (noting that SBC allows free linking of home page to Yahoo! Auctions, but charges for identical links to eBay).

56 LESSIG, FUTURE OF IDEAS, at 39.

57 Wu, *Network Neutrality,* at 148.

58 *See id.* at 150-51.

59 *See, e.g.,* WILLAM BAUMOL & ALAN BLINDER, ECONOMICS: PRINCIPLES AND POLICY 248-52 (8th ed. 2000) (discussing "monopolistic competition").

60 CARL SHAPIRO & HAL R. VARIAN, INFORMATION RULES 300 (Harv. Bus. School Press, 1998).

61 Jerry Hausman & Jeffrey MacKie-Mason, *Price Discrimination and Patent Policy,* 19 RAND J. ECON. 253, 257 (1988).

62 Richard A. Posner, *The Chicago School of Antitrust Analysis,* 127 U. PA. L. REV. 925, 926–28 (1979).

63 Yoo, *Mandating Broadband Network Neutrality,* at 29.

64 *See, e.g.,* Nancy Victory, Net Neutrality: Let's Look Before We Leap, Address to the Progress and Freedom Foundation (June 27, 2003) (urging caution against mandating any specific regulations without an empirical basis for concern) (http://www.pff.org/publications/communications/pop10.22netneutrality.pdf).

65 Remarks of Michael K. Powell, Preserving Internet Freedom: Guiding Principles for the Industry, Feb. 8, 2004 (http://hraunfoss.fcc.gov/edocs_public/attachmatch/ DOC-243556A1.pdf) (*"Powell Internet Freedom Speech"*); *see also* Michael K. Powell, *Preserving Internet Freedom: Guiding Principles for the Industry*, 3 J. TELECOMM. & HIGH TECH. L. 5, 11-12 (2004)

66 *Powell Internet Freedom Speech* at 4.

67 *See* Steven Hetcher, *The FTC as an Internet Privacy Norm Entrepreneur*, 53 VAND. L. REV. 2041, 2046, 2056 (2000); *see also* Complaint, *Eli Lilly and Company*, FTC Dkt. No. C4047 (http://www.ftc.gov/os/2002/05/elilillycmp.htm).

68 *See* Philip J. Weiser, *Toward a Next Generation Regulatory Strategy*, 35 LOY. U. CHI. L.J. 41, 65-84 (2003) (detailing how the FCC could announce a non-discrimination standard and enforce it in adjudication-like proceedings that would enable platform providers to justify their discriminatory policies with respect to legitimate business practices).

69 *See* United States Telecom Ass'n. v. FCC, 290 F.3d 415, 428-29 (D.C. Cir. 2002) (*"USTA I"*); Report and Order and Order on Remand and Further Notice of Proposed Rulemaking, *Review of the Section 251 Unbundling Obligations of Incumbent Local Exchange Carriers*, 18 FCC Rcd 16,978, ¶ 292 (2003) (*"Triennial Review Order"*) (subsequent judicial history discussed in the text).

70 *Triennial Review Order*, ¶¶ 43-54.

71 *See* Notice of Proposed Rulemaking, *Review of Regulatory Requirements for Incumbent LEC Broadband Telecommunications Servs.*, 16 FCC Rcd 22,745 (2001); *see also* Memorandum Opinion and Order, *Review of Regulatory Requirements for Incumbent LEC Broadband Telecommunications Servs.*, 17 FCC Rcd 27,000 (2002) (granting limited relief for SBC's separate advanced services affiliate).

72 *See, e.g.*, Yankee Group, Cable and DSL Battle for Broadband Dominance 4-5 (Feb. 2004).

73 *See, e.g.*, Joint Petition for Declaratory Ruling, *The American ISP Ass'n and BestWeb Corp.* (filed Feb. 20, 2004). As of this writing, the FCC has not acted on this petition.

74 *See generally* 2A PHILLIP E. AREEDA, ET AL., ANTITRUST LAW ¶ 423, at 81-82 (2002); United States v. Aluminum Co. of America, 148 F.2d 416, 424-25 (2d Cir. 1945) (L. Hand); DOJ/FTC, *Horizontal Merger Guidelines*, ¶¶ 1.31-1.32.

75 As a business matter, the ILEC often leases the entire unbundled loop to the voice CLEC, which in turn leases the high frequency portion to the data CLEC. Of course, the ILEC plays some role in engineering this split.

76 *USTA I*, 290 F.3d at 428-30.

77 *Id.* at 429.

78 *Triennial Review Order*, ¶¶ 255-269.

79 *Triennial Review Order*, at 17,505 (Separate Statement of Chairman Michael K. Powell, Approving in Part and Dissenting in Part).

80 Alfred Kahn, *Regulatory Politics As Usual*, Pol'y Matters (Mar. 2003) (http://www.aei-brookings.org/policy/page.php?id=127). The experience abroad can be instructive as well. In Japan, for example, line sharing has enabled one competitor to gain 30%of the market and is said to have pressured the incumbent (NTT) to respond aggressively. *See* David Howard, *The All-IP Broadband Network: What The US Can Learn From the Rest of the World*, Internet Telephony (November 2003) (http://www.tmcnet.com/it/1103/1103f-utstar.htm).

81 United States Telecom Ass'n v. FCC, 359 F.3d 554, 584-85 (D.C. Cir.) (*"USTA II"*), *cert. denied*, 2004 WL 2152860 (2004).

82 *See ILEC Court Challenges to Interim UNE Order Mark Bid to Keep Case in D.C.*, Telecomm. Rep. (Sept. 1, 2004) (2004 WL 69683450).

83 Notably, the FCC adopted a different set of rules for fiber ("high capacity") loops deployed to *enterprise* business customers. Although it insulated the very highest capacity loops of this sort from any unbundling obligation, it entered a nationwide presumption, rebuttable by the states under various conditions, of "impairment" for dark fiber loops, DS1 loops, and up to two DS3 loops per CLEC per customer location. *Triennial Review Order*, ¶¶ 298-340. "DS1" and "DS3" are measures of capacity: a DS1's capacity is equivalent to 24 voice-grade ("DS0") circuits, and a DS3 is equivalent to 28 DS1s. After the D.C. Circuit invalidated the unbundling rules applicable to transport in *USTA II* (see chapter 3), the FCC raised the "impairment" threshold for enterprise loops, transport, and dark fiber. *See* pp. 109, 550, *supra*; *see also* Order and Notice of Proposed Rulemaking, *Unbundled Access to Network Elements*, WC Dkt. No. 04-313, CC Dkt. No. 01-338, 2004 WL 1900394, ¶ 1 n.4 (Aug. 20, 2004).

It is difficult to reconcile the *Order's* strikingly different analyses in the "enterprise" and "mass market" subsections of the *Order's* loop unbundling discussion. Indeed, the D.C. Circuit, in upholding the more restrictive mass market rules, seemed to credit the CLECs' contention that the two sets of rules are mutually inconsistent. *See USTA II*, 359 F.3d at 583. Perhaps the best rationale for the divergence in treatment, which the FCC itself did not develop until later, *see* Order on Reconsideration, *Review of the Section 251 Unbundling Obligations of Incumbent Local Exchange Carriers*, CC Dkt. No. 01-338, 2004 WL 1774552, ¶ 8 (Aug. 9, 2004) ("MDU Order"), is that the investment-deterring costs of overregulation are greater in the mass market, where much less fiber has already been deployed and where the risks of stranded investment (due to low customer demand) are most severe.

84 For the initial FTTP ruling, see *Triennial Review Order*, ¶¶ 285-297. After the *Triennial Review Order* was issued, BellSouth and other ILECs sought reconsideration of the FCC's ruling that, to be treated for these purposes as an FTTP loop (rather than a hybrid copper-fiber loop), the fiber portion of the loop must actually extend all the way to the "demarcation point" marking the boundary between the ILEC's facilities and the "inside wire" in a customer's home. *See id.*, ¶ 275

n.811, ¶ 288 n.832. In the view of these ILECs, it makes no policy sense to distinguish between these loops and FTTC loops, which contain copper in the final few hundred feet from the street to a customer's building. The FCC granted this reconsideration request as this book went to press, entitling ILECs to the same favorable treatment as is applicable to FTTP loops for any mass market loop in which fiber extends to within 500 feet of all customers served by that loop. *See* Order on Reconsideration, *Review of the Section 251 Unbundling Obligations of Incumbent Local Exchange Carriers*, CC Dkt. No. 01-338 (Oct. 18, 2004) (http://hraunfoss.fcc.gov/edocs_public/attachmatch/FCC-04-248A1.pdf).

The FCC had separately clarified that a fiber loop would be eligible for deregulatory treatment as a full-fledged FTTP loop when the fiber portion is deployed to the "minimum point of entry" in a "multiple dwelling unit" (MDU) that is "predominantly residential" (e.g., an apartment building), no matter who owns the inside wiring between that point and particular subscribers. *See MDU Order, supra.* This issue has considerable commercial significance because, as the Commission found, "millions of Americans today live in MDUs, constituting perhaps as much as one-third of the population." *Id.,* ¶ 7.

85 In more technical terms, the *Triennial Review Order* provides that CLECs cannot invoke section 251 unbundling rights to use the fiber portion of an incumbent's hybrid loop for the transmission of packetized data from an end user all the way to the central office. Instead, if they want to provide DSL services of their own to customers served by hybrid loops, they will have to build their own fiber links to the remote terminal and install their own electronic equipment there alongside the ILEC's—which can sometimes be a costly proposition subject to various logistical obstacles. At the same time, the Commission required ILECs, as before, to continue providing a direct *circuit-switched* pathway from end users all the way to the central office over the ILEC's legacy "TDM" (time-division multiplexing) electronics also located at the remote terminal. *See id.,* ¶¶ 288-89. In its October 2004 order, however, the FCC clarified that ILECs have no obligation to build TDM capability into networks that have never had it.

86 *Id.,* ¶ 286.

87 *See id.,* ¶ 291.

88 Pub. L. 104-104, Title VII, § 706(a), Feb. 8, 1996, 110 Stat. 153 (reprinted at 47 U.S.C. § 157 note).

89 *Triennial Review Order,* ¶¶ 288, 292.

90 *Id.,* ¶¶ 295, 272.

91 *Id.,* ¶ 292.

92 *See, e.g., USTA II,* 359 F.3d at 581 ("The Commission says little in the Order or in its brief to respond [to] the assertion that ILECs would invest in fiber feeder [for hybrid loops] even without revenue from broadband. Indeed, the Commission appears to concede that ILECs are already investing heavily in fiber feeder loops, and offers no specific evidence suggesting that unbundling the broadband capabilities of these loops would have a substantial negative impact on this investment. (Nor, to be sure, do the CLECs offer any sort of sophisticated econometric analysis demonstrating the likely marginal impact on investment.)") (citation omitted), 583 ("While the CLECs' objections [to the FCC's impairment finding for fiber-to-

the-premises loops] are convincing in many respects, they are ultimately unavailing. Even if the CLECs are impaired with respect to [FTTP] deployment (a point we do not decide), the § 706 considerations that we upheld as legitimate in the hybrid loop case are enough to justify the Commission's decision not to unbundle [FTTP].").

93 *Id.* at 580.

94 *Id.* at 582 (emphasis added).

95 *Id.* at 585.

96 *See Triennial Review Order,* ¶¶ 649-67.

97 *See USTA II,* 359 F.3d at 589. The "just and reasonable" standard permits regulators to take account of many factors other than the economic cost of providing service, and agencies have wide discretion to let market forces ensure a "just and reasonable" rate. *See, e.g.,* In re Permian Basin Area Rate Cases, 390 U.S. 747, 798 (1968); Consumers Energy Co. v. FERC, 367 F.3d 915, 922-23 (D.C. Cir. 2004); Orloff v. FCC, 352 F.3d 415, 420-21 (D.C. Cir. 2003); Natural Gas Pipeline Co. of Am. v. FERC, 765 F.2d 1155, 1168 (D.C. Cir. 1985); *see generally* Win Whittaker, *A Price-Level (Incentive) Regulation Proposal for Oil Pipelines,* 46 OKLA. L. REV. 415, 429-30 (1993).

98 *See* Memorandum Opinion and Order, *Petition for Forbearance of the Verizon Telephone Companies Pursuant to 47 U.S.C. § 160(c),* WC Docket No. 01-338 (October 27, 2004) (http://hraunfoss.fcc.gov/edocs_public/attachmatch/FCC-04-254A1.pdf). The FCC previously missed an October 2003 statutory deadline for deciding this issue on the merits. *See Verizon Tel. Cos. v. FCC,* 374 F.3d 1229 (D.C. Cir. 2004).

99 *See USTA II,* 359 F.3d at 580-81 (describing CLEC position).

Chapter Six

1 JOSEPH SCHUMPETER, CAPITALISM, SOCIALISM AND DEMOCRACY 82-85 (Harper, 1975) (1942).

2 *See* Jeff Bertolucci, *Internet Phones: Clear Winners,* PC WORLD, May 1, 2004 (http://www.pcworld.com/reviews/article/0,aid,115053,00.asp).

3 SIP is not the only signaling protocol available for VoIP communications, but it is the standard embraced by the Internet Engineering Task Force. *See* http://www.ietf.org/html.charters/sip-charter.html. An earlier standard endorsed by the International Telecommunications Union, "H.323," is now fading in popularity. *See* Philip Manchester, *Telecoms Standards—Opening the Door to New Applications,* FIN. TIMES (March 19, 2002) (http://specials.ft.com/fttelecoms/march2002/FT33D0YMZYC.html) (praising SIP and calling H.323 "cumbersome, inflexible, and difficult to program"). Moreover, other standards for VoIP, such as PacketCable (developed by CableLabs) and 3GPP, are incorporating SIP, underscoring the importance of that standard.

4 Scott Cleland et al., SIP Happens: How VoIP Technology "Re-unbundles" Telecom, Precursor Research (April 12, 2004).

5 *See* Peter Heywood, *Softswitches: The Gateway to Profitability*, Light Reading, Feb. 20, 2003 (http://www.lightreading.com/document.asp?site=lightreading& doc_id=28649).

6 According to one estimate, about a fifth of all U.S. businesses had either begun the transition to VoIP by mid-2004 or had announced plans to do so. Ben Charny, *Customers Clamor For Net Telephony Extras*, CNET News.com, June 21, 2004 (http://news.com.com/Customers+clamor+for+Net+telephony+extras/2100-1037_3-5242255.html).

7 Ken Belson, *Hackers Are Discovering a New Frontier: Internet Telephone Service*, N.Y. Times, Aug. 2, 2004, at C4 (http://www.nytimes.com/2004/08/02/technology/02virus.html?adxnnl=1&adxnnlx=1091459511uk7MNbfnUziNrUIh/qA1Ag&pa gewanted=print&position=) ("Internet phones and the routers and servers that steer and store the digitized calls are susceptible to the bugs, viruses and worms that have plagued computer data systems for years.").

8 Ben Charny, *AT&T Slashes Net-Phoning Prices*, CNET News.com, June 15, 2004 (http://news.com.com/AT&%2338%3BT+slashes+Net-phoning+prices/2100-7352_3-5235242.html?part=rss&tag=5235242&subj=news.7352.20); *see also* Dinesh C. Sharma, *VoIP Picks Up Momentum*, CNET News.com, August 30, 2004 (http://news.com.com/VoIP+picks+up+momentum/2100-7352_3-5330123.html?type=pt&part=inv&tag=feed&subj=news) (predicting 17.5 million VoIP customers by 2008).

9 J. Hodulik et al., UBS, Cable Telephony Competition: Who Gets It? at 1 (Aug. 7, 2003); *see also* Peter Rojas, *Bon Vonage, Baby Bells*, Slate, Dec. 17, 2002 (http://slate.msn.com/?id=2075534&device=) ("[W]ith Vonage, Internet users with a high-speed connection (28 percent of the country and growing) really don't need their local phone company anymore. . . . Vonage means that you can finally call up Verizon or Pacific Bell or Ameritech and tell them you don't need them or their poor customer service, inflated prices, and bloated bureaucracies.").

10 Although the FCC has decided not to ban this practice, Third Report and Order, *Deployment of Wireline Services Offering Advanced Telecommunication Capability*, 16 FCC Rcd 2101, ¶¶ 13-16 (2001), some claim that it is evidence that the incumbents maintain market power in the provision of bundled voice and data services. Despite claims of federal preemption, a number of state commissions have forced ILECs to unbundle their retail DSL offerings from their voice telephone services, thereby removing a practical impediment to a CLEC's acquisition of new voice customers. *See, e.g.*, BellSouth Telecomm., Inc. v. Cinergy Communications Co., 297 F. Supp.2d 946, 953 (E.D. Ky. 2003) (upholding ruling). In response, BellSouth has sought the FCC's intervention to establish that the Commission's own decision not to require the provision of DSL services on an unbundled basis preempts any such requirements imposed by a state commission. *See* Public Notice, *Pleading Cycle Established for BellSouth's Request for Declaratory Ruling*, 18 FCC Rcd 26,169 (2003). Competitors have also filed antitrust complaints against incumbents for engaging in this practice. Over the long term, however, the increasing availability of VoIP as an alternative to circuit-switched telephone service will likely—for the reasons discussed in the text—resolve these concerns without the need for regulatory intervention.

11 George Mannes, *Comcast Faces Long Haul on Phone Push*, THESTREET.COM, July 6, 2004 (http://www.thestreet.com/pf/tech/georgemannes/10169214.html).

12 Ken Brown, *Cablevision to Offer Internet Phone-Call Bundle*, WALL ST. J., June 21, 2004, at B5 (emphasis added) (http://online.wsj.com/article_print/ 0,,SB108777034073042332,00.html).

13 *See* Ken Brown & Almar Latour, *Phone Industry Faces Upheaval as Ways of Calling Change Fast*, WALL ST. J., August 25, 2004, at A1.

14 *See, e.g.*, Daniel Klein, *Why Vonage Is Just a Fad*, ZDNET (May 19, 2004) (discussing Yankee Group Study) (http://techupdate.zdnet.com/techupdate/stories/ main/Why_Vonage_Just_Fad.html?tag=tu.arch.link); Dinesh C. Sharma, *Study: Cable Giants to Flex VoIP Muscle*, CNET NEWS.COM (Aug. 3, 2004) (http://news.com.com/Study%3A+Cable+giants+to+flex+VoIP+muscle/2100-7352-5295023.html?part=dtx&tag=ntop) (describing Yankee Group study predicting that established broadband providers will soon overcome the early lead of the unaffiliated VoIP providers like Vonage); Dinesh C. Sharma, *VoIP Picks Up Momentum*, CNET NEWS.COM, August 30, 2004 (http://news.com.com/VoIP+picks+up+mo mentum/2100-7352_3-5330123.html?type=pt&part=inv&tag=feed&subj=news) (predicting that cable providers will gain a 56% market share at the end of 2004, with alternative voice providers continuing to fall from their 66% 2003 market share to a 19% market share in 2005).

15 As a Yankee Group analyst suggests: "It may seem like a dodgy competitive tactic, but broadband network operators could slow down Vonage's service. As subscribers increase their use of latency sensitive and graphic-rich IP traffic, broadband providers could give network precedence to their own revenue-generating services. Unless Vonage pays fees to the network provider, there is no reason that the operator should not make the service a lower priority on the network." Klein, *supra*.

16 47 U.S.C. § 230(b)(2). Although section 230(b)(2) has gained much currency among supporters of an unregulated Internet, some have argued, on the basis of legislative context, that section 230's purpose is solely to restrict "content" regulation and that the provision should not be construed to preclude state or federal common carrier regulation. In fact, section 230 was enacted with legislation intended not to restrict content regulation, but to regulate "indecent" content on the Internet. *See* 47 U.S.C. §§ 223, 231; *see generally* Reno v. ACLU, 521 U.S. 844 (1997) (invalidating section 223 on First Amendment grounds).

17 Memorandum Opinion and Order, *Petition for Declaratory Ruling That Pulver.com's Free World Dialup Is Neither Telecommunications Nor a Telecommunications Service*, 19 FCC Rcd 3307, ¶ 9 (Feb. 19, 2004) ("*Pulver Order*").

18 As the FCC has explained, "'[p]eer-to-peer' is a communications model in which each party has the same capabilities and either party can initiate a communication session. In recent usage, peer-to-peer has come to describe applications in which users can use the Internet to, for example, exchange files with each other directly or through a mediating server." *Id.* at ¶ 5 n.13.

19 *Id.*, at ¶ 11.

20 *Id.*, at ¶ 15.

21 *Id.*, at ¶ 21.

22 In 1998, the FCC had defined a "phone-to-phone" VoIP provider as one that has the following four characteristics: "(1) it holds itself out as providing voice telephony or facsimile transmission service; (2) it does not require the customer to use [customer premises equipment] different from that CPE necessary to place an ordinary touch-tone call (or facsimile transmission) over the public switched telephone network; (3) it allows the customer to call telephone numbers assigned in accordance with the North American Numbering Plan, and associated international agreements; and (4) it transmits customer information without net change in form or content." Report to Congress, *Federal-State Joint Board on Universal Service*, 13 FCC Rcd 11,501, ¶ 88 (1998) (*"1998 Report to Congress"*). AT&T's service met all four of these criteria.

23 Order, *Petition for Declaratory Ruling that AT&T's Phone-to-Phone IP Telephony Services Are Exempt from Access Charges*, 19 FCC Rcd. 7457, at ¶ 12 (2004) (*"AT&T Phone-to-Phone Order"*).

24 *See* http://www.vonage.com/products_tour.php

25 If the customer wishes to cut the cord to his regular telephone company but keep his existing telephone number, he can often direct that company to "port" his existing telephone number to Vonage (or, more precisely, Vonage's CLEC partner).

26 To take the same idea one step further, Vonage also permits subscribers to set up 800 numbers at which a caller can reach them, again "for free," from anywhere in the United States or Canada. These are effectively collect calls, except that Vonage charges subscribers only $5.00 a month for the first 100 minutes of these in-bound long distance calls—again, a fraction of what a circuit-switched telephone company would charge.

27 Vonage Holdings Corp. v. Minn. Pub. Utils. Comm'n, 290 F. Supp. 2d 993, 994, 1003 (D. Minn. 2003), *appeal pending,* No. 04-1434 (8th Cir.). Other states, including New York, soon adopted similar regulatory policies. *See* Vonage Holdings Corp. v. N. Y. State Pub. Serv. Comm'n, No. 04 Civ. 4306 (DFE) (July 16, 2004) (enjoining New York regulations, largely following reasoning of Minnesota court).

28 The *Vonage* Order was released as we completed work on the galleys for this book. *See* Memorandum Opinion and Order, *Vonage Holding Corporation Petition for Declaratory Ruling Concerning an Order of the Minnesota Public Utilities Commission*, WC Docket 03-211 (November 12, 2004) (http://hraunfoss.fcc.gov/edocs_public/attachmatch/FCC-04-267A1.pdf) (*"Vonage Order"*). The broader inquiry into IP-enabled services was initiated in Notice of Proposed Rulemaking, *IP-Enabled Services*, 19 FCC Rcd 4863 (2004) (*"IP-Enabled Servs. NPRM"*). The FCC likewise folded into that broader proceeding petitions by SBC Communications for wide-ranging "unregulation" of "IP platform services" (in WC Dkt. No. 04-29).

29 *Pulver Order, supra*; Declaratory Ruling and Notice of Proposed Rulemaking, *Inquiry Concerning High-Speed Access to the Internet over Cable and Other Facilities*, 17 FCC Rcd 4798, ¶ 59 (2002) (*"Cable Modem Order"*) (subsequent judicial history discussed in previous chapter); Order on Remand and Report and Order, *Implementation of the Local Competition Provisions in the Telecommunications Act of 1996*, 16 FCC Rcd 9151, ¶ 58 & n.115 (2001) (*"ISP Recip. Comp. Remand Order"*) (subsequent judicial history discussed in chapter 9); Memorandum Opinion and Order, *GTE Tel. Operating Cos.*, 13 FCC Rcd 22,466,

¶ 5 (1998) (*"GTE Order"*); *1998 Report to Congress,* ¶ 88; *see also* Southwestern Bell Tel. Co. v. FCC, 153 F.3d 523, 543 (8th Cir. 1998); *cf.* California v. FCC, 39 F.3d 919, 931-33 (9th Cir. 1994) (*"California III"*) (noting limiting principles); *California v. FCC,* 905 F.2d 1217, 1244 (9th Cir. 1990) (*"California I"*) (same).

30 *ISP Recip. Comp. Remand Order,* ¶ 58 (Internet communications entail "interact[ions] with a global network of connected computers" and thus "computers in multiple locations, often across state and national boundaries"); *GTE Order,* ¶ 22 ("In a single Internet communication, an Internet user may, for example, access websites that reside on servers in various state[s] or foreign countries, communicate directly with another Internet user, or chat on-line with a group of Internet users located in the same local exchange or in another country, and may do so either sequentially or simultaneously").

31 *See, e.g., Pulver Order,* ¶ 20 (a service is subject to exclusive federal jurisdiction if it is not "practically and economically possible to separate [its] interstate and intrastate components . . . without negating federal objectives for the interstate component"); *see also* note 30, *supra; see generally* La Pub. Serv. Comm'n v. FCC, 476 U.S. 355, 375 n.4 (1986) (noting inseparability issue); Ill. Bell Tel. Co. v. FCC, 883 F.2d 104, 114-15 (D.C. Cir. 1989); Pub. Util. Comm'n of Tex. v. FCC, 886 F.2d 1325, 1331 (D.C. Cir. 1989); N.C. Utils. Comm'n v. FCC, 552 F.2d 1036, 1045-46 (4th Cir.), *cert. denied,* 434 U.S. 874 (1977).

32 47 U.S.C. § 230(b)(2).

33 *See AT&T Phone-to-Phone Order,* ¶ 4 & n.13.

34 47 U.S.C. § 153(20).

35 *See* Randy May, *The Metaphysics of VoIP,* CNET NEWS.COM (Jan. 5, 2004) (urging a focus on marketplace realities, not metaphysical distinctions) (http://news.com.com/2010-7352-5134896.html).

36 As noted in chapter 9, the Commission generally employs an "end-to-end" (or "one call") analysis in determining whether particular Internet-related transmissions are "interstate" or "intrastate." This means that, in the dial-up context, the jurisdictional inquiry turns not on whether your ISP's access number is in another state, but on whether the website (or other Internet address) you're visiting is outside of your state. The courts have generally accepted the FCC's use of this end-to-end principle for purposes of determining jurisdiction, though not necessarily for purposes of determining the rules for reciprocal compensation. *See* Bell Atl. Tel. Cos. v. FCC, 206 F.3d 1, 5-7 (D.C. Cir. 2000); *cf. California III, supra.* The same principle applies *a fortiori* in the broadband context, where end users do not place distinct "calls" to their ISPs to begin with. In the *Pulver Order,* the FCC muddied the waters a bit, using loose language to the effect that the end-to-end analysis has little or no relevance to the analysis of the jurisdictional treatment of at least some VoIP services. *See Pulver Order,* ¶ 21. What the Commission meant—as it later made clear in the *Vonage Order*—is simply that identifying the geography of an Internet-related transmission is so difficult as to be unworthy of the effort. *See*

Vonage Order, ¶ 25. The basic point of the end-to-end analysis thus remains intact: the ends matter, and if they are difficult to pinpoint, the service will fall within the FCC's jurisdiction if the ends can be presumed to fall within different states a substantial percentage of the time.

37 *Id.*, ¶¶ 21, 24.

38 Similarly, enforcement of the federally mandated "slamming" rules, which bar carriers from switching customers to their services without the customers' consent, relies heavily on the participation of state commissions. *See* Second Report and Order, *Implementation of the Subscriber Carrier Selection Changes Provisions of the Telecommunications Act of 1996*, 14 FCC Rcd 1508, ¶ 90 (1998) (noting that section 258 of the Act expressly grants the state agencies the authority to enforce the relevant federal rules).

39 *See* VoIP Regulatory Freedom Act of 2004, S. 2281, 108th Cong. (2004); Advanced Internet Communications Services Act of 2004, H.R. 4757, 108th Cong. (2004); *see also* VoIP Regulatory Freedom Act of 2004, H.R. 4129, 108th Cong. (2004). H.R. 4757 has received more attention than H.R. 4129, and we thus refer to it in the text as the leading House bill. The text of these bills and other legislative materials can be found at http://thomas.loc.gov/home/thomas.html.

40 Declan McCullagh, *Senate Panel Embraces State VoIP Taxes*, CNET NEWS.COM (July 22, 2004) (http://news.com.com/2100-1028-5280118.html).

41 *See, e.g.*, Rob Frieden, *Adjusting the Horizontal and Vertical in Telecommunications Regulation: A Comparison of the Traditional and a New Layered Approach*, 55 FED. COMM. L.J. 207, 215 (2003) ("The horizontal orientation . . . makes better sense in a convergent, increasingly Internet-dominated marketplace and also provides a more intelligent model than the existing vertical orientation that creates unsustainable service and regulatory distinctions."); Craig McTaggert, *A Layered Approach to Internet Legal Analysis*, 48 McGILL L. J. 571 (2003); Philip J. Weiser, *Toward a Next Generation Regulatory Strategy*, 35 LOY. U. CHI. L.J. 41 (2003) ("*Next Generation Strategy*"); Kevin Werbach, A *Layered Model for Internet Policy*, 1 J. TELECOMM. & HIGH TECH. L. 37, 38 (2002) (arguing that communications regulation should be based on "the technical architecture of the Internet itself"); Douglas C. Sicker & Joshua L. Mindel, *Refinements of a Layered Model for Telecommunications Policy*, 1 J. TELECOMM. & HIGH TECH. L. 69, 71 (2002); John T. Nakahata, *Regulating Information Platforms: The Challenges of Rewriting Communications Regulation from the Bottom Up*, 1 J. TELECOMM. & HIGH TECH. L. 95, 98 (2002).

42 *1998 Report to Congress*, ¶ 95; *see also IP-Enabled Servs. NPRM* at ¶ 37 (seeking comment on the feasibility of a "layered" model of regulation).

43 Testimony of George Gilder before the Senate Committee on Commerce, Science & Transportation, Apr. 28, 2004 (http://commerce.senate.gov/hearings/testimony.cfm?id=1166&wit_id=3340).

44 *Id.*

45 *See* NEW MILLENNIUM RESEARCH COUNCIL, FREE RIDE: DEFICIENCIES OF THE MCI "LAYERS" POLICY MODEL AND THE NEED FOR PRINCIPLES THAT ENCOURAGE

COMPETITION IN THE NEW IP WORLD (July 2004) ("FREE RIDE") (http://www.newmillenniumresearch.org/news/071304_report.pdf).

46 Richard S. Whitt, *A Horizontal Leap Forward: Formulating a New Communications Public Policy Framework Based on the Network Layers Model*, 56 FED. COMM. L.J 587 (2004). Whitt is MCI's Senior Director of Global Policy and Planning.

47 *Cf.* Andrew Odlyzko, *Layer Architectures and Regulation in Telecommunications, in* FREE RIDE, *supra*, at 16-19.

48 *See id.* at 16; *see also* Richard N. Langlois, *Modularity in Technology and Organization*, 49 J. ECON. BEHAVIOR & ORG. 19, 25 (2000) (noting that "[t]he problem of defining boundaries of encapsulation becomes even more challenging in a dynamic setting" and that, in some cases, "improving the functioning of a system calls for remodularization rather than recombination").

49 *See, e.g.*, Virgin Is. Tel. Corp. v. FCC, 198 F.3d 921, 922 (D.C. Cir. 1999).

50 Not every carrier that wishes to operate as a private carrier will be permitted to do so. *See* Nat'l Ass'n of Regulatory Comm'rs v. FCC, 525 F.2d 630, 642 (D.C. Cir. 1976) (to determine whether a telecommunications offering should be treated as a common carrier service, regulators must "inquire, first, whether there will be any legal compulsion . . . to serve [the public] indifferently, and if not, second, whether there are reasons implicit in the nature of [the] operations to expect an indifferent holding out to the eligible user public"); Declaratory Ruling, *NORLIGHT Request for Declaratory Ruling*, 2 FCC Rcd 132, ¶¶ 19-21 (1987) (relevant factors for determining whether provider may operate as a private carrier include (1) whether the provider will engage in "individualized" negotiations resulting in contracts "tailored to the needs of particular customers"; (2) whether the customers are sophisticated business entities; (3) whether the contracts will be "medium-to-long range"; and (4) whether the provider possesses "market power" with respect to the services at issue).

51 *Brand X*, 345 F.3d at 1129 (internal quotations omitted).

52 *IP-Enabled Servs. NPRM*, ¶ 24 (citing 47 U.S.C. §§ 201, 202). The statutory definition of "common carrier" is notoriously circular: "any person engaged as a common carrier for hire, in interstate or foreign communication by wire or radio." 47 U.S.C. § 153(10).

53 *IP-Enabled Servs. NPRM*, ¶ 26 (citing 47 U.S.C. §§ 251(c)(3), 255(c)).

54 47 U.S.C. § 254(d) (emphasis added).

55 *See generally* Order, *Motion of AT&T Corp. to be Reclassified as a Non-Dominant Carrier*, 11 FCC Rcd 3271 (1995); Order, *Motion of AT&T Corp. to be Declared Non-Dominant for International Service*, 11 FCC Rcd 17,963 (1996).

56 *See generally* MCI WorldCom, Inc. v. FCC, 209 F.3d 760 (D.C. Cir. 2000) (discussing history); *see also* 47 U.S.C. § 211 (filing requirement for non-tariffed contracts). For a discussion of the implications of detariffing, see Jim Rossi, *Lowering*

The Filed Tariff Shield: Judicial Enforcement for A Deregulatory Era, 56 VAND. L. REV. 1591 (2003).

57 *See* MCI Telecomm. Corp. v. Am. Tel. & Tel. Co., 512 U.S. 218 (1994).

58 47 U.S.C. § 160. As discussed in chapter 8, the Commission had preexisting authority to forbear from the application of common carrier regulations to cellular telephone providers. *See* 47 U.S.C. § 332(c)(1).

59 *Id.* § 160(a)(1)-(3).

60 *Id.* § 160(d). In October 2004, the FCC concluded that section 271's checklist requirements are "fully implemented" once a section 271 application is granted for a given state. *See* p. 569 n. 98, *supra*, and accompanying text.

61 *Cable Modem Order*, ¶ 95 (subsequent judicial history discussed in previous chapter).

62 47 U.S.C. §§ 151, 152(a).

63 *See, e.g.*, Motion Picture Ass'n of America, Inc. v. FCC, 309 F.3d 796, 806-07 (D.C. Cir. 2002).

64 47 U.S.C. § 154(i); *cf.* U.S. CONST. art. I, § 8.

65 In justifying one of the conditions it placed on its approval of the AOL-Time Warner merger, the Commission asserted Title I jurisdiction over instant messaging services as a form of interstate communications. *See* Memorandum Opinion and Order, *Applications for Consent to the Transfer of Control of Licenses and Section 214 Authorizations by Time Warner Inc. and America Online, Inc., Transferors, to AOL Time Warner Inc., Transferee*, 16 FCC Rcd 6547, ¶ 148 (2001). For a discussion of the instant messaging interconnection debate, see chapter 1.

66 Analogously, courts implement the Copyright Act with similar flexibility in evaluating whether new technologies—ranging from cable television to the VCR to Napster—facilitate unlawful infringement. Lotus Dev. Corp. v. Borland Int'l, Inc., 49 F.3d 807, 820 (1st Cir. 1995) (Boudin, J., concurring) (explaining that "the heart of copyright doctrine—what may be protected and with what limitations and exceptions—has been developed by the courts through experience with individual cases"), *aff'd by an equally divided Court*, 516 U.S. 233 (1996).

67 United States v. Southwestern Cable, 392 U.S. 157, 178 (1968).

68 United States v. Midwest Video Corp., 406 U.S. 649, 665 n.23 (1972) (*"Midwest Video I"*) (quoting Gen. Tel. Co. of Cal. v. F.C.C., 413 F.2d 390, 398 (D.C. Cir. 1969)); *see also* Glen O. Robinson, *The Federal Communications Act: An Essay on Origins and Regulatory Purposes, in* A LEGISLATIVE HISTORY OF THE COMMUNICATIONS ACT OF 1934 24 (Oxford Univ. Press, Max D. Paglin, ed. 1989) (commenting, with respect to the FCC's role, that "with each passing era [the F.C.C.'s statutory charter] is beginning to look more like a 'living constitution' than a fixed statutory mandate"); Philip J. Weiser, *Federal Common Law, Cooperative Federalism, and the Enforcement of the Telecom Act*, 76 N.Y.U. L. REV. 1692, 1753-57 (2001) (explaining rationale for agency leeway in implementing regulatory statutes). For a seminal early discussion of the FCC's ancillary jurisdiction, see

Thomas G. Krattenmaker and A. Richard Metzger, Jr., *FCC Regulatory Authority over Commercial Television Networks: The Role of Ancillary Jurisdiction*, 77 Nw. U.L. Rev. 403 (1982).

69 *Southwestern Cable*, 392 U.S. at 178.

70 FCC v. Midwest Video Corp., 440 U.S. 689, 706 (1979) (*"Midwest Video II"*).

71 *Midwest Video I, supra*.

72 *Id.* at 676 (Burger, C.J., concurring).

73 440 U.S. 689 (1979).

74 *Id.* at 702-08. Congress perceived no such tension as a policy matter: it responded to the Supreme Court's decision by subsequently including similar public access requirements in the Cable Act of 1984, which added Title VI. *See* 47 U.S.C. § 531.

75 Motion Picture Ass'n. of Am., Inc. v. FCC, 309 F.3d 796, 805 (D.C. Cir. 2002) ("The FCC's position seems to be that the adoption of rules mandating video description is permissible because Congress did not expressly foreclose the possibility. This is an entirely untenable position.").

76 *Id.* at 805-06.

77 Computer & Communications Indus. Ass'n v. FCC, 693 F.2d 198, 206 (D.C. Cir. 1982); *but cf.* GTE Serv. Corp. v. FCC, 474 F.2d 724, 735-36 (2d Cir. 1973) (invalidating FCC's rule regarding the use of a common carrier's name on its information services affiliate because this regulation did not relate to communications and thus constituted an impermissible extension of the FCC's authority).

78 *See* Jacobellis v. Ohio, 378 U.S. 184, 197 (1964) (Stewart, J., concurring).

79 *See* Weiser, *Next Generation Strategy, supra*, at 61-65.

80 *See, e.g.*, AT&T v. City of Portland, 216 F.3d 871, 878 (9th Cir. 2000) (stating, imprecisely, that information services "have never been subject to regulation").

81 Separate Statement of Commissioner Michael K. Powell, at 11,625-26, in *1998 Report to Congress, supra* (arguing against imposing legacy regulations on new entrant in the name of competitive neutrality); Kathleen Q. Abernathy, The Nascent Services Doctrine (July 11, 2002) (http://www.fcc.gov/Speeches/Abernathy/2002/spkqa217.html) (tolerating "short-term regulatory disparities" to facilitate long-term competition).

82 "Competitive markets are superior mechanisms for protecting consumers by ensuring that goods and services are provided to consumers in the most efficient manner possible and at prices that reflect the cost of production. Accordingly, where competition develops, it should be relied upon as much as possible to protect consumers and the public interest. In addition, using a market-based approach should minimize the potential that regulation will create and maintain distortions in the investment decisions of competitors as they enter local telecommunications markets." First Report and Order, *Access Charge Reform*, 12 FCC Rcd 15,982, 16,094 ¶ 263 (1997).

83 *See* 47 U.S.C. §§ 222 (privacy safeguards for "customer proprietary network information"), 229 ("Communications Assistance for Law Enforcement Act," or "CALEA"), 255 (governing access to telecommunications services by persons with disabilities).

84 *Cf.* Lawrence Lessig, *Fidelity in Translation*, 71 TEX. L. REV. 1165 (1993).

85 *See IP-Enabled Servs. NPRM,* ¶¶ 51-57.

86 47 U.S.C. §§ 229, 1001 et seq.; *see also* Third Report and Order, *Communications Assistance for Law Enforcement Act,* 14 FCC Rcd 16,794, ¶¶ 55-57 (1999), *aff'd in part,* USTA v. FCC, 227 F.3d 450, 464-66 (D.C. Cir. 2000).

87 *See, e.g.,* 47 U.S.C. §§ 1001(8), 1002.

88 Notice of Proposed Rulemaking, *Communications Assistance for Law Enforcement Act and Broadband Access and Services,* ET Docket 04-295 (August 9, 2004) (http://hraunfoss.fcc.gov/edocs_public/attachmatch/FCC-04-187A1.pdf).

89 *Id.,* ¶41; *see* 47 U.S.C. § 1001(8) (defining "telecommunications carrier" for purposes of CALEA).

90 *See* John B. Horrigan, Data Memo—Pew Internet Project & New Millennium Research Council, 27% of Online Americans Have Heard of VoIP Telephone Service; 4 Million Are Considering Getting It At Home (June 27, 2004) (http://www.pewinternet.org/pdfs/PIP_VOIP_DataMemo.pdf).

Chapter Seven

1 Nicholas Negroponte, *Wireless Revisited,* WIRED (Aug. 1997) (http://www.wired.com/wired/archive/5.08/negroponte_pr.html).

2 We are indebted to Kevin Werbach for noting the significance of this quote for current policy debates. *See* Kevin Werbach, *Supercommons: Toward a Unified Theory of Wireless Communication,* 82 TEX. L. REV. 863, 882 & n.97 (2004) (*"Supercommons"*). It is quite possible, however, that the original attribution to Einstein is apocryphal.

3 Thomas W. Hazlett, *The Wireless Craze, the Unlimited Bandwidth Myth, the Spectrum Auction Faux Pas, and the Punchline to Ronald Coase's "Big Joke": An Essay on Airwave Allocation Policy,* 14 HARV. J.L. & TECH. 335, 338 (2001) (*"Wireless Craze"*).

4 NBC v. United States, 319 U.S. 190, 216 (1944). The Supreme Court reaffirmed this conclusion in its more famous decision in Red Lion Broad. Co. v. FCC, 395 U.S. 367 (1969). In that case, the Court relied on the same scarcity rationale to uphold the FCC's now-defunct "fairness doctrine," which obligated broadcasters to

give equal time to opposing viewpoints on matters of public interest. Although *Red Lion* technically remains good law, the Court has subsequently expressed skepticism about whether the scarcity rationale still justifies an exception to otherwise applicable First Amendment restrictions on content-based regulation. *See, e.g.,* Turner Broad. Sys., Inc. v. FCC, 512 U.S. 622, 637 (1994) ("the rationale for applying a less rigorous standard of First Amendment scrutiny to broadcast regulation, whatever its validity in the cases elaborating it, does not apply in the context of cable regulation"); *see also* Christopher S. Yoo, *The Rise and Demise of the Technology-Specific Approach to the First Amendment*, 91 Geo. L.J. 245 (2003) (comprehensively critiquing *Red Lion*).

5 *See* Matthew L. Spitzer, *The Constitutionality of Licensing Broadcasters*, 64 N.Y.U. L. Rev. 990, 1017-1021 (1989); *see also* Stuart M. Benjamin, *The Logic of Scarcity: Idle Spectrum as a First Amendment Violation*, 52 Duke L.J. 1 (2002); Yochai Benkler & Lawrence Lessig, *Net Gains: Is CBS Unconstitutional*, New Republic, Dec. 14, 1998, at 12 (arguing that changes in technology make the potential uses of spectrum more plentiful and government regulation less justifiable under the First Amendment).

6 Ronald Coase, *The Federal Communications Commission*, 2 J. Law & Econ. 1, 2 (1959) (quoting S. Rep. No. 659, 61st Cong., 2d Sess. 4 (1910)).

7 Lawrence Lessig, The Future of Ideas 73 (Basic Books, 2001).

8 *See* Radio Act of 1927, 44 Stat. 1162; United States v. Zenith Radio Corp., 12 F.2d 614 (N.D. Ill. 1926) (no authority to impose restrictions on license); Hoover v. Intercity Radio Co., 286 F. 1003 (D.C. Cir. 1923) (no discretion to deny licenses).

9 47 U.S.C. § 301; *see also* Note, *Federal Control of Radio Broadcasting*, 39 Yale L.J. 244, 250 (1929) (the premise that the "'the government owns the ether' was an idée fixee in the debates of Congress" over the Radio Act of 1927).

10 FCC Frequency Allocations and Radio Treaty Matters; General Rules and Regulations, 47 C.F.R. § 2.1.

11 General Accounting Office, Telecommunications: Comprehensive Review of U.S. Spectrum Management with Broad Stakeholder Involvement Is Needed 11 (2003).

12 For a critique of the United States' preparations for international spectrum policy proceedings, see Briefing Memo for Subcommittee on National Security, Emerging Threats, and International Relations, U.S. Preparation for the World Radio Conferences: Too Little, Too Late (March 17, 2004) (http://reform.house.gov/UploadedFiles/WRCBACKGROUNDMEMOFINAL.pdf).

13 The GAO recently underscored this concern, noting that government users rarely make an effort to use their spectrum efficiently. *See* General Accounting

Office, Better Knowledge Needed to Take Advantage of Technologies that May Improve Spectrum Efficiency (2004).

14 General Accounting Office, History and Current Issues Related to Radio Spectrum Management (2002).

15 Press Release, The White House, Fact Sheet on Spectrum Management (June 5, 2003) (http://www.whitehouse.gov/news/releases/2003/06/20030605-5.html); DEPARTMENT OF COMMERCE, SPECTRUM POLICY FOR THE TWENTY FIRST CENTURY – THE PRESIDENT'S SPECTRUM POLICY INITIATIVE (JUNE 2004) (http://www.ntia.doc.gov/reports/specpolini/presspecpolini_report1_06242004.pdf).

16 ROBERT CARO, MEANS OF ASCENT 89-105 (Knopf, 1990).

17 THOMAS G. KRATTENMAKER & LUCAS A. POWE, JR., REGULATING BROADCAST PROGRAMMING 148 (MIT Press, 1994).

18 *See* Ashbacker Radio Corp. v. FCC, 326 U.S. 327 (1945).

19 Report and Order, *An Inquiry Relative to the Future Use of the Frequency Band 806-960 MHz*, 46 F.C.C.2d 752 (1974); Second Report and Order, *An Inquiry into the Use of the Bands 825 – 845 MHz and 870 – 890 MHz for Cellular Communications Systems*, 86 F.C.C.2d 469 (1981).

20 47 U.S.C. § 309(i); *see* Report and Order, *Amendment of the Commission's Rules to Allow the Selection from Among Mutually Exclusive Competing Cellular Applications Using Random Selection or Lotteries Instead of Comparative Hearings*, 98 F.C.C.2d 175 (1984).

21 *See* Hazlett, *Wireless Craze*, at 399.

22 Omnibus Budget Reconciliation Act of 1993, Pub. L. No 103-66, § 6002, 107 Stat. 312, 379-86 (codified at 47 U.S.C. § 309(j) (2000)).

23 SYLVIA NASAR, A BEAUTIFUL MIND 374-78 (Simon & Schuster, 1998).

24 For an excellent discussion of such issues, *see* JOHN McMILLIAN, REINVENTING THE BAZAAR 80-85 (W.W. Norton & Co., 2003); *see also Beyond Discovery: The Bidding Game* (http://www.beyonddiscovery.org/content/view.txt.asp?a=3681).

25 *See* 47 U.S.C 309(j) (delineating exceptions); Report and Order, *Implementation of Sections 309(j) and 337 of the Communications Act of 1934 As Amended*, 15 FCC Rcd 22,709 (2000).

26 Paul Klemperer, *How Not To Run Auctions: The European 3G Auctions*, 46 EUR. ECON. REV. 829, 837-39 (2002) (http://www.nuff.ox.ac.uk/users/klemperer/hownot.pdf).

27 FCC v. NextWave Personal Communications, Inc., 537 U.S. 293 (2003). Before the Supreme Court ruled, the FCC sought to broker a sale of the licenses that would resolve the litigation and enable the spectrum to be used promptly. It proposed that the licenses be transferred to those firms that had bid the highest for them at a sec-

ond auction (in an amount exceeding $15 billion), with the proceeds split between NextWave and the U.S. Treasury. But Congress, whose legislative intervention was needed to preserve this compromise from legal challenge, was unwilling to sign off on any such deal. In the eyes of many, such as Senator John McCain (who led the Senate Commerce Committee), any deal that left NextWave with close to $6 billion constituted an unthinkable spectrum "giveaway." The result, however, was that the spectrum remained idle for longer than it otherwise would have—a significant loss for consumer welfare.

28 Michael K. Powell, Broadband Migration III: New Directions in Wireless Policy 6 (Oct. 30, 2002) (*"Broadband Migration III"*) (http://hraunfoss.fcc.gov/edocs_public/attachmatch/DOC-227944A1.pdf).

29 Memorandum Opinion and Order on Reconsideration, *Creation of Low Power Radio Service*, 15 FCC Rcd 19,208 (2000).

30 Stephen Labaton, *F.C.C. Heads for Showdown with Congress Over Radio Plan*, N.Y. TIMES, March 27, 2000, at C1.

31 Hazlett, *Wireless Craze*, at 432 n.308 (quoting wire report).

32 Patrick Ross, *Kennard Defends FCC Against Illegal Lobbying Charges*, COMM. DAILY, Apr. 19, 2000. The Justice Department eventually balked at Tauzin's request for a formal criminal investigation.

33 Pub. L. No. 106-553 § 632, 114 Stat. 2762, 2762A-111 (2000).

34 S. 2505, 108th Cong., § 1(13) (2004) (see http://thomas.loc.gov/home/thomas.html). When it blocked the FCC's initiative in December 2000, Congress required the Commission to conduct an "independent" study to determine whether any noticeable inference would result from the low power transmissions. After the Mitre Corporation performed such a study, the results came back almost identical to the FCC's original tests, showing that, even in the worst case, any minimal interference would be within 1.1 kilometers around the low-power transmission facility and that any such concerns could be dealt with effectively through a license modification process (as the FCC had originally envisioned). The report thus concluded that there "appears to be no public interest reason" for Congress's radical restrictions on low power licenses and recommended that Congress revisit the need for those restrictions. *See Report to the Congress on the Low Power FM Interference Testing Program*, Pub. L. No. 106-553 (February 19, 2004) (http://hraunfoss.fcc.gov/edocs_public/attachmatch/DOC-244128A1.pdf). In the words of the McCain-Leahy bill: "After 2 years and the expenditure of $2,193,343 in taxpayer dollars to conduct this study, the broadcasters' concerns were demonstrated to be unsubstantiated." S. 2505, § 1(13).

35 *Id.*, § 1(11).

36 LESSIG, FUTURE OF IDEAS, at 223.

37 Coase, *The Federal Communications Commission, supra*. This critique followed an earlier piece by a University of Chicago law student, Leo Herzel, who made a similar argument in favor of a market-based system. *See* Leo Herzel, *"Public Interest" and the Market in Color Television Regulation*, 18 U. CHI. L. REV. 802 (1951). Subsequently, numerous economists and legal scholars have advanced versions of this argument. *See* Ellen P. Goodman, *Spectrum Rights in the Telecosm to Come*, 41 SAN DIEGO L. REV. 269, 271 n.3 (2004) (*"Spectrum Rights"*) (listing property rights advocates).

38 Coase, *The Federal Communications Commission*, at 14.

39 Hazlett, *The Wireless Craze*, at 405-453.

40 Douglas W. Webbink, *Frequency Spectrum Deregulation Alternatives*, FCC WORKING PAPER 10 (October 1980) (http:/www.fcc.gov/Bureaus/OPP/working_papers/oppwp2.pdf).

41 Report and Order, *Formulation of Policies Relating to the Broadcast Renewal Applicant, Stemming from the Comparative Hearing Process*, 66 F.C.C.2d 419, 432 n.18 (1977) (Separate Statement of Commissioners Benjamin L. Hooks and Joseph R. Fogarty).

42 Hazlett, *The Wireless Craze*, at 427 (quoting O. CASEY CORR, MONEY FROM THIN AIR 235 (Crown, 2000)) (internal quotations omitted).

43 *Id.* at 427 (emphasis deleted).

44 Nextel has moved well beyond its scrappy origins, as "[t]he big carriers now covet Nextel's business, which has strong growth, low subscriber turnover and the highest per-customer revenue in the industry." Ken Belson, *The Voice of the Worker*, N.Y. TIMES, July 12, 2004 (http://www.nytimes.com/2004/07/12/technology/12nextel.html?8br).

45 As Thomas Hazlett put it, "[b]ringing radio spectrum out of an unproductive employment should not be such a tricky business. . . . Entrepreneurs should have to make their mark innovating in the marketplace, inventing technologies or marketing 'killer apps,' not out-foxing competing lawyers. The countless other businesses that have flunked this test—most of them unknown and deterred from the start—constitute economic carnage without offsetting social advantage." Hazlett, *The Wireless Craze*, at 428.

46 47 C.F.R. § 24.3.

47 Public Notice, *Nonbroadcast and General Action Report No. 1142*, 12 F.C.C.2d 559, 560 (1963) (aka *"Intermountain Microwave Decision"*).

48 Report and Order, *Promoting Efficient Use of Spectrum Through Elimination of Barriers to the Development of Secondary Markets*, 18 FCC Rcd 20,604 (2003) (*"Secondary Markets Order"*).

49 In particular, Commissioner Michael Copps dissented because he found it inconsistent with section 310(d) of the Communications Act, 47 U.S.C. § 310(d), which provides that "[n]o . . . station license, *or any rights thereunder,* shall be transferred, assigned, or disposed of in any manner . . . except upon application to the Commission and upon finding by the Commission that the public interest, convenience, and necessity will be served thereby." Copps argued: "[T]oday we allow licensees to transfer a significant right—the right to control the spectrum on a day-to-day basis—without applying to the Commission and without the requirement of any Commission public interest finding. How can this be legal under Section 310(d)?" *Id.* at 20,797.

50 *See* Second Report and Order, *Promoting Efficient Use of Spectrum Through Elimination of Barriers to the Development of Secondary Markets,* WT Docket 00-230 (September 2, 2004) (http://hraunfoss.fcc.gov/edocs_public/attachmatch/FCC-04-167A1.pdf).

51 For example, Commissioner Copps qualifiedly endorsed the policy goals of the *Secondary Markets Order* with the observation that "[g]enerally we limit our actions to commercial telecommunications providers that paid for their spectrum licenses at auction. Allowing leasing by companies that have already compensated the public for the use of spectrum is both significantly different and far more defensible than allowing companies that were given their spectrum rights for free to lease it and reap windfall profits." *Secondary Markets Order, supra,* at 20,797; *see also* Norman Ornstein & Michael Calabrese, *A Private Windfall for Public Property,* WASH. POST, Aug. 12, 2003, at A13.

52 This analogy comes from Eli Noam, *Spectrum Auctions: Yesterday's Heresy, Today's Orthodoxy, Tomorrow's Anachronism,* 41 J.L. & ECON. 765, 765-66 (1998). Similarly, Judge Stephen Williams has explained that spectrum is "government property only in the special sense that it simply has not been allocated to any real 'owner' in any way." Time Warner Entm't Co. v. FCC, 105 F.3d 723, 727 (D.C. Cir. 1997) (dissent from denial of hearing en banc).

53 Thomas Hazlett & Gregory Rosston, *Why the Airwaves Should Be Deregulated,* CNET NEWS.COM, February 11, 2004 (http:/news.com.com/2102-1039_3-5156846.html).

54 Robert M. Entman, Spectrum and Network Policy for Next Generation Telecommunications: A Report on the Eighteenth Annual Aspen Institute Conference on Telecommunications Policy 7 (2004). Some broadcasters freely acknowledge this point. *See* Scott Woolley, *Dead Air,* FORBES (Nov. 25, 2002) (http://www.forbes.com/forbes/2002/1125/138_print.html).

55 Third Report and Order, *Service Rules for the 746-764 and 776-794 MHz Bands,* 16 FCC Rcd 2703 (2001) (*"700 MHz Order"*), *clarified,* 16 FCC Rcd 21,633 (2001). The transition to the more efficient use of this spectrum remains a

work in progress, however, for several possible reasons. These include complications confronted by new entrants in setting up service in the spectrum at issue; the delays and transaction costs they face in negotiating for many local licenses to cover larger territories for new services; and strategic "holdout" behavior by incumbents: i.e., delays in their sale of licenses to interested buyers in the hope that, if they wait long enough, the licenses will become indispensable components of the buyers' developing spectrum portfolios and will thus command above-market rates. *See generally id.*, ¶¶ 54-56 (discussing "lone holdout" issue).

In the context of negotiating spectrum transactions with *governmental* users, the effort has also moved more slowly than anticipated, as the parties have failed to agree on the amount of money necessary for relocation. To expedite such re-banding efforts, Congress enacted in late 2004 a proposal to establish a "spectrum trust fund" to cover all such costs and avoid the need for negotiation. And the FCC's larger strategy for clearing spectrum for broadband ("3G") wireless services involves a series of interrelated decisions involving spectrum relocation. *See* Second Report and Order, *Amendment of Part 2 of the Commission's Rules to Allocate Spectrum Below 3GHz for Mobile and Fixed Services to Support the Introduction of New Advanced Wireless Services, including Third Generation Systems*, 17 FCC Rcd 23,193 (2002); Report and Order, *Service Rules for Advanced Wireless Services in the 1.7 GHz and 2.1 GHz Bands*, 18 FCC Rcd 25,162, ¶¶ 47-56 (2003). In general, such relocation decisions involve negotiation between the parties involved as to the amount of money necessary to reimburse any relevant equipment expenses, with procedures for non-binding arbitration where the parties cannot agree. *See Reimbursement Rules for Frequency Band or Geographic Relocation of Federal Spectrum-Dependent Systems*, 67 Fed. Reg. 41,182 (2002).

56 Evan Kwerel & John Williams, *A Proposal for a Rapid Transition to Market Allocation of Spectrum*, OPP WORKING PAPER SERIES NO. 38, at iv (FCC 2002) (http://hraunfoss.fcc.gov/edocs_public/attachmatch/DOC-228552A1.pdf).

57 *Id.*

58 Nextel's wireless rivals proposed that any brokered deal involve a relocation of Nextel's spectrum to the 2.1 GHz band instead because, as the *Wall Street Journal* reported, the 1.9 GHz band "is considered by some to be more valuable because existing cellphone equipment would need only slight alterations to work on it. Standard cellphone service isn't currently offered over [2.1 GHz]." Jesse Drucker and Anne Marie Squeo, *Nextel's Maneuver for Wireless Rights Has Rivals Fuming*, WALL ST. J., Apr. 19, 2004, at A1.

59 Report and Order, *Improving Public Safety Communications in the 800 MHz Band*, 19 FCC Rcd 14,969 (2004).

60 *Id.* (Separate Statement of Chairman Michael Powell) (http://hraunfoss.fcc.gov/edocs_public/attachmatch/DOC-249414A2.pdf).

61 Letter from William Barr, General Counsel, Verizon to Chairman Michael K. Powell, at 1 (Jun 28, 2004) (emphasis added) (http://gullfoss2.fcc.gov/prod/ecfs/retrieve.cgi?native_or_pdf=pdf&id_document=6516282241). Lest there be any confusion about the implication of this message, Verizon added: "[T]hese proscriptions . . . hold [an] official accountable in his personal, individual capacity" and, in this case, give rise to "a substantial probability of criminality." *Id.* at 6.

62 *See* Report and Order, *Flexibility for Delivery of Communications by Mobile Satellite Service Providers in the 2 GHz Band, the L-Band, and the 1.6/2.4 GHz Bands,* 18 FCC Rcd 1962 (2003), *appeal filed sub nom.* AT&T Wireless Servs., Inc. v. FCC, No. 03-1191 (D.C. Cir. July 8, 2003); *see generally* 47 U.S.C. § 765f ("the Commission shall not have the authority to assign by competitive bidding orbital locations or spectrum used for the provision of international or global satellite communications services"). The FCC adopted a middle ground approach in this dispute, permitting the satellite providers to integrate "terrestrial components" in their services but only so long as those components "remain[] ancillary to the principal [mobile satellite service] offering." *Id.,* ¶ 1.

63 Fresno Mobile Radio, Inc. v. FCC, 165 F.3d 965, 969 (D.C. Cir. 1999) (citations omitted).

64 Report and Order, *Flexibility for Delivery of Communications by Mobile-Satellite Service Providers in the 2 GHz Band, the L-Band, and the 1.6/2.4 GHz Band,* 18 FCC Rcd 1962, ¶ 39 (2003) (footnotes and internal quotations omitted).

65 *Id.*

66 *See generally* Notice of Proposed Rulemaking, *Facilitating Opportunities for Flexible, Efficient, and Reliable Spectrum Use Employing Cognitive Radio Technologies,* 18 FCC Rcd 26,859, ¶ 36 (2003); Notice of Proposed Rulemaking, *Unlicensed Operation in the TV Broadcast Bands,* 19 FCC Rcd 10,018 (2004); New America Foundation & Shared Spectrum Company, Dupont Circle Spectrum Utilization During Peak Hours (http://www.newamerica.net/Download_Docs/pdfs/Doc_File_183_1.pdf) (finding that two-thirds of studied spectrum was unused during peak hours in a dense urban area).

67 For a good discussion of such developments, see Kenneth R. Carter et al., *Unlicensed and Unshackled: A Joint OSP-OET White Paper on Unlicensed Devices and Their Regulatory Issues* (2003) (http://hraunfoss.fcc.gov/edocs_public/attachmatch/DOC-234741A1.pdf).

68 Although our discussion of unlicensed spectrum focuses on "intentional radiators" (i.e., devices that are intended to emit radio-frequency radiation), there are also "unintentional" radiators (such as personal computers that generate internal

radiation, which is sometimes emitted into the outside world) and "incidental" radiators (like electric motors, which are not designed to transmit radio-frequency radiation at all, but still may do so through their operation). The FCC has authority to address the radiation emitted by these devices as well.

69 Under its current Part 15 rules, the FCC regulates access to unlicensed spectrum through *ex ante* rules that require all equipment designed for use in such bands to be certified as compliant with certain technical standards (e.g., maximum power limits and listen-before-talk protocols). *See, e.g.,* 47 C.F.R. § 15.209 (2002) (power level limitations); 47 C.F.R. §15.321 (2002) (imposing listen-before-talk etiquette). To expedite the process of certifying such equipment, the FCC has authorized private organizations (known as Telecommunication Certification Bodies) to perform this function. In some cases, where there are notable reasons for concern, the FCC has gone even further to devise special protective rules to govern specific unlicensed uses, such as the Commission's recent decision to make radar detectors comply with specified emissions levels to avoid interference with licensed uses. Notice of Proposed Rulemaking, *Revision of Parts 2 and 15 of the Commission's Rules to Permit Unlicensed National Information Infrastructure (U-NII) Devices in the 5 GHz Band,* 18 FCC Rcd 11,581 (2003). Finally, to police compliance with all relevant requirements (special ones and otherwise), the FCC's Enforcement Bureau identifies, investigates, and addresses violations; as a practical matter, however, most such issues come to the FCC's attention through complaints by competitors. *See, e.g.,* Transp. Intelligence, Inc. v. FCC, 336 F.3d 1058, 1060 (D.C. Cir. 2003).

70 First Report and Order, *Revision of Part 15 of the Rules Regarding the Operation of Radio Frequency Devices Without an Individual License,* 4 FCC Rcd 3493, ¶ 130 (1989).

71 Alex Salkever, *Before Wi-Fi Can Go Mainstream,* Bus. Wk., Feb. 18, 2004 (www.businessweek.com/technology/content/feb2004/tc20040218_4891_tc140.htm).

72 *See* Claude E. Shannon, *A Mathematical Theory of Communications,* 27 Bell Sys. Tech. J. 623 (1948) (continuing discussion of issue initiated at 27 Bell Sys. Tech. J. 379 (1948)).

73 Yochai Benkler, *Some Economics of Wireless Communications,* 16 Harv. J.L. & Tech. 25, 41 (2002) (*"Some Economics"*).

74 *See, e.g.,* Bob Brewin, *Airlines Alarmed By Planned Tests of Ultrawideband Devices,* Computerworld, July 28, 2000 (http://www.computerworld.com/governmenttopics/government/policy/story/0,10801,47703,00.html) (noting airline industry concern that "if the FCC eventually authorizes widespread use of UWB devices, it could lead to the proliferation of wireless networks in 'the tens of thousands in a major metropolitan area,' operating without any safeguards in the aircraft navigation bands").

75 First Report and Order, *Revision of Part 15 of the Commission's Rules Regarding Ultra-Wideband Transmission Systems*, 17 FCC Rcd 7435 (2002) ("UWB Order").

76 *Id.* at 7551 (Separate Statement of Commissioner Michael J. Copps); *see also id.*, ¶ 5 (noting that authorization for ultrawideband includes limits that are "significantly more stringent than those imposed on other Part 15 devices").

77 Rudy L. Baca, FCC Approval of Ultra-Wideband: The Next "New Thing," Precursor Group Independent Research (Jan. 2, 2002) (emphasis omitted).

78 Benkler, *Some Economics*, at 36-37.

79 *See* Yochai Benkler, *Overcoming Agoraphobia: Building the Commons of the Digitally Networked Environment*, 11 HARV. J.L. & TECH. 287 (1998).

80 Richard Shin, *City of Brotherly Love May Embrace Wi-Fi*, CNET NEWS.COM (Sept. 1, 2004) (http://news.com.com/City+of+Brotherly+Love+may+embrace+Wi-Fi/2100-1039_3-5342286.html?part=rss&tag=5342286&subj=news.1039.5).

81 Garrett Hardin, *The Tragedy of the Commons*, 162 SCI. 1243, 1244-45 (1968).

82 Stuart Benjamin, *Spectrum Abundance and the Choice Between Private and Public Control*, 78 N.Y.U. L. REV. 2007, 2031 (2003).

83 *Id.* at 2032.

84 For an excellent discussion of the challenges inherent in adjudicating disputes under either a property or commons-based system of spectrum management, see Goodman, *Spectrum Rights*, at 398-403.

85 Hazlett, *Wireless Craze*, at 495-509; James B. Speta, *A Vision of Internet Openness By Government Fiat*, 96 Nw. L. REV. 1553, 1572 (2002) ("Where there is a single licensee either operating its own service or acting as a bandwidth manager, that licensee can mandate the use of equipment or protocols that fully utilize the spectrum"); Durga P. Satapathy & Jon M. Peha, *Etiquette Modification for Unlicensed Spectrum: Approach and Impact*, 1 PROC. IEEE VEHIC. TECHNOLOGIES CONF. 272 (1998) (www.contrib.andrew.cmu.edu/usr/dsaq/vtc_conf.pdf) ("It has been shown, for both fluid flow and bursty traffic, that while greed may benefit a device even with contention for spectrum, it always degrades performance of other devices, forcing them to also resort to greed, in order to regain their performance"). Critics of the commons model also argue that, to the extent the commons approach is efficient, spectrum licensees can establish "private commons," as the FCC has authorized. *See* Second Report and Order, *Promoting Efficient Use of Spectrum Through Elimination of Barriers to the Development of Secondary Markets*, WT Docket 00-230, ¶¶ 91-99 (July 8, 2004) (http://hraunfoss.fcc.gov/edocs_public/attachmatch/FCC-04-167A1.pdf). Whether market forces will often produce this outcome, however, is still unclear.

86 LESSIG, FUTURE OF IDEAS, at 222.

87 Werbach, *Supercommons*, at 964.

88 *See* Gerald R. Faulhaber & David Farber, *Spectrum Management: Property Rights, Markets, and the Commons* (2003) (http://rider.wharton.upenn.edu/~faulhabe/SPECTRUM_MANAGEMENTv51.pdf) (*"Spectrum Management"*); *accord* Benjamin, *supra*, at 2097-2101.

89 LESSIG, FUTURE OF IDEAS, at 230.

90 Faulhaber and Farber, *Spectrum Management*, at 16-19.

91 Federal Communications Commission, Spectrum Policy Task Force Report, ET Docket No. 02-135, 39 (Nov. 15, 2002) (http://hraunfoss.fcc.gov/edocs_public/attachmatch/DOC-228542A1.pdf).

92 *Id.* at 55.

93 *Id.* at 57.

94 *See* Policy Statement, *Principles for Promoting Efficient Use of Spectrum By Encouraging the Development of Secondary Markets,* 15 FCC Rcd 24,178, ¶ 8 (2000) ("[T]he best way to realize the maximum benefits from the spectrum is to permit and promote the operation of market forces in determining how spectrum is used"); *see also* News Release, *FCC Issues Guiding Principles for Spectrum Management* (Nov. 18, 1999) (not even mentioning unlicensed uses) (http://www.fcc.gov/Bureaus/Engineering_Technology/News_Releases/1999/nret9007.html).

95 *See* Goodman, *supra*, at 389 n.384.

96 Benkler, *Some Economics*, at 38.

97 Hazlett, *Wireless Craze*, at 432-33.

98 Notice of Proposed Rulemaking, *Establishment of an Interference Temperature Metric to Quantify and Manage Interference and to Expand Available Unlicensed Operation in Certain Fixed, Mobile and Satellite Frequency Bands,* 18 FCC Rcd 25,309, ¶¶ 29-51 (2003).

99 *See, e.g.,* Notice of Inquiry, *Interference Immunity Performance Specifications for Radio Receivers; Review of the Commission's Rules and Policies Affecting the Conversion to Digital Television,* 18 FCC Rcd 6039, ¶ 2 (2003) (noting importance of upgrading quality of receivers and suggesting that "it is preferable to rely primarily on market incentives and voluntary industry programs").

100 *See* Powell, *Broadband Migration III*, at 4 ("[I]nterference is often more a product of receivers; that is receivers are too dumb or too sensitive or too cheap to filter out unwanted signals. Yet, our decade-old rules have generally ignored receivers.").

101 For a good discussion of the importance of and challenges in developing a regime along these lines, see R. Paul Margie, *Can You Hear Me Now?: Getting Better Reception From The FCC's Spectrum Policy*, 2004 STAN. TECH. L. REV. 5.

Chapter Eight

1 Ninth Report, *Implementation of Section 6002(b) of the Omnibus Budget Reconciliation Act of 1993*, WT Docket No. 04-11, ¶ 5 (Sept. 28, 2004) (http://hraunfoss.fcc.gov/edocs_public/attachmatch/FCC-04-216A1.pdf) (*"Ninth Wireless Report"*); *compare* Eighth Report, *Implementation of Section 6002(b) of the Omnibus Budget Reconciliation Act of 1993*, 18 FCC Rcd 14,783, ¶ 17 (2003) (*"Eighth Wireless Report"*) (noting a nationwide penetration rate of roughly 49%).

2 *See Ninth Wireless Report,* ¶¶ 5, 21.

3 *See generally* Nat'l Cable & Telecomm. Ass'n v. Gulf Power Co., 534 U.S. 327, 339-42 (2002) (discussing statutory right to use utility poles for this purpose).

4 47 U.S.C. § 332(c)(7)(B); *see generally* Timothy J. Tryniecki, *Cellular Tower Siting Jurisprudence Under the Telecommunications Act of 1996—The First Five Years*, 37 REAL PROP. PROB. & TR. J. 271 (2002).

5 PrimeCo v. City of Mequon, 352 F.3d 1147, 1149 (7th Cir. 2003) (Posner, J.) (citations omitted).

6 47 U.S.C. § 332(d)(1)-(2).

7 47 U.S.C. § 332(d)(3).

8 *Eighth Wireless Report,* ¶ 38 ("Because these licensees offer mobile telephone services that are essentially interchangeable from the perspective of most consumers, they are discussed in this report as a cohesive industry sector.").

9 *See* Report and Order, *Gen. Mobile Radio Serv.*, 13 F.C.C. 1190, 1212 (1949); Fourth Report and Order, *Amendment of Section 3.606 of the Commission's Rules and Regulations*, 41 F.C.C. 131 (1951).

10 JEFFREY H. ROHLFS ET AL., ESTIMATE OF LOSS TO THE UNITED STATES CAUSED BY THE FCC'S DELAY IN LICENSING CELLULAR COMMUNICATIONS, NATIONAL ECONOMIC RESEARCH ASSOCIATES (Nov. 8, 1991).

11 *See generally* Ill. Bell Tel. Co., 63 F.C.C.2d 655 (1977), *aff'd sub nom*, Rogers Radio Commun. Sys., Inc. v. FCC, 593 F.2d 1225 (D.C. Cir. 1978).

12 *See* chapter 7; *see generally* Philip Palmer McGuigan et al., *Cellular Mobile Radio Telecommunications: Regulating An Emerging Industry*, 1983 BYU L. REV. 305. When the FCC granted these initial cellular licenses, the telecommunications world was preoccupied with the impending break-up of the wireline Bell System, and few in the broader industry recognized just how commercially significant mobile telephony would become. Indeed, at a 1982 news conference announcing AT&T's divestiture of its local exchange operations, the company's own CEO was

unable to answer a question about which set of companies would inherit the cellular licenses: AT&T proper or the newly independent Bell companies. The consent decree ultimately assigned them to the Bell companies, along with some initial restrictions on their ability to offer service across exchange area boundaries. U.S. v. W. Elec. Corp., 578 F. Supp. 643, 648-49 (D.D.C 1983). Ironically, just ten years after AT&T divested its wireless properties to the local Bells, it paid dearly for this mistake, buying the extensive wireless network of McCaw Communications for $11 billion in 1994. To come full circle, AT&T later spun off "AT&T Wireless" in 2001, concluding that the business could succeed better on its own than as part of an integrated telephone company. In the spring of 2004, AT&T made yet another 180 degree turn, contracting to resell Sprint PCS services under its own brand name on the theory that the availability of wireline-wireless product bundles may be important to consumers after all. *See* Jesse Drucker, *Sprint's Role as Wholesaler: "Arms Dealer" to the Industry*, WALL ST. J., May 21, 2004, at B1.

13 For a succinct telling of the rise of the cellular industry, see Stephanie N. Mehta, *Cellular Evolution*, FORTUNE (Aug. 9, 2004) (http://www.fortune.com/fortune/fortune500/articles/0,15114,678704,00.html).

14 47 C.F.R. § 24.202 (defining these terms, which are based on Rand McNally concepts).

15 Cincinnati Bell Tel. Co. v. FCC, 69 F.3d 752, 766-67 (6th Cir. 1995).

16 *See* Report and Order, *Competitive Serv. Safeguards for LEC Provision of CMRS*, 12 FCC Rcd 15,668 (1997), *clarified*, 12 FCC Rcd 17,983 (1997), *aff'd*, GTE Midwest, Inc. v. FCC, 233 F.3d 341, 348 (6th Cir. 2000).

17 As discussed in chapter 7, Congress authorized the Commission in 1996 to "forbear from applying any regulation or any provision of this [Act] to a telecommunications carrier or telecommunications service" in a wide range of circumstances. 47 U.S.C. § 160.

18 47 U.S.C. § 332(c)(1).

19 Second Report and Order, *Implementation of Sections 3(n) and 332 of the Communications Act; Regulatory Treatment of Mobile Services*, 9 FCC Rcd 1411, ¶¶ 124-219 (1994).

20 Orloff v. FCC, 352 F.3d 415, 420 (D.C. Cir. 2003) (emphasis omitted), *aff'g* Orloff v. Vodafone AirTouch Licenses LLC d/b/a Verizon Wireless, 17 FCC Rcd 8987 (2002).

21 Final Decision, *Amendment of Section 64.702 of the Commissions's Rules and Regulations* (Second Computer Inquiry), 77 F.C.C.2d 384, ¶ 149, *modified on recon.*, 84 F.C.C.2d 50 (1980), *further modified*, 84 F.C.C.2d 50, *aff'd sub. nom.*, Computer and Communications Indus. Ass'n v. F.C.C., 693 F.2d 198 (D.C. 1982), *cert. denied*, 461 U.S. 938 (1983). For a discussion of the complex antitrust considerations presented by the bundling practices of dominant firms, see 3 PHILLIP E. AREEDA & HERBERT HOVENKAMP, ANTITRUST LAW 136-137, ¶ 749 (2003 Supp.). For a controversial judicial decision on that topic, see LePage's Inc. v. 3M Co., 324 F.3d 141 (3d Cir. 2003) (en banc), *cert. denied*, 124 S. Ct. 2932 (2004).

22 *See, e.g.*, Yannis Bakos & Erik Brynjolfsson, *Bundling Information Goods in Pricing, Profits, and Efficiency*, 45 MGMT. SCI. 1613, 1619 (1999) ("Bundling can create significant economies of scope even in the absence of technological economies in production, distribution, or consumption").

23 *See* Report and Order, *Bundling of Cellular Customer Premises Equipment and Cellular Service*, 7 FCC Rcd 4028 (1992).

24 *See* Report and Order, *Regulatory Policies Concerning Resale and Shared Use of Common Carrier Services and Facilities*, 60 F.C.C.2d 261 (1976), *aff'd*, AT&T v. FCC, 572 F.2d 17 (2d Cir. 1978); *see also* Report and Order, *Resale and Shared Use of Common Carrier Domestic Public Switched Network Services*, 83 F.C.C.2d 167 (1980).

25 For example, there are many circumstances in which a firm will wish to target its discounts narrowly to a particular class of customers that might otherwise take their business elsewhere. Requiring such a firm to accommodate resale arbitrageurs in extending those discounts to consumers at large may discourage it from offering such discounts to anyone in the first place, resulting in a net loss of consumer welfare. Of course, this concern arises only in markets with less than perfect competition, but that characterizes virtually all competitive markets in the economy. For a discussion of the complex economics of price discrimination, see 8 PHILLIP AREEDA & HERBERT HOVENKAMP, ANTITRUST LAW 226, ¶ 1616f (2d ed. 2002) ("[P]rohibition [of price discrimination] would worsen consumer welfare if—as I tend to believe—prohibiting the restraint would lead the manufacturer . . . to maintain the higher wholesale price while adopting more costly or less effective strategies for reaching low-price customers, or even . . . to abandon his efforts to reach those customers altogether. I therefore regard price discrimination in aid of deep market penetration as a benefit."); William J. Baumol, *Predation and the Logic of the Average Variable Cost Test*, 39 J.L. & ECON. 49, 65-67 & n.17 (1996) (noting circumstances in which economic efficiency requires the use of differential pricing); In re Brand Name Prescription Drugs Antitrust Litig., 288 F.3d 1028, 1032 (7th Cir. 2002) ("[s]ince price discrimination is not (in general) unlawful, neither are efforts to prevent arbitrage"); *see also* chapter 5, *supra* (discussing price discrimination in broadband context). Curiously, a quite different rule applies in the wireline context, where the 1996 Act requires even the least competitively significant CLEC to make its services available for resale. *See* 47 U.S.C. § 251(b)(1).

26 *See* First Report and Order, *Interconnection and Resale Obligations Pertaining to Commercial Mobile Radio Servs.*, 11 FCC Rcd. 18,455 (1996), *aff'd* Cellnet Commun., Inc. v. FCC, 149 F.3d 429 (6th Cir. 1998); *see also* Fourth Report and Order, *Interconnection and Resale Obligations Pertaining to Commercial Mobile Radio Servs.*, 15 FCC Rcd 13,523, ¶ 1 (2000) ("deny[ing] requests for mandatory interconnection between resellers' switches and CMRS providers' networks") (*"Fourth Report"*).

27 *See* Third Report and Order, *Implementation of Section 3(n) and 332 of the Communications Act*, 9 FCC Rcd 7988, ¶16 (1994).

28 *See* Report and Order, *2000 Biennial Regulatory Review Spectrum Aggregation Limits for Commercial Mobile Radio Services*, 16 FCC Rcd 22,668 (2001); *see also* Memorandum Opinion and Order, *Applications of AT&T Wireless Services, Inc. and Cingular Wireless Corp.*, WT Docket No. 04-70 (October 26, 2004) (http://hraunfoss.fcc.gov/edocs_public/attachmatch/FCC-04-255A1.pdf) (*"AT&T Wireless Merger Order"*).

29 47 U.S.C. § 332(c)(3)(A).

30 For an instructive case study in the tortuous preemption issues that arise in this area, see *Application of Western Wireless Holding Co., Inc. for Designation as an Eligible Telecommunications Carrier,* Decision No. C04-0545, ¶¶ 66-86 (Colo. PUC May 26, 2004) (*"Colo. Western Wireless Order"*) (requiring submission of pricing plans by ETC to ensure that they are affordable, just and reasonable) (http://www.dora.state.co.us/puc/decisions/2004/C04-0545_03A-061T.doc).

31 *See, e.g.,* Conn. Dep't of Pub. Util. Control v. FCC, 78 F.3d 842 (2d Cir. 1996) (upholding FCC denial of state petition).

32 Memorandum Opinion and Order, *Wireless Consumers Alliance, Inc.,* 15 FCC Rcd 17,021, ¶¶ 28-36 (2000) (discussing case law); Leonard J. Kennedy & Heather A. Purcell, *Wandering Along the Road to Competition and Convergence—The Changing CMRS Roadmap,* 56 FED. COMM. L.J. 489, 500-511 (2004) (same).

33 *Wireless Consumers Alliance,* ¶39. For its part, the FCC has exempted wireless carriers from some of its "truth-in-billing" rules, given the paucity of relevant consumer complaints. First Report and Order, *Truth-in-Billing Format,* 14 FCC Rcd 7492, ¶¶ 13-19 (1999).

34 *See* Interim Decision, *Order Instituting Rulemaking on the Commission's Own Motion to Establish Consumer Rights and Consumer Protection Rules Applicable to All Telecommunications Utilities* (May 27, 2004) (http://www.cpuc.ca.gov/word_pdf/FINAL_DECISION/37166.pdf). To some extent, these states are filling a regulatory void left by the statutory exclusion of the Federal Trade Commission from regulating "common carriers." 15 U.S.C. § 45(a)(2); *see also* FTC v. Miller, 549 F.2d 452 (7th Cir. 1977) (applying exception).

35 *See* CTIA Consumer Code for Wireless Service (http://files.ctia.org/pdf/The_Code.pdf).

36 2 ALFRED E. KAHN, THE ECONOMICS OF REGULATION: PRINCIPLES AND INSTITUTIONS 119 (1989).

37 The FCC ordered such interconnection in the form of requiring telephone companies to provide access to wireless networks as *customers* rather than fellow *carriers.* The distinction between a customer's access to a network and a co-carrier's access to a network largely reflects (1) where interconnection may occur; (2) whether interconnection is comparable to what the carrier gives its own affiliates; and (3) what price the carrier may charge for interconnection. Under the prevailing rule that emerged in the common law of common carriage, a carrier could refuse to interconnect with a rival, making the regulation of interconnection—and the resolution of the associated issues—a matter for the regulatory authorities. *See, e.g.,* Pac. Tel. & Tel. Co. v. Anderson, 196 F. 699, 703 (D.C. Wash. 1912); *see also* James B. Speta, *A Common Carrier Approach to Internet Interconnection,* 54 FED. COMM. L.J. 225, 258 (2002) (discussing issue); Report and Order, *Cellular Communications Systems,* 86 F.C.C.2d 469, ¶ 56 (1981) (in mandating interconnection for cellular providers, noting that "[a] cellular system operator is a common carrier and not merely a customer" and requiring that interconnection arrangements should be designed to minimize "unnecessary duplication of switching facilities").

38 Report and Order, *Cellular Communications Systems*, 86 F.C.C.2d 469, ¶¶ 53-57 (1981). Specifically, the Commission provided that the "particular arrangements involved in interconnection of a given cellular system should be negotiated among the carriers involved," but mandated that interconnection should be provided upon "reasonable demand" and at "terms no less favorable than those offered to the cellular systems of affiliated entities or independent telephone companies." *Id.*, ¶¶ 56-57.

39 *See, e.g.*, Third Report and Order, *Interconnection and Resale Obligations Pertaining to Commercial Mobile Radio Services*, 15 FCC Rcd 15,975, ¶ 24 (2000) (terminating consideration of "automatic roaming" rules); Notice of Proposed Rulemaking, *Automatic and Manual Roaming Obligations Pertaining to Commercial Mobile Radio Services*, 15 FCC Rcd 21,628, ¶ 32 (2000) (tentatively concluding that any roaming rules should sunset).

40 47 CFR § 20.12(c).

41 *Spread Betting*, THE ECONOMIST TECH. Q. (June 19, 2003) (http://www.economist.com/science/tq/displayStory.cfm?story_id=1841059).

42 Year 2000 Biennial Regulatory Review, *Amendment of Part 22 of the Commission's Rules to Modify or Eliminate Outdated Rules Affecting the Cellular Radiotelephone Service and Other Commercial Mobile Radio Services*, 17 FCC Rcd 18,401, ¶¶ 9-21 (2002).

43 *See* Marlon A. Walker & Jesse Drucker, *Wireless Carriers Leave Many Callers in Dead Zone*, WALL ST. J., at A1 (Aug. 9, 2004).

44 *See How The Radio Changed Its Spots*, THE ECONOMIST TECH. Q. (Dec. 6, 2003) (http://www.economist.com/science/tq/displayStory.cfm?story_id=2246155).

45 For a discussion of the two approaches, see Neil Gandal et al., *Standards in Wireless Telephone Networks*, 27 TELECOMM. POL'Y. 325 (2003).

46 *See Time For Plan B*, THE ECONOMIST (Sept 26, 2002) (www.economist.com/business/PrinterFriendly.cfm?Story_ID=1353050).

47 *See* Report and Order, *Service Rules for Advanced Wireless Services in the 1.7 GHz and 2.1 GHz Bands*, 18 FCC Rcd 25,162 (2003); Ben Charny, *Verizon Wireless Brings 3G to More Cities*, CNET NEWS.COM (Sept. 22, 2004) (http://news.com.com/Verizon+Wireless+brings+3G+to+more+cities/2100-1039_3-5378121.html).

48 *See* Aldo Morri, *3G Migration: Waiting the Wave*, WIRELESS REV. (May 1, 1999) (http://wirelessreview.com/ar/wireless_migration_waiting_wave/) (noting that upgrading to 3G from CDMA can be as simple as "a matter of channel-card plug-ins with the same base stations, power amplifiers, and filters"); Peggy Albright, *Charting the Course to 3G*, WIRELESS WK., Jan. 8, 2001, at 25; Lynette Luna, *Battle of the Standards*, TELEPHONY, Feb. 19, 2001, at 62. On the more efficient spectrum usage qualities of CDMA in particular (and spread spectrum more generally), see chapter 7; *see also* MARTIN LIBICKI ET AL., SCAFFOLDING THE NEW WEB: STANDARDS AND STANDARDS POLICY FOR THE DIGITAL ECONOMY 8, 10 (2000) (http://www.rand.org/publications/MR/MR1215).

49 Written Statement of Michael K. Powell on Competition Issues in the Telecommunications Industry, Before the Committee on Commerce, Science, and Transportation, United States Senate, at ii (Jan. 14, 2003) (http://hraunfoss.fcc.gov/edocs_public/attachmatch/DOC-230241A1.pdf); *see also AT&T Wireless Merger Order*, ¶ 242.

50 47 U.S.C. § 153(26), (47). Congress authorized the FCC to include wireless carriers within the definition of "local exchange carrier" at its discretion, *see* 47 U.S.C. § 153(26), but the FCC has not exercised that authority. As a technical matter, the exclusion of wireless carriers from the category of "LECs" exempts them from the formal *obligations* of section 251(b), although, as in the case of number portability (discussed below), the Commission has ample independent authority to impose the same obligations on them without formally classifying them as "LECs." *See* Cellular Telecomm. & Internet Ass'n v. FCC, 330 F.3d 502, 505 (D.C. Cir. 2003) (*"CTIA"*). This definitional issue has no direct effect on a wireless carrier's *right* to lease an ILEC's network elements under section 251(c)(3), since that provision extends such leasing rights to "any requesting telecommunications carrier," and wireless carriers indisputably qualify as such. Because wireless carriers operate their own switches and use spectrum as a surrogate for physical loops, the primary ILEC elements they might wish to lease are transport links. In the *Triennial Review Order* (see chapter 3), the FCC clarified that wireless carriers could lease those links at "cost" as network elements on a par with other CLECs. But the D.C. Circuit subsequently vacated that portion of the *Order* on the grounds that wireless carriers could lease the same links in the form of a higher priced special access services and that the availability of those services casts doubt on whether these network elements satisfy the "impairment" standard of section 251(d)(2). *USTA II*, 359 F.3d at 575-577.

51 *AT&T Wireless Merger Order*, ¶ 241.

52 Report and Order and Order on Remand and Further Notice of Proposed Rulemaking, *Review of the Section 251 Unbundling Obligations of Incumbent Local Exchange Carriers*, 18 FCC Rcd 16,978, ¶ 53 n.184 (2003) (subsequent judicial history discussed in chapter 3).

53 ITAA e-Letter, Consumers Abandon Landlines and Increase Mobile Call Volumes, Creating Strong Growth in the Wireless Market (Sept. 2002) (http://www.itaa.org/isec/pubs/e20029-09.pdf) (citing Yankee Group study).

54 Of course, no consumer has a property right in any particular number—as one enterprising person discovered when he logged onto eBay and tried to sell, within the 212 area code, the number "867-5309" of the famed Tommy Tutone song. Monty Phan, *Jenny's Phone Number—From the Song—For Sale*, MIAMI HERALD, (Feb. 15, 2004) (http://www.miami.com/mld/miamiherald/news/nation/7957736.htm?1c); *see also* In re Starnet, 355 F.3d 634, 637 (7th Cir. 2004) ("No one has a property interest in a phone number.").

55 For a concise history of the FCC's wireless-to-wireless number portability rules, see *CTIA*, 330 F.3d at 504-07.

56 For competing views of the need for governmental intervention in the market to counteract switching costs and the associated phenomenon of *path dependence*, compare Joseph Farrell & Garth Saloner, *Installed Base and Compatibility: Innovation, Product Preannouncements, and Predation*, 76 AM. ECON. REV. 940 (1986); Michael Katz & Carl Shapiro, *Technology Adoption in the Presence of Network Externalities*, 92 J. POL. ECON. 822 (1986) with STAN LIEBOWITZ & STEPHEN MARGOLIS, WINNERS, LOSERS, AND MICROSOFT (1999).

57 Memorandum Opinion and Order, *Verizon Wireless's Petition for Partial Forbearance from the Commercial Mobile Radio Services Number Portability Obligation*, 17 FCC Rcd. 14,972, ¶ 18 (2002) (voicing fear that, absent portability rules, consumers "will find themselves forced to stay with carriers with whom they may be dissatisfied because the cost of giving up their wireless phone number in order to move to another carrier is too high").

58 *CTIA, supra.*

59 *See* Memorandum Opinion and Order, *Carrier Requests for Clarification of Wireless-Wireless Porting Issues*, 18 FCC Rcd 20,972 (2003).

60 Memorandum Opinion and Order, *Telephone Number Portability—CTIA Petitions for Declaratory Ruling on Wireline-Wireless Porting Issues*, 18 FCC Rcd 23,697, ¶ 27 (2003).

61 Kathleen Q. Abernathy, Regulating Wireless: How Much and By Whom? 4 (May 13, 2004)(http://hraunfoss.fcc.gov/edocs_public/attachmatch/DOC247211A1.pdf).

62 *See* Report and Order, *Revision of the Commission's Rules to Ensure Compatibility with Enhanced 911 Emergency Calling Systems*, 11 FCC Rcd 18,676, ¶¶ 24-91 (1996); 47 C.F.R. § 20.18(d), (e), (h).

63 Michael K. Powell, Second Meeting of the FCC's Wireless E911 Coordination Initiative 3 (October 29, 2003) (http://hraunfoss.fcc.gov/edocs_public/attachmatch/DOC-240493A1.pdf).

64 Dale N. Hatfield, *A Report on Technical and Operational Issues Impacting the Provision of Wireless Enhanced 911 Services* (Oct. 15, 2002) (http://gullfoss2.fcc.gov/prod/ecfs/retrieve.cgi?native_or_pdf=pdf&id_document=6513296239).

65 *See, e.g.*, Order, *Cingular Wireless LLC*, 18 FCC Rcd 11,746 (2003) (consent decree with agreement to pay a fine and be subject to compliance program); *see also* Edward Wyatt, *Albany Diverts Funds Billed For 911 Cellphone Safety*, N.Y. TIMES, May 10, 2004, at A22.

66 General Accounting Office, Uneven Implementation of Wireless Enhanced 911 Raises Prospect of Piecemeal Availability for Years to Come (2003).

67 *See, e.g., Colo. Western Wireless Order, supra.*

68 *See, e.g.*, Order and Order on Recons., *Federal-State Joint Board on Universal Service*, 18 FCC Rcd 15,090, 15,115 (2003) (separate statement of Commissioner

Kevin Martin). For a critique of this position, see Recommended Decision, *Federal State Joint Board on Universal Service*, 17 FCC Rcd 14,095, 14,132-35 (July 10, 2002) (Separate Statement of Commissioner Kathleen Q. Abernathy).

Chapter Nine

1 Patrick Brogan, Intercarrier Compensation Reform (ICR) Framework for Gauging Investment Impact, Precursor Research (April 19, 2004).

2 Stephen Labaton, *MCI Faces Federal Fraud Inquiry on Fees for Long Distance Calls*, N.Y. TIMES, July 27, 2003, at A1.

3 *Id.*

4 In February 2004, AT&T dropped a lawsuit based on claims of such wrongdoing—in the face of MCI's own investigation "of AT&T's routing practices," which "found several cases of alleged improper routing on AT&T's part," according to sources cited by the *Wall Street Journal. See* Shawn Young & Almar Latour, *AT&T Drops Lawsuit Against MCI*, WALL ST. J., Feb. 24, 2004, at A3.

5 The amount of money paid in access charges each year is enormous. In 2002, AT&T alone racked up access charge obligations in the neighborhood of $10 billion, which constitutes about 30% of its operating expenses *See* AT&T's 2002 Annual Report 12 (http://www.att.com/ar-2002/docs/ar2002.pdf). On the other end, SBC, one of the Bell companies that relies on these fees for its bottom line, reportedly took in over $2 billion in 2002 (for approximately 5% of its revenue). Kevin Maney et al., *Straightening Out The Story In Telecom's Routing Game*, USA TODAY (Aug. 26, 2003) (www.usatoday.com/money/industries/telecom/2003-08-26-mcicover_x. htm).

6 Before the 1990s, most of the local calls that crossed different networks were those that linked adjacent rural communities, each of which was served by a different local monopolist. In cases involving a symmetrical exchange of local traffic between adjacent LECs, regulators generally imposed a bill-and-keep regime (i.e., no money changed hands) on the theory that the number of calls from monopolist X to monopolist Y would be roughly equivalent to the number of calls from monopolist Y to monopolist X. Regulators sometimes devised more nuanced intercarrier compensation arrangements for more complex scenarios involving adjacent Bell companies, "independent" ILECs, and long distance companies.

7 47 U.S.C. §§ 251(b)(5), 252(d)(2)(A)(ii). By its terms, the provision containing the "additional costs" language applies only to ILECs, but the FCC has extended the requirement to all carriers terminating local calls.

8 47 U.S.C. § 252(d)(2)(B)(i).

9 *See* First Report and Order, *Implementation of the Local Competition Provisions*

of the Telecommunications Act of 1996, 11 FCC Rcd 15,499, ¶¶ 1111-12 (1996) (*"Local Competition Order"*). The FCC recognized an exception in the special case where the call volume from carrier A to carrier B is so similar to the call volume from carrier B to carrier A that the carriers' mutual obligations all but cancel out—in which event the FCC permitted bill-and-keep as a simplifying mechanism.

10 Susan Polyakova, *Wireless Carriers Criticized As Major Sources of "Phantom Traffic,"* COMM. DAILY, April 8, 2004 (2004 WL 60705626).

11 Maney et al., *supra.*

12 Similar calls date back to the 1980s, when providers offered information services ranging from Lexis-Nexis to email (MCIMail, for example) to online services like Prodigy. But these services were fairly small compared to those later offered by AOL or Earthlink, which benefited from the World Wide Web's emergence in the mid-1990s and signed up millions of subscribers.

13 *See generally* Bell Atl. Tel. Cos. v. FCC, 206 F.3d 1, 5 (D.C. Cir. 2000) (noting that there is "no dispute that the Commission has historically been justified in relying on this method when determining whether a particular communication is jurisdictionally interstate").

14 *See* Memorandum Opinion and Order, *MTS and WATS Market Structure*, 97 F.C.C.2d 682, ¶¶ 76-83 (1983) (*"MTS/WATS Market Structure Order"*); Notice of Proposed Rulemaking, *Amendments of Part 69 of the Commission's Rules Relating to Enhanced Service Providers*, 2 FCC Rcd 4305, ¶ 2 (1987); *see generally* Notice of Proposed Rulemaking, *IP-Enabled Services*, 19 FCC Rcd 4863 (2004) (*"IP-Enabled Servs. NPRM"*).

15 The counterparts to terminating access charges in international calling are known as *settlement rates*. Many countries, viewing the opportunity to "tax" incoming international calls with high settlement rates as an easy form of revenue, historically set these charges very high, sometimes at levels exceeding one U.S. dollar per minute. Consequently, as late as 1997, U.S. consumers paid on average 88 cents per minute for an international call, with much of that price reflecting a subsidy from U.S. consumers to foreign providers or to the foreign governments that often owned the incumbent telephone companies. *See* http://www.fcc.gov/Bureaus/International/News_Releases/1997/nrin7028.html. To address this issue, the FCC developed a set of benchmark rates to bring settlement rates down to 15-23 cents per minute, depending on the country at issue. Report and Order, *International Settlement Rates*, 12 FCC Rcd 19,806, ¶ 19 (1997); *see also* First Report and Order, *International Settlements Policy Reform*, 19 FCC Rcd 5709, ¶ 82 (2004) (reiterating importance of benchmarks policy, declining to eliminate it, and declining to initiate proceeding to revise benchmarks downward). In so doing, the FCC recognized that, while inefficient, high settlement rates constitute an implicit social policy to subsidize less well-off nations through telecommunications regulation. As with inflated access charges, those rates face pressures not simply from FCC regulatory reforms, but also from various arbitrage mechanisms, including "call back" technologies and, as discussed here, VoIP. *See generally* JEAN-JACQUES LAFFONT & JEAN TIROLE, COMPETITION IN TELECOMMUNICATIONS 184-86 & n.7 (MIT Press, 2000) (citing literature).

16 *See Local Competition Order,* ¶ 1054.

17 Note that this phenomenon arose principally in the case of dial-up ("narrow-band") Internet calls, not broadband DSL connections. In the latter context, as discussed in chapter 5, there is typically only one carrier between the end user and the Internet: either the ILEC itself or a CLEC, such as Covad, that may have leased the loop (or the "high frequency" portion of it) from the ILEC. Also, there is often no independent ISP either; because a broadband connection avoids the circuit-switched network altogether, there is no need for any entity other than the broad-band carrier to perform the "protocol conversion" functions usually associated with an ISP. The carrier itself typically performs the other ISP-type functions, such as storing e-mails and arranging for transmission paths to the broader Internet.

18 The only other remedy available to the ILECs—short of a change in the "recip-rocal compensation" rules themselves—would be an increase in the monthly local-service rates for everyone, irrespective of a given end user's actual use of the Internet. In the late 1990s, some ILECs argued, without success, that the skyrock-eting use of the public telephone network for Internet access had placed unprece-dented strains on the capacity of existing facilities, had required unforeseen capital expenditures on facility upgrades, and thus justified higher retail rates. Even apart from the political unsustainability of that argument, however, raising everyone's monthly rate would be problematic even as a theoretical matter, because it would exacerbate the existing cross-subsidy flowing from non-users of the Internet to heavy users of the Internet.

19 Order on Remand and Report and Order, *Implementation of the Local Competition Provisions in the Telecommunications Act of 1996; Intercarrier Compensation for ISP-Bound Traffic,* 16 FCC Rcd 9151 (2001) (*"ISP Reciprocal Compensation Remand Order"*), *remanded,* WorldCom, Inc. v. FCC, 288 F.3d 429 (D.C. Cir. 2002), *cert. denied sub nom.* Core Communications, Inc. v. FCC, 538 U.S. 1012 (2003).

20 *Id.,* ¶ 7.

21 *See* WorldCom, Inc. v. FCC, 288 F.3d 429 (D.C. Cir. 2002); Bell Atl. Tel. Cos. v. FCC, 206 F.3d 1 (D.C. Cir. 2000).

22 *Bell Atl.,* 206 F.3d at 7.

23 *WorldCom,* 288 F.3d at 434.

24 *See generally IP-Enabled Servs. NPRM,* ¶ 61 & n.179 (posing this question).

25 *See id.* (citing FCC precedent).

26 Similarly, the CLEC and any wireless carrier with an interconnection agreement must pay the opting-out ILEC that same TELRIC-based rate for completing what-ever "local" calls they originate. *See Local Competition Order,* ¶ 1036 ("traffic to or from a [commercial mobile wireless] network that originates and terminates within the same [Major Trading Area] is subject to transport and termination rates under section 251(b)(5), rather than interstate and intrastate access charges"); *see also* 47 C.F.R. § 51.701(b)(2).

27 Notice of Proposed Rulemaking, *Interconnection Between Local Exchange Carriers and Commercial Mobile Radio Service Providers*, 11 FCC Rcd 5020, ¶¶ 115-16 (1996).

28 *See* Declaratory Ruling, *Petitions of Sprint PCS and AT&T Corp. for Declaratory Ruling Regarding CMRS Access Charges*, 17 FCC Rcd 13,192 (2002), *appeal dismissed sub nom.* AT&T Corp. v. FCC, 349 F.3d 692 (D.C. Cir. 2003). A wireless carrier's inability to impose terminating access charges by tariff can present significant practical obstacles to collecting such charges. Those obstacles are particularly severe in the transiting context (discussed immediately below in the text), where the wireless carrier may not even know which carrier originated a given call, let alone have a contractual arrangement with that carrier.

29 *See* Eighth Report and Order and Fifth Order on Reconsideration, *Access Charge Reform; Reform of Access Charges Imposed by Competitive Local Exchange Carriers*, 19 FCC Rcd 9108, ¶¶ 10-19 (2004) (*"Eighth Report"*) (permitting long distance carrier to refuse full payment in these circumstances); *cf.* Public Notice, *Comment Sought on Petitions for Declaratory Ruling Regarding Intercarrier Compensation for Wireless Traffic*, 17 FCC Rcd 19046 (2002) (*"2002 Public Notice"*) (US LEC petition).

30 *See, e.g.*, Memorandum Opinion and Order, *Texcom, Inc. v. Bell Atl. Corp.*, 16 FCC Rcd 21,493, ¶¶ 4, 6, *recon. denied*, 17 FCC Rcd 6275 (2002).

31 *Id.*, ¶ 6.

32 Report and Order and Order on Remand and Further Notice of Proposed Rulemaking, *Review of the Section 251 Unbundling Obligations of Incumbent Local Exchange Carriers*, 18 FCC Rcd 16,978, ¶ 534 n.1640 (2003) (subsequent judicial history discussed in chapters 3 and 5) ("To date, the Commission's rules have not required incumbent LECs to provide transiting."); *see generally* Iowa Network Servs., Inc. v. Qwest Corp., 363 F.3d 683 (8th Cir. 2004) (addressing transiting dispute).

33 This problem applies equally in both three-carrier transiting scenarios and traditional two-carrier scenarios and, specifically, arises whenever the terminating carrier is either (i) a wireless carrier or CLEC, which (unlike an ILEC) owes no obligations to wireless carriers under section 252, *see* 47 U.S.C. § 252(a)(1), (d)(2); or (ii) a "rural telephone company" to the extent it is exempt under section 251(f) from the relevant provisions of sections 251 and 252. In the absence of a section 252 interconnection agreement, such a carrier will often file tariffs specifying rates for terminating local traffic. Those tariffed rates are normally much higher than the TELRIC-based rates charged for reciprocal compensation, and they often bear no resemblance to the underlying cost. As to their legality, at least one state has controversially deemed them binding on the wireless carriers that originate this traffic. *See* Sprint Spectrum LLP v. Missouri Pub. Serv. Comm., 112 S.W.3d 20, 26 (Mo. Ct. App. 2003) (finding no preemption but remanding for redetermination of just and reasonable rate); *cf.* 3 Rivers v. Qwest, 2003 U.S. Dist. LEXIS 24871 (D. Mont. 2003).

34 *See* 2002 Public Notice, *supra* (seeking comment on T-Mobile petition).

35 *See* Notice of Proposed Rulemaking, *Developing a Unified Intercarrier Compensation Regime*, 16 FCC Rcd 9610 (2001) (*"Intercarrier Comp. NPRM"*).

36 *See* Seventh Report and Order and Further Notice of Proposed Rulemaking, *Access Charge Reform*, 16 FCC Rcd 9923 (2001) (*"CLEC Access Charge Order"*); *see also Eighth Report, supra.*

37 *See Local Competition Order*, ¶¶ 1042, 1087.

38 After an initial setback in court, see AT&T Corp. v. FCC, 292 F.3d 808 (D.C. Cir. 2002), the FCC recently reimposed obligations on long distance carriers to terminate traffic to CLECs that charge FCC-approved terminating access rates. *See Eighth Report, supra*, ¶¶ 59-61.

39 *See Local Competition Order*, ¶ 1054.

40 Of course, policymakers will confront the indeterminacy of this inquiry anyway to the extent they continue obligating ILECs to lease switching and shared transport as network elements, since those elements are priced in essentially the same manner as the transport and termination function. *See id.* The difference is that, whereas those obligations can be eliminated as sufficient competition develops, the terminating access monopoly will always present a need for intercarrier compensation rules no matter how competitive the landscape. Adherence to the calling-network-pays regime would thus require this regulatory indeterminacy in perpetuity.

41 *See, e.g.,* Order, *Cost-Based Terminating Comp. for CMRS Providers*, 18 FCC Rcd 18,441 (2003) (opening door for wireless carriers to argue for higher termination rates than wireline ILECs), *pet. for review filed sub nom.* SBC Communications Inc. v. FCC, No. 03-4311 (3d Cir. Nov. 3, 2003). In its 1996 *Local Competition Order*, the FCC established a rebuttable presumption that, with the limited exception of paging companies, any given carrier has termination costs equivalent to the ILEC's termination costs. *Local Competition Order*, ¶¶ 1085-93; *see also Intercarrier Comp. NPRM*, ¶¶ 102-04.

42 The same economic indeterminacy has spawned parallel disputes about how much an ILEC should be able to charge CLECs under the TELRIC pricing standard for leasing capacity on its switches.

43 *See Local Competition Order*, ¶ 1064; *ISP Reciprocal Compensation Remand Order*, ¶ 76. This is an issue not just for intercarrier compensation for call termination services, but also for retail pricing plans. In truly competitive markets (such as wireless), carriers offer their subscribers a continuously changing menu of options featuring different combinations of flat and usage-sensitive rates. If the carrier's executives are doing their jobs, these payment plans will produce an income flow that manages to cover the carrier's costs. But such carriers succeed despite the absence of any determinate answer to the problem of recovering their high fixed costs over time. And they succeed because, unlike regulators, they have the flexibility to use several different compensation options at once and to change their customers' menu of options as soon as the need arises.

44 *See* Texas Office of Public Util. Counsel v. FCC, 265 F.3d 313, 328-29 (5th Cir. 2001); United States Tel. Ass'n v. FCC, 188 F.3d 521 (D.C. Cir. 1999).

45 Here we are using the terms "transport" and "termination" in their distinct, more technical senses.

46 *See generally* Patrick DeGraba, *Bill and Keep at the Central Office as the Efficient Interconnection Regime*, OPP WORKING PAPER NO. 33, at 17-19 (2000) (http://www.fcc.gov/Bureaus/OPP/working_papers/oppwp33.pdf).

47 *See Local Competition Order,* ¶ 1112; *cf. ISP Reciprocal Compensation Remand Order,* ¶¶ 72-73 (adopting contrary position).

48 *See* DeGraba, *supra.*

49 Under the FCC's current approach, that geographic region is defined as the "local access and transport area," or "LATA," derived from the 1984 AT&T consent decree. *See, e.g.,* Memorandum Opinion and Order, *Application by Verizon Maryland Inc. et al. for Authorization to Provide In-Region, InterLATA Services in Maryland, Washington, D.C., and West Virginia,* 18 FCC Rcd 5212, ¶ 103 (2003).

50 Alternatively, regulators might prescribe actual physical points of interconnection between carriers across a range of scenarios, at least as default arrangements subject to negotiated alternatives. Depending on how the requirement is framed, however, this approach might be subject to challenge on the ground that section 251(c)(2) entitles CLECs to interconnect at "any technically feasible point" on the ILEC's network. *See generally* US West Commun., Inc. v. Jennings, 304 F.3d 950, 961 (9th Cir. 2002); MCI Telecomm. Corp. v. Bell Atl.-Pa., 271 F.3d 491, 517-18 (3d Cir. 2001).

51 AT&T Corp. v. Iowa Utils. Bd., 525 U.S. 366 (1999) (discussed in chapter 3).

52 *Id.* at 397.

53 *Local Competition Order,* ¶¶ 1111-12.

54 *WorldCom,* 288 F.3d at 434.

55 *See Local Competition Order,* ¶¶ 1042, 1087. As a belt-and-suspenders approach, the FCC could also assert its authority under section 10 to "forbear" from section 251(b)(5) or section 252(d)(2) to the extent that either provision could be read to preclude bill-and-keep for unbalanced traffic. *See* 47 U.S.C. § 160. That approach would present some complications, however. First, because bill-and-keep requires continuing regulatory oversight, critics might argue that substituting bill-and-keep for a calling-network-pays rule simply replaces one regulatory scheme with another and therefore does not constitute "forbearance" from regulation in the first place. Second, item 13 on the section 271 checklist (see chapter 3) requires each Bell company to provide "[r]eciprocal compensation arrangements in accordance with the requirements of section 252(d)(2)." 47 U.S.C. § 271(c)(2)(B)(xiii). To the extent that section 252(d)(2) is construed to prohibit bill-and-keep for the relevant classes of traffic, the FCC might conceivably need to forbear not just from that provision, but from checklist item 13 itself, lest the Bell companies later be deemed to fall out of compliance with their checklist obligations if they adopt bill-

and-keep for that traffic. *See generally* 47 U.S.C. § 160(d); p. 569 n. 98, *supra*, and accompanying text.

56 *See* 47 U.S.C. § 152(b); La. Pub. Serv. Comm'n v. FCC, 476 U.S. 355 (1986). This traditional jurisdictional divide is discussed in chapters 2 and 3.

57 *See ISP Reciprocal Compensation Remand Order*, ¶¶ 34, 37 n.66, 45; *compare Local Competition Order*, ¶¶ 1033-34.

58 *Cf. ISP Reciprocal Compensation Remand Order*, ¶ 37 & n.66.

59 *Local Competition Order*, ¶ 1041.

60 *See* Philip J. Weiser, *Cooperative Federalism and Its Challenges*, 2003 MICH. ST. DCL L. REV. 727, 734-37 (discussing options for state implementation of intercarrier compensation reform).

61 *See generally* Qwest Corp. v. FCC, 258 F.3d 1191, 1203-04 (10th Cir. 2001); Comsat Corp. v. FCC 250 F.3d 931, 939 (5th Cir. 2001) ("the FCC cannot maintain any implicit subsidies whether on a permissive or mandatory basis") (internal quotations omitted). On the interstate side of the cost ledger, the FCC itself engaged in analogous universal service reform in the 2000 *CALLS* order, discussed in chapter 10, where it reduced interstate access charges and increased the size of the federal universal service fund, subsidized by competitively neutral contributions by all carriers.

Chapter Ten

1 *See generally* ROBERT CRANDALL & LEONARD WAVERMAN, WHO PAYS FOR UNIVERSAL SERVICE? WHEN TELEPHONE SUBSIDIES BECOME TRANSPARENT 21 (Brookings Inst. Press, 2000) ("Most studies of universal service subsidies conclude that they have minimal effect on telephone subscriptions . . . they do not address the real causes of nonsubscription—installation fees and excessive past fees for long distance calling.").

2 In addition to these universal service programs, there are other government initiatives that also seek to ensure widespread access to telecommunications services. For example, the Rural Utilities Service has traditionally provided loans and other benefits to rural providers in order to increase access to telecommunications services. *See* http://www.usda.gov/rus/telecom/rtb/index_rtb.htm.

3 By 2002, the total cost of these programs reached almost $6 billion and was projected to reach $6.34 billion in 2003. A little under half of the 2002 funding went to the high cost fund ($2.9 billion). The Schools and Library Fund received a capped level of $2.25 billion to support Internet connections. *See* Statement of Michael Powell, Committee on Commerce, Science, and Transportation (Oct. 30, 2003) (http://hraunfoss.fcc.gov/edocs_public/attachmatch/DOC-240507A1.pdf). The Lifeline/Link-Up and the rural health care programs, which receive the remain-

ing support, are underutilized in the sense that many potential beneficiaries have not taken advantage of them. The FCC has redoubled its efforts to address this issue, particularly for Lifeline/Link-Up, which is used only by approximately one-third of eligible households. Report and Order, *Lifeline and Link-Up,* 19 FCC Rcd 8302 (2004). To promote adoption of this program, which provides up to a $10 per month subsidy and $30 discount on the installation of telephone service, the FCC has removed some administrative obstacles and enforced the requirement that carriers publicize the availability of subsidies for low income subscribers. *Id.* (revising rules); *Pend Oreille Tel. Co.,* File No. EB-030-TC-123 ¶ 1 (May 24, 2004) (http://hraunfoss.fcc.gov/edocs_public/attachmatch/DA-04-1447A1.pdf) (penalizing carrier for "willfully and repeatedly failing to publicize the availability of Lifeline and Link-Up services 'in a manner reasonably designed to reach those likely to qualify' for the services"). To give an added boost to telephone adoption on Indian reservations, where only 47% of households currently have telephone service, the FCC has adopted a special Lifeline and Link-Up initiative, including an additional $25 per month subsidy and an additional $70 subsidy to offset initial connection charges. *See* Report and Order, *Federal State Board on Universal Service,* 15 FCC Rcd 12,208, ¶¶ 2, 12 (2000).

4 Eli M. Noam, *Will Universal Service and Common Carriage Survive The Telecommunications Act of 1996,* 97 COLUM. L. REV. 955, 956 (1997) ("For all its pro-competitive rhetoric, [the 1996 Act] is a solid commitment to redistributive universal service to rural areas, the poor, the middle class, and the educational system.").

5 *See* W. KIP VISCUSI ET AL., ECONOMICS OF REGULATION AND ANTITRUST 352 (MIT Press, 3d ed. 2000) ("The Ramsey pricing 'rule' that gives the prices that minimize the deadweight losses is to raise prices in inverse proportion to demand elasticities"); *see also* AT&T Corp. v. Iowa Utils. Bd., 525 U.S. 366, 426 (1999) (Breyer, J., concurring in part and dissenting in part).

6 *See* H.R. Rep. No. 204, 104th Cong., 2d Sess. 80 (1995) (recognizing need to reform universal service support "in the context of a local market changing from one characterized by monopoly to one of competition").

7 *See, e.g.,* Jerry Hausman & Howard Shelanski, *Economic Welfare and Telecommunications Regulation: The E-Rate Policy for Universal-Service Subsidies,* 16 YALE J. REG. 19, 30 (1999) ("[t]he alternative of subsidizing universal services through general tax revenues" is "a good option from the standpoint of efficient public finance"); ROBERT HAHN ET AL., CHEAP NET PHONES FACE THE THREAT OF A TAX HANGUP (June 2004) (http://aei-brookings.org/policy/page.php?id=189) ("Telecom taxation-by-regulation was never a good way for government to raise revenues: It costs the economy more than three times as much as the same amount of money raised through general income taxes.").

8 *See* Yochi Dreazen, *New Taxes, Fees Hit Phone Bills,* WALL ST. J., Sept. 18, 2002, at D1. For a general discussion of such issues, including the ones related to the Internet taxation moratorium, see Heather Forsgren Weaver, *Lawmakers Push to Classify VoIP as "Info" Service,* RCR WIRELESS NEWS, April 12, 2004 (available at 2004 WL 63048528).

9 Howard Gleckman, *Net Taxes: Here Comes A Battle Royal*, BUS. WK. ONLINE (December 1, 2003) (http://www.businessweek.com/bwdaily/dnflash/dec2003/nf2003121_7035_db015.htm). In mid-2004, the Internal Revenue Service began to investigate whether the 3% excise tax should extend to VoIP calls. *See* Declan McCullagh, *IRS Eyes Net Phone Taxes*, CNET NEWS.COM (July 6, 2004) (http://news.com.com/IRS+eyes+Net+phone+taxes/2100-7352_3-5258809.html?part=rss&tag=5258809&subj=news.7352.20).

10 For an example of such confusion, see Don Oldenburg, *The Hidden Cost of High-Speed Internet*, WASH. POST, June 15, 2004, at C10 ("Many . . . broadband providers are now charging their customers the [universal service] fees as separate line items in their bills. Customers often mistake them for 'some sort of federal tax,' as one online complaint put it. They're not. And the feds do not require DSL providers to charge their customers the fee as they do taxes.").

11 Richard Posner, *Taxation by Regulation*, 2 BELL J. ECON. & MGMT. SCI. 22, 29 (1971).

12 *See* chapter 2. The origins of the modern commitment to universal service are detailed in MILTON L. MUELLER, JR., UNIVERSAL SERVICE: MONOPOLY IN THE MAKING OF AMERICAN TELEPHONE SYSTEM (MIT Press, 1996). Notably, the initial deployment of ubiquitous telephone service arose in a competitive environment without governmental support. *Id.* at 60-67. And even when Theodore Vail, the early AT&T CEO who championed "universal service," pressed the concept, he did not mean "rate subsidies to make telephone service more affordable"; rather, he meant "the unification of telephone service under regulated monopolies." *Id.* at 92. Nonetheless, AT&T's Bell System succeeded in establishing the opposition between competition and universal service, using the system of "taxation by regulation" as a basis for barring competitive entry into telecommunications markets.

13 *See generally* Smith v. Ill. Bell Tel. Co., 282 U.S. 133, 148 (1930).

14 Under a federal-state compact known as the "Ozark Plan," a disproportionate amount of the costs of telephone service were placed in the federal jurisdiction. *See* Report and Order, *Prescription of Procedures for Separating and Allocating Plant Investment, Operating Expenses, Taxes and Reserves Between the Intrastate and Interstate Operations of Telephone Companies*, 26 F.C.C.2d 247 (1970). At the time, the proportion allocated to the respective jurisdictions worked out to a 66/33 split, but the FCC ultimately migrated to a fixed 75/25 ratio. *See* Decision and Order, *Amendment of Part 67 of the Commission's Rules and Establishment of a Joint Board*, 96 F.C.C.2d 781 (1984).

15 *See* 47 U.S.C. § 221(c) (empowering FCC to "determine what property of said carrier shall be considered as used in interstate or foreign telephone toll service"); *id.* at § 410 (requiring use of a Joint Board to address separations); *see also* Hawaiian Tel. Co. v. Pub. Util. Comm., 827 F.2d 1264, 1277-78 (9th Cir. 1987) (making clear that FCC may oversee separations rules). The FCC has investigated the possibility of fundamentally reforming the traditional separations regime, but has yet to take action and is unlikely to do so anytime soon. *See* Report and Order, *Jurisdictional Separations and Referral to the Federal-State Joint Board*, 16 FCC Rcd 11,382, ¶ 1 (2001); *cf.* Notice of Proposed Rulemaking, *Jurisdictional Separations Reform and Referral to the Federal-State Joint Board*, 12 FCC Rcd

22,120, ¶ 3 (1997) (seeking comment "on whether some form of separations must exist under the 1930 Smith v. Illinois decision, or whether statutory, regulatory and market changes since that decision have been so pronounced and persuasive as to make its holding inapplicable in our new deregulatory environment").

16 *See* Nat'l Ass'n of Regulatory Utils. Comm'rs v. FCC, 737 F.2d 1095 (D.C. Cir. 1984).

17 *See* 47 U.S.C. § 214(e)(3).

18 *See* Qwest Corp. v. FCC, 258 F.3d 1191, 1203-04 (10th Cir. 2001).

19 *See* 47 U.S.C. §§ 254(a), 410(c). The Joint Board is composed of several FCC commissioners, several members of state public utility commissions, and a designated consumer advocate. Its recommendations cannot bind the FCC in any legal sense, but they do carry political significance.

20 *See* 47 U.S.C. § 254(b)(4).

21 *See* 47 U.S.C. §§ 214(e), 254(e).

22 *See generally* Recommended Decision, *Federal-State Joint Board on Universal Service*, 19 FCC Rcd 4257, ¶¶ 5-55 (2004) (*"Joint Board Recommended Decision"*).

23 Sixth Report and Order, *Access Charge Reform*, 15 FCC Rcd 12,962 (2000) (*"CALLS Order"*). The exact amount of the needed increase in the size of the federal fund has been subject to some dispute. Although the FCC originally increased the fund size by $650 million, the Fifth Circuit reversed that portion of the *CALLS Order* on the ground that the Commission had essentially picked the number out of a hat, and it remanded for a recalculation. *See* Texas Office of Public Utility Counsel v. FCC, 265 F.3d 313, 327-28 (5th Cir. 2001). On remand, the FCC conducted further cost proceedings and concluded that the right number is $650 million after all, though this time it purported to offer greater justification. *See* Order on Remand, *Access Charge Reform*, 18 FCC Rcd 14,976 (2003).

24 As in the unbundling context, the FCC has defined "cost" for these purposes on the basis of a "forward-looking" methodology that, in essence, looks to replacement costs rather than book costs. *See* chapter 3 and appendix A. That methodological choice has less significance than might appear at first blush because the FCC uses the same forward-looking cost methodology in both the numerator (average state costs) and the denominator (average national costs) of the cost calculus.

25 *See Qwest*, 258 F.3d at 1203-04.

26 Order on Remand, *Federal-State Joint Board on Universal Service*, 18 FCC Rcd 22,559, ¶¶ 76-79; 93-96; 126-32 (2003), *pet. for review filed sub nom.* Qwest Communications Int'l, Inc. v. FCC, Nos. 03-9617 *et al.* (10th Cir. Dec. 29, 2003).

27 For an argument about how universal service policy lends itself to cooperative federalism, see Christopher Wyeth Kirkham, Note, *Busting the Administrative*

Trust: An Experimentalist Approach to Universal Service Administration in Telecommunications Policy, 98 COLUM. L. REV. 620 (1998).

28 *See, e.g.,* Tex. Office of Pub. Util. Counsel v. FCC, 183 F.3d 393, 437 (5th Cir. 1999) (*"TOPUC"*) ("Where the statutory language does not explicitly command otherwise, we defer to the agency's reasonable judgment about what will constitute 'sufficient' support during the transition period from one universal service system to another."); Alenco Communications, Inc. v. FCC, 201 F.3d 608, 615 (5th Cir. 2000) (the aspirational principles set forth by Congress "reflect [the] congressional intent to delegate [the] difficult policy choices to the Commission's discretion").

29 *See, e.g., TOPUC,* 183 F.3d at 424 (discussed below).

30 *See generally* 47 U.S.C. § 153(37) (defining "rural telephone company"); *see also* chapter 2 (describing rate-of-return and price cap regimes).

31 *See, e.g.,* ACS of Alaska, Inc. v. Regulatory Comm'n. of Alaska, 81 P.3d 292 (Alaska 2003).

32 Report and Order, *Federal-State Joint Board on Universal Service, Multi-Association Group (MAG) Plan for Regulation of Interstate Services of Non-Price Cap Incumbent Local Exchange Carriers and Interexchange Carriers,* 16 FCC Rcd 11,244 (2001) (*"Rural Task Force Order"*); *see also* Second Report and Order, *Federal-State Joint Board on Universal Service, Multi-Association Group (MAG) Plan for Regulation of Interstate Services of Non-Price Cap Incumbent Local Exchange Carriers and Interexchange Carriers,* 16 FCC Rcd. 19,613 (2001).

33 *See Alenco,* 201 F.3d at 617.

34 *Rural Task Force Order,* ¶¶ 8-10. Again, for a discussion of the difference between forward-looking and embedded "historical" costs, see chapter 3 and appendix A.

35 *Id.* at ¶¶ 5, 11.

36 *See* 47 U.S.C. §§ 214(e), 254(e).

37 *Rural Task Force Order,* ¶¶ 207.

38 *Id.* at ¶ 211.

39 *Joint Board Recommended Decision,* ¶ 67 n.183.

40 *Id.,* Separate Statement of Billy Jack Gregg, at 4314.

41 *Joint Board Recommended Decision,* ¶¶ 56-87.

42 *Id.,* Separate Statement of Commissioner Abernathy, at 4306-07.

43 *Id.,* Dissenting Statement of Commissioners Adelstein, Thompson and Rowe, at 4318-25. Permitting a customer to designate a single carrier as the provider of her "primary" connection for support purposes would, to that extent, convert the universal service regime into a voucher system for telecommunications services. In the

debates prior to 1996 Act, Congress rejected Senator McCain's proposal for the express adoption of such a system. *See.* S. Rep. No. 1276, 141 Cong. Rec. 8266 (1995) (text of McCain Amendment); No. 251, 104th Cong., 1st Sess., 141 Cong. Rec. D719 (1995) (recording vote).

44 *Joint Board Recommended Decision*, ¶ 96.

45 *Id.*, Separate Statement of Commissioner Abernathy, at 4307.

46 *Id.*

47 Report and Order, *Federal-State Joint Board on Universal Service*, 12 FCC Rcd 8776, ¶ 808 (1997) (*"First Universal Service Order"*).

48 *TOPUC*, 183 F.3d at 447-48.

49 *See* Further Notice of Proposed Rulemaking, *Federal-State Joint Board on Universal Service*, 17 FCC Rcd 3752, ¶ 5-13 (2002) (*"Further Notice"*); Ken Belson, *Trying To Revive Struggling AT&T: A Job Made, It Seems, for Sisyphus*, N.Y. TIMES, June 1, 2004, at C1 (reporting on the decline in revenue from the long distance market from $100 billion to $80 billion from 2000 to 2002). Determining which traffic should be deemed "interstate" for these purposes often presents exceptionally difficult implementation problems, particularly for wireless and other carriers that offer calling plans that do not charge extra for long distance. The FCC has adopted various presumptions about the percentage of wireless revenues that count as "interstate," and, as a general matter, wireless carriers tend to contribute less for the interstate calls they place than do wireline carriers. *See* Report and Order and Second Further Notice of Proposed Rulemaking, *Federal-State Joint Board on Universal Service*, 17 FCC Rcd 24,952, ¶¶ 20-26 (2002) (*"Second Further Notice"*).

50 *See* Public Notice, *Proposed Third Quarter 2004 Universal Service Contribution Factor*, 19 FCC Rcd 10,194 (2004); *see also* Written Statement of FCC Commissioner Kathleen Q. Abernathy, Preserving and Advancing Universal Service, Senate Subcommittee on Communications (Apr. 2, 2003) (www.fcc.gov/commissioners/abernathy/speeches2003.html).

51 *Second Further Notice*, ¶ 3 (footnotes omitted).

52 *See Further Notice*, ¶¶ 37-63.

53 *See Second Further Notice*, ¶¶ 71-95.

54 *See id.*, ¶¶ 96-99.

55 *First Universal Service Order*, ¶ 796. See chapter 6 for a discussion of the difference between "common carriers" and "private carriers."

56 *See generally* Report to Congress, *Federal-State Joint Board on Universal Service*, 13 FCC Rcd 11,501 (1998); *see also* Notice of Proposed Rulemaking, *IP-Enabled Services*, 19 FCC Rcd 4863, ¶¶ 63-66 (2004).

57 *See* Recommended Decision, *Federal State Joint Board on Universal Service*, 17 FCC Rcd 14,095, ¶¶ 9-19 (2002) (recommending that broadband not be included within universal service); Order and Order on Reconsideration, *Federal State Joint Board on Universal Service*, 18 FCC Rcd 15,090, ¶¶ 8-13 (2003) (adopting recommendation).

58 Rural interests began championing such programs at the turn of the millennium. *See, e.g.*, Kathy Koch, *Riding The Internet Express*, CQ OUTLOOK 6, 11-12 (March 11, 2000).

59 47 U.S.C. § 254(c)(1). The reference to "telecommunications service" in the quoted language, combined with restrictions on universal service expenditures in section 254(e), suggests that federal subsidies for broadband services may require legal gymnastics to the extent that the FCC succeeds in classifying those services as pure "information services" or "private carriage" under Title I rather than "telecommunications services" under Title II. On the other hand, before section 254 was enacted, the Commission had long administered universal service programs under its more general Title I authority "to make available, so far as possible, to all the people of the United States . . . a rapid, efficient, Nation-wide, . . . wire and radio communication service with adequate facilities at reasonable charges." 47 U.S.C. § 151; *see, e.g.*, Rural Tel. Coalition v. FCC, 838 F.2d 1307 (D.C. Cir. 1988) (upholding the FCC's pre-statutory version of the universal service fund as part of its Title I authority). It is by no means clear that section 254 should be read to curtail any aspect of that authority.

60 *Federal State Joint Board on Universal Service*, 17 FCC Rcd 14,095 (2002) (http://hraunfoss.fcc.gov/edocs_public/attachmatch/FCC-02J-1A1.doc) (Separate Statement of Commissioner Michael J. Copps).

61 *See* NAT'L RESEARCH COUNCIL, BROADBAND: BRINGING HOME THE BITS 25 (National Academies Press, 2002) ("Once a mass market [in broadband] is achieved—which brings with it prospects of new applications and business opportunities—there is a likelihood that demand and willingness to pay will increase."); *id.* at 115 ("Without a mass market of consumer with broadband access, it is hard to develop a business model that justifies investment in new content (or translating old content)."); JEFFREY H. ROHLFS, BANDWAGON EFFECTS IN HIGH-TECH INDUSTRIES 4 (MIT Press, 2001) (noting how "bandwagon markets" are different from conventional markets in that "[t]hey are quite difficult to get started and often end up in a ditch before they can get underway").

62 President George W. Bush, Remarks at the American Association of Community Colleges Annual Convention, Minneapolis, Minn. (April 26, 2004) (www.whitehouse.gov/news/releases/2004/04/20040426-6.html).

63 *See* Gerald Faulhaber, *Broadband Deployment: Is Policy In The Way?* in BROADBAND: SHOULD WE REGULATE HIGH-SPEED INTERNET ACCESS? 226-27 (Brookings Inst. Press, Crandall & Alleman eds., 2002).

64 We say "generally successful" because, although the program has helped to spur broadband access in public schools (enabling 87% of them to gain access by 2001) and libraries (enabling 95% to gain access by 2002), it has been plagued by allegations of fraud and poor oversight. *See* Marguerite Reardon, *Fraud Threatens Internet Programs For U.S. Schools*, CNET NEWS.COM (June 17, 2004) (http://news.com.com/Eroding+E-rate/2009-1028_3-5236723.html).

65 For these reasons, there is no strong political constituency for subsidizing broadband deployment in poor and rural areas. Indeed, a 2004 poll showed that nearly 70% of Americans oppose paying additional fees to underwrite such a program.

See Charles Cooper, *Poll Shows Tough Road for Broadband*, CNET NEWS.COM (July 26, 2004) (http://news.com.com/Poll+shows+tough+road+for+broad band/2100-1034_3-5273082.html?tag=mainstry).

66 *See, e.g.*, Kathy Koch, *Riding The Internet Express*, CQ OUTLOOK 6, 8-9 (March 11, 2000).

67 Austan Goolsbee observes that subsidies designed to encourage investment where it is not already occurring are far more cost-effective than subsidizing usage where individuals might well either adopt broadband without the subsidies or not value it at all. *See* Austan Goolsbee, *Subsidies, The Value of Broadband, and the Importance of Fixed Costs in* BROADBAND: SHOULD WE REGULATE HIGH-SPEED INTERNET ACCESS? 292-93 (Brookings Inst. Press, Crandall & Alleman eds., 2002).

68 Congress's sole initiative to date in this area seeks to facilitate market-based efforts to drive broadband deployment by affording low interest loans to rural broadband providers—although the administering agency (the Rural Utilities Service of the Department of Agriculture) has had difficulty finding qualified applicants. *RUS Having Trouble Finding Broadband Loan Applicants*, COMM. DAILY, May 28, 2004.

69 For an examination of some of the challenges of reforming the health care system, see Sharona Hoffman, *Unmanaged Care: Towards Moral Fairness in Health Care Coverage*, 78 IND. L.J. 659 (2003).

70 This explains, for example, why the economically appealing concept of an "auction model" for supporting universal service has yet to gain much traction among policymakers. *See* Dennis Weller, *Auctions for Universal Service Obligations*, 23 TELECOM. POL'Y 645 (1999); Gregory L. Rosston & Bradley S. Wimmer, *The ABC's of Universal Service: Arbitrage, Big Bucks, and Competition*, 50 HASTINGS L.J. 1585, 1613-14 (1999).

Chapter Eleven

1 *See, e.g.*, Thomas W. Hazlett, *All Broadcast Regulation Politics Are Local: A Response To Christopher Yoo's Model of Broadcast Regulation*, 53 EMORY L.J. 233, 235 (2004) ("Licenses are awarded without competitive bidding, and when rival technologies (such as cable or satellite television) pose a competitive threat, regulators first attempt to thwart the new entrants and, at the point that they lose that battle, enforce rules mandating that the new rivals help broadcast licensees distribute their programs. . ."). Indeed, at the direction of the D.C. Circuit, the FCC expressly rejected competition for 30 years in favor of a protectionist policy towards local broadcasters as part of the "*Carroll* doctrine," which prevented the assignment of additional stations that could endanger the vitality of current ones. *See Carroll Broadcasting Co. v. FCC*, 258 F.2d 440 (D.C. Cir. 1958); Report and Order, *Regarding Detrimental Effects of Proposed New Broadcasting Stations on Existing Stations*, 3 FCC Rcd 638 (1988) (abolishing *Carroll* doctrine).

2 As Cass Sunstein has put it: "There is a large difference between the public interest and what interests the public. This is so especially in light of the character and consequences of the communications market. One of the central goals of the system of broadcasting, private as well as public, should be to promote the American aspiration to deliberative democracy." Cass R. Sunstein, *Television and the Public Interest*, 88 CAL. L. REV. 499, 501 (2000); *see also* Mark Cooper, *Open Communications Platforms: The Physical Infrastructure As The Bedrock of Innovation and Democratic Discourse in the Internet Age*, 2 J. TELECOMM. & HIGH TECH. L. 177, 193 (2003) (arguing that speech is not just "an economic commodity").

3 *See, e.g.,* Prometheus Radio Project v. FCC, 373 F.3d 372, 414 (3rd Cir. 2004) ("The Commission ensures that license transfers serve public goals of diversity, competition, and localism, while the antitrust authorities have a different purpose: ensuring that merging companies do not raise prices above competitive levels.").

4 This quote appeared as part of an interview in the Nov. 1, 1981 issue of *Reason* magazine and can be found at http://www.conservativeforum.org/authquot.asp?ID=775. *See also* C. EDWIN BAKER, MEDIA, MARKETS, AND DEMOCRACY 3 (Cambridge Univ. Press, 2002).

5 For years, telephone companies were banned from providing cable television service. 47 U.S.C. § 533(b) (repealed); *see, e.g.,* Gen. Tel. v. United States, 449 F.2d 846 (5th Cir. 1971) (upholding ban); *but see* Chesapeake & Potomac Tel. Co. v. United States, 42 F.3d 181, 202 (4th Cir. 1996) (invalidating ban), *vacated as moot*, 516 U.S. 415 (1996). In the 1996 Act, Congress repealed this ban. *See* 1996 Act, Pub. L. 104-104, § 302(b)(1). Although Congress authorized telephone companies and cable overbuilders to enter video delivery markets under an experimental regulatory model known as "open video systems," *see* 47 U.S.C. § 573, a subsequent Fifth Circuit ruling, among other factors, limited the attractiveness of that model. *See* City of Dallas v. FCC, 165 F.3d 341, 347-48 (5th Cir. 1999). Telephone companies remain free, however, to provide cable television service over their networks subject to the Title VI regime applicable to traditional cable operators.

6 As noted in chapter 7, the FCC and its predecessor (the Federal Radio Commission) have long held an expansive view of the statutory "public interest" standard for licensing broadcast applicants. As Justice Frankfurter explained in upholding this view, "the Act does not restrict the Commission merely to supervision of the [radio] traffic. It puts upon the Commission the burden of determining the composition of that traffic. The facilities of radio are not large enough to accommodate all who wish to use them. Methods must be devised for choosing from among the many who apply." Nat'l. Broad. Co. v. United States, 319 U.S. 190, 215-16 (1943) (*"NBC v. U.S."*); *see also* Red Lion Broad. Co. v. FCC, 395 U.S. 367

(1969). The traditional view has always been that "programming is the essence" of the public interest standard. *See, e.g.,* Johnston Broad. Co. v. FCC, 175 F.2d 351, 359 (D.C. Cir. 1949); *see generally En Banc Programming Inquiry,* 44 F.C.C. 2303, 2311 (1960). The FCC has further attributed particular significance to each licensee's obligation to air programming on issues of *local* importance, given the Commission's obligation under section 307(b) of the Communications Act "to provide a fair, efficient, and equitable distribution" of service "among the several States and communities."

7 The relationships between networks and affiliates can be quite complex. The classic study is contained in Network Inquiry Special Staff, *An Analysis of the Network-Affiliate Relationship in Television,* reprinted in *New Television Networks,* vol. II, 106-292 (1980); *see also* BRUCE M. OWEN & STEVEN S. WILDMAN, VIDEO ECONOMICS 151-210 (Harvard Univ. Press, 1992); STANLEY M. BESEN, ET AL., MISREGULATING TELEVISION (Univ. of Chicago Press, 1984). The FCC is often asked to intervene in these relationships, as demonstrated most recently in the proceeding commenced by the National Affiliated Stations Alliance ("NASA") in 2001, which concerns, among other things, an affiliate's right to reject network programming. *See* Public Notice, *Comment Sought on Petition for Inquiry Into Network Practices,* 16 FCC Rcd 10,939 (2001).

8 In the Cable Act of 1992, Congress barred municipalities from awarding *exclusive* monopoly franchises. *See* 47 U.S.C. § 541(a)(1).

9 The leading national overbuilder, RCN, filed for bankruptcy in 2004, underscoring the difficulties that such providers have in servicing their debt burdens. *See* Colin C. Hadley, *Debt-Saddled RCN Files Ch. 11,* INTERNETNEWS.COM (May 27, 2004) (http://www.internetnews.com/fina-news/article.php/3360131).

10 *See* Hearing Designation Order, *Application of EchoStar Communications Corp., General Motors Corp., and Hughes Electronics Corp., and EchoStar Corp.,* 17 FCC Rcd 20,559 (2002) (*"EchoStar-DirecTV Hearing Designation Order"*).

11 *See* Memorandum Opinion and Order, *General Motors Corp. and Hughes Electronics Corp., Transferors, and News Corp. Ltd., Transferee,* 19 FCC Rcd 473 (2004) (*"News Corp.-DirectTV Merger Order"*).

12 Malrite T.V. v. FCC, 652 F.2d 1140, 1144 (2d Cir. 1981). Thomas Hazlett has similarly described this regime as "a textbook example of anticompetitive regulation." Thomas W. Hazlett, *The Wireless Craze, The Unlimited Bandwidth Myth, the Spectrum Auction Faux Pas, and the Punchline to Ronald Coase's "Big Joke": An Essay on Airwave Allocation Policy,* 14 HARV. J.L. & TECH. 335, 420 (2001) (*"Wireless Craze"*); *see also* Stanley Besen & Robert Crandall, *The Deregulation of Cable Television,* 44 LAW & CONTEMP. PROB. 77 (1981) (criticizing early regulation of cable television); Nat'l Ass'n of Broad. v. FCC, 740 F.2d 1190, 1195 (D.C. Cir. 1984) (acknowledging criticisms and upholding deregulated status of DBS). Over time, the FCC abandoned some of these rules, such as the ones mandating program origination, and the courts invalidated others as unconstitutional or beyond the scope of the FCC's statutory authority. *See* Report and Order, *Amendment of Part 76, Subpart G of Comm'n Rules and Regulations Relative to Program Origination by Cable Television Sys.,* 49 F.C.C.2d 1090 (1974); FCC v. Midwest Video Corp.

440 U.S. 689 (1979) (invalidating, as beyond FCC's Title I authority, pre-Cable Act requirements for "leased access" channels and channels dedicated to "public, educational, and governmental" ("PEG") programming); Home Box Office v. FCC, 567 F.2d 9 (D.C. Cir. 1977) (invalidating restrictions on pay television).

13 *See generally* PAUL STARR, THE CREATION OF THE MEDIA: POLITICAL ORIGINS OF MODERN COMMUNICATIONS (Basic Books, 2004).

14 Fortnightly Corp. v. United Artists Television, Inc., 392 U.S. 390 (1968); Teleprompter Corp. v. CBS, Inc., 415 U.S. 394 (1974). Ironically, the National Association of Broadcasters, which spearheaded the litigation, had been founded as part of an effort to defend broadcasters from copyright actions brought by record companies, which objected to their music being played on the radio. *See* ERIK BARNOUW, A TOWER IN BABEL (HISTORY OF BROADCASTING IN THE UNITED STATES) 120-21 (American Philological Assoc., 1967).

15 For thoughtful discussions of the rationales behind this regime, see Tim Wu, *Copyright's Communications Policy*, __ MICH. L. REV. __ (2004); Stanley M. Besen et. al, *Copyright Liability for Cable Television: Compulsory Licensing*, 21 J. L. & ECON. 67 (1978).

16 Copyright Revision Act of 1976, 17 U.S.C. §§ 101-08, 111 (1976).

17 Library of Congress, *Distribution of 1998 and 1999 Cable Royalty Funds*, 69 Fed. Reg. 3606, 3607 (2004).

18 *See* Neil Weinstock Netanel, *Impose A Noncommercial Use Levy to Allow Free Peer-to-Peer File Sharing*, 17 HARV. J. L & TECH. 1 (2003); William Fisher, *Don't Beat Them, Join Them*, N.Y. TIMES, June 25, 2004, at A25.

19 47 U.S.C. § 325(b)(1)(A); *see* United Video v. FCC, 890 F.2d 1173, 1187 (D.C. Cir. 1989) (confessing surprise that Congress would institute compulsory license alongside rules akin to retransmission consent, but upholding FCC rules according broadcasters related rights).

20 *See generally* Charles Lubinsky, *Reconsidering Retransmission Consent: An Examination of The Retransmission Consent Provision (47 U.S.C. §325(b)) of The 1992 Cable Act*, 49 FED. COMM. L.J. 99 (1996).

21 *See* Mike Musgrove, *Dish Network Drops Viacom Channels*, WASH. POST, March 10, 2004, at E1 (www.washingtonpost.com/wp-dyn/articles/A44561-2004Mar9.html).

22 47 C.F.R. § 76.92. For a history of this and related provisions, see Christopher S. Yoo, *Rethinking the Commitment to Free, Local Television*, 52 EMORY L.J. 1579, 1646 n.189 (2003).

23 *See* Notice of Proposed Rulemaking, *Carriage of Transmissions of Digital Broad. Stations*, 13 FCC Rcd 15,092, ¶ 33 & n.92 (1998) (observing that 80% of the major network affiliates enter into "retransmission consent" arrangements, whereas 20% of independent stations invoke "must carry" rights).

24 47 U.S.C. §§ 534, 535. The FCC had laid the groundwork for this statutory "must carry" requirement by developing a regulatory scheme of its own in the 1960s "to ameliorate the adverse impact of [cable] competition upon local stations, existing and potential." First Report and Order, *Rules Re Microwave-Service CATV,* 38 F.C.C. 683, ¶ 77 (1966). While the FCC adhered to that scheme over the ensuing decades, the D.C. Circuit invalidated it in 1985 on the grounds that the agency's purported justification—the preservation of local over-the-air television—was "fanciful" and that the rules were overbroad in any event because they indiscriminately protected all broadcasters regardless of whether they aired local content. *See* Quincy Cable TV, Inc. v. FCC, 768 F.2d 1434, 1454-62 (D.C. Cir. 1985), *cert. denied,* 476 U.S. 1169 (1986). The FCC then adopted a narrower form of "must carry" and a modified rationale, but the D.C. Circuit invalidated the new rules too. *See* Century Communications v. FCC, 835 F.2d 292 (D.C. Cir. 1987), *clarified,* 837 F.2d 517 (D.C. Cir. 1987).

25 *See* Turner Broad. Sys. v. FCC, 520 U.S. 180 (1997). In that case, Justice Breyer provided the crucial fifth vote, reasoning that even though the must carry regime hurt cable subscribers by restricting their available programming choices, it helped the over-the-air viewers more by expanding their array of local programming options. *Id.* at 228-29 (Breyer, J., concurring).

26 *See generally* Thomas W. Hazlett, *Digitizing "Must Carry" Under Turner Broadcasting v. FCC,* 8 Sup. Ct. Econ. Rev. 141, 172 (2000); Glen O. Robinson, *The Electronic First Amendment: An Essay for the New Age,* 47 Duke L.J. 899, 937 (1998).

27 Robinson, *supra,* 47 Duke L.J. at 941.

28 17 U.S.C. § 119(d)(10)(a).

29 *See, e.g.,* ABC, Inc. v. PrimeTime 24, 17 F. Supp. 2d 478 (M.D.N.C.), *aff'd,* 184 F.3d 348 (4th Cir. 1999).

30 *See* Satellite Broad. and Communications Ass'n v. FCC, 275 F.3d 337, 348 (4th Cir. 2001) (quoting EchoStar executive), *cert. denied,* 536 U.S. 922 (2002).

31 *Id.* at 350 n.5.

32 *See* Pub. L. No. 102-385, 106 Stat. 1460 (1992); *see also* Report and Order, *Implementation of Sections of the Cable Television Consumer Protection and Competition Act of 1992 Rate Regulation,* 8 FCC Rcd 5631 (1993).

33 *See* 47 U.S.C. § 543(b)(1), (c)(4); *see also* General Accounting Office, Issues Related to Competition and Subscriber Rates In the Cable Television Industry 8 (October 2003) (relating history).

34 17 U.S.C. § 122(a), (f), (j)(2).

35 *See* 47 U.S.C. § 338.

36 *See Satellite Broad. and Communications Ass'n,* 275 F.3d at 366.

37 *See* 47 U.S.C. § 548. In particular, these rules assure rival MVPD platforms access to affiliated programming on non-discriminatory terms and conditions, prohibit the use of "exclusive contracts," and bar "unfair methods of competition or

unfair or deceptive acts or practices" designed to limit entry. *See* 47 U.S.C. § 548(b), (c); Report and Order, *Development of Competition and Diversity In Video Programming Distribution and Carriage*, 8 FCC Rcd 3359, ¶¶ 36-41 (1993). These rules apply only to programming delivered by means of wholesale satellite transmissions, however, and not to programming transmitted over terrestrial fiber-optic lines. This loophole enables Comcast, for example, to avoid the program access requirements by using terrestrial means to deliver its local sports programming (Comcast SportsNet). *See* EchoStar Communications Corp. v. FCC, 292 F.3d 749 (D.C. Cir. 2002).

38 In general, antitrust law tolerates such self-dealing unless it effectively "forecloses" rival firms from the markets for either distribution or production. Antitrust courts evaluate a variety of factors to judge whether the practice suppresses competition, including the duration of the exclusivity arrangement and the availability of reasonable alternatives. *See, e.g.,* Twin City Sportservice v. Charles O. Finley & Co., 676 F.2d 1291, 1302 (9th Cir. 1982). In the 1990s, before direct-to-home satellite providers had obtained significant market share, antitrust officials concluded on a couple of occasions that vertically integrated cable providers had both the incentive and opportunity to exclude entry by new video distribution platforms. *See United States v. Tele-Communications, Inc. and Liberty Media Corp.*, Competitive Impact Statement, 59 Fed. Reg. 24,723 (1994); *United States v. Primestar Partners, L.P.*, Competitive Impact Statement, 58 Fed. Reg. 33944 (1993).

39 47 U.S.C. § 548(c)(5).

40 *See* Report and Order, *Implementation of the Cable Television Consumer Protection and Competition Act of 1992*, 17 FCC Rcd 12,124, ¶ 4 (2002) ("*2002 Program Access Order*").

41 *Id.* at 12,175 (Dissenting Statement of Commissioner Abernathy).

42 *Id.* at 12,177 (Dissenting Statement of Commissioner Abernathy) (emphasis added).

43 For a compelling critique of the traditional restrictions on vertical integration in the media industry, see Christopher Yoo, *Vertical Integration and Media Regulation in the New Economy*, 19 YALE J. REG. 171 (2002). For an explanation of when vertical integration questions pose valid antitrust concerns, see Michael Riordan & Steven Salop, *Evaluating Vertical Mergers: A Post-Chicago Approach*, 63 ANTITRUST L.J. 513 (1995).

44 *See* United States v. Paramount Pictures, 334 U.S. 131 (1948).

45 *See generally* OLIVER WILLIAMSON, THE MECHANISMS OF GOVERNANCE (Oxford Univ. Press, 1996).

46 *See* RONALD COASE, THE FIRM, THE MARKET, AND THE LAW (Univ. of Chicago Press, 1990).

47 *See* Bill Carter, *Ailing ABC Turns to HBO in Search of TV Hits*, N.Y. TIMES, Aug. 5, 2002, at C1.

48 *See, e.g.,* Time Warner Entertainment, Co. v. FCC, 240 F.3d 1126, 1138 (D.C. Cir. 2001) (*"Time Warner"*) ("even where an unaffiliated supplier offered a better cost-quality trade-off, a company might be reluctant to ditch or curtail an inefficient in-house operation because of the impact on firm executives or other employees, or the resulting spotlight on management's earlier judgment").

49 Associated Press v. United States, 326 U.S. 1, 20 (1945).

50 Schurz Communications, Inc. v. FCC, 982 F.2d 1043, 1051 (7th Cir. 1992); *see generally* BESEN ET AL., MISREGULATING TELEVISION, *supra*, at 127-46.

51 *Schurz*, 982 F.2d at 1051.

52 *See, e.g.,* FCC v. Nat'l Citizens Comm. for Broad., 436 U.S. 775 (1978) (*"NCCB"*).

53 *Schurz*, 982 F.2d at 1054-55.

54 *Id.* at 1050.

55 Ted Turner, *Monopoly or Democracy*, WASH. POST A23 (May 30, 2003); Ted Turner, *My Beef With Big Media*, WASH. MONTHLY (July/August 2004) (www.washingtonmonthly.com/features/2004/0407.turner.html). Lawrence Lessig also argues that finsyn's repeal has had a "narrowing effect" on what programs are produced. LAWRENCE LESSIG, FREE CULTURE: HOW BIG MEDIA USES TECHNOLOGY AND THE LAW TO LOCK DOWN CULTURE AND CONTROL CREATIVITY 166 (Penguin Press, 2004). He acknowledges, however, that "the efficiencies [from vertical integration] are important, and the effect on culture is hard to measure." *Id.*

56 Michael J. Copps, Remarks at the Future of Music Coalition Policy Summit 3 (May 3, 2004) (http://hraunfoss.fcc.gov/edocs_public/attachmatch/DOC-246862A1.doc).

57 *See* Report and Order, *2002 Biennial Regulatory Review—Review of the Commission's Broadcast Ownership Rules and Other Rules Adopted Pursuant to Section 202 of the Telecommunications Act of 1996*, 18 FCC Rcd 13,620, ¶¶ 45, 640-656 (2003) (rejecting "source diversity" as a valid goal for media policy and declining to reinstitute finsyn rules).

58 47 U.S.C. § 533.

59 47 U.S.C. § 533(f)(1).

60 *See* Third Report and Order, *Implementation of Section 11(c) of the Cable Television Consumer Protection and Competition Act of 1992*, 14 FCC Rcd 19,098 (1999) (*"3d R&O"*).

61 *Time Warner*, 240 F.3d at 1137-40.

62 While the digital future where viewers can control what video programming they watch is still years away, developments like MSN's carriage of major league baseball games, Hollywood's creation of a Movielink platform for delivering movies, and the effort to link personal video recorders with programs available on the Internet all suggest that the possible dawn of a new era is near. *See* Saul Hansell, *Selling "Nemo" Online, Trying to Repel Pirates*, N.Y. TIMES, June 14, 2004, at C1 (reporting on Starz Ticket on Real Movies, which sells a service allowing for down-

loading movies via the Internet for $12.95 per month); J. William Gurley, *One Nation Under Internet Protocol*, CNET NEWS.COM (April 6, 2004) (http://news.com.com/One+nation+under+Internet+Protocol/2010-7352_3-5185413.html) (noting opportunities, within the next ten years, for firms to offer video content over broadband).

63 *See 3d R&O,* ¶ 1.

64 *Time Warner,* 240 F.3d at 1130-36.

65 *YES Network, Cablevision Break Off Talks,* ESPN.COM (March 28, 2003) (http://espn.go.com/mlb/news/2003/0328/1530781.html); Len Maniace, *YES-Cablevision Dispute Settled,* THE JOURNAL NEWS (March 13, 2003) (http://www.nynews.com/newsroom/031303/a01p13yes.html)

66 YES subsequently won an arbitration battle with Cablevision, preventing Cablevision from establishing a separate regional sports tier—i.e., separate from the basic tier—that would include the YES Network. *See* News Release, Cablevision Reacts to YES Network Arbitration Ruling (March 24, 2004) (http://www.cablevision.com/index.jhtml?id=2004_03_24).

67 *Time Warner,* 240 F.3d at 1134-36.

68 *Prometheus,* 373 F.3d at 414; *see also NBC v. U.S., supra.*

69 *Compare, e.g.,* C. Edwin Baker, *Media Concentration: Giving Up on Democracy,* 54 FLA. L. REV. 839 (2002) (*"Media Concentration"*) (arguing for greater role for FCC regulation) *with* Bruce M. Owen, *Regulatory Reform: The Telecommunications Act of 1996 and the FCC Media Ownership Rules,* 2003 MICH. ST. L. REV. 671 (2003) (arguing for antitrust review alone).

70 Notice, *Time Warner, Inc.,* 61 FED. REG. 50,301 (Sept. 25, 1996).

71 Sharon Waxman, *Independent Producers Wary of Proposed Deal,* N.Y. TIMES, Feb. 14, 2004, at C1, C2.

72 Case-by-case merger review has likewise played an important role in ensuring cross-platform competition between cable and satellite TV providers. As noted above, the FCC effectively blocked the proposed combination of EchoStar and DirecTV in 2002 because it would have left just one major satellite provider to compete with the cable companies. *See EchoStar-DirecTV Hearing Designation Order, supra.* And, in the 1990s, the Justice Department similarly blocked the efforts of a consortium of cable operators (in a partnership known as Primestar) to purchase a set of DBS licenses. *See* http://www.usdoj.gov/atr/cases/ f1700/1757.htm (Justice Department complaint); STEPHEN KEATING, CUTTHROAT (Johnson Books, 1999).

73 *See News Corp.-DirectTV Merger Order.*

74 *See Rules Governing Standard and High Frequency Broadcast Stations,* 5 FED. REG. 2382, 2384 (1940) (FM radio); *Rules Governing Standard and High Frequency Broadcast Stations,* 6 FED. REG. 2282, 2284-85 (1941) (TV); *Rules*

Governing Standard and High Frequency Broadcast Stations, 8 FED. REG. 16065 (1943) (AM radio). The Supreme Court upheld the FCC's authority to impose such restrictions in U.S. v. Storer Broadcasting, 351 U.S. 192 (1956).

75 *See, e.g.,* Second Report and Order, *Rules Relating to Multiple Ownership of Standard, FM, and Television Broadcast Stations*, 50 F.C.C.2d 1046 (1975).

76 *NCCB*, 436 U.S. at 796.

77 *See* Report and Order, *Multiple Ownership of AM, FM and Television Broadcast Stations*, 100 F.C.C.2d 17 (1984); *see also* Mark S. Fowler & Daniel L. Brenner, *A Marketplace Approach to Broadcast Regulation*, 60 TEX. L. REV. 207 (1982).

78 *See* Second Supplemental Appropriations Act, Pub. L. No. 98-396, Sec. 304, 98 Stat. 1369 (1984); *Multiple Ownership of AM, FM and Television Broadcast Stations*, 100 F.C.C.2d 74 (1984).

79 *See, e.g.,* Second Report and Order, *Amendment of Section 73.3555 of the Commission's Rules, the Broadcast Multiple Ownership Rules*, 4 FCC Rcd 1741, ¶ 76 (1988).

80 Pub. L. No. 104-104, § 202(c)(1)(B), 110 Stat. 56, 110 (1996).

81 *Id.*, § 202(c)(2), (h).

82 Report and Order, *Review of the Commission's Regulations Governing Television Broadcasting*, 14 FCC Rcd 12,903, ¶ 64 (1999) (TV); *see also id.* ¶ 100 (TV-radio). The D.C. Circuit invalidated portions of these rules in Sinclair Broadcasting Group, Inc. v. FCC, 284 F.3d 148, 162 (D.C. Cir. 2002), and remanded the matter back to the FCC for further proceedings.

83 Biennial Review Report, 1998 *Biennial Regulatory Review - Review of the Commission's Broadcast Ownership Rules and Other Rules Pursuant to Section 202 of the Telecommunications Act of 1996*, 15 FCC Rcd 11,058, ¶ 25 (2000).

84 280 F.3d 1027, 1044 (D.C. Cir. 2002).

85 *Id.*

86 *See* BENJAMIN M. COMPAINE & DOUGLAS GOMERY, WHO OWNS THE MEDIA?: COMPETITION AND CONCENTRATION IN THE MASS MEDIA INDUSTRY 135, 136 (Dimension, 3d ed. 2000).

87 *See* Baker, *Media Concentration, supra; see also* MARK COOPER, MEDIA OWNERSHIP AND DEMOCRACY IN THE DIGITAL INFORMATION AGE 31 (Gillis Pub. Group, 2003) (http://cyberlaw.stanford.edu/blogs/cooper/archives/mediabooke. pdf) (discussing public disquiet with media mergers).

88 Report and Order, *2002 Biennial Regulatory Review—Review of the Commission's Broadcast Ownership Rules and other Rules Adopted Pursuant to Section 202 of the Telecommunications Act of 1996*, 18 FCC Rcd 13,620 (2003) ("*2003 Media Ownership Decision*"). Our discussion does not address the

Commission's efforts in the same order to amend its restrictions on the ownership of multiple broadcast radio stations in the same community. *See Prometheus,* 373 F.3d at 421-35 (upholding some aspects of FCC's analysis but invalidating others).

89 *See 2003 Media Ownership Decision,* ¶¶ 499-500.

90 *See* 2004 Consolidated Appropriations Act, Pub. L. No. 108-199, § 629, 118 Stat. 3, 99 (2004); *see also* Ben Scott, *The Politics and Policy of Media Ownership,* 53 AM. U. L. REV. 645 (2004).

91 Scott, *supra,* at 674 (noting that the compromise simply "legalized the status quo," which stemmed from earlier waivers of the 35% limit).

92 *2003 Media Ownership Decision,* ¶¶ 368-69 (abolishing newspaper-TV cross ownership rule); *id.,* ¶ 390 (abolishing radio-TV cross ownership rule); *id.,* ¶¶ 432-498 (instituting cross media limits).

93 *Id.,* ¶¶ 185-87.

94 *Id.,* ¶ 327.

95 *See* COOPER, *supra,* at 215.

96 373 F.3d 372; *see also* Prometheus Radio Project v. FCC, No. 03-3388, 2003 WL 22052896 (3d Cir. Sept. 3, 2003) (staying application of rules pending further review). The Third Circuit also dealt at length with threshold questions about whether the statute required the FCC to apply a presumption of deregulation when considering proposals to relax its media ownership rules. The Third Circuit concluded that the answer to this question is no, despite mixed signals on the subject from the D.C. Circuit. *See* 373 F.3d at 393-94 (concluding that discussion of issue in Cellco Partnership v. FCC, 357 F.3d 88, 96-98 (D.C. Cir. 2004), trumped earlier suggestions in *Fox* and *Sinclair* that a deregulatory presumption should apply).

97 *Id.* at 397-412.

98 *Id.* at 415.

99 *Id.* at 418-20. Chief Judge Scirica dissented, arguing that "[p]reserving the 'marketplace of ideas' does not easily lend itself to mathematical certitude," *id.* at 436, of the type the majority was demanding and that "[i]t is not the role of the judiciary to second-guess the reasoned policy judgments of an administrative agency acting within the scope of its delegated authority," *id.* at 435.

100 *See generally* Roger G. Noll, The FCC'S New Television Ownership Rules, Stanford Institute for Economic Policy Research Policy Brief (June 2003) (http://siepr.stanford.edu/papers/briefs/policybrief_jun03.pdf) ("Television is among the least suitable communications media for success in producing genuinely local products.").

101 *See, e.g.,* Anne Applebaum, *Rather Irrelevant,* WASH. POST, Sept. 22, 2004, at A31 (noting that, as a group, post-baby boomers "have no emotional attachment to ABC, NBC and CBS," and looking forward to "the death throes of network news") (http://www.washingtonpost.com/wp-dyn/articles/A40119-2004Sep21.html).

Chapter Twelve

1 For a discussion of standard-setting dilemmas, see generally Kathleen M.H. Wallman, *The Role of Government in Telecommunications Standard Setting*, 8 COMMLAW CONSPECTUS 235, 251 (2000); Dale N. Hatfield, Challenges of Network Design in an Increasingly Deregulated, Competitive Market, Remarks at the IEEE International Symposium (March 27, 2003) (http://www.comsoc.org/confs/im/ 2003/presentation%20files/RemarksDH_IM2003.doc).

2 *See* CARL SHAPIRO & HAL R. VARIAN, INFORMATION RULES 263-64 (Harvard Bus. Sch. Press, 1999) (arguing that FCC indecision played a part in the failure of AM stereo); Bruce C. Klopfenstein & David Seidman, *Technical Standards and the Marketplace: The Case of AM Stereo*, 34 J. BROADCASTING & ELEC. MEDIA 171 (1990) (same); *but see* Michael I. Kraus, *Regulation vs. Markets in the Development of Standards*, 3 S. CAL. INTERDISC. L. J. 781 (1994) (rejecting argument).

3 For a narrative of this episode from the perspective of an RCA engineer, see GEORGE BROWN, AND PART OF WHICH I WAS: RECOLLECTIONS OF A RESEARCH ENGINEER (Angus Cupar, 1982).

4 Joseph Farrell & Carl Shapiro, *Standard-Setting in High Definition Television*, BROOKINGS PAPERS ON ECONOMIC ACTIVITY, at 57 (Brookings Inst. Press, 1992).

5 *See* MICHAEL A. HILTZIK, DEALERS OF LIGHTNING: XEROX PARC AND THE DAWN OF THE COMPUTER AGE (Harper Collins, 1999).

6 First Report and Order, *Interstate and Foreign Message Toll Tel. Serv.*, 56 F.C.C.2d 593, ¶¶ 3-8 (1975), *modified*, 58 F.C.C.2d 716, *modified*, 58 F.C.C.2d 736 (1976), *aff'd sub nom.* N.C. Utils. Comm'n v. FCC, 552 F.2d 1036 (4th Cir. 1977).

7 Report and Order, *2000 Biennial Regulatory Review of Part 68 of the Commission's Rules and Regulations*, 15 FCC Rcd 24,944 (2000) ("*2000 Biennial Review*").

8 *Id.* at ¶¶ 23-31. Although the FCC, as an independent regulatory agency, is not subject to the Office of Management and Budget's directive in Circular No. A-119 regarding the importance of relying on *de jure* standard-setting bodies, its approach follows the spirit of that directive. *See* Office of Management and Budget, Federal Participation in the Development and Use of Voluntary Consensus Standards and in Conformity Assessment Activities, Circular No. A-119, Feb. 10, 1998 (http://www.whitehouse.gov/omb/circulars/a119/a119.html). To some scholars of administrative law, however, the FCC's willingness to delegate authority to standard-setting bodies compromises on public accountability concerns. *See* Jody Freeman, *Private Parties, Public Functions and the New Administrative Law*, 52 ADMIN. L. REV. 813, 816-18 (2000) ("*Private Parties*"); Jody Freeman, *The Private Role in Public Governance*, 75 N.Y.U. L. REV. 543, 556-64 (2000). For its part, the FCC considered such arguments in favor of direct standard-setting—or the use of Federal Advisory Committee Act committees (like that used in the digital television

context, as discussed later in this chapter)—and rejected them in the Part 68 context on the ground that setting up such a committee would undermine the "goals of reduced governmental involvement in the standards process and expedited development of technical criteria for new technology." *2000 Biennial Review*, ¶ 35.

9 For discussions of this issue, see James C. DeVellis, *Patenting Industry Standards: Balancing The Rights of Patent Holders With The Need For Industry-Wide Standards*, 31 AIPLA Q. J. 301 (2003); Mark A. Lemley, *Intellectual Property Rights and Standard-Setting Organizations*, 90 CAL. L. REV. 1889 (2002); Michael J. Schallop, *The IPR Paradox: Leveraging Intellectual Property Rights to Encourage Interoperability in the Network Computing Age*, 28 AIPLA Q.J. 195 (2000).

10 For example, as noted in chapter 7, disputes between rival factions continue to stall the development of a consensus standard for ultra-wideband technologies. *See* Paul Davidson, *Fight Over Ultrawideband Standards Turns Into Morass*, USA TODAY 1B (August 25, 2004) (http://www.usatoday.com/tech/news/techinnovations/2004-08-24-ultrawideband_x.htm). Although the ethic of participation in standard-setting bodies like those sponsored by the IEEE is for participants to vote their conscience and to select technologies on merit alone, this approach is increasingly obeyed only in the breach. After all, many employees of firms with a stake in the outcome "'may feel that their jobs wouldn't be secure if they didn't vote as told.'" *Id.* (quoting Bob Heile, Chairman of the IEEE's UWB panel).

11 This dynamic can frustrate efforts to facilitate interoperability between rival technologies. For a recent challenge of this type, consider the case of "Web services," in which a faction led by Sun Microsystems battled another faction led by Microsoft. *See* Martin LaMonica, *Rivalry Bogs Down Web Services*, CNET NEWS.COM (July 17, 2003) (http://news.com.com/2102-1012_3-1026889.html?tag=ni_print). For a discussion of the changing nature of the IETF, see Philip J. Weiser, *The Internet, Innovation, and Intellectual Property Policy*, 103 COLUM. L. REV. 534, 542 n.24 (2003).

12 For the Justice Department's Business Review Letter approving this patent pool, see http://www.usdoj.gov/atr/public/busreview/1170.htm.

13 Although we will not venture into discussing their antitrust aspects, it is worth noting that, like formal standard-setting bodies, patent pools can be either procompetitive, when used to develop new technologies that otherwise would not be created, or anticompetitive, when used to facilitate collusion between would-be rivals. *See* Carl Shapiro, *Setting Compatibility Standards: Cooperation or Collusion?* in EXPANDING THE BOUNDARIES OF INTELLECTUAL PROPERTY (Oxford Univ. Press, Rochelle Cooper Dreyfus et al., eds., 2001).

14 The business and economic dimensions of these issues are discussed masterfully in SHAPIRO & VARIAN, *supra*, at 261-296.

15 *See* RICHARD CORNES & TODD SANDLER, THE THEORY OF EXTERNALITIES, PUBLIC GOODS, AND CLUB GOODS 240–326. (Cambridge Univ. Press, 2d ed. 1996) (describing the public goods concept in general and the intersection of public goods and game theory); U.S. Congress, Office of Technology Assessment, Global Standards: Building Blocks for the Future 14 (1992) (discussing standards as a public good).

16 *See* Jonathan M. Barnett, *Cultivating the Genetic Commons: Imperfect Patent Protection and the Network Model of Innovation*, 37 SAN DIEGO L. REV. 987, 1004 (2000) ("In the absence of some form of state intervention, the market is likely to underinvest in fundamental innovation projects that generate a large stream of inappropriable spillovers."); Michael L. Katz & Carl Shapiro, *Systems Competition and Network Effects*, 8 J. ECON. PERSP., 93, 102-03 (1994).

17 This is often described as a concern about "excess inertia"—i.e., a concern that high "switching costs" will lead users to remain locked into an inferior technology. The classic, and controversial, case in point remains the continuing use of the QWERTY standard for typewriter (and now computer) keyboards. Some have argued that this standard maintained its dominance over supposedly superior alternatives (such as a rival DVORAK standard) because of the difficulties in convincing users to switch en masse. *See* Joseph Farrell and Garth Saloner, *Installed Base and Compatibility: Innovation, Product Preannouncements, and Predation*, 76 AM. ECON. REV. 940 (1986); Michael Katz and Carl Shapiro, *Technology Adoption In The Presence of Network Externalities*, 92 J. POL. ECON. 822 (1986); *cf.* chapter 8 (discussing number portability rules). Others have challenged this version of the story and, more generally, have expressed skepticism about such claims of "path dependence" as a basis for government intervention in the market. *See, e.g.,* STAN LIEBOWITZ & STEPHEN MARGOLIS, WINNERS, LOSERS, AND MICROSOFT (Independent Inst., 1999).

18 *See* Bruce C. Klopfenstein & David Seidman, *Technical Standards and the Marketplace: The Case of AM Stereo,* 34 J. BROADCASTING & ELEC. MEDIA 171 (1990).

19 *See* Michael I. Kraus, *Regulation vs. Markets in the Development of Standards,* 3 S. CAL. INTERDISC. L. J. 781 (1994).

20 *See* STEPHEN BREYER, REGULATION AND ITS REFORM 105 (Harvard Univ. Press, 1982). Of course, the distinction between these two types of standards can collapse when a particular design is necessary to achieve a particular function.

21 *See, e.g.,* A. Michael Froomkin, *Habermas@discourse.net: Toward a Critical Theory of Cyberspace,* 116 HARV. L. REV. 749 (2003); *see also* PRESIDENT WILLIAM J. CLINTON & VICE PRESIDENT ALBERT GORE JR., A FRAMEWORK FOR GLOBAL ELECTRONIC COMMERCE § 9 (1997) (http://www.w3.org/TR/NOTE-framework-970706.html); Mark A. Lemley, *Standardizing Government Standard-Setting Policy for Electronic Commerce,* 14 BERKELEY TECH. L.J. 745 (1999) (noting contradictory government policy vis-à-vis standard-setting activity).

22 As Justice Breyer once put it, "four types of problems—information, enforcement, competition, and judicial review—explain to a considerable degree why the standard-setting process so often deviates from the policy planner's ideal." Stephen Breyer, *Analyzing Regulatory Failure: Mismatches, Less Restrictive Alternatives, and Reform,* 92 HARV. L. REV. 549, 575 (1979).

23 The role of the National Association of Broadcasters in initiating the transition to digital television is recounted in JOEL BRINKLEY, DEFINING VISION (Harvest Books, 1998).

24 Notice of Inquiry, *Advanced Television Systems and Their Impact on Existing Television Broadcast Service,* 2 FCC Rcd 5125 (1987); *see also* Richard E. Wiley, *The Challenge of Choice,* 47 FED. COMM. L.J. 401 (1994).

25 *See generally* Farrell & Shapiro, *supra,* at 17.

26 Fourth Report and Order, *Advanced Television Systems and Their Impact upon the Existing Television Broadcast Service,* 11 FCC Rcd 17,771 ¶ 24 (1996) ("*Fourth Report and Order*") (noting availability of licensing fees and explaining that all relevant patent-holders have agreed to a "reasonableness" limitation on royalties).

27 BRINKLEY, *supra,* at 176-78.

28 For a discussion of this debate, see Ellen P. Goodman, *Digital Television and the Allure of Auctions: The Birth and Stillbirth of DTV Legislation,* 49 FED. COMM. L.J. 517 (1997). The terms "digital spectrum" and "analog spectrum" denote only the uses for which the FCC has allocated particular frequency bands; they do not refer, of course, to any inherent technical characteristics of the spectrum itself.

29 *See* 47 U.S.C. § 309(j)(14). Relatedly, Congress instructed the FCC to design rules concerning the terms on which licensees may use digital spectrum to provide certain non-broadcast ("ancillary") services, subject to a licensee's obligation to pay fees to the federal government if it earns revenues from such services. *See* 47 U.S.C. § 336; Memorandum Opinion and Order, *Fees for Ancillary or Supplementary Use of Digital Television Spectrum Pursuant to Section 336(e)(1) of the Telecommunications Act of 1996,* 14 FCC Rcd 19,931 (1999).

30 47 U.S.C. § 309(j)(14)(B)(iii)(I).

31 Fifth Further Notice of Proposed Rulemaking, *Advanced Television Systems and Their Impact Upon Existing Television Broadcast Service,* 11 FCC Rcd 6235 (1996).

32 *Id.,* ¶¶ 29-36. The FCC flirted with precisely those perils, however, when it accommodated the eleventh-hour concerns of the computer industry by allowing for some differentiation and potential incompatibility within the basic standard. *Fourth Report and Order,* ¶¶ 7, 61; *see also* BRINKLEY, *supra,* at 390-91.

33 *See, e.g.,* Second Report and Order, *Review of the Commission's Rules and Policies Affecting the Conversion to Digital Television,* 17 FCC Rcd 15,978, ¶ 51 (2002); *see also* Notice of Proposed Rulemaking, *Review of the Commission's Rules and Policies Affecting The Conversion to Digital Television,* 15 FCC Rcd 5257 (2000) (outlining buildout requirements to facilitate transition).

34 Bill McConnell, *Ferree TV: FCC Defends DTV Plan,* BROADCASTING & CABLE (April 14, 2004) (http://www.broadcastingcable.com/article/CA410640.html).

35 Fifth Report and Order, *Advanced Television Systems and Their Impact upon the Existing Television Broadcast Service,* 12 FCC Rcd 12,809, ¶ 85 (1997) (*"Fifth Report and Order"*).

36 Report and Order, *Remedial Steps for Failure to Comply with Digital Television Construction Schedule,* 18 FCC Rcd 7174 ¶ 21 (2003).

37 *Fifth Report and Order,* ¶ 41. The FCC initially required that each broadcaster transmit its analog programming on its digital channel on a transitional timetable scheduled to culminate in 2005, *id.,* ¶ 54, but it subsequently suspended that requirement. Report and Order, *Second Periodic Review of the Commission's Rules and Policies Affecting the Conversion to Digital Television,* FCC No. 04-192, MB Dkt. No. 03-15, ¶¶ 125-31 (Sept. 7, 2004) (*"Second Periodic Review Order"*).

38 Ken Ferree, From Dead to Dynamo, Address to the 53rd Annual Broadcast Symposium, October 16, 2003 (http://hraunfoss.fcc.gov/edocs_public/attachmatch/DOC-240054A1.pdf). This category of television sets should not be confused with the overlapping category of television sets that take advantage of digital technology to provide higher quality images from other digital inputs—say, the signals delivered by DVD players. Sets in this latter category are not necessarily capable of receiving over-the-air DTV signals. For a discussion of the increasing use of digital technology in consumer electronic devices (whether or not related to DTV), see William J. Gurley, *Watching the Digital Hand,* CNET NEWS.COM (October 8, 2003) (http://news.com.com/Watching+the+'digital+hand'/2010-7355_3-5088457.html).

39 General Accounting Office, Additional Federal Efforts Could Help Advance Digital Television Transition 15 (November 2002).

40 Proposal for Voluntary Industry Action to Speed Digital Television Transition (April 4, 2002) (http://www.fcc.gov/commissioners/powell/mkp_proposal_to_speed_dtv_transtion.pdf).

41 Second Report and Order, *Review of the Commission's Rules and Policies Affecting the Conversion to Digital Television,* 17 FCC Rcd 15,978 (2002).

42 Consumer Elec. Ass'n v. FCC, 347 F.3d 291, 301 & n.6 (2003).

43 First Report and Order, *Carriage of Digital Television Broadcast Signals,* 16 FCC Rcd 2598, ¶¶ 2-3 (2001).

44 *Id.* at ¶¶ 27-29.

45 *See* W. Kenneth Ferree, Advancing The DTV Transition: An Examination of the FCC Media Bureau Proposal, Statement Before The Subcommittee on Telecommunications and The Internet (June 2, 2004) (http://energycommerce.house.gov/108/Hearings/06022004hearing1289/Ferree2037.htm). In 2003, the FCC sought comment on how to define the statutory 85% standard under existing law, but as of this writing, it had not begun resolving the issue. *See Second Periodic Review Order,* ¶ 6; Notice of Proposed Rulemaking, *Second Periodic Review of the Commission's Rules and Policies Affecting the Conversion to Digital Television,* 18 FCC Rcd 1279 (2003).

46 *See, e.g.,* Edward C. Fritts, Statement Before The Subcommittee on Telecommunications and The Internet, Advancing The DTV Transition: An Examination of the FCC Media Bureau Proposal (June 2, 2004) (http://energycommerce.house.gov/108/Hearings/06022004hearing1289/Fritts2038.htm); Bill McConnell, *Searching For Solutions: FCC Staffers Are Trolling For Plan B for DTV Transition,* BROADCASTING AND CABLE, Apr. 19, 2004, at 24 (calling plan, according to Capitol Hill and industry sources, "dead on arrival").

47 Congress could, for example, set up a spectrum trust fund (or authorize tax credits) that would subsidize the purchase of digital-analog converters for poor families (as was done in Germany)—and recoup those subsidies once the FCC auctioned off the returned spectrum. For a proposal along these lines, see J. H. Snider & Michael Calabrese, A Consumer Tax Credit Can Unplug Analog TV, Reduce the Deficit, and Redeploy Low-Frequency Spectrum For Wireless Broadband, New America Foundation (May 2004) (http://www.newamerica.net/Download_Docs/pdfs/Pub_File_1575_1.pdf); *see also* General Accounting Office, German DTV Differs in Many Respects, but Certain Key Challenges Are Similar (July 21, 2004). Or Congress could focus on the producer side of things and provide certain incentives for broadcasters to give up their analog spectrum before a date certain. In a plan along these lines, the Association of Public Television Stations has proposed that public stations making such a transition be rewarded by a trust fund to support public broadcasting. *See, e.g.,* John M. Lawson, Testimony Before the U.S. Senate Committee on Commerce, Science, and Transportation, Hearing on Completing the Digital Television Transition (June 9, 2004) (http://commerce.senate.gov/hearings/testimony.cfm?id=1220&wit_id=3514). Another model would be to grant flexible rights to broadcasters to lease their spectrum for other uses (while allowing them to keep their must carry rights). *See* Thomas W. Hazlett, Testimony Before the U.S. Senate Committee on Commerce, Science, and Transportation, Hearing on Completing the Digital Television Transition (June 9, 2004) (http://commerce.senate.gov/pdf/hazlett060904.doc). In a reminder of the obstacles to passing any program opposed by the broadcasters, they ensured the defeat in the Senate Commerce Committee of a plan offered by John McCain that included subsidies to spur the transition. *See* Michael Grebb, *Broadcasters Gut Digital TV Bill,* WIRED (Sept. 23, 2004) (http://www.wired.com/news/politics/0,1283,65056,00.html).

48 Statement of Michael K. Powell, Implementing the 9-11 Commission's Recommendations to Expeditiously Provide Spectrum to Public Safety Organizations, Hearing of the Senate Committee on Commerce, Science, and Transportation 7 (September 8, 2004) (http://hraunfoss.fcc.gov/edocs_public/attachmatch/DOC-251933A1.pdf).

49 *See* A&M Records, Inc. v. Napster, Inc., 239 F.3d 1004, 1016-17 (9th Cir. 2001). Critics note that the content industry, like other established industries, has histori-

cally balked at new technologies. For example, Jack Valenti, the leader of the Motion Picture Association of America, famously claimed in 1982 that the VCR was "to the American film producer and the American public as the Boston strangler is to the woman home alone." *Home Recording of Copyrighted Works, Hearings Before the Subcommittee on Courts, Civil Liberties, and the Administration of Justice, of the Senate Judiciary Committee,* 97th Cong., 2d Sess., No. 97, Pt. 1, at 8 (1982) (http://cryptome.org/hrcw-hear.htm). Valenti turned out to be wrong, of course, and the film industry continues to do quite well, in part *because of* the lucrative secondary market for renting and selling videotapes to consumers who miss the initial release of movies in theaters or who want to see them again. *See generally* Sony Corp. of Am. v. Universal City Studios, Inc., 464 U.S. 417, 456 (1984).

50 *Fixing Spectrum Policy Is Among Powell's Top Priorities,* COMM. DAILY, Jan. 13, 2003 ("Intellectual property is the Achilles heel of overall digital transition and FCC is 'groping its way through what role it can play.'") (quoting Michael Powell, FCC Chairman).

51 Second Report and Order, *Implementation of Section 304 of Telecommunications Act of 1996; Commercial Availability of Navigation Devices,* 18 FCC Rcd 20,885 (2003) ("*Plug-and-Play Order*"). The FCC concluded that it had jurisdiction to impose such rules, invoking its authority under 47 U.S.C. § 549(a) to regulate set-top boxes.

52 *See* Report and Order, *Digital Broadcast Content Protection,* 18 FCC Rcd 23,550, ¶¶ 22-24 (2003) ("*Broadcast Flag Decision*").

53 We will use the more familiar term, but technically speaking, the flag is known as the "Redistribution Control Descriptor." *ATSC Standard A/65B: Program and System Information Protocol for Terrestrial Broadcast and Cable,* Revision B 78 (March 18, 2003) (http://www.atsc.org/standards/a_65b.pdf).

54 *Broadcast Flag Decision,* ¶ 20. Notably, the "broadcast flag" is ineffective in plugging the "analog hole"—i.e., in preventing users from converting digital television broadcasts to an analog format (such as that used for a VCR) and then re-converting them back to a digital format for purposes of widespread distribution.

55 *Id.,* ¶ 46.

56 In an early such decision, the FCC concluded that a service offered by TiVo satisfied the broadcast flag standard. *See* News Release, FCC Protects Digital Output Protection Technologies and Recording Method Certifications (August 4, 2004) (http://hraunfoss.fcc.gov/edocs_public/attachmatch/DOC-250532A1.pdf) (finding "sufficient evidence" that the TiVo Guard technology (among others) is "technically sufficient to adequately protect digital broadcast television from indiscriminate redistribution"); Rob Pegoraro, *TiVo vs. the Broadcast Flag Wavers,* WASH. POST, Aug. 1, 2004, at F6.

57 Similar legal questions have arisen concerning the relationship between the FCC's DRM rules and copyright law. The Commission has no jurisdiction over copyright policy *per se*. But it does have jurisdiction over any signals transmitted

by air or wire. The Commission thus invokes the legal fiction that, because "communications law and copyright law can create independent rights," its DRM rulings are "not intended in any way to change or affect existing copyright law" (*Plug-and-Play Order,* ¶ 54, ¶ 9)—although they often have precisely that effect.

58 *Broadcast Flag Order,* ¶ 28 n.66 (citing 1962 All Channel Receiver Act (codified at 47 U.S.C. §§ 303(s), 330(a)) (television frequencies); 1990 Television Decoder Circuitry Act (codified at 47 U.S.C. §§ 303(u), 330(b)) (closed-caption transmissions); Parental Choice in Television Programming provisions of the 1996 Telecommunications Act (codified at 47 U.S.C. §§ 303(x), 330(c)) (V-Chip); Section 624A of the Communications Act, 47 U.S.C. § 544a (cable compatibility); Section 629 of the Communications Act, 47 U.S.C. § 549 (navigation devices)).

59 *Id.* at ¶ 29 (quoting 47 U.S.C. § 153(33)). *But cf.* Motion Picture Ass'n of Am., Inc. v. FCC, 309 F.3d 796, 805 (D.C. Cir. 2002) (invalidating attempted exercise of ancillary authority to impose "video description" rules for television programming).

60 For a copy of the petition for review of the FCC's order, filed in the D.C. Circuit by a number of public interest organizations, see http://www.ala.org/ala/washoff/WOissues/copyrightb/regulatorymatters/BFPetitionforReview.pdf.

61 *Cf.* Thomas W. Hazlett, Testimony Before the U.S. Senate Committee on Commerce, Science, and Transportation, Hearing on Completing the Digital Television Transition (June 9, 2004) (http://commerce.senate.gov/pdf/hazlett060904.doc).

Chapter Thirteen

1 For a further discussion of airline deregulation and its parallels to the 1996 Act, see James B. Speta, *Deregulating Telecommunications In Internet Time*, 61 WASH. & LEE L. REV. 1063, 1071-75 (2004).

2 *See* Richard D. Cudahy, *Whither Deregulation: A Look at the Portents*, 58 N.Y.U. ANN. SURV. AM. L. 155, 166 (2001); Michael E. Levine, *Airline Competition in Deregulated Markets: Theory, Firm Strategy, and Public Policy*, 4 YALE J. ON REG. 393, 394 (1987) ("by the mid-1970's it was probably fair to say that no impartial academic observer of any standing doubted that the airline business, if unregulated, would reach something that more or less resembled a competitive equilibrium").

3 *See, e.g.,* Alfred E. Kahn, *The Theory and Application of Regulation*, 55 ANTITRUST L.J. 177, 178 (1986).

4 *See* Airline Deregulation Act of 1978, Pub. L. No. 95-504, 92 Stat. 1705 (codified in scattered sections of 49 U.S.C.).

5 H.R. Rep. No. 204, 104th Cong., 1st Sess. 48, *reprinted in* 1996 U.S.C.C.A.N. 10, 11.

6 For an explanation of this new model, and its parallels in other regulated industries, see Joseph D. Kearney & Thomas W. Merrill, *The Great Transformation of Regulated Industries Law*, 98 COLUM. L. REV. 1323 (1998); *see also* Joseph Farrell, *Creating Local Competition*, 49 FED. COMM. L.J. 201, 211-212 (1996) (noting that procompetitive interconnection and unbundling rules take significant regulatory effort to implement).

7 ALFRED KAHN, LETTING GO: DEREGULATING THE PROCESS OF DEREGULATION 70 (Inst. of Pub. Utils. and Network Indus., 1998).

8 *Id.*

9 Stephen Breyer, *Anticipating Antitrust's Centennial: Antitrust, Deregulation, and the Newly Liberated Marketplace*, 75 CALIF. L. REV. 1005, 1018 (1987).

10 *See* Verizon Communications Inc. v. FCC, 535 U.S. 467, 539 (2002) (Breyer, J., dissenting); AT&T v. Iowa Utils. Bd., 525 U.S. 366, 413 (1999) (Breyer, J., dissenting); STEPHEN G. BREYER, ECONOMIC REASONING AND JUDICIAL REVIEW 8-10 (American Enterprise Institute Press, 2004) (amplifying his criticisms of FCC decisions) (http://www.aei.brookings.org/admin/authorpdfs/page.php?id=840); *see also* Brown Shoe Co. v. United States, 370 U.S. 294, 320 (1962) (emphasizing that antitrust law serves to protect "competition, not competitors").

11 PETER W. HUBER, LAW AND DISORDER IN CYBERSPACE: ABOLISH THE FCC AND LET COMMON LAW RULE THE TELECOSM (Oxford Univ. Press, 1997).

12 Andrew Odlyzko, Telecom Dogma and Spectrum Allocations 7 (June 20, 2004) (http://wirelessunleashed.com/papers/TelecomDogmas.pdf).

13 Michael K. Powell, Remarks at the Wireless Communications Association International 1 (June 3, 2004) (http://hraunfoss.fcc.gov/edocs_public/attachmatch/DOC-248003A1.pdf); *see* Andrew Odlyzko, *The Many Paradoxes of Broadband*, 8 FIRST MONDAY Sec. 14 (September 2003) (http://firstmonday.org /issues/issue8_9/odlyzko/index.html); *see also* Kevin Fitchard, *Broadband Wireless Wins Endorsement*, TELEPHONY ONLINE (June 7, 2004) (reporting on Craig McCaw's new broadband wireless venture) (http://telephonyonline.com/ar/telecom _broadband_wireless_wins).

14 Scott Woolley, *Into Thin Air*, FORBES (April 26, 2004) (http://forbes.com/forbes/2004/0426/098_print.html) (stock market decline); Todd Rosenbluth, *Costly Growth For the Bells*, BUS. WK. (May 7, 2004) (http://www.businessweek.com/investor/content/may2004/pi2004057_0898_pi041 .htm) (noting continuing local line loss); *Beyond The Bubble*, THE ECONOMIST (October 9, 2003) (http://www.economist.com/displaystory.cfm?story_id =2098913) (same). One expert estimated that the total capacity of fiber networks increased by 500-fold from 1998 to 2002 (i.e., the years of the Internet gold rush), whereas demand merely increased four-fold during the same period—reflecting a $150 billion investment in unnecessary telecommunication networks. *Id.*

15 Scott Woolley, *Into Thin Air*, FORBES (April 26, 2004) (www.forbes.com/forbes/2004/0426/098_print.html); *see also* Adam Quinton, The Current State of the Communications Marketplace, Testimony to the House Commerce Committee, February 4, 2004 (http://energycommerce.house.gov/108/Hearings/02042004hearing1164/Quinton1852.htm) (noting that, in early 2004, 80% of the revenues—but only 20% of the traffic in terms of bits—stems from voice communications and that, over time, the voice revenues will disappear as the industry is reshaped around IP networks).

16 *See* Almar Latour, *Verizon to Launch Nationwide Plan for Internet Calls*, WALL ST. J., July 22, 2004, at B7.

17 *See* Scott Woolley, *Roaming Free*, FORBES.COM (July 15, 2004) (http://www.forbes.com/wireless/2004/07/15/cz_sw_0715wireless.html); Woolly, *Into Thin Air, supra*; Paul Davidson, *IDT Uses Wi-Fi To Offer Cheaper Cell Service But Service Limited To Certain Areas*, USA TODAY, April 22, 2004, at 1B (http://www.usatoday.com/tech/wireless/data/2004-04-21-idt-wifi_x.htm) (reporting on IDT's experimental VoIP over Wi-Fi offering).

18 Saul Hansell, *Selling "Nemo" Online, Trying to Repel Pirates*, N.Y. TIMES, June 14, 2004, at C1 (reporting on Starz Ticket on Real Movies, which sells a service allowing for downloading movies via the Internet for $12.95 per month); J. William Gurley, *One Nation Under Internet Protocol*, CNET NEWS.COM (April 6, 2004) (http://news.com.com/One+nation+under+Internet+Protocol/2010-7352_3-5185413.html) (noting opportunities, within the next ten years, for firms to offer video content over broadband).

19 Philip J. Weiser, *Law and Information Platforms*, 1 J. TELECOMM. & HIGH TECH. L. 1, 12 n.51 (2002); *see, e.g.*, Marguerite Reardon, *Rumble in the "Triple Play" Jungle*, CNET NEWS.COM (June 21, 2004) (http://news.com.com/2100-1037-5242738.html).

20 Burnet v. Coronado Oil & Gas Co., 285 U.S. 393, 406 (1932) (Brandeis, J., dissenting). This intuition is an application of the Coase Theorem (discussed in chapter 7), which holds that parties can order their behavior efficiently within a given legal framework if, but only if, transaction costs are low and that framework is reasonably clear and stable.

21 Indeed, Congress's inability to move quickly in the face of industry change is the established justification for the FCC's broad ancillary jurisdiction (see chapter 6). As for why and how Congress delegates authority to regulatory agencies, there is a substantial legal and policy science literature on the topic. *See, e.g.*, Kathleen Bawn, *Political Control Versus Expertise: Congressional Choices About Administrative Procedures*, 89 AMER. POLI. SCI. REV. 62 (1995); Cass R. Sunstein, *Law and Administration After* Chevron, 90 COLUM. L. REV. 2071 (1990).

22 AT&T Corp. v. Iowa Utils. Bd., 525 U.S. 366, 397 (1999) ("It would be gross understatement to say that the 1996 Act is not a model of clarity. It is in many important respects a model of ambiguity or indeed even self-contradiction. That is most unfortunate for a piece of legislation that profoundly affects a crucial segment

of the economy worth tens of billions of dollars."). This problem seems to have eluded the legislation's congressional sponsors. Senator Larry Pressler, for example, maintained that the FCC's rulemaking tasks were straightforward because "Congress has already done the heavy lifting when it comes to policy choices in telecommunications reform." *A New FCC Dawns in the Wake of the Telecom Act,* FCC REPORTS, 1996 WL 8542600 (June 19, 1996) (quoting Sen. Larry Pressler).

23 PETER HUBER ET AL., FEDERAL TELECOMMUNICATIONS LAW 402-03 (2d ed.) (Aspen, 1999); *see also* HUBER, LAW AND DISORDER IN CYBERSPACE, *supra.*

24 *See* Joseph D. Kearney, *From the Fall of the Bell System to the Telecommunications Act: Regulation of Telecommunications Under Judge Greene,* 50 HASTINGS L.J. 1395 (1999).

25 SBC Communications, Inc. v. FCC, 981 F. Supp. 996 (N.D. Tex. 1997), *rev'd,* 154 F.3d 226 (5th Cir.1998). Judge Kendall's opinion is perhaps best remembered for its characterization of Laurence Tribe, whom the Bell companies had hired as their counsel in that case, as "probably the most respected Constitutional law scholar alive." *Id.* at 1003 n.5.

26 15 U.S.C. § 1.

27 Frank H. Easterbrook, *When Does Competition Improve Regulation,* 52 EMORY L. REV. 1297, 1297 (2003); *see also* Richard A. Posner, *Antitrust in the New Economy,* 68 ANTITRUST L.J. 925, 937 (2001) (noting challenge in antitrust cases).

28 *See, e.g.,* STEPHEN BREYER, ECONOMIC REASONING, *supra,* at 11-13 (discussing use of specialist courts and experts and embracing latter option).

29 United States v. Microsoft Corp., 147 F.3d 935, 954-56 (D.C. Cir. 1998).

30 Reviews of Huber's argument have made this same point, explaining that his failure to explain how antitrust courts would oversee "non-discriminatory and reasonably priced interconnection . . . is a notable shortcoming." Joseph D. Kearney, *Twilight of the FCC?,* 1 GREEN BAG 2D 327, 329 (1998). The government of New Zealand reached a similar conclusion and adopted a sector-specific regulatory regime after experimenting with an antitrust-like approach for telecommunications deregulation. In particular, it found that antitrust courts are ill-suited to manage the ongoing challenges of ensuring reliable cooperation between an incumbent and new entrants (as to, say, interconnection) and develop stable rules in a cost-effective fashion. *See* Mary Newcomer Williams, *Comparative Analysis of Telecommunications Regulation: Pitfalls and Opportunities,* 56 FED. COMM. L.J. 269, 277 (2003); *see also* JEAN-JACQUES LAFFONT & JEAN TIROLE, COMPETITION IN TELECOMMUNICATIONS 34 (MIT Press, 2000) (examining New Zealand case and concluding that it demonstrates the "difficulty of ensuring competition in the absence of regulation").

31 For a discussion of the rationale for delegation of lawmaking authority to agencies as opposed to courts, see Philip J. Weiser, *Federal Common Law, Cooperative Federalism, and the Enforcement of the Telecom Act,* 76 N.Y.U. L. REV. 1692, 1718-20 (2001) (*"Federal Common Law"*).

32 124 S. Ct. 874 (2004).

33 United States v. Am. Tel. & Tel. Co., 552 F. Supp. 131, 168 (D.D.C. 1982). In 1975, AT&T's argument had earlier persuaded Greene's predecessor on the case, Judge Joseph Waddy, to halt further discovery until this jurisdictional point was resolved, thereby winning the company several years of delay. *See* STEVE COLL, THE DEAL OF THE CENTURY 79-82 (1986).

34 Pub. L. No. 104-104, § 601(b)(1), 110 Stat. 56 (1996); *see also* H.R. CONF. REP. NO. 104-458, at 201 (1996) (explaining that the clause "prevents affected parties from asserting that the [Act] impliedly pre-empts other laws.").

35 *See, e.g.*, Goldwasser v. Ameritech Corp., 222 F.3d 390, 401 (7th Cir. 2000); James B. Speta, *Antitrust and Local Competition Under the Telecommunications Act*, 71 ANTITRUST L.J. 99 (2003).

36 *See, e.g.*, Law Offices of Curtis V. Trinko, L.L.P. v. Bell Atl., 305 F.3d 89 (2d Cir. 2002), *rev'd*, 124 S.Ct. 872 (2004); Philip J. Weiser, Goldwasser, *The Telecom Act, and Reflections on Antitrust Remedies*, 55 ADMIN. L. REV. 1 (2003); Steven Semeraro, *Speta on Antitrust and Local Competition Under the Telecommunications Act: A Comment Respecting the Accommodation of Antitrust and Telecom Regulation*, 71 ANTITRUST L.J. 147 (2003).

37 As noted in chapter 3, the essential facilities doctrine was most famously applied to the telecommunications industry in MCI's own private antitrust case against AT&T, which proceeded parallel to the litigation handled by Judge Greene. In that case, the Seventh Circuit ruled that a competitor states a claim under the essential facilities doctrine where (1) a monopolist exercised control of an essential facility; (2) a competitor cannot practically or reasonably duplicate the facility; (3) the monopolist has denied the competitor access to the facility; and (4) the monopolist could feasibly provide access to the facility. MCI Communications Corp. v. Am. Tel. & Tel. Co., 708 F.2d 1081, 1132-33 (7th Cir. 1983). Many have criticized this doctrine on the ground that it requires antitrust courts to manage access to monopoly facilities and invites overbroad applications. *See, e.g.*, Phillip Areeda, *Essential Facilities: An Epithet in Need of Limiting Principles*, 58 ANTITRUST L.J. 841 (1989). Antitrust courts have also relied on the related claim that incumbent providers owe a duty to deal with the new entrants "where some cooperation is indispensable to effective competition." Olympia Equip. Leasing Co. v. W. Union Tel. Co., 797 F.2d 370, 379 (7th Cir. 1986), *cert. denied*, 480 U.S. 934 (1987); *see, e.g.*, Covad Communications Co. v. BellSouth Corp., 299 F.3d 1272 (11th Cir. 2002), *vacated*, 124 S. Ct. 1143 (2004); *see also* Aspen Skiing Co. v. Aspen Highlands Skiing Corp., 472 U.S. 585, 605 (1985) (noting that antitrust laws prevent firms from "exclud[ing] rivals on some basis other than efficiency") (internal quotations omitted); Otter Tail v. United States, 410 U.S. 366, 380 (1973) (mandating cooperation from an incumbent electric utility to facilitate entry). *But see* Dennis W. Carlton, *A General Analysis of Exclusionary Conduct and Refusal to Deal—Why* Aspen *and* Kodak *Are Misguided*, 68 ANTITRUST L.J. 659, 659 (2001) (criticizing such theories).

38 *Trinko*, 124 S. Ct. at 878.

39 *Id*. at 879, 882.

40 *Id*. at 879.

41 *Id*. at 881. For a discussion of the Act's wireline competition provisions and their enforcement mechanisms, see chapter 3 and appendixes A and B.

42 *See, e.g.,* Covad Communications Co. v. BellSouth Corp., 374 F.3d 1044 (11th Cir. 2004) (concluding that *Trinko* does not bar traditional "price squeeze" claims); Z-Tel Communications, Inc. v. SBC Communications, Inc., 331 F. Supp. 2d 513, (E.D. Tex. 2004) (denying motion to dismiss (among other things) Sherman Act claims resting on theories other than essential facilities).

43 THE OXFORD DICTIONARY OF QUOTATIONS 150 (Oxford Univ. Press, 3d ed. 1979) (quoting Winston Churchill, speech before the House of Commons (Nov. 11, 1947)).

44 Am. Broad. Co. v. FCC, 191 F.2d 492, 501 (D.C. Cir. 1951); *see also* Radio-Television News Dirs. Ass'n v. FCC, 229 F.3d 269, 272 (D.C. Cir. 2000) (issuing writ of mandamus where the Commission "failed to act for nine months" after "acknowledg[ing] the need for a prompt decision," and "its response consists of an order that further postpones a final decision without any assurance of a final decision"); In re Monroe Communications Corp., 840 F.2d 942, 945-46 (D.C. Cir. 1988) (noting that "an undesirably large amount of time has passed during this [FCC] proceeding; the three years of administrative limbo following the *Initial Decision* have benefited neither the parties nor the public"); Sierra Club v. Thomas, 828 F.2d 783, 795 (D.C. Cir. 1987) (noting that "[t]he classic example of [delay depriving parties of rights granted by Congress] is the undue length of rate proceedings conducted by the Federal Communications Commission," which "deprive[s] ratepayers of their statutory right to [just and reasonable] rates"); So. Pac. Communications Co. v. Am. Tel. and Tel. Co., 740 F.2d 980, 1000 (D.C. Cir. 1984) ("At minimum, long regulatory delays often have preceded final FCC approval or disapproval of AT&T's allegedly predatory rates, refusals to interconnect, or unreasonable and discriminatory terms and conditions of access to local distribution facilities."); Telecomm. Research and Action Ctr. v. FCC, 750 F.2d 70, 80 (D.C. Cir. 1984) (noting "serious" delays and retaining jurisdiction over case until final agency disposition "in light of the Commission's failure to meet its self-declared prior deadlines for these proceedings"); Nader v. FCC, 520 F.2d 182, 206-07 (D.C. Cir. 1975) (cautioning Commission, again, "in the strongest terms" about its "dilatory pace" because court "foresee[s] the breakdown of the regulatory process if the public and the regulated carriers must wait as long as ten years to have important issues decided").

45 *See* 47 U.S.C. § 251(d)(1).

46 47 U.S.C. § 271(d)(3). Beneath the surface, those proceedings lasted much longer than 90 days. A Bell company often spent months or years winning state commission support and then obtaining the FCC's own informal indication that a section 271 application would receive serious consideration. Then, if concerns

remained that the FCC considered too serious to resolve by the deadline, the Bell company typically withdrew the application ("voluntarily") and refiled it with updated information, thereby restarting the 90-day clock.

47 Verizon Tel. Cos. v. FCC, 374 F.3d 1229 (D.C. Cir. 2004).

48 47 U.S.C. § 154(b)(5), (c) (specifying rules on party affiliation and term of office).

49 A notable such recommendation came in the famous Landis Report on Regulatory Agencies. *See* JAMES M. LANDIS, REPORT ON REGULATORY AGENCIES TO THE PRESIDENT-ELECT (1960).

50 Any theoretical deliberative benefits of this multi-member structure go largely unrealized because the Sunshine Act generally prohibits the FCC's members from discussing substantive matters as a group outside of formal public hearings. 5 U.S.C. §552b(e)(1); *see also* 5 U.S.C. §552b(c) & (d)(1) (allowing closed meetings only when a majority of a commission votes to hold one). Among its other unintended consequences, this restriction increases the importance of each commissioner's "legal advisors," who are subject to no such bar. For a critical look at the Sunshine Act, see Jim Rossi, *Participation Run Amok: The Costs of Mass Participation for Deliberative Agency Decisionmaking*, 92 NW. U. L. REV. 173 (1997).

51 A few categories of orders can be appealed only to the D.C. Circuit, whereas the remainder can be appealed either to that court or to any of the eleven regional circuits in which the appealing party resides or has its principal office. 47 U.S.C. § 402; 28 U.S.C. § 2343. Under 28 U.S.C. § 2342, known as the Hobbs Act, challenges to FCC orders *must* be filed in a court of appeals; they may not be filed in federal district court. That provision is generally construed to mean that when one private party sues another in district court, that court must assume the statutory validity of any FCC order that has not been vacated by a reviewing court of appeals. *See* US West Communications, Inc. v. Hamilton, 224 F.3d 1049, 1054-55 (9th Cir. 2000); Wilson v. A.H. Belo Corp., 87 F.3d 393, 400 (9th Cir. 1996); *see generally* FCC v. ITT World Communications, Inc., 466 U.S. 463, 468 (1984).

52 467 U.S. 837, 866 (1984); *see also* Weiser, *Federal Common Law*, at 1715-18.

53 *See* 5 U.S.C. § 706 (Administrative Procedure Act; directing courts to invalidate, inter alia, agency actions that are "arbitrary, capricious, an abuse of discretion, or otherwise not in accordance with law").

54 Weiser, *Federal Common Law*, at 1725 n.177 (discussing, among other things, the Tenth Circuit's approach in *Qwest Corp. v. FCC*, 258 F.3d 1191, 1199-1202 (10th Cir. 2001)).

55 *See* Cass Sunstein & Adrian Vermeule, *Interpretation and Institutions*, 101 MICH. L. REV. 885, 926 (2003) ("We think that the best defenses of *Chevron* attempt to read ambiguous congressional instructions in a way that is well-attuned to institutional considerations.").

56 Some courts have similarly invoked the First Amendment not to combat the evils of state-sponsored viewpoint discrimination, but simply as a back-door mechanism for substituting their own policy judgments for those of the expert agency. *See, e.g.,* Comcast Cablevision of Broward County, Inc. v. Broward County, 124 F.Supp. 2d 685, 696 (S.D. Fla. 2000) (invalidating access requirement on First Amendment grounds); *see also* Stuart Benjamin, *Proactive Legislation and The First Amendment,* 99 MICH. L. REV. 281 (2000).

57 To be sure, the Act does not literally conscript the state agencies into service. Under section 252(e)(5), any state is free to opt out of this entire framework for implementing the local competition provisions, in which event the FCC stands in the state's shoes, sets the wholesale rates, and resolves any other disputes. So far, however, states have only rarely declined to participate in this regulatory scheme. Starpower Communications LLC v. FCC, 334 F.3d 1150 (D.C. Cir. 2003) (reviewing FCC decision rendered in the place of the Virginia State Corporation Commission).

58 Weiser, *Federal Common Law,* at 1731-33.

59 Jonathan E. Nuechterlein, *Incentives to Speak Honestly About Incentives: The Need for Structural Reform of the Local Competition Debate,* 2 J. TELECOMM. & HIGH TECH. L. 399, 402-05 (2003).

60 By longstanding tradition, the Justice Department, rather than the FTC, reviews mergers between telecommunications carriers. But the FTC has taken the lead in reviewing several major mergers in the communications industry involving firms other than telecommunications carriers, such as Time Warner's merger with AOL in 2000-01. Open questions about which of these two agencies should review a particular merger are generally decided after informal interagency consultation.

61 Brent Shearer, *Who Will Survive The Telecom Shakeout?,* MERGERS & ACQUISITIONS 13 (May 2004) (quoting analyst Raul Katz).

62 Matt Richtel, *Qwest Steps Up to Lure AT&T's Customers,* N.Y. TIMES, July 24, 2004 (http://www.nytimes.com/2004/07/24/business/24bell.html) (citing analyst Daniel Zito). The *Times* article added: "An executive at one Bell company, who insisted on anonymity, said there was interest in a takeover of AT&T," albeit not in the very short term. *Id.*

63 *See* Reed Hundt, Thinking About Why Some Communications Mergers Are Unthinkable, Address to the Brookings Institution, June 19, 1997 (http://www.fcc.gov/Speeches/Hundt/spreh735.html).

64 Yochi Dreazen, *FCC, Faced With Telecom Crisis, Could Let a Bell Buy WorldCom,* WALL ST. J., July 15, 2002, at 1.

65 15 U.S.C. § 18. As a technical matter, the standard generally focuses on the goal of preventing a firm from creating "monopoly power" through merger. As defined by a classic antitrust law precedent, "monopoly power" represents the "power to control prices or exclude competition." United States v. DuPont & Co., 351 U.S. 377, 391 (1956). In practice, antitrust authorities judge whether a merger creates monopoly power through a series of fact-specific factors related to the nature of the

marketplace. *See* ABA SECTION OF ANTITRUST LAW, ANTITRUST LAW DEVELOPMENTS 238 (4th ed. 1997) (listing factors relevant to monopoly power determinations such as "presence and degree of barriers to entry or expansion, technological superiority resulting in cost advantages, economies of scale and scope, ability to price discriminate, the relative size of competitors, competitors' performance, pricing trends and practices, homogeneity of products, potential competition, and the stability of market shares over time").

66 Complaint, United States v. Worldcom (D.D.C.) (No. 00-CV-1526) (http://www.usdoj.gov/atr/cases/f5000/5051.pdf). The post-1996 ILEC combinations include SBC and Pacific Telesis (1996), Bell Atlantic and NYNEX (1997), SBC and Ameritech (1999), and Bell Atlantic and GTE (2000).

67 Joel Klein, Making The Transition From Regulation To Competition: Thinking About Merger Policy During the Process Of Electric Power Restructuring (January 21, 1998) (http://www.usdoj.gov/atr/public/speeches/1332.htm).

68 *See, e.g.*, United States v. Marine Bancorporation, Inc., 418 U.S. 602 (1974) (turning away potential competition argument).

69 47 U.S.C. §§ 214, 310(d) (public interest authority to review license transfers); *see* 15 U.S.C. § 21 (a) (FCC authorized to act under Clayton Act); James R. Weiss & Martin L. Stern, *Serving Two Masters: The Dual Jurisdiction of the FCC and the Justice Department over Telecommunications Transactions*, 6 COMM. L. CONSPECTUS 195, 198 (1998) (noting that the FCC rarely exercises its Clayton Act authority).

70 Memorandum Opinion and Order, *Application of Nynex Corp., Transferor, and Bell Atlantic Corp., Transferee*, 12 FCC Rcd 19,985, ¶ 7 (1997) ("*BA/NYNEX Merger Order*").

71 15 U.S.C. § 25.

72 *BA/NYNEX Merger Order*, ¶ 3.

73 *See, e.g.*, Memorandum Opinion and Order, *Application of Ameritech Corp. and SBC Comm., Inc.*, 14 FCC Rcd 14,712 (1999); Memorandum Opinion and Order, *Applications of GTE Corp. and Bell Atlantic Corp.*, 15 FCC Rcd 14,032 (2000).

74 *BA/NYNEX Merger Order*, ¶ 185-86; *see also* Bryan Tramont, *Too Much Power, Too Little Restraint: How the FCC Expands Its Reach Through Unenforceable and Unwieldy "Voluntary" Agreements*, 53 FED. COMM. L.J. 49 (2000).

75 Memorandum Opinion and Order, *Applications of Ameritech Corp., Transferor, and SBC Communications, Inc., Transferee*, 14 FCC Rcd 14,712, 15,197 (1999) (Statement of Commissioner Michael K. Powell, Concurring in Part and Dissenting in Part).

76 *Id*. at 15,201

77 *See* Hearing Designation Order, *Application of EchoStar Communications Corporation, General Motors Corporation, and Hughes Electronics Corp.*, 17 FCC Rcd 20,559 (2002).

78 *See* Donald J. Russell & Sherri Lynn Wolson, *Dual Antitrust Review of Telecommunications Mergers by the Department of Justice and the Federal Communications Commission*, 11 Geo. Mason L. Rev. 143 (2002); Rachel E. Barkow & Peter W. Huber, *A Tale of Two Agencies: A Comparative Analysis of FCC and DOJ Review of Telecommunications Mergers*, 2000 U. Chi. Legal F. 29 (2000).

79 *See* Phil Weiser, *Paradigm Changes in Telecommunications Regulation*, 71 U. Colo. L. Rev. 819, 839-840 (2000) (*"Paradigm Changes"*) (contrasting approach of Illinois commission in SBC-Ameritech merger with that of the New York commission in the Bell Atlantic-NYNEX merger); *see also* Ill. Bell Tel. Co. v. Ill. Commerce Comm'n, 816 N.E.2d 379 (Ill. App. 2004) (invalidating a condition of merger approval).

80 *See* 47 U.S.C. § 572 (d)(6)(A)(iii) (limiting cable-telephone company mergers to situations where the FCC concludes that "the anticompetitive effects of the proposed transaction are clearly outweighed in the public interest by the probable effect of the transaction in meeting the convenience and needs of the community to be served"); *see also* 141 Cong. Rec. S8,464 (June 15, 1995) (Senator Leahy) (explaining rationale for heightened standard for proposed combinations between cable and telephone companies on the ground that allowing "telephone companies to buy out cable companies—their most likely competitor—in the telephone companies' local service areas . . . would destroy the best hope of developing competition in both local telephone service and cable television markets").

81 *See, e.g.*, H.R. 4019, 106th Cong. (2000) (see http://thomas.loc.gov for text).

82 Schurz Comm, Inc. v. FCC, 982 F.2d 1043, 1050 (7th Cir. 1992).

83 Philip J. Weiser, *Regulatory Challenges and Models of Regulation*, 2 J. Telecomm. & High Tech. L. 1, 14-15 (2003); Weiser, *Paradigm Changes, supra*, at 837-838.

84 Kahn, Letting Go, *supra*, at 70 (1998).

85 As discussed in appendix B, existing law significantly complicates the FCC's ongoing efforts to develop a more professional and effective approach to enforcement.

86 First Report and Order, *Rules Re Microwave-Served CATV*, 50 F.C.C. 683 (1966).

87 The change in the regulatory mentality over the last two generations has been nothing short of revolutionary. As Harold Demsetz summarized the old model of public utility regulation, "regulation has often been sought because of the inconvenience of competition." Harold Demsetz, *Why Regulate Utilities?*, 11 J. L. & Econ. 55, 61 (1968).

Appendix A

1 47 U.S.C. § 252(d)(1).

2 535 U.S. 467.

3 The basic idea of the efficient component pricing rule is that a CLEC leasing network elements should make an incumbent scrupulously whole for its loss of market share by covering (among other things) the incumbent's "opportunity costs"—i.e., the net revenues the incumbent forgoes by ceding to the entrant the retail relationship with the customer. The incumbents unsurprisingly advocated this approach, and CLECs opposed it. In August 1996, the FCC rejected adoption of the efficient component pricing rule largely on the ground that, in important respects, it would arbitrarily perpetuate the traditional retail pricing structure of the industry, which is laden with various cross-subsidies and is largely divorced from any rigorous conception of the underlying costs of providing service. *See* First Report and Order, *Implementation of the Local Competition Provisions of the Telecommunications Act of 1996*, 11 FCC Rcd 15,499, ¶¶ 708-11 (1996) (*"Local Competition Order"*).

The FCC made similarly short work of Ramsey pricing, named after the brilliant Cambridge mathematician Frank Ramsey, who died in 1930 at the age of 26. As briefly discussed in chapter 2, telephone companies and other natural monopolies tend to have high "common costs" that are not specific to (and could not be avoided by discontinuing) any particular service but that nonetheless must be recovered somehow. As applied to regulated ratemaking, Ramsey pricing holds that it is economically efficient to allocate the greatest percentage of such costs to the services with the lowest demand elasticity: i.e., those that purchasers would be *least* likely to give up with any incremental price increase. The FCC concluded that, whatever its abstract merits in other contexts (such as taxation), Ramsey pricing would make little sense as a tool for promoting local competition because it would impose disproportionately prohibitive costs on CLECs precisely when they lease the bottleneck elements (such as the loop) that they need *the most* in order to compete. *Id.*, ¶ 696.

4 Notice of Proposed Rulemaking, *Review of the Commission's Rules Regarding the Pricing of Unbundled Network Elements and the Resale of Service by Incumbent Local Exchange Carriers*, 18 FCC Rcd 20,265, ¶ 30 (2003) (*"TELRIC NPRM"*).

5 *Local Competition Order*, ¶ 679.

6 PAUL A. SAMUELSON & WILLIAM D. NORDHAUS, ECONOMICS 167 (McGraw-Hill, 16th ed. 1998).

7 1 ALFRED KAHN, THE ECONOMICS OF REGULATION: PRINCIPLES AND INSTITUTIONS 26-27 (MIT Press, reissue ed. 1988).

8 In reality, the question of historical cost recovery through retail rates is quite complicated. That is because, among other reasons, most incumbents are now governed by price cap regulation (as discussed in chapter 2) rather than classic rate-of-return regulation. Also, universal service policies tend to spread recovery of network costs over an incumbent's entire customer base, further attenuating the links between actual expenditures and how they are recovered.

9 *See* 1 KAHN, *supra*, at 63-122.

10 "Marginal" cost refers to the cost of one additional unit of service or capacity, whereas "incremental" cost refers more broadly to variously sized increments of the same. For present purposes, the two concepts are interchangeable.

11 Technically, TELRIC measures the forward-looking costs attributable to the element itself, and network element prices are then based on the sum of those costs and an appropriate share of an efficient firm's forward-looking "common costs" (i.e., costs that cannot be attributed specifically to a given element). *See* 47 C.F.R. § 51.505. TELRIC is similar to a pricing methodology, developed in the years before 1996, known as "TSLRIC" (pronounced "tee ess lyric"). The ostensible difference is that the latter is designed to recover the total costs of a "service," such as a retail service, whereas the former is designed to recover the total costs of an "element."

12 *TELRIC NPRM*, ¶ 4.

13 Southwestern Bell Tel. Co. v. Pub. Serv. Comm'n, 262 U.S. 276, 312 (1923) (Brandeis, J., concurring in the judgment).

14 AT&T Communications of Illinois, Inc. v. Illinois Bell Tel. Co., 349 F.3d 402, 404 (7th Cir. 2003). Justice Breyer's lone dissent in the *Verizon* case struck a similar note: "The Commission's system will tend to create instances in which (1) the incumbent's *actual* future cost of maintaining an element (say, a set of wires) will exceed (2) the [CLEC's] cost of building or buying elsewhere (say, through wireless or buying elsewhere (say, through wireless or wires in electrical conduits) which, in turn, will equal (or even exceed), (3) the *hypothetical* future 'best practice' cost (namely, what the experts decide will, in general, be cheapest)." 535 U.S. at 550 (Breyer, J., dissenting).

15 *See* 47 C.F.R. § 51.505(b); *see also Local Competition Order*, ¶¶ 683-85.

16 *See Verizon*, 535 U.S. at 523. In so doing, the Court formally reserved the question of whether the use of an historical cost methodology might be relevant to a suit for just compensation under the Takings Clause. *Id.* at 527; *compare, e.g.,* J.

GREGORY SIDAK & DANIEL F. SPULBER, DEREGULATORY TAKINGS AND THE REGULATORY CONTRACT (Cambridge Univ. Press, 1997) (arguing that a forward-looking cost methodology gives rise to takings concerns) *with* William J. Baumol & Thomas W. Merrill, *Deregulatory Takings, Breach of the Regulatory Contract, and the Telecommunications Act of 1996*, 72 N.Y.U. L. REV. 1037 (1997) (challenging takings argument).

17 *See, e.g.,* Chevron USA Inc. v. Natural Resources Defense Council, Inc., 467 U.S. 837 (1984).

18 *TELRIC NPRM, supra.*

19 *Local Competition Order,* ¶ 620.

20 *TELRIC NPRM,* ¶¶ 6-7.

21 *See, e.g.,* Debra J. Aron and William Rogerson, *The Economics of UNE Pricing* 4-5 (Dec. 16, 2003) (submitted to FCC on behalf of SBC Communications Inc.).

22 *TELRIC NPRM,* ¶ 50

23 *Id.,* ¶ 51.

24 *See generally* WILLIAM J. BAUMOL ET AL., CONTESTABLE MARKETS AND THE THEORY OF INDUSTRY STRUCTURE (Harcourt, rev. ed., 1988).

25 *Cf.* WILLIAM J. BAUMOL, THE FREE-MARKET INNOVATION MACHINE: ANALYZING THE GROWTH MIRACLE OF CAPITALISM 166-67 (Princeton Univ. Press, 2002) (noting that "the threat of entry," even in highly contestable markets, "will not prevent the innovating firms in the field from recovering their sunk costs" because "[e]ntry will occur and drive down prices only if those prices are above the levels needed to cover these costs").

26 *TELRIC NPRM,* ¶ 4.

Appendix B

1 *See* 47 U.S.C. §§206-207; Memorandum Opinion and Order, *Just Aaron v. GTE Cal., Inc.,* 10 FCC Rcd 11,519, ¶ 9 (1995) ("We lack authority, however, under the congressional mandate accorded by our governing statute to award the punitive damages and legal expenses sought by Aaron.").

2 47 U.S.C. §§ 202(c), 203. These figures are subject to inflation adjustments.

3 47 U.S.C. §§ 503(b)(1)(A), (B), 503(b)(2)(B). The FCC has interpreted "willful" in this context to include any case in which a carrier knew that it was taking the action in question, not that it knew that action would have the negative effect that it had. *See* Memorandum Opinion and Order, *Application for Review of Southern*

California Broadcasting Co., 6 FCC Rcd 4387, ¶5 (1991). Whether this aggressive interpretation of the penalty-enhancing "willfulness" provision will be upheld remains to be seen.

4 The D.C. Circuit only recently made clear that a carrier could appeal a "forfeiture order" directly to it (after the carrier paid the penalty), rather than waiting to challenge the merits of such a decision after the United States commenced a proceeding to claim the forfeiture in federal district court. *See* AT&T Corp. v. F.C.C., 323 F.3d 1081, 1085 (D.C. Cir. 2003); *see also* SBC Communications, Inc. v. FCC, 373 F.3d 140, 146-47 (D.C. Cir. 2004) (*"SBC v. FCC"*). While it had always been clear that a carrier could appeal an order entered after an adjudication by an administrative law judge, the FCC tended to use the "notice of apparent liability" procedure as opposed to the more formal method, thus leaving uncertain whether a direct appeal to a circuit court could be taken. *Id.*

5 MCI Telecomm. Corp. v. Am. Tel. & Tel. Co., 512 U.S. 218, 230 (1994); *see also* Cahnmann v. Sprint Corp., 133 F.3d 484, 489 (7th Cir. 1998) (Posner, J.).

6 *See* STEPHEN COLL, THE DEAL OF THE CENTURY 373 (1986) (describing testimony of former Common Carrier Bureau Chiefs Bernard Strassburg and Walter Hinchman in the AT&T case).

7 Indeed, commentators have debated whether the FCC could have managed this effort effectively without the structural relief provided by the AT&T consent decree. *Compare* Robert W. Crandall, *The Failure of Structural Remedies in Sherman Act Monopolization Cases*, 80 OR. L. REV. 109, 179–92 (2001) (arguing that equal access regulations alone, without divestiture and quarantine, would have ensured the decree's intended competitive benefits) *with* Joseph D. Kearney, *From the Fall of the Bell System to the Telecommunications Act: Regulation of Telecommunications Under Judge Greene*, 50 HASTINGS L.J. 1395, 1415–16 (1999) (discussing the Justice Department's objections to a pure conduct remedy).

8 BellSouth Telecomm., Inc. v. MCIMetro Access Transmission Services, Inc., 317 F.3d 1270, 1274 (11th Cir. 2003); *id.* at 1275-76 (collecting cases).

9 *See generally* Memorandum Opinion and Order, *Core Communications, Inc. v. SBC Communications, Inc.*, 18 FCC Rcd 7568, ¶¶ 19, 20 & n.48 (2003); *id.* at 7583-84 (Separate Statement of Commissioner Abernathy); *see also* AT&T Corp. v. Iowa Utils. Bd., 525 U.S. 366, 386 (1999) (declining to reach issue on merits).

10 *See* 47 U.S.C. § 271(d)(6); *SBC v. FCC, supra.*

11 Michael K. Powell, Chairman, Federal Communications Commission, Statement on Competition Issues In The Telecommunications Industry Before The Senate Committee on Commerce, Science, and Transportation 12 (Tuesday, Jan. 14, 2003) (http://hraunfoss.fcc.gov/edocs_public/attachmatch/DOC-230241A1.pdf).

12 *See* William E. Kennard, Remarks Before the Competitive Carrier Summit 2000 (January 19, 2000) (http://www.fcc.gov/Speeches/Kennard/2000/spwek003.html).

13 News Release, FCC Chairman Powell Recommends Increased FCC Enforcement Powers for Local Telephone Competition (May 7, 2001) (http://www.fcc.gov/Bureaus/Common_Carrier/News_Releases/2001/nrcc0116.html).

14 Forfeiture Order, *SBC Communications, Inc. Apparent Liability for Forfeiture*, 17 FCC Rcd 19,923, 19,935, ¶ 24 (2002) (*"SBC Forfeiture Order"*), aff'd, SBC v. FCC, *supra*.

15 Apparent Liability for Forfeiture, *Qwest Corporation*, 19 FCC Rcd. 5169 (2004) (*"Qwest Order"*).

16 *See* Report and Order, *Commission's Forfeiture Policy Statement and Amendment of Section 1.80 of the Rules to Incorporate the Forfeiture Guidelines*, 12 FCC Rcd 17087 (1997).

17 *See, e.g., Qwest Order*, ¶ 50 (concluding that the fine was not "excessive under the circumstances"); *id.*, ¶ 51 (concluding that, "[f]or a company of this size, a $9 million forfeiture is not excessive"); *see also* Qwest Corp. v. Minnesota Pub. Util. Comm'n, 2004 WL 1920970 (D. Minn. 2004) (upholding $25.9 million fine imposed by state agency).

18 *See SBC v. FCC, supra.*

19 US West Communications, Inc. v. TCG Or., 31 F. Supp. 2d 828, 837 (D. Or. 1998).

20 *See, e.g.*, Indiana Bell Tel. Co. v. Indiana Util. Reg. Comm., 359 F.3d 493, 497 (7th Cir. 2004); *but cf.* Qwest Corp. v. Worldcom, Inc., 380 F.3d 367 (8th Cir. 2004) (upholding state-mandated wholesale service quality standards).

21 The relevant source of law governing such proceedings, for example, is yet to be determined. One possibility is that the measure of damages for violating interconnection agreements will be a matter of state contract law. *See* Memorandum Opinion and Order, *Starpower Communications LLC v. Verizon Virginia, Inc.*, 17 FCC Rcd 6873, ¶ 24 (2002) (suggesting that contract rules govern interpretation of agreement, though not discussing their applicability to appropriate remedies), *remanded*, 334 F.3d 1150 (D.C. Cir. 2003). On this view, a new entrant seeking punitive damages for a willful breach of an interconnection agreement would almost certainly be out of luck because contract law generally does not provide for punitive damages. *See* Wisconsin Bell, Inc. v. Public Service Comm., 670 N.W.2d 97, 106 (Wisc. 2003) (holding that Wisconsin PSC possesses authority only to provide compensatory damages, precluding any effort to impose penalties for inadequate service not pegged to actual harm).

22 In 2002, the Supreme Court held that legal challenges to the formation of interconnection agreements can proceed in federal court. *See* Verizon Maryland, Inc. v. Public Serv. Comm'n of Md., 535 U.S. 635 (2002). Since then, all federal courts to consider the matter have concluded that challenges to the enforcement of interconnection agreements should be heard in federal court as well, but some judges have dissented from this position. *See* Verizon Md., Inc. v. Global Naps, Inc., 377 F.3d 355, 370 (4th Cir. 2004) (Niemeyer, J., dissenting) (arguing for state court review);

BellSouth Telecommunications, Inc. v. MCIMetro Access Transmission Services, Inc., 317 F.3d 1270, 1288 (11th Cir. 2003) (Tjoflat, J., dissenting) (same). For a more detailed discussion of the Act's jurisdictional architecture, see Philip J. Weiser, *Federal Common Law, Cooperative Federalism, and the Enforcement of the Telecom Act*, 76 N.Y.U. L. REV. 1692, 1731-33 (2001); Philip J. Weiser, *Towards A Constitutional Architecture For Cooperative Federalism*, 79 N.C. L. Rev. 663 (2001); Philip J. Weiser, Chevron, *Cooperative Federalism, and Telecommunications Reform*, 52 VAND. L. REV. 1 (1999).

Index

Glossary of Acronyms

2G: second generation (wireless networks)

3G: third generation (wireless networks)

ADSL: Asymmetric Digital Subscriber Line

AMPS: Advanced Mobile Phone System

ANSI: American National Standards Institute

ATM: Asynchronous Transfer Mode

ATSC: Advanced Television Services Committee

BOCs: Bell Operating Companies

CALEA: Communication Assistance to Law Enforcement Act

CALLS: Coalition for Affordable Local and Long Distance Service

CAPS: Competitive Access Providers

CATV: Community Antenna Television (i.e., cable television)

CCIS: Common Channel Interoffice Signaling

CDMA: Code Division Multiple Access

CEI: Comparatively Efficient Interconnection

CLECs: Competitive Local Exchange Carriers

CMRS: Commercial Mobile Radio Services

CMTS: Cable Modem Termination System

CPE: Customer Premises Equipment

CPNI: Customer Proprietary Network Information

DARPA: Defense Department's Advanced Research Project Administration

DBS: Direct Broadcast Satellite

DHCP:	Dynamic Host Configuration Protocol
DLEC:	Data Local Exchange Carrier
DNS:	Domain Name Server
DoJ:	Department of Justice
DRM:	Digital Rights Management
DS0:	Digital Service Level 0
DS1:	Digital Service Level 1
DS3:	Digital Service Level 3
DSL:	Digital Subscriber Line
DSLAM:	Digital Subscriber Loop Access Multiplexer
ECPR:	Efficient Component Pricing Rule
EEL:	Enhanced Extended Link
ESP:	Enhanced Service Provider
ETC:	Eligible Telecommunications Carrier
FCC:	Federal Communications Commission
finsyn:	Financial Interest and Syndication Rules
FTC:	Federal Trade Commision
FTP:	File Transfer Protocol
FTTH:	Fiber To The Home (or **FTTP:** Fiber To The Premises)
FTTN:	Fiber To The Node
FX:	Foreign Exchange
GHz:	gigahertz (billion cycles per second)
GSM:	Global System for Mobile
HFC:	Hybrid Fiber Coax
HDSL:	High speed (or bit rate) Digital Subscriber Line
HDTV:	High Definition Television
HTML:	Hypertext Markup Language
HTTP:	Hypertext Transport Protocol
ICANN:	Internet Corporation for Assigned Names and Numbers
iDEN:	Integrated Digital Enhanced Network
IEEE:	Institute of Electrical and Electronics Engineers

IETF:	Internet Engineering Task Force
ILECs:	Incumbent Local Exchange Carriers
IM:	Instant Messaging
IP:	Internet Protocol
IPv6:	upgraded version of IP addressing scheme
ISDN:	Integrated Services Digital Network
ISP:	Internet Service Provider
ITU:	International Telecommunications Union
IXC:	Interexchange Carrier
kbps:	kilobits (thousand bits) per second
kHz:	kilohertz (thousand cycles per second)
LAN:	Local Area Network
LATA:	Local Access and Transport Area
LEC:	Local Exchange Carrier
LRIC:	Long-Run Incremental Cost
Mbps:	megabits (million bits) per second
MHz:	megahertz (million cycles per second)
MFJ:	Modification of Final Judgment
MPLS:	Multi Protocol Label Switching
MSA:	Metropolitan Statistical Area
MSC:	Mobile Switching Center
MTA:	Major Trading Area
MVPD:	Multi-Video Programming Distribution
NTSC:	National Television Systems Committee
ONA:	Open Network Architecture
OVS:	Open Video Systems
PBX:	Private Branch Exchange
PCS:	Personal Communications Service
POI:	Point of Interconnection
POP:	Point of Presence
POTS:	Plain Old Telephone Service

PSTN:	Public Switched Telephone Network
PUC:	Public Utilities Commission
PVR:	Personal Video Recorder
QoS:	Quality of Service
RBOC:	Regional Bell Operating Company
SGAT:	Statement of Generally Agreed Terms
SHVA:	Satellite Home Viewers Act
SHVIA:	Satellite Home Viewers Improvement Act
SIP:	Session Initiation Protocol
SLC:	Subscriber Line Charge
SMR:	Specialized Mobile Radio
SMTP:	Simple Mail Transport Protocol
SONET:	Synchronous Optical Network
SS7:	Signaling System 7
TCP/IP:	Transmission Control Protocol/Internet Protocol
TDMA:	Time Division Multiple Access
TELRIC:	Total Element Long Run Incremental Cost
TSLRIC:	Total Service Long-Run Incremental Cost
UMTS:	Universal Mobile Telephone System
UNE:	Unbundled Network Element
UNE-L:	UNE loop
UNE-P:	UNE platform
URL:	Uniform Resource Locator
USF:	Universal Service Fund
VDSL:	Very high speed (or bit rate) Digital Subscriber Line
VoIP:	Voice over Internet Protocol
VPN:	Virtual Private Network
W3C:	World Wide Web Consortium
WATS:	Wide Area Telecommunications/Telephone Service
Wi-Fi:	wireless fidelity
WiMAX:	next generation Wi-Fi standard

JONATHAN E. NUECHTERLEIN AND PHILIP J. WEISER

DIGITAL CROSSROADS

American Telecommunications Policy in the Internet Age

WITH A NEW PREFACE FOR THE 2007 PAPERBACK EDITION

Telecommunications policy profoundly affects the economy and our everyday lives. It sets the ground rules for how people send and receive information, whether through telephones or television or the Internet. Yet accounts of important telecommunications issues tend to be either superficial (and inaccurate) or mired in jargon and technical esoterica. In *Digital Crossroads*, Jonathan Nuechterlein and Philip Weiser offer a clear, balanced, and accessible analysis of how the Internet is transforming not just the economics of the telecommunications industry, but also the legal and policy debate about how—and whether—that industry should be regulated.

JONATHAN E. NUECHTERLEIN is a partner at Wilmer Cutler Pickering Hale and Dorr LLP in Washington, D.C. He served as Deputy General Counsel of the Federal Communications Commission in 2000–2001 and as Assistant to the Solicitor General in 1996–2000. **PHILIP J. WEISER** is Professor of Law and Telecommunications at the University of Colorado and Executive Director and Founder of the Silicon Flatirons Telecommunications Program. He was principal telecommunications adviser to former Assistant Attorney General Joel Klein during the Clinton administration. Both authors previously served as law clerks on the U.S. Supreme Court: Nuechterlein for Justice Souter, and Weiser for Justice White and Ginsburg.

"*Digital Crossroads* brings fresh clarity to a complex subject. It is thorough, comprehensive, and insightful, and will prove invaluable to anyone trying to navigate the tumultuous changes of the digital age."
   FORMER FCC CHAIRMAN MICHAEL K. POWELL

"A magnificent achievement. . . . This is a marvelous book, and well worth working through from cover to cover, as I have done."
   ALFRED E. KAHN, ROBERT JULIUS THORNE PROFESSOR, EMERITUS, OF POLITICAL ECONOMY AT CORNELL UNIVERSITY, AND AUTHOR OF *THE ECONOMICS OF REGULATION: PRINCIPLES AND INSTITUTIONS* (MIT PRESS, 1988).

"An impressive work that will be useful to anyone desiring an advanced understanding of telecommunications law and policies."
   THE LAW AND POLITICS BOOK REVIEW

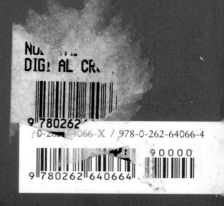

THE MIT PRESS
Massachusetts Institute of Technology
Cambridge, Massachusetts 02142
http://mitpress.mit.edu

0-262-64066-X / 978-0-262-64066-4

9 780262 640664

90000